ONE GAME SEASON

92 Games of College Football's Greatest Rivalry Ohio State vs. Michigan

Compiled by
STEVE WHITE

game stories 1897-1978 written by
Thomas Kiess
game stories 1979-1995 written by
Brent Bowen

Brent Bowen

STEVE WHITE, the compiler of ONE GAME SEASON, has been a fan of Ohio State and Michigan football for many years. Most of his adult life has been spent in the world of publishing. Through business, he has traveled throughout the two states, sharing his enthusiasm with fellow fans.

Recently, Steve has begun pursuit of a second career in Minnesota. He expects to be ordained in 1998 as a Roman Catholic priest for the Diocese of Duluth.

THOMAS KIESS was a high school coach, teacher and avid fan. He wrote the game stories from 1897 through 1978.

BRENT BOWEN is a professional in publication sales and management training. He has a strong background in sports writing and promotion. Game stories from 1979 through 1995 have been written by Bowen.

This book is dedicated to
THOMAS M. KIESS
1947-1983
a good friend and fellow
fan who is greatly missed.

Second Edition

Published by
ONE GAME SEASON
PO Box 5633
Collegeville, MN 56321

Printed in United States of America

ISBN 0-9643228-0-3
LCCCN 94-090404

cover and dust jacket design by BILL HINSCH

FOREWORD

Rivalry is hardly an adequate term to describe the University of Michigan—Ohio State University confrontations on the gridiron. In the previous sentence Michigan is mentioned first simply because "M" comes before "O" in the alphabet. Throughout the remainder of this volume the schools will alternate positions to eliminate any implication to determine which is number one. Such is the intensity not only between the schools, not only between the alumni, but also between the fans. For this reason the annual battle between Ohio State and Michigan has become one of the greatest spectacles in college football.

The skill and courage of all of the players who fought for the Maize and Blue and the Scarlet and Gray deserve praise and gratitude from fans of either persuasion. The superb All-Americans from both sides showcase the superior talent which is attracted to these schools and have highlighted these first 92 games in, what is hoped, a never ending tradition of spirited competition. One enchanting sidelight has been the personalities of the coaches who have guided the various teams through the years. The respect these men have garnered from their players, fans, and peers is overshadowed only by the impact they have had on the actual development of football into a sophisticated game of finesse and strategy.

Your personal enjoyment with this book is limited only by your own imagination as you huddle with the Buckeyes or the Wolverines during that game-winning drive. Remember it's only a game, but to us it's a **One Game Season.**

SIDELINE RIVALRY

ROSES
FOR
WOODY
GATOR FOR BO
BOWL

Ohio State
THIS IS BUCKEYE COUNTRY

BEAT BLUE

UR SHORTS
e Says: "Go- Blue"

BUCKS LOVE
SMELL OF ROSES
BETTER THAN

M CLUB SUPPORTS YO

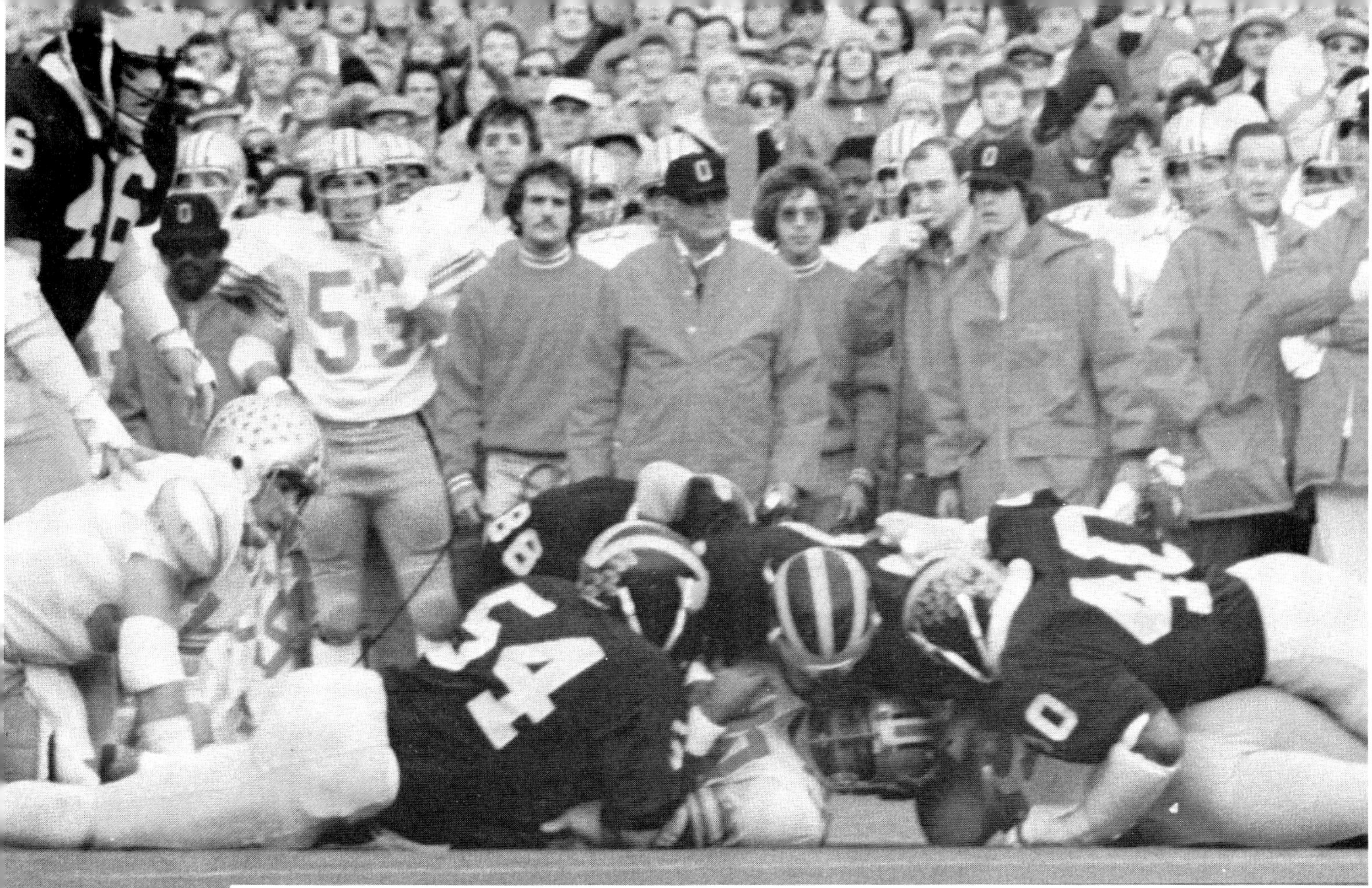

John Cooper
Head Coach

John Cooper has compiled the best overall record in the Big Ten the past three years, a combined mark of 27-8-2 that includes a 17-5-2 ledger in league play, a conference championship and two second-place finishes. Cooper, who received a new five-year contract at the end of last season, is in his eighth year at Ohio State.

After a 4-6-1 record his first year, his last six teams have a combined record of 50-20-3, including a 32-12-3 record in Big Ten play. His overall record with the Buckeyes is 54-26-4 and his seven-year Big Ten record is 35-17-4.

Each of Cooper's last six teams has won at least seven games and five of those teams have won at least eight. Since 1989, the Buckeyes have finished third, fifth, third, second, first and second, respectively, in the Big Ten. In 1993, the Buckeyes posted a 10-1-1 record and were one of the top teams in college football. In 1994, theoretically in the midst of a rebuilding year, OSU went 9-4, defeated both Wisconsin and Michigan and took Alabama down to the wire before losing a seven-point decision in the Florida Citrus Bowl. The latter game, incidentally, was Ohio State's second appearance in three years in Orlando. Overall, Cooper has taken Ohio State to six bowl games, including four New Year's Day contests.

Cooper is in his 19th year as a head coach on the collegiate level. His 18-year record of 136-66-6 includes a 57-31 mark at Tulsa between 1977 and 1984, and a 25-9-2 record at Arizona State between 1985 and 1987.

Cooper has won numerous national honors. He was National Coach of the Year in 1986 when he led ASU to its first-ever Pac-10 title, a win over Michigan in the Rose Bowl and a 10-1-1 record. He was selected by the American Football Coaches Association as District Coach of the Year and was one of four finalists for the Paul "Bear" Bryant National Coach of the Year award in 1993.

Cooper grew up in Powell, Tennessee, a rural community near Knoxville. After graduating from high school, he spent two years in the Army and then enrolled at Iowa State. An outstanding high school athlete, Cooper resumed his athletic career at Iowa State, playing four years of football for the Cyclones. He was team captain and MVP as a senior.

Cooper graduated from Iowa State in the spring of 1962. He embarked upon his coaching career the following fall as the Cyclones' freshman coach.

In 1963, Cooper left his alma mater to become an assistant coach at Oregon State under Tommy Prothro. In 1964, the Beavers won the Pac-8 title and played in the Rose Bowl. Following the 1964 season, Cooper accompanied Prothro to UCLA. In his first year there, the Bruins won the Pac-8 championship and again played in the Rose Bowl.

Cooper left UCLA following the 1967 campaign to become defensive coordinator for Pepper Rodgers at Kansas. He spent five years on the Jayhawks staff, none more memorable than 1969, when Kansas won the Big Eight title and played in the Orange Bowl.

Cooper's last stop as an assistant coach was at the University of Kentucky in 1972. He left Kentucky to become head coach at Tulsa in 1977.

Cooper quickly breathed new life into the Tulsa program. After a 3-8 record his first year, the rookie head coach led the Golden Hurricane to six straight winning seasons, including five consecutive Missouri Valley Conference championships between 1980 and 1984.

At the end of the 1984 season, Cooper's record at Tulsa was an impressive 57-31 and included a 33-6 mark in league play. The Golden Hurricane had won 21 straight and 31 of its last 34 conference games. His eight-year stay at Tulsa was a golden era for the Golden Hurricane.

Having accomplished all that he could at Tulsa and eager for a new challenge, Cooper accepted an offer to become head coach at Arizona State University in 1985. As he had done at Tulsa, he quickly established himself at ASU, leading his first Sun Devil team to an 8-4 record and a berth in the Holiday Bowl. A loss to arch-rival Arizona on the last day of the regular season cost ASU its first-ever Pac-10 football championship. But the Sun Devils made history the following year by winning that elusive title and making their first-ever trip to Pasadena, where they capped off a 10-1-1 season with a 22-15 win over Michigan.

Despite heavy graduation losses in 1986, Arizona State went to a school-record third straight bowl game in 1987. A win over Air Force in the Freedom Bowl put the wraps on a 7-4-1 season and gave Cooper a three-year record of 25-9-2 with the Sun Devils.

With a resume that included a combined record of 82-40-2, six league championships and three bowl appearances, Cooper became the 21st head football coach in Ohio State history on Dec. 31, 1987. As he has done throughout his coaching career, Cooper attacked the Ohio State job with unrelenting enthusiasm and energy. The results of his efforts are reflected in his record, particularly in the accomplishments of his last three teams.

Now in his 33rd year of college coaching, Cooper has coached in several all-star games, including the Japan and Hula bowls and the East-West Shrine game.

In addition to his coaching responsibilities, Cooper, born July 2, 1937, is extremely active in the Columbus community and is involved with several charities, including Big Brothers/Big Sisters, United Way, the Alzheimer's Foundation, the Arthur James Cancer Hospital and Children's Hospital.

John and his wife, Helen, have two children, John Jr. and Cindy, both of whom live in Columbus.

The Cooper Family: John, John Jr, Cindy and Helen.

LLOYD CARR, Head Football Coach

Lloyd Carr once said he had the greatest assistant coaching job in the country, at the University of Michigan.

For 15 years, under Bo Schembechler (1980-1989) and Gary Moeller (1990-94), Carr served that role as defensive secondary coach and most recently assistant head coach and defensive coordinator.

Now, Carr has moved into one of the best *head* coaching jobs in the country. On May 16, 1995, Michigan Athletic Director Joe Roberson named Carr as the 1995 head coach of the Wolverines, after the resignation of Moeller.

Carr said he is ready for the challenge of leading the most successful college football program of all time.

"I am excited about the opportunity to lead this team in the 1995 season," said Carr, shortly after being named the 17th football coach in Michigan history. "I am confident in my preparation and my ability to do so. I am thankful for the support I have from the people here at Michigan."

Carr takes over a team coming off consecutive 8-4 seasons, the latter capped by a 24-14 win over Colorado State in the 1994 Holiday Bowl. It was a triumphant game for Michigan's Carr-led defense, which shut down a potent Ram offense.

In 1995, Carr will oversee a program which has won six of the last 10 Big Ten Conference titles.

"I'm not afraid to make decisions," said Carr. "I have great support, good coaches and players that are special guys ... There is a standard at Michigan that's special. I have all the support we need to win."

Carr brings much experience to his familiar spot on the Michigan Stadium sidelines. A coach at the high school and college levels for more than 25 years, Carr has also led teams on the field as a player.

Carr was a three-sport athlete at Riverview (Mich.) High School, where he was an all-state performer in football. Carr spent his first three years of college at the University of Missouri, and was back-up quarterback on the Tigers' 1966 Sugar Bowl championship squad.

Carr transferred back to his home state the following season, and quarterbacked Northern Michigan University to a perfect 9-0 regular season in 1967. He graduated from NMU in 1968, and earned a master's degree in education administration from NMU in 1970 under a Mott Fellowship.

Carr began his coaching career as a high school assistant at Nativity (Detroit) High School (1968-69) and Belleville (Mich.) High School (1970-73). He moved up to the head coaching ranks in 1973, coaching at Westland (Mich.) John Glenn High School until 1975.

At John Glenn, Carr was named Regional Class A Coach of the Year after leading the Rockets to an 8-1 mark in 1975.

Carr began his college coaching career at Eastern Michigan University, where he coached defensive backs from 1976-77. He assumed the same position at the University of Illinois from 1978-79, before joining Schembechler's staff at Michigan in 1980.

From his experiences as both a player and coach, Carr knows a balanced attack is necessary to have a winning football program.

"A great offense is one that can score quickly, but also control the ball when the situation dictates," said Carr. "Defensively, you have to be able to play a different style when you are ahead and when you are behind."

Ahead is where Carr hopes to be in 1995. He is now the head coach at an institution that expects success. According to Carr, this season should be no different.

"We're going to have no excuses for failure," said Carr, who will open his head coaching tenure August 26 against Virginia in the Pigskin Classic at Michigan Stadium. "We expect to play Ohio State in the last game of the year for the Big Ten Championship."

Carr is married to the former Laurie McCartney. They have six children, Melissa, Jason, Emily, Brett, Ryan and Jarrett. Jason is a fifth-year senior quarterback for the Wolverines, and Emily is a sophomore at U-M and was a member of the 1994 volleyball team.

BIRTHDATE: 7/30/45
YEARS ON 'M' STAFF: Starting 17th
ASSIGNMENT: Head Coach
FAMILY: Wife Laurie,
Children - Melissa, Jason, Emily, Brett, Ryan and Jarrett
COLLEGE: Northern Michigan '68 & '70

COLLEGE COACHING EXPERIENCE:

Eastern Michigan	1976-77
Illinois	1978-79
Michigan	1980-94
Michigan Head Coach	1995

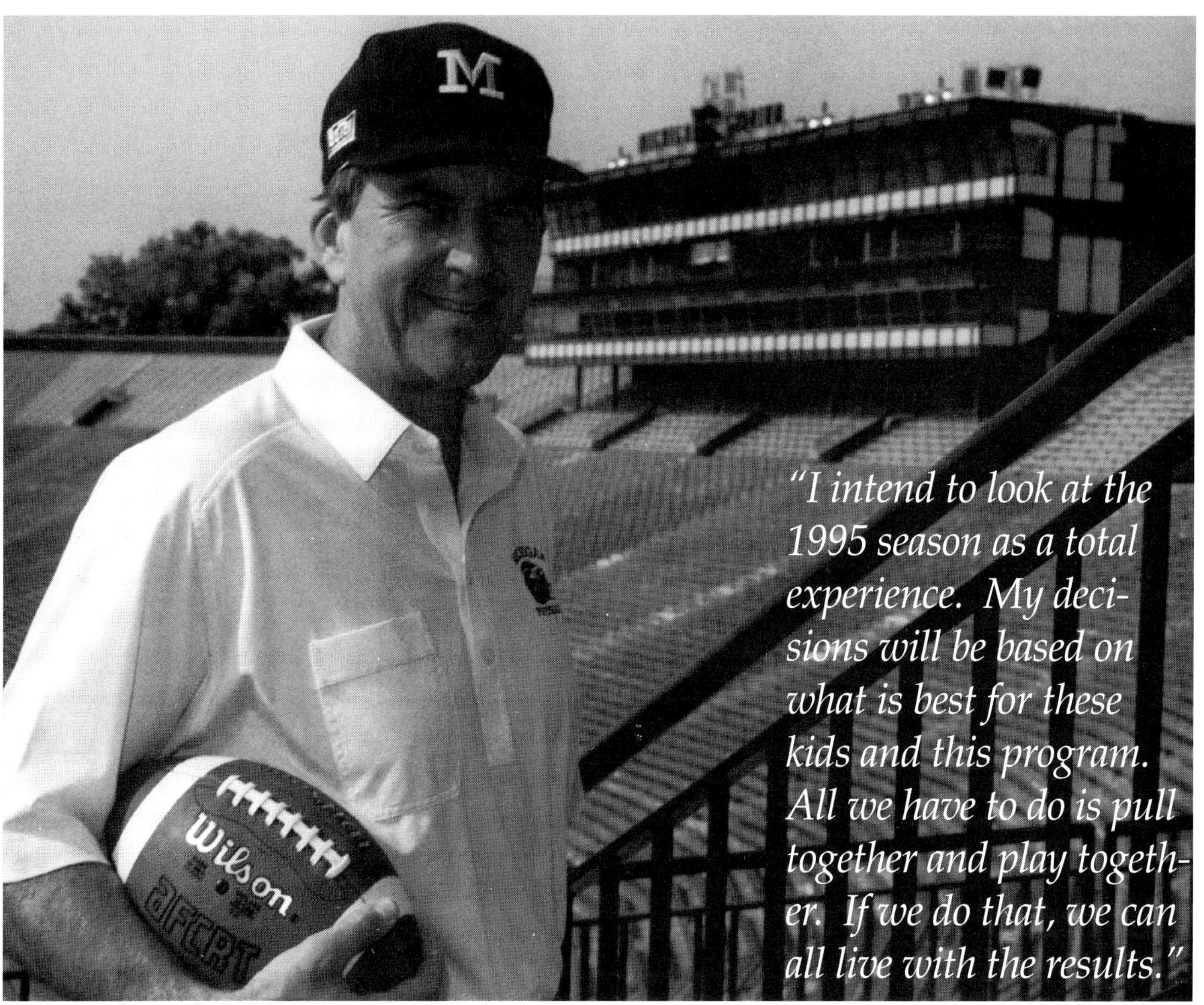

THE MICHIGAN COACHES

Years	Coach	Record	Pct.	First Season	Record	Pct.
1879-90	No Coaches	23-10-1	.691	—	—	—
1891	Mike Murphy / Frank Crawford	4-5-0	.444	1891	4-5-0	.444
1892-93	Frank E. Barbour (Yale '92)	14-8-0	.632	1892	7-5-0	.583
1894-95	William L. McCauley (Princeton '94)	17-2-1	.875	1894	9-1-1	.864
1896	William Douglas Ward (Princeton '95)	9-1-0	.900	1896	9-1-0	.900
1897-99	Gustave H. Ferbert (Michigan'97)	24-3-1	.875	1897	6-1-1	.813
1900	Langdon 'Biff' Lea (Princeton)	7-2-1	.750	1900	7-2-1	.750
1901-23, 25-6	Fielding H. Yost (W. Virginia)	165-29-10	.833	1901	11-0-0	1.000*
1924	George Little (Ohio Wesleyan '12)	6-2-0	.750	1924	6-2-0	.750
1927-28	Elton E. 'Tad' Wieman (Michigan '21)	9-6-1	.593	1927	6-2-0	.750
1929-37	Harry G. Kipke (Michigan '24)	46-26-4	.631	1929	5-3-1	.611
1937-49	H.O.'Fritz' Crisler (Chicago '22)	71-16-3	.805	1938	6-1-1	.813
1948-58	Bennie G. Oosterbaan (Michigan '28)	63-33-4	.650	1948	9-0-0	1.000*
1959-68	Chalmers W.'Bump' Elliott (Michigan '48)	51-42-2	.547	1959	4-5-0	.444
1969-89	Glenn E. 'Bo' Schembechler (Miami '51)	194-48-5	.796	1969	8-3-0	.727*
1990-94	Gary O. Moeller (Ohio State '63)	36-9-3	.781	1990	9-3-0	.750*
1995	Lloyd H. Carr (Northern Michigan '68 & '70)	—	—	—	—	—

** Won Big Ten Championship in inaugural season*

An Ohio State practice session in 1892. In the center, wearing the dark jersey, is Coach Jack Ryder.

OHIO STATE SCORES THROUGH THE EARLY YEARS

1890

		Opponent	
Ohio	20	OH Wesleyan	14
Ohio	0	Wooster	64
Ohio	0	Denison	14
Ohio	10	Kenyon	18

Season Summary
Games Won, 1; Lost, 3

1891

		Opponent	
Ohio	6	Western Reserve	50
Ohio	0	Kenyon	26
Ohio	8	Denison	4
Ohio	6	Akron	0

Season Summary
Games Won, 2; Lost, 2

1892

		Opponent	
Ohio	0	Oberlin	40
Ohio	62	Akron	0
Ohio	80	Marietta	0
Ohio	32	Denison	0
Ohio	42	Dayton YMCA	4
Ohio	18	Western Reserve	40
Ohio	26	Kenyon	10

Season Summary
Games Won, 5; Lost, 2

1893

		Opponent	
Ohio	16	Otterbein	22
Ohio	36	Wittenberg	10
Ohio	10	Oberlin	38
Ohio	6	Kenyon	42
Ohio	16	Western Reserve	30
Ohio	32	Akron	18
Ohio	38	Cincinnati	0
Ohio	40	Marietta	8
Ohio	8	Kenyon	10

Season Summary
Games Won, 4; Lost, 5

1894

		Opponent	
Ohio	6	Akron	12
Ohio	0	Wittenberg	6
Ohio	32	Antioch	0
Ohio	6	Wittenberg	18
Ohio	30	Columbus Barracks	0
Ohio	4	Western Reserve	24
Ohio	10	Marietta	4
Ohio	0	Case	38
Ohio	6	Cincinnati	4
Ohio	46	17th Regiment	4
Ohio	20	Kenyon	4

Season Summary
Games Won, 6; Lost, 5

1895

		Opponent	
Ohio	14	Akron	6
Ohio	6	Otterbein	14
Ohio	6	Oberlin	12
Ohio	4	Denison	4
Ohio	8	OH Wesleyan	8
Ohio	4	Cincinnati	0
Ohio	8	Kentucky	6
Ohio	0	Central KY	18
Ohio	0	Marietta	24
Ohio	12	Kenyon	10

Season Summary
Games Won, 4; Lost, 4; Tied, 2

1896

		Opponent	
Ohio	24	OH Medical	0
Ohio	6	Cincinnati	8
Ohio	12	Otterbein	0
Ohio	0	Oberlin	16
Ohio	30	Case	10
Ohio	4	OH Wesleyan	10
Ohio	10	Columbus Barracks	2
Ohio	0	OH Medical	0
Ohio	6	Wittenberg	24
Ohio	12	OH Medical	0
Ohio	18	Kenyon	34

Season Summary
Games Won, 5; Lost, 5; Tied, 1

ALEXANDER S. LILLEY
Ohio State Head Coach
1890-1891

JACK RYDER
Ohio State Head Coach
1892-1895 and 1898

Pictures are not available for;
COACH CHARLES HICKEY - 1896
COACH DAVID EDWARDS - 1897

"**The Football Team, 1890**. Thirteen strong young men and their manager pose in front of the Grotto at the edge of Mirror Lake. This is the University's first football team and this rather formal group portrait looks like an image found in the family album of nearly every institution of higher education in America. In 1890, a faculty committee recommended improvements in the athletic fields and the construction of a grandstand, arguing: 'In an institution of the size and scope of our University, suitable provision for physical development and maintenance of health should be provided . . . The University domain is ample enough to meet all reasonable demands in the direction of a suitable athletic field, without interfering with class room work or detracting to any considerable extent from the orderly appearance on the campus.' The players are, from left to right: in the back row, Richard T. Ellis (Manager), Walter 'Kansas' Miller, Paul M. Lincoln, Arthur H. Kennedy, Frank W. Rane, Hamilton H. Richardson, Jesse Jones (Captain), Hiram E. Rutan, Edward D. Martin, Charles W. Foulk, David S. Hegler, and John E. Huggins; in the front row, Herbert L. Johnston and Charles B. Morrey." —Test and illustration reprinted from **The First Hundred Years: A Family Album of the Ohio State University, 1870-1970**, a collection of one hundred historic photographs compiled and edited by the Department of Photography and Cinema, and published in observance of the centennial of the founding of the University.

A game in Columbus, 1891.

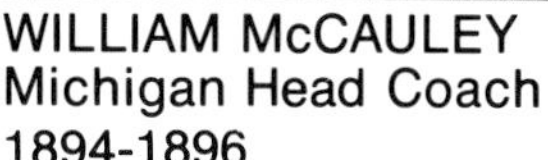

WILLIAM McCAULEY
Michigan Head Coach
1894-1896

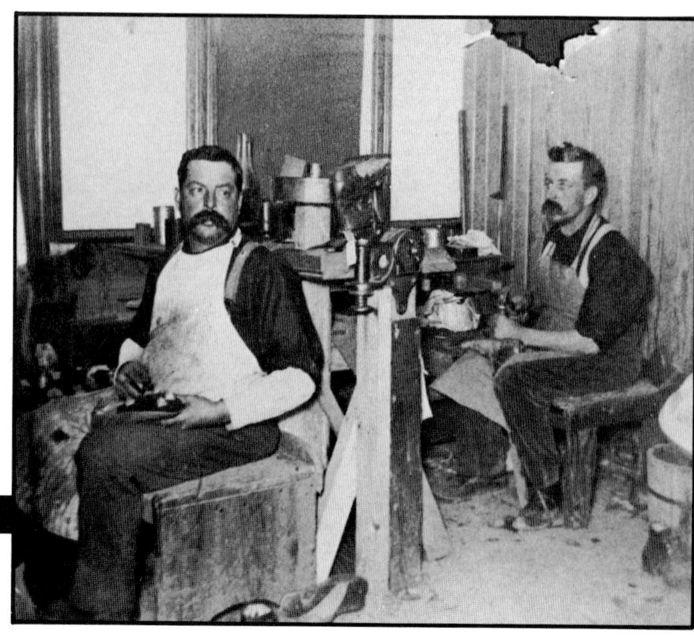

Official football shoemaker in 1890's

MICHIGAN SCORES DURING THE EARLY DAYS

May 30, 1879

Michigan	1	Racine College	0

Fall, 1879

Michigan	0	Toronto	0

Season Summary
Games Won, 1; Lost, 0; Tied, 1

1880

Michigan	13	Toronto	6

Season Summary
Games Won, 1

1881

Michigan	0	Harvard	4
Michigan	0	Yale	11
Michigan	4	Princeton	13

Season Summary
Games Won, 0; Lost 3

1882

No regular team or outside games.

1883

Michigan	0	Yale	46
Michigan	0	Harvard	3
Michigan	6	Wesleyan	14
Michigan	5	Stevens Inst.	1
Michigan	40	Detroit Ind.	5

Season Summary
Games won, 2; Lost, 3

1884

Michigan	18	Albion	0
Michigan	18	Chicago U Club	10

Season Summary
Games Won, 2

1885

Michigan	10	Windsor Club	0
Michigan	30	Windsor Club	0
Michigan	42	Peninsulars, Det.	0

Season Summary
Games Won, 3

1886

Michigan	50	Albion	0
Michigan	24	Albion	0

Season Summary
Games Won, 2

1887

Michigan	32	Albion	0
Michigan	8	Notre Dame	0
Michigan	26	Harvard of Chic.	0

Season Summary
Games Won, 3

1888

Michigan	4	Chic. U Club	26
Michigan	26	Notre Dame	6
Michigan	10	Notre Dame	4
Michigan	14	Detroit A. C.	6
Michigan	76	Albion	4

Season Summary
Games Won, 4; Lost, 1

1889

Michigan	33	Albion	4
Michigan	0	Cornell	56
Michigan	0	Chicago A.A.	20

Season Summary
Games Won, 1; Lost; 2

1890

Michigan	56	Albion	10
Michigan	16	Albion	0
Michigan	18	D.A.C.	0
Michigan	34	Purdue	6
Michigan	5	Cornell	20

Season Summary
Games Won, 4; Lost, 1

1891

Michigan	26	Oberlin	6
Michigan	18	Olivet	6
Michigan	4	Albion	10
Michigan	12	Cornell	58
Michigan	0	Chicago A. C.	10
Michigan	42	Butler	6
Michigan	0	Cornell	10
Michigan	4	Cleveland A.A.	6
Michigan	62	Ann Arbor High	0

Season Summary
Games Won, 4; Lost, 5

1892

Michigan	74	Michigan A.A.	0
Michigan	68	Michigan A.A.	0
Michigan	10	Wisconsin	6
Michigan	6	Minnesota	14
Michigan	18	DePauw	0
Michigan	8	Northwestern	10
Michigan	0	Purdue	24
Michigan	60	Albion	8
Michigan	0	Cornell	44
Michigan	10	Cornell	30
Michigan	18	Chicago	10
Michigan	26	Oberlin	24

Season Summary
Games Won, 7; Lost, 5

1893

Michigan	6	D.A.C.	0
Michigan	26	D.A.C.	0
Michigan	6	Chicago	10
Michigan	20	Minnesota	34
Michigan	18	Wisconsin	34
Michigan	46	Purdue	8
Michigan	34	DePauw	0
Michigan	72	Northwestern	6
Michigan	22	Kansas	0
Michigan	28	Chicago	10

Season Summary
Games Won, 7; Lost, 3

1894

Michigan	12	Orchard Lake	12
Michigan	26	Albion	10
Michigan	48	Olivet	0
Michigan	40	Orchard Lake	6
Michigan	46	Adrian	0
Michigan	18	Case	8
Michigan	0	Cornell	22
Michigan	22	Kansas	12
Michigan	14	Oberlin	6
Michigan	12	Cornell	4
Michigan	6	Chicago	4

Season Summary
Games Won, 9; Lost, 1; Tied, 1

1895

Michigan	34	M.M.A.	0
Michigan	42	D.A.C.	0
Michigan	64	Adelbert	0
Michigan	40	Lake Forest	0
Michigan	42	Oberlin	0
Michigan	0	Harvard	4
Michigan	12	Purdue	10
Michigan	20	Minnesota	0
Michigan	12	Chicago	0

Season Summary
Games Won, 8; Lost, 1

1896

Michigan	18	Normal	0
Michigan	44	Grand Rapids	0
Michigan	28	C. of P & S	0
Michigan	66	Lake Forest	0
Michigan	16	Purdue	0
Michigan	40	Lehigh	0
Michigan	6	Minnesota	4
Michigan	10	Oberlin	0
Michigan	28	Wittenberg	0
Michigan	6	Chicago	7

Season Summary
Games Won, 9; Lost, 1

Pictures were not available of Michigan Head Coaches;
Mike Murphy and Frank Crawford - 1891, Frank Babour, 1892-93

1895-96 Hall, Baird, Carr and Hooper

Michigan's First Uniformed Football Team (1879)

Top Row, Left to Right: "Jack" Green, '80; W. W. Hannan, '80; "Dave" DeTar, '78, Med. '80; C. S. Mitchell, '80; Frank Reed, '80; A. S. Pettit, '79. **Middle Row**: Irving K. Pond, '79; Tom Edwards, '79; John Chase, '79; Charlie Campbell, '80. **Bottom Row**: Collins H. Johnstone, '81; Gay Depuy, '79; Edmund H. Barmore, '82

Members of the first Michigan Intercollegiate Football Team. All except Collins H. Johnstone were in Chicago for the game with Racine College on May 1879. Pettit was substitute and did not get into the game. Touchdown by Pond. Field goal by DeTar.

Photo presented by Irving K. Pond, C. E., Hon., 1911, 1930, designer of the Michigan Union and Michigan League Buildings and of the Student Publications Building. Irving K. Pond, '79 and Allen B. Pond, '80, composed the architectural firm of Pond and Pond, Chicago (A. B. P. died in 1929) which was responsible for the above mentioned buildings.

1897: OHIO STATE TEAM

Front row (left to right): Brophy, Mackey, Leonard, Engensberger, Richards, Stienie, Waite. **Second row:** Purdy, Urban, Captain Hawkins, Saxby, Scott. **Third row:** Butcher, Benedict, Segrist. **Back row:** Culbertson, King, Sykes, Enos, Dyer, Miller, Segrist.

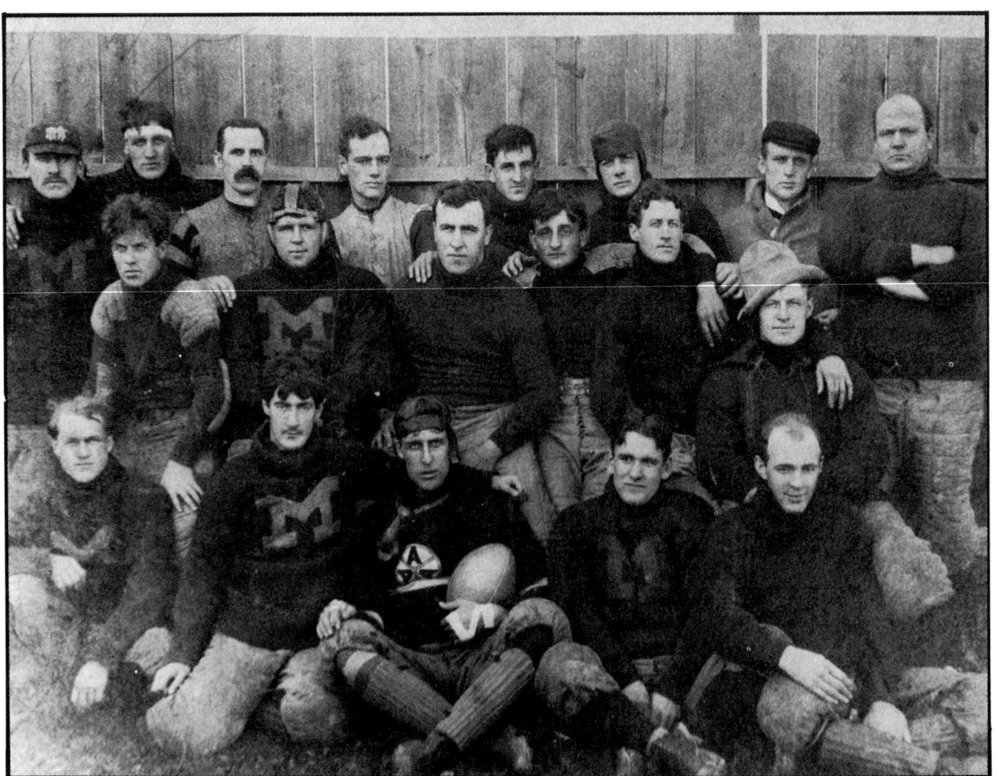

This picture of the 1897 Michigan Team was presented to the authors by The Bentley Historical Library. Unfortunately, the players are unidentified.

A picture is not available of Michigan Head Coach, Gustave Ferbert, 1897-1899.

OHIO

1897

Ohio	6	Ohio Medical	0
Ohio	0	Case	14
Ohio	0	Michigan	34
Ohio	12	Otterbein	12
Ohio	0	Columbus Barracks	6
Ohio	0	Oberlin	44
Ohio	0	W. Virginia	28
Ohio	0	Cincinnati	24
Ohio	0	OH Wesleyan	6

Season Summary

Games Won, 1; Lost, 7; Tied, 1

1898

Ohio	17	Heidelberg	0
Ohio	0	Ohio Medical	10
Ohio	34	Denison	0
Ohio	0	Marietta	10
Ohio	0	Western Reserve	49
Ohio	5	Case	23
Ohio	0	Kenyon	29
Ohio	24	OH Wesleyan	0

Season Summary

Games Won, 3; Lost, 5

1899

Ohio	30	Otterbein	0
Ohio	28	Wittenberg	0
Ohio	5	Case	5
Ohio	41	Ohio University	0
Ohio	6	Oberlin	0
Ohio	6	Western Reserve	0
Ohio	17	Marietta	0
Ohio	12	Ohio Medical	0
Ohio	34	Muskingum	0
Ohio	5	Kenyon	0

Season Summary

Games Won, 9; Lost, 0; Tied, 1

MICHIGAN

1897

Michigan	24	Normal	0
Michigan	0	OH Wesleyan	0
Michigan	36	O.S.U.	0
Michigan	16	Oberlin	6
Michigan	34	Purdue	4
Michigan	14	Minnesota	0
Michigan	34	Wittenberg	0
Michigan	12	Chicago	21
Michigan	0	Varsity Alumni	15

Season Summary

Games Won, 6; Lost, 1; Tied, 1

1898

Michigan	21	Normal	0
Michigan	29	Kenyon	0
Michigan	39	M.A.C.	0
Michigan	18	Western Reserve	0
Michigan	23	Case	5
Michigan	23	Notre Dame	0
Michigan	6	Northwestern	5
Michigan	12	Illinois	5
Michigan	22	Beloit	5
Michigan	12	Chicago	11
Michigan	11	Varsity Alumni	2

Season Summary

Games Won, 10; Lost, 0

1899

Michigan	11	Hillsdale	0
Michigan	26	Albion	0
Michigan	17	Western Reserve	0
Michigan	12	Notre Dame	0
Michigan	5	Illinois	0
Michigan	38	Virginia	0
Michigan	10	Pennsylvania	11
Michigan	28	Case	6
Michigan	24	Kalamazoo	9
Michigan	5	Wisconsin	17
Michigan	0	Varsity Alumni	0

Season Summary

Games Won, 8; Lost, 2

Michigan's First All-American, William Ralph Cunningham 1898, is holding the ball for Neil Snow.

October 16, 1897

Ann Arbor, Michigan

Ohio State University Defeated By Michigan Eleven, 34 To 0

Wolverines Outclass Buckeyes

O.S.U. and the University of Michigan met on Athletic Field and for the first half, the Michigan boys had it all their own way. They completely outclassed the Ohio team scoring six touchdowns, while Hogg kicked five goals, scoring 34 points for Michigan. When play was called, there was a high wind blowing from the west, so Captain Hawkins took that goal, taking advantage of the breeze. Michigan kicked off and downed Saxbe on the 20-yard line. After two ineffectual attempts to gain, Hawkins punted. From that time the ball was in Michigan's possession until the last of the half when OSU got it. After making a good gain by bucking the line, time was called with the ball on OSU's 15-yard line.

The second half was quite different as Michigan put in several subs, and OSU making a brace, held their own. The ball changed hands several times, neither side being able to make a touchdown. The halves were 20 and 15 minutes in length. There was not a bit of slugging or dirty playing on either side. The Michigan team had taken quite a brace, and the work that day was fine, so the Ohio team should not have been too disappointed. The Michigan backs played a nice game, each of the four making nice runs. Those that distinguished their team most were Hogg, Stuart, Pingree, Teetzel, and Bennett. Michigan's line did far better work than they had earlier in the year, while the interference was nearly perfect. OSU, though beaten, was not disgraced and had the reputation of playing clean amateur football. For Ohio, Butcher, Blose, Miller, and Hawkins did the best work. Butcher bucked the line well and tackled nicely, as did Miller and Blose. Hawkins' punting was a feature of the game, as several times he handled bad passes well and sent the ball down into Michigan's territory. Taking all in all, the Ohio boys played well especially in the second half against a Michigan team which was far superior and stronger in the field.

Michigan Team

Name	Pos.	Name	Pos.
J. W. F. Bennett	E	N. B. Ayers	E
C. T. Teetzel	E	W. C. Steckle	T
W. P. Baker	T	R. S. Lockwood	T
C. F. Juttner	T	M. B. Snow	G
J. E. Egan	G	W. H. Caley	G
H. E. Lehr	G	W. R. Cunningham	C
Howard Felver	QB	J. D. Richards	QB
J. R. Hogg	HB	G. D. Stewart	HB
H. S. Pingree, Jr.	HB	C. A. Barabee	HB
F. C. Hannan	FB	L. S. Kenna	FB

Reserves

Kasper, Capt.	Talcott	Savage	Armstrong
Hampton	Thomas	Allen	McLean
Welz	Bain	Moore	Gordon
Marks	Pagelson	Simons	Wickes
Anderson	Kennedy	Richardson	Henry
Bell	Hodgman	Ganshaw	

Ohio Team

Name	Pos.	Name	Pos.
Hawkins, Capt.	FB	Segrist, L. T.	C
Segrist, L. T.	LG	Urban	RG
Miller	RT	Richards	LT
Scott	RE	Waite	LE
Mackey	LT	Saxby	QB
Engensberger	E-RHB	Brophy	LHB
Benedict	T-HB	Purdy	RHB
Butcher	HB	Leonard	E
Dyer	T	King	G
Sykes	T	Culbertson	HB
Steinle	HB	Enos	Mgr.

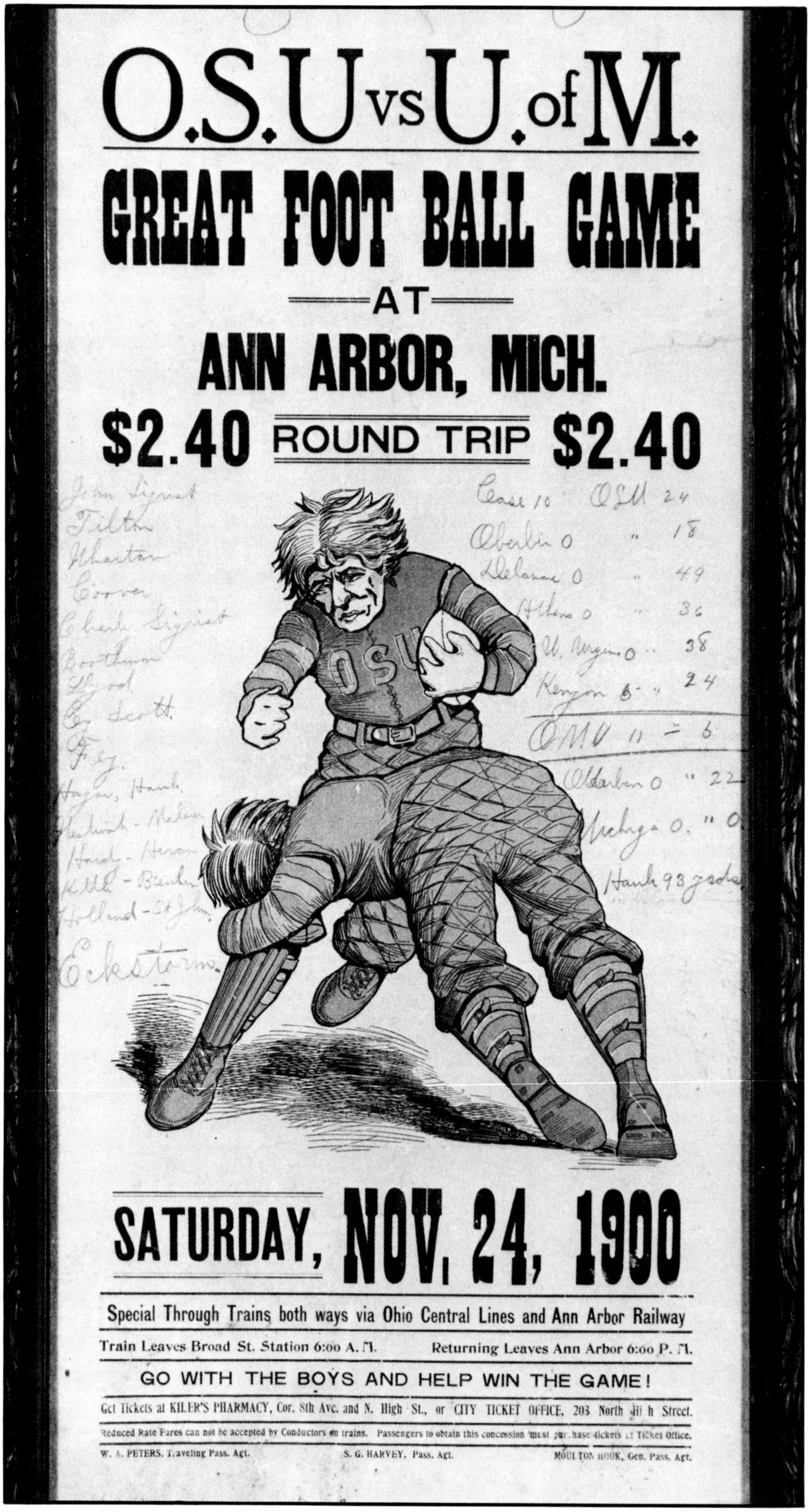

O.S.U vs U. of M.

GREAT FOOT BALL GAME

AT

ANN ARBOR, MICH.

$2.40 ROUND TRIP $2.40

SATURDAY, NOV. 24, 1900

Special Through Trains both ways via Ohio Central Lines and Ann Arbor Railway

Train Leaves Broad St. Station 6:00 A. M. Returning Leaves Ann Arbor 6:00 P. M.

GO WITH THE BOYS AND HELP WIN THE GAME!

Get Tickets at KILER'S PHARMACY, Cor. 8th Ave. and N. High St., or CITY TICKET OFFICE, 203 North High Street.

Reduced Rate Fares can not be accepted by Conductors on trains. Passengers to obtain this concession must purchase tickets at Ticket Office.

W. A. PETERS, Traveling Pass. Agt. S. G. HARVEY, Pass. Agt. MOULTON HOOK, Gen. Pass. Agt.

1900			
Michigan	29	Hillsdale	0
Michigan	11	Kalamazoo	0
Michigan	24	Case	6
Michigan	11	Purdue	6
Michigan	12	Illinois	0
Michigan	12	Indiana	0
Michigan	5	Iowa	28
Michigan	7	Notre Dame	0
Michigan	0	Ohio State	0
Michigan	6	Chicago	15

Season Summary
Games Won, 7; Lost, 2; Tied, 1

1900			
Ohio	20	Otterbein	0
Ohio	20	Ohio U.	0
Ohio	29	Cincinnati	0
Ohio	47	OH Wesleyan	0
Ohio	17	Oberlin	0
Ohio	27	W. Virginia	0
Ohio	24	Case	10
Ohio	6	OH Medical	11
Ohio	0	Michigan	0
Ohio	23	Kenyon	5

Season Summary
Games Won, 8; Lost, 1; Tied, 1

The most successful coach in the early days was Dr. John B. Eckstorm. His teams of 1899-1900-1901 won 22 games, lost only 4, and tied 3. The 1899 team was undefeated but tied Case 5 to 5. It was OSU's first undefeated season, and the next one did not occur until 1916.

Michigan's 1900 Center Trio, King Kelly, Tug Wilson and Barkenbus.

November 24, 1900

Ann Arbor, Michigan

Michigan Played To A Standstill By Ohio State

Fierce Game On Regents' Field Ends In Scoreless Tie

Ohio State played Michigan to a standstill in one of the fiercest games ever played on Regent's Field. Neither team was able to score in two 25-minute halves. The game was played in a driving snowstorm and on a slippery field, which was greatly to the advantage of Michigan's heavy team, but the Ohioans gained more than twice as much ground as their opponents. In the first half the ball was in Michigan territory nearly all the time. In the second half a blocked kick gave Michigan the ball on OSU's seven-yard line, but the Buckeye's defense was too strong to be battered down. About one thousand Columbus people saw the game.

Ohio outplayed the husky Michiganders in all departments of the game save one, and clearly demonstrated their right to a place among the leading elevens of the West. For the first time during the year Michigan was held scoreless. Their powerful line, instructed in the art of charging by that famous coach, Biffy Lee of Princeton, bent back and yielded before the fierce attacks of the Ohio backs. The Buckeye team was helped by the crowd of OSU rooters which lined both sides of the field and cheered continuously. Never before in the history of Ohio State had there been such a demonstration of college spirit. Almost the entire student body was present on Regents' Field when the whistle blew. President Thompson was there and Professors Thomas, Gondy, Magruder, Knight, McPherson, Caldwell, Barrows, Captain Cope, Dr. Linhart and many others. Lots of co-eds, too, made the long trip and added their voices to the deeper notes of the masculine section of the crowd. No such crowd of rooters ever before visited Ann Arbor to cheer a visiting team. The Michigan people were surprised and they expressed their surprise in no measured terms. The streets of the pretty college town were lined with spectators as the visitors marched to the hotel where the team was quartered. The first section of the excursion train arrived in Ann Arbor shortly after 11 o'clock and the second came in 15 minutes later. Then the big crowd, more than 900 strong, and headed to the Cook House, each man anxious to see the players who were to fight for the honor of O.S.U. in the afternoon. The guests held the keys of the city during their stay and the privilege was not abused.

There was very little betting on the game. Michigan followers were far from confident and refused to give anything but even money, while OSU financiers demanded odds. As a result of this difference of opinion, there was little money up, and consequently little had to be taken down after the game was over.

The only long gain made during the game went to the credit of O.S.U. In the first half, after securing the ball on downs on their own 30-yard line, McLaren was sent around the famous end rush, Snow, for a pretty run of 28 yards. He got by everybody but Sweeley and might have gone the length of the field if he had not slipped and fallen. Ohio had carried the ball 60 yards, without losing it, and Michigan was on the wagon. But the eye of Robert Wrenn detected John Segrist in the act of embracing his opponent with both arms, and the ball was given to Michigan for holding. Sweeley promptly punted to the center of the field and Michigan's danger was over.

Michigan's Sweeley controlled the game in the entire second half with his magnificent kicking. Twice Michigan, by tandem plays and line-bucking, carried the ball to the 15-yard line, but each time Ohio rallied and took the ball on downs. The best play of the game was near disaster for the Buckeyes. It was Michigan's ball near the center of the field and Sweeley punted 40 yards. McLaren fumbled the ball, which rolled on toward the goal line. Hardy picked it up and was thrown heavily by Snow just 2 yards from the fatal line. A little more and Michigan would have had a safety.

With the exception of the handling of punts and getting down under them, O.S.U., fairly and squarely, outplayed the former champions of the West. O.S.U. was credited with carrying the ball forward about 136 yards, all told, while the Wolverines gained about 74 yards.

Michigan

No.	Name	Wt.	No.	Name	Wt.
1	Snow	180	2	Weber	170
3	Sweeley	180	4	Begle	165
5	Graver	176	6	Shaw	168
7	Weeks	160	8	Frank	150
9	Wilson	189	10	White, H.	190
11	Sims	185	12	Brookfield	175
13	Kelly	218	14	Bliss	194
15	Sterry	160	16	Shorts	153
17	Redden	185	18	Woodard	180
19	McGinnis	165	20	Brown, H.	230
21	Marks	195	22	Hernstein	175
23	White, M.	176	24	Durant	180
25	Burns	175	26	Walker, W. F.	165
27	Weeks, W.	152	28	Broeseme	220
29	Barkeubus	219	30	Urquhart	160
31	Redner	175	32	Brown	163
33	Hinchs		34	Jones	
35	Engelhard				

Ohio

Name	Pos.	Name	Pos.
Lloyd	E	Coover	T
Wharton	G	Fay	C
Tilton	G	C. Segrist	T
J. Segrist	E	Hardy	QB
Westwater	HB	Hagar	HB
Bulen	FB		

The 'Tally-Ho,' 1901. The Spartan costumes of the gladiators of the gridiron contrast with the correct social attire of the spectators who enjoy the vantage point of the Tally-Ho wagon at the sporting event of the year. This is the University of Michigan's first appearance on old Ohio Field in what was soon to develop into a fierce and classic football rivalry between the Maize and Blue and the Scarlet and Gray. In this first, historic encounter on its home territory, it must be reported, OSU went down to defeat, 21-0." —Text and illustration reprinted from **A Family Album of the Ohio State University, 1870-1970,** a collection of one hundred historic photographs compiled and edited by the Department of Photography and Cinema, and published in observance of the centennial of the founding of the University. Copyright© 1970 by the Ohio State University Press. All rights reserved.

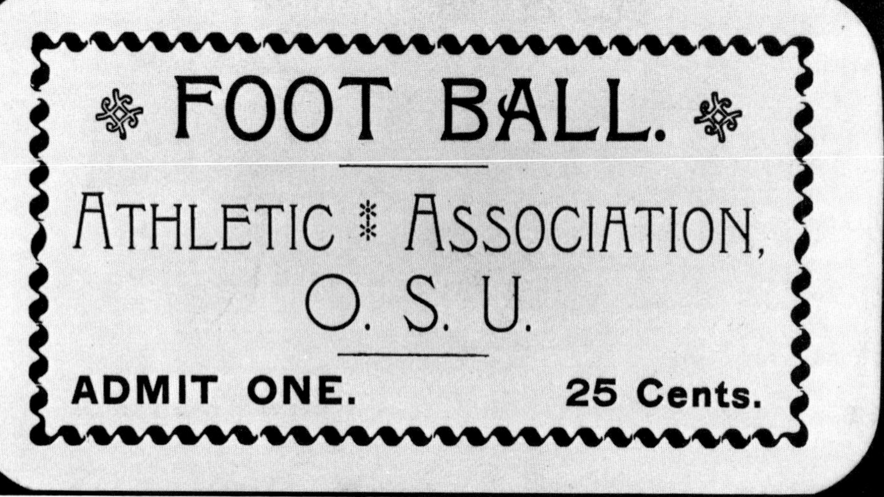

1901

Michigan	50	Albion	0
Michigan	57	Case	0
Michigan	33	Indiana	0
Michigan	29	Northwestern	0
Michigan	128	Buffalo	0
Michigan	22	Carlisle	0
Michigan	21	O.S.U	0
Michigan	22	Chicago	0
Michigan	89	Beloit	0
Michigan	50	Iowa	0
Michigan	49	Leland S. J.	0

Season Summary

Games Won, 11; Lost, 0; Tied, 0

1901

Ohio	0	Otterbein	0
Ohio	30	Wittenberg	0
Ohio	17	OH University	0
Ohio	24	Marietta	0
Ohio	6	Western Reserve	5
Ohio	0	Michigan	21
Ohio	0	Oberlin	6
Ohio	6	Indiana	18
Ohio	11	Kenyon	6

Season Summary

Games Won, 5; Lost, 3; Tied, 1

November 9, 1901

Columbus, Ohio

Michigan Team Defeats Battered Buckeyes

Ohio State Eleven Downed 21-0

Coach Yost of Michigan—"The score would have been twice as large if O.S.U. had not insisted on taking out so much time. With time called after nearly every play, it was practically impossible for our men to show their speed. It was a practice game for Michigan. The defensive work of OSU's Westwater and McLaren was very fine."

Coach Eckstorm of O.S.U.—"The game showed me that I have a team of fighters, and I am very proud of the work of my players. A defeat is a defeat, and I have no excuses to offer. Under the discouraging conditions of the past two weeks, the boys did remarkably well. Michigan did not play so strongly as I had expected, and I think they have been overrated."

The game was frustrating for both teams. Michigan felt hampered by the unusual number of time outs taken by Ohio State which destroyed UM's momentum. Ohio State was suffering from a week without practice and the absence of four good players. As a result Michigan won the game but was limited to the smallest score made by the Ann Arbor eleven in any game that year.

The defense of O.S.U. was superb whenever their goal line was threatened. Four times they held the powerful Michiganders inside the five yard line and secured the ball on downs or fumbles. UM's Sweeley was often forced to punt, and his kicking, interspersed with end runs by Heston, was mainly responsible for the touchdowns. Michigan played an intelligent kicking game, using Sweeley's skill to great advantage. They never attempted to carry the ball the length of the field by rushing, but always punted it into O.S.U. territory and waited until they got possession of it within scoring distance before trying for a touchdown. They proved the great advantage of playing a kicking game when it can be properly done.

For Michigan, Heston was the star ground-gainer. He forced his way past the tackles by main strength and seldom failed to gain, whether he had any interference or not. Snow also did some effective handling of the line and was a power on the end where he played on defense.

The teams were prompt in coming on to the field, Michigan appearing first, 17 strong, at three minutes after 2 o'clock. The O.S.U. squad arrived five minutes later. Then ensued an annoying and entirely unnecessary delay while the coaches and captains wrangled about the length of halves. Eckstorm, scenting defeat for his cripples, wanted only 20 minutes, while Yost held out for the legal time of 35 minutes per half. The O.S.U. leader finally rose to 25, but would go no higher. It took 25 minutes to come to an agreement that halves should be of 30 minute duration.

Nearly 5000 people surrounded the field and enjoyed the struggle. A special from Ann Arbor brought 375 who, with a band at their head, marched on to the field and took seats in the east bleachers. The O.S.U. rooters were in full force, also with a band. The day was perfect for football and all the conditions most excellent for the contest.

1901

Michigan

Name	Pos.	Name	Pos.
Hernstein, Knight	E	Shorts	T
Wilson	G	Gregory	C
McGugin	G	White, Captain	T
Redden	E	Weeks, Graver	QB
Sweeley, Redner	HB	Heston, Shaw	HB
Snow	FB		

Ohio

Name	Pos.	Name	Pos.
Fay	C	Tangeman	G
Riddle	G	Coover	T
Tilton, Westwater	T	Jackson, Hardy	QB
Kittle, Birdseye	FB	McLaren	HB
Diel, Lloyd	HB		

Michigan's Second All-American
NEIL SNOW (End)

Windsprints at Ann Arbor

Harrison Weeks was Michigan's outstanding captain 1901-02.

Perry Hale was OSU head coach in 1902-03, during which his team won 14, lost 5 and tied 2.

1902

Michigan	88	Albion	0
Michigan	48	Case	6
Michigan	119	M.A.C.	0
Michigan	60	Indiana	0
Michigan	23	Notre Dame	0
Michigan	86	O.S.U.	0
Michigan	6	Wisconsin	0
Michigan	107	Iowa	0
Michigan	21	Chicago	0
Michigan	63	Oberlin	0
Michigan	23	Minnesota	6

Season Summary

Games Won, 11; Lost, 0; Tied, 0

1902

Ohio	5	Otterbein	0
Ohio	17	OH University	0
Ohio	30	W. Virginia	0
Ohio	34	Marietta	0
Ohio	0	Michigan	86
Ohio	51	Kenyon	5
Ohio	12	Case	23
Ohio	0	Illinois	0
Ohio	17	OH Wesleyan	16
Ohio	6	Indiana	6

Season Summary

Games Won, 6; Lost 2; Tied, 2

October 25, 1902

Ann Arbor, Michigan

Nothing Left Of Ohio State As Michigan Wins 86-0

Only Once Did The Columbus Players Hold For Downs

Everett Sweeley kicking.

The most pessimistic rooter for the scarlet and gray had looked for nothing worse than a defeat by a margin of four or five touchdowns. But Michigan crossed the Ohio goal line 15 times in 60 minutes of play, averaging a touchdown every four minutes. From all but four of these TD's, goals were kicked. The score at the end of the first half was 45 to 0. Almost as many points were rolled up in the 10 minutes less playing time after the intermission. The final score was 86 to 0, a figure which had seldom been excelled during the previous decade since the method of starting off by kicking the ball instead of by a wedge play, was introduced.

The Buckeyes were outplayed from the start. Outclassed would perhaps be a more accurate way of putting it. Not once during the hour of play did the scarlet and gray eleven have the remotest chance of scoring a point.

On the other hand, there was scarcely a moment when a Michigan gain was not to be expected. Coach Yost's machine tore up and battered down the Ohio line. The heavy forwards got the charge on their opponents and bent back the line like pasteboard, while the backs, behind fast and compact interference, careered around the Ohio wings.

Michigan's star ground-gainer was Heston, the husky left halfback. He ran beautifully with his peculiar galloping stride somewhat like that of Snake Hines and Bum McClurg in the old days. Herrnstein also ran well, particularly in a broken field, and Maddoch plunged for many yards around O.S.U.'s right end.

118 pound Foss was Ohio's only hero. When the rest of the team was displaying terrible tackling, Little Foss was bringing down the mighty Michigan backs. He also handled punts with great nerve and accuracy.

O.S.U.'s McLaren was in poor form and of no use whatsoever to the team. He could make no gains of importance and did nothing on defense. For trying to stamp on a Michigan man's face, apparently hoping to be put out of the game, he was roundly hissed.

Coach Hale of O.S.U.—"Michigan played a faster and more aggressive game than she did against Notre Dame. Her line changed more quickly and carried our boys off their feet. One trouble was that we had not had a hard game to uncover our weak points. I think the officials gave us a little the worst of it on several occasions, which may have affected the score, but, of course, not the result."

Coach Yost of Michigan—"It was scarcely a practice game for us. We couldn't score that many points on our own scrubs if we played four halves of an hour each. O.S.U. showed the poorest form in tackling I have ever seen."

1902

Ohio

lame	Pos.	Name	Pos.
anney	E	Coover	T
incoln	G	Thrower	C
ay	G	Maaker	T
laynard	E	Fess	QB
ill	HB	McLaren	HB
ownshend	FB		

Michigan

lame	Wt.	Name	Wt.
Veeks	158	Heston	174
errnstein	166	Sweeley	164
edden	172	Gregory	189
lcGugin	181	Graver	161
ones	166	Maddock	182
awrence	191	Carter	235
ohnson	178	Forrest	184
ole	168	Gooding	189
idston	166	Dunlop	171
aker	181	Dickey	154
terry	164	Cooley	152
Vill Weeks	142	Drake	161

FIELDING H. YOST
Michigan Head Coach
1901-1923 and 1925-1926

Yost as he is remembered in Ann Arbor, carrying the only piece of equipment he ever needed - a football.

1903

Michigan	31	Case	0
Michigan	79	Beloit	0
Michigan	66	Ohio Northern	0
Michigan	51	Indiana	0
Michigan	88	Ferris Inst.	0
Michigan	47	Drake	0
Michigan	76	Albion	0
Michigan	6	Minnesota	6
Michigan	36	O.S.U.	0
Michigan	16	Wisconsin	0
Michigan	42	Oberlin	0
Michigan	28	Chicago	0

Season Summary

Games Won, 11; Lost, 0; Tied, 1

1903

Ohio	18	Otterbein	0
Ohio	28	Wittenberg	0
Ohio	24	Denison	5
Ohio	30	Muskingum	0
Ohio	59	Kenyon	0
Ohio	0	Case	12
Ohio	34	W. Virginia	6
Ohio	0	Michigan	36
Ohio	27	Oberlin	5
Ohio	29	OH Wesleyan	6
Ohio	16	Indiana	17

Season Summary

Games Won, 8; Lost 3

WILLIAM HESTON
All-American Fullback

November 7, 1903

Ann Arbor, Michigan

Wolverines Win Again, 36-0

Two Entirely Different Halves of Football

The first half of the game on Ferry Field looked like it was going to be a repeat of the previous year as Michigan scored all of its 36 points before the half-time gun sounded. With the discouragement of 36 to 0 staring them in the face, O.S.U. played Michigan to a standstill in the second half.

Once again the lack of a kicking game hurt the Buckeyes. When Ohio had the ball they could not gain and instead of punting, they lost the ball on downs at critical junctures.

In the first half the Michigan offense bulled through Ohio State time after time. Graven, Heston, Redden, Dad Gregory relentlessly bucked and blocked the Ohio eleven.

Graver scored the first of his five touchdowns on a five yard run around left end. Hammond kicked goal and the score was 6 to 0 after only a minute and 20 seconds' play. Graver did it again with a sensational run around his left end and again Hammond was good making the score 12 to 0.

A series of fumbles stalled action as neither team could produce any momentum until Ohio lost the ball on downs on their own 40-yard line. Graver was once again the man of the hour as he circled right end and scored Michigan's third touchdown with Hammond converting to raise the score to 18-0.

Michigan held O.S.U. and forced them to punt. The Wolverines had the ball at mid field. Graver with the able assistance of the rest of the backfield and line ripped off 10 yards through right tackle. On the next play Curtis broke away through the line and ran 40 yards for a touchdown. Hammond kicked the goal moving Michigan ahead 24-0. Graver scored two more TD's, both on end sweeps, and Hammond converted the goals to make the score 36-0.

The second half saw several players switch positions which seemed to benefit Ohio as the Buckeyes had some luck moving the ball against Michigan. The Michigan defense rose to the occasion and repelled the Ohio onslaughts. Ohio had several opportunities to try field goals but passed them up in efforts to score touchdowns.

Coach Yost of Michigan—"You can't expect a team to keep keyed up to concert pitch all the time. The men showed the effects of the Minnesota game. O.S.U. made a fine showing and a better one than I expected. The game was clean and the second half was thoroughly good football."

Coach Hale of Ohio State—"The men did nobly and I am proud of them. The way the rushes of Michigan were stopped in the second half was pleasant to see. We were in great form.

Attendance at the game was 3500.

Michigan

ame	Wt.	Name	Wt.
regory	188	Curtis	197
ooding	187	Maddock	185
ongman	180	C. Redden	178
raver	165	James	142
eston	178	T. Hammond	176
ePree	158	E. Hammond	187
arnett	192	Schulte	187
yke	182	Garrels	178
oty	160	F. Redden	162
ead	158	Wolfe	163
orcross	148	Person	152
. Weeks	162	Thomson	154
igelow	182	Bill Weeks	158
idston	178	Dunlap	172
endell	162	Clark	168
cClure	192	Crawford	178
ingeman	182	Schule	152
dmunds	172	Fulton	168
horts	161		

Ohio

ame	Pos.	Name	Pos.
yde	E	Lincoln	T
unington	G	Powell	C
ilts	G	Thrower	T
alker	E	Foss	QB
ones	HB	Marker	HB
awrence	FB		

O.S.U. Crosses Michigan Line

SOME INCIDENTS OF THE GAME

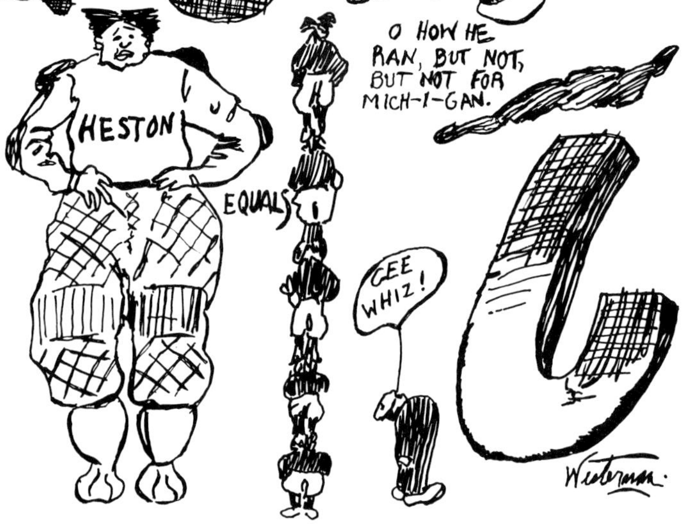

CASE
WHAT AM I UP AGAINST?
O.S.U.
MICH
MARQUARDT
SHE'S YOURS.
EARTH
MICHIGAN O.S.U. SCORE
O.S.U.
O HOW HE RAN, BUT NOT, BUT NOT FOR MICH-I-GAN.
HESTON
EQUALS
GEE WHIZ!

E. R. SWEETLAND
OSU Coach 1904-05

1904			
Ohio	34	Otterbein	0
Ohio	80	Miami	0
Ohio	24	Denison	0
Ohio	46	Muskingum	0
Ohio	6	Michigan	31
Ohio	16	Case	6
Ohio	0	Indiana	8
Ohio	0	Illinois	46
Ohio	2	Oberlin	4
Ohio	11	Kenyon	5
Ohio	0	Carlisle	23

Season Summary

Games Won, 6; Lost, 5

1904			
Michigan	33	Case	0
Michigan	48	O. Northern	0
Michigan	95	Kalamazoo	0
Michigan	72	P & S	0
Michigan	31	O.S.U.	6
Michigan	72	Am. Col M & S.	0
Michigan	130	W. Virginia	0
Michigan	28	Wisconsin	0
Michigan	36	Drake	4
Michigan	22	Chicago	12

Season Summary

Games Won, 10; Lost, 0; Tied, 0

WILLIAM HESTON
All-American Halfback

October 15, 1904

Columbus, Ohio

Michigan Downs Ohio State, 31 To 6

Heston and Norcross of UM Star In The Closing Moments Of Play

For a while it seemed that the Buckeyes had a chance. Ohio actually led by one point at one time during the struggle. But the Wolverines were not to be denied as they came roaring back to smother the Ohio contingent 31 to 6.

Michigan's forwards were splendid chargers since only once did the O.S.U. team make a first down. Generally the Ohio backs went down for small losses. The inability to gain ground forced Ohio's Jackson to try his luck at punting. His first effort went up in the air and Michigan gained two yards as a result of that fluke.

All interest of the first half centered on the last ditch stands made by Ohio when Michigan threatened their goal. The first Michigan series was stalled on Ohio's five-yard line.

Michigan finally got started again on the 50-yard line. Heston was worked when it was necessary to gain the distance and in 24 minutes of play Harry Hammond was shoved over the line. Tom Hammond missed the goal and the score was Michigan 5, Ohio State 0 at half time.

With Michigan in possession at the start of the second half the big break for Ohio occurred. Michigan's Longman was sent into the line. He fumbled the ball and it rolled out of the swirling mass into the arms of Marquardt of Ohio. In a flash the long fullback was off for the Michigan goal line. His touchdown tied the score and Hoyer's accurate work in kicking the goal put Ohio State ahead 6 to 5.

About six minutes later, during which time Longman had been disqualified for fighting with Jackson, Heston went over for Michigan's second touchdown. Tom Hammond kicked the goal giving the lead back to Michigan 11 to 6.

Tom Hammond added a 31 yard field goal moments later after Michigan had gained excellent field position. An exciting punt return by Heston set up another Hammond field goal. This time from 18 yards out making the score 19 to 6 in Michigan's favor.

Norcross and Heston provided the leg work for the next touchdown. A penalty against Ohio's Jackson for fighting caused his ejection from the game and moved the ball in close where Heston easily bulled over. Heston added the goal making the score a rout 25 to 6.

Michigan scored one last time on long runs by Norcross, McGoffin, and Heston who covered the small yardage remaining for the score and Hammond was good again making the final score 31 to 6.

One of Yost's early "Wonder" teams, 1904.

OHIO ROSTER

Name	Pos.	Name	Pos.
Walters	LE	Gill	LT
Clark	LG	Dunsford	LG
Hoyer	C	Diltz	RG
Marker	RT	Curran	RT
Remsnyder	RE	Thrower	QB
Jones	QB	Swan	LHB
Carver	LHB	Warwick	LHB
Marquardt	FB	Schory	FB

MICHIGAN ROSTER

Name	Pos.	Name	Pos.
Schulz	C	Schulte	G
Carter	G	Curtis	T
Graham	T	Clarke	E
H. Hammond	E	Weeks	E-HB
Stuart	E-HB	T. Hammond	HB
Heston	HB	Norcross	QB
Longman	FB		

1904

Center Germany Schultz, far left, leads the Michigan backfield through a drill as quarterback Fred Norcross hands off to Tom Hammond.

1905

Michigan	65	OH Wesleyan	0
Michigan	44	Kalamazoo	0
Michigan	36	Case	0
Michigan	23	OH Northern	0
Michigan	18	Vanderbilt	0
Michigan	31	Nebraska	0
Michigan	70	Albion	0
Michigan	48	Drake	0
Michigan	33	Illinois	0
Michigan	40	O.S.U.	0
Michigan	12	Wisconsin	0
Michigan	75	Oberlin	0
Michigan	0	Chicago	2

Season Summary

Games Won, 12; Lost, 1; Tied, 0

1905

Ohio	6	Otterbein	6
Ohio	28	Heidelberg	0
Ohio	40	Muskingum	0
Ohio	17	Wittenberg	0
Ohio	2	Denison	0
Ohio	32	DePauw	6
Ohio	0	Case	0
Ohio	23	Kenyon	0
Ohio	0	Michigan	40
Ohio	36	Oberlin	0
Ohio	15	Wooster	0
Ohio	0	Indiana	11

Season Summary

Games Won, 8; Lost, 2; Tied, 2

Michigan

Name	Wt.	Name	Wt.
Norcross	154	Longman	187
Curtis	218	T. Hammond	185
Schulte	194	Schultz	192
Graham	234	H. Hammond	180
Clark	184	H. Weeks	160
Stuart	161	Magoffin	160
Garrels	183	Dunlap	180
Love	190	Patrick	180
Pierce	178	Chandler	175
Rheinschilds	183	Miller	187
Rumney	160	Newton	175
Doty	157	Eyke	180
Workman	150	Clement	180
Barlow	145	Kanaga	165
Van Ness	180	Embs	172
Bartlett	158	Work	162

Ohio

Name	Pos.	Name	Pos.
eemsnyder	E	Brindle	T
unsford	G	Hoyer	C
effleman	G	Woodbury	T
eonard	E	Barrington	QB
tolp	HB	Kirby	HB
chory	FB		

November 11, 1905

Ann Arbor, Michigan

Michigan Scores 40, Ohio State 0

Long Run Of 110 Yards By Barlow Excites Crowd

Spectacular play featured the game from start to finish. Michigan's maize and blue machine was in fine form as its linemen opened up yawning gaps in the Ohio line and sent some 200 pounds of beef shooting through for 6, 8, 10, or 12 yards at a crack. Ohio's offense looked good at times, plowing up the sod and Yost's line for good gains.

Michigan scored their first touchdown on an Ohio miscue. The Wolverines had threatened to score, but the Buckeyes held. Ohio could not move and Kirby dropped back to punt. Michigan's Curtiss got through and blocked the kick. Curtiss, Hammond, and Jones mixed it up in association tactics, booting the ball from one to another until Curtiss fell across the line on the ball. Hammond kicked goal for a 6-0 lead.

Ohio's next series moved the ball to Michigan's 25-yard line with Lincoln and Kirby and Stolp doing the running. The drive stalled when Lincoln fumbled and Michigan's Garrells recovered. That was as close as the Buckeyes could come the entire game.

From their own 25 Michigan began a drive that did not end until Embs made the final yard for the score. Curtiss and Hammond did much of the running during the march. Curtiss kicked the goal, while the Michigan band played "O, Ain't It Great."

Shortly thereafter Michigan crossed Ohio's goal again on a 38-yard end sweep by Garrells. Once again the lack of a good kicking game had given Michigan excellent field position. Hammond kicked goal for an 18-0 half-time lead.

The start of the second half saw the ball exchanged hands when neither team could move. Michigan then began a long, steady march with gains varying from 1 to 8 yards. With both bands playing "Wahoo" and the bleachers singing different tunes, Ohio took a stone wall brace on their 2-yard line. Clark and Embs gained nothing, but Curtiss cleared the line by inches. Hammond kicked goal at 12 minutes into the second half.

Curtiss blocked another Ohio punt with Clarke falling on the ball. Clarke made a first down and Steward 4, but Curtiss lost and Hammond fell back to the 19-yard line for a place kick which he made. Score 28-0.

Ohio's Leonard attempted a drop kick from about 35 yards out. The field goal was not good but the ball traveled over the line where Michigan's Barlow caught the ball. State was bunched on the edge of the field. Barlow shot to the right, cleared the entire Ohio team in the most spectacular 110-yard run of the season on Ferry Field and fell exhausted behind the goal posts. Hammond kicked goal making the score 34-0.

Garrells added the final TD when he broke outside of tackle, shook off 5 tacklers, ran 40 yards, and added 5 points to the score. Hammond kicked goal which made the final score 40-0.

A. E. Herrnstein
Ohio State Coach 1906-09

1906

Ohio	41	Otterbein	0
Ohio	52	Wittenberg	0
Ohio	16	Muskingum	0
Ohio	0	Michigan	6
Ohio	6	Oberlin	0
Ohio	6	Kenyon	0
Ohio	9	Case	0
Ohio	12	Wooster	0
Ohio	11	OH Medical	8

Season Summary

Games Won, 8; Lost, 1

1906

Michigan	28	Case	0
Michigan	6	O.S.U.	0
Michigan	28	Illinois	9
Michigan	10	Vanderbilt	4
Michigan	0	Pennsylvania	17
Michigan	0	Varsity Alumni	0

Season Summary

Games Won, 4; Lost, 1; Tied, 0

Ohio

ame	Wt.	Hgt.	Age
laflin	153	5-7	19
incoln	190	6-2	23
aurence	180	5-10	23
heldon	175	5-10	22
illie	189	6-3	24
chory	183	6-1	21
arr	165	5-9	20
arrington	145	5-7	19
ibson	168	6-0	19
racy	170	6-0	20
tolp	170	5-11	20
cDonald	160	5-11	19
verage	170 2/3	5-11	20 3/4

Michigan

ame	Pos.	Name	Pos.
S. Curtis	T	W. L. Eyke	G-T
D. Graham	G	C. H. Clement	C
C. Garrels	FB	F. R. Newton	E-T
P. Magoffin	HB	H. A. Workman	QB
S. Hammond	E	M. P. Rumney	HB
E. Patrick	T	S. J. Davison	G
L. Loell	C-E-T	H. S. Bishop	QB-HB

October 20, 1906

Columbus, Ohio

Michigan Stops Ohio State 6-0

Mighty Michigan Unable To Cross Ohio's Goal Line

Michigan could not cross the goal line which Ohio State's varsity team defended for one solid hour. Six thousand people saw the Wolverines fail to score a touchdown on the Buckeye eleven and yet Yost's proteges won 6 points to 0. No points were scored until the final four minutes of the game.

Johnny Garrels of Michigan booted a thirty-five yard field goal which gave the Wolverines the upper hand just in the nick of time. Misfortune and slow thinking by Ohio caused two more points to be credited to the Michigan account. After the Garrels' goal from placement, he kicked the ball into Ohio State's possession and but fifteen yards from her last line. Because of a replacement at the center position, Claggett for Lawrence, the ball was snapped over Gibson's head. Instead of coming out into fair territory and availing himself of another chance to kick, the fullback downed himself behind his own line and thus without the hand of a Michigan man being laid upon him, made the safety that gave the Wolverines the final one-third of her half dozen points.

The fight waged at "U" field was between the gamest team Ohio State had had in years on one side and the greenest eleven Yost had ever fetched into the Buckeye capital.

Although Michigan won the game, the Ohio rooters howled with glee to see a Michigan team actually being thrown for losses. To be sure it was unusual considering the complete Michigan domination displayed by the previous Wolverine teams.

During the interim between halves, Michigan shouters sat silent but quite confident. The final period of play started and although O.S.U.'s offense was gone, the defense was still there. UM's quarterback Bishop tried all the plays at his command but the OSU eleven held. When the halt was called at the 25-yard line and Garrels dropped back, the Michigan rooters arose en masse to cheer for success. He made good and the UM fans tore loose. Victory over such a worthy rival as Ohio State was sweet to the delegation from Ann Arbor.

1906

Ohio Field

1907

Michigan		Opponent	
Michigan	9	Case	0
Michigan	46	M.A.C.	0
Michigan	22	Wabash	0
Michigan	22	O.S.U.	0
Michigan	8	Vanderbilt	0
Michigan	0	Pennsylvania	6

Season Summary

Games Won, 5; Lost, 1; Tied, 0

1907

Ohio		Opponent	
Ohio	28	Otterbein	0
Ohio	16	Muskingum	0
Ohio	28	Denison	0
Ohio	6	Wooster	6
Ohio	0	Michigan	22
Ohio	12	Kenyon	0
Ohio	22	Oberlin	10
Ohio	9	Case	11
Ohio	23	Heidelberg	0
Ohio	16	OH Wesleyan	0

Season Summary

Games Won, 7; Lost, 2; Tied, 1

ADOLPH GERMANY SCHULTZ
All-American Center

October 26, 1907

Ann Arbor, Michigan

Wolverines Make Four Trips Over Ohio State Line

Forward Passes Work Twice In Second Half For UM

YOST, 1907

When the annual contest between Ohio State and Michigan ended at Ferry Field, the Wolverines were victorious over the Buckeyes by a score of 22-0.

The Ohio State rooters who numbered 965 had a great time in Ann Arbor town. When the field was reached, the best of feeling prevailed. Yells and cheers were exchanged across the field, Ohio cheered for the Wolverines and Michigan cheered for the Buckeyes.

Luck favored O.S.U. at the beginning of the game. Michigan supporters were treated to a great period of apprehension in the following 26 minutes, for that is the length of time it took for the first UM touchdown.

Michigan's Graham tried to break the ice with a field goal, but he couldn't turn the trick. "Octy" was not a bit successful on the kicks for he fell down on four chances. Allerdice, who succeeded him, also missed several attempts.

It was straight football that Michigan used in the first half with the three backs and tackle Rheinschild carrying the ball. "Rheiny" was the real goods as an advancer, but O.S.U.'s Gibson stopped him many times later in the game.

Michigan scored its first touchdown on a sustained march after a Buckeye punt. A forward pass to Rheinschild made 15. He bucked for 11 more. Douglas made seven, and the ex DePauw player made a first down on State's 10-yard line. Magoffin made a yard. On second down Loell went through the hole Schulz opened for a touchdown. Graham kicked goal.

In the second half Michigan marched 45 yards for their second TD. O.S.U.'s Gibson punted to Douglas on State's 50-yard line and he returned 15, but was penalized for hurdling, bringing the ball to Ohio's 45-yard line. Magoffin was dumped by Secrest for a loss of 4. A forward pass to Rheinschild gained 15. A fake place kick which ended in a forward pass to Magoffin was caught by the captain on the 25 yard line from where he ran for a touchdown. Graham missed the goal.

Michigan scored the final touchdown following a Gibson punt which UM's Wasmund returned 20 yards. Allerdice made four. Sullivan couldn't gain. Allerdice got off an onside kick from the 46-yard line that Michigan's Runney recovered on the 12-yard line. "Rheiny" made six yards and then went the necessary distance to the line. Allerdice missed goal. That ended the scoring for the day. The final score remained Michigan 22, Ohio State 0.

1907

Michigan

Name	**Pos.**
P. P. Magoffin	HB
D. W. Allerdice	HB
Jas. K. Watkins	FB
J. L. Loell	FB
Wm. Wasmund	QB
Adolph Schulz	C
Wm. Embs	G
Wm. M. Casey	T
M. P. Rumney	E
W. D. Graham	G
W. M. Rheinschild	T
Harry Hammond	E

Ohio

Name	**Pos.**
Claflin	E
McAllister	T
Schachtel	G
Clagget	C
Sanzenbacher	G
Schory	T
Carr	T
Barrington	QB
Secrist	HB
Bryce	HB
Gibson	FB

"HERRNIE"

The 1908 Football Season and its Greater Significance to Ohio State

The results of the games throughout the 1908 football season were to a very great extent unexpected. The average observer, looking over the heavy schedule at the beginning of the season, would never have predicted that State would lose the games that were lost, and would scarcely have expected the Varsity to make her most creditable showing against Michigan and Vanderbilt instead of against her natural enemies here in Ohio.

The unexpected reverses in the early part of the season tested to the limit the spirit of the team and its followers; and it was the grit of the boys on the field and the loyalty of the boys in the bleachers that made possible our unlooked for victories.

In our Michigan game, when Gibson started on his long trip to Michigan's goal, he was apparently stopped several times, but shook himself free on each occasion, and went through the entire Michigan team for a touchdown. In the Vanderbilt game, after several substitutions had been made, including that of Jones for Captain Barrington, Vanderbilt expected to more than gain back the ground that they had lost, — the score standing 11 to 6 against them. They had not reckoned with our Tommie, however. In the briefest space of time, while the umpire's whistle was blowing for a foul committed by Vanderbilt, taking advantage of a slight hesitancy on the part of the other team, Tommie carried the ball from well out in the field to within one yard of their goal, and soon converted this gain into a touchdown, bringing certain victory to Ohio State.

"RUBE" SCHORY

These unexpected results, brought about by the fighting spirit of the team, made a success of that part of the season's work which we want to remember. Our victory over Vanderbilt, our fine showing against Michigan, and the complete blotting out of the good records of Oberlin and Kenyon established us in a high position in the football world. The brilliant climax of the season has probably wiped out all recollection of the early reverses from the minds of the rooters, although it still remains in the hearts of the coaches and players. Of the results of the Michigan, Vanderbilt, Oberlin, and Kenyon games we can be justly proud; and of the rest of the season, the least said the better. The unexpected reverses taught us to take our defeats with courage, and our unexpected success in the other games taught us to take our victories with modesty.

At home, — here within the University circle, — we had throughout the season the one thing which every rooter, player, captain, manager, and coach of every university team in the country wishes for most, especially in the moments of saddest defeat, — a perfect demonstration of loyalty, which came direct from the SPIRIT of the men and women of the University.

The granting of a half-holiday by the president and faculty of this university, the co-operation of the Athletic Board, the presence of nearly 1,000 students in the line of the snake dance from the University to the Union Station, on the afternoon the team left Columbus for Nashville to play Vanderbilt, will always stand as a record for Spirit. That display of loyalty and enthusiasm in the face of defeat and adverse conditions has never been equaled anywhere, and can always be pointed to as a standard which future rooters should strive to live up to.

Next year we are going to have a hard row to hoe; but with that spirit always possessing the minds and hearts of all University men, victory should be the only result of our efforts.

1908

Michigan	16	Case	6
Michigan	0	M.A.C.	0
Michigan	12	Notre Dame	6
Michigan	10	O.S.U.	6
Michigan	24	Vanderbilt	6
Michigan	62	Kentucky	0
Michigan	0	Pennsylvania	29
Michigan	4	Syracuse	28

Season Summary

Games Won, 5; Lost, 2; Tied, 1

1908

Ohio	18	Otterbein	0
Ohio	0	Wooster	8
Ohio	16	Denison	2
Ohio	0	West. Reserve	18
Ohio	6	Michigan	10
Ohio	20	OH Wesleyan	9
Ohio	8	Case	18
Ohio	17	Vanderbilt	6
Ohio	14	Oberlin	12
Ohio	19	Kenyon	9

Season Summary

Games Won, 6; Lost, 4

October 24, 1908

Columbus, Ohio

Michigan Beats Ohio State 10-6

Ranney's Receipt of Wasmund's Forward Pass Pulls Yost's Team Out Of Hole

Michigan

Name	Pos.	Name	Pos.
Embs	E	Casey	T
Primeau	G	Schultz	C
Brennan	C	Benbrook	G
Crumpacker	T	Ranney-Lillie	E
Wasmund	QB	Douglas-Green	HB
Allerdice	HB	Davidson	FB

Ohio

Name	Pos.	Name	Pos.
Clark	E	Schactel	T
McAllister	G	Wetzel	C
Sanzenbacher	G	Powell	T
Jones-Bachman	E	Barrington-Jones	QB
Wells-Funkhouser	HB	Eberle	HB
Gibson	FB		

Columbus had her portion of Saturday's football unexpectedness as Michigan had to extend herself to win 10 to 6. Although the Buckeyes lost one more to the Wolverines, the Ohio State fans thoroughly enjoyed the 75 yard touchdown run of Millard Gibson, the Buckeye fullback. It was only the second time in nine years that Ohio State had been able to cross Michigan's goal line. Barrington added a point by a goal kick.

Michigan had scored the first points of the game on a 35-yard field goal by Allerdice moments before Gibson's run. There was no more scoring before the half ended, so Ohio carried a 6-4 lead into the second half.

Michigan's play in the second half improved. Allerdice was able to make a couple of efforts at shoving his team ahead by the field goal route. Since these efforts failed as did line plunging, another scheme was tried as a last resort. A forward pass from a kicking formation won the game.

Wasmund hurled the ball some 35 yards through the air to Rammey. Unfortunately for Ohio, there was no defender to bowl him over and cause the ball to hit the ground as had been the case half a dozen times previously. Rammey made his catch cleanly. Whirling, he ran 15 yards before Wells laid him low with the Ohio line within reach less than five yards away. One plunge was not enough, but Allerdice, on the second, went over for the winning score. He also kicked the goal.

Michigan had been expected to prance to an easy victory over an Ohio State team that seemed rusty as a result of the earlier Western Reserve disaster. Ohio had no offensive attack outside Gibson's run, but the defense performed brilliantly most of the game.

Michigan's line had first half problems as there were numerous penalties called for illegal hand use. The second half showed improved line play and was the ultimate formula for victory.

FOOTBALL

In reviewing the football season just past, many facts are obvious, the summarization of which, on the whole, give a satisfactory conclusion. Football at Ohio State, as in most of the larger colleges, over towers all other sports in importance and, coming as it does, at a time when the students have returned for the year, full of enthusiasm, Ohio Field becomes a mecca every Saturday for practically the whole college, the effects of which are never really lost before another year rolls around.

Looking at it, however, from the point of view of the man to whom victory is the all-important thing, the past season was only one of moderate success. One must admit that the two most important Ohio games were lost, yet the splendid victory over Vanderbilt, to a certain degree, atoned for those reverses. The men from whom Herrnstein had to select his team were what the "up-state" papers characterized as "a bunch of recruits," and, in a sense, that was undoubtedly true. These men, however, were whipped into a team that was at all times a factor in the race for state honors. Every team of any importance in the state was successfully defeated until the Case game, when on a slippery field the Scientists won undisputed claim to the Trophy Cup. Two out of the three remaining games were victories. The other was the defeat at Oberlin, but the team came back to true form on Thanksgiving Day and gave Kenyon one of the worst drubbings of the year. Among many, at least two things were demonstrated conclusively last fall. In the first place, it became evident that a change was needed in our playing schedule. for we had arrived at the point where we should drop most of the Ohio teams and fill these dates with out of state elevens, or confine our schedule to the colleges within the state. The time was evidently not at hand, in view of the unsettled championship of the last two years, to take the former step, and as a consequence, the latter has been adopted in its entirety. Our schedule for the coming season includes but one out of state game. At present this is commendable, but the time is at hand when finally demonstrating our superiority by one of possibly two championship teams, we shall step out into a broader field and make Ohio State the great Middle Western football power that everyone feels she should be—that everyone knows she can be.

In the second place, no one that witnessed such examples of college spirit as were displayed last fall on more than one occasion, both on the field and from the stands, can but realize that Ohio State has a new fighting spirit. For this we are greatly indebted to the man who, for the past four years has been our coach, and who in all places, at all times, in defeat as well as in victory, has stood for high athletic ideals and absolutely clean sport. This year ends Coach Herrnstein's engagement at Ohio State and the coming season will see the Eastern style of coaching inaugurated. Extremely fortunate, it seems, has the Atheltic Board been in securing as Mr. Herrnstein's successor, Mr. Jones, head coach at Yale last season, who will be assisted by Mr. Farrell, present track coach, in the capacity of trainer, and by Mr. Welch, of Ohio Wesleyan, who will have charge of the new men. The outlook for next fall is bright and it must be admitted, that barring none but the very impossible, Howard Jones will give Ohio State one of the very best teams in her history.

1909

Michigan	3	Case	0
Michigan	33	O.S.U.	6
Michigan	6	Marquette	5
Michigan	44	Syracuse	0
Michigan	3	Notre Dame	11
Michigan	12	Pennsylvania	6
Michigan	15	Minnesota	6

Season Summary

Games Won, 6; Lost, 1; Tied, 0

1909

Ohio	14	Otterbein	0
Ohio	39	Wittenberg	0
Ohio	74	Wooster	0
Ohio	6	Michigan	33
Ohio	29	Denison	0
Ohio	21	OH Wesleyan	6
Ohio	3	Case	11
Ohio	5	Vanderbilt	0
Ohio	6	Oberlin	26
Ohio	22	Kenyon	0

Season Summary

Games Won, 7; Lost, 3

ALBERT BENBROOK
All-American Guard

Artwork from OSU Programs 1909

October 16, 1909

Ann Arbor, Michigan

Michigan Rolls For 33 to Beat Buckeyes

Allerdice Stars For Wolverines

Captain Allerdice of the Michigan Wolverines was largely responsible for the defeat of the visiting Buckeyes. During the game he negotiated successfully three field goals and two showy 40-yard runs through a broken field which made two more touchdowns possible. Lawton, Freeney, and Wells shared Michigan's honor with the captain.

Wells, Jones, and Hatfield did the bulk of the brilliant work for the Buckeyes and, by their fast field work and excellent interference, kept the goal line of Yost's men in constant danger throughout the greater part of the game.

Before the game the sun went behind the clouds and a cold drizzle began to fall. This change in the weather kept hundreds of local fans at home and, as a consequence, the Michigan rooters were nearly outnumbered by the supporters of Herrnstein's men. Time and time again the rooting of the visiting enthusiasts called forth applause from the stands of yellow and blue.

Early in the game after an exchange of punts and two line plays by Lawton and Freeney, Michigan lost the ball to Ohio on the Buckeyes' 20-yard line. Wells dropped back to punt out of danger. McCarthy made a miserable pass, heaving the ball over the kicker's head, and Wells of Michigan fell on it. With but 10 yards to go, Michigan's backfield tore through the line for small but consistent gains and Lawton went over for the first touchdown. Allerdice kicked goal for a 6-0 lead.

After a fumble by O.S.U.'s Wells, Michigan marched for their second score. Wells of Michigan gained several yards, then Lawton made a first down. On the next play from a left shift play, Allerdice ran 40 yards through Hall for a touchdown. This second count came 10 minutes after the kickoff, and with the goal which Allerdice made, made the score Michigan 12; Ohio State, 0.

After an unsuccessful onside kick attempt, Wells recovered for Michigan in Ohio territory. A moment later Allerdice kicked a field goal which made the score 15 to 0.

Allerdice kicked off to O.S.U.'s Eberle and the ball was returned 10 yards. Jones put an onside kick through with Powell recovering. The ball went over to the Wolverines on downs. Lawton gained four with Freeney adding six more. Allerdice plunged three and followed this up with a spurt from O.S.U.'s 38-yard line to a point three yards from the goal line. Lawton carried the ball over for a touchdown on the second try. The PAT was good and the half ended with Michigan in front 21-0.

The second half opened with a rush and, after a few minutes of play, the Wolverines had carried the ball to within striking distance and Allerdice made his second field goal.

Lawton's knee began to trouble him and he gave way to Clark who put new life into his teammates. He scooted for 10 then 15 yards. After a fumble and an aborted onside kick, Michigan had the ball on Ohio's 20-yard line. Watkins made a hole through center for Clark and Freeney completed the necessary gain for a touchdown. That score gave Michigan 30 points.

Ohio then scored its 6 points when a punt sailed over the head of UM's Freeney who was playing defensive quarter. He appeared too exhausted to follow the ball and O.S.U.'s Boon fell on it for a touchdown.

During the last three minutes of play Clark, Magidsohn, and Allerdice brought the ball to Ohio's 30-yard line on successive end runs and line bucks and from there Captain Allerdice completed a great day's game by kicking his third field goal. Final score for the day was Michigan 33, Ohio State 6.

OHIO

No.	Name	Pos.	No.	Name	Pos.
10	Summeers	E	14	Gease	E
8	Powell	T	17	McClain	T
6	Portz	G	19	Olds	G
5	McCarty	C	19	Olds	C
7	Parmelee	G	15	Boesel	G
22	Geib	G	9	Perry	T
11	Bachman	E	18	Wright	E
20	Beatty	E	1	Jones	QB
12	Hines	QB	13	Schaffer	QB
2	Wells	HB	12	Hines	HB
3	Hatfield	HB	17	McClain	HB
4	Eberle	FB	16	Cox	FB
21	Schieber	FB			

MICHIGAN

Name	Pos.	Name	Pos.
Rogers	E	Edmunds	T
Benbrook	G	Watkins	C
Smith	G	Wells	T
Borleske	E	Wasmund	QB
Magidsohn	HB	Freeney	HB
Allerdice, Capt.	HB	Lawton	FB

1910

Ohio	14	Otterbein	5
Ohio	62	Wittenberg	0
Ohio	23	Cincinnati	0
Ohio	6	West. Reserve	0
Ohio	3	Michigan	3
Ohio	5	Denison	5
Ohio	10	Case	14
Ohio	6	OH Wesleyan	0
Ohio	0	Oberlin	0
Ohio	53	Kenyon	0

Season Summary

Games Won, 6; Lost, 1; Tied 3

1910

Michigan	3	Case	3
Michigan	6	M.A.C.	3
Michigan	3	O.S.U.	3
Michigan	11	Syracuse	0
Michigan	0	Pennsylvania	0
Michigan	6	Minnesota	0

Season Summary

Games Won, 3; Lost, 0; Tied, 3

Coach Howard Jones came to OSU in 1910. He later coached at Iowa, Duke and Southern California.

ALBERT BENBROOK
All-American Guard

STANFIELD WELLS
All-American End

October 22, 1910

Columbus, Ohio

Ohio State, Michigan Tie, 3-3

Conklin of UM and Wells of O.S.U. Boot Field Goals

Daring and determination, set upon a foundation of football skill, had its proper reward at Ohio Field where Ohio State played the Michigan eleven even, three to three.

Both scoring feats were performed in the second period of the first half. With these eliminated, the game resolved itself into a punting frolic and repeated failures of Michigan eleven to get a sturdy runner loose by use of the forward pass. All the way through Ohio was on the defense, a successful one, through the ability of players to link together when necessary or do individual work at the proper time.

If one without knowing the home of either eleven, was to pick, after having seen them pass in review, he would certainly select the Michigan eleven as the one to run for him. Beside the Wolverines, the Buckeyes looked somewhat out of place in their tattered togs, but beneath the surface there was spirit of the right sort.

By having more power generally in her backfield where Thompson and Magidsohn were best, the Michigan eleven was able to sweep along with the goal line some distance away. Just once was the Ann Arbor line able to crush Ohio's forwards, and from the result, that flash of attack did not carry clear through. It did lead up to Conklin's placement success, however.

Thompson, about whom the Michigan system of attack centered, punted well and faked for gains. He had little success when it came to making forward passes, either having too much power behind the heave or else not being able to toss to a teammate out in the open. Ohio players were thick about Michigan ends and backs whenever they were into the clear.

Complacency that came with the wind-up of the first period was routed by Ohio fear almost instantly after the second installment was underway. An exchange of kicks started it off and then Michigan began to march from Ohio's 50-yard line. Snaps into the tackles or outside them brought consistent five yard gains. After three first downs had been secured, Michigan was some 15 yards from a touchdown. Like a life line was the rush of O.S.U.'s Powell upon the powerful Magidsohn as the big Michigander tried to skirt Ohio's left wing. He lost some yardage and Michigan was penalized for being offside. A forward pass went through, but not as good as desired. Finally Conklin was forced to the placement attempt and there was no doubt about the success he achieved. Michigan 3, Ohio State, 0.

Shortly thereafter, due to a free ball recovery and some punting equal to that of Michigan, and Ohio State's Wells and Egbert gaining some valuable yardage, the Buckeyes were threatening Michigan. With a spur of the moment decision, Wells faded back and drop-kicked the ball through to tie the score at 3-3.

In the third period Ohio outplayed Michigan but could not score. When the fourth period began, Ohio knew their work was cut out for them as Michigan tried desperately to score. Using forward passes, end sweeps, and line bucks, the Wolverines battled valiantly, but the Ohio defense withstood the onslaught and preserved the tie.

Ohio State Line-Up

ame	Pos.	Name	Pos.
eaty	E	Sheiber	E
eat	E	Markley	T
aymond	T	Hall	G
cClain	G	Pavey	G
ds	C	Foss	QB
gbert	QB	Boesel	G
aine	G	Powell	T
ariklow	T	Bachman	E
mners	E	Leyburne	HB
nith	HB	Wright	FB
ox	FB	Wells	HB
are	HB		

Michigan Line-Up

me	Pos.	Name	Pos.
ttengill	E	Edmunds	T
nklin	G	Bogle	C
nbrook (Capt.)	G	Wells	T
rleske	E	McMillan	QB
agidson	HB	Green	HB
omas	FB	Wenner	FB

1910

1911

Michigan		Opponent	
Michigan	24	Case	0
Michigan	15	M.A.C.	3
Michigan	19	O.S.U.	0
Michigan	9	Vanderbilt	8
Michigan	6	Syracuse	6
Michigan	0	Cornell	6
Michigan	11	Pennsylvania	9
Michigan	6	Nebraska	6

Season Summary

Games Won, 5; Lost, 1; Tied, 2

1911

Ohio		Opponent	
Ohio	6	Otterbein	0
Ohio	3	Miami	0
Ohio	0	West. Reserve	0
Ohio	0	Michigan	19
Ohio	3	OH Wesleyan	0
Ohio	0	Case	9
Ohio	24	Kenyon	0
Ohio	0	Oberlin	0
Ohio	0	Syracuse	6
Ohio	11	Cincinnati	6

Season Summary

Games Won, 5; Lost, 3; Tied 2

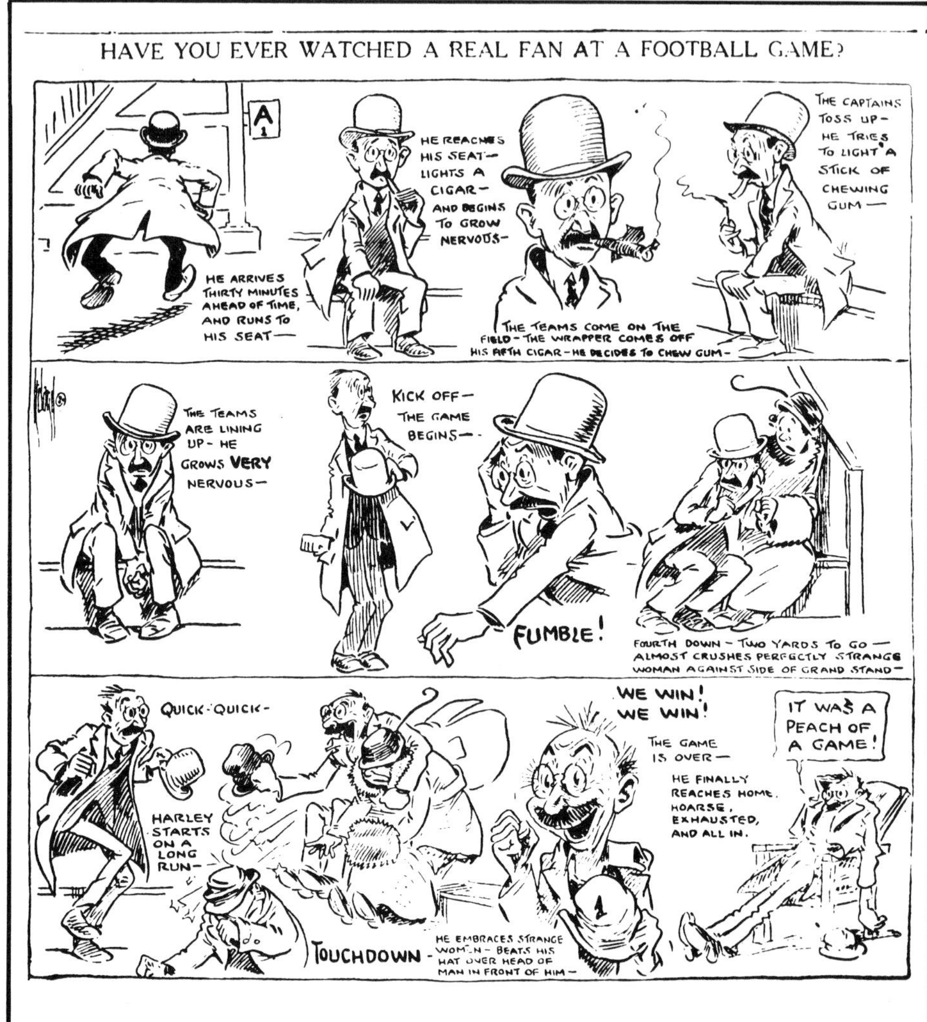

Neil McMillan, outstanding Michigan fullback, shows the latest in playing equipment.

October 21, 1911

Ann Arbor, Michigan

Michigan 19, Ohio State 0

Wolverine Size And Speed Too Much For Buckeyes

When Michigan rushed on the field, the team looked about twice the size of the toilers from Columbus. The line and backfield, despite its beef, was very speedy. The heavy team also played an open game, only at times sending plays directly at their smaller opponents.

Ohio State actually outplayed Michigan for the first 12 minutes. The Buckeyes made one first down and got three cracks at drop-kicking goals, Foss being the kicker. One of his attempts was very close, while the other two failed in both direction and height. The O.S.U. defense stopped the Wolverines in their tracks during the first period. The line of Ohio, Darst, Geib, Geissman, Stover, McCoy, and Raymond were all over the field.

The rest of the first half was a battle with Ohio holding its own fairly well. The Scarlet and Gray spent most of the time on defense and generally punted on the first play, but then Michigan was not able to gain when dangerous territory was reached.

The second half belonged to Michigan. After an O.S.U. punt went out of bounds on their own 28-yard line and two plays gained little, Michigan decided to try Bogle's toe on a placekick. It was a wise decision and the ball sailed over the bar from the 37-yard line.

Moments later, Ohio's Wright attempted to punt from his own six, but the ball was blocked and Conklin made an easy touchdown by falling on it. The PAT was good.

Michigan got its last score in the final period. An exchange of punts, in which UM's Thomson bettered O.S.U.'s Wright, and an offside play by Ohio, gave the ball to Michigan on the 25-yard line. Terrific plunging, in which the ball was carried by Wells and Thomson, sent the ball to the half-yard line. Thomsom bucked it over easily enough, but Bogle missed the goal.

With five minutes remaining, Ohio opened their line of offensive play. Their forward passes netted 55 yards and the team was running smoothly with Foss using wonderful headwork. Barricklow missed the fourth straight forward pass and Ohio State's attack fizzled. One last chance to score was nullified when Michigan intercepted a Foss aerial. When the game ended, Michigan was only inches from the goal line of Ohio State. Final score: Michigan 19, Ohio State 0.

Michigan Roster

F. L. Conklin
Geo. C. Thomson
Thos. Bogle
S. M. Wells
C. P. Quinn
Neil McMillan
M. H. Pontius
F. A. Picard
J. B. Craig
G. C. Paterson
H.S. Kaynor
O. C. Carpell
A. E. Garrells
H. H. Huebel
R. C. Meek
R. H. Torbet

Ohio State Roster

Hoss Markley
C. L. Baer
Don Barricklow
Ernie Blaine
Ike Carroll
Cooley
Joe Cox
Lester Darst
Hen Feldwisch
Whitie Foss
Gardy Gardner
Dad Geib
J. R. Geise
Irving Geismann
L. W. Hunt
Jones
Stan Kerr
Mac McCoy
Ed Morrissey
Baldy Pavey
Bugs Raymond
Ralph Shafor
Earl Smith
Hack Smith
Dutch Stover
Red Trautman
Willie Willaman
Bill Wright

Without previous coaching experience Harry Vaughn, a Yale law student, had charge of the 1911 Ohio State team. He did an outstanding job, winning five games, losing three, and tying two.

1912

Ohio		Opponent	
Ohio	55	Otterbein	0
Ohio	34	Denison	0
Ohio	0	Michigan	14
Ohio	45	Cincinnati	7
Ohio	31	Case	6
Ohio	23	Oberlin	17
Ohio	0	Penn State	37
Ohio	36	OH Wesleyan	6
Ohio	20	Mich. State	35

Season Summary

Games Won, 6; Lost, 3

John R. Richards
Ohio State Coach 1912

1912

Michigan		Opponent	
Michigan	34	Case	0
Michigan	55	M.A.C.	7
Michigan	14	O.S.U.	0
Michigan	7	Syracuse	18
Michigan	7	S. Dakota	6
Michigan	21	Pennsylvania	27
Michigan	20	Cornell	7

Season Summary

Games Won, 5; Lost, 2; Tied, 0

Football Reflections

THE notable feature of the past football season was the increased spirit shown by the men that did come out for the team. But more men should have come out. The entire squad was made up of willing workers. The Freshmen were especially devoted and worked with the Varsity after their season was over. This enthusiasm was in large measure due to Coach Harry Vaughn. He was at all times with the men and one of them. The team when in battle stood their ground manfully. However that was not sufficient to win games. The rules as they were in 1911 were a great handicap to the Scarlet and Gray. As the season came toward its close an offense that was effective was finally developed. The opening quarter of the Michigan game was a hummer. Ohio State looked like the goods, but the defeat that came, 19-0, was not terrific. Some day when dreams come true Case will lack a Roby and we will win. Let's have a true dream this Fall. The Syracuse game was a revelation to the Eastern delegation. They expected at least an 18-0 victory. They were asked by a St. Louis team not to defeat us too badly. At this point in the season our offense began to get into effective action. The final game at Cincinnati was the test of the season and should have been more overwhelmingly ours. This Fall—1912—we have the hardest schedule yet. We also have the ground work of an excellent team. Our football coach will, as has been so often the case, have the handicap of being a comparative stranger to the men. The permanent coach should increase the team's efficiency tremendously. Next Fall every man of brains should come out for the team. Harry Vaughn had a poster put up in the football room in 1911: "To H——l with weight, it's BRAINS that counts in Football."

Ohio

Name	Pos.	Name	Pos.
Cherry	LE	Barricklow	LE
Feldswich	LG	Ward	LG
Geismann	RG	Raymond	RT
Darst	RE	McClure	QB
Morrissey	LH	Ryan	RH
Graf	FB	Geib	LG
Schwartzbaugh	RE	Briggs	QB
Shafer	FB	Stover	RE
Pavey	LE	Gardner	RE
Fritz	HB	Godfrey	RE
Carroll	QB	Trautman	LH

Michigan

Geo. C. Thompson	Michael H. Boyle
Geo. C. Patterson	Thomas H. Bushnell
Clement C. Quinn	Ernest J. Allmendinger
Miller H. Pontius	James C. Musser
James B. Craig	James W. Raynsford
Otto C. Carpell	Charles P. Barton
Herbert H. Huebel	H. M. Cole
Roy M. Torbet	William H. Collette
Ernest F. Highitt	

October 19, 1912

Columbus, Ohio

Fumble Helps Michigan Over Ohio State, 14-0

Michigan's Craig Is Hero After O.S.U. Miscue

No one went away from the field and said that Michigan ever had Ohio State on the run. The Wolverines won because Craig was able to take advantage of one golden chance and then doubled their total because their team was fitted out with a man, Thomson, who could gather himself together and batter ahead for a few needed yards.

Ohio's team was not as well equipped. Its forwards could not brush aside their opponents and a close match of tackles was made favorable to Michigan by the power of the ends, Pontius and Barton. No matter how many different schemes were tried, an Ohio State runner could not be carried into the clear. At driving straight ahead and at cutting in after feinting at a flank, better results were obtained.

The toss of the coin to start the game was won by Captain Thomson of Michigan over Captain Barricklow of Ohio State and he chose to kick off to Ohio. After several punt exchanges, Ohio was marching aided by two Michigan penalties. Ryan of Ohio made a first down at mid-field. Graf was thrown by Allmendinger for no gain. On the next play, McClure uncorked the Minnesota shift, but on a delayed pass, Graf fumbled the ball on the 50-yard line. Michigan's Craig was on the job, and picking it up, he ran 50 yards for the first touchdown of the contest. Patterson kicked the goal and gave Michigan a 7-0 advantage.

That concluded the scoring until the fourth period. At the end of third quarter Ohio's McClure punted and Craig made a 5-yard return. This put the ball on the 50-yard line. McClure downed Craig after he ran 20 yards around right end. A fake forward pass started that run. Highitt failed to gain. Godfrey went in for Gardner at end, and the third quarter ended with Michigan in possession of the ball on Ohio's 20-yard line.

For the fourth quarter Barricklow went to left tackle for Ohio. Chery and Darst went to the ends for the same team. Thomson made five and Craig carried the ball for a first down inside the ten. Thomson was stopped on two plays, but on the next and telltale one he went through Raymond for a touchdown. Patterson kicked the goal. The time for this count was two minutes.

In Ohio's next series of plays, they moved to within 20 yards of Michigan's goal but a McClure pass was intercepted by Collette to end the threat. Ohio attempted a 35-yard drop kick before the game concluded.

1912

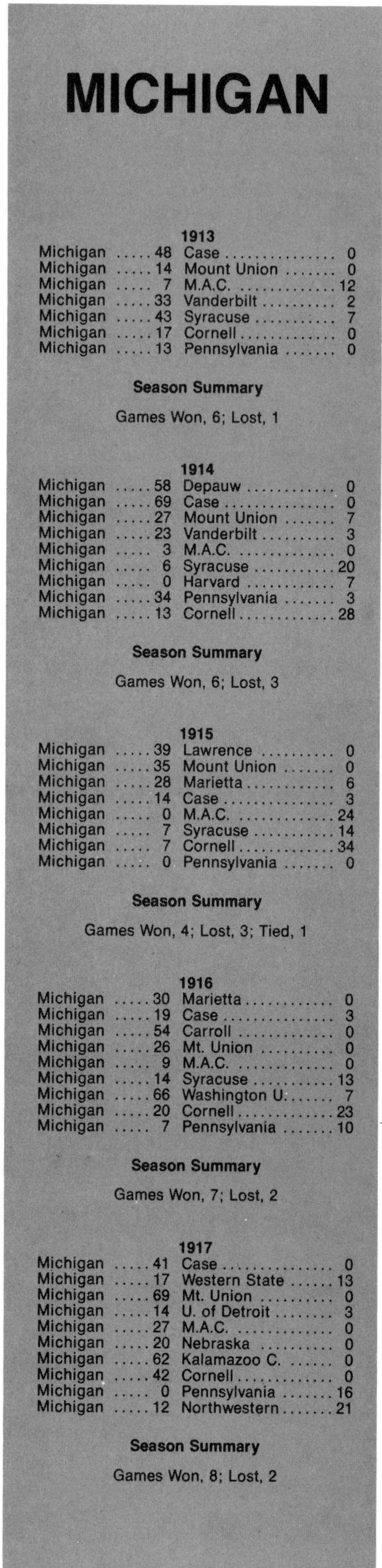

MICHIGAN

1913

Michigan	48	Case	0
Michigan	14	Mount Union	0
Michigan	7	M.A.C.	12
Michigan	33	Vanderbilt	2
Michigan	43	Syracuse	7
Michigan	17	Cornell	0
Michigan	13	Pennsylvania	0

Season Summary

Games Won, 6; Lost, 1

1914

Michigan	58	Depauw	0
Michigan	69	Case	0
Michigan	27	Mount Union	7
Michigan	23	Vanderbilt	3
Michigan	3	M.A.C.	0
Michigan	6	Syracuse	20
Michigan	0	Harvard	7
Michigan	34	Pennsylvania	3
Michigan	13	Cornell	28

Season Summary

Games Won, 6; Lost, 3

1915

Michigan	39	Lawrence	0
Michigan	35	Mount Union	0
Michigan	28	Marietta	6
Michigan	14	Case	3
Michigan	0	M.A.C.	24
Michigan	7	Syracuse	14
Michigan	7	Cornell	34
Michigan	0	Pennsylvania	0

Season Summary

Games Won, 4; Lost, 3; Tied, 1

1916

Michigan	30	Marietta	0
Michigan	19	Case	3
Michigan	54	Carroll	0
Michigan	26	Mt. Union	0
Michigan	9	M.A.C.	0
Michigan	14	Syracuse	13
Michigan	66	Washington U.	7
Michigan	20	Cornell	23
Michigan	7	Pennsylvania	10

Season Summary

Games Won, 7; Lost, 2

1917

Michigan	41	Case	0
Michigan	17	Western State	13
Michigan	69	Mt. Union	0
Michigan	14	U. of Detroit	3
Michigan	27	M.A.C.	0
Michigan	20	Nebraska	0
Michigan	62	Kalamazoo C.	0
Michigan	42	Cornell	0
Michigan	0	Pennsylvania	16
Michigan	12	Northwestern	21

Season Summary

Games Won, 8; Lost, 2

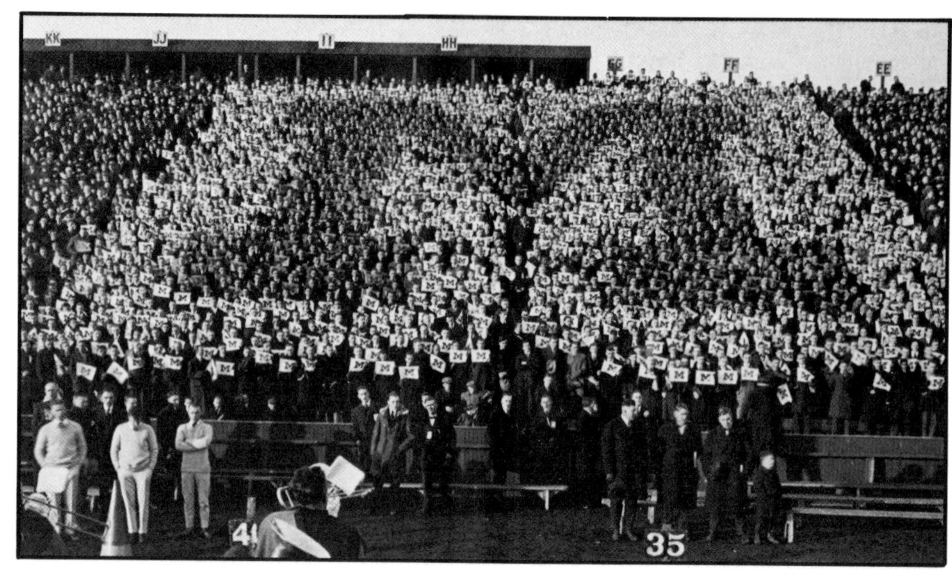

BLOCK "M", 1916

MILLER PONTIUS
All-American Tackle 1913

JOHN MAULBETSCH
All-American Halfback 1914

JAMES CRAIG
All-American Halfback 1913

FRANK CULVER
All-American Guard 1917

ERNEST ALLMENDINGER
All-American Guard 1917

CEDRIC SMITH
All-American Fullback 1917

Ohio State and Michigan did not meet during the seasons from 1913 to 1917.

One of Ohio's First All-Americans
ROBERT KARCH
All-American Tackle 1916

Second of Ohio's First All-Americans
CHARLES HARLEY
All-American Back 1916 and 1917

CHARLES BOLEN
All-American End 1917

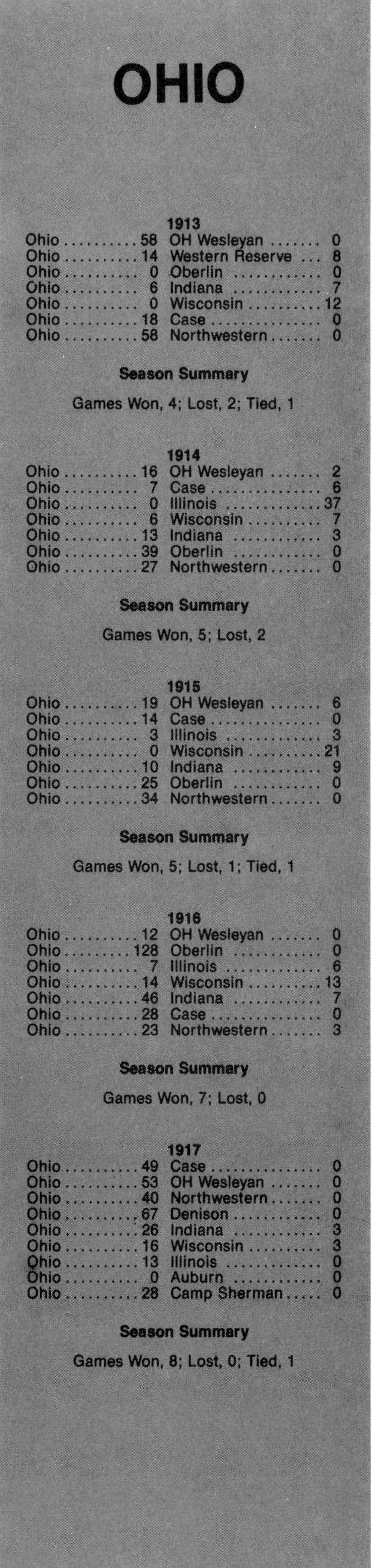

OHIO

1913

Ohio	58	OH Wesleyan	0
Ohio	14	Western Reserve	8
Ohio	0	Oberlin	0
Ohio	6	Indiana	7
Ohio	0	Wisconsin	12
Ohio	18	Case	0
Ohio	58	Northwestern	0

Season Summary

Games Won, 4; Lost, 2; Tied, 1

1914

Ohio	16	OH Wesleyan	2
Ohio	7	Case	6
Ohio	0	Illinois	37
Ohio	6	Wisconsin	7
Ohio	13	Indiana	3
Ohio	39	Oberlin	0
Ohio	27	Northwestern	0

Season Summary

Games Won, 5; Lost, 2

1915

Ohio	19	OH Wesleyan	6
Ohio	14	Case	0
Ohio	3	Illinois	3
Ohio	0	Wisconsin	21
Ohio	10	Indiana	9
Ohio	25	Oberlin	0
Ohio	34	Northwestern	0

Season Summary

Games Won, 5; Lost, 1; Tied, 1

1916

Ohio	12	OH Wesleyan	0
Ohio	128	Oberlin	0
Ohio	7	Illinois	6
Ohio	14	Wisconsin	13
Ohio	46	Indiana	7
Ohio	28	Case	0
Ohio	23	Northwestern	3

Season Summary

Games Won, 7; Lost, 0

1917

Ohio	49	Case	0
Ohio	53	OH Wesleyan	0
Ohio	40	Northwestern	0
Ohio	67	Denison	0
Ohio	26	Indiana	3
Ohio	16	Wisconsin	3
Ohio	13	Illinois	0
Ohio	0	Auburn	0
Ohio	28	Camp Sherman	0

Season Summary

Games Won, 8; Lost, 0; Tied, 1

LINE UP
Ohio State

			F. B.			
			Matheny			
	R. H.		Q. B.		L. H.	
	Rife		Wiper		Davies	
R. E.	R. T.	R. G.	C.	L. G.	L. T.	L. E.
Slyker	Addison	Sneddon	Gillam or Friedman	Pixley	Huffman	McDonald

LINE UP
Michigan

			F. B.			
			Steketee			
	R. H.		Q. B.		L. H.	
	Perrin		Knode		Cohn	
R. E.	R. T.	R. G.	C.	L. G.	L. T.	L. E.
Bovill Morrison	Fortune Young	Freeman	Vick	Adams	Goetz	Dunne

JOHN W. WILCE
Ohio Head Coach
1913-1928

Ohio State Roster

1. Addison
2. Sneddon
3. Wiper, H.
4. Kerr
5. Myers
6. Lieberman
7. Pixley
8. Huffman
9. McCune
10. Haines
11. Howell
12. Slyker
13. Howenstine
14. Early
15. Farcasin
16. Wiper, D.
17. Taylor
18. Shackson
19. Matheny
20. Klein
21. McDonald
22. Friedman
23. Davies
24. Gross
25. Gillam
26. Clarke
27. Elgin
28. Assman
29. Boland
30. Loofbourrow
31. Miller
32. Rife
33. Moeller

Michigan Roster

1. Goetz
2. Karpus
3. Cruse
4. Perrin
5. Cohn
6. Knode
7. Adams
8. Wilson
9. Steketee
10. Freeman
11. Jordan
13. Walker
18. Genebach
19. Vick
22. Dunne
23. Carter
24. Bovill
25. Baines
26. Cartwright
27. Czysz
28. Morrison
29. Olken
33. Hendershot
34. Hodder
35. Fortune
36. Usher

1918			
Ohio	41	OH Wesleyan	0
Ohio	34	Denison	0
Ohio	0	Michigan	14
Ohio	56	Case	0
Ohio	0	Illinois	13
Ohio	3	Wisconsin	14

Season Summary

Games Won, 3; Lost, 3

1918			
Michigan	33	Case	0
Michigan	13	Chicago	0
Michigan	15	Syracuse	0
Michigan	21	M.A.C.	6
Michigan	14	Ohio State	0

Season Summary

Games Won, 5; Lost, 0; Tied, 0.

FRANK STEKETEE
All-American Fullback

December 1, 1918

Columbus, Ohio

Michigan Crosses Twice, 14-0 Over Ohio State

Blockade Of Punt Sets The Wolverines Scoring

The regularly scheduled game between Michigan and Ohio State was postponed due to the death of Ohio State's 1917 captain, Hap Courtney who died while in the service of his country. Other games in the midwest were postponed or cancelled due to a Spanish influenza epidemic.

The game was finally played on December 1 in Columbus with the result being the same as it had been for many years, Michigan on top. Michigan paired touchdowns in the fourth quarter of the game played on Ohio Field. With a couple of goal kicks the total number of points was 14.

Spirit of the Ohio State players was high and discovery of the fact that they could not gain ground, even if special pains had been taken to have Rife run from a kicking formation, did not destroy their power to resist. They fought the larger Wolverines to a standstill during the first half and caused F. H. Yost to deliver a bitter tirade to his players during the intermission. For the final half the Michigan backfield was changed and allowed to remain so until it was all over.

Michigan played with the most assurance and no glaring mistakes were made. Once Steketee had to punt from back of his own goal line and made a perfect job of it. On defense Ohio was held to only one first down which was the result of a 28-yard pass from Wiper to Davies. The UM offense gained good yardage most of the afternoon which resulted in many first downs, but not many TD's.

The first half of play was marked by many exchanges. Punts were numerous and O.S.U.'s Rife got away a kick that travelled 70 yards and was downed on Michigan's one-yard line.

Between halves Coach Yost issued an order for more speed and sent in Usher and Van Wagner as halfbacks to fill it. Michigan with Steketee kicking off, soon was on the offensive, and the first trial at counting came up when Steketee missed a place-kicking trial from the 40-yard line. He had the right direction, but the ball did not carry high enough to get even against the cross-bar.

At the start of the fourth period there was a barter of punts, Steketee making the second of the set and getting the ball off on its roll to almost the Ohio goal line. Ohio's Rife attempted to kick out of danger, but what looked like a Michigan human wall blocked the kick and U.M.'s Goetz beat all others to the ball and did whatever was necessary to gain the touchdown that had been so long in coming. Steketee kicked the goal.

After a pass interception by the Wolverine's Van Wagner, Ohio began to crumble. Van Wagner and Usher made a string of plays straight into the line for 18 yards. On the eighth of the series driving was discontinued and Steketee punted. The Buckeyes' Rife returned the kick. Knode of Michigan snatched the ball and returned it to Ohio's 32. Ohio's Elgin piled up after coming in from behind on a play that was stopped and he was banished from the game. That penalty moved the ball to Ohio's 12-yard line. The Wolverines could not rush for the remaining yardage, so Dunne ducked over the goal line and caught the ball that Steketee passed forward to him. Steketee kicked an easy goal to end the scoring. The game ended shortly and the final score remained 14-0 in Michigan's favor.

Above: Action in Ann Arbor.
At Left: Scoreboard parties were the place to be in Columbus when the game was in Michigan.

October 25, 1919

Ann Arbor, Michigan

Ohio State Wins 13 to 3

Chic Harley Stars in Victory and Buckeyes Rooters Go Wild

Ohio celebrated the burial rites for the Michigan jinx. Led by the sensational playing of Captain Chic Harley, famous All American halfback, the great Buckeye machine triumphed over Michigan 13 to 3.

Conclusively and sensationally after twenty-two years of defeat, the Buckeyes celebrated their supremacy over the Wolverines. The plays of the Columbus line far surpassed that of the Michigan forwards. The maize and blue backs were unable to gain except at infrequent intervals.

Four thousand OSU fans reached the border of insanity, yelling themselves hoarse after the famous Harley dashed around end, sidestepped Cruse, stiff-armed Vick, and slipped out of the grasp of Sparks, enroute to a fifty yard touchdown run. The kickout failed, touching the ground, leaving the final score 13 to 3.

The scarlet and gray registered its first touchdown on a fluke when left tackle Huffman broke through the line and blocked one of Sparks punts. The oval rolled over the line with the Bucks after it. Three men dove for the pill, but right end Jim Flower achieved the glory by getting the firmest grasp on it. Harley kicked goal.

It was not the fault of Cliff Sparks, Yost's nifty quarterback, that the Buckeyes achieved their goal. Sparks was the only man who could gain at all through Ohio. It was he that dropped over a field goal from the 43 yard line in the second period that resulted in Michigan's only score.

Columbus fans who came here en masse on a special train or freight, loaded with money to bet on their football team, rode back in Pullmans.

After an early fumble by Ohio's Stinchcomb, Michigan's right end Harold Rye fractured his right leg above the knee. Peach who had been playing guard took Rye's place, while Czysz took Peach's guard.

Coach Yost sought to counteract the effective ground control game of Ohio State with forward passes. Michigan tried eighteen aerial heaves during the game, but none were successful. Time and time again Vick, Peach, and Sparks threw the ball forty yards, but Harley, Stinchcomb, or Davies would block the throws or intercept them. The State defense was perfect.

Fully 25,000 persons attended the game, one-fifth of these were Ohio partisans. Before the start of the game, the Michigan band, garbed in the regimental uniforms of blue with yellow steamers, paraded up and down the field. Shortly after, the Ohio band, clad in khaki of the R O T C, marched on. The bands played the school songs, the "Yellow and Blue" and "Carmen Ohio" while the crowd stood with bared heads. Between halves, a collection for the Roosevelt memorial fund was taken up, the crowd tossing silver into two big American flags that were stretched out in front of the bleachers.

1919

Ohio	38	OH Wesleyan	0
Ohio	46	Cincinnati	0
Ohio	49	Kentucky	0
Ohio	13	Michigan	3
Ohio	20	Purdue	0
Ohio	3	Wisconsin	0
Ohio	7	Illinois	9

Season Summary

Games Won, 6; Lost, 1

OHIO

No.	Name	Pos.
1	Meyers	E
2	Huffman	T
3	Pixley	G
4	Trott	C
5	Holtkamp	G
6	Spiers	T
7	Flower	E
8	Stinchcomb	QB
9	Davies	HB
10	Harley (Capt.)	HB
11	Willaman	FB

Substitutes:

12	Bliss	24	Ewart
13	McDonald	25	Gillam
14	Friedman	26	Churches
15	Wiche	27	Volzer
16	Nemecek	28	H. Wiper
17	Johnson	29	D. Wiper
18	Addison	30	Taylor
19	Farcasin	31	Sweitzer
20	Slyker	32	Matheny
21	Weaver	33	DeMore
22	Cott	34	Newlum
23	Johnston	35	Weiss
		36	Navin

CHARLES HARLEY
All-American Back third time in four years

MICHIGAN

No.	Name	Pos.
10	Peach	E
1	Goetz (Capt.)	T
7	Fortune	G
16	Johnson	C
14	Wilson	G
2	Dunn	T
22	R. J. Dunne	E
5	Sparks	QB
3	Cruse	HB
11	Weston	HB
19	Vick	FB

Substitutes:

6	Knode	17	Eades
8	Froemke	18	Henderson
9	Rye	20	Schumacher
12	McGrath	21	Loucks
15	Cress	23	Barnes
24	Czysz	31	Stewart
25	Hammels	32	Van Wagoner
28	Campbell	33	Hamilton
29	Timchac	34	Culver
30	Breakey	35	Cary
		36	Weadock

1919

Michigan	34	Case	0
Michigan	26	M.A.C.	0
Michigan	3	Ohio State	13
Michigan	16	Northwestern	13
Michigan	0	Chicago	13
Michigan	7	Illinois	29
Michigan	7	Minnesota	34

Season Summary

Games Won, 3; Lost, 4; Tied, 0

1-5

November 6, 1920

Columbus, Ohio

Ohio State Beats Michigan 14 to 7 For Second Time In Two Years

Buckeyes Given Stiff Battle By Wolverines

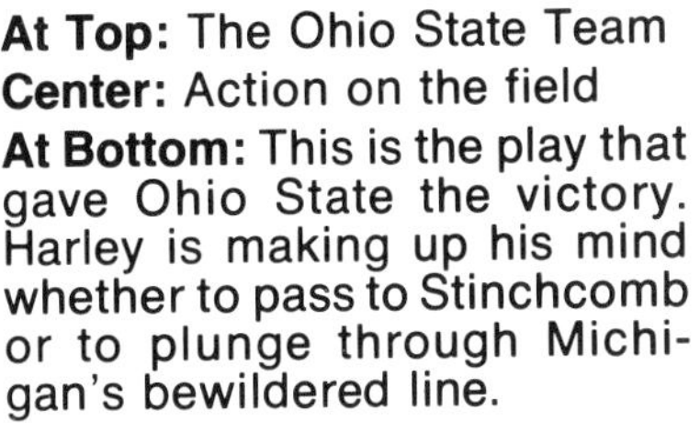

At Top: The Ohio State Team
Center: Action on the field
At Bottom: This is the play that gave Ohio State the victory. Harley is making up his mind whether to pass to Stinchcomb or to plunge through Michigan's bewildered line.

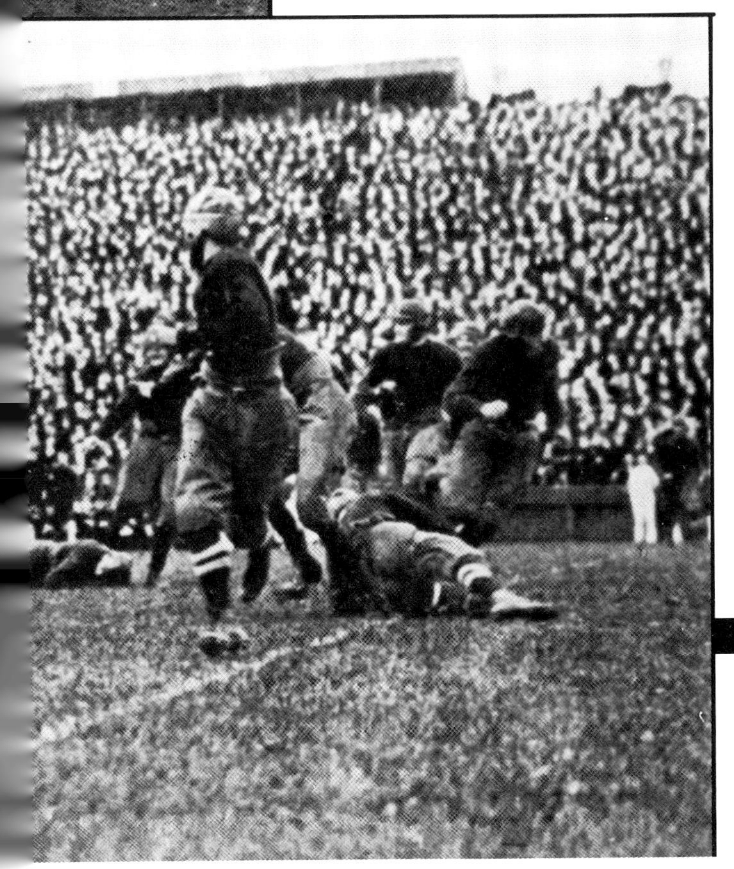

Ohio State's football team defeated Michigan 14-7 and as a result OSU did battle with Illinois for the football championship of the Western Conference. Neither of the championship contenders had lost a game.

Ohio State outplayed Michigan in every department of the game, although Michigan drew first blood with a touchdown in the second period. Ohio retaliated almost immediately with a touchdown tieing the score. In the fourth period Ohio State players blocked Steketee's punt behind Michigan's goal line and fell on the ball for a second touchdown.

In the second period Michigan threatened Ohio moving the ball to the one yard line where T. Taylor stopped Usher on the one foot line on fourth down. OSU's Workman punted 36 yards to Dunn who signaled for a fair catch. Workman did not see the signal and tackled him. Ohio was penalized 20 yards, Michigan's ball on the 17 yard line of Ohio. Usher made ten on a delayed pass. Usher hit for two and a half yards, putting the ball on Ohio's six inch line. Dunn sneaked the six inches for the touchdown. Steketee kicked goal.

OSU scored after a Steketee punt was returned to Michigan's 24 yard line by Workman. Stinchcomb made four, then lost six. After a pass from Workman to Noel and a 22 yard run by Workman, the ball was on the Wolverine's three yard line. Willaman smashed for one, then failed to gain. Workman sneaked for one. With one yard to go Henderson crashed through for a touchdown. Workman kicked goal. The half ended 7 to 7.

The third period saw no scoring, but the fourth period started with Michigan on their own three yard line. Steketee attempted to punt but Huffman and Meyers blocked it behind Michigan's goal line and Huffman fell on the ball for a touchdown. Stinchcomb kicked goal. The play occurred only twenty seconds after the fourth period started.

The game ended with neither team threatening to score.

1920

1920

Michigan	35	Case	0
Michigan	35	M.A.C.	0
Michigan	6	Illinois	7
Michigan	21	Tulane	0
Michigan	7	Ohio State	14
Michigan	14	Chicago	0
Michigan	3	Minnesota	0

Season Summary

Games Won, 5; Lost, 2; Tied, 0

MICHIGAN

No.	Name	Pos.
1	Goetz (Capt.)	T
2	Weiman	T
3	D. Dunn	G
4	Wilson	G
5	Perrin	HB
6	Steketee	FB
7	Usher	HB
8	Vick	C
9	J. Dunn	QB
10	Goeble	E
11	Gappen	E
12	Nelson	FB
14	Johns	T
15	Banks	G
16	Paper	HB
17	Petro	G
18	Planck	G
19	Gilmore	HB
20	Van Orden	G
21	Cohn	HB
21	Searle	HB
23	Rowland	E
23	Czoyz	G
24	Andrew	E
25	Lehman	E
26	Wachter	G
27	Bailey	HB
28	Fortune	G

OHIO

No.	Name	Pos.	No.	Name	Pos.
1	Nemecek	C	27	Weaver	FB
2	Kaplow	C	29	McGregor	
3	Trott	G	30	Lusk	C
4	Weiche	G	31	Patchel	
5	Tayler	G	32	Weiss	
6	Huffman (Capt.)	T	33	Campbell	
7	Spiers	T	34	Volzer	
8	Jackson	T	35	Rumer	G
9	Johnson	T	36	C. MacGinnis	G
10	Pauley		37	Lakin	
11	Slyker	E	38	Navin	
12	Myers	E	39	Miller	
13	Blair	E	40	Alcorn	
14	Speed		41	Lightner	
15	N. Workman	E	42	Walker	
16	Johnson		43	Osburn	
17	H. Workman	QB	44	Craig	
18	D. Wiper	QB	45	Patterson	
19	Stinchcomb	HB	46	Albl	
20	Cott	HB	47	Nesbitt	
21	Henderson	HB	48	DeMore	
22	Bliss	HB	49	Early	
24	Taylor	HB	51	Blumenthal	
24	Miller		53	D. MacGinnis	
25	Isabell	FB	54	Failer	
25	Wilder		55	Duell	
26	Willaman	FB		Doig	

1920

Ohio	55	OH Wesleyan	0
Ohio	37	Oberlin	0
Ohio	17	Purdue	0
Ohio	13	Wisconsin	7
Ohio	7	Chicago	6
Ohio	14	Michigan	7
Ohio	7	Illinois	0
Ohio	0	California	28

Season Summary

Games Won, 7; Lost, 1

IOLAS HUFFMAN
All-American Guard

GAYLORD STINCHCOMB
All-American Back

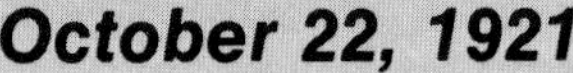

October 22, 1921

Ann Arbor, Michigan

Ohio State Beats Michigan 14-0

Stuart's 34 Yard Dash Sets Stage In Second Period

Michigan's football team went to sleep for one short moment in the second quarter of the game with Ohio State on Ferry Field and when it was aroused the Buckeyes had scored the touchdown that started them on the path to a 14-0 victory over the heavier Wolverines.

Johnny Stuart's name was on the lips of every Ohio State rooter that night. It was the curly haired halfback from Huntington, West Virginia, who used his brains as well as feet and arms at the psychological moment and swept past the entire astonished and dumbfounded Michigan team for a touchdown.

After an opening period of even football, the second period provided the big thrill. Stuart drove Michigan back to its twenty with a splendid punt. State killed the rushes of the Wolvernines' backs so quickly that Steketee again punted. The boot was a poor one, going only a few yards and then bounding back toward the Michigan goal line. Michigan players rushed around the ball waiting for it to stop bounding and the Ohio players grouped with them. As the ball was seemingly on its last bounce there was a rush of scarlet and Stuart scooped the ball cleanly and set out at lightning speed for the Michigan line, 34 yards away. There was no one between the Ohioan and the Wolverine goal except Uteritz who was playing a deep defensive fullback. He bounded across the field and hurled himself in Stuart's path, groping wildly to make the tackle, but his arms encountered only the cool air of Ferry Field, for Stuart with a tremendous leap, easily went over Uteritz's head and landed heavily on his shoulders, but with the ball clutched in his arms behind the goal line. A better piece of brain work and physical co-ordination seldom had been seen in Big Ten football.

The Wolverines refused to lose courage and fought fiercely until late in the third period, both sides again punting frequently. When the watch was ticking off the closing minutes of the quarter, Ohio State started a smash that did not halt until Charlie Taylor was over the Michigan line. Straight line plays, interspersed with one forward pass that was good for twenty yards, advanced the ball to Michigan's ten yard line. Buck Weaver crushed the Michigan wall for five yards and put the leather on Michigan's half-yard stripe which ended the third period.

On the resumption of play Taylor plowed past center and over the line on the third play of the fourth quarter. The Buckeye line was a stone wall when danger threatened, every man doing his tasks, with Huffman and Spiers the outstanding figures. Ohio did not open its aerial attack until the second half, and then with less than usual success, only four of the Buckeyes throws finding their mark. But Michigan was a failure at passing and completed only two of thirteen. State made seven first downs to six for Michigan, but here the figures do not show the superiority of Ohio.

What was probably the longest punt in recent years was kicked by Wilbur Isabel, Ohio State halfback. In the third period Isabel punted from his own ten yard line and when the ball stopped rolling it was a good twelve yards behind the Michigan goal line. The ball with the wind behind it, carried over 85 yards and falling in a clear field, rolled the remainder of the distance.

The battle was witnessed by a crowd of 15,000. A gale like wind blew through the stadium all afternoon and made an open game too perilous to attempt.

1921

Ohio	28	OH Wesleyan	0
Ohio	6	Oberlin	7
Ohio	27	Minnesota	0
Ohio	14	Michigan	0
Ohio	7	Chicago	0
Ohio	28	Purdue	0
Ohio	0	Illinois	7

Season Summary

Games Won, 5; Lost, 2

OHIO

No.	Name	Pos.	No.	Name	Pos.
1	Huffman	T	28	Harter	HB
2	Dunlap	T	29	McGregor	T
3	Pauley	C	30	Trott	G
4	Pixley	G	31	Wasson	G
5	Petcoff	G	32	Wallace	G
6	Spiers	T	33	Wormser	T
7	Steele	T	34	Addison	T
8	Young	C	35	Friend	E
9	Jackson	T	36	Conklin	E
10	Myers	E	37	Gwinn	E
11	Gillam	G	38	Siebert	E
12	Kaplow	C	39	Colvin	E
13	Blair	FB	40	Metzger	QB
14	Cott	HB	41	Lincoln	QB
16	Honaker	HB	42	Slyker	E
17	Isabel	HB	43	Kruse	G
18	Lightner	HB	44	Anderson	T
19	Moorehead	HB	45	Hamilton	E
20	Stuart	HB	47	Mesloh	E
21	Taylor	FB	48	Speed	E
22	Weaver	FB	49	Patchell	G
23	Wiper	QB	50	Kissell	HB
24	Workman	QB	51	Connell	HB
25	Diamond	HB	52	Thompson	HB
26	Oberlin	FB	56	Moseley	G
27	Higgins	HB	61	Roff	T

MICHIGAN

Name	Pos.	Name	Pos.
Kirk	LE	Cappon	LT
Van Orden	LG	Vick	C
Wilson	RG	Muirhead	RT
Goebel	RE	Banks	QB
Kipke	HB	Uteritz	HB
Usher	FB	Johns	LT
Dunne	LG	Steketee	HB
Roby	FB	Petro	LG

1921

Michigan	44	Mt. Union	0
Michigan	65	Case	0
Michigan	30	M.A.C.	0
Michigan	0	Ohio State	14
Michigan	3	Illinois	0
Michigan	7	Wisconsin	7
Michigan	38	Minnesota	0

Season Summary

Games Won, 5; Lost, 1; Tied, 1

HENRY VICK
All American Center

Michigan Gov
President Burt
tified)

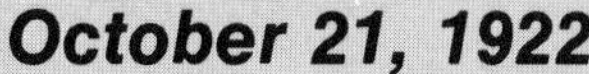

October 21, 1922

Columbus, Ohio

Ohio State Is No Match For Wolverines, 19 To 0

Buckeyes' Forward Pass Attack Fails. Kipke's Long Runs Give Michigan Two Touchdowns

›sbeck, Ohio Governor H. L. Davis, University of Michigan
›tate University President Thompson (man on right uniden-

A tall, gangling boy with hair the color of straw bleached by a hot summer sun, and a little mite of a fellow, speedy and elusive as a rabbit, led the Blue hurricane from Michigan into the new stadium and blasted Ohio's hopes for an auspicious opening of the new structure and another champion eleven. The tall blond lad was Paul Goebel, captain of the Michigan foemen, and one of the greatest ends on the gridiron that day. It was Goebel who sounded the first gun in the attack against State when he kicked a goal from placement early in the opening period. Little Harry Kipke did the rest, scoring two touchdowns and kicking another field goal.

Michigan was a small odds favorite when it entered the game due to its more veteran team. It did precisely as the Michigan coaches had expected, ripped the green Buckeye line to shreds and stopped the vaunted State forward pass. After the rush was completely stalled by Michigan, Workman went to the air, but ten out of the twenty times State attempted a pass, the Michigan ends charged in so quickly that Workman was forced to hurry his throws so much that they were incomplete. Only seven times did State's throws connect and then only one made any appreciable gain. Two were intercepted and one of those caught by Michigan led to a touchdown.

After several exchanges of punts in the first period, Goebel blocked Workman's punt on State's 37 yard line. That paved the way for the third score. Robey broke around State's left end and had a clear path for the goal when he was brought down after a sidelong tackle by Hoge Workman. Then after two line plays Goebel went into the backfield and kicked a goal from placement, the ball clearing the bars by two feet.

In the second period after OSU's Isabel fumbled and Goebel recovered, the ball was on State's 26 yard line. The next play saw Kipke circle left end on a double pass play for a touchdown. The same Goebel, who seemed to have been equal to the entire State team, kicked for the extra point.

The third peirod saw Michigan score once more, this time on a pass interception. It came after Kipke had punted out of bounds on Ohio's 27 yard line. Workman resorted to passing. His long shot went straight into the arms of Kipke who legged it forty yards down the field for a touchdown. This time the kick by Goebel failed.

Late in the fourth quarter, with Goebel out of the game from injuries, Kipke took a shot at the crossbars from the 30 yard line and drove the ball over the timber for the final points.

1922

MICHIGAN

1922

Michigan	48	Case	0
Michigan	0	Vanderbilt	0
Michigan	19	Ohio State	0
Michigan	24	Illinois	0
Michigan	63	M.A.C.	0
Michigan	13	Wisconsin	6
Michigan	16	Minnesota	7

Season Summary

Games Won, 6; Lost, 0; Tied, 1

Varsity

No.	Name	Pos.	Wt.	No.	Name	Pos.	Wt.
1	Goebel (Capt.)	E	195	6	Kipke	HB	155
2	Johns	G	175	7	Kirk	E	184
3	Vandervoort	T	208	11	Muirhead	T	180
4	Roby	HB	188	12	Blott	C	180
5	Cappon	FB	195	21	Steele	G	182
				25	Uteritz	QB	152

Reserves

No.	Name	Pos.
8	Knode	QB
9	Neisch	E
10	Slaughter	C
13	Rosatti	G
14	Blahnik	T
15	Dunleavy	FB
16	Gunther	FB
17	Henderson	E
18	Keefer	HB
20	Heath	G
22	Steger	HB
23	Swan	G
24	Van Orden	G
26	Curran	E
27	Garfield	T
28	Allen	C
30	Rankin	HB
31	Murray	G
32	Carter	HB
33	Foster	QB
34	White	T
35	Tracy, F. S.	QB

Average Weight Of Michigan Team - 181 lbs. Line - 186 lbs. Backfield - 172 lbs.

HARRY KIPKE
All-American Halfback

PAUL GOEBEL
All-American End

OHIO

Varsity

No.	Name	Pos.	Wt.	No.	Name	Pos.	Wt.
1	Pixley	G	242	15	Blair	FB	171
4	Isabel	HB	167	16	Schweinsberger	E	173
5	Young	T	180	17	Kutler	G	175
7	Petcoff	T	210	22	Michaels	FB	175
8	Honaker	E	200	31	Pauley	C	188
9	Klee	HB	152	40	H. Workman	QB	163

Reserves

No.	Name	Pos.	No.	Name	Pos.
3	Kaplow	C	48	Patchell	C
6	Lightner	HB	49	Murphy	C
10	Kyle	E	50	Speed	E
11	Hamilton, Ian B.	FB	51	Skeele	T
12	Elgin	E	52	Studabaker	E
13	Schulist	T	53	Guild	G
14	Farcasin	HB	54	Williston	FB
18	Harter	HB	54	Knickerbocker	FB
19	Gwinn	E	55	Van Scoyk	T
20	Fioretti	E	56	Lindauer	QB
23	Wasson	T	57	Jisa	T
24	Moorehead	HB	58	Butler	G
25	Cameron	QB	59	Calhoun	T
26	A. Klein	C	60	Croft	G
27	Oberlin	G	61	Donham	HB
28	Steel	T	62	Fox	HB
29	Hollingsworth	G	64	H. L. Hamilton	C
30	Wilson	E	65	Holmes	HB
32	Addison	T	67	Marts	QB
33	Dunlap	G	68	F. H. Milliken	QB
34	Long	G	68	Lincoln	QB
36	Jackson	T	69	Myers	E
38	Schaffer	QB	70	Nida	G
41	Judy	E	70	Chambers	G
42	Kissell	HB	71	Reiser	HB
43	Lemley	E	72	Scanlon	T
44	D. Klein	HB	74	E. D. Watts	HB
45	McNamer	QB	75	R. P. Wood	HB
46	E. C. Milliken	HB	76	Zaenglein	HB
47	Sandrock	E			

Average Weight of Ohio State Team - 183 lbs. Line - 194 lbs. Backfield - 164 lbs.

1922

Ohio	5	OH Wesleyan	0
Ohio	14	Oberlin	0
Ohio	0	Michigan	19
Ohio	0	Minnesota	9
Ohio	9	Chicago	14
Ohio	9	Iowa	12
Ohio	6	Illinois	3

Season Summary

Games Won, 3; Lost, 4

ELOISE FROMME
Stadium Queen

SCORE
SCORE
DOWN
NICHOLS
WINDLER
KAROW
HESS
CLARK
ROWAN
FLORA
HAWKINS
GREGORY
FRIEDMAN
BROWN
MOLENDA
EDWARDS
OOSTERBAAN
KICK OFF FORWARD PASS
END RUN PUNT GOAL KICK THRU LINE
INTERCEPTED BLOCKED RECOVERED
TOUCH DOWN FAILED TOUCH BACK
PENALTY FAKE FUMBLE
TIME OUT

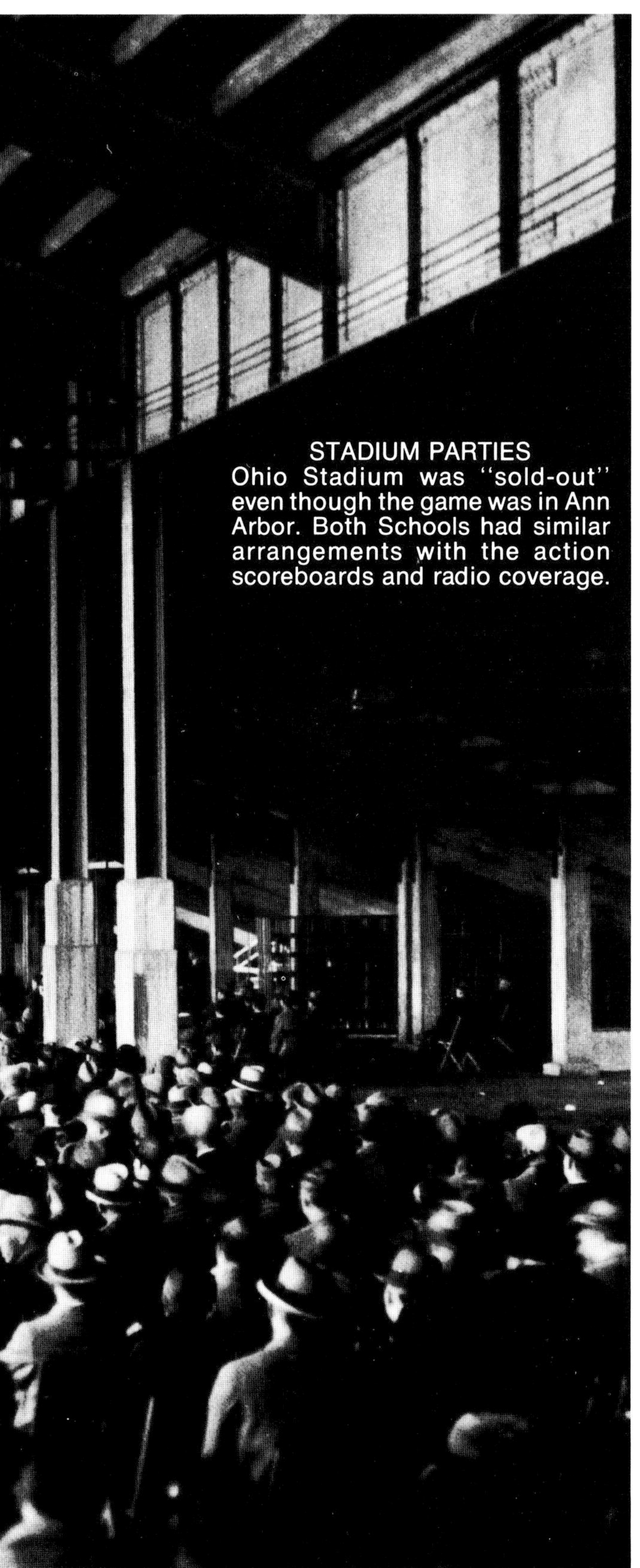

STADIUM PARTIES
Ohio Stadium was "sold-out" even though the game was in Ann Arbor. Both Schools had similar arrangements with the action scoreboards and radio coverage.

October 20, 1923

Ann Arbor, Michigan

Ohio State, Playing Pitiful Football, Bows To Michigan

Buckeyes Are No Match For Wolverines In 23 to 0 Game

Showing wonderful all around form and outplaying Ohio State in every department, Michigan crushed the Buckeye eleven and chalked up a 23 to 0 victory. Ohio looked good in the first quarter. The Bucks faded completely in the last period and staged an awful exhibition, the only question being in regard to the number of points the Wolverines would amass.

State's pass defense could not contain quarterback Uteritz's cleverly executed aerial attacks ably assisted by Curran, Kipke, and Steger as receivers. Uteritz completed all but two passes which were blocked by fullback Devoe, the only State back who seemed to have any idea of how to stop the heaves.

Blott scored the first points credited to Michigan, booting a goal from placement in the second period. Kipke twice went over for touchdowns, both times getting perfect throws from Uteritz and scampering on the remaining yards for a score.

The game, which eliminated Ohio State as a contender for Western Conference honors, opened with State being the victim of a bad break, quarterback Marts misjudging a punt and letting the ball roll almost to the State goal. But State came right back and throughout the quarter played real football, recording two first downs while Michigan made none. Then Michigan started its real attack. With that start State began to waver. As the game went on Coach Wilce rushed in man after man in substitutions. But his efforts to stave off defeat went for nothing. State was up against a better team, a team that knew its plays and how to use them.

1923

1923

Ohio	24	OH Wesleyan	7
Ohio	23	Colgate	23
Ohio	0	Michigan	23
Ohio	0	Iowa	20
Ohio	42	Denison	0
Ohio	32	Purdue	0
Ohio	3	Chicago	17
Ohio	0	Illinois	9

Season Summary

Games Won, 3; Lost, 4; Tied, 1

OHIO

Name	Pos.	Wt.	Hgt.	Age	Home Town
Bradshaw, Jas. B.		150	6-0	19	Columbus
Brashear, Richard	QB	145	5-8	20	Columbus
Bruck, H. J.		210	5-11	19	Columbus
Cameron, Geo. D.	QB	150	5-10	24	Cleveland
Carlson, Herbert R.	HB	166	6-1	22	Cleveland
Croft, Daniel R.	C	176	6-½	20	Elkton
Cunningham, Harold	E	183	6-2	18	Mt. Vernon
Dobeleit, Richard	HB	145	5-4	20	Dayton
De Voe, Keith E.	FB	179	5-10	19	Lima
Dunlap, Nelson	T	196	5-10	21	Columbus
Edmiston, Charles		186	5-10	19	Columbus
Friend, Dwight	E	165	6-0	23	Columbus
Fioretti, A. R.	E	171	5-11½	22	Cleveland
Guild, W. P.	G	190	6-1	19	Columbus
Gorrill, C. V.	E	160	5-11	20	Fostoria
Hamilton, Ian B.	FB	155	5-11	20	Louisville, OH
Hamilton, Howard	C	150	6-0	20	Columbus
Harter, Albert G.	HB	167	5-9½	23	Akron
Hollingsworth, Morris	G	214	5-10	21	Columbus
Hendershott, L. W.	QB	148	5-8½	19	Columbus
Holmes, Paul M.		160	5-6½	25	Columbus
Honaker, Frank	FB	182	5-11	23	Huntington, W. Va.
Howell, Raymond S.		144	5-8½	24	Columbus
Judy, Edwin	QB	161	5-10	21	Martins Ferry
Klee, Ollie	QB	153	5-8	23	Dayton
Kyle, George S.	E	153	5-9½	21	Cortland
Kutler, R. J.	G	180	5-8½	21	Cleveland
Lusk, Homer D.		166	6-0	23	Bainbridge
Long, Thomas N.	G	156	6-0	24	Columbus
Lang, Robert A.	FB	183	6-2	26	Muncie, IN
Mack, Carl	T	232	6-3½		Belle Center
Marts, R. J.	QB	142	5-7	26	Middletown
Marion, A. W.	T	180	6-1½	19	Circleville
Miller, J. B.		146	5-9	19	Portsmouth
Miller, E. P.	C	157	5-8	19	Lima
Murphy, Loren A.	FB	186	6-0	20	Columbus
NcNamer, A. V.	HB	160	5-7½	22	Columbus
Nichols, John H.	T	183	6-0		La Grange
Nopper, Arnold	T	176	5-10	24	Toledo
Oberlin, R. W.	T	161	5-8	23	Navarre
Ort, Paul		146	5-9	18	Columbus
Paul, Charles E.		140	5-8	20	Columbus
Petcoff, Boni (Capt.)	T	195	5-10	23	Toledo
Peterson, Archie	E	168	5-10½	23	Cedar Rapids, IA
Place, Graham	HB	138	5-7	19	Bowling Green
Pothoff, William	G	254	5-9	22	Sharonville
Poling, Luther	E	166	5-11	20	Marysville
Rader, O. W.		138	5-9	19	Columbus
Roesch, Karl O.	G	195	5-11½	19	Cleveland
Rogers, John	G	164	5-9	18	Columbus
Ross, J. G.		132	5-7	22	Sandusky
Rogers, R. J.		165	5-9	20	Cincinnati
Schulist, B. N.	G	168	5-10	19	Cleveland
Schweinsberger, H.	G	175	5-10	21	Columbus
Southern, Clarence	HB	150	5-9	22	Evansville, IN
Snyder, Lawrence	HB	155	6-0	26	Columbus
Sobul, Sanford	QB	137	5-8	20	Cleveland
Seiffer, Ralph E.	E	164	6-1	19	Evansville, IN
Steel, Harry D.	T	201	6-3	24	East Sparta
Van Scoyk, E. N.		171	6-0	23	Dayton
Walther, L. R.	C	170	6-0	21	Canton
Watkins, E. H.	G	164	5-8	19	Mansfield
Watts, R. S.	C	145	5-7	22	Columbus
Wasson, Harold	T	190	6-1	21	Columbus
Wisterman, John M.	QB	150	5-8½	20	Galion
Wilson, John F.	E	167	6-1	20	Milan
Workman, Harry	HB	166	5-10½	23	Huntington, W. Va.
Wendler, Harold	HB	146	5-10	21	Fremont
Wood, Rolland P.		147	5-9	19	Columbus
Woodruff, Charles	G	205	5-5	25	Columbus
Young, Frank D.	C	178	6-0	24	Toledo
Zaenglein, C. M.	HB	153	5-7	21	Botkins

MICHIGAN

No.	Name	Pos.	Wt.	Hgt.	Year	Prep School
1	Kipke, Captain	HB	158	5-9	'24	Lansing High
2	Blott	C	185	6-0	'24	Girard, OH
3	Miller	FB	170	5-10	'25	Grand Rapids Central
4	Muirhead	T	180	6-0	'24	Detroit Northern
5	Uteritz	QB	150	5-8	'24	Oak Park
6	Van Dervoort	T	198	6-1	'24	Lansing High
7	Steele	G	175	5-10	'25	Sioux City
8	Neisch	E	178	6-1	'24	Detroit Eastern
9	Steger	HB	170	5-10	'25	Oak Park
10	Marion	E	180	5-9	'24	Detroit Northeastern
11	Herrnstein	HB	157	5-11	'26	Chillicothe, OH
12	Grube	HB	155	5-10	'26	Arthur Hill, Saginaw
13	Witherspoon	E	170	5-11	'25	Detroit Northwestern
14	Vick	HB	155	5-8	'26	Scott High, Toledo
15	Babcock	T	180	5-11	'26	Royal Oak, MI
16	Curran	E	165	5-10	'24E	Louisville, KY
17	Hawkins	G	185	6-0	'26E	Arthur Hill, Saginaw
18	Heston	HB	170	5-11	'26E	Detroit
19	Kunow	T	204	6-0	'25	Detroit Eastern
20	Ingle	G	190	6-2	'25	Ann Arbor High
21	Donnelly	T	185	5-11	'24	Cadillac
22	Brown	C	178	5-10	'26	Ypsilanti
24	Parker	HB	150	5-8	'26	Hastings
25	Palmer	E	170	6-1	'26E	Grand Rapids Central
26	Rockwell	QB	160	5-9	'25	Jackson
27	White	G	195	6-2	'24	Reed City, MI
28	Swan	G	175	5-10	'24E	Detroit Central
29	Wall	C	170	5-11	'24	Birmingham
30	Slaughter	G	190	5-10	'25E	Louisville, KY
31	Ferenz	E	163	5-10	'26E	Flint
32	Parker	QB	148	5-7	'26	Kalamazoo Central

1923

Michigan	36	Case	0
Michigan	3	Vanderbilt	0
Michigan	23	Ohio State	0
Michigan	37	M.A.C.	0
Michigan	9	Iowa	3
Michigan	26	Quantico Mar	6
Michigan	6	Wisconsin	3
Michigan	10	Minnesota	0

Season Summary

Games Won, 8; Lost, 0; Tied, 0

JACK BLOTT
All-American Center

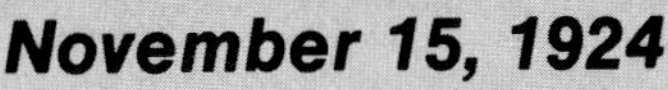

Michigan's Tod Rockwell

November 15, 1924

Columbus, Ohio

Victory Goes To Michigan, 16 To 6

Friedman's Passes Put Buckeyes Down

A monstrous crowd of 70,000, the west's greatest football crowd, blinked unbelievingly as long "Cookie" Cunningham raced 68 yards to a touchdown for Ohio State in the first minute and a half of play. A fighting, irresistible Michigan eleven tried in vain for three periods to shake off that early handicap. Late in the third period they were in sight of the objective and then galloped on to 16 points and a decisive, clean-cut conquest in the twilight session of a most spectacular contest.

It was the forward flips of Friedman, almost twenty of them, that gave the massive throngs its greatest thrills. It was forward passes and intercepted forward passes that paved the way for every tally. There have been better games, no doubt, in State's huge plant, but none so colorful, none more nerve tingling, than that overhead struggle.

After the first period score, there came about a see-saw battle for three periods with Michigan, for the most part, in Ohio territory. Only the slippery fingers of Friedman's receivers prevented a cake walk for the strongly favored Wolverine array.

Benny shot a dozen of those forwards into the air, eight of that number perfect, before one connected. That started Ohio on the waiting skids. Soon Marion plunged over for the Michigan touchdown and Rockwell kicked the goal.

Then came an Ohio kickoff, an exchange of punts, a Buckeye forward throw intercepted by Rockwell and the young gentleman's expert piece of toe marksmanship from the 40 yard stripe. Another kickoff, more trading of punts, another interception pass flung by Cameron of the Buckeyes and the Wolverines were on the trail again. Benny Friedman's accurate arm, several line plunges, and an end skirt by Rockwell provided the final touchdown. But the never-say-die Bucks blocked his extra point attempt.

Michigan most assuredly deserved to win, but Ohio State threw away a golden opportunity in the final period when Hunt dashed off right tackle for 56 yards to the enemy's 20 yard line. After an attempt by Hunt through the line, a forward pass was ordered and Slaughter intercepted for the Yostmen and carried it back 45 yards.

The Wolverines achieved more than twice as many first downs as the Bucks. The Wolverines had the edge — quite something of an edge — in punting. It took them a long time to get there — their frantic forays in the last minutes of the third session making possible their score at the outset of the final verse — but they were due to get there. And they could not be stopped.

1924

1924			
Michigan	55	Miami	0
Michigan	7	M.A.C.	0
Michigan	14	Illinois	39
Michigan	21	Wisconsin	0
Michigan	13	Minnesota	0
Michigan	27	Northwestern	0
Michigan	16	Ohio State	6
Michigan	2	Iowa	9

Season Summary

Games Won, 6; Lost, 2; Tied, 0

E. R. SLAUGHTER
All-American Guard

MICHIGAN

No.	Name	Pos.	Wt.	Home Town
36	Babcock, R. G.	T	180	Detroit, MI
23	Brown, Robert	C	182	Ypsilanti, MI
28	Domhoff, Victor	QB	160	Toledo, OH
65	Edwards, T. L.	T	180	Central Lake MI
37	Flora, William	T	176	Muskegon, MI
47	Froemke, Harlan	B	160	Sheldon, N.D.
63	Grube, C. W.	E	165	Saginaw, MI
38	Hawkins, Harry	G-T	185	Saginaw, MI
52	Hall, Foster	T	190	Ann Arbor, MI
43	Heath, William	B	180	Corning, N.Y.
39	Herrnstein, Wm.	B	160	Chillicothe, OH
47	Kunow, Walter	T	210	Detroit, MI
63	Lovette, John H.	B	180	Saginaw, MI
56	Madsen, Edgar	E-C	180	Oak Park, IL
59	Marion, P. E.	E	180	Detroit, MI
34	Miller, J. K.	B	180	Grand Rapids, MI
69	Parker, H. F.	B	165	Hastings, MI
53	Rockwell, F.	Q	165	Ann Arbor, MI
46	Samson, Paul C.	T	190	Ypsilanti, MI
32	Slaughter, E. R.	G	200	Louisville, KY
35	Steger, Herbert	B	175	Oak Park, IL
29	Stamman, Carl	B	160	Toledo, OH
25	Steele, Harold O.	G	172	Sioux City, IA
42	White, H. S.	G	198	Ashton, MI
68	Gregory, Bruce	B	165	Ann Arbor, MI
71	Baker, Merle	B	155	Kalamazoo, MI
72	Davis, Russel	B	155	Flint, MI
73	Dewey, Sidney	G	185	Monroe, MI
74	Friedman, Ben	B	170	Cleveland, OH
77	McIntyre, Kent	C	170	Detroit, MI
78	Palmer, Lowell	E	165	Grand Rapids, MI
79	Ullman, Wm. S.	G	172	Elmhurst, IL
81	Langguth, Elmer	L	170	Cleveland, OH
82	Coventry, W. D.	C	165	Duluth, MN

GEORGE LITTLE
Michigan Head Coach
1924

OHIO

Name	Pos.	Wt.	Hgt.	Home Town
Beck, Herbert R.	E	163	5-11	Columbus
Blanchard, Bruce	QB	145	5-9	Columbus
Bloser, Parker G.	E	177	6-0	Columbus
Blumer, Gabe	HB	158	5-11	Sandusky
Boxwell, Paul	HB	172	5-9½	Xenia
Bradley, R. T.	T	182	5-11	Woodstock
Cameron, George D.	QB	152	5-10	Cleveland
Carlson, Herbert R.	HB	186	6-1	Cleveland
Cervenka, Laddie F.	E	168	5-11½	Lorain
Clark, Myers A.	HB	168	5-11½	Gettysburg
Cook, James M.	HB	150	5-9	West Dover
Cunningham, Harold B.	E	197	6-2	Mt. Vernon
De Voe, Keith	FB	180	5-10	Lima
Dreyer, Carl A.	G	203	6-1½	Toledo
Evans, Benjamin F.	T	176	5-11¾	Windham
Galbraith, M. H.	E	160	6-1½	Columbus
Gorrill, Charles V.	E	162	5-10¾	Fostoria
Griffith, William N.	G	168	5-8	Bluffton
Harrison, H. C.	T	175	6-0	Columbus
Hess, Edwin	T	179	6-0	Chardon
Hunt, Howser C.	HB	153	5-10	Richwood
Hunt, William	HB	153	5-8	Toledo
Jackson, George H.	G	231	6-0	Columbus
Jenkins, William R.	G	188	6-2	Columbus
Jones, A. D.	G	164	5-10	Columbus
Jones, Norman K.	G	193	5-11	London
Karow, Marty	FB	173	5-10	Cleveland
Klee, Ollie	HB	164	5-8	Dayton
Kreglow, James J.	G	217	6-1	De Graff
Kromer, Philip F.	T	166	5-9	Columbus
Kutler, Rudolph J.	G	186	5-8½	Cleveland
Mackey, F. C.	T	183	5-9½	Galion
Manchester, Frank	T	175	6-0	Perry
Marion, A. W.	T	190	6-1½	Circleville
Marr, Joseph E.	HB	158	5-10	Hamilton
McCarthy, Tim	T	185	6-2	Fremont
McNamer, Arthur	HB	156	5-6½	Columbus
Meacham, Howard	G	198	6-1½	Atwater
Miller, A. R.	C	177	5-11½	Canton
Murphy, Loren A.	C	188	6-0	Columbus
Nichols, John H.	T	193	6-0	La Grange
Ort, Paul J.	E	149	5-7½	Columbus
Packard, Ralph	G	167	6-2	Columbus
Penrod, James L.	G	192	5-10	Lewisburg
Peterson, Archie L.	HB	174	5-10¾	Cedar Rapids, IA
Poling, Luther	E	174	5-11	Marysville
Pothoff, William	G	264	5-9	Sharonville
Price, Charles R.	E	159	6-0	Dayton
Roesch, Karl A.	G	191	5-11	Cleveland
Rosofsky, Jacob	E	146	5-8	Columbus
Royer, John	G	180	5-9	Columbus
Scheiderer, Paul F.	G	150	5-10	Columbus
Schulist, Bernard	E	187	5-10	Cleveland
Schweinsberger, H.	HB	185	5-10	Columbus
Seiffer, Ralph E.	E	173	6-0	Evansville, IN
Shifflette, Don F.	FB	166	5-11	Columbus
Slemmons, R. H.	QB	149	5-8	Columbus
Slough, H. R.	C	177	5-10½	Mansfield
Smith, R. G.	QB	133	5-9	Columbus
Stewart, William E.	G	170	5-10	Columbiana
Tanner, Charles C.	E	158	6-0	London
Watkins, Ed H.	G	170	5-8	Mansfield
Wilson, J. B.	E	176	6-0	Milan
Watts, Robert	C	148	5-7	Columbus
Wendler, Harold	HB	153	5-10	Fremont
Wentz, Burke	HB	158	5-8½	Kenton
Winters, Paul C.	E	169	5-9	Briggsdale
Wisterman, John M.	QB	161	5-9	Galion
Woerlein, George	HB	157	5-10½	Groveport
Woods, G. C.	T	183	5-11	Port William
Young, Frank D.	C	188	6-0	Toledo

1924

Ohio	7	Purdue	0
Ohio	0	Iowa	0
Ohio	10	OH Wesleyan	0
Ohio	3	Chicago	3
Ohio	7	Wooster	7
Ohio	7	Indiana	12
Ohio	6	Michigan	16
Ohio	0	Illinois	7

Season Summary

Games Won, 2; Lost, 3; Tied 3

HAROLD CUNNINGHAM
All-American End

Coachman's Dinner, November 30, 1925. Glenn Warner, Knute Rockne, Babe Ruth, Christy Walsh, T.A.D. Jones and Fielding Yost.

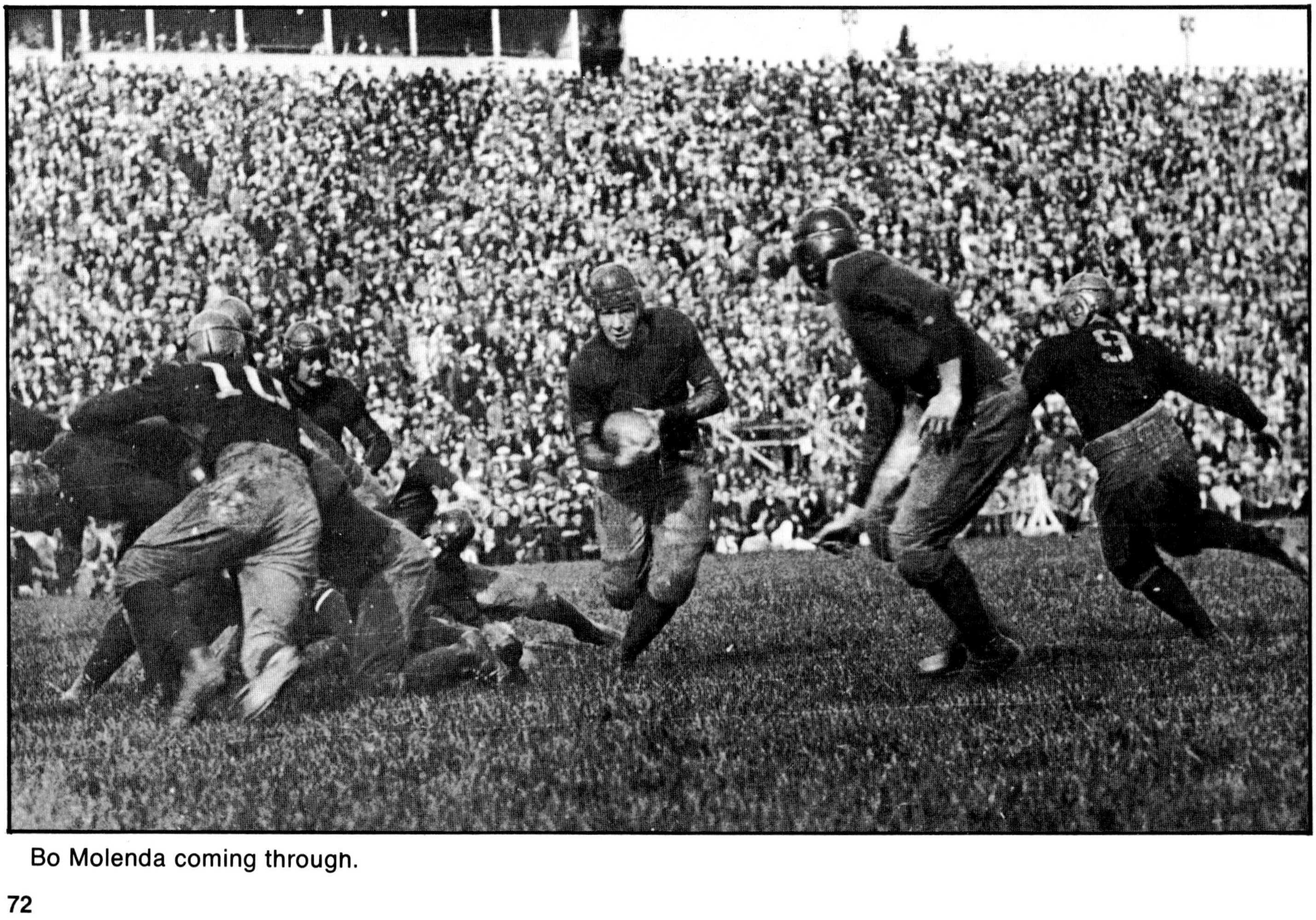

Bo Molenda coming through.

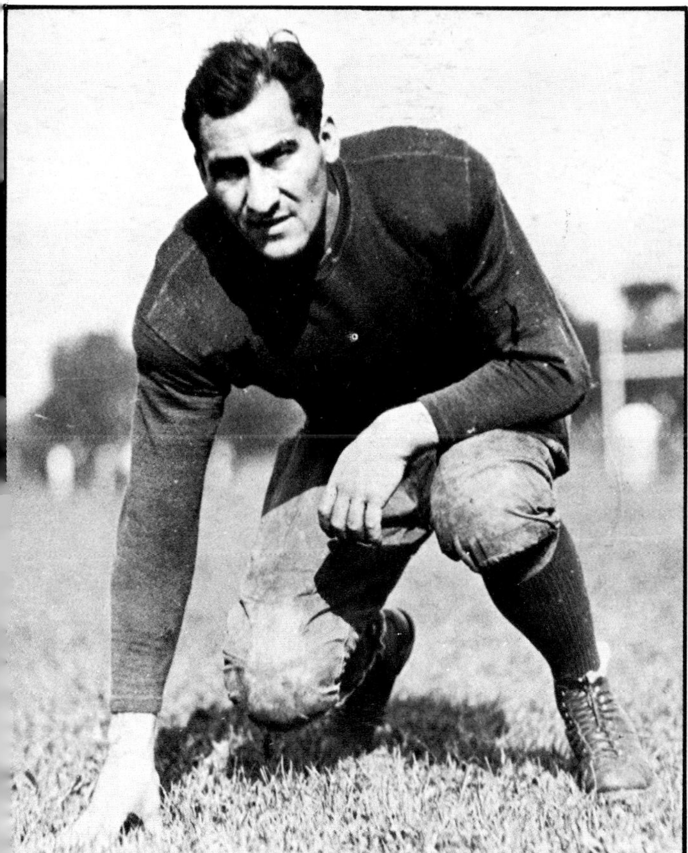

ROBERT FLORA
Michigan right end.

At right, "Cookie" Cunningham

November 14, 1925

Ann Arbor, Michigan

Wolverines Down Buckeyes, 10 To 0, Karow Game Hero

Molenda Smashes Line For Single Touchdown

For the fourth successive year, the maize and blue of Michigan triumphed over the scarlet and gray of Ohio State, but Michigan had to toil much harder than it had expected to score its victory, 10 to 0. The Wolverines had counted on three touchdowns, at least, from the Buckeyes, but the latter, crippled as they were and handicapped by the absence of Elmer Marck, star halfback, fought gamely throughout and threw the Michigan offense back time and again. Michigan, in fact, was lucky to score the lone touchdown and but for a break of the game, the count would merely have been 3 to 0 in favor of the Yostmen.

It was a blocked punt on Ohio's 20 yard line in the first quarter that gave Michigan its chance to score that touchdown. An attempt to kick a goal from placement, that fell short, had given OSU the ball on its own 20 yard line. After three rushes failed to gain, Wendler dropped back to kick. Right end Flora of Michigan shot in and blocked it, the ball bounding back to Ohio's 3 yard line where OSU's Clark fell on it, but Michigan getting possession.

After three futile attempts to cross the Bucks' goal, Molenda smashed over on the fourth. Benny Friedman kicked the extra point. Michigan did add three more points in the second quarter when Oosterbaan intercepted a forward pass, and thus gave Friedman the chance to kick a goal from placement from the 38 yard line, a noble effort, distance and bad angle considered.

Defense was the name of the game on both sides. Ohio was held to one first down during the entire contest, that being the result of a forward pass, Grim to Karow, in the second quarter. From scrimmage, Michigan gained 299 yards and yet neither march of 46 or 53 yards resulted in a touchdown, Ohio being found a most stubborn antagonist inside its own twenty yard line. Ohio gained only 62 yards through the game.

Marty Karow, a Cleveland boy, was the hero for OSU as he stopped the Michigan smashes through the line and also spilled the famous Friedman pass attack repeatedly. Michigan tried 21 passes and only completed 4. Ohio completed 2 of 9.

1925			
Ohio	10	OH Wesleyan	3
Ohio	9	Columbia	0
Ohio	3	Chicago	3
Ohio	0	Iowa	15
Ohio	17	Wooster	0
Ohio	7	Indiana	0
Ohio	0	Michigan	10
Ohio	9	Illinois	14

Season Summary

Games Won, 4; Lost, 3; Tied 1

OHIO

No.	Name	Pos.	Wt.	Home Town
11	Marek	B	170	Cedar Rapids, IA
46	Grim	B	160	Toledo, OH
48	Bell, Robin	QB	173	Erie, PA
49	Williman	B	157	Cleveland, OH
50	Ullery	C	184	Bradford, OH
51	Slough	C	182	Mansfield, OH
52	Ackerman	E	164	Wauseon, OH
54	Uridil	T	174	Cedar Rapids, IA
55	Jenkins	T	188	Columbus, OH
56	Reed	G	180	Columbus, OH
57	Hess	G	185	Chardon, OH
58	Seiffer	E	170	Evansville, IN
59	Harrison	T	173	Columbus, OH
60	Nichols	T	190	LaGrange, OH
61	Clark	B	170	Gettysburg, OH
62	McCarthy	T	180	Fremont, OH
63	Bell, Bob	FB	185	Columbus, OH
66	Karow	FB	175	Cleveland, OH
67	Wentz	B	165	Kenton, OH
68	Rowan	E	180	Chillicothe, OH
69	Klein	C	175	Lorain, OH
70	Meyers	G	190	Cleveland, OH
75	Griswold	B	170	Erie, PA
76	Joseph	E	175	Columbus, OH
77	Cunningham	E	193	Mt. Vernon, OH
78	Jeffrey	E	178	Toledo, OH
80	Mackey	T	178	Galion, OH
81	Lacksen	T	194	Ashtabula, OH
82	Bradley	C	188	Woodstock, OH
84	Young	T	180	Kenton, OH
85	Mitchell	B	162	Lima, OH
87	Hunt	B	160	Toledo, OH
88	Kraglow	G	220	DeGraf, OH
91	Hieronymus	FB	202	Columbus, OH
95	Wendler	B	152	Fremont, OH
96	Gorrill	E	165	Fostoria, OH
97	Blanchard	QB	144	Columbus, OH

EDWIN HESS
All-American Guard

Benny's backfield

ROBERT BROWN
All-American Center

MICHIGAN

No.	Name	Pos.	Wt.	Home Town
11	Hoffman	QB	147	Richmond Hill, N.Y.
14	Babcock, R.	T	181	Royal Oak, MI
15	Garber	B	152	Enid, OK
16	Gilbert	B	159	Kalamazoo, MI
17	Babcock, S.	B	157	Detroit, MI
18	Baer	G	181	Louisville, KY
19	Brown	C	183	Ypsilanti, MI
20	Coventry	C	172	Duluth, MN
22	Dewey	G	197	Monroe, MI
23	Domhoff	Q	169	Toledo, OH
24	Gregory	B	160	Ann Arbor,MI
25	Edwards	T	180	Central Lake, MI
26	Grinnell	T	184	Grosse Isle, MI
27	Friedman	Q	174	Cleveland, OH
28	Grube	E	174	Saginaw, MI
29	Gabel	T	192	Detroit, MI
30	Hawkins	G	198	Saginaw, MI
31	Flora	E	185	Muskegon, MI
32	Herrnstein	B-E	163	Chillicothe, OH
33	Heston	B	180	Ann Arbor, MI
34	Fuller	B	173	Jackson, MI
40	Lovette	B	190	Saginaw, MI
41	McIntyre	G	168	Detroit, MI
42	Miller	Q	162	Adrian, MI
43	Molenda	FB	187	Detroit, MI
45	Nickerson	E	187	Oak Park, IL
46	Oade	T	186	Lansing, MI
47	Oosterbaan	E	182	Muskegon, MI
48	Palmeroli	G	183	Highland Park, MI
49	Palmer	E	181	Grand Rapids, MI
50	Parker	B	165	Hastings, MI
51	Puckolwartz	QB	152	Chicago, IL
53	Schoenfeldt	C	184	Detroit, MI
55	Stamman	E	165	Toledo, OH
56	Thisted	C	185	Great Falls, MT
57	Webber, H.	G	194	Mt. Clemens, MI
58	Webber, W.	FB	181	Mt. Clemens, MI
61	Heath	FB	184	Corning, NY

1925

Michigan	39	M.A.C.	0
Michigan	63	Indiana	0
Michigan	21	Wisconsin	0
Michigan	3	Illinois	0
Michigan	54	Navy	0
Michigan	2	Northwestern	3
Michigan	10	Ohio State	0
Michigan	35	Minnesota	0

Season Summary

Games Won, 7; Lost, 1; Tied 0

BENNIE OOSTERBAAN
All-American End

BENNY FRIEDMAN
All-American Quarterback

TOM EDWARDS
All-American Tackle

HARRY HAWKINS
All-American Guard

ABOVE; OSU Captain Karow greets his counterpart. BELOW; Friedman dodges through a field of Ohio players.

November 13, 1926

Columbus, Ohio

Ohio Loses Chance To Tie Score Near End When Goal Kick Fails

Michigan Survives Scare, 17 To 16

Tears streamed down the cheeks of Myers Clark, Buckeye quarterback, when the great gridiron struggle ended and the scarlet and gray clad warriors were downheartedly stumbling off the field, for his failure to kick a goal after touchdown that had given Michigan the victory, 17 to 16.

90,411 wild fans saw a monumental struggle between two evenly matched teams. Clark of the Buckeyes played brilliantly, as did Oosterbaan with his passing surprises.

Taking advantage of the breaks in the first period, Ohio dashed off in front with a lead of ten points. But coolly as a chess master opposed to a mere beginner, Captain Oosterbaan opened his famous air attack with uncanny precision and actually swept clear down the field to spring the best trick in his possession, a forward pass when the Buckeyes were looking for a place kick. And the same master of the gridiron, thirty seconds before the half ended, dazzled 90,000 spectators with a most phenomenal place kick for a goal that tied the score. The kick actually traveled a total distance of sixty yards ending between the posts and over the crossbars.

The first half ended in a 10 to 10 tie and each great eleven was battling the other to a standstill, when Marek of Ohio State was guilty of a double error, one mental, the other mechanical, fumbling a punt he should have let roll. As it happened to be on Ohio's 5 yard line, Michigan was given its chance to score another touchdown that spelled victory.

At the start of the fourth quarter Oosterbaan outwitted the Buckeyes again when he again passed over the line for the touchdown that put the Wolverines six more points out in front. But there was no more "quit" in the make-up of the Buckeyes than there had been in the gladiators from Ann Arbor. Back came Ohio, fighting even more fiercely than at any time, eager to overcome the lead of seven points.

As the Wolverines had swept down the famous gridiron in the second quarter, so swept the Buckeyes in the fourth. Starting well up in their own territory and inspired by Byron Eby, they never stopped until Eby had darted across the line for the touchdown that left Ohio but one little point behind their hated rivals. The crowd went wild as they figured Myers Clark's trusty right foot would knot the score. The kick, however, instead of clearing the crossbar, merely cleared the heads of the opposing linemen, and crossed the goal line a yard or so below the bar. With it went Ohio's hopes of a Big Ten championship, hopes that had been raised to great heights in view of the fighting spirit inspired by Captain Marty Karow and the victories over Iowa and Chicago.

It was a contest that was decided by the "breaks of the game."

1926

1926		
Michigan .. 42	OK A & M	3
Michigan .. 55	M.S.C.	3
Michigan .. 20	Minnesota	0
Michigan .. 13	Illinois	0
Michigan .. 0	Navy	10
Michigan .. 37	Wisconsin	0
Michigan .. 17	Ohio State	16
Michigan .. 7	Minnesota	6

Season Summary

Games Won, 7; Lost, 1; Tied, 0

BENNIE OOSTERBAAN
All-American End

BENNY FRIEDMAN
All-American Quarterback

MICHIGAN

Name	Pos.	Wt.	Home Town
Babcock, S.	HB	155	Detroit, MI
Baer, R.	G-T	186	Louisville, KY
Black, D.	FB-HB	170	Poland, OH
Boden, M.	E	171	Detroit, MI
Cook, A.	HB	165	Muskegon, MI
Cowell, G.	HB-FB	170	Coldwater, MI
Cragin, R.	C	169	Leominster, MA
Dahlem, A. G.	QB-HB	147	Jackson, MI
Dewey, S.	G	192	Monroe, MI
Domhoff, V.	QB-HB	175	Toledo, OH
Flora, Wm.	E	182	Muskegon, MI
Friedman (Capt.)	QB	182	Cleveland, OH
Gabel, N	G-T	195	Detroit, MI
Gilbert, L.	HB	157	Kalamazoo, MI
Greenwald, H. T.	HB	156	Chicago, IL
Grinnell, H. S.	T	188	Detroit, MI
Harrigan, Frank	HB	180	Grand Rapids, MI
Heath, W. H.	T-FB	178	Corning, NY
Heston, L. G.	E	175	Detroit, MI
Hoffman, L.	QB-HB	152	Allegan, MI
Hughes, A. M.	FB-HB	164	Gary, IN
Kelly, J. J.	QB-HB	160	Latrobe, PA
Lovette, J.	G	185	Saginaw, MI
McIntyre, K. C.	G	166	Detroit, MI
Meese, F. E.	G-T	174	Toledo, OH
Miller, J. F., Jr.	HB	165	Adrian, MI
Molenda, J.	FB	195	Detroit, MI
Nicholson, G. A.	G-T	197	Kansas City, MO
Nickerson, M.	T	187	Oak Park, IL
Nyland, H. Z., Jr.	E	170	Grand Haven, MI
Oade, J.	T	177	Lansing, MI
Oosterbaan, B. G.	E	192	Muskegon, MI
Palmeroli, J.	G-T	188	Highland Park, MI
Pommerening, O	G-T	176	Ann Arbor, MI
Puckelwartz, W.	QB	157	Chicago, IL
Rich, G.	HB-FB	180	Lakewood, OH
Rose, H.	T	178	Detroit, MI
Schoenfeld, J.	C	191	Bartlesville, OK
Stienecker, C.	C	193	Toledo, OH
Squier, G.	G	192	South Haven, MI
Totzke, H. G.	HB	166	Benton Harbor, MI
Truskowski, J.	C	190	Detroit, MI
Weber, H.	G	194	Mt. Clemens, MI
Weber, W.	FB	188	Mt. Clemens, MI
Whittle, J. D.	QB	146	Chicago, IL

OHIO

Name	Pos.	Wt.	Hgt.	Home Town
Ackerman, Cornelius	E	170	5-10	Wauseon
Alber, George	E	175	5-10	Toledo
Bell, Robert	FB	170	5-9	Columbus
Bell, Robin	E	176	6-0	Erie, PA
Blanchard, Bruce	QB	148	5-10	Columbus
Bloser, Parker	E	175	6-0	Columbus
Bonser, Thomas	E	138	5-7½	Dayton
Carlin, Oscar E.	G	170	5-11	Bryan
Carter, Dave	G	175	6-0	Springfield
Chambers, H. E.	QB	140	5-8	Sold. Summit, UT
Clark, Myers	HB	170	5-11½	Gettysburg
Conklin, Robert	HB	170	6-½	Chicago, IL
Cox, Joe	T	177	6-2	Dayton
Dunlap, John	G	170	5-11½	Williamsport
Eby, Byron	HB	170	6-0	Chillicothe
Fenner, Harry	E	149	5-10	Dayton
Freeman, Eddie	QB	152	5-8½	Canal Winchester
Glenn, C. L.	E	195	6-4	Columbus
Grim, Fred	HB	163	5-10½	Toledo
Griswold, Francis	HB	168	5-10	Erie, PA
Hamilton, Clarence	HB	150	5-11	Louisville
Hardway, L. E.	T	185	6-1½	Columbus
Hess, Ed	G	178	6-½	Columbus
Hunt, William	HB	160	5-8½	Toledo
Jeckell, Charles	E	157	6-2½	Youngstown
Karow, Marty	FB	170	5-10½	Cleveland
Klein, Alex	C	175	5-11	Lorain
Kreglow, Julius	G	223	6-2	DeGraff
Kriss, Howard	QB	164	5-7½	East Cleveland
Kruskamp, Harold	HB	185	6-0	Wellston
Lacksen, Frank	T	195	6-4	Ashtabula
McCarthy, Tim	T	185	6-2	Fremont
McMillen, Harold	T	205	6-0	Bellpoint
Mackey, Fred	T	175	5-10	Galion
Marek, Elmer	HB	165	5-10½	Cedar Rapids, IA
Meacham, H. C.	T	200	6-1½	Atwater
Meyer, Ted	G	180	5-11	Cleveland
Moler, William	G	193	5-11	Columbus
esser, John	G	187	6-0	Columbus
hsner, Clarence	HB	175	5-10	Columbus
reston, Fred	C	184	5-10	Lancaster
askowski, Leo	T	199	6-3	Cleveland
eed, William	G	178	5-9	Columbus
oshon, Ray	G	180	5-10½	Basil
owan, Deb	E	181	6-1	Chillicothe
chmidt, Walter	E	177	6-2	Cleveland
hifflette, Don	HB	167	6-0	Columbus
lemmons, Robert	QB	153	5-8	Columbus
lough, Herb	C	183	5-11½	Mansfield
urina, Cyril	E	167	5-10½	Cleveland
hone, Franklin	G	175	5-11	Columbus
rombetti, Raymond	G	220	5-10	Steubenville
llery, Jack	C	185	6-1	Bradford
ridil, Leo	T	180	6-0	Cedar Rapids, IA
iswell, Owen	T	181	6-1	Columbus
oerlein, George	HB	166	5-11	Groveport
ingling, Walter	C	154	5-8	Lima

1926

Ohio	40	Wittenberg	0
Ohio	47	OH Wesleyan	0
Ohio	32	Columbia	7
Ohio	23	Iowa	6
Ohio	18	Chicago	0
Ohio	13	Wilmington	7
Ohio	16	Michigan	17
Ohio	7	Illinois	6

Season Summary

Games Won, 7; Lost, 1

EDWIN HESS
All-American Guard

MARTIN KAROW
All-American Offensive Back

Michigan Stadium was dedicated in 1927. With later additions, it is now (1978) the largest college owned football structure in the nation with a seating capacity of over 101,000.

ELTON "TAD" WIEMAN
Michigan Head Coach
1927-1928

October 23, 1927

Ann Arbor, Michigan

Michigan Men Victors Over Ohio, 21 To 0

87,000 Fill Wolverines' New Stadium As Oosterbaan And Gilbert Show Grid Ability

The Wolverines composed a machine. They had the interference, the punch, and tackled desperately. When they hit a Buckeye ball carrier, said ball carrier knew he was hit. Ohio, on the other hand, suffered because of high tackles coupled with poor interference. The Wolverines' trick plays also had Ohio puzzled. In short, the contest looked like a Big Ten eleven opposed to one from the Ohio Conference.

With the first period and five minutes of the second period scoreless, Eby punted to Ohio's 47 yard line. Michigan's Gembis tore through the line for four yards while a Gilbert to Oosterbaan netted 16 yards. An end run worked only a yard. Michigan did not care as the play merely was to set the stage for a trick play, the "dead man" trick.

One of the Michigan backs remained all alone on the east side of the field as if Michigan hoped Ohio would overlook and fail to guard him. It worked. With Ohio's attention turned toward the lone wolf, Oosterbaan dropped back and passed to Gilbert right down the west side close to the line. The pass was straight as a die, the catch was perfect, and Eby missed the tackle, Gilbert going over for the touchdown Gilbert kicked goal for a 7 to 0 lead.

The third quarter was fairly well along when Gilbert caught a punt and, aided by highbrow tackling of the Buckeyes, brought the ball back to Ohio's 40 yard line. Ohio made two changes and Michigan's smashing attack failed. Another trick play — Domhoff dropped back as if to forward pass, but Oosterbaan whirled, circled Domhoff, grabbed the ball and passed to Gilbert, who, tackled by Ohsner, stumbled across the line for the second touchdown, a gain of 50 yards from where the ball was thrown by Oosterbaan.

The final period saw the Buckeyes open an unexpected offensive attack that fairly swept the Wolverines off their feet. Taking possession in their own territory, Grim, Eby, Ohsner and Alber passed, ran, and plunged until the Michigan 13 yard line was reached. There Grim fumbled but recovered for a loss. A forward pass was grounded over the line and the Ohio threat was a thing of the past.

Not long afterward the Michigan attack again carried the ball to Ohio's 15 yard line. A lateral from Oosterbaan allowed Gilbert to score his third T.D. He also kicked goal for Michigan's 21 to 0 lead.

Ohio shot Kriss, its speed merchant, into the game, and the Buckeyes opened up a running and passing attack that inside of two minutes took the ball to Michigan's 3 yard line. But again, a forward pass over the line was incomplete and the contest ended with the Michigan goal line still uncrossed.

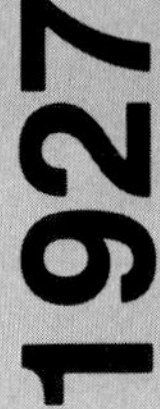

1927

Ohio	31	Wittenberg	0
Ohio	13	Iowa	6
Ohio	13	Northwestern	19
Ohio	0	Michigan	21
Ohio	13	Chicago	7
Ohio	0	Princeton	20
Ohio	61	Denison	6
Ohio	0	Illinois	13

Season Summary
Won 4, Lost 4

LEO RASKOWSKI
All-American Tackle

OHIO

No.	Name	Pos.	Wt.	Home Town
1	Huston, Arthur	HB	160	Findlay
2	Fry, Edgar Allen	G	172	Columbus
3	Carlin, Oscar E.	G	167	Bryan
4	Marek, Elmer	HB	167	Cedar Rapids, IA
5	Eby, Byron	HB	179	Chillicothe
6	Penrod, James L.	T	205	Lewisburg
7	Ullery, Jack	C	187	Bradford
8	Griswold, Francis	HB	167	Erie, PA
9	Alber, George	E	177	Toledo
10	Schear, Herbert	C	174	Dayton
12	Ackerman, Cor.	E	170	Wauseon
13	Cory, Lincoln	FB	176	Coon Rapids, IA
14	Hess, Albert	E	158	Cleveland
15	Young, William	G	189	Kenton
16	Fouch, George	QB	160	Columbus
17	Coffey, Chas. B.	HB	159	Salem
18	Nesser, John P.	T	180	Columbus
19	Bell, Robert	FB	173	Columbus
20	Grim, Fred	HB	163	Toledo
22	Uridel, Leo	T	173	Cedar Rapids, IA
23	Kriss, Howard	QB	166	E. Cleveland
24	Cox, Joe	T	177	Dayton
25	Schmidt, Walter	E	180	Cleveland
26	Redman, F. A.	QB	160	Chillicothe
27	Meyer, Theo. (Capt.)	G	182	Cleveland
28	Bruck, John	G	224	Columbus
29	Barklow, Carson	G	177	Portsmouth
30	Dunn, D. L.	FB	150	Curtice
31	Buechsenschuss, A.	T	176	Toledo
32	Moler, William	G	195	Columbus
33	Ohsner, Clarence	HB	171	Columbus
34	Surina, Cyril	E	165	Cleveland
35	Tarr, Robert	T	168	Russell Point
36	Popp, Milton F.	T	179	Fort Wayne, IN
37	Weprin, Abram	T	185	Dayton
38	Glasser, Chester	T	185	Youngstown
39	Wiswell, Owen	G	181	Columbus
40	Raskowski, Leo	T	212	Cleveland
41	Hieronymus, Theo.	FB	190	Columbus
42	Bell, Robin	E	182	Erie, PA
43	Chambers, H. E.	QB	135	Summit, UT
44	Rowan, Deb.	E	181	Chillicothe
46	McClure, Donald	HB	165	Toledo
48	Weaver, William	C	160	Cleveland
50	Mitchel, Joe	G	198	Van Wert
51	Moore, James H.	HB	160	Struthers
52	Brozic, Andrew	T	197	Midland, PA
53	Sandman, Russell	HB	170	Cincinnati
54	Harris, George	HB	162	Cincinnati
55	Heppberger, C. E.	QB	162	Akron
56	Henninger, W.	E	160	Wapakoneta
57	Walker, Gordon	C	168	Columbus
58	Yingling, W.	C	151	Lima

MICHIGAN

No.	Name	Pos.	Wt.	Home Town
4	Carter, C. F.	E	172	Bay City
5	Crego, W. B.	T	190	Saginaw
6	Drabicki, J. J.	FB	190	Detroit
7	Flajole, Paul	G	140	Bay City
8	Kanitz, G.	H	170	Milan
9	Roderick, H.	E	170	Elkhart, IN
10	Shantz, Fred B.	C	165	Detroit
11	Hoffman, Leo	Q	152	Allegan
12	Schwarze, Bruce	H	160	Birmingham
14	Sims, A. H.	H	165	Frederick, OK
15	Sullo, Dominic	G	198	Detroit
16	Gilbert, Louis	H	160	Kalamazoo
17	Babcock, Sam	H	155	Detroit
18	Baer, Ray	T	185	Louisville, KY
19	Boden, M. H.	E	177	Detroit
20	Cook, Paul A.	H	160	Muskegon
21	Bovard, A. J.	C	174	Ann Arbor
22	Dansby, William J.	FB	183	Monroe
23	Domhoff, Victor	Q	170	Toledo, OH
24	Greenwald, H. T.	H	158	Chicago, IL
25	Fuller, Fred	FB	170	Grand Rapids
26	Grinnell, Henry	T	187	Detroit
27	George, Edward	G	160	Kalamazoo
28	Harrigan, Frank	E	184	Grand Rapids
29	Gabel, Norman	T	198	Detroit
30	Geistert, W. E.	H	159	Grand Rapids
31	Taylor, L. H.	E	180	Ann Arbor
32	Kerr, Douglas	E	169	Gary, IN
33	Heston, L. G.	E	180	Detroit
34	McBride, Jennings	Q	165	Oklahoma City, OK
35	Ketz, W. H.	T	191	Detroit
36	Meese, Frank	T	175	Toledo, OH
37	Parker, Roy	G	170	Fordson
38	Poe, H. W.	G	185	Toledo, OH
39	Poorman, E. B.	T	178	Chicago Heights, IL
40	Robbins, J. S.	T	190	Highland Park, IL
41	Straub, G. H.	Q	155	Toledo, OH
42	Miller, James F., Jr.	Q	165	Adrian
43	Gembis, J. G.	FB	190	Vicksburg
44	Nicholson, Geo., Jr.	G	195	Kansas City, MO
45	Nickerson, Max	T	185	Chicago, IL
46	Thisted, C. E.	C	188	Great Falls, MT
47	Oosterbaan, B. (Capt.)	E	186	Muskegon
48	Palmeroli, John	G	185	Highland Park
49	Nyland, H., Jr.	E	168	Grand Haven
50	Pommerening, O. P.	T	178	Ann Arbor
51	Puckelwartz, Wm.	H	160	Chicago, IL
52	Rich, George	H	180	Lakewood, OH
53	Shoenfeld, John	C	195	Bartesville, OK
54	Walder, Harold	T	188	Jackson
55	Whittle, John	Q	153	Chicago, IL
56	Williams, R. J.	G	190	Detroit
57	Weber, H. A.	G	194	Mt. Clemens
58	Wolff, John S., Jr.	G	185	Detroit
64	Cragin, Ray	C	182	Leominster, MA

1927

Michigan	33	Ohio Wesleyan	0
Michigan	21	M.S.C.	0
Michigan	14	Wisconsin	0
Michigan	21	Ohio State	0
Michigan	0	Illinois	14
Michigan	14	Chicago	0
Michigan	27	Navy	12
Michigan	7	Minnesota	13

Season Summary

Games Won, 6; Lost, 2; Tied, 0.

BENNIE OOSTERBAAN
All-American End
Third Consecutive Year

Notice the scoreboard in the Bend.

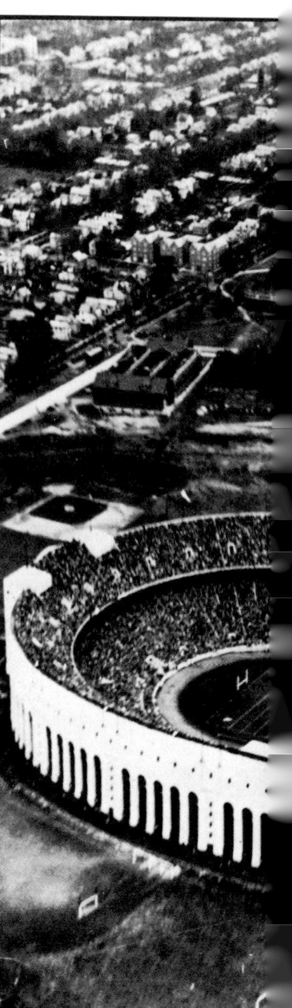

Michigan and Ohio crowds join as they enter the stadium.

October 21, 1928

Columbus, Ohio

Ohio State Crushes Michigan, 19 To 7 In Hard Fight

Wilce Has Football Victory Over 'Old Enemy For First Time In Seven Years

Ripped by the fangs of an infuriated cornered Wolverine — stunned and stopped for a moment — Jack Wilce's last Ohio State football team came fighting back to an overwhelming victory. A crowd of 72,723 banked to the skies of the giant Buckeye Stadium saw the scarlet wave of Ohio at last go pouring over Michigan, 19 to 7.

A versatile attack — Coffee and Eby like wraiths around the ends, Cory pounding the line, and Holman throwing passes — rolled up thirteen first downs for Ohio to Michigan's scant one. Twice Ohio scored on passes, Holman to Fesler and Holman to Coffee.

Wounded and shaky from two previous defeats, the Wolverines came to Columbus hopeful of a break. It got the break, a real one, and scored on it, but nevertheless it was dubbed anyhow.

After an opening period touchdown pass from Holman to Fesler and a missed extra point try, the score stood 6 to 0. That set the stage for Michigan's big break. Since Michigan could not move from its own 45 yard line, Jack Wheeler dropped back to kick and booted a beauty. The ball went bounding toward the goal line. On it went, with Michigan forwards tearing down upon it, and Charley Coffee, the Buckeye safety man, watching it roll. With the ball inches from the line, Coffee plunged for it and it skidded like a greased pig, struck him, glancing away and went scooting over the end zone. Leo Draveling, Michigan end fell upon it for a Wolverine touchdown. Big Joe Gembis booted the placement for the extra point.

The Michigan score awakened the Bucks and Lincoln Cory and Byron Eby smashed the Wolverines with Eby scoring from 21 yards out on a sweep around left end. Barratt's place kick was blocked so the half ended 12 to 7, Ohio favor.

The final onslaught by the Buckeyes came in the final period and began on their own 37 yard line. Coffee and Hieronymous banged down to the Michigan 35 yard line. Two passes from Holman to Coffee provided the final T.D. for Ohio and Barrett added the point after.

Nine of Ohio's first downs were by rushing and four by passing. Ohio was 5 for 14 through the air for 79 yards with none intercepted. Michigan connected on only two of six, with two interceptions.

1928

1928

Michigan	7	Ohio Wesleyan	17
Michigan	0	Indiana	6
Michigan	7	Ohio State	19
Michigan	0	Wisconsin	7
Michigan	3	Illinois	0
Michigan	6	Navy	6
Michigan	3	M.S.C.	0
Michigan	10	Iowa	7

Season Summary

Games Won, 3; Lost, 4; Tied, 1

OTTO POMMERENING
All-American Tackle

MICHIGAN

Name	Pos.	Wt.	Hgt.	Home Town
Ashbeck, Fred	E	210	6-6½	Lakewood, OH
Avery, Leslie	HB	170	5-10	South Haven
Barley, A.	HB	165	5-11	Marion, IN
Bator, Kalman, Jr.	HB	178	5-11	Detroit
Bauer, Carl J., Jr.	G	198	5-8	Saginaw
Bergman, Milton	T	178	5-9	Clarence, NY
Biedenweg, C.	HB	165	5-10	Fort Wayne, IN
Boden, Marshall	E	175	6-2	Detroit
Bovard, Alan	C	178	5-11	Ann Arbor
Bovard, Theo.	E	175	6-1	Ann Arbor
Brown, Frank P.	QB	190	6	Elgin, IL
Brown, William A.	C	200	5-10	Sandusky
Carter, Clare F.	E	170	6	Bay City
Cooke, Thomas M.	C	197	6-6	Chicago, IL
Cornwell, Francis	E	185	5-10½	Grand Rapids
Cragin, Raymond	C	188	5-11	Leominster, MA
Dahlem, Alvin G.	HB	155	5-8	Jackson
Dansby, William J.	FB	182	5-11¼	Monroe
Decker, Art W.	G	200	5-11	Flint
Dobbin, John	HB	157	5-10	State Center, IA
Draveling, Leo	T	200	6-1	Port Huron
Duff, Robert	G	200	5-9	Canton, OH
Fish, Willard	G	180	5-9	Battle Creek
Gambis, Joe	FB	210	5-11½	Vicksburg
Geistert, Walter	HB	156	5-7	Grand Rapids
Gitman, William	T	190	5-9	Dayton, OH
Grodsky, Isadore	HB	170	5-10	New Haven, CT
Gundry, George	HB	160	5-7	Grand Blanc
Hager, H.	T	190	6-1	Lansing
Holmes, Danny W.	QB	165	5-11	Canton, OH
Hozer, Stanley	FB	170	5-10	Muskegon
Hughes, A. Morris	FB	174	5-10½	Gary, IN
Kanitz, Tharel	HB	170	5-10	Milan
Keene, Clifford	T	175	6	Buffalo, NY
Kerr, Douglas	E	170	5-10	Gary, IN
Kubicek, Louis	T	194	5-11	Chicago, IL
Lytle, Richard	FB	156	5-8	Valparaiso, IN
McBride, Jennings	HB	170	5-7	Oklahoma City, OK
McCormick, Wilson	HB	155	5-11	Ann Arbor
McCoy, Earnest	E	170	6-1	Detroit
Meese, Frank	T	200	5-11	Toledo, OH
Morgan, Robert	G	180	5-11	Toledo, OH
Moyer, Chas. P.	T	201	6-1	Detroit
Olson, Joel E.	G	172	6	Escanaba
Orwig, James	E	172	6	Ann Arbor
Parker, C. F.	E	175	5-11	Wray, CO
Parker, Ray	G	170	5-9¾	Ann Arbor
Patton, Robert J.	C	200	6-1	Springfield, IL
Poe, Howard	G	185	5-11½	Toledo, OH
Poorman, Edwin	T	184	6	Chicago Heights, IL
Pommerening, Otto	T	178	5-11½	Ann Arbor
Precobb, G. W.	HB	150	5-10	Detroit
Reichman, Gerson	FB	195	5-11	New York City
Rich, Geo. (Capt.)	HB	180	6	Lakewood, OH
Risk, Robert D.	E	183	5-11½	Muskegon
Schurrer, Chas.	G	185	5-11	Highland Park
Sherwood, Marion	C	170	6	Grand Haven
Simrall, James O.	QB	155	5-10	Lexington, KY
Slater, Roger	T	195	6-½	Webster Grove, MO
Squier, George	T	205	5-10	South Haven
Smith, Harsen A.	E	168	5-10	Algonac
Straub, Harvey	QB	158	5-8	Toledo, OH
Steinke, Al	G	182	6	St. Joseph
Sukupchak, Paul	HB	163	5-7	Bridgman
Totzke, John H.	HB	170	6	Benton Harbor
Truskowski, Joe	E	188	5-11½	Detroit
Wheeler, C. Jack	QB	152	5-11¼	Bay City
Widman, John C.	HB	160	5-10	Detroit
Whittle, J. Dallas	HB	158	5-9	Chicago, IL
Williams, R.	G	190	5-11	Detroit

OHIO

Name	Pos.	Wt.	Hgt.	Home Town
Alber, George	E	177	5-11	Toledo
Barratt, F. W.	C	236	6-1½	Lansing, MI
Beck, P. E.	C	180	5-10	Columbus
Buechsenschuss, A.	T	174	5-11	Toledo
Carlin, Oscar	G	166	5-10½	Bryan
Cahen, Herman	HB	158	5-10	Cleveland Heights
Carter, David W.	T	172	6-1	Springfield
Cory, Lincoln	FB	171	5-10	Coon Rapids, IA
Coffee, Chas.	HB	161	5-10½	Salem
Cox, Joe	T	184	6-2	Dayton
Dill, M. R.	E	171	6-1	Lakewood
Eby, Byron	HB	175	6	Chillicothe
Evans, Robert	E	170	6	Columbus
Ferral, Walter	T	181	6	Columbiana
Fesler, W.	E	173	5-11½	Youngstown
Fisher, Max M.	C	168	6-1	Salem
Fivaz, Robert	HB	157	5-10	Sunbury
Fouch, George	QB	159	5-10	Columbus
Freppel, F.	QB	145	5-7	Napoleon
George, Samuel	FB	168	5-10	Youngstown
Gerhard, Maurice	FB	181	5-11½	Hamilton
Glasser, Chester	T	186	6-1½	Youngstown
Griffith, Wm.	T	218	5-11½	Cleveland
Hess, Albert	HB	162	5-11	Cincinnati
Hieronymous, Theo.	T	200	6-3	Columbus
Holman, Allen	QB	171	5-10½	Fairfield, IA
Horn, R.	HB	175	6	Columbus
Hudson, A. M.	E	172	6-1	Columbus
Humberstone, H. J.	G	177	6-1	Columbus
Huston, Arthur	HB	161	5-10½	Findlay
Idle, Ralph	E	166	5-10½	Wapakoneta
Kriss, Howard	HB	168	5-8	Cleveland
Kruskamp, Harold	FB	189	6	Wellston
Larkins, R.	T	180	6	East Liverpool
Lemon, George D.	G	189	6-2	Toledo
McConnell, A. L.	HB	174	6-1½	Massillon
McClure, Donald	FB	167	5-10½	Toledo
Neidert, John	C	158	5-9	Akron
Nesser, John	T	191	6	Columbus
Nesser, Wm.	HB	158	5-7	Columbus
Neubreckt, K.	HB	170	5-10½	Toledo
Nichlaus, F. E.	T	175	6-2½	Columbus
North, D. W.	G	171	6	Groveport
O'Shaughnessy, J. J.	E	182	6-1	Columbus
Oster, Harvey	T	190	6	Cleveland
Popp, Milton	T	182	5-11	Fort Wayne, IN
Ray, Ernest	G	225	5-10	Akron
Raskowski, Leo	T	208	6-3	Cleveland
Reboulet, Laverne	T	173	5-10½	Dayton
Reese, D.	T	177	6	Findlay
Rose, Milton	T	170	5-10½	Cleveland
Sack, Irving A.	QB	164	5-7	Toledo
Sattler, C. L.	G	188	5-9½	Findlay
Schear, Herbert	C	170	5-8	Dayton
Selby, Sam	G	174	5-11	Middletown
Sundra, John	E	175	5-11	Cleveland
Surina, Cyril	E	175	5-10¾	Cleveland
Taylor, R. E.	FB	157	5-10½	Sandusky
Tuttle, George	HB	—	5-10	Columbus
Ujhelyi, Joe	G	191	5-11	Lorain
Van Heyde, Geo.	E	164	6-3	Columbus
Walker, Gordon	C	170	—	Columbus
Walkup, Mos. K.	HB	156	5-10½	Columbus
Weprin, Abram	T	196	6-1	Dayton
Wiragos, Lewis	FB	175	5-10½	Cleveland
Wilson, Franklin	QB	153	5-8	Dayton
Wyer, P. H.	QB	169	5-10½	Orrville
Yingling, Walter	C	153	5-8	Lima
Young, Wm.	G	190	5-10½	Kenton

1928

Ohio	41	Wittenberg	0
Ohio	10	Northwestern	0
Ohio	19	Michigan	7
Ohio	13	Indiana	0
Ohio	6	Princeton	6
Ohio	7	Iowa	14
Ohio	39	Muskingum	0
Ohio	0	Illinois	8

Season Summary

Won, 5; Lost, 2; Tied, 1

WESLEY FESLER
All-American End

October 19, 1929

Ann Arbor, Michigan

87,000 See Fighting Ohio Turn Back Michigan

O.S.U. Scores On Pass Early In Battle

A vast throng of 87,000, rising tier upon tier in the giant Michigan Stadium saw a great bunch of never say die scrappers from Columbus play football for Ohio State that day. In a slashing, dramatic battle in which cool heads and brave hearts conquered muscle and might, those dauntless Buckeyes overcame the mastodonic and ferocious Wolverines, 7 to 0.

The long arms of Wesley Fesler, reaching into the air above Michigan's goal line, brought down the long forward pass from Allen Holman to score the only touchdown of the afternoon. Dropping over the goal, with a mass of Wolverine brawn diving on top of him, Fesler brought Ohio its second consecutive victory over the old foe it has battled generally with poor success, since the flying wedge days of 1897. Fred Barratt, Ohio's 240-pound center from Lansing, place kicked the extra point that settled the issue.

Many things were to transpire before that afternoon was over. A gallant Ohio line, outweighed and outrushed, was to stand with its back to the wall, again and again, hoping and battling, tearing in with everything at its command, fighting for every inch. When the game ended those big Wolverines had just completed their last ferocious assault. They had brought the ball to within 6 yards of the Ohio goal and had failed to make it first down by the margin of an inch.

Willie Heston, Jr. led the Michigan attack with 76 yards in sixteen attempts, putting on a dazzling display of running. Dynamite Joe Gembis rammed the Ohio line for 48 yards. But the other huge Michigan backs were helpless against the determined Bucks.

The magnificent punting of Ohio's McConnell and Horn saved the Bucks more than once and those fine boots would have given the Buckeyes a chance for another touchdown, except for Heston.

Michigan gained 207 yards and made eleven first downs. Ohio made six first downs and gained only 110 yards, passes and all, but then Ohio wasn't trying anything fancy in the second half.

1929

1929

Ohio	19	Wittenberg	0
Ohio	7	Iowa	6
Ohio	7	Michigan	0
Ohio	0	Indiana	0
Ohio	2	Pittsburgh	18
Ohio	6	Northwestern	18
Ohio	54	Kenyon	0
Ohio	0	Illinois	27

Season Summary

Games Won, 4; Lost, 3; Tied, 1

WESLEY FESLER
All-American End

OHIO

No.	Name	Pos.	Wt.	Home Town
2	Farrier, Marvin E.	E	180	Dayton, OH
3	Doyle, Burton L.	HB	170	Mishawaka, IN
4	Buechsenschuss, Al.	T	170	Toledo, OH
5	Campbell, Charles A.	G	165	Coshocton, OH
6	Huston, Arthur	HB	163	Findlay, OH
7	Holcomb, Stuart K.	FB	165	Erie, PA
8	Dill, M. Reese	E	175	Lakewood, OH
9	Fouch, George	QB	170	Columbus, OH
10	Holman, Allen	HB	177	Fairfield, IA
11	Follett, Richard	T	175	Cleveland, OH
12	McClure, Donald L.	FB	172	Toledo, OH
13	Horn, Robert L.	HB	181	Columbus, OH
14	Grady, Robert	HB	160	Columbus, OH
15	Benis, Joseph	QB	164	Cleveland, OH
16	Baker, Morgan W.	QB	171	Youngstown, OH
17	Nesser, William H.	HB	163	Reynoldsburg, OH
18	Peterson, L. B., Jr.	E	171	Steubenville, OH
19	Reboulet, Laverne	G	170	Dayton, OH
20	Coffee, Charles	HB	164	Salem, OH
21	Larkins, Richard C.	T	184	East Liverpool, OH
23	Taylor, Russell E.	FB	168	Sandusky, OH
24	Weaver, J. Edward	E	185	Lima, OH
26	Worstell, Hillis	T	178	Bloomdale, OH
27	Kabealo, Charles L.	G	176	Youngstown, OH
28	Kile, Eugene M.	G	185	Marysville, OH
29	Selby, Sam	G	180	W. Middletown, OH
30	Fesler, Wesley E.	E	183	Youngstown, OH
31	Carter, David	C	175	Springfield, OH
32	Von Derau, John	C	168	Dayton, OH
33	Hall, John E.	C	180	Mansfield, OH
34	Griffith, William A.	G	212	E. Cleveland, OH
35	McConnell, Arden	HB	170	Massillon, OH
36	Slaughter, David R.	G	170	Louisville, KY
37	Haubrich, Robert C.	T	190	Columbus, OH
38	Carlin, Oscar	G	166	Bryan, OH
39	Marsh, George C.	T	208	Cleveland, OH
40	Ohsner, Clarence S.	FB	186	Columbus, OH
41	O'Shaughnessy, Joe	E	184	Columbus, OH
42	Bell, William	T	177	Akron, OH
43	Uhjelyi, Joseph	F	198	Lorain, OH
44	Barratt, Fred W.	C	239	Lansing, MI
45	Glasser, Chester	T	192	Youngstown, OH
46	Humberstone, H. J.	G	180	Columbus, OH
47	Larson, Harry E.	G	206	Bridgeport, CT
48	Fisher, Max	C	175	Cleveland, OH

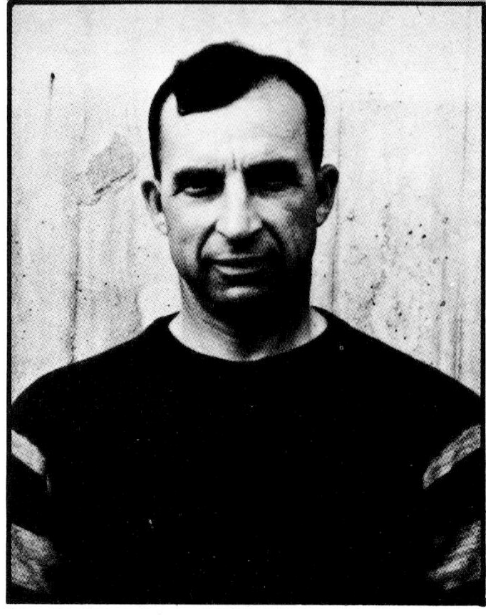

SAM S. WILLAMAN
Ohio State Head Coach
1929-1933

MICHIGAN

No.	Name	Pos.	Wt.	Home Town
4	Jones, William	E	176	Bay City, MI
5	Hodgson, Harold	B	160	River Forest, IL
6	Hayden, E.	T	200	Chicago, IL
7	Miller, Wallace	T	190	Wilmette, IL
8	Bauer, Carl, Jr.	G	200	Saginaw, MI
9	Hayes, Nyol	E	182	Grosse Isle, MI
10	Renner, John	E	175	Youngstown, OH
11	Dahlem, Alvin	B	152	Jackson, MI
12	Schantz, Fred B.	B	170	Detroit, MI
13	Berkowitz, Albert	B	165	Granville, MI
14	Holmes, Danny W.	B	165	Canton, OH
15	Justice, Thos. G.	E	169	Youngstown, NY
16	Heston, Wm.	B	165	Detroit, MI
17	Simrall, Jas. Jr.	QB	163	Lexington, KY
18	Wills, Ralph	B	154	Flint, MI
19	Priest, Ray	B	168	Battle Creek, MI
20	Williams, Everett	B	165	Yale, MI
21	Bovard, Alan	C	195	Ann Arbor, MI
22	Bergman, Milton	T	178	Clarence, NY
24	Anderson, Jack	QB	150	Ann Arbor, MI
25	Brown, Frank P.	B	188	Elgin, IL
26	Brown, Wm.	C	200	Sandusky, MI
27	Draveling, Leo	E	205	Port Huron, MI
28	Cornwell, Francis	E	180	Grand Rapids, MI
29	Ricketts, Girard	E	178	Covington, KY
30	Holland, Kirk	QB	150	Evanston, IL
31	Hudson, Roy	B	195	Girard, OH
32	Daniels, Norman	E	168	Detroit, MI
33	Dierberger, Wesley	E	170	Great Falls, MT
34	McBride, Jennings	B	180	Oklahoma City, OK
35	Steinke, Alfred	G	184	St. Joseph, MI
37	Parker, Ray	G	168	Ann Arbor, MI
38	Poe, Howard	G	190	Toledo, OH
39	Poorman, Edwin	T	185	Chicago Heights, IL
40	Blowney, Henry	T	190	Toledo, OH
41	Straub, Harvey	QB	160	Toledo, OH
42	Gitman, Wm.	T	190	Dayton, OH
43	Gembis, Joe	FB	200	Vicksburg, MI
44	Wilson, Donald	QB	140	Jefferson, IA
45	Morgan, Robert	G	180	Toledo, OH
48	Grinnell, Ira	G	195	Detroit, MI
49	Miller, Harold	B	165	Ann Arbor, MI
50	Auer, Howard	T	193	Bay City, MI
51	Sakupckak, Paul	B	163	Bridgman, MI
52	Smith, Ivan	E	185	Toledo, OH
53	Patton, Robert	C	205	Springfield, IL
55	Roach, Tom	T	190	Grand Rapids, MI
56	Hewitt, Wm.	E	175	Bay City, MI
57	Morrison, Maynard	FB	210	Royal Oak, MI
58	LaJeunesse, Omer	FB	168	Iron Mountain, MI
59	Parker, Orville	B	163	Detroit, MI
60	Mosser, Murray	E	168	Detroit, MI
61	Richardson, Karl	G	190	Ottawa, IL
63	Lindsay, Harold	B	140	Detroit, MI
64	Wheeler, Jack	B	154	Bay City, MI
65	Widman, John	B	165	Detroit, MI
66	Truskowski, J., Capt.	E	190	Detroit, MI
68	Samuels, Tom	G	196	Canton, OH
69	Sikkenga, Jay	E	180	Muskegon, MI
70	Sorensen, Thorwald	T	197	Marquette, MI
71	Wolff, John	G	185	Detroit, MI
72	Heath, Charles	T	190	Cedar Rapids, IA

1929

Michigan	39	Albion	0
Michigan	16	Mt. Union	6
Michigan	17	M.S.C.	0
Michigan	16	Purdue	30
Michigan	0	Ohio State	7
Michigan	0	Illinois	14
Michigan	14	Harvard	12
Michigan	7	Minnesota	6
Michigan	0	Iowa	0

Season Summary

Games Won, 5; Lost, 3; Tied, 1

HARRY G. KIPKE
Michigan Head Coach
1929-1937

October 18, 1930

Columbus, Ohio

Passes By Newman Rout Bucks 13 To 0

68,000 See Big Ten Battle At Columbus; Chizek Is Star In Defeat

Harry Newman, who was hailed as a new Benny Friedman, rose behind a mighty wall of Wolverines to shatter Ohio State's dream of a third straight victory over the Maize and Blue of Michigan.

Only a couple of minutes remained in the first half when disaster began for the Buckeyes. The ball was Michigan's on its 46 yard line, first down. Ohio was caught napping. Newman ran well back of the burly Wolverine line and threw a long, bullet-like pass to the right. The pass was about 25 yards and Capt. Jim Simrall raced to receive it. On the run, and closely pursued by an Ohio defender, he leaped into the air, caught the ball, and down he came whirling toward the goal line. The Buckeyes rushed in pursuit and Stuart Holcomb finally felled Simrall on the one yard line. On the next play Harry Newman stuck his head into a clawing mass of young humanity and squeezed the ball over. He then coolly kicked the extra point. Thus ended the first half.

The second half began with Ohio unable to make yardage so Fesler punted to Simrall who returned to the Ohio 46. A Newman to Wheeler pass clicked and Michigan was on Ohio's 19 yard line. A rush put the ball on the 16 where Roy Hudson from a half punt formation, took the ball and plunged through a gaping hole at center straight through for a touchdown. Newman's place kick was partially blocked.

Dave Chizek attempted to bring the Bucks back, once to the Michigan 13 yard line, but the green O.S.U. team could not score. In the sadness of defeat, Ohio found a bright spot in the passing of Chizek. Once more, as in games by the half dozens, since he first donned a varsity uniform in 1928, Wesley Fesler, Ohio's All-American right end was a tremendous player and complemented the passing of Chizek.

Ohio made 13 first downs to Michigan's 6, and gained 272 yards to Michigan's 224, but remember that Michigan after its two touchdowns, was playing a defensive game. It wasn't any debacle—it was just defeat suffered by a fair team at the hands of a smarter one.

1930

MICHIGAN

1930

Michigan	33	Denison	0
Michigan	7	MI St. Norm.	0
Michigan	0	MSC	0
Michigan	14	Purdue	13
Michigan	13	OH State	0
Michigan	15	Illinois	7
Michigan	6	Harvard	3
Michigan	7	Minnesota	0
Michigan	16	Chicago	0

Season Summary

Games Won, 8; Lost, 0; Tied, 1

No.	Name	No.	Name
4	Jordan, William	35	Avery, Leslie
5	Ochmann, Ward	36	O'Neil, William
6	Bremen, George	39	Williamson, Ivan
7	Miller, Wallace B.	40	Berkowitz, Albert
8	Kuijala, Walfred	41	Marcovsky, Abe
9	Hayes, Nyol	42	Gitman, William
10	Manuel, Kenneth	43	Purdum, Claire
12	Clohset, Fred	45	Morgan, R. C.
13	Hudson, Roy	46	Newman, Harry
14	Holmes, Danny	48	Grinnell, Ira
15	Justice, Tom	49	Markley, J. Charles
16	Heston, William	50	Auer, Howard
17	Simrall, Harrison (Capt.)	51	Stoll, Claude
18	Wills, Ralph	52	Smith, Ivan
19	Eastman, Harry	53	Castle, Carl
20	DeBaker, Charles	54	Unger, William
22	Frisk, Leslie	55	Cox, Roderick
23	Kutsche, A.	56	Hewitt, William
24	Tessmer, Estil	57	Morrison, Maynard
25	O'Neil, Emmett	58	LaJeunesse, Omer
26	Damm, Russell	60	Yost, Fielding, Jr.
27	Draveling, Leo	61	Richardson, Karl
28	Cornwell, F. M.	62	Podlewski, Arthur
29	Douglass, Leslie	63	Lindsay, Harold
30	Winston, J. Leo	64	Wheeler, Jack
31	Shea, Sylvester	66	Hozer, Stanley
32	Daniels, Norman	68	Samuels, Thomas
33	Turner, Edward	69	Sikkenga, Jay
34	Soelberg, Carlton	70	Horwitz, Gilbert
		70	Goldsmith, DuVal

OHIO

No.	Name	No.	Name
1	Hoffer, Joseph	27	Kabealo, Charles
2	Farrier, Marvin	28	Kile, Eugene
3	Bough, Clarence	29	Selby, Sam
4	Rabenstein, Howard	30	Fesler, Wesley
5	Peterson, L. B.	31	Ferrall, Junius
6	Chizek, David	32	Roth, Michael
7	Holcomb, Stuart	33	Hall, John
9	Hinchman, Lewis	34	Campbell, Charles
10	Hodnick, Paul	35	Weaver, Edward
11	Bryant, John	36	Baumgarten, Eugene
12	Sola, Olavi	37	Haubrich, Robert
13	Horn, Robert	38	Lukz, Frank
14	Grady, Robert	39	Smith, Richard
15	Benis, Joseph	40	Varner, Martin
16	Greenberg, Jack	41	Gardner, James
18	Bauer, Robert	42	Bell, William
20	Carroll, William	43	Fried, Lawrence
21	Larkins, Richard	44	Ehrensberger, Carl
22	Idle, Ralph	45	Nasman, Bert
23	Taylor, Russell	46	Mandula, George
24	Mazaika, John	47	Griffith, William
25	VanBlaricom, Robert	48	Hudson, Addison
26	Wingert, Charles	51	Diehl, William
		52	Peppe, Louis

1930

Ohio	59	Mt. Union	0
Ohio	23	Indiana	0
Ohio	2	Northwestern	19
Ohio	0	Michigan	13
Ohio	0	Wisconsin	0
Ohio	27	Navy	0
Ohio	16	Pittsburgh	7
Ohio	12	Illinois	9

Season Summary

Games Won, 5; Lost, 2; Tied, 1

WESLEY FESLER
All-American End
Third Consecutive Year

October 17, 1931

Ann Arbor, Michigan

Ohio State Turns Back Michigan, 20 To 7

Carroll Scores Twice As 72,000 Watch Midwest's Annual Classic

t left: Carroll scores Ohio's first touchdown at Michigan

elow: Lou Hinchman carries the ball

The scarlet wave of Ohio State, battered down to the merest ripple the week before, rose again in its old might to sweep over its ancient gridiron enemy, Michigan, 20 to 7, the largest score by which an Ohio State eleven had ever beaten the Maize and Blue.

Out of the victory rose new Ohio heroes that promised much for the future Buckeye teams. A sturdy little quarterback, Carl Cramer of Dayton; Mike Vauchinich, fullback; and Joe Galius, guard; all sophomores rose to great heights in the pinches that pulled Ohio out of danger on several occasions.

The first Buckeye score was the result of a Michigan fumble by Heston. Smith, Ohio center, recovered on the Wolverines' 31 yard line. Bill Carroll, a hometown Columbus favorite, replaced Capt. Stu Holcomb at right half. He drove off tackle for 3. Then Lew Hinchman, the great left half, fought his way for 9 yards and a first down on the 19. Three more line plunges and it was fourth and one at the ten yard line. Behind good interference, Carroll came racing out around Michigan's right end, ten yards and over for the score. Bob Haubrich booted the extra point.

After several exchanges Ohio had put the ball in play on its 20 yard line after a punt over the goal line. Cramer went back to punt and Ivan Williamson, Michigan right end, who once starred for Bowling Green High School in Ohio, came ploughing in to block it. The ball rolled to within 3 yards of the goal. Williamson, hot on the trail, dove, squirmed to his feet with the ball, and was over, tying the score at 7 all.

The newly found flash for Ohio State, Bill Carroll, led the attack for the Buckeye's second touchdown also. Shortly after the second half started, Ohio took the ball on its 45 yard line and by end runs, hard line plunging by Vauchinich, a forward and a lateral pass, Ohio took the ball to the 2 yard line. From there, Carroll plunged through. Haubrich missed the kick by a hair, but Ohio was back on top 13 to 7.

Another unsuspected hero for Ohio, Cramer, supplied the thrill and the longest run of the day. He caught Heston's punt on the Michigan 45 yard line in the fourth period. Hesitating just long enough to be sure of the catch, Cramer was off down the right side of the field, whirling, dancing, side stepping. At least six Wolverine players had a chance to nail him, but he eluded them.

With the Michigan stands aghast, Cramer was darting over the goal line. Then it was Louis Peppe who added the point after touchdown. The final score was 20 to 7.

Ohio gained a total of 175 yards, 109 from scrimmage, 21 by passes, and 45 on penalties. Michigan gained 47 on rushing, 95 by passes, the desperate yet successful advance at the tail end of the game helping that total, and 25 on penalties, for a total of 167. Ohio made nine first downs and Michigan seven. Ohio tried only three forward passes, connecting on two; one was intercepted. The Wolverine attack was demolished by Ohio, intercepting six of twelve. Four were completed.

1931

1931			
Ohio	67	Cincinnati	6
Ohio	21	Vanderbilt	26
Ohio	20	Michigan	7
Ohio	0	Northwestern	10
Ohio	13	Indiana	0
Ohio	20	Navy	0
Ohio	6	Wisconsin	0
Ohio	40	Illinois	0
Ohio	7	Minnesota	19

Season Summary

Games Won, 6; Lost, 3

OHIO

No.	Name	Class	Pos.	Wt.	Home Town
1	Hoffer, Joseph	'33	HB	160	Youngstown
2	Fisher, Jerome	'34	HB	168	Cleveland
3	Vidis, Martin	'34	HB	158	Youngstown
4	Rabenstein, H.	'32	E	168	Lockland
5	Fuggit, John	'34	HB	157	Portsmouth
6	Cron, Robert	'34	HB	153	Piqua
7	Holcomb, Stuart	'32	HB	174	Erie, PA
8	Ramsey, Robert	'34	HB	167	Columbus
9	Hinchman, Lewis	'33	HB	172	Columbus
10	Cramer, Carl	'34	HB	168	Dayton
12	Welever, Watson	'34	FB	186	Toledo
13	Wilson, Donald	'34	E	184	Garfield Heights
14	Grady, Robert	'32	HB	162	Columbus
15	Benis, Joseph	'32	HB	165	Cleveland
16	Greenberg, Jack	'33	HB	163	Detroit, MI
17	Embrey, Russell	'34	HB	165	Dayton
18	Vauchinich, M.	'33	HB	190	Southwest, PA
19	Russ, Donald	'34	E	168	Toledo
20	Carroll, William	'33	HB	173	Columbus
21	Kull, Herbert	'34	HB	179	Columbus
22	Oliphant, Marshall	'34	HB	164	Cleveland Heights
23	Keefe, Thomas	'34	HB	176	Toledo
24	McKinney, William	'34	T	185	New Rochelle, NY
25	Van Blaricom, R.	'33	T	190	Salem
26	Kirk, James	'34	E	179	Canton
27	Gillman, Sidney	'34	E	180	Minneapolis, MN
28	Kile, Eugene	'32	G	170	Marysville
29	Allen, Robert	'33	G	176	Columbus
30	Delich, Peter	'33	C	180	Gary, IN
31	Ferrall, Junius	'33	E	167	Canton
32	Galius, Joseph	'33	G	188	Vandergrift, PA
33	Fitzgerald, Fred	'33	E	168	Detroit, MI
34	Conrad, Frederick	'34	E	200	Wooster
35	Weaver, Edward	'33	E	186	Columbus
36	Baumgarten, E.	'32	T	215	Louisville, KY
37	Haubrich, Robert	'32	T	195	Columbus
38	Lukz, Frank	'33	G	180	Niles
39	Smith, Richard	'33	C	204	E. Chicago, IL
40	Varner, Martin	'33	G	198	Lima
41	Cochran, Kenneth	'32	C	205	Mt. Vernor
42	Bell, William	'32	T	192	Akron
45	Nasman, Bert	'33	E	175	Youngstown
46	Mandula, George	'33	HB	190	Cleveland
47	Rosequist, Ted	'34	T	208	Warrensville
50	Drakulich, Samuel	'34	HB	133	Salem
51	Bompeidi, Carl	'34	G	160	Cleveland
54	Tanski, Victor	'34	G	188	Cleveland
57	Diehl, William	'33	G	185	Columbus
58	Hosket, Wilmer	'34	E	194	Dayton
60	Johnson, Earl	'34	G	178	Mount Iron, MN

MICHIGAN

No.	Name	Class	Pos.	Wt.	Home Town
4	Savage, Carl	'33	T	188	Flint
5	Oehmann, Ward	'33	G	170	Washington, D. C.
6	Bremen, George K.	'33	HB	185	Detroit
7	Miller, Wallace	'33	T	195	Wilmette, IL
8	Hazen, Francis	'32	T	182	Bellingham, WA
9	Westover, Louis	'34	HB	160	Bay City
10	Ellerby, Harold	'34	E	180	Birmingham
11	Wistert, Francis	'34	E	196	Chicago, IL
12	Clohset, Fred	'33	T	185	Bay City
13	Hudson, Roy, Capt.	'32	FB	185	Girard, OH
14	Holland, Kirk	'32	HB	150	Evanston, IL
16	Heston, William	'32	HB	165	Detroit
17	Petoskey, Fred	'34	E	175	Saginaw
18	Stone, Charles	'34	E	170	Detroit
19	Eastman, Harry	'32	HB	168	Detroit
20	De Baker, Charles	'33	HB	165	Muskegon
21	Heston, John P.	'34	HB	170	Detroit
22	Frisk, Leslie	'33	T	178	Rock Island, IL
23	Kutsche, Arthur	'33	QB	155	Monroe
24	Tessmer, Estil	'33	QB	165	Ann Arbor
26	Damm, Russell	'33	T	186	Muskegon
27	Bernard, Charles	'34	C	215	Benton Harbor
28	Cantrill, Cecil	'33E	T	195	Lexington, KY
29	Douglass, Leslie	'32	G	185	Gary, IN
30	Winston, J. Leo	'33	C	155	Washington, D. C.
31	Everhardus, Herm	'34	HB	175	Kalamazoo
32	Daniels, Norman	'32	E	175	Detroit
34	Chapman, Harvey	'34	T	178	Detroit
35	Fay, Stanley	'34	HB	175	Detroit
39	Williamson, Ivan	'33	E	180	Toledo, OH
40	Meldman, Leonard	'34	T	175	Detroit
41	Marcovsky, Abe	'33	G	163	Pittsburgh, PA
42	McCrath, L. E.	'32	T	215	Grand Rapids
43	Schmid, Herbert	'34	HB	182	Grand Rapids
45	Kowalik, John	'34	G	190	Chicago, IL
46	Newman, Harry	'32	QB	174	Detroit
48	McGuire, Donald	'34	E	183	South Haven
49	Miller, Robert	'33	T	180	Highland Park
50	Auer, Howard	'32E	T	198	Bay City
51	Horner, William	'33E	E	155	Jackson
52	Conover, James	'34E	G	202	Ann Arbor
54	Singer, Oscar	'34	G	185	Jackson Hgts., NY
55	Cox, Roderick	'33	FB	196	Birmingham
56	Hewitt, William	'32	E	185	Bay City
57	Morrison, Maynard	'32	C	210	Royal Oak
58	LaJeunesse, Omer	'32	G	185	Iron Mountain
60	Yost, Fielding H.	'32	E	168	Ann Arbor
61	Cooke, Thomas	'33	T	195	Chicago, IL
62	Kelley, Bethel	'34	E	164	Bardstown, KY
63	Renner, William	'34	HB	165	Youngstown, OH
64	Stinespring, Harry	'34	QB	140	Chicago, IL
66	Hozer, Stanley	'32	E	187	Muskegon
68	Samuels, Tom	'32	T	190	Canton, OH
69	Sikkenga, Jay	'32	G	182	Muskegon Hgts.
72	Goldsmith, Duval	'33	T	200	Christiansburg, VA

1931

Michigan	27	Cen. St. Tch.	0
Michigan	34	MI St. Norm	0
Michigan	13	Chicago	7
Michigan	7	Ohio State	20
Michigan	35	Illinois	0
Michigan	21	Princeton	0
Michigan	22	Indiana	0
Michigan	0	MSU	0
Michigan	6	Minnesota	0
Michigan	16	Wisconsin	0

Season Summary

Games Won, 8; Lost, 1; Tied, 1

MAYNARD MORRISON
All-American Center

Gerald Ford began playing this year and went on to become "Most Valuable Player" in 1934.

October 15, 1932

Columbus, Ohio

Michigan Beats Ohio State, 14 To 0

Newman's Passes Bewilder Buckeyes; Clevelander Oliphant Shines

Opening the way with its wizard air attack-spreading destruction behind the magic throwing arm of Harry Newman — Michigan's mighty Wolverines rolled over their old and bitter enemy, Ohio State, 14 to 0. With Newman's bullet like heaves demoralizing the Buckeye defenses right at the outset, the hardy and mobile Wolverines scored their two touchdowns in the first half. Then, battered and hammered by a bruising Ohio attack that fought with the fury of desperation, the husky men of the maize and blue courageously and skillfully defended their lead.

A crowd of 42,038, considered pretty good in those times of high tariffs, streamed in Ohio's giant horseshoe stadium to watch the 29th battle between the traditional foes. The battle was not more than three minutes old when Newman, standing near Ohio's 20-yard line, fired a pass to the right to fullback John Regeczi, the phenomenal Michigan sophomore. Regeczi, completely uncovered, gathered in the ball and loped five yards or so for the touchdown. Newman put the place kick squarely between the uprights and Michigan led 7 to 0.

The second Wolverine TD, midway of the second period, was just as spectacular. This time it was a 30 yard pass by "Dead-Eye" Newman, hurled almost over the center of the line. Ivan Williamson, the Wolverines captain and right end, reached up and snatched the ball in his fingers, three yards from the Buckeyes' goal and galloped over. Newman again place kicked perfectly, and the issue was decided. It was 14 to 0 and all that was left for Ohio was to make it look good.

After a fumble by Michigan on their own 29 yard line, recovered by Ohio's Sid Gillman, Ohio kept the Wolverines backed up on defense the rest of the game. At least three times the Buckeyes piled the ball down near the goal line, but they could not put it over. With no forward passing threat to open the secondary, the aroused but frustrated Ohioans were helpless.

Ohio State did have several bright moments, one being the performance of Marshall Oliphant. Subbing for Carl Cramer, Ohio's regular field general, Oliphant made a showing that ranked only behind that of Michigan's Harry Newman. Oliphant was the leading ground gainer of the day with a total of 54 yards. O.S.U.'s Hinchman added another 44.

STATISTICS

	UM	OSU
First Downs	7	8
First Downs Rushing	2	6
First Down Passing	4	1
First Down Penalties	1	1
Yards gained rushing	46	144
Yards gained passing	81	53
Passes Attempted	6	11
Passes Completed	4	1
Passes Inter. By	2	0
Fumbles Rec. By	0	1
Punting Average	35	33

1932			
Michigan	26	MSU	0
Michigan	15	Northwestern	6
Michigan	14	Ohio State	0
Michigan	32	Illinois	0
Michigan	14	Princeton	7
Michigan	7	Indiana	0
Michigan	12	Chicago	0
Michigan	3	Minnesota	0

Season Summary

Games Won, 8; Lost, 0; Tied, 0

TED PETOSKEY
All-American End

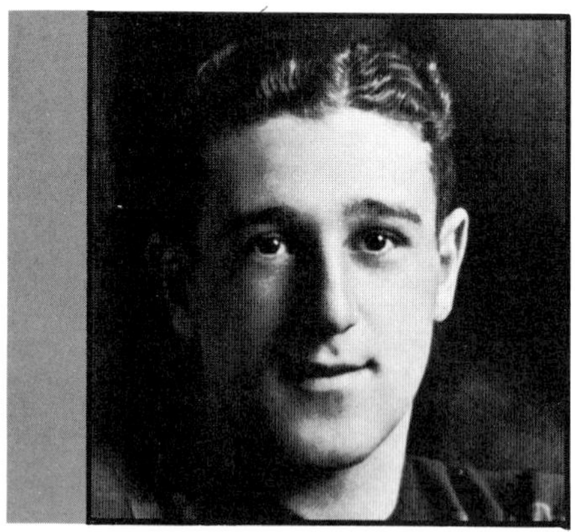

HARRY NEWMAN
All-American Quarterback

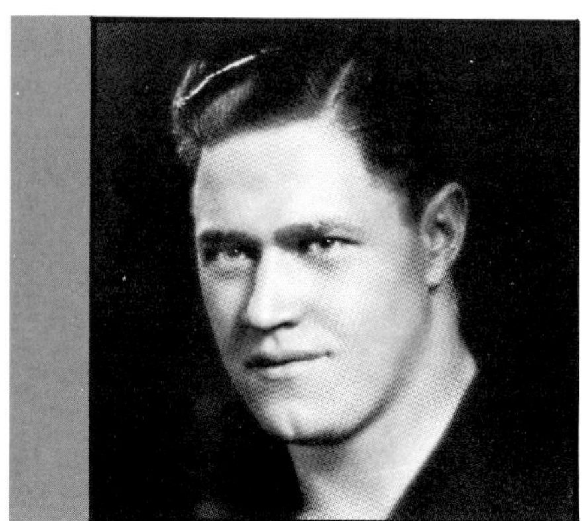

CHARLES BERNARD
All-American Center

MICHIGAN

Name	Pos.	Wt.	Year	Home Town
Antell, Gunnard	E	168	Jr.	Negaunee
Austin, Thomas D.	T	200	Jr.	Columbus, OH
Bernard, Charles	C	215	Jr.	Benton Habor
Borgmann, William	G	180	So.	Ft. Wayne, IN
Cantrill, Cecil, Jr.	T	195	Sr.	Lexington, KY
Chapman, Harvey	T	178	Jr.	Detroit
Clohset, Fred	T	185	Sr.	Bay City
Cox, Roderick	FB	196	Sr.	Birmingham
Damm, Russell	T	186	Sr.	Muskegon
DeBaker, Charles	HB	165	Sr.	Fruitport
Everhardus, Herman	HB	175	Jr.	Kalamazoo
Fay, Stanley E.	HB	175	Jr.	Detroit
Ford, Gerald	C	187	So.	Grand Rapids
Frisk, Leslie L.	T	178	Sr.	Rock Island, IL
Fuog, Russell	G	185	So.	Chicago, IL
Heston, John P.	HB	170	Jr.	Ann Arbor
Hildebrand, Willard	T	187	Jr.	Saginaw
Jacobs, Benjamin	QB	155	So.	Sault Ste. Marie
Jacobson, Tage	T	193	So.	Detroit
Kelly, Bethel B.	E	164	Jr.	Beardstown, KY
Kowalik, John	G	190	Sr.	Chicago, IL
Madden, Francis L.	T	234	So.	Lockport, NY
Marcovsky, Abe	G	163	Sr.	Pittsburgh, PA
Meldman, Leonard	FB	175	Jr.	Detroit
Miller, Robert E.	T	180	Sr.	Highland Park
McClintic, William	C	216	So.	Detroit
Newman, Harry	QB	174	Sr.	Detroit
Oliver, Russell D.	FB	190	So.	Pontiac
Ottoman, Louis J.	E	163	So.	Chicago, IL
Palmeroli, Peter	FB	170	So.	Highland Park, IL
Petoskey, Fred	E	175	Sr.	St. Charles
Ponto, Hilton A.	G	170	Jr.	Ann Arbor
Regeczi, John	FB	180	So.	Muskegon Heights
Renner, William	HB	165	Jr.	Youngstown, OH
Savage, Carl M.	T	188	Sr.	Flint
Shaw, Lee C.	QB	150	So.	Coldwater
Shea, Sylvester	E	178	Jr.	Detroit
Singer, Oscar A.	G	186	Jr.	Jackson Heights, NY
Stewart, Thomas	HB	170	Jr.	Detroit
Ward, Willis	E	185	So.	Detroit
Westover, Louis	HB	160	Jr.	Bay City
Williamson, I. (Capt.)	E	180	Sr.	Toledo, OH
Wistert, Francis	T	196	Jr.	Chicago, IL
Zendzian, Frank P.	HB	170	So.	Providence, RI

OHIO

Name	Pos.	Wt.	Hgt.	Year	Home Town
Allen, Robert	G	176	5-10	Sr.	Columbus
Bompiedi, Carl	E	170	5-9	Jr.	Cleveland
Burger, Carl	E	150	5-11	Sr.	Columbus
Carmody, Clarence	E	180	5-11½	So.	Middletown
*Carroll, William	HB	173	5-10	Sr.	Columbus
*Conrad, Frederick	T	208	6-4	Jr.	Wooster
Cox, Budd	E	165	5-10	So.	Springfield
*Cramer, Carl	QB	168	5-10	Jr.	Dayton
Cron, Robert	HB	164	5-9½	Jr.	Piqua
*Delich, Peter	G	180	5-10	Jr.	Gary, IN
Diehl, William	G	195	5-11½	Sr.	Columbus
Drakulich, Sam	QB	132	5-7	Jr.	Salem
*Ferrall, Junius	E	168	5-10	Sr.	Canton
Fisher, Jerome	HB	172	6-0	Jr.	Cleveland
Ford, Samuel	E	180	6-0½	So.	Columbus
Fugitt, John	HB	170	5-11½	Jr.	Portsmouth
*Gailus, Joseph	G	192	6-1	Jr.	Vandergrift, PA
*Gillman, Sidney	E	185	5-11	Jr.	Minneapolis, MN
Granger, Ralph	E	196	6-3	So.	Columbus
*Greenberg, Jack	HB	173	5-9	Sr.	Detroit, MI
Greenblatt, Louis	C	182	5-11½	Jr.	Massena, NY
Griffith, Eugene	HB	182	6-0	So.	N. Baltimore
Heekin, Richard	HB	193	6-0	So.	Cincinnati
Heyman, Joseph	C	175	5-11	So.	Toledo
*Hinchman, L. (Capt.)	HB	178	5-11	Sr.	Columbus
Hosking, John	T	206	5-11½	So.	Ft. Thomas, KY
Johnson, Earl	T	243	6-3	Jr.	Prospect
Jones, Dave	HB	164	5-10	So.	Jackson
Kabealo, Charles	FB	178	5-10	Sr.	Youngstown
Kabealo, George	C	180	5-9¾	So.	Youngstown
Karcher, James	FB	188	5-11	So.	Forest
*Keefe, Tom	HB	172	6-0	Jr.	Toledo
Kirk, James	E	183	6-0	Jr.	Canton
Livorno, Joseph	G	170	5-10	So.	Bellaire
*Lukz, Frank	G	180	5-10	Sr.	Niles
*Mandula, George	FB	190	6-0½	Jr.	Cleveland
McAfee, John	QB	168	5-9½	So.	Ironton
McCombs, Alton	T	202	6-1	Jr.	Middletown
McKenney, John	QB	180	5-11	So.	Cleveland
McKinney, William	T	200	6-0	Jr.	New Rochelle, NY
Monahan, Regis	T	209	5-11	So.	Lorain
*Nasman, Bert	C	178	6-1	Sr.	Youngstown
Neal, George	G	187	6-0	So.	Dayton
Nelson, Harry	T	220	6-0	So.	Gary, IN
*Oliphant, Marshall	QB	171	6-0	Jr.	Cleveland
O'Shaughnessey, T.	G	218	6-0	Jr.	Columbus
Padlow, Max	E	190	6-0	So.	Dayton
Ramsey, Robert	HB	162	5-10½	So.	Bloomfield, IN
Reilly, Robert	QB	171	5-8	So.	Columbus
Rose, James	QB	155	5-9	So.	Wilmington
Rosequist, Ted	T	207	6-4½	So.	Warrensville
Salvaterra, Joe	E	165	6-0	Sr.	Bellaire
Scherer, Belden	HB	155	6-0	Sr.	Cleveland
Scott, James	E	185	6-2	So.	Toledo
Smith, Jack	HB	182	6-0	So.	Hamilton
*Smith, Richard	C	204	6-2	Sr.	E. Chicago, IN
Tanski, Victor	G	188	5-10	Jr.	Cleveland
*Thies, Wilford	T	196	6-4	Jr.	Norwood
Thomas, Joe	HB	170	5-11	Sr.	Columbus
Van Blaricom, Robert	T	190	6-1	Sr.	Salem
*Varner, Martin	G	212	5-11	Sr.	Lima
Vidis, Martin	HB	158	5-8	Jr.	Youngstown
*Vuchinich, Michael	FB	192	6-0	Jr.	Southwest, PA
Weaver, J. H.	C	163	6-0	So.	Hilliards
Werner, Irving	E	168	5-10	Sr.	Newark, NJ
Wetzel, Damon	FB	188	5-10½	So.	Columbus
Yards, Ludwig	T	195	6-3	So.	Gary, IN

*indicates letters won

1932

Ohio	34	OH Wesleyan	7
Ohio	7	Indiana	7
Ohio	0	Michigan	14
Ohio	0	Pittsburgh	0
Ohio	7	Wisconsin	7
Ohio	20	Northwestern	6
Ohio	19	Pennsylvania	0
Ohio	3	Illinois	0

Season Summary

Games Won, 4; Lost, 1; Tied, 3

JOSEPH GAILUS
All-American Guard

4
18

October 22, 1933

Ann Arbor, Michigan

Michigan Whips Ohio State, 13 To 0

Bucks Held To Three First Downs At Ann Arbor

In one of the mighty football spectacles of all time—with a host of 93,508 fans, the official Big Ten attendance record, piled to the skies in Michigan's great stadium—Ohio State's challenge for a place in the national gridiron spotlight ended in saddening, crushing defeat.

Ohio stopped Michigan backs, but it never stopped the ball. In a maze of lateral passes—worked with such dazzling execution that the hand was a thousandfold quicker then the eye—Ohio was chased right out of the Western Conference picture. Michigan's Bill Renner, on the squad two years, but never a regular until that day, was the lightning-handed instrument with which magic was accomplished. He was helped by the indomitable, quick-thinking Jack Heston, second son of the immortal Willie Heston.

The first period was a punting duel. Amazed Michigan cohorts watched Carl Cramer, using his head as well as his foot, hold his own on three kicks with the great John Regeczi, Michigan fullback and wonder booter. John Kabealo took over the punting duties for Cramer and did an excellent job.

Starting from their own 49 yard line, Michigan began their first scoring drive with Renner at the helm. With Heston, Everhardus, and Regenczi supplying the finesse and power, the Wolverines moved the ball down to O.S.U.'s three yard line. The big Ohio line stopped the next two rushes, but on the third, Renner went through a hole on the left side of the Buckeye line for the score. Everhardus missed the point after touchdown by inches.

The third period was a matter of Kabealo kicking the ball, time and time again, in a desperate effort to boot the Wolverines back into their own territory.

The details of Michigan's second touchdown was the old, old story of desperation passing by an Ohio team that had nothing in the way of an aerial attack. Michigan's Willis Ward intercepted Stan Pincura's pass and raced down toward the Buckeye goal line. Pincura, with a dive and a desperate clutch, just caught one of the flying Ward's shoes and the big end sprawled head-long 24 yards from the goal. Although the Wolverines did not score, because of missed field goal, a second touchdown was only a matter of time.

Chuck Bernard, Michigan's All American center, intercepted a pass and was downed on O.S.U.'s 23 yard line. Renner, Oliver, and Petoskey pounded up to the 10 yard line for a first down. Petoskey, befuddling Ohio completely; came around the Buck's left side for nearly 9 yards. Everhardus missed on the first plunge, but on the second went to his left. Just as he stepped on the goal line, he was knocked back two yards. The official ruled he had been over, and it was a touchdown. Renner held the ball, Savage placekicked the point, and a somber day for Ohio State was all but at an end. A minute more the gun popped the death knell of Ohio's Big Ten chances.

Above: Michigan's Ted Petoskey
Top Left: Ohio's Jack Smith
Left: Scott attempts a field goal

STATISTICS

	UM	OSU
First Downs	9	3
Yards Gained, Rushing	174	30
Yards Gained Passing	48	37
Passes, Attempted	7	12
Passes, Completed	3	3
Passes, Intercepted	1	5
Punts	12-37	15-39
Fumbles	5	2
Fumbles Lost	2	1
Yards Penalized	15	15

1933			
Ohio	75	Virginia	0
Ohio	20	Vanderbilt	0
Ohio	0	Michigan	13
Ohio	12	Northwestern	0
Ohio	21	Indiana	0
Ohio	20	Pennsylvania	7
Ohio	6	Wisconsin	0
Ohio	7	Illinois	6

Season Summary

Games Won, 7; Lost, 1

OHIO

No.	Name	Pos.	Wt.	Class	Home Town
1	Pincura, Stanley	QB	157	'36	Lorain
2	Jones, David L.	HB	168	'35	Jackson
3	Vidis, Martin S.	HB	160	'34	Youngstown
4	Smith, Jack E.	HB	189	'35	Hamilton
5	Lightburn, Robert	E	172	'36	Crestline
6	Heekin, Richard F.	HB	195	'36	Cincinnati
7	Thomas, Joseph A.	HB	175	'34	Columbus
8	Boucher, Franklin A.	HB	172	'36	Kent
9	Beltz, Richard H.	HB	163	'36	Findlay
10	Cramer, Carl F.	QB	163	'34	Dayton
11	Liptak, Steve	E	178	'36	Cleveland
12	Rees, Trevor J.	E	180	'36	Dover
13	Wilson, Don A.	E	185	'34	Garfield Hts.
14	McAfee, John N.	FB	170	'35	Ironton
15	Vogelgesang, James	HB	174	'36	Lima
16	Kabealo, John	FB	183	'36	Youngstown
17	Wetzel, Damon H.	FB	182	'35	Columbus
18	Vuchinich, Michael	C	190	'34	Southwest, PA
19	Karcher, James M.	FB	198	'35	Forest
20	Pipoly, James E.	E	170	'36	Struthers
21	Whinnery, Glenn	HB	170	'34	Salem
22	Oliphant, Marshall T.	QB	170	'34	Cleveland
23	Keefe, Thomas C.	HB	182	'34	Toledo
24	Fisch, Frank	HB	182	'34	Mansfield
25	Brungard, Geo. H.	FB	170	'36	North Lima
26	Heyman, Joseph	E	170	'34	Toledo
27	Gillman, Sidney (C)	E	188	'34	Minneapolis, MN
28	Cox, M. Budd	E	168	'35	Springfield
29	Padlow, Max	E	187	'35	Dayton
30	Delich, Pete B.	C	185	'34	Gary, IN
31	Busich, Sam	C	185	'36	Lorain
32	Gailus, J. T. (C)	G	197	'34	Vandergrift, PA
33	Jones, Gomer T.	G	200	'36	Cleveland
34	Conrad, Frederick B.	T	208	'34	Wooster
35	Scott, James	T	190	'35	Toledo
36	Neal, George V.	C	206	'35	Dayton
37	Phillips, Clyde	QB	160	'36	Columbus
38	Romoser, James W.	G	185	'36	Lorain
40	Fisher, Jerome	HB	176	'34	Cleveland
41	Monahan, J. Regis	G	210	'35	Lorain
42	Roush, Ernest	G	200	'36	Black Lick
43	Yards, Ludwig	T	182	'35	Gary, IN
44	Johnson, Earl	T	240	'34	Prospect
45	Kleinhaus, John L.	G	190	'36	Maumee
46	Fleming, Mark	T	190	'36	Columbus
47	Rosequist, T.	T	209	'34	Cleveland
48	Harre, Gilbert	T	207	'36	Toledo
49	Zirkle, Lewis G.	T	210	'36	Defiance
50	Drakulich, Sam	QB	155	'34	Salem
51	Greenblatt, Louis	C	170	'34	Massena, NY
52	Livorno, Joseph	G	170	'34	Bellaire
53	Thies, Wilfred	T	200	'34	Norwood
54	Kabealo, George	C	185	'35	Youngstown
55	Cashell, Jack	C	195	'36	Columbus
56	Bompeidi, Carl J.	E	170	'36	Cleveland
57	Benton, Julian	HB	160	'36	Columbus
58	Miller, Robert	C	175	'36	Cleveland
59	Barrows, Arthur	G	175	'36	Columbus

MICHIGAN

No.	Name	Pos.	Wt.	Class	Home Town
4	Savage, Carl M.	G	200	'34	Flint
5	Remias, Steve	FB	175	'36Ed	Chicago, IL
6	Borgmann, W. F.	G	180	'35	Ft. Wayne, IN
7	Kidston, James A.	FB	170	'36	La Grange, IL
8	Stetson, Parker F.	HB	160	'36	Milford, CT
9	Westover, Louis W.	QB	167	'34E	Bay City
10	Beard, Chester C.	G	178	'35	Youngstown, OH
11	Wistert, Francis M.	T	205	'34	Chicago, IL
12	Raymond, Henry T.	HB	165	'36	Lapeer
14	Paulson, Herbert C.	HB	168	'35Ed	Winnetka, IL
15	Frankowski, Wallace	E	173	'35	Chicago, IL
16	Regeczi, John M.	FB	185	'35Ed	Muskegon Hts.
17	Petoskey, Fred L.	E	182	'34Ed	St. Charles
18	Fuog, Russell J.	C-G	195	'35Ed	Chicago, IL
19	Jacobs, Benjamin P.	QB	155	'35	Sault St. Marie
20	Triplehorn, Howard	HB	165	'36	Bluffton, OH
21	Heston, John P.	HB	170	'34Ed	Ann Arbor
23	Dauksza, Antone	QB	163	'36E	Grand Rapids
24	Tessmer, Estel S.	QB	170	'34Ed	Ann Arbor
25	Wells, Robert L.	G	167	'34E	Grand Rapids
27	Bernard, Charles J.	C	215	'34	Benton Harbor
29	Hildebrand, Willard	T-G	187	'35	Saginaw
30	Bolas, George	QB	158	'36	Chicago, IL
31	Everhardus, Herman	HB	174	'34	Kalamazoo
32	Stone, Edward A.	T	172	'36	Chicago, IL
33	Ratterman, L. F.	QB	160	'34	Cincinnati, OH
34	Chapman, Harvey E.	E	180	'35	Detroit
35	Fay, Stanley E. (C.)	'34Ed	HB	175	Detroit
36	Nelson, Winfred	HB	175	'36Ed	Greenville
37	Rudness, George	HB	153	'36Ed	Negaunee
38	Soodik, Eli	C	165	'34Ed	New Brighton, PA
40	Shea, Sylvester C.	E	178	'34	Detroit
41	McGuire, Donald T.	T	190	'34	South Haven
42	Viergiver, John D.	T	220	'35Ed	Algonac
43	Oliver, Russell D	FB	190	'35	Pontiac
44	Swanson, Robert G.	T	187	'34	Detroit
45	Kowalik, John F.	G	190	'34Ed	Chicago, IL
48	Ford, Gerald	C-G	195	'35	Grand Rapids
49	Schmidt, Herbert T.	FB	190	'35	Grand Rapids
50	Singer, Oscar A.	G	180	'34	Jackson Hts., NY
52	Austin, Thomas D.	T	200	'35	Columbus,OH
53	Johnson, Ernest C.	E	170	'36Ed	Grand Rapids
54	Ponto, Hilton A.	G	175	'34Ed	Ann Arbor
55	Lewis, D. King	HB	175	'36	Mt. Pleasant
56	Hunn, David S.	QB	160	'36	Elkhart, IN
61	Ward, Willis F.	E	183	'35	Detroit
62	Malashevich, M.	E	196	'36Ed	Dearborn
63	Renner, William W.	HB-QB	165	'34	Youngstown, OH
64	Shaw, Lee Charles	QB	150	'35	Coldwater
66	Tomagno, Chelso	E	177	'36Ed	Chicago, IL
67	James, Richard	QB	162	'36E	Detroit
68	Patchin, Arthur B.	FB	175	'35	Detroit
70	Semeyn, Roy A.	T	198	'36E	Muskegon
72	Jacobson, Tage O.	T	210	'35E	Detroit

1933

Michigan	20	MSU	6
Michigan	40	Cornell	0
Michigan	13	Ohio State	0
Michigan	28	Chicago	0
Michigan	7	Illinois	6
Michigan	10	Iowa	6
Michigan	0	Minnesota	0
Michigan	13	Northwestern	0

Season Summary

Games Won, 7; Lost, 0; Tied, 1

CHARLES BERNARD
All-American Center

TED PETOSKEY
All-American End

FRANCIS WISTERT
All-American Tackle

FRANCIS A. SCHMIDT
Ohio State Coach
1934-40

November 17, 1934

Columbus, Ohio

Ohio State Circus Parades Through Feeble Michigan

Air Spectacle Buries Wolverines 34 To 0

Before a vast host of 68,678 spectators, who rubbed their eyes and peered down from the heights wondering if it could be true, Ohio State finally brought Michigan to judgment. With five touchdowns, with lateral and forward passes, and ball-crushing power, the aroused and inspired Scarlet Buckeyes of High Street wrought that long delayed vengeance upon their ancient enemy.

Dick Heekin plunged through the shattered left side of the Michigan line for Ohio's first touchdown after only five minutes of the game. Next, Buzz Wetzel rammed over for the second TD again through the Michigan line that was once so impregnable. The third touchdown resulted from a dying fumble recovered by Frank Antenucci behind the Michigan goal in the fourth quarter. Captain Regis Monahan rifled over the extra points. Frank Fisch winged a tremendous pass to Merle Wendt for another score. The final TD was scored on a pass from Tippy Dye to Frank Cumisky.

Michigan had been beaten five times previous to the game with O.S.U. and their weariness was evident. From the opening kickoff, it was evident that the maize and blue jinx over the Buckeyes was buried for good. The victory for Ohio State was complete, devastating, and oh so sweet.

STATISTICS

	OSU	UM
First Downs	24	3
First Downs Rushing	21	0
First Downs Passing	3	2
First Down Penalties	0	1
Rushing Yardage	319	6
Forward Passes	5-8	2-11
Forward Passes Inter.	0	2
Passing Yardage	141	34
Punts - Average	10-37	12-45
Kickoff Return, Yards	120	0
Fumbles - Lost	5-3	0-0
Total Yardage	638	86

1934	
Michigan 0	Mich. State 16
Michigan 0	Chicago 27
Michigan 9	Georgia Tech . 2
Michigan 6	Illinois 7
Michigan 0	Minnesota 34
Michigan 0	Wisconsin 10
Michigan 0	Ohio State 34
Michigan 6	Northwestern . . 13

Season Summary

Games won, 1; Lost, 7; Tied, 0

MICHIGAN

No.	Name	Pos.	Ht.	Wgt.	Years on Squad	Home Town
24	Amrine, Robert O.	HB	6	189	0	London, OH
35	Aug, Vincent J.	HB	5-11½	175	0	Cincinnati, OH
52	Austin, T. D. (Capt.)	T	6-1	207	2	Columbus, OH
21	Barnett, David G.	HB	5-11	165	0	Detroit
10	Beard, Chester C.	G	5-9	191	2	Youngstown, OH
68	Bissell, Frank	G	5-8	162	0	Pittsburgh, PA
30	Bolas, George	QB	5-7	162	1	Chicago, IL
6	Borgman, Wm. F.	G	5-10	198	2	Fort Wayne, IN
50	Brandman, Charles	QB	5-6	162	0	Findlay, OH
26	Carr, Carl W., Jr.	T	6-2	189	0	Saline
49	Ellis, Joseph O.	Q-HB	6	178	0	Eagle River, WI
31	Everhardus, Chris	HB	6-1	169	0	Kalamazoo
54	Fisher, Joe	T	5-11	197	0	Ann Arbor
48	Ford, Gerald	C	6	198	2	Grand Rapids
18	Fuog, Russell J.	C	5-11	193	2	Chicago, IL
25	Garber, Jesse G.	G	5-8½	187	0	New York, NY
34	Graper, Robert	E	6-1½	188	0	Maumee, OH
66	Hanshue, Cloyce E.	G	5-11	202	0	Kalamazoo
29	Hildebrand, W. H.	G-T	6	195	2	Saginaw
19	Jacobs, Phillip H.	HB	5-10½	160	0	Sault Ste. Marie
72	Jacobson, Tage O.	T	6-1	199	2	Detroit
67	James, Richard H.	QB	5-9	164	1	Detroit
64	Jennings, Ferris	QB	5-10	137	0	Ann Arbor
53	Johnson, Ernest C.	E	6	181	1	Grand Rapids
70	Lett, Franklin	E	6	197	0	Battle Creek
23	Liffiton, Jack K.	FB	5-11	180	0	Lakewood, OH
14	Meyers, Earl J.	E	5-11½	188	0	Detroit
40	Mumford, John	FB	5-10½	180	0	Highland Park
36	Nelson, Winfred	HB	5-10	176	1	Greenville
43	Oliver, Russell D.	FB	5-10½	181	2	Pontiac
45	Oyler, Thomas T.	E	5-11¼	190	0	Cincinnati, OH
17	Patanelli, Matt	E	6-1	202	0	Elkhart, IN
55	Pederson, Ernest A.	G	5-10½	175	0	Grand Blanc
15	Pillinger, Harry J.	QB	5-8½	155	0	Whitehall
16	Regeczi, John M.	FB	6	186	2	Muskegon Hts.
5	Remias, Steve	FB	5-11	190	1	Chicago, IL
63	Renner, William W.	QB	5-10½	159	2	Youngstown, OH
9	Rieck, John A.	E	5-11	161	0	Detroit
37	Rudness, George	HB	5-8	160	1	Negaunee
62	Savage, Michael	E	6-3	210	1	Dearborn
41	Schuman, Stanton J.	C	5-9	189	0	Winnetka, IL
11	Sears, Harold W., Jr.	G	5-8	202	0	Grand Rapids
38	Soodik, Eli	G	5-7	168	2	New Brighton, P
32	Stone, Edward A.	T	6	185	1	Chicago, IL
60	Sweet, Cedric C.	FB	6	192	0	Fremont
20	Triplehorn, Howard	HB	5-10½	166	1	Bluffton, OH
42	Viergever, John D.	T	6-1	233	1	Algonac
61	Ward, Willis F.	E	6-1	185	2	Detroit
27	Wright, Harry T.	T	6-2¾	242	0	Mt. Clemens

OHIO

No.	Name	Pos.	Ht.	Wgt.	Class	Home Town
7	Antenucci, Frank	HB	5-9	176	So.	Niles
9	Beltz, Dick	HB	6-1	167	Jr.	Findlay
10	Bettridge, John	FB	5-10	178	So.	Toledo
56	Bittel, Robert	G	6-½	177	So.	Cleveland
8	Boucher, Frank	HB	6-1	177	Jr.	Kent
15	Boston, William	C	6	185	So.	Cleveland
25	Brungard, George	HB	6	191	Jr.	North Lima
31	Busich, Sam	E	6-2	187	Jr.	Lorain
28	Cox, Budd	E	5-11	174	Sr.	Springfield
27	Cumiskey, Frank	E	6-1	186	So.	Youngstown
11	Dobbs, Bennie	E	6-½	180	Jr.	Columbus
5	Dorris, Victor	FB	5-9	178	So.	Bellaire
50	Dye, William	QB	5-6	138	So.	Pomeroy
24	*Fisch, Frank	QB	6-½	189	Jr.	Mansfield
46	Fleming, Mark	G	6	190	Jr.	Columbus
47	George, August	T	6-4½	224	So.	Dayton
60	Georgepoulos, Tom	C	6-1½	181	Jr.	Cleveland
26	Greider, Robert	T	6-2	202	So.	Cleveland
59	Haddad, George	G	5-5½	161	So.	Toledo
34	Hamrick, Charles	T	6-½	230	So.	Gallipolis
48	Harre, Gilbert	T	6-2½	213	Jr.	Toledo
6	*Heekin, Dick	HB	6-1	196	Jr.	Cincinnati
51	Heiser, Vern	C	5-11	175	So.	Mansfield
37	Horwitz, Sam	QB	5-8½	147	So.	Columbus
2	Jones, Dave	HB	5-10	162	Sr.	Jackson
33	Jones, Gomer	C	5-8½	207	Jr.	Cleveland
54	Kabealo, George	C	5-9	195	Jr.	Youngstown
16	*Kabealo, John	FB	5-9	203	Jr.	Youngstown
19	Karcher, James	G	5-10	192	Sr.	Forest
45	Kleinhans, John	E	6-1½	195	Jr.	Maumee
39	Lightburn, Robert	E	6	166	Jr.	Crestline
55	Luckino, Angelo	G	5-6	175	Jr.	Wellsville
14	*McAfee, John	FB	5-10	165	Sr.	Ironton
53	Miller, James	HB	5-11	178	So.	Shelby
58	Miller, Robert	C	5-11	180	Jr.	Cleveland
41	*Monahan, Regis (C)	G	5-10½	203	Sr.	Lorain
40	Nagy, John	HB	5-11	160	So.	Cleveland
36	Neal, George	G	6	*219	Sr.	Dayton
52	Novotny, George	T	5-11¾	193	So.	Elyria
1	Pincura, Stan	QB	5-11	163	Jr.	Lorain
20	Pipoly, James	E	5-9	176	Jr.	Struthers
12	*Rees, Trevor	E	6	183	Jr.	Dover
30	Roberts, Vernell	G	5-11	195	So.	Wellsville
42	Roush, Ernest	G	5-9	210	Jr.	Blacklick
44	Scholl, Millard	T	5-9	224	So.	Lorain
35	Scott, James	T	6-1½	201	Sr.	Toledo
29	Smith, Inwood	G	5-11	191	So.	Mansfield
4	*Smith, Jack	HB	6	183	Sr.	Hamilton
3	Stump, Wilson	QB	5-8	153	So.	Alliance
21	Thomas, Earl	E	6-1	186	So.	Ashland
32	Torrance, James	E	6-1	186	So.	Cleveland
18	Wendt, Merle	E	5-10	191	So.	Middletown
17	*Wetzel, Damon	C-FB	5-10	185	Sr.	Columbus
43	*Yards, Ludwig	T	6-3	188	Sr.	Gary, IN
49	Zirkle, Lewis	T	6-4½	214	Jr.	Defiance

* Denotes letterman

1934

Ohio	33	Indiana	0
Ohio	13	Illinois	14
Ohio	10	Colgate	7
Ohio	28	Northwestern	6
Ohio	76	Western Res.	0
Ohio	33	Chicago	0
Ohio	34	Michigan	0
Ohio	40	Iowa	7

Season Summary

Won, 7; Lost, 1

MERLE WENDT
All-American End

REGIS MONAHAN
All-American Guard

Coach Kipke and Fritz Crisler (Princeton) inspect the new Wilson mesh, marked grip fast, perfect balance football

November 23, 1935

Ann Arbor, Michigan

Ohio State Annihilates The Wolverines, 38 To 0

Dye Streaks 73 Yards In Six-Touchdown Avalanche

Above and Left: Practice outside Ohio Stadium

Life was worth living after all. A Scarlet Scourge at last, a great football team arose in might and wrath to its full worth, Ohio State annihilated Michigan and tied for the Big Ten title. Scoring six touchdowns, piling insult upon injury, pounding pell-mell for 60 minutes, Ohio displayed their superiority over the dismayed maize and blue.

Two Ohio touchdowns, one on a 50-yard run by Frank Boucher, and another on a forward pass, Wee Tippy Dye to Sam Busich, were ruled out by penalties. In a blaze of glory, heroic to the last man and inspired by Gomer Jones and Dick Heekin, Ohio's seniors played their hearts out. Every one of those veterans, Heekin, Pincura, Boucher, Jones, Busich, Kabaelo, gave everything he had to pile up the score. They tied it all up in one package and let Michigan have it, entirely and completely with justice.

The game started auspiciously for the Wolverines when early in the first period they recovered a fumble on the Ohio 17. But the Bucks were equal to the challenge as a Michigan field goal attempt fell short. O.S.U. then began the assault with a vicious ground attack that led to the first score with Heekin going over from the two-foot line. Dick Beltz missed the point after.

A Michigan punt by Renner, Tippy Dye of O.S.U. receiving, produced one of the biggest thrills of the day, a 73 yard punt return for the second Ohio State touchdown. Sam Busich converted the extra point.

Just before the end of the first half Ohio State scored again on a great effort by Pincura and Bettridge. On a third down Pincura dropped back and ducking a tackler who all but had him, fired a pass into the end zone to Bettridge who, although surrounded, made a clean catch and the score was 19 to 0 as Kabealo missed the conversion.

On the third play of the second half, Boucher departed 50 yards around end for a TD which was called back by a penalty. Early in the fourth quarter O.S.U. scored their fifth touchdown on a double lateral with Nick Wasylik going over. Again the extra point fizzled, but the score was 31 to 0. Heekin scored the final TD with four yard plunge. Busich converted the extra point for a final score of 38 to 0.

STATISTICS

	OSU	UM
First Downs	20	5
Rushing Yardage	295	12
Passing Yardage	152	73
Total Yards	447	85
Passes	10-26	7-16
Yards Penalized	35	5
Punts, Average	4-36½	12-38
Fumbles, Lost	2-0	3-2

1935

1935

Ohio	19	Kentucky	6
Ohio	85	Drake	7
Ohio	28	Northwestern	7
Ohio	28	Indiana	6
Ohio	13	Notre Dame	18
Ohio	20	Chicago	13
Ohio	6	Illinois	0
Ohio	38	Michigan	0

Season Summary
Won, 7; Lost, 1

GOMER JONES
All-American Center

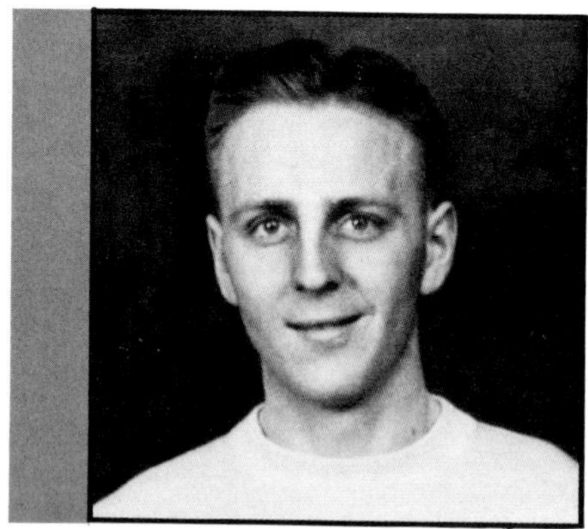

INWOOD SMITH
All-American Guard

MERLE WENDT
All-American End

OHIO

No.	Name	Pos.	Ht.	Wgt.	Years on Squad	Home Town
1	Pincura, Stanley	Q	5-10	167	3	Lorain
3	Stump, Wilson	Q	5-7	156	1	Alliance
4	West, Edward	E	6-1	181	1	Springfield
5	Dorris, Victor	F	5-8	175	1	Bellaire
6	Heekin, Richard	H	6	189	3	Cincinnati
7	Antenucci, Frank	F	5-10	174	2	Niles
8	Boucher, Frank	H	6-1	180	3	Kent
9	Beltz, Richard	H	6	171	3	Findlay
10	Bettridge, John	H	5-8½	177	2	Toledo
11	Waller, Francis	G	5-9	162	1	Columbus
12	Rees, Trevor	E	6	182	3	Dover
13	Williams, Joseph	H	5-5	165	1	Barberton
14	Belli, Roxie	G	5-10½	176	1	Martins Ferry
15	Boston, William	C	5-10	185	1	Lakewood
16	Kabealo, John	F	5-10	188	3	Youngstown
17	Van Meter, Howard	E	6-1	176	2	Struthers
18	Wendt, Merle	E	5-11	188	2	Middletown
19	Karcher, James	G	6	189	2	Forest
20	Gales, Charles	T	5-11	190	1	Niles
21	Thomas, Earl	E	6-3	193	2	Ashland
23	Crow, Fred	E	6-4	180	1	Pomeroy
24	Fisch, Frank	Q	6-½	189	3	Mansfield
25	Brungard, George	G	5-10½	187	2	North Lima
26	Zarnas, Gus	G	5-10	190	1	Youngstown
27	Cumiskey, Frank	E	6	185	2	Youngstown
29	Smith, Inwood	G	5-11	189	2	Mansfield
31	Busich, Sam	E	6-1	178	3	Lorain
33	Jones, Gomer (C)	C	5-8	200	3	Cleveland
34	Hamrick, Charles	T	6-1	216	2	Gallipolis
35	McDonald, James	F	6-1	181	1	Springfield
37	Waslik, Nicholas	Q	5-10	147	1	Astoria, L.I.
39	Nardi, Richard	H	5-10	182	1	Cleveland
40	Maggied, Sol	G	5-10	189	1	Columbus
41	Monahan, Thomas	G	5-8	174	1	Lorain
42	Roush, Ernest	T	5-10½	198	3	Blacklick
44	Hargraves, William	E	6-2	190	1	Akron
46	Wolf, Ralph	C	6-2	187	1	Youngstown
47	George, August	T	6-4	208	2	Dayton
48	Harre, Gilbert	T	6-2	205	3	Toledo
49	Ross, Robert	T	6-2	223	1	Troy
50	Dye, William H. H.	Q	5-8	142	2	Pomeroy
51	Chrissinger, Warren	G	5-9	185	1	Springfield
52	Cook, Donald	H	5-11	185	1	Columbus
53	Miller, James	H	5-11½	170	1	Shelby
57	Ream, Charles	T	6-2	191	1	Navarre
58	Miller, Robert	C	5-10½	181	2	Cleveland
59	Haddad, George	G	5-6	169	1	Toledo
60	Georgopoulos, Tom	E	6-1	185	3	Cleveland

MICHIGAN

No.	Name	Pos.	Ht.	Wgt.	Home Town
5	Remias, Steve	F	5-11	183	Chicago, IL
6	Olds, Frederic C.	G	5-11	186	East Lansing
8	Rieck, John	E	5-11	158	Detroit
9	Gray, Charles	Q	5-6	140	Lombard, IL
10	Babbin, George	H	5-6	166	Pentwater
11	Valpey, Arthur L.	E	6-2	188	Detroit
12	Kramer, Melvin G.	T	6	194	Toledo, OH
13	Ellis, Joseph O.	H	6	181	Eagle River, WI
14	Meyers, Earl J.	H	6	183	Detroit
15	Pillinger, Harry J.	H	5-9	165	Whitehall
16	Cooper, Robert E.	F-Q	6	188	Detroit
17	Barasa, Joseph L.	Q	5-9	161	Chicago, IL
19	Lillie, Walter I.	G	5-11	187	Grand Haven
20	Barclay, William C.	Q-H	5-11	153	Flint
21	Barnett, David G.	H-E	5-10	169	Detroit
23	Campbell, Robert D.	H	5-10	175	Ionia
24	Amrine, Robert Y.	C	6	179	London, OH
25	Garber, Jesse G.	G	5-8½	185	New York, NY
26	Carr, Carl W.	T	6-2	196	Saline
27	Wright, Harry T.	C	6-2¾	242	Mt. Clemens
29	Greenwald, Edward U.	T	6-3	203	Whiting, IN
30	Bolas, George A.	Q-H	5-8	161	Chicago, IL
31	Everhardus, Chris	H	6-1	172	Kalamazoo
32	Shakarian, George	C	6-½	177	Dearborn
33	Ritchie, C. Stark	H	5-10	170	Battle Creek
34	Hinshaw, Joseph M.	G	5-9½	192	Bloomfield Hills
35	Aug, Vincent	H	6	177	Cincinnati, OH
36	Nelson, Winfred	H	5-10	170	Greenville
37	Lutomski, Harry J.	F	5-9	187	Detroit
40	Mumford, John	F	5-10½	181	Birmingham
41	Schuman, Stanton J.	C-G	5-9	191	Winnetka, IL
42	Viergever, John D.	T	6-1	228	Algonac
43	Smithers, John A.	H	5-11	188	Elkhart, IN
44	Luby, Earle B.	T	5-11½	199	Chicago, IL
45	Oyler, Thomas T.	C	5-11½	190	Cincinnati, OH
49	Ziem, Fred C.	G	5-10	167	Pontiac
50	Brandman, Charles	Q	5-7	175	Findlay, OH
51	Murray, Charles A.	T	6-1	218	Butte, MT
52	Lincoln, James H.	T	6	193	Harbor Beach
53	Johnson, Ernest C.	E	6-½	182	Grand Rapids
54	Cushing, Frederick	C	5-11	191	Birmingham
55	Pederson, Ernest A.	G	5-10½	184	Grand Blanc
56	Stabovitz, Chester C.	E	5-11	180	Chicago, IL
60	Sweet, Cedric C.	F	6	197	Fremont
61	Rinaldi, Joseph M.	C	5-11	195	Elkhart, IN
62	Savage, Michael	E	6-3	218	Dearborn
63	Muzyk, Alexander F.	E	6-1	180	Pittsburgh, PA
64	Jennings, Ferris G.	Q	5-10	144	Ann Arbor
65	Renner, Wm. (Capt.)	Q	5-10½	159	Youngstown, OH
66	Hanshue, Cloyce E.	G	5-11	200	Kalamazoo
67	Patanelli, Matthew L.	E	6-1½	203	Elkhart, IN
68	Bissell, Frank S.	G	5-8	164	Hyannisport, MA
69	Warns, James	E	6-5	198	Ann Arbor
70	Farmer, Douglas A.	F	6	181	Hinsdale, IL
72	Sobsey, Solomon	E	6	186	Brooklyn, NY

1935

Michigan	6	Mich. State	25
Michigan	7	Indiana	0
Michigan	20	Wisconsin	12
Michigan	19	Columbia	7
Michigan	16	Pennsylvania	6
Michigan	0	Illinois	3
Michigan	0	Minnesota	40
Michigan	0	Ohio State	38

Season Summary

Games Won, 4; Lost, 4; Tied, 0

CUMISKEY, OHIO
RITCHIE—MICH.
M. WENDT, OHIO
RINALDI—MICH.
SMICK—MICH.
RABB, OHI

November 21, 1936

Columbus, Ohio

Ohio State Destroys Michigan 21 To 0

Tippy Dye Ends Grid Career In Glory As Wolves Fall Third Time In Row

As 56,202 fans looked on, a fearless Mickey Mouse among a bunch of ferocious glowering tiger men, little William Henry Harrison (Tippecanoe) Dye, played his last grand football for Ohio State. The Pomeroy bantamweight — a 145 pounder, dripping wet — threw a forward pass to Red Cumiskey for one touchdown. He whirled a shovel pass, a short forward behind the line, to set sophomore Johnny Rabb off on a 31-yard dash for another score. He ran 55 yards returning a punt to the Michigan 6 for what should have been yet another TD.

The third O.S.U. touchdown was scored by Nick Wasylik on a run of seven yards around Michigan's left end. Ohio missed all of its placements for extra points. The three points that made it 21 to 0, came from a place kick from 12 yards out booted for a field goal by Bill Booth.

Dye threw nine forward passes and completed six of them, one for a TD. In the second period Dye connected on four of five in a sensational 76-yard march, finally flinging a 20-yarder to Cumiskey for the score. Through the first half, which ended 6-0 for the Bucks, the game had been a fight — a real, old-fashioned Michigan-Ohio donnybrook. The third period established Ohio's superiority. There was an exchange of punts, punctuated by a nice 12-yard but fruitless gallop by Cedric Sweet. Then from its 31, Ohio went 69 yards in seven plays for the touchdown.

Detroit writers, sympathetic to Michigan, loved to call the Ohio coach "Close the Gates of Mercy Schmidt." But that day Schmidt did open the gates as he took Dye out for most of the final quarter.

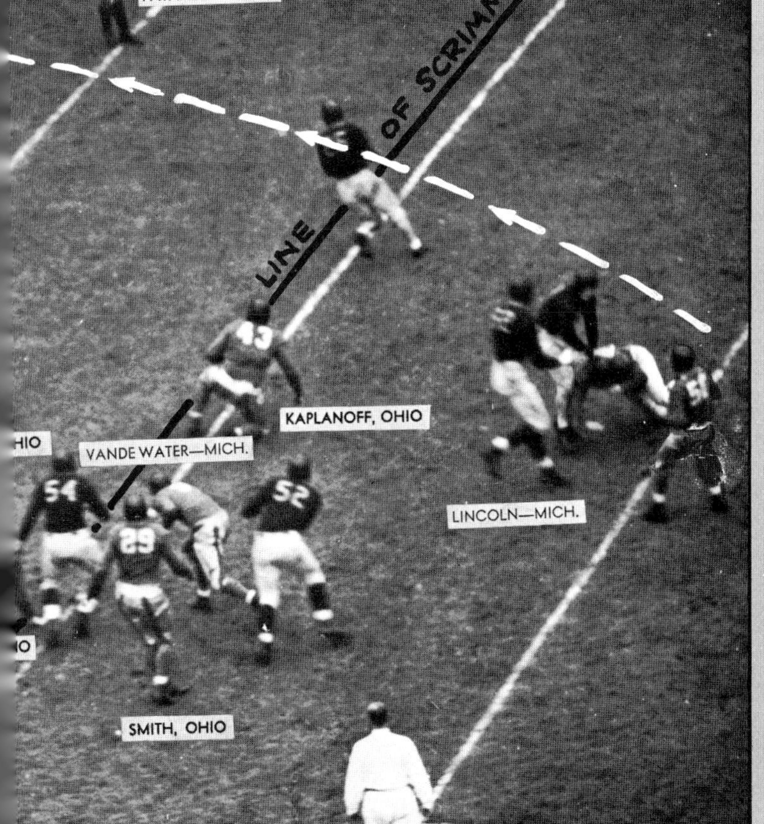

STATISTICS

	OSU	MU
First Downs	18	5
Yards Rushing	168	73
Yards Passing	173	44
Total Yards	356	127
Passes	11-19	2-12
Passes Intercepted	1	0
Punts, Average	9-44½	14-37
Fumbles, Lost	1-1	0-0
Yards Penalized	10	15

1936

MICHIGAN

1936			
Michigan	7	Mich. State	21
Michigan	3	Indiana	14
Michigan	0	Minnesota	26
Michigan	13	Columbia	0
Michigan	6	Illinois	9
Michigan	7	Pennsylvania	27
Michigan	0	Northwestern	9
Michigan	0	Ohio State	21

Season Summary

Games Won, 1; Lost, 7; Tied, 0

Williams, Kabealo, Birkholtz and Booth

No.	Name	Pos.	Ht.	Wgt.	Years on Squad	Home Town
17	Barasa, J. Laurence	QB	5-8½	160	2	Chicago, IL
20	*Barclay, William C.	QB	5-11	160	2	Flint
21	Barnett, James A.	G	5-8½	168	1	Detroit
50	Belsky, Jerome	G	6	190	1	Woodcliff, NJ
68	Bissell, Frank S.	G	5-8½	165	3	Hyannisport, MA
45	Brennan, John C.	T	6-1	199	1	Racine, WI
23	*Campbell, Robert D.	HB	5-9½	174	2	Ionia
16	Cooper, Robert E.	QB	6	187	2	Detroit
40	Curren, Robert B.	FB	5-11	190	1	Warren, PA
70	Farmer, Douglas A.	FB	6	183	2	Hinsdale, IL
32	Floersch, Harold J.	E	6-2	185	1	Wyandotte
63	Frost, Kenneth D.	HB	5-9	170	1	Willoughby, OH
25	*Garber, Jesse G.	G	5-9	190	3	Brookline, MA
51	Gedeon, Elmer J.	E	6-3	180	1	Cleveland, OH
9	Gray, Charles	QB	5-6	140	2	Lombard, IL
29	Greenwald, Edward	T	6-3	203	2	Whiting, IN
36	Heikkinen, Ralph I.	G	5-8	187	1	Ramsay
13	Hook, R. Wallace, Jr.	HB	5-9	170	1	Grand Rapids
66	Janke, Fred C.	T	6-½	200	1	Jackson
64	*Jennings, Ferris G.	QB	5-10	140	2	Ann Arbor
26	Jordan, Forrest R.	G	6-2	195	1	Clare
27	Jordan, John D.	C	6-2	228	1	Evanston, IL
12	*Kramer, Melvin G.	T	6	196	2	Toledo, OH
48	Leadbeater, Arthur	HB	5-10½	180	2	Belleville, NJ
37	Levine, Louis	QB	5-10½	180	1	Muskegon
52	*Lincoln, James H.	T	6	190	2	Harbor Beach
5	Loiko, Alex	HB	6-¼	188	1	Hamtramck
44	*Luby, Earle B.	T	5-11½	195	2	Chicago, IL
8	Mark, Martin	G	5-9	180	1	New York, NY
19	Marzonie, George A.	G	5-9	178	2	Flint
72	Maurer, George J.	FB	5-11	180	1	Toledo, OH
34	Nickerson, N. J.	FB	6-¼	182	1	Detroit
15	Ochs, Lilburn M.	HB	5-9	175	2	Univ. City, MO
6	Olds, Fredric C.	G-T	5-11	185	2	E. Lansing
14	Paquette, Donald M.	HB	6-1½	190	1	Superior, WI
67	*Patanelli, Matt (C)	E	6-1	200	3	Elkhart, IN
55	*Pederson, E. A., Jr.	G	5-10	190	2	Grand Blanc
35	Phillips, E. J., Jr.	HB	5-10	177	1-	Bradford, PA
30	Piotrowski, R. P.	HB	5-10	157	1	Manistee
65	Purucker, N. B.	HB	5-10	168	1	Poland, OH
61	*Rinaldi, Joe M.	C	5-11	190	2	Elkhart, IN
33	*Ritchie, C. Stark	HB	5-11	180	2	Battle Creek
41	Rosenthal, S. C.	T	6-2½	200	1	Blue Island, IL
53	Shakarian, George	C	6-½	180	2	Dearborn
62	Siegel, Don J.	T	6-4	199	1	Royal Oak
42	Smick, Dan	E	6-4	198	1	Hazel Park
43	*Smithers, John A.	HB	5-11	188	2	Elkhart, IN
56	Stabovitz, C. C.	E	5-11	180	3	Chicago, IL
24	Stanton, Edward C.	FB	6	183	1	Charleston, WV
60	*Sweet, Cedric C.	FB	6	200	3	Fremont
11	*Valpey, Arthur L.	E	6-2½	190	2	Detroit
54	VandeWater, C.	G	5-11	185	1	Holland
49	Ziem, Fred C.	G	5-10	162	2	Pontiac

OHIO

No.	Name	Pos.	Ht.	Wgt.	Year on Squad	Home Town
22	Aleskus, Joseph	C	6-2½	190	1	Piqua
7	*Antenucci, Frank	RH	5-10	178	3	Niles
60	Belli, Roxie	RG	5-11	182	2	Martins Ferry
6	*Bettridge, John	RH	5-10	182	3	Sandusky
4	Birkholtz, Paul	LH	6	179	1	Youngstown
19	Bliss, Keith	FB	5-11	170	1	Columbus
9	Booth, William	LH	5-11	177	1	E. Liverpool
52	Boughner, R.	LE	5-11	172	1	Akron
54	Bullock, William	QB	5-10	167	1	Kent
12	Cartwright, E.	RH	6	175	1	Tiffin
51	Chrissinger, W.	RG	5-11	192	2	Springfield
21	Cook, Donald	RH	5-11	175	2	Columbus
23	Crow, Fred	LE	6-3	189	2	Pomeroy
27	*Cumiskey, Frank	RE	6	187	3	Youngstown
5	Dorris, Victor	RH	5-10	180	2	Bellaire
50	*Dye, William	QB	5-7½	145	3	Pomeroy
20	*Gales, Charles	RT	5-11	192	2	Niles
47	*George, August	LT	6-3	212	3	Dayton
59	Haddad, George	RG	5-6	170	2	Toledo
34	*Hamrick, Charles	LT	6	243	3	Gallipolis
44	Hargreaves, Wm.	RT	6-2	196	1	Akron
55	Hofmayer, E.	RG	5-10	175	1	Columbus
48	Hohenberger, C.	RT	5-11	218	1	Defiance
1	Hull, James	QB	5-10	165	1	Greenfield
16	Kabealo, Michael	LH	5-9	161	1	Youngstown
43	Kaplanoff, Carl	RT	5-10	215	1	Bucyrus
61	Kinel, Tony	QB	5-7	143	1	Newton Falls
25	Kleinfelder, K.	RE	6-1	188	1	Sandusky
45	Kleinhans, John	LE	6-2	195	3	Maumee
17	Knecht, John	LH	5-10	175	1	Chillicothe
31	Lind, Jack	LE	6	183	1	Columbus
56	Lohr, Wendell	RE	6	174	1	Massillon
40	*Maggied, Sol	LG	5-10	192	2	Columbus
32	Masoner, Robert	RE	5-11½	175	1	Middletown
8	*McDonald, James	FB	6	186	2	Springfield
58	*Miller, Robert	C	5-11	182	3	Cleveland
41	Monahan, T.	FB	5-10	176	2	Lorain
11	Nardi, Richard	RH	5-11	183	2	Cleveland
62	Novotny, George	LG	5-11	187	1	Elyria
10	Phillips, William	QB	5-10	176	1	Columbus
3	Rabb, John	FB	5-11	175	1	Akron
57	*Ream, Charles	LT	6	196	2	Navarre
64	Robinson, James	C	6-1	184	1	Columbus
49	Ross, Robert	LT	6-1	239	2	Troy
24	Rutkay, Nicholas	LG	6	189	1	Youngstown
42	Schoenbaum, A.	RT	5-11	210	1	Cleveland
29	*Smith, Inwood	LG	5-11	190	3	Mansfield
67	Stump, Wilson	QB	5-9	157	2	Alliance
2	*Wasylik, Nicholas	QB	5-8	151	2	Astoria, L.I.
14	Wedebrook, H.	RH	6-1	189	1	Portsmouth
65	Welbaum, T.	LH	5-10	165	1	Akron
35	Wendt, Emerson	RE	6-1	191	1	Middletown
18	*Wendt, Merle (C)	LE	5-10	190	3	Middletown
28	West, Edward	RE	6	195	2	Springfield
13	*Williams, Joseph	LH	5-7	166	2	Barberton
33	Wolf, Ralph	C	6-2	191	2	Youngstown
66	Wuellner, Richard	C	5-11	180	1	Columbus
30	Young, Louis	LG	5-10½	193	1	Massillon
26	*Zarnas, Gust	RG	5-10	193	2	Youngstown

* Indicates letterman

1936

Ohio	60	New York Univ.	0
Ohio	0	Pittsburgh	6
Ohio	13	Northwestern	14
Ohio	7	Indiana	0
Ohio	2	Notre Dame	7
Ohio	44	Chicago	0
Ohio	13	Illinois	0
Ohio	21	Michigan	0

Season Summary

Won, 5; Lost, 3

November 20, 1937

Ann Arbor, Michigan

Ohio State, 21 To 0, Over The Wolverines

60,000 Frozen Fans Watch State Trounce Michigan For Fourth Straight Year

H. O. "FRITZ" CRISLER
Michigan Head Coach
1937-1947

Ohio State's big rough-housing line, at its farewell appearance of a great season, once more manhandled fallen Michigan, 21 to 0. For the fourth straight year, by a score that hardly measured the Scarlet superiority, Ohio completely routed and overwhelmed its oldest and most bitter Big Ten rival. The battle was waged in bitter cold as snow fell throughout the second half, reaching blizzard proportions as the game ended.

Jim Miller of Shelby piled over the Michigan line for two touchdowns. His first score, in the last second of the first half, came on a blast through Michigan's left tackle from the two yard line. His second TD came on a superb forward pass play, good for 44 yards, from Nick Wasylik in which Miller raced 17 yards through fluffy snowfall. Not a Michigan man was near him.

The other touchdown belonged to Nick Nardi, the Collinwood right halfback and the drivingest pile-driver in the whole Scarlet ensemble. On a pass from Wasylik from 11 yards out, the crashing Nardi carried a Michigan tackler three yards with him and over the goal.

Jim McDonald, the fullback, quarterback, and co-captain, kicked one of the three extra points. Ohio's other two points in the second quarter, were on a safety in which Charley Ream, senior end, tackled intrepid Norm Purucker, Michigan halfback, behind the goal line.

Purucker, 170 pound junior from Poland, Ohio, played a tremendous, heroic game for the lost cause of Michigan. His great punting time and time again hurled back the charging Ohio giants. A dozen times, after his kick, he tore down the field and made the tackle of the Ohio receiver.

The size of the victory represented the hardest, most ferocious football that Ohio State could play. Never had an Ohio team, that might have been over-confident, looked in better mental condition. The great charging Ohio line, featured by such stalwarts as Gus Zarnas, Carl Kaplanoff, and Ralph Wolf, spared Michigan not at all. The Buckeyes were in there to win and by the biggest possible score.

Ohio, though making only seven first downs, gained 194 yards by rushing and 101 yards through the air. Michigan's net gain against Ohio's line from rushing was exactly 8 yards. In passing the Wolves gained 37 yards.

1937

1937

Ohio	14	Texas Christian	0
Ohio	13	Purdue	0
Ohio	12	Southern Calif.	13
Ohio	7	Northwestern	0
Ohio	39	Chicago	0
Ohio	0	Indiana	10
Ohio	19	Illinois	0
Ohio	21	Michigan	0

Season Summary
Won, 6; Lost, 2

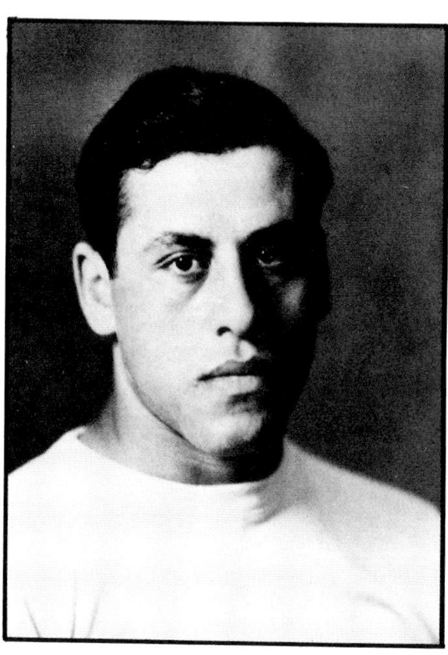

GUST ZARNAS
All-American Guard

OHIO

No.	Name	Pos.	Ht.	Wgt.	Years on Squad	Home Town
2	*Wasylik, Nicholas	LH	5-9	160	3	Astoria, L.I.
3	*Rabb, John	FB	5-11	178	2	Akron
5	Dorris, Victor	FB	5-10	185	3	Bellaire
6	Zadworney, Frank	RH	5-10	195	1	Cleveland
7	Fordham, Forrest	FB	5-8	172	1	Toledo
8	*McDonald, J. (CC)	QB	6	190	3	Springfield
10	Phillips, William	QB	5-10	180	2	Columbus
11	Nardi, Richard	RH	5-11	193	3	Cleveland
12	Miller, James	LH	5-11	182	3	Shelby
14	*Wedebrook, Howard	RH	6-1	191	2	Portsmouth
15	Simione, John	QB	5-8	162	1	Youngstown
16	*Kabealo, Michael	LH	5-9	170	2	Youngstown
17	Bartschy, Ross	LE	6	185	1	Orrville
18	Smith, Francis L.	FB	5-10	190	1	Quincy, MA
19	Bliss, Keith	RE	5-11	180	2	Columbus
20	*Gales, Charles	RT	5-11	205	3	Niles
21	Moloney, Robert	LH	6	173	1	Columbus
22	Aleskus, Joe	LT	6-2	197	2	Columbus
23	*Crow, Fred	LE	6-3	189	3	Pomeroy
24	Rutkay, Nicholas	RG	6	212	1	Youngstown
25	Sarkkinen, Esco	LE	6	176	1	Fairport Harbor
26	*Zarnas, Gust	RG	5-10	198	3	Brackenridge, P.
27	Spears, Jerry	RE	6-1	191	1	Columbus
28	Whitehead, Stuart	RE	6-1	196	1	Columbus
29	Clair, Frank	LE	6	193	1	Hamilton
30	Young, Louis	LG	5-11	199	2	Massillon
31	Smith, Frank	RG	5-10	190	1	Columbus
33	*Wolf, R. (CC)	C	6-2	194	3	Youngstown
34	Shaffer, Bernard	LT	6-2	265	1	Cincinnati
35	Wendt, Emerson	LT	6-1	195	1	Middletown
36	Andrako, Steve	C	6	184	1	Trinway
37	White, Claude	C	5-11	181	1	Portsmouth
39	Dietrich, Russell	C	6-1	185	1	Bay Village
40	*Maggied, Sol	LG	5-10	197	3	Columbus
41	Monahan, Thomas	FB	5-10	180	3	Lorain
42	*Schoenbaum, Alex	LT	5-11	215	2	Huntington, WV
43	*Kaplanoff, Carl	RT	5-10	210	2	Bucyrus
44	Hargreaves, William	RT	6-3	192	2	Akron
46	Mastako, Frank	RT	6	190	1	New Philadelphi
48	Barren, Henry	LT	6	215	1	Shaker Heights
49	Tucci, Amel	RG	5-9	186	1	Zanesville
50	Marino, Victor	LG	5-7	178	1	Youngstown
51	*Chrissinger, Warren	RG	5-11	196	3	Springfield
52	Boughner, Richard	LE	5-11	178	2	Akron
53	Graf, Campbell	RG	5-9	170	1	Columbus
54	Bullock, William	QB	5-10	174	2	Kent
55	Hofmayer, Edward	LG	5-10	180	2	Columbus
56	Lohr, Wendell	RE	6	178	2	Massillon
57	*Ream, Charles	RE	6	208	3	Navarre
58	Howe, Frank	RH	5-10	190	1	Columbus
59	Haddad, George	LG	5-6	173	3	Toledo
61	Coyer, William	QB	5-8	157	1	Orrville
62	Novotny, George	RT	6-1	198	2	Elyria
63	Hull, James	QB	5-10	165	2	Greenfield
64	Kopach, Stephen	RG	5-8	160	1	Youngstown
65	Welbaum, Thomas	LH	5-10	156	2	Akron
66	Wuellner, Richard	C	5-11	181	2	Columbus
71	Madro, Joseph	LG	5-7	175	1	Wellington

* Indicates letterman

MICHIGAN

No.	Name	Pos.	Ht.	Wgt.	Home Town
2	Bennett, Arthur L.	G	5-9	170	Schenectady, NY
3	Vial, A. Burgess	G	6	164	LaGrange, IL
4	Bowers, Charles L.	E	5-11	165	Pontiac
6	Kinsey, John H.	FB	6	194	Plymouth
7	Penvenne, Paul F.	FB	6-½	190	Lenox, MA
9	Laskey, Derwood D.	HB	5-9	155	Milan
11	Valpey, Arthur L.	E	6-2	201	Detroit
12	Kramer, Melvin G.	T	6	200	Toledo, OH
13	Hook, R. Wallace, Jr.	HB	5-9	175	E. Grand Rapids
14	Hutton, Thomas G.	C	5-11	174	Bay City
15	Sukup, Milo F.	HB	5-7½	176	Muskegon Hgts.
16	Marzonie, George A.	G	5-9	185	Flint
17	Renda, Hercules	HB	5-4	152	Jochin, WV
19	Trosko, Fred	HB	5-9	154	Flint
20	Barclay, William C.	QB	5-11	163	Flint
21	Nielsen, Paul	E	6	182	Ann Arbor
22	Gates, David W.	G	5-10	174	Plymouth
23	Campbell, Robert D.	HB	5-9½	170	Ionia
24	Stanton, E. Cramon	FB	6-½	183	Charleston, WV
25	Ziem, Frederick C.	G	5-10	161	Pontiac
27	Kuhn, Dennis A.	T	6-2	207	River Rouge
29	Savilla, Roland	T	6-3½	195	Gallagher, WV
30	Piotrowski, Robert P.	HB	5-11	157	Manistee
32	Floersch, Harold J.	E	6-2½	188	Wyandotte
33	Ritchie, C. Stark	HB	5-11	173	Battle Creek
34	Nickerson, Norman J.	FB	6-¼	192	Detroit
36	Heikkinen, Ralph I.	G	5-9	180	Ramsay
37	Levine, Louis	QB	5-11	186	Muskegon Hgts.
40	Curren, Robert B.	FB	6	198	Warren, PA
41	Bilbie, James N.	T	6-1	200	South Lyon
42	Smick, Dan	E	6-4	198	Hazel Park
43	Smith, William A.	T	6-2	203	Brooks Field, TX
44	Luby, Earle B.	T	6	204	Chicago, IL
45	Brennan, John C.	G	6-2	201	Racine, WI
49	Frutig, Edward C.	E	6-1	176	River Rouge
50	Belsky, Jerome	G	6	184	Woodcliff, NJ
51	Gedeon, Elmer J.	E	6-3	192	Cleveland, OH
52	Lincoln, James H.	T	6	191	Harbor Beach
53	Kodros, Archie J.	C-G	5-8	191	Alton, IL
54	Vande Water, C. H.	G	5-10	183	Holland
55	Pederson, Ernest A.	G	5-11	185	Grand Blanc
56	Valek, Vincent	E	6-2	170	Holly
59	Mulholland, Harry K.	FB	5-11	191	Bay City
60	Steen, Kenneth	T	6-2	196	Detroit
61	Rinaldi, Joseph (Capt.)	C	5-11	190	Elkhart, IN
62	Siegel, Donald J.	T	6-4	205	Royal Oak
63	Frost, Kenneth D.	HB	5-9	170	Willoughby, OH
64	Tinker, Horace C.	C	5-10	173	Battle Creek
65	Purucker, Norman B.	HB	5-10	170	Poland, OH
66	Janke, Fred C.	FB	6-1	208	Jackson
67	Nicholson, John E., Jr.	E	6-4	186	Elkhart, IN
69	Rogers, Joseph C.	E	6-3	190	Royal Oak
70	Farmer, Douglas A.	FB	6-1	182	Hinsdale, IL
71	Ulevitch, Herman H.	G	5-8	188	Cleveland, OH
72	Sobsey, Solomon	E	6	189	W. New York, NJ
75	Olds, Fred C.	GT	6	192	East Lansing

1937

Michigan	14	Michigan State	19
Michigan	0	Northwestern	7
Michigan	6	Minnesota	39
Michigan	7	Iowa	6
Michigan	7	Illinois	6
Michigan	13	Chicago	12
Michigan	7	Pennsylvania	0
Michigan	0	Ohio State	21

Season Summary

Games Won, 4; Lost, 4; Tied, 0

November 19, 1938

Columbus, Ohio

Michigan Breaks Four Year Jinx Of Buckeyes

Wolves, Led By Kromer, Snap Four-Year Domination Of Scarlet And Gray, 18 To 0

A Michigan team like that of the best good old days, staunch, resourceful, always alert, closed its year of Renaissance with a smashing victory over Ohio State, 18 to 0.

Before 67,554 Ohio State was beaten largely by an Ohioan. Paul Kromer, the Lorain tornado, wearing on his back the significant number of one of Michigan's famed plays — No. 83 — was the balance wheel and man of all work as the Wolverine attack raged in triumph. Although he did not figure in the scoring, he wound up gloriously his first season of college competition.

Tom Harmon, the Hoosier hot shot from Gary, Indiana, also a sophomore, scored the first Wolverine touchdown, on a plunge in the second period. Harmon winged a beautiful forward pass to end Ed Furtig in the fourth period for the second touchdown.

With one minute and 58 seconds of the game left, the blow that made it a rout was delivered by little Fred Trosko of Flint, 154-pound halfback. Through the demoralized and sagging Ohio forces, Trosko departed 36 yards around the Ohio right end and over the line. All three tries for extra points were missed.

Michigan had the line as figured — a great line with Janke, Kodros, Heikkinen, and others. They also had the backs — Harmon and Kromer — just as expected. Michigan lost the Big Ten title by one point — the 7-6 loss in Minnesota, in a game that according to the figures and run of the game, Michigan should have won. It was a fair year's work for Fritz Crisler, the rejuvenator.

STATISTICS

	UM	OSU
First Downs Rushing	8	7
First Downs Passing	2	2
Rushing Yards	205	72
Passing Yards	64	37
Total Yards	269	109
Passing	6-13-0	3-17-3
Punts-Average	12-34	13-34½
Fumbles-Lost	1-0	5-1
Yards Penalized	45	5

1938

1938			
Michigan	14	Michigan State	0
Michigan	45	Chicago	7
Michigan	6	Minnesota	7
Michigan	15	Yale	13
Michigan	14	Illinois	0
Michigan	19	Pennsylvania	13
Michigan	0	Northwestern	0
Michigan	18	Ohio State	0

Season Summary

Games Won, 6; Lost, 1; Tied, 1.

RALPH HEIKKINEN
All-American Guard

Michigan Helmet Goes Back to '38

Michigan's famed winged football helmet dates back to 1938 when Fritz Crisler arrived from Princeton with his penchant for detail and style.

"Michigan had a plain black helmet and we wanted to dress it up a little," Fritz recalls. "We added some color (maize and blue) and used the same basic helmet I had designed at Princeton."

There was one other consideration. Fritz thought this unique helmet could be helpful to his passers when they tried to spot their receivers downfield. There was a tendency to use different colored helmets just for receivers in those days, but I always thought that would be as helpful for the defense as for the offense," Fritz explained.

MICHIGAN

No.	Name	Pos.	Ht.	Wgt.	Year	Home Town
19	Bennett, Arthur L.	G	5-8	170	2	Schenectady, NY
74	Bennett, Richard C.	HB	5-10	170	1	Springfield, IL
65	*Brennan, John C.	G	6-2	200	3	Monroe
96	Christy, Edward	FB	5-10	185	1	Gary, IN
40	Czak, Edward	E	5-11	180	1	Elyria, OH
69	Evashevski, Forest	C-QB	6-1	198	1	Detroit
5	Fabyan, August E.	HB	5-8	165	1	Muskegon Hts.
32	Floersch, Harold	E	6-3	188	3	Wyandotte
73	Flora, Robert L.	T	6-1	213	1	Muskegon
57	Ford, Thomas G.	C	6-1	185	1	E. Grand Rapids
63	Fritz, Ralph	G	5-9	198	1	New Kensington, PA
49	Frutig, Edward	E	6	176	1	River Rouge
51	*Gedeon, Elmer J.	E	6-4	192	3	Cleveland, OH
98	Harmon, Tom	HB	6	194	1	Gary, IN
36	*Heikkinen, Ralph	G	5-10	180	3	Ramsey
79	*Hook, R. Wallace, Jr.	FB	5-11	176	3	E. Grand Rapids
76	Hook, Robert M.	T	6-3	205	1	E. Grand Rapids
14	Hutton, Thomas	C	5-11	185	2	Bay City
66	*Janke, Fred (Capt.)	T	6-1	205	3	Jackson
26	Jordan, Forrest	G	6-2	200	3	Clare
50	Kelto, Reuben	C	6-1	195	1	Bessemer
6	Kinsey, John	FB	6	194	2	Plymouth
39	Kitti, Walter	QB	5-10	170	1	Calumet
53	*Kodros, Archie	C	5-8	190	2	Alton, IL
7	Kohl, Harry E.	QB	5-6	147	1	Dayton, OH
83	Kromer, Paul S.	HB	5-10	160	1	Lorain, OH
27	Kuhn, Dennis	T	6-2	207	2	River Rouge
9	Laskey, Derwood	HB	5-9	155	2	Milan
46	*Levine, Louis	QB	5-11	188	3	Muskegon Hts.
10	Luther, William	HB	5-11	165	1	Toledo, OH
61	Megregian, Michael	HB	5-8	190	1	Detroit
22	Mehaffey, Howard	FB	6	177	1	Pittsburgh, PA
77	Meyer, Jack	QB	5-9	195	1	Elyria, OH
59	Mulholland, Harry	FB	5-11	195	2	Bay City
54	Nielsen, Paul	E	6	182	2	Ann Arbor
67	*Nicholson, John	E	6-4	190	2	Elkhart, IN
34	Nickerson, Norman J.	E	6-1	192	1	Detroit
56	*Olds, Frederick	G	6	192	2	East Lansing
70	Paddy, Arthur	G	5-7	160	1	Benton Harbor
18	Parfet, William	E	6-1	190	2	Golden, CO
30	Persky, Lester	QB	5-10	170	1	Cleveland Hgts., OH
21	*Phillips, Edward J.	FB	5-10	180	3	Bradford, PA
58	*Purucker, Norman B.	HB	5-11	180	3	Youngstown, OH
85	*Renda, Hercules	HB	5-4	163	2	Jochin, WV
29	*Savilla, Roland	T	6-1	206	2	Gallagher, WV
72	Scott, Virgil	G	5-11	175	2	Hazel Park
62	*Siegel, Don	T	6-4	210	3	Royal Oak
38	*Smick, Danny	E	6-4	205	3	Hazel Park
43	*Smith, William A.	T	6-2	210	2	Riverside, CA
31	Steketee, Jack N.	C	6	185	1	Detroit
88	Strong, David A.	HB	5-8	155	2	Helena, MT
15	Sukup, Milo	G	5-8	176	2	Muskegon Hts.
64	Tinker, Horace	C	5-10	173	2	Battle Creek
55	*Trosko, Fred	HB	5-9	154	2	Flint
71	Ulevitch, Herman	G	5-8	188	2	Cleveland, OH
33	Valek, Vincent	E	6-2	170	2	Holly
17	Vial, A. Burgess	FB	5-9	175	2	LaGrange, IL
41	Vollmer, William E.	T	6	200	1	Manistee
16	Wickter, Larry	FB	5-10	170	1	Toledo, OH
80	Zielinski, Ernest P.	E	6-1	185	2	Bay City

* Indicates letterman

OHIO

No.	Name	Pos.	Wt.	Hgt.	Year	Home Town
22	*Aleskus, Joseph	LT	230	6-2	3	Columbus
36	Andrako, Steve	C	185	6	2	Trinway
52	Arnold, James	RG	184	5-8	1	Akron
17	*Bartschy, Ross	LE	187	6	2	Orrville
41	Bennet, William	RT	204	6	1	Willoughby
19	*Bliss, Keith	RE	192	5-10	3	Columbus
60	Bolser, Harvey	RT	228	6-2	1	Lockland
54	Bullock, William	QB	184	5-11	3	Kent
29	Clair, Frank	RE	200	6	1	Hamilton
61	Coyer, William	QB	170	5-8	1	Orrville
68	Crabbe, Jack	FB	186	5-8	1	Columbus
11	Elliott, Roy	RH	176	5-11	1	Grindstone, PA
7	*Fordham, Forrest	RH	170	5-9	2	Toledo
20	*Gales, Charles	LG	202	5-10	3	Niles
53	Graf, Campbell	LG	168	5-9	1	Columbus
34	Grundies, Jerry	LT	235	6-2	1	Cleveland
55	Hofmayer, Edward	RG	191	6	2	Columbus
70	Hodick, Mike	C	173	5-11	1	Martins Ferry
58	Howe, Frank	RH	176	5-10	1	Columbus
16	*Kabealo, Michael (Co-Capt.)	QB	175	5-8	3	Youngstown
43	*Kaplanoff, Carl, (Co-Capt.)	RT	245	5-11	3	Bucyrus
8	Langhurst, James	FB	187	5-10	1	Willard
56	*Lohr, Wendell	RE	186	5-10	3	Massillon
33	Maag, Charles	C	206	6-3	1	Sandusky
71	Madro, Joseph	LG	185	5-9	1	Wellington
50	*Marino, Victor	LG	189	5-7	2	Youngstown
59	Masoner, Robert	LE	185	5-11	2	Middletown
48	Monas, Alfons	LT	265	6-3	1	Dayton
72	Newlin, John	LE	192	6	1	St. Clairsville
26	Nosker, William	RG	200	5-11	1	Columbus
44	Oman, Donald	RT	190	6	1	Richwood
40	Rosen, Andy	RT	204	6-1	1	Isabella, PA
24	*Rutkay, Nicholas	RG	220	6	2	Youngstown
32	Santschi, John	LE	180	6	1	Akron
35	Sarkkinen, Eino	LE	172	6	1	Fairport Harbor
25	*Sarkkinen, Esco	LE	191	6	2	Fairport Harbor
42	*Schoenbaum, Alex	LT	219	5-11	3	Huntington, WV
9	Scott, Donald	LH	200	6-1	1	Canton
5	Sexton, James	QB	184	5-10	1	Middletown
5	Simione, John	QB	168	5-8	1	Youngstown
8	Smith, Francis	RE	190	5-10	2	Quincy, MA
1	Smith, Frank	RG	203	5-10	2	Columbus
4	Strausbaugh, James	LH	172	5-10	1	Chillicothe
7	Spears, Jerry	LG	219	6	1	Columbus
1	Tobik, Andy	RG	175	5-10	1	Cleveland
9	Tucci, Amel	RG	195	5-9	1	Zanesville
3	Vittek, Paul	LG	185	5-10	1	Columbus
4	*Wedebrook, Howard	RH	196	6-1	3	Portsmouth
5	Welbaum, Thomas	FB	165	5-9	2	Akron
7	White, Claude	C	190	6	2	Portsmouth
3	Whitehead, Stuart	LE	195	6	2	Columbus
6	Wuellner, Richard	C	186	5-11	2	Columbus
[illegible]	Young, Lewis	RT	220	5-10	3	Massillon
6	*Zadworney, Frank	RH	190	5-11	2	Cleveland
2	Zuchegno, Albert	FB	166	5-8	1	Dover

*indicates letterman

1938

Ohio	6	Indiana	0
Ohio	7	USC	14
Ohio	0	Northwestern	0
Ohio	42	Chicago	7
Ohio	32	NYU	0
Ohio	0	Purdue	12
Ohio	32	Illinois	14
Ohio	0	Michigan	18

Season Summary

Won, 4; Lost, 3; Tied, 1

Tom Harmon punting.

Fritz Crisler confers with Evashevski, Westfall, Harmon and Trosko.

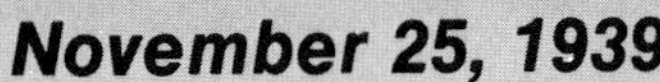

November 25, 1939

Ann Arbor, Michigan

Ohio State Upset In Final Minute

Buckeyes Gain Undisputed Title Despite Loss To Michigan, 21 To 14

The stout heart and the strong arm of mighty Michigan wrought one of the most heroic feats of all time. Up from the pit of near despair, a frenzied Michigan team reached the pinnacle of valor to strike down Ohio State, 21 to 14 before a monster host of 80,227 fans. In a football struggle filled with incredible drama and bravery, Michigan, trailing 14 to 0 at the end of the first period, rallied to conquer the Scarlet Buckeyes in the final minute of play.

The light of the big stadium clock had passed the last minute mark as 154-pound Fred Trosko, in the final minute of the last game of his college career, set up the ball for a supposed place kick, just beyond Ohio's 30-yard line. The scrimmage line was the 23. The score was 14-14. Behind Trosko the great Tom Harmon swung his foot as if to get the line for the field goal. The ball passed from center. Trosko hesitated one instant as if to set it up, then seized the ball in his arms and darted down the side line. With superb blocking Trosko carried the pigskin over the goal without a hand being laid on him.

The game established beyond any doubt the All American eminence of Tom Harmon. Every time he took the ball, he was dangerous. He made repeated gains through the clutches of the baffled Ohioans. He completed twelve of twenty forward passes, most of them to Forest (One-man Gang)) Evashevski.

Ohio's two first period touchdowns were both by passing. The first was on a fooler from the 5-yard line of Michigan when Doug Scott threw to guard Vic Marino who had moved out to end and had become eligible. The second connected for 20 yards from Scott to end Frank Clair who made a masterful catch in the end zone.

Michigan moved from their own 35-yard line down the field to score. Harmon went the last 16 yards for the Wolverine TD. Much as Ohio had been cautioned, Michigan's "Old 83" play was at its best as it provided the second Michigan score, tying the Bucks at 14-14. The score remained deadlocked until the final minute when Trosko scored on the fake place kick.

STATISTICS

	UM	OSU
First Downs	11	11
Rushing	5	8
Passing	6	2
Penalties	0	1
Total Net Yards	265	208
Rushing	119	172
Passing	146	36
Passing	12-20-4	5-15-2
Punts-Average	8-41	5-44
Fumbles-Lost	3-1	7-4
Yards Penalized	20	0

1939

1939			
Ohio	19	Missouri	0
Ohio	13	Northwestern	0
Ohio	23	Minnesota	20
Ohio	14	Cornell	23
Ohio	24	Indiana	0
Ohio	61	Chicago	0
Ohio	21	Illinois	0
Ohio	14	Michigan	21

Season Summary
Won, 6; Lost, 2
Big Ten Champions

ESCO SARKKINEN
All-American End

DONALD SCOTT
All-American Back

OHIO

No.	Name	Pos.	Ht.	Wgt.	Home Town
1	Daniell, James	T	6-1	210	Mt. Lebanon, PA
2	Fisher, Richard	HB	5-10	185	Columbiana
3	Rabb, John	FB	5-10	178	Akron
4	Strausbaugh, James	HB	5-10	179	Chillicothe
5	Sexton, James	QB	5-10	185	Youngstown
6	Zadworney, Frank	HB	6	190	Cleveland
8	Langhurst, James	FB	5-11	191	Willard
9	Scott, Don	QB	6-1	208	Canton
10	Terry, Carl	HB	6-2	212	Ironton
11	Graf, Jack	QB	6	196	Columbus
12	Hallabrin, John	FB	5-10	194	Mansfield
14	Wedebrook, Howard	HB	6-1	195	Portsmouth
15	Simione, John	QB	5-9	170	Youngstown
16	Kinkade, Thomas	HB	6-1	190	Toronto
17	Bartschy, Ross	E	6	185	Orrville
18	Wansack, Andy	HB	5-10	171	Campbell
19	Moloney, Robert	HB	6	185	Columbus
20	Bell, William	C	5-11	195	Steubenville
21	Carlin, Earl	G	5-10	182	Bryan
22	Anderson, Charles	E	5-11	189	Massillon
23	Howard, Fritz	G	5-11	194	Toledo
24	Zavistoske, George	HB	5-10	160	Racine, WI
25	Sarkkinen, Esco	E	6	192	Fairport
26	Nosker, William	G	6	194	Columbus
27	Spears, Jerry	G	6	204	Columbus
28	Whitehead, Stuart	G	6	192	Columbus
29	Clair, Frank	E	6	198	Hamilton
30	Bruckner, Edwin	G	5-11	193	Sandusky
31	Smith, Frank	G	5-10	195	Columbus
32	Santschi, John	E	6	178	Akron
33	Maag, Charles	T	6-3	210	Sandusky
34	Grundies, Jerome	T	6-2	228	Cleveland
35	Sarkkinen, Eino	HB	6	172	Fairport
36	Andrako, Stephen (C)	C	6	192	Trinway
37	White, Claude	C	6	196	Portsmouth
38	Fox, Sam	E	6	188	Washington, D.C.
39	Oman, Donald	T	6	189	Richwood
40	Rosen, Andy	T	6-1	210	Isabella, PA
41	Bennet, William	T	6	211	Willoughby
42	Piccinini, James	T	6	229	Cleveland
43	Stephenson, Jack	T	6-1	214	Marion
44	Dixon, Thornton	T	5-11	212	Toledo
45	Heffelfinger, Clifford	E	5-10	184	Martins Ferry
46	Thom, Leonard	T	6	196	Sandusky
47	Hecklinger, Harold	E	6	181	Toledo
48	Gustavson, Carl	T	6-2	230	Erie, PA
49	Tucci, Amel	G	5-9	190	Zanesville
50	Marino, Victor	G	5-7	178	Youngstown
51	Tobik, Andy	G	5-10	180	Cleveland
52	Scarberry, William	C	6-1	193	Columbus
53	Graf, Campbell	QB	6	196	Columbus
56	Herschberger, Peter	E	6	185	Columbus
57	Williams, Quentin	E	6-2	187	Cincinnati
58	Howe, Frank	HB	5-10	180	Columbus
61	Coyer, William	HB	5-8	172	Orrville
62	Karvasales, James	HB	5-8	160	Columbus
65	Welbaum, Thomas	FB	5-9	165	Akron
66	Wuellner, Richard	C	5-11	190	Columbus
67	Eastlake, Charles	E	5-11	180	Youngstown
68	Parry, Ward	HB	6	171	Augusta, KS
69	Lindsay, Jean	E	5-11	182	Columbus
71	Madro, Joseph	G	5-9	180	Wellington
72	Newlin, John	E	5-11	190	St. Clairsville

MICHIGAN

No.	Name	Pos.	Ht.	Wgt.	Home Town
7	Kohl, Harry E.	QB	5-6	150	Dayton, OH
10	Luther, William A.	HB	5-11	165	Toledo, OH
15	Wilson, John L.	C	5-9	188	Monroe
16	Wickter, Larry D.	FB	5-11	175	Toledo, OH
17	Funk, William	HB	5-10	160	Athens
18	Laine, John T.	G	5-11	185	Puritan
19	Nelson, David	HB	5-8	165	Detroit
24	Galles, James	G	5-11	180	Chicago, IL
26	Jordan, Forrest R.	G	6-2	202	Clare
27	Kuhn, Dennis	T	6-2	207	Ann Arbor
28	Zimmerman, Robert	FB	5-10	180	Chicago, IL
29	Savilla, Roland	T	6-2	206	Gallagher, WV
31	Bosza, Joseph J.	E	6	170	Pittsburgh, PA
33	Kennedy, Theodore, Jr.	E	6-2	190	Saginaw
34	Cunningham, Leo P.	G	6	184	Revere, MA
35	Weber, Marwood A.	HB	5-10	164	Saginaw
36	Fraumann, Harlin E.	E	6-3	190	Pontiac
38	Butler, Jack W.	G	6	185	Port Huron
39	Kitti, Walter I.	HB	5-10	170	Calumet
40	Czak, Edward W.	E	5-11	180	Elyria, OH
41	Vollmer, William E.	T	6-1	200	Manistee
42	Salvaterra, Arnold	HB	5-11	173	Bellaire, OH
43	Smith, William A.	T	6-2	217	Riverside, CA
45	Grissen, James	FB	5-11	180	Holland
48	Melzow, William	G	5-11	185	Flint
49	Frutig, Edward C.	E	6-1	186	River Rouge
53	Kodros, Archie (Capt.)	C	5-8	202	Alton, IL
54	Nielsen, Paul	E	6	185	Ann Arbor
55	Trosko, Fred	HB	5-9	154	Flint
56	Olds, Frederick C.	G	6	192	East Lansing
57	Ford, Thomas G.	C	6-2	193	E. Grand Rapids
58	Kelto, Reuben	T	6-1	195	Bessemer
59	Sukup, Milo	G	5-8	182	Muskegon Hgts.
60	Call, Norman	HB	6-1	170	Norwalk, OH
61	Purcell, George A.	E	6-3	200	Marshall
62	Ostroot, George	T	6-4	215	Viborg, SD
63	Fritz, Ralph	G	5-9	198	New Kensington, PA
64	Tinker, Horace	C	5-10	173	Battle Creek
65	Morrow, Ned	G	5-10	185	Elkhart, IN
66	Ingalls, Robert D.	C	6-3	200	Marblehead, MA
67	Nicholson, John E., Jr.	E	6-4	190	Elkhart, IN
68	Wistert, Albert A.	T	6-2	205	Chicago, IL
69	Evashevski, Forest	QB	6-1	198	Detroit
70	Paddy, Arthur	G	5-7	160	Benton Harbor
71	Roberts, Harris W.	QB	6	185	Shaker Hgts., OH
73	Flora, Robert L.	T	6-1	212	Muskegon
74	Thomas, Robert	G	5-11	176	Muskegon
76	Gannatal, Paul	HB	6	198	Detroit
77	Meyer, Jack	QB	5-9	195	Elyria, OH
78	Rogers, Joseph C.	E	6-3	193	Royal Oak
80	Zielinski, Ernest	T	6-1	195	Bay City
83	Kromer, Paul	HB	5-10	160	Lorain, OH
85	Renda, Hercules	HB	5-4	163	Jochin, WV
86	Westfall, Robert B.	FB	5-7	178	Ann Arbor
88	Strong, David A.	HB	5-8	185	Helena, MT
96	Christy, Edward	FB	5-10	185	Gary, IN
98	Harmon, Tom	HB	6	194	Gary, IN

1939

Michigan	26	Mich. State	13
Michigan	27	Iowa	7
Michigan	85	Chicago	0
Michigan	27	Yale	7
Michigan	7	Illinois	16
Michigan	7	Minnesota	20
Michigan	19	Pennsylvania	17
Michigan	21	Ohio State	14

Season Summary

Games Won, 6; Lost, 2

THOMAS HARMON
All-American Halfback

Tom Harmon, in his last game for Michigan, demonstrates the best defense against passing; the interception.

FRUSTRATION

ELATION

November 23, 1940

Columbus, Ohio

Michigan Smears Ohio State, 40-0

Rout Is Worst Since 1913; Harmon Sets Record

Victim of one of the greatest halfbacks of all time, Tom Harmon, and a great Michigan team, the Buckeyes were demolished in a smashing, terrific loss, 40-0. Before a vast crowd of 73,648 packed in fog and rain in Ohio Stadium, the Buckeyes were cut to pieces and scattered like a bunch of leaves by a gust of wind.

The great Harmon, in his collegiate final, was magnificent. He ran, he passed, he kicked. He scored three touchdowns, bringing his all-time touchdown total to 33, and surpassed by two the Big Ten record set by the great Red Grange 15 years earlier. In his finale he kicked four extra points, his total points for the game was 22. In his collegiate career, Harmon scored 237 points, carried the ball 398 times averaging four and one half yards a carry. He gained a total of 2,134 by rushing and including passing, amassed 3,533 yards.

Michigan had a 13-0 lead at the end of the first quarter on a 7-yard dash through guard by Harmon, a dazzling 80-yard touchdown run by Kromer, and an extra point boot by Harmon. In the second period Harmon threw a 17-yard scoring pass to Forest Evashevski, and then kicked another extra point to make it 20-0 at the half.

The debacle continued through the third period as Harmon heaved another TD pass to end Ed Frutig 15 yards into the end zone. Harmon ran 18 yards around end for his second touchdown and his team's fifth. It was 33 to 0 going into the final quarter.

With the Ohio line-up plentifully filled with substitutes, the Buckeyes looked better in the last quarter, but finally, with the end nearing, Michigan got started on a final 40-yard march over the line. This was when Harmon brought his exhibition to the supreme climax with his touchdown in the last minute. Thus, of the six touchdowns, Harmon scored three personally and passed for two others.

Though he did not figure in the scoring, there was another luminary in the Michigan attack — fullback Bob Westfall who continually plowed through the Ohio line for huge gains.

Except for the kicking of Don Scott, Ohio had very little of anything, offense or defense. It was not the same Buckeye team that made such a great losing fight against Minnesota, 13 to 7, earlier in the season. At times there were flashes of fire, but for the most part, Ohio looked like a team just out enjoying the afternoon.

1940

1940			
Michigan	41	California	0
Michigan	21	Mich. State	14
Michigan	26	Harvard	0
Michigan	28	Illinois	0
Michigan	14	Pennsylvania	0
Michigan	6	Minnesota	7
Michigan	20	Northwestern	13
Michigan	40	Ohio State	0

Season Summary

Games Won, 7; Lost, 1

THOMAS HARMON
All-American Halfback

EDWARD FRUTIG
All-American End

MICHIGAN

No.	Name	Pos.	Ht.	Wgt.	Years on Squad	Home Town
45	Anderson, Harry	C	5-11	210	1	Chicago, IL
31	Bosza, Joseph	E	6	170	2	Pittsburgh, PA
48	Butler, Jack	T	6	193	2	Port Huron
55	Call, Norman	B	6-1	170	2	Norwalk, OH
89	Ceithaml, George	B	6	190	1	Chicago, IL
67	Chady, Otto	E	6-1	195	1	Highland Park
36	Cunningham, Leo	G	6	188	2	Revere, MA
84	*Czak, Edward	E	5-11	180	3	Elyria, OH
41	Dawley, Fred	B	5-8	175	1	Detroit
10	Day, Frank	B	5-8	165	1	Detroit
19	Denise, Theodore	G	5-11	187	1	Lansing
69	*Evashevski, Forest	B	6-1	198	3	Detroit
73	*Flora, Robert	T	6-2	215	3	Muskegon
68	Fraumann, Harlin	E	6-3	190	2	Pontiac
63	*Fritz, Ralph	G	5-9	202	3	New Kensington, PA
87	*Frutig, Edward	E	6-1	180	3	River Rouge
76	Gannatal, Paul	B	6	185	3	Detroit
54	Grissen, James	B	5-11	185	2	Holland
49	Hall, Clarence	E	6	192	1	Raynham, MA
98	*Harmon, Tom	B	6	195	3	Gary, IN
82	Hildebrandt, G.	G	5-11	185	1	Hamburg, NY
26	Hook, Robert	T	6-3	205	3	E. Gr. Rapids
66	*Ingalls, Robert	C	6-3	200	2	Marblehead, MA
34	Ireland, Glenn	G	5-10	175	1	Benton Harbor
39	Karwales, John	E	6-1	180	1	Chicago, IL
65	Keating, Wallace	C	6-2	192	1	Detroit
58	*Kelto, Reuben	T	6-1	195	3	Bessemer
33	Kennedy, Ted	C	6-2	185	2	Saginaw
88	Kohl, Harry	B	5-6	150	3	Dayton, OH
96	Kolesar, Robert	G	5-10	198	1	Cleveland, OH
80	Krejsa, Robert	B	5-10	190	1	Shaker Hgts., OH
83	*Kromer, Paul	B	5-10	165	3	Lorain, OH
27	Laine, John	G	5-11	185	2	Puritan
42	Lockard, Harold	B	5-9	180	1	Canton, OH
64	Madar, Elmer	B	5-11	180	1	Detroit
7	Manalakas, George	B	5-9	160	3	Detroit
71	Megregian, Michael	B	5-8	180	2	Detroit
22	*Melzow, William	G	5-11	185	2	Flint
23	Nelson, David	B	5-8	165	2	Detroit
78	*Rogers, Joseph	E	6-8	200	3	Plymouth
70	Seltzer, Holbrooke	G	5-9	165	3	Chicago, IL
56	Sengel, Rudolph	T	6-2	217	1	Louisville, KY
57	Sharpe, Philip	E	6-2	185	1	Lakewood, OH
53	Shwayder, Irving	C	5-9	185	1	Denver, CO
38	Smeja, Rudy	E	6-1	200	1	Chicago, IL
43	Smith, Robert	T	6-3	210	1	Riverside, CA
59	*Sukup, Milo	G	5-8	190	3	Muskegon Hts.
74	Thomas, Robert	G	5-11	180	2	Muskegon
86	*Westfall, Robert	B	5-8	175	2	Ann Arbor
60	Wise, Clifford	B	5-11	170	1	Spring Lake
11	Wistert, Albert	T	6-2	212	2	Chicago, IL
40	Woytek, Louis	C	5-9	170	1	Johnson City, NY
28	*Zimmerman, R.	B	5-10	180	2	Chicago, IL

* Denotes letterman

OHIO

No.	Name	Pos.	Wt.	Hgt.	Home Town
27	Adams, William	E	191	6-1	Steubenville
19	Alexinas, Edward	B	171	6-1	Dayton
22	*Anderson, Charles	E	189	5-11	Massillon
60	Arnold, James	G	190	5-8	Akron
20	Bell, William	C	190	5-11	Steubenville
30	Bruckner, Edwin	G	191	5-11	Sandusky
21	Carlin, Earl	G	180	5-10	Bryan
29	*Clair, Frank	E	198	6	Hamilton
68	Correll, John	B	172	5-11	Canton
1	*Daniell, James	T	209	6-1	Mt. Lebanon, PA
44	*Dixon, Thornton	T	212	5-11	Toledo
2	*Fisher, Richard	B	181	5-10	Columbiana
38	Fox, Sam	E	188	6	Washington, D. C.
11	*Graf, Jack	B	190	6	Columbus
34	*Grundies, Jerry	T	210	6	Cleveland
48	Gustavson, Carl	T	215	6	Erie, PA
12	*Hallabrin, John	B	187	5-10	Mansfield
47	Hecklinger, Harold	E	182	6	Toledo
45	Heffelfinger, Clifford	G	184	5-10	Martins Ferry
56	Hershberger, Peter	E	185	6	Columbus
53	Horvath, Leslie	B	169	5-10	Parma
23	*Howard, Fritz	G	193	5-11	Toledo
16	*Kinkade, Thomas	B	184	6-1	Toronto
8	*Langhurst, J. (Capt.)	B	193	5-11	Willard
54	Linkins, Arthur	C	180	5-11	Middletown
6	Lynn, George	B	185	5-11	Niles
33	*Maag, Charles	T	208	6-3	Sandusky
14	Massie, Edmund	E	192	5-11	Wellston
25	McCafferty, Don	E	198	6-2	Cleveland
63	Mires, David	T	204	5-11	Liberty Center
72	Newlin, Jack	E	192	5-11	St. Clairsville
17	Nichols, Harold	B	177	5-11	Marietta
26	*Nosker, William	G	191	5-11	Columbus
18	Novak, Joseph	B	178	5-9	Chardon
42	*Piccinini, James	T	215	6	Cleveland
59	Pitton, Robert	T	194	6	Columbus
66	Placas, John	T	197	5-11	Cleveland
13	Richey, Frank	B	151	5-10	Columbus
28	Roman, Nicholas	E	198	6	Canton
40	*Rosen, Andy	G	199	6	Isabella, PA
32	Santschi, John	E	178	6	Akron
35	Sarkkinen, Eino	B	173	6	Fairport Harbor
31	Sayers, Peter	G	193	5-11	Columbus
50	Schimke, Louis	G	190	5-9	Massillon
9	*Scott, Donald	B	208	6-1	Canton
5	*Sexton, James	B	184	5-10	Middletown
67	Siferd, Charles	G	187	5-11	Wapakoneta
15	*Simione, John	B	170	5-9	Youngstown
43	Stephenson, Jack	T	214	6-1	Marion
4	*Strausbaugh, James	B	180	5-10	Chillicothe
3	Sweeney, Paul	B	179	5-9	Cleveland
46	*Thom, Leonard	G	196	6	Sandusky
51	Tobik, Andy	G	179	5-10	Cleveland
36	Vickroy, William	C	182	5-11	Toledo
37	*White, Claude	C	196	6	Portsmouth
57	Williams, Quent	E	190	6-2	Cincinnati
7	Wynn, Herbert	B	182	5-11	Canton
24	Zavistoske, George	B	161	5-10	Racine, WI

* Denotes lettermen.

1940

Ohio	30	Pittsburgh	7
Ohio	17	Purdue	14
Ohio	3	Northwestern	6
Ohio	7	Minnesota	13
Ohio	7	Cornell	21
Ohio	21	Indiana	6
Ohio	14	Illinois	6
Ohio	0	Michigan	40

Season Summary

Games Won, 4; Lost, 4

Howard is called in for Ohio State.

Coach Crisler and Westfall

November 22, 1941

Ann Arbor, Michigan

Ohio State - Michigan In Stalemate, 20-20

Wolverines Trail Twice, But Break Even In Last Period

The Buckeyes of Ohio State more than held their own against the mighty Wolverines of Michigan. Coach Paul Brown of OSU won his spurs as the rejuvenated Buckeyes almost defeated the heavily favored rival from Michigan.

In the first quarter of play the Bucks, starting from the 50-yard line, marched to their first touchdown. On a third play situation a briskly executed shovel pass from Graf to Fisher moved the ball to the Michigan 33. After several line plunges, Graf sailed a forward pass to Fox who made the catch on the 15-yard line for a first down. Several more rushes by Graf and one by Fisher put the ball on the 4-yard line and another first down. Then after one plunge was stopped, the Buckeye fullback, Graf, bulled through a good opening and was over for the touchdown. Hallabrin kicked the extra point for a 7-0 Ohio lead.

In the closing minutes of the second quarter, Michigan got on track. Starting from Ohio's 42, the Wolverines began making yardage through a tiring Buckeye line. In the drive White had one gain of 17 yards and Westfall gained 13 to the three yard line and a first down. Two more Westfall plunges put the ball on the one. Then Kuzuma took the ball, raged into a pile around center, slid off to his left and was over with only 30 seconds left in the half. Melzow converted the PAT for a 7-7 half time score.

The third period saw Michigan score first on a beautiful play from Ohio's 17-yard line. Ceithami took the ball from center, lateraled to Kuzma, and the sophomore star raced to the right. Then, on the lope, he threw a pass toward the end zone. End Fraumann, waiting on the goal line, was in the clear and made the catch for the TD. Melzow kicked the point and the score was 14 to 7.

Ohio fought back. Mixing running and passing to perfection, the Buckeyes drove steadily down the field with Graf, Kinkade, and Fisher making good gains. With first down and only two feet from Michigan pay dirt, Kinkade hurtled into left guard for the score. Hallabrin's perfect placement tied the score at 14-14.

Michigan stormed back but the Buckeyes stopped the Maize and Blue on the Ohio 4-yard line. Then Ohio broke forth on a great surging attack that nearly won the game. After moving the ball out to the Ohio 48 on grinding ground plays, OSU's Graf hurled the ball to Fisher in the flat. He grabbed the ball on the Michigan 45, whirled and sized up the situation and was gone. Hallabrin's missed point left Ohio leading 20-14 with 12 minutes left in the game.

Back down the field came the Michigan juggernaut. Line smashes by Westfall, Kuzma, and White, plus a 19 yard pass from Kuzma to Ceithami moved the ball to Ohio's five yard line. Westfall then cut back through Ohio's right side and over the goal. Tie or victory hinged on Melzow's placement and he missed it.

Although there were still six minutes and forty seconds left in the game, neither team culd sustain any type of scoring drive. The game closed with all the red-shirted Ohioans and blue-clad Michigan players milling around on the field. Evidently it was just a battle for the ball, but it looked like a free-for-all Donnybrook. Even from the height of the press box, you could see a few haymakers kissing Buckeye and Wolverine chins. There is no kiss-and-make-up in this series.

STATISTICS

	OSU	UM
First Downs	15	19
Yards Rushing	179	271
Yards Passing	124	104
Passes	6-11	7-11
Punting Average	37	37

Michigan	0	7	7	6	20
Ohio State	7	0	7	6	20

1941

1941			
Ohio	12	Missouri	7
Ohio	33	USC	0
Ohio	16	Purdue	14
Ohio	7	Northwestern	14
Ohio	21	Pittsburgh	14
Ohio	46	Wisconsin	34
Ohio	12	Illinois	7
Ohio	20	Michigan	20

Season Summary

Games won, 6; Lost, 1; Tied, 1

PAUL E. BROWN
Ohio State Head Coach
1941-43

OHIO

No.	Name	Pos.	Wt.	Hgt.	Home Town
22	Anderson, Charles	E	196	6-0	Massillon
80	Bruckner, Ed	G	188	5-11	Sandusky
24	Burgett, Richard	FB	178	5-11	Columbus
26	Coleman, Kenneth	E	180	6-0	Brooklyn, NY
28	Cheroke, George	G	183	5-9	Shadyside
60	Csuri, Charles	T	197	6-1	Cleveland
99	Daniell, James	T	219	6-2	Mt. Lebanon, PA
84	Dean, Harold	G	185	6-0	Wooster
86	Dixon, Thornton	T	202	5-11	Toledo
33	Fisher, Dick	HB	188	6-0	Columbiana
34	Fox, Sam	E	197	6-1	Washington, D.C.
36	Frye, Robert	FB	180	6-0	Crestline
44	Graf, Jack	FB	190	6-0	Columbus
55	Hallabrin, John	QB	190	5-10	Mansfield
42	Hecklinger, Robert	FB	185	5-11	Toledo
70	Hershberger, Peter	E	187	6-1	Columbus
48	Horvath, Leslie	HB	157	5-10	Cleveland
72	Howard, Fritz	G	195	6-0	Toledo
96	Houston, Lindell	G	192	6-0	Massillon
66	Kinkade, Thomas	HB	190	6-2	Toronto
11	Lynn, George	QB	191	6-0	Niles
98	McCafferty, Don	T	200	6-3	Cleveland
50	Martin, Earl	C	200	6-3	Massillon
52	McCormick, Robert	T	202	6-0	Columbus
58	Novak, Joe	HB	175	5-9	Chardon
62	Palmer, Richard	QB	190	5-10	Cleveland
68	Placas, John	QB	195	5-10	Cleveland
74	Roe, John	C	180	5-11	Steubenville
10	Rosen, John	C	185	5-11	Isabella, PA
88	Sarringhaus, Paul	HB	190	6-0	Hamilton
12	Schneider, Wilbur	G	175	5-8	Gahanna
82	Schoenbaum, Leon	E	187	6-0	Huntington, WV
14	Sedor, William	E	188	6-2	Shadyside
40	Shaw, Robert	E	198	6-3	Fremont
46	Steinberg, Don	E	190	6-0	Toledo
90	Stephenson, Jack	T	212	6-1	Marion
16	Sweeney, Paul	HB	178	5-9	Cleveland
32	Staker, Loren	HB	180	5-10	Columbus
18	Vickroy, William	C	190	6-0	Toledo
20	Zavistoske, George	HB	172	5-10	Racine, WI
30	Zimmerman, Dick	T	210	6-1	Columbus

MICHIGAN

No.	Name	Pos.	Wt.	Hgt.	Class	Home Town
10	Lockard, Harold C.	HB	186	5-9	'43	Canton, OH
11	Wistert, Albert A.	T	206	6-2	'43	Chicago, IL
14	Morrison, Robert L.	HB	160	5-10	'44	Minocqua, WI
15	Brown, James J.	HB	156	5-9	'44	St. Ignace
16	White, Paul G.	HB	184	6-1	'44	River Rouge
18	Sowers, Ray B.	HB	193	6-0	'44	Bay City
19	Kennedy, Chas. F.	HB	180	6-1	'44	Van Wert, OH
22	Harrigan, John F.	QB	165	5-8	'44	Detroit
23	Nelson, David M.	HB	156	5-7	'42	Detroit
24	Greene, John J.	QB	191	6-0	'44	Pittsburgh, PA
26	Haslam, Charles J.	QB	190	6-1	'44	Duluth, MN
27	Shemky, Robert W.	E	177	6-0	'44	Crystal Falls
28	Madar, Elmer F.	QB	170	5-10	'43	Detroit
29	Dawley, Fred M.	QB	178	5-8	'44	Detroit
33	Kennedy, Ted	C	190	6-2	'42	Saginaw
34	Miller, Austin S.	FB	169	5-7	'44	Mt. Pleasant
36	Stenberg, Robert P.	FB	168	5-7	'44	Chicago, IL
38	MacConnachie, Wm.	E	181	6-1	'44	Upper Mt. Clair, NJ
39	Boor, Donald P.	FB	185	5-11	'44	Dearborn
42	Thomas, Alfred S.	HB	162	5-10	'42	Detroit
45	Kuzma, Thomas G.	HB	196	6-1	'44	Gary, IN
46	Robinson, Don W.	HB	167	5-11	'44	Detroit
48	Call, Norman D.	HB	170	6-1	'42	Norwalk, OH
54	Pritula, William	C	198	6-0	'44	Detroit
55	McFaddin, Robert L.	C	173	6-0	'44	Detroit
60	Amstutz, Ralph H.	G	168	5-11	'44	Oak Park, IL
61	Trogan, Angelo E.	G	202	5-8	'44	Saginaw
62	Franks, Julius S.	G	187	6-0	'44	Hamtramck
64	Laine, John T.	G	196	6-0	'43	Puritan
65	Melzow, William	G	190	5-11	'42	Flint
66	Ingalls, Robert D.	C	190	6-3	'42	Marblehead, MA
67	Pregulman, Mervin	G	207	6-3	'44	Lansing
68	Kolesar, Robert C.	G	193	5-10	'43	Cleveland, OH
71	Caswell, Harry H.	T	190	6-2	'44	Ann Arbor
72	Kuyper, William E.	T	201	6-0	'44	Newtonville, MA
73	Denise, Theodore E.	T	188	5-11	'43	Lansing
74	MacDougall, Wm. J.	T	190	6-3	'43	Highland Park
75	Hildebrandt, Geo. H.	T	181	5-11	'43	Hamburg, NY
76	Flora, Robert L.	T	216	6-2	'42	Muskegon
77	Secontine, Vincent C.	T	193	6-0	'44	Detroit
78	Kelto, Reuben W.	T	198	6-1	'42	Bessemer
79	Cunningham, Leo P.	T	187	6-0	'42	Revere, MA
80	Freihofer, Walter B.	E	180	5-11	'44	Indianapolis, IN
81	Chady, Otto E.	E	191	6-1	'42	Highland Park
82	Karwales, John J.	E	190	6-1	'44	Chicago, IL
83	Smeja, Rudy M.	E	185	6-2	'43	Chicago, IL
84	Fraumann, Harlin E.	E	190	6-3	'42	Pontiac
85	Sharpe, Philip E.	E	188	6-2	'43	Lakewood, OH
86	Westfall, Robert B.	FB	186	5-8	'42	Ann Arbor
87	Rogers, Joseph C.	E	184	6-3	'42	Plymouth
88	Petroskey, Jack E.	E	167	5-11	'44	Dearborn
89	Ceithaml, George F.	QB	184	6-0	'43	Chicago, IL

1941

Michigan	19	Michigan State	7
Michigan	6	Iowa	0
Michigan	40	Pittsburgh	0
Michigan	14	Northwestern	7
Michigan	0	Minnesota	7
Michigan	20	Illinois	0
Michigan	28	Columbia	0
Michigan	20	Ohio State	20

Season Summary

Games won, 6; Lost, 1; Tied, 1

ROBERT WESTFALL
All-American Fullback

November 21, 1942

Columbus, Ohio

Ohio State Trips Michigan, 21 To 7

Air Attack Knocks Out Wolverines

Halfback Gene Derricotte holds for "Automatic" Jim Brieske, star place kicker.

The Michigan team that a week earlier had shattered Notre Dame, that had been heralded as the comfortable favorite in this decisive battle for the conference title, was practically overwhelmed. Mighty Michigan hardly had a chance. As the game ended, the hysterically delighted players hoisted Coach Paul Brown on their shoulders while a drenched mob of 71,896 stood and cheered the definite arrival of the new football era in Columbus.

The first period saw Sarringhaus of OSU and Kuzma of Michigan exchange punts in a scoreless battle. The Michigan mishap that brought Ohio's first touchdown came in the first minute of the second period. The Wolverines had the ball on their 31. Kuzma dropped back to kick and as the pass came from center, the Buckeyes swarmed in on him. The kick was blocked by Csuri and the ball wobbled outside on the Michigan 35. In three plays Ohio was over the line. On the scoring play Horvath did the passing. Sarringhaus, who had caught only one aerial all year, was wide open in the end zone. Fekete's placement was good and Ohio State led 7 to 0.

A strong surge by Michigan just before the half on the accurate arm of Bob Chappuis who completed five of six passes in the drive, ended on the Ohio two as the first half gun sounded. After the kickoff in the third quarter, Michigan could not get started and was forced to punt.

With the ball on their own 40-yard line, OSU sent Sarringhaus on a wide run. He cut loose with another of his great passes. Bob Shaw got behind his interferer and took the ball almost on the side line. He whirled and was gone down the white stripe. Fekete's PAT made it 14 to 0.

Michigan then made an impressive comeback. Mixing an accurate passing attack with an efficient running game moved the ball from the Michigan 36 to the Ohio one yard line. From there Bob Wiese broke through for the TD. Jim Brieske booted the extra point and the score at the end of three quarters stood at 14-7.

After an exchange of punts Michigan made a fatal error. White tried a pass which was intercepted by Shaw who carried it back to the Michigan 33. Although the drive ended with a missed field goal, it took valuable time. Soon after, White fumbled and Jabbusch recovered on the Michigan 32. On the next play Horvath went down the left, got himself wide open and Sarringhaus whipped the ball to him. Horvath breezed over and Fekete was again perfect and it was 21-7.

Two more drives by Michigan were spoiled, one by a fumble, the other by an interception. It was Ohio State's first victory over Michigan since 1937 and its 11th in all time. For the first time the Buckeyes gave the coaching regime of Fritz Crisler a pasting – and it was a pasting.

STATISTICS

	OSU	UM
First Downs	9	17
Rushes-Yards	48-106	42-120
Passing Yards	142	148
Return Yards	21	15
Passes	6-8-0	10-22-2
Punts-Average	10-31	8-30
Fumbles-Lost	0-0	3-3
Yards Penalized	5	25

OSU	0	7	7	7	21
UM	0	0	7	0	7

1942			
Michigan	9	Great Lakes	0
Michigan	20	Michigan State	0
Michigan	14	Iowa PreFlight	26
Michigan	34	Northwestern	16
Michigan	14	Minnesota	16
Michigan	28	Illinois	14
Michigan	35	Harvard	7
Michigan	32	Notre Dame	20
Michigan	7	Ohio State	21
Michigan	28	Iowa	14

Season Summary

Games won, 7; Lost, 3; Tied, 0

ALBERT WISTERT
All-American Tackle

JULIUS FRANKS
All-American Guard

MICHIGAN

No.	Name	Pos.	Wt.	Hgt.	Class	Home Town
10	Avery, Charles B.	HB	170	6	So.	Antigo, WI
11	Wistert, Albert A.	T	205	6-2	Sr.	Chicago, IL
14	Keenan, William C.	HB	175	5-11	So.	Cleveland, OH
16	White, Paul G.	HB	184	6-1	Jr.	River Rouge
17	Petoskey, Jack E.	E	167	5-11	Jr.	Dearborn
18	Wardley, Frank L.	HB	180	6-1	So.	Joliet, IL
26	Vernier, Robert W.	QB	184	5-11	So.	Toledo, OH
28	Kiesel, George C.F.	QB	165	5-10	So.	Detroit
29	Pergament, Milton	QB	185	6	So.	Chicago, IL
33	Lund, Donald A.	FB	193	6	So.	Detroit
36	Stenberg, Robert P.	FB	168	5-7	Jr.	Chicago, IL
38	Wiese, Robert L.	FB	193	6-2	So.	Jamestown, ND
39	Boor, Donald P.	FB	185	5-11	Jr.	Dearborn
40	Myll, Clifton O.	E	175	6	So.	St. Clair Shores
42	Yaap, Warren E.	HB	165	5-11	So.	Chicago, IL
45	Kuzma, Tom G.	HB	196	6-1	Jr.	Gary, IN
46	Robinson, Don W.	HB	168	5-11	Jr.	Detroit
48	Wise, Clifford C.	HB	170	5-11	Jr.	Jackson
49	Chappuis, Robert R.	HB	174	6	So.	Toledo, OH
54	Pritula, William	T	195	6	Jr.	Detroit
55	Marcellus, Phillip	T	205	6-2	Jr.	Rockford, IL
56	Brieske, James F.	C	194	6-2	So.	Harbor Beach, MN
57	Kuyper, William E.	T	201	6	Jr.	Boston, MA
58	Mooney, Philip K.	C	182	6	So.	Marion, IN
60	Amstutz, Ralph H.	G	167	5-10	Jr.	Oak Park, IL
61	Trogan, Angelo E.	G	202	5-8	Jr.	Saginaw
62	Freihofer, Walter B.	G	185	6	Jr.	Indianapolis, IN
63	Franks, Julius	G	187	6	Jr.	Hamtramck
64	Hartrick, James G.	G	175	5-8	So.	Royal Oak
65	Gage, Robert J.	T	185	6	So.	Reading
66	Gans, William	G	165	5-9	Sr.	Poland Mines, PA
67	Pregulman, Mervin	C	207	6-3	Jr.	Lansing
68	Kolesar, Robert C.	G	193	5-10	Sr.	Cleveland, OH
69	Rohrbach, William R.	G	185	5-8	Jr.	E. Aurora, NY
70	Bryan, Fred J.	E	200	6-2	Jr.	Melvindale
72	Karwales, John J.	T	190	6	Jr.	Chicago, IL
73	Oren, Robert A.	E	197	6-4	So.	Evart
74	Gritis, Peter	T	200	5-10	So.	Chicago, IL
75	Greene, John J.	T	193	6	Jr.	Pittsburgh, PA
76	Baldwin, William W.	T	208	6-4	So.	Lansing
77	Secontine, Vincent C.	T	191	6	Jr.	Detroit
78	Derleth, Robert J.	T	203	6-1	Jr.	Marquette
79	Cady, Donald J.	T	190	6-2	So.	Saginaw
80	Grey, William	E	172	6-1	So.	Arlington, VA
81	Van Summern, J. S.	E	180	5-10	Jr.	Kenmore, NY
82	Kennedy, Charles F.	HB	180	6-1	Jr.	Van Wert, OH
83	Smeja, Rudy M.	E	187	6-2	Sr.	Chicago, IL
84	Shemky, Robert W.	E	178	6	Jr.	CrystalFalls
85	Sharpe, Philip E.	E	185	6-2	Sr.	Lakewood, OH
87	Chady, Otto E.	E	191	6-1	Sr.	Highland Park
88	Madar, Elmer F.	E	170	5-10	Sr.	Detroit
89	Ceithaml, George F.	QB	184	6	Sr.	Chicago, IL

OHIO

No.	Name	Pos.	Wt.	Hgt.	Class
50	Appleby, Gordon	C	181	5-11	So.
92	Amling, Martin	G	180	5-9	So.
82	Antennucci, Thomas	E	178	5-11	So.
78	Cleary, Thomas	HB	188	5-11	So.
26	Coleman, Kenneth	C	185	6-1	Jr.
60	Csuri, Charles	T	195	6	Jr.
84	Dean, Hal	G	190	6	Jr.
68	Drake, Phillip	QB	185	6	So.
94	Dugger, Jack	T	205	6-4	So.
20	Durtschi, William	HB	172	5-8	Jr.
48	Eichwald, Kenneth	E	181	6-4	So.
44	Fekete, Gene	FB	192	6-1	So.
36	Frye, Robert	HB	161	5-10	Jr.
28	Hackett, William	G	185	5-9	So.
22	Horvath, Leslie	HB	160	5-11	Sr.
96	Houston, Lindel	G	198	5-11	Jr.
72	Jabbusch, Robert	G	187	5-10	So.
66	James, Thomas	HB	155	5-9	So.
76	Lipaj, Cyril	FB	180	5-10	So.
33	Lavelli, Dante	E	185	6-1	So.
11	Lynn, George (C)	QB	195	6	Jr.
98	McCafferty, Don	T	202	6-4	Sr.
52	McCormick, Bob	T	198	5-10	Jr.
24	MacDonald, W.	G	182	5-10	So.
10	Matus, Paul	E	178	5-11	So.
86	Naples, Carmen	G	185	5-11	Jr.
62	Palmer, Richard	FB	192	5-10	Jr.
30	Priday, Paul	QB	180	5-10	So.
90	Rees, James	T	199	6	So.
74	Roe, Jack	C	180	5-11	Jr.
88	Sarringhaus, Paul	HB	190	5-10	Jr.
12	Schneider, Wib	G	175	5-8	Jr.
14	Sedor, William	E	188	6-2	Jr.
54	Selby, Paul	QB	198	5-10	So.
40	Shaw, Robert	E	199	6-3	Jr.
42	Slusser, George	HB	170	5-11	So.
80	Souders, Cecil	E	189	6	So.
32	Staker, Loren	HB	160	5-11	Sr.
46	Steinberg, Don	E	190	6	Jr.
55	Vickroy, William	C	190	6	Sr.
99	Willis, William	T	202	6-2	So.
70	White, John	E	190	6-3	So.
64	Taylor, Tom	T	195	6-1	So.

1942

Ohio	59	Fort Knox	0
Ohio	32	Indiana	21
Ohio	28	USC	12
Ohio	26	Purdue	0
Ohio	20	Northwestern	6
Ohio	7	Wisconsin	17
Ohio	59	Pittsburgh	19
Ohio	44	Illinois	20
Ohio	21	Michigan	7
Ohio	41	Iowa Seahawks	12

Season Summary

Games won, 9; Lost, 1

ROBERT SHAW
All-American End

CHARLES CSURI
All-American Tackle

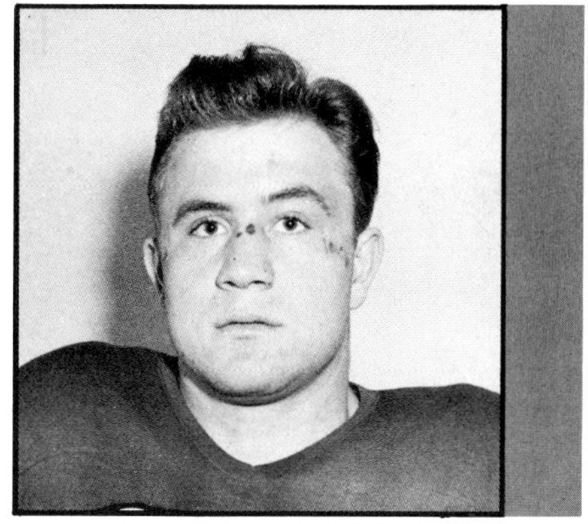

LINDELL HOUSTON
All-American Guard

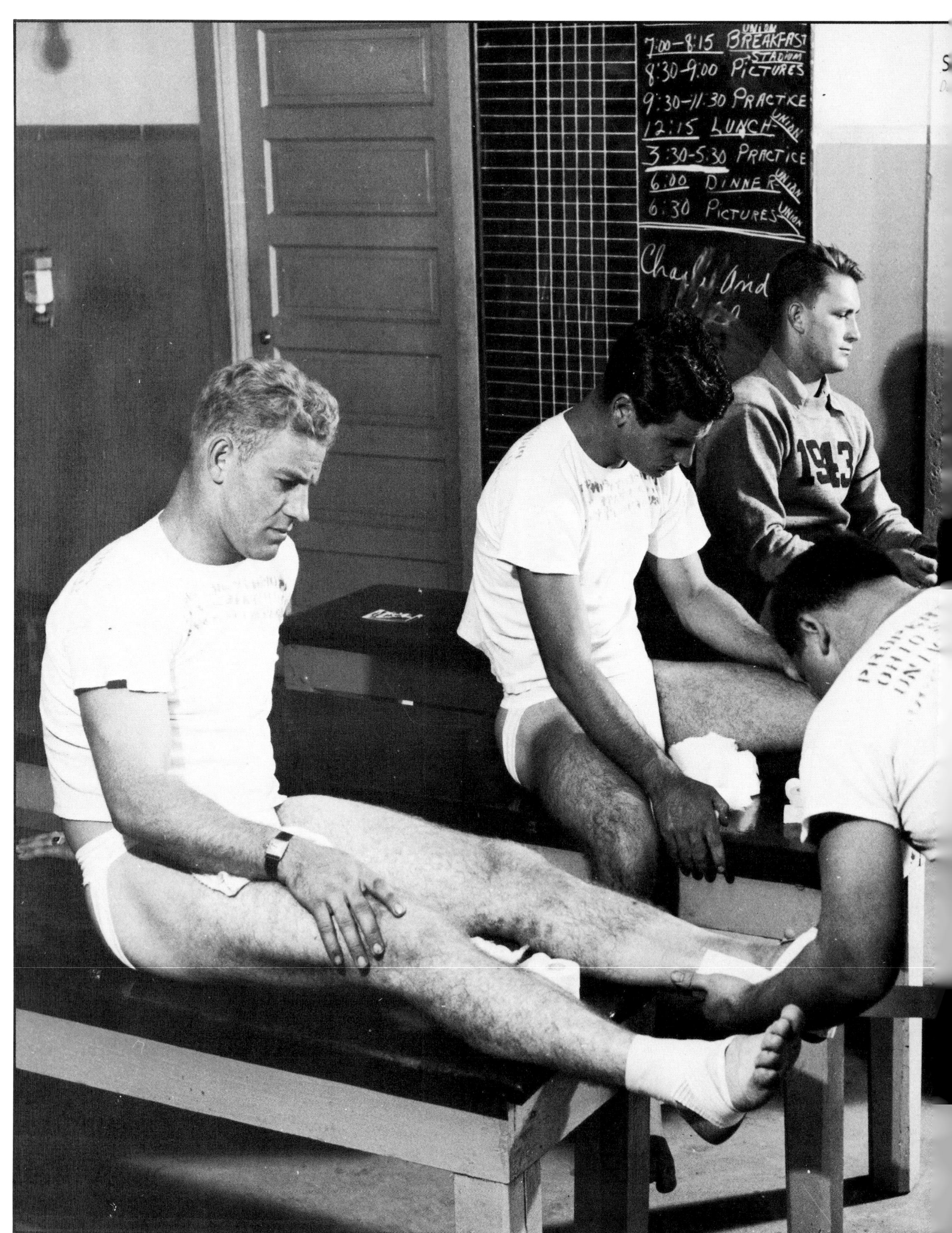

Ohio State Training Room before the Big Game.

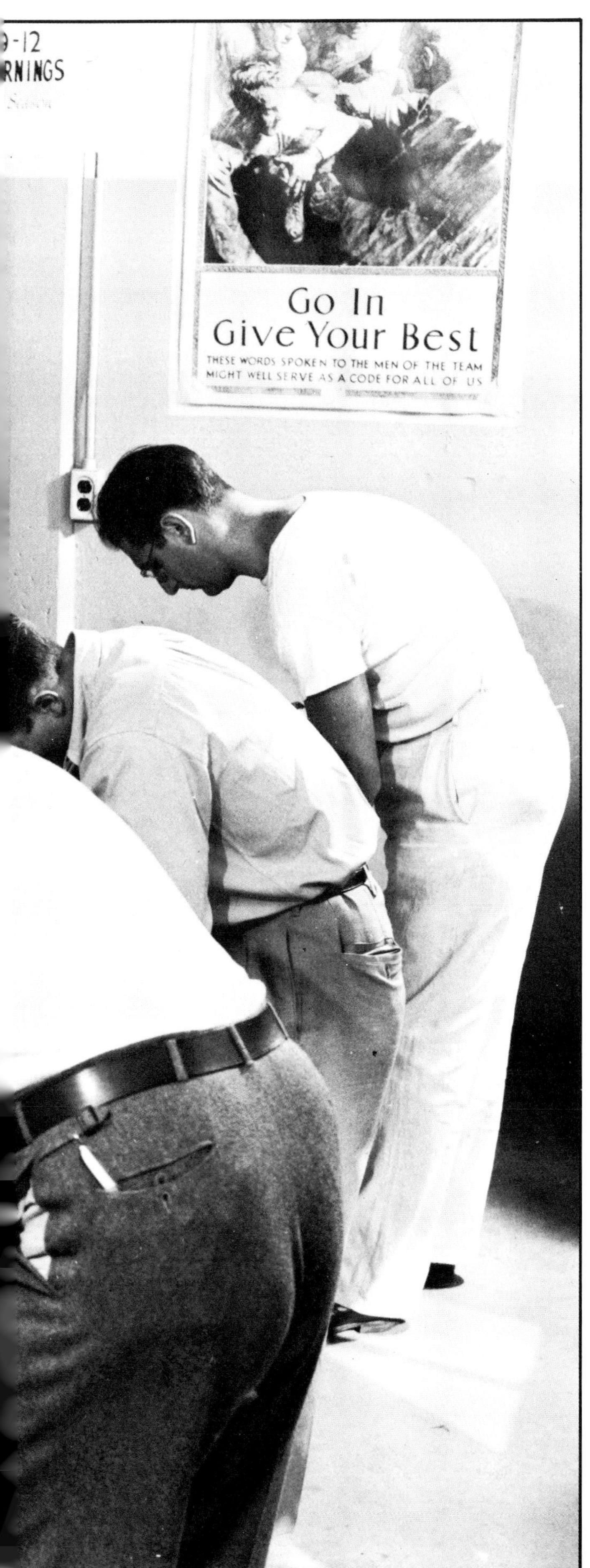

November 20, 1943

Ann Arbor, Michigan

Wolves' Five Touchdowns In Last Half Jar Ohio State, 45 To 7

Parks Races 36 Yards For Bucks' Only TD

Michigan had the men and Ohio State did not. That was the whole story as the high powered Wolverines ran away from the sadly outclassed Buckeyes, 45 to 7. It was the first perfect Big Ten season for Michigan since 1932 and its first cut of the championship since 1933. Michigan and Purdue, unbeaten and untied in conference play, shared the pennant.

Michigan scored twice in the first period, first on a forward march indirectly as the result of an Ohio fumble, with fullback Bob Wiese going over, and next on a 42-yard drive after an Ohio gamble on fourth down had failed to make the yardage. This time Wally Dreyer carried it over. In the weird second quarter, a rassle of fumbles in which Michigan always seemed to get the ball, kept the struggling Buckeyes in trouble. But the half time score was 13 to 0.

On the ninth play of the third quarter, Big Ernie Parks galloped 36 yards around right end for an Ohio touchdown. The anything but confident Ohio coherts began to have some hope. John Stungis' extra point made it 13-7.

That was the beginning of the end for the tired and bruised Bucks. In a crunching drive Michigan moved to the Ohio one where Wiese took it over and Wells converted the PAT making it 20-7. On the last play of the third quarter Nussbaumer took a lateral from Wink and sped 31 yards for the fourth Michigan TD. Hirsch, with a helpless arm from an injury, missed the conversion and the score remained 26-7.

Next, going 60 yards in six plays, Wink threw a 10-yard pass to Mroz for a touchdown. Ohio tried the Statue of Liberty play rather than kicking on fourth down and the Wolves took over on the Buckeye 23. Maves scored through tackle from the seven on the third play. The final TD was scored on a 20-yard dash by Don Lund.

Ohio, having had only one regular from the previous year, tackle Bill Willis, and forced to rely largely on a couple dozen freshmen, won three games in nine starts. No official attendance was announced, but it was estimated at 45,000.

STATISTICS

	UM	OSU
First Downs	23	2
Rushes - Yards	76-426	32-68
Passing Yards	105	27
Return Yards	134	8
Passing	7-11-1	3-11-3
Punts - Average	2-27	5-39
Fumbles - Lost	6-1	7-4
Penalties - Yards	5-65	0-0

1943

1943	
Ohio ... 13	Iowa Seahawks ... 28
Ohio ... 27	Missouri 6
Ohio ... 6	Great Lakes....... 13
Ohio ... 7	Purdue (Cleveland) 30
Ohio ... 0	Northwestern 13
Ohio ... 14	Indiana 20
Ohio ... 46	Pittsburgh 6
Ohio ... 29	Illinois 26
Ohio ... 7	Michigan 45

Season Summary
Won, 3; Lost 6

OHIO

No.	Name	Pos.	Wgt.	Home Town
11	Williams, Albert	QB	184	Canton
14	Pearson, Myron	T	195	Malvern
20	Hecker, Bob	RH	160	Olmsted Falls
21	Plank, Ernest	LE	189	Bexley
22	Parks, Ernest	RH	190	Canton
24	Marker, Jim	LT	188	Columbus
25	Yerges, Howard	QB	160	Grandview
26	McCarty, Bill	QB	158	Hilliards
28	Meinke, Dick	LT	187	Elyria
30	Harris, Jasper	LH	162	Canton
32	Davis, Paul	LH	171	Middletown
33	Sensanbaugher, Dean	LH	175	Uhrichsville
34	Lehman, Ernest	RT	190	Toledo
35	Redd, Jack	LG	170	Columbus
36	McQuade, Bob	LH	157	Columbus
38	Lonjak, Bill	LH	165	Cleveland
40	Brown, Matthew	FB	162	Canton
44	Oliver, Glen	FB	162	Columbus
45	Slough, Gene	LH	155	Findlay
50	Appleby, Gordon	C	175	Massillon
55	Dugger, Jack	LE	189	Canton
60	Hefflinger, Ronnie	RG	174	Napoleon
64	Hall, Bob	LG	182	Toledo
65	Parenti, Frank	RG	164	Dayton
66	Souders, Cecil	RE	188	Bucyrus
68	Dunivant, Bill	C	157	Cuyahoga Falls
70	Miller, William	LG	174	Wapakoneta
72	Stungis, John	QB	180	Powhatan Point
74	Swartzbaugh, Jack	RT	187	Toledo
75	Cunningham, Lee	RG	180	Revere, MA
76	Teifke, Howard	C	174	Fremont
80	Kay, Don	LT	186	Marion
82	Clark, Gene	RE	170	Columbus
84	Kessler, Bud	RE	181	Worthington
86	Maltinsky, Paul	C	180	Wheeling, WV
87	Komer, Stuart	T	190	Detroit, MI
92	Stackhouse, Ray	RT	199	Dayton
93	Stora, Joe	RH	152	Shadyside
94	Neff, George	RG	184	Bellaire
95	Fedderson, Jerry	LE	190	Sandusky
96	Hackett, Bill	RG	177	London
98	Thomas, Russell	RT	199	Charleston, WV
99	Willis, Bill	LT	199	Columbus

MICHIGAN

No.	Name	Pos.	Ht.	Wgt.	Home Town
10	Nussbaumer, R. J.	HB	5-11	160	Oak Park, IL
14	Dreyer, Walter O.	HB	5-9	158	Milwaukee, WI
15	Sturges, Ray E.	G	5-11	169	Detroit
22	Powers, Jerome E.	HB	6-3	180	Green Bay, WI
24	Wink, Jack S.	QB	5-10	185	Milwaukee, WI
26	Ponsetto, Joe L.	QB	6	175	Flint
28	Kiesel, George C.	QB	5-10	172	Detroit
29	Aliber, James J.	QB	5-11	185	Detroit
33	Lund, Donald A.	FB	6	180	Detroit
34	Maves, Earl C.	FB	5-10	180	Stanley, WI
38	Wiese, Robert L.	FB	6-2	190	Jamestown, ND
39	Frisco, Frank P.	FB	5-10	170	Detroit
40	Hirsch, Elroy L.	HB	6-1	182	Wausau, WI
42	Hilkene, Bruce L.	E	6-1	180	Indianapolis, IN
43	LeRoux, Arthur N.	T	6	190	Muskegon Hts.
46	Culligan, W. L.	HB	5-10	160	Detroit
48	Wikel, Howard	HB	5-10	170	Ann Arbor
49	Alberti, Larry R.	HB	6-1	162	Chicago, IL
51	Negus, Fred W.	C-T	6-2	196	Martins Ferry, OH
54	Welch, George	HB	5-10	175	Lansing
55	Kern, Frank J.	C	5-11	190	Detroit
58	Watts, Harold	C	5-10	176	Birmingham
61	Gallagher, John M.	G	5-9	176	Eau Claire, WI
62	Kraeger, George W.	G	6-1	190	Indianapolis, IN
64	Sigler, William	G	6	210	Toledo, OH
65	Fischer, Robert H.	G	5-10	176	Benton Harbor
66	Trump, Jack	G	5-10	202	Battle Creek
69	Rohrbach, Wm. R.	G	5-8	185	East Aurora, NY
70	Bryan, Fred J.	T	6-2	192	Melvindale
71	Mroz, Vincent P.	E	6-2	191	E. Chicago, IN
72	Bauman, Clement L.	T	6-3	200	Dayton, OH
73	Kennedy, Robert W.	T	6	198	Riverside, IL
75	Greene, John J.	T	6	193	Pittsburgh, PA
76	Wheeler, Lewis	T	6-4	215	Roosevelt, NY
77	Hanzlik, Robert L.	T	6-1	195	Chippewa Falls, WI
78	Derleth, Robert J.	T	6-1	203	Marquette
80	Renner, Arthur W.	E	6-2	172	Sturgis
81	Cook, Thomas C.	E	6	178	Detroit
82	Olshanski, Henry S.	E	6-1	180	Wausau, WI
83	Smeja, Rudy M.	E	6-2	187	Chicago, IL
84	Schwartz, Alan E.	E	6-1	173	Detroit
85	Crane, Fenwick J.	E	6-3	201	Pleasant Ridge
86	Wells, Rex C.	G	6-1	178	Twin Falls, ID
87	Johnson, Farnham J.	E	6	188	Appleton, WI
88	Rennebohm, R. B.	E	5-11	183	LaCrosse, WI
89	Myll, Clifton O.	E	6	180	St. Clair Shores

1943

Michigan	26	Camp Grant	0
Michigan	57	Western Mich.	6
Michigan	21	Northwestern	7
Michigan	12	Notre Dame	35
Michigan	49	Minnesota	6
Michigan	42	Illinois	6
Michigan	23	Indiana	6
Michigan	27	Wisconsin	0
Michigan	45	Ohio State	7

Season Summary

Games Won, 8; Lost, 1

WILLIAM DALEY
All-American Fullback

MERVIN PREGUIMAN
All-American Tackle

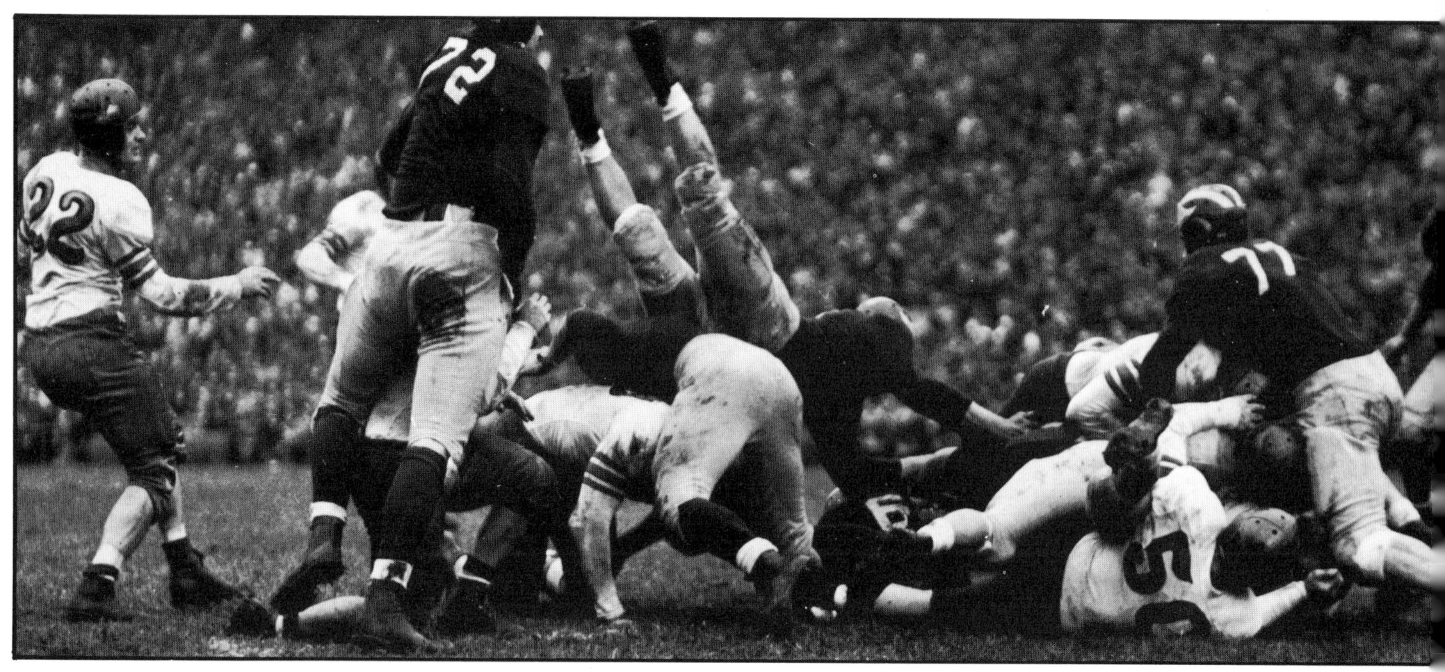

November 25, 1944

Columbus, Ohio

Ohio's Last-Period Rally Topples Michigan, 18-14

Horvath Scores Two Touchdowns As Bucks Compile First Perfect Record in 24 Years

HOMECOMING GAME ACTION

CARROLL C. WIDDOES
Ohio State Head Coach
1944-45

At long last the great dream came true. After nearly a quarter century of painful disappointments, Ohio State went all the way. Led by that terrific one-man Parma typhoon, Les Horvath, one of the greatest college halfbacks in the country, the brilliant Buckeyes of 1944 completed their first perfect record in 24 years by defeating a big, rough, and courageous Michigan team, 18 to 14.

The second time the Bucks got hold of the ball in the first quarter, they unleashed their driving power and marched 56 yards to a touchdown with fullback Ollie Cline hitting through guard for the score. Jack Dugger's kick for the point was blocked by Harold Watts, the Michigan center.

Ohio continued to hold the upper hand until late in the second period when an intercepted pass by Ralph Chubb paved the way for a Michigan touchdown scored by Bill Culligan with only 22 seconds left in the half. Quarterback Joe Ponsetto's kick for the point sent the Wolverines ahead 7-6 for halftime.

After two fumbles in the third period by Michigan, Ohio moved in for their second score. The Buckeyes went 23 yards to take the lead, Horvath plunging for the last yard. Tom Keane missed the PAT this time and the score was 12-7 in Ohio's favor.

As the last quarter opened, it was the Wolverines' turn. They were underway with a masterful, smashing rush that went 83 yards during which they completed the only forward pass of the game, Culligan to Ponsetto for 28 yards. Culligan ripped off tackle for the score with 8:29 left. Ponsetto's placement was good for the point making it 14-12.

After a botched on-side kick that went out of bounds on the Ohio 48, the Buckeyes began their march. With Horvath, Flanagan, Brugge, and Cline doing the leg work, the Bucks steadily moved toward the Michigan goal. With the ball on the one yard line, Horvath dove high over right guard and came down with the ball over the goal line. The clock showed 3:16 left to go. Dugger tried again for the extra point and once more he missed. The kick was high and close, but just wide of the uprights.

Michigan still had ample time to go for another score. On their own 38 Culligan tried to pass. It was not thrown too well and Ohio's Flanagan came down with it. That was the end for Michigan and an undefeated, perfect season for Ohio State. OSU ended up with 73 rushes for 235 yards while UM had 41 rushes for 151 yards.

1944

1944		
Michigan .. 12	Iowa Pre-Flight	7
Michigan .. 14	Marquette	0
Michigan .. 0	Indiana	20
Michigan .. 28	Minnesota	13
Michigan .. 27	Northwestern	0
Michigan .. 40	Purdue	14
Michigan .. 41	Pennsylvania	19
Michigan .. 14	Illinois	0
Michigan .. 14	Wisconsin	0
Michigan .. 14	Ohio State	18

Season Summary

Games won, 8; Lost, 2; Tied, 0

Elroy Hirsch earned four letters during the 1943-44 season, the only Michigan athlete ever to accomplish that feat

MICHIGAN

No.	Name	Pos.	Wt.	Hgt.	Home Town
10	DeMark, Richard	HB	160	5-8	Detroit
15	Powers, Ward	FB	175	5-10	Jonesville
16	Chubb, Ralph	HB	180	5-11	Ann Arbor
18	Bentz, Warren	HB	165	5-11	Washington, D.C.
19	Roper, William	HB	170	6-0	Napa, CA
22	Mahaffey, Howard	G	185	5-11	Pittsburgh, PA
24	Yerges, Howard	QB	172	5-9	Pt. Pleasant, WV
26	*Ponsetto, Joe	QB	185	6-0	Flint
33	*Lund, Donald	FB	190	5-11	Detroit
34	Peterson, Tom	FB	180	5-9	Racine, WI
39	Babyak, John	FB	198	6-0	Campbell, OH
41	Derricotte, Eugene	HB	172	5-10	Defiance, OH
46	Culligan, William	HB	166	5-10	Detroit
48	Weisenburger, Jack	HB	181	6-0	Muskegon Hgts.
53	Wahl, Charles	C	190	5-9	Defiance, OH
55	Drake, Donald	C	176	5-10	Ypsilanti
56	Lintol, John	C	185	6-0	Detroit
58	*Watts, Harold	C	180	5-11	Birmingham
60	Mantho, Henry	G	185	5-9	Alliance, OH
61	Babe, George	G	174	5-8	Sharon Hill, PA
62	Sickels, Quentin	G	190	6-2	Benton Harbor
63	Swift, Thomas	G	170	5-11	Kansas City, MO
64	Nakamura, Frank	G	185	5-6	Ann Arbor
65	Kerr, William	G	170	5-10	Melbourne, FL
66	Sohacki, Edward	G	180	6-0	Detroit
67	Burg, George	G	186	5-11	Winnetka, IL
68	Chaeverini, Roger	G	180	5-11	Detroit
69	Weyers, John	G	175	5-11	Page, ND
70	Fate, Donald	T	204	6-3	Bellaire
71	Redmond, William	QB	170	6-0	Kalamazoo
72	*Bauman, Clement L.	T	210	6-4	Dayton, OH
73	LeRoux, Arthur	T	200	5-10	Muskegon Hgts.
74	Dunne, Maurice	T	190	6-1	Winnetka, IL
77	Lazetich, Milan	T	200	6-0	Anaconda, MT
78	Brielmaier, Jerry	T	190	6-1	Detroit
79	Milczuk, Henry	T	185	5-11	Hamtramck
80	*Renner, Arthur	E	175	6-2	Sturgis
81	Greer, Edward	E	170	5-11	Wayzata, MN
82	Abbott, George	E	170	6-1	Lansing
83	Freihofer, Cecil	E	175	6-1	Indianapolis, IN
85	Hilkene, Bruce	E	190	6-2	Indianapolis, IN
86	Honigsbaum, Frank	E	185	6-2	Troy, NY
87	Sampson, Charles	E	180	6-3	Wausau, WI
96	Wiltse, Robert	G	176	6-0	Walled Lake

* indicates letters won

OHIO

No.	Name	Pos.	Wt.	Class	Home Town
90	Amling, Warren	RT	196	So.	Pana, IL
50	*Appleby, Gordon	C	182	Sr.	Massillon
28	Boxwell, Kenneth	FB	178	Fr.	Xenia
40	*Brown, Matthew	FB	168	So.	Canton
11	Brugge, Robert	HB	188	Fr.	Parma
33	Cline, Ollie	FB	194	Fr.	Fredericktown
92	Cottrell, Ernest	LT	214	Fr.	Curtice
82	Dendiu, Traian	RE	182	Fr.	Campbell
73	Diamond, Charles	LT	194	Fr.	Ashtabula
68	DiPierro, Ray	LG	192	Fr.	Toledo
45	Dove, Robert	QB	165	Fr.	Ashland
55	*Dugger, Jack	LE	210	Sr.	Canton
26	Ehrsam, John	FB	168	Fr.	Toledo
27	Flanagan, Richard	HB	189	Fr.	Sidney
46	Gordon, George	QB	153	Fr.	Maumee
88	Graper, Frank	RT	204	Fr.	Maumee
96	*Hackett, William	RG	191	Jr.	London
84	Hamilton, M.N.	RE	174	Fr.	Toledo
52	Herron, Kendall	C	183	Fr.	Willoughby
22	*Horvath, Leslie	RH	167	Sr.	Parma
87	Jackson, Richard	LE	181	Fr.	Wellsville
36	Janecko, Gene	LH	156	Fr.	Campbell
44	Keane, Tom	QB	178	Fr.	Bellaire
34	Klofta, Dan T.	FB	178	Fr.	Toledo
86	*Maltinsky, Paul	LG	188	Jr.	Wheeling, WV
14	Mascio, Joe	RH	192	Fr.	Ravenna
80	Motejzik, John	LE	188	Fr.	Parma
72	McElheny, Norman	RT	194	Fr.	Tiffin
74	McGinnis, Robert	LT	194	Fr.	Wyoming
94	*Neff, George	LG	198	So.	Bellaire
12	Powelson, Myron	RH	158	Fr.	Zanesville
60	*Redd, Jack	RG	181	Jr.	Columbus
54	Renner, Charles	C	178	Fr.	Akron
56	Ryan, Robert	C	185	So.	Columbus
58	Schnittker, Max	C	188	Fr.	Sandusky
64	Snyder, Tom	LG	187	Fr.	Upper Sandusky
10	Stranges, Tony	RH	157	Fr.	St. Clairesville
98	*Thomas, Russell	RT	220	So.	Huntington, WV
65	Toneff, George	RG	175	Fr.	Barberton
42	Tuttle, Jerry	QB	176	Fr.	Kent
85	Wallace, Robert	LE	167	Fr.	Massillon
24	Wandke, Richard	LH	185	Fr.	Toledo
99	*Willis, William	LT	205	Sr.	Columbus

* indicates letters won

1944

Ohio	54	Missouri	0
Ohio	34	Iowa	0
Ohio	20	Wisconsin	7
Ohio	26	Great Lakes	6
Ohio	34	Minnesota	14
Ohio	21	Indiana	7
Ohio	54	Pittsburgh	19
Ohio	26	Illinois	12
Ohio	18	Michigan	14

Season Summary

Games won, 9; Lost, 0

JACK DUGGER
All-American End

WILLIAM WILLIS
All-American Tackle

WILLIAM HACKETT
All-American Guard

LESLIE HORVATH
All-American Back

November 24, 1945

Ann Arbor, Michigan

Wolverines Roll In Final Minutes To Defeat Bucks, 7 To 3

Schnittker's Field Goal Almost Enough As 85,143 Frozen Fans Look On

Short on experience, long on grit, Michigan's youngest football team since its beginning finished its season with a dramatic and victorious climax. Beaten for three periods, Coach Fritz Crisler's band of youthful Wolverines smashed their way to a fourth quarter touchdown to defeat Ohio State 7 to 3. Ohio was not badly beaten. On the contrary it was one of the closest games of the long series of which this was the 42nd.

Smart, alert, using every bit of strategy to the utmost, the resourceful Michigan attack came up from nowhere to drive 44 yards for the game's only touchdown with six minutes and 45 seconds left of the final period. Halfback Henry Fonde, 165-pound, 21 year-old naval trainee from Knoxville, Tenn., and a track sprinter, drove through the Ohio right tackle for the winning score. George Criames, one of the Michigan crop of 17-year-olds, kicked the extra point on his second try after his first attempt, a miss, had been nullified by a delay of game penalty on Michigan which could not be declined.

It was a luckless Ohio team that went down to defeat. A crushing break just before the Michigan touchdown—an offside penalty that took the ball from Ohio's five to the one yard line, first down—wrecked the Buckeye's chances for a goal line stand that might have saved the day.

A 16-yard field goal by tackle Max Schnittker, Ohio's field goal specialist, had given the Buckeyes the lead early in the third quarter. Ohio looked the winner as that fatal last quarter opened. But after an exchange of punts Michigan began their march which decided the contest.

A Pete Elliott to Henry Fonde pass was good for 25 yards to the OSU 19. Quarterback Howard Yerges ran to the right and just as he was tackled, popped a short lateral pass to Elliott who carried it to the 12. Two bucks by Elliott made the 10-yard line and on fourth down, Yerges ran left and lateralled to Fonde for enough yardage to make the first down. The scoring play was a reverse close to the line with Fonde hurling himself into the Ohio right side for the score. It was the first touchdown Fonde had ever scored for Michigan.

The Bucks had two more chances but could not take advantage of them. So the score was to remain Michigan 7, Ohio State 3.

STATISTICS

	UM	OSU
First Downs	11	11
Rushes-Yards	46-105	48-143
Passing Yards	63	35
Return Yards	56	33
Passing	4-12-2	1-6-2
Punts-Average	9-29.7	5-31.8
Fumbles-Lost	1	2
Penalties-Yards	1-15	3-14

UM	0	0	0	7	7
OSU	0	0	3	0	3

1945

1945			
Ohio	47	Missouri	6
Ohio	42	Iowa	0
Ohio	12	Wisconsin	0
Ohio	13	Purdue	35
Ohio	20	Minnesota	7
Ohio	16	Northwestern	14
Ohio	14	Pittsburgh	0
Ohio	27	Illinois	2
Ohio	3	Michigan	7

Season Summary

Games won, 7; Lost, 2

WARREN AMLING
All-American Guard

OHIO

No.	Name	Pos.	Wt.	Home Town
90	*Amling, Warren	LG	197	Pana, IL
55	Baker, Ray	C	182	Akron
64	Barna, Joseph	RG	197	Cleveland
12	Biel, William	RHB	177	Canton
40	*Brown, Matt	FB	169	Canton
33	*Cline, Ollie	FB	195	Fredericktown
56	Crane, James	LE	183	Columbus
46	Daugherty, Harold	LHB	164	Weirton, WV
73	*Dixon, Thornton	RT	204	Toledo
45	*Dove, Robert	QB	162	Ashland
26	*Ehrsam, John	QB	178	Toledo
72	Fazio, Charles	RT	203	Marion
17	*Fisher, Richard	RHB	198	Columbiana
28	Fout, James	QB	174	Portsmouth
18	Galbraith, James	C	159	Toledo
34	Gandee, Charles	FB	188	Berea
30	Gorby, Herbert	LE	193	East Palestine
93	Gunther, Don	LE	188	LaCrosse, WI
96	*Hackett, William (C)	RG	189	South Solon
76	Hamilton, Forest	LT	204	Cleveland
87	*Jackson, Richard	LE	182	Wellsville
89	Keane, Michael	RE	175	Bellaire
95	Kelsey, Thomas	RE	172	Lakewood
80	*Kessler, Bud	LE	189	Worthington
44	Krall, Jerry	LHB	179	Toledo
54	Lininger, Jack	C	193	Van Wert
74	*McGinnis, Robert	LG	200	Wyoming
14	McKenna, James	RHB	174	Mingo Junction
86	*Maltinsky, Paul	RT	195	Wheeling, WV
16	Marshall, Clyde	RHB	181	Mingo Junction
94	Merrell, Bob	RE	181	Geneva
92	Nicolls, Donald	LE	182	Poland
50	O'Dea, Stephen	C	196	Campbell
27	*Priday, Robin	QB	190	West Jefferson
60	*Redd, Jack	RG	177	Columbus
66	Roe, Jack	LG	204	Steubenville
52	Ryan, Robert	C	191	Columbus
78	Santora, Ernest	LG	207	Cleveland
88	*Sarringhaus, Paul	LHB	184	Hamilton
70	Schnittker, Max	LT	209	Sandusky
42	Smith, Harley	LHB	183	Akron
85	*Steinberg, Don	RE	190	Toledo
98	*Thomas, Russell	LT	223	Griffithsville, WV
11	Verdova, Alex	RHB	177	Lakewood
65	Walbolt, George	LG	192	Toledo
24	Wambold, Ed	FB	184	Perrysburg
82	Watson, Thomas	RE	185	Urbana
67	Wible, Cal	RG	176	Lakewood
75	Winters, Samuel	LT	198	East Liverpool
83	Wright, Ward	RE	201	Huntington, WV
68	Zangara, Don	LG	191	Youngstown

* indicates letters won

MICHIGAN

No.	Name	Pos.	Wt.	Hgt.	Home Town
15	Ott, John A.	HB	180	6-0	Traverse City
16	Coleman, Horace	HB	180	5-10	Hamtramck
18	*Bentz, Warren W.	HB	167	5-11	Washington, D.C.
19	Fonde, Henry	HB	165	5-8	Knoxville, TN
22	Doty, Howard R.	QB	165	5-9	Downers Grove, IL
24	*Yerges, Howard F., Jr.	QB	175	5-10	Pt. Pleasant, WV
26	*Ponsetto, Joe L. Jr., Capt.	QB	190	6-0	Flint
28	Hutter, George	QB	173	5-10	Fond du Lac
33	Chiames, George J.	FB	180	5-10	Freeport, IL
36	Foltz, James H.	FB	185	5-9	Toledo, OH
39	Dworsky, Daniel	FB	206	6-0	Sioux Falls, SD
40	*Nussbaumer, Robert	HB	165	5-11	Oak Park, IL
42	Teninga, Walter H.	HB	180	5-10	Chicago, IL
45	Elliott, Peter R.	HB	187	6-0	Bloomington, IL
46	Robinson, Don	HB	168	5-11	Detroit
48	*Weisenburger, Jack	HB	176	6-1	Muskegon Hgts.
49	Muelder, Wesley W.	HB	165	5-11	Colfax, IL
51	Kavanaugh, Russell L.	C	175	6-1	Detroit
54	Sauls, Reginald	HB	175	5-11	Bayonne, NJ
55	Swanson, Robert	C	180	6-4	Lansing
56	Momsen, Anton, Jr.	C	205	6-2	Toledo, OH
58	*Watts, Harold M.	C	176	5-10	Birmingham
60	*Weyers, John	G	180	5-11	Page, ND
62	*Freihofer, Cecil	G	187	6-0	Indianapolis, IN
63	Smith, Jack E.	G	195	6-0	Muncie, IN
64	Nakamura, Frank	G	185	5-6	Ann Arbor
65	Tomasi, Dominic	G	180	5-10	Flint
66	*Lintol, John F.	G	187	6-1	Detroit
68	Wilkins, F. Stuart	G	187	5-10	Canton, OH
69	Soboleski, Joseph R.	G	182	5-11	Grand Rapids
72	Johnson, C. Robert	T	192	6-2	Dearborn
73	Derleth, Robert	T	200	6-1	Marquette
74	Prashaw, Michael	T	200	6-0	Massena, NY
75	Callahan, Robert F.	T	200	6-0	St. Louis, MO
76	Wahl, R. Allen	T	210	6-3	Oak Park, IL
77	Johnson, George	T	190	6-2	Columbus, OH
78	Hinton, Eugene	T	233	6-2	Drumright, OK
79	Pratt, William	T	200	6-1	Traverse City
80	Renner, Arthur	E	175	6-2	Sturgis
81	Andersen, John M.	E	185	6-5	Manistee
82	Grenkoski, Edward	E	165	6-0	Saginaw
83	Hershberger, Donovan	E	180	6-1	Freeport, IL
84	Ford, Leonard	E	195	6-5	Washington, D.C.
85	McNeill, Edward D.	E	190	6-1	Toledo, OH
86	Brunsting, Louis A., Jr.	E	175	6-2	Rochester, MN
87	Youngblood, Dennis E.	E	185	6-0	Rochester
88	Rabbers, Norman	E	165	6-0	Kalamazoo
89	Kuick, Stanley J.	E	195	6-4	Midland

* indicates letters won

1945

Michigan	27	Great Lakes	2
Michigan	7	Indiana	13
Michigan	40	Michigan State	0
Michigan	20	Northwestern	7
Michigan	7	Army	28
Michigan	19	Illinois	0
Michigan	26	Minnesota	0
Michigan	7	Navy	33
Michigan	27	Purdue	13
Michigan	7	Ohio State	3

Season Summary

Games won, 7; Lost, 3; Tied, 0

JOE PONSETTO
Quarterback-Captain

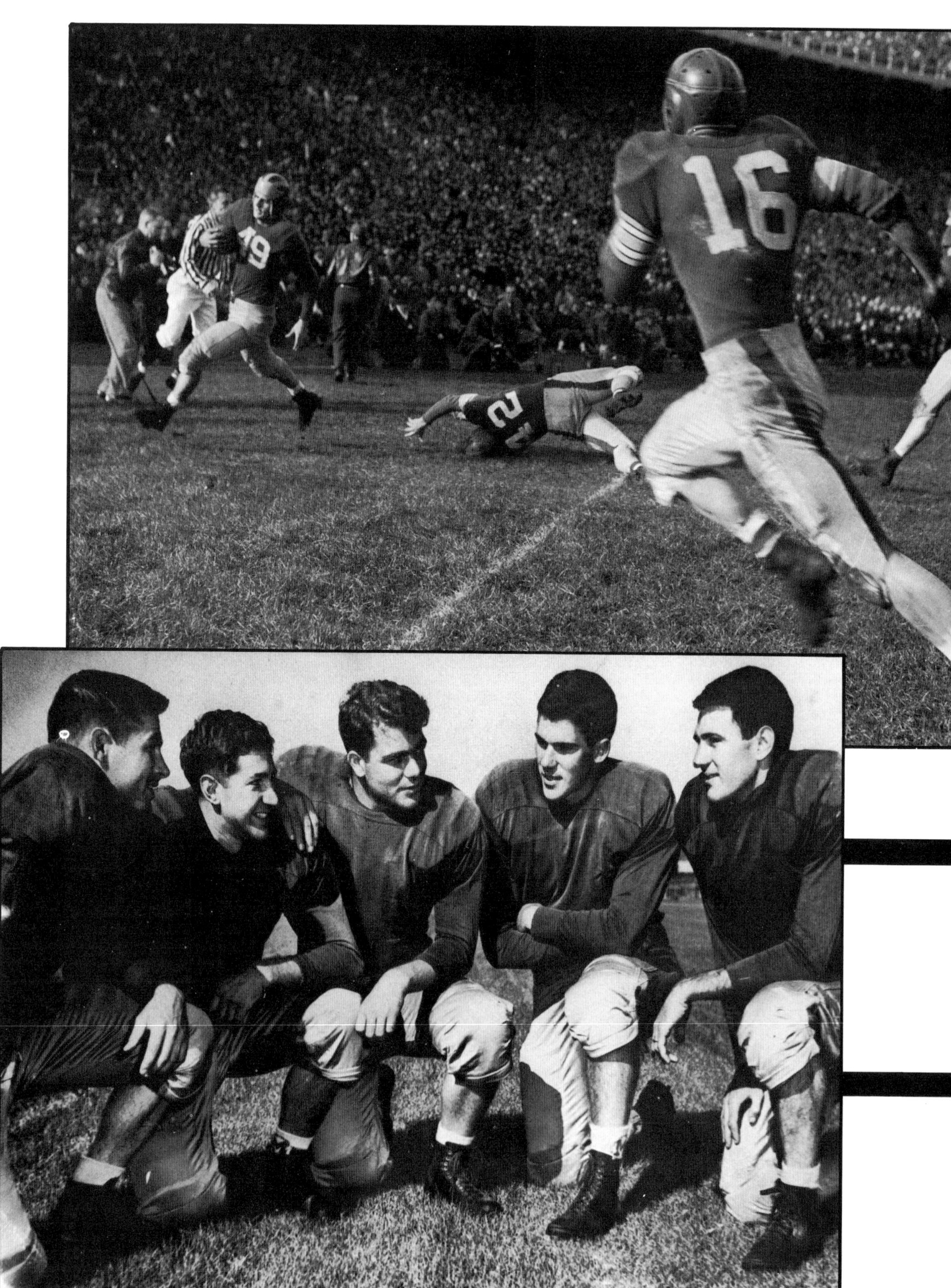

Five former Wolverines returned from the services to rejoin the year's team. Left to right: White (1932), Wiese (1944), Ponsetto (1945), Hilkene (1944) and Renner (1944)

November 23, 1946

Columbus, Ohio

Michigan Annihilates Buckeyes, 58 To 6

Chappuis Is Star In Worst Beating Ever

The worst collapse in modern Ohio State football history went into the records as a band of Michigan Wolverines, led by halfback Bob Chappuis, rolled up one of its most impressive Big Nine victories of all times. Before 78,634 astounded fans, the rampant maize-and-blue machine rioted through a hapless and demoralized squad of bewildered Buckeyes, 58 to 6.

Michigan marched 64 yards for a touchdown on its very first series. Fonde's running was the feature of that drive and he finally galloped over from the one-yard line, off tackle. After Ohio failed to take advantage of a Michigan fumble recovered by Whisler on the Michigan 24, the Wolverines began another scoring drive on the strong, accurate arm of Chappuis. This one covered 81 yards and included a 48-yard heave to Mann. The combination clicked again for a 16-yard TD toss.

Next to Chappuis' passing, Michigan's chief weapon was its much publicized end-around play, mainly with the slippery Mann and Len Ford doing the carrying. Ford's 36-yard gallop on this play led up to the third TD, taking the ball to Ohio's 27. Chappuis passed to end Art Renner on the 13. Then Fonde, out to the left, gathered in a flat pass from Chappuis and dashed for the goal line. Brieske missed the PAT and it was 20-0.

Michigan got one more before the half started by an Ohio fumble. Another Chappuis aerial to Howard Yerges put the ball on the Ohio 5. Chappuis rounded end for the score and Brieske made it 27-0 at the half.

Six plays into the second half Michigan had touchdown number 5 after a whirlwind 61-yard assault. Mann galloped 21 yards for the score, a result of an end-around play.

Ten minutes later four Michigan plays made 67 yards for the sixth score. The payoff punch was a Chappuis aerial to Paul White, southpaw right halfback, good for 32 yards. It was 41-0 going into the final period.

With the second string now doing the damage, Michigan scored again. UM's Elmer Madar recovered an OSU fumble on the Buckeye 40. Culligan, now throwing for the Wolverines, fired to end Rifenburg good for six more points.

First play after the next kickoff, Tommy Phillip's pass was intercepted by Michigan's Derricotte who raced back to Ohio's 16. Dan Dworsky and Ralph Chubb plunged the ball to the four where Culligan went around end for the score.

Another pass interception, this time by Pete Elliott, set up the ball on Ohio's six. Ohio held and Brieske came on to kick a 13-yard field goal.

With only 1:30 remaining, Ohio escaped a skunking. The "sleeper" play with Doolittle to Swinehart pass good for 62 yards and a Buckeye touchdown, provided Ohio State's only points as the PAT was not good.

STATISTICS

	UM	OSU
First Downs	22	4
Rushes-Yards	50-209	31-47
Passing Yardage	300	78
Return Yardage	78	174
Passing	16-29-2	4-18-5
Punts	4-30	7-43
Fumbles Lost	1	2
Yards Penalized	35	10

PAUL O. BIXLER
Ohio State Head Coach
1946

1946

1946	
Michigan 21	Indiana 0
Michigan 14	Iowa 7
Michigan 13	Army 20
Michigan 14	Northwestern 14
Michigan 9	Illinois 13
Michigan 21	Minnesota . . . 0
Michigan 55	MSU 7
Michigan 28	Wisconsin . . . 6
Michigan 58	Ohio State . . . 6

Season Summary

Games Won, 6; Lost, 2; Tied, 1

ELMER MADAR
All-American End

MICHIGAN

No.	Name	Pos.	Wt.	Hgt.	Age	Home Town
82	Bahlow, Edward	E	196	6-2	26	Springfield, IL
74	Ballau, Robert	T	192	6-0	21	Springfield, VT
56	*Brieske, James	C	201	6-2	23	Harbor Beach
76	Brown, Richard	T	203	6-1	21	Detroit
67	*Burg, George	G	187	5-11	21	Winnetka, IL
57	Callahan, Robert	C	198	5-11	23	St. Louis, MO
78	Carpenter, Jack	T	226	6-0	23	Kansas City, M
49	*Chappuis, Robert	HB	183	6-0	23	Toledo, OH
18	*Chubb, Ralph	HB	182	5-11	22	Ann Arbor
77	Crane, Fenwick	T	195	6-3	23	Pleasant Ridge
40	*Culligan, William	HB	158	5-10	22	Detroit
73	*Derleth, Robert	T	206	6-3	24	Marquette
41	*Derricotte, Gene	HB	172	5-11	20	Defiance, OH
39	*Dworsky, Daniel	FB	198	6-0	18	Sioux Falls, SD
42	Elliott, Chalmers	HB	170	5-10	21	Bloomington, I
45	*Elliott, Peter	HB	186	6-0	19	Bloomington, I
19	*Fonde, Henry	HB	162	5-8	22	Knoxville, TN
87	*Ford, Leonard	E	207	6-4	20	Washington, D.
63	Freihofer, Walter	G	180	6-0	21	Indianapolis, I
61	Heneveld, Lloyd	G	180	6-0	22	Holland
83	*Hershberger, D.	E	183	6-1	19	Freeport, IL
75	*Hilkene, Bruce	T	193	6-2	22	Indianapolis, I
79	Honigsbaum, F.	T	198	6-3	19	Troy, NY
53	Kample, Kurt	G	181	5-9	23	Detroit
59	Keeler, Walter	C	190	6-0	21	Bay City
64	*Kraeger, George	G	178	6-1	23	Indianapolis, I
15	Kuick, Donald	HB	173	6-1	17	Midland
66	Lintol, John	G	185	6-1	21	Detroit
81	Mann, Robert	E	167	5-10	21	New Bern, NC
88	*Madar, Elmer	E	172	5-10	25	Detroit
85	*McNeill, Edward	E	185	6-1	18	Toledo, OH
60	Phillips, Elmer	G	185	5-10	20	Big Bend, WV
72	*Pritula, William	T	189	5-11	24	Pittsburgh, PA
80	*Renner, Arthur (C)	E	172	6-2	22	Sturgis
89	*Rifenburg, Richard	E	191	6-3	20	Saginaw
46	*Robinson, Donald	QB	168	5-11	24	Detroit
62	*Sickels, Quentin	G	194	6-2	19	Benton Harbor
69	Soboleski, Joseph	G	187	6-0	20	Grand Rapids
65	*Tomasi, Dominick	G	180	5-8	18	Flint
44	Traugott, Alan	HB	180	5-11	22	Indianapolis, I
25	*Vernier, Robert	QB	183	5-11	22	Toledo, OH
58	*Watts, Harold	C	173	5-10	21	Birmingham
48	*Weisenburger, J.	FB	178	6-1	18	Muskegon Hts
16	*White, Paul	HB	180	6-0	24	River Rouge
55	White, J. T.	C	189	6-2	26	River Rouge
38	*Wiese, Robert	FB	193	6-2	23	Jamestown, N
68	*Wilkins, Stuart	G	183	5-10	18	Canton, OH
14	Wisniewski, Irvin	E	190	6-3	21	Toledo, OH
33	Yedinak, Michael	FB	182	5-7	22	Flint
24	*Yerges, Howard	QB	172	5-10	21	Pt. Pleasant,

* indicates letters won

OHIO

No.	Name	Pos.	Wt.	Hgt.	Age	Home Town
3	Adamle, Anthony	C	206	6-0	22	Cleveland
0	*Amling, Waren	T	197	5-11½	21	Pana, IL
8	Bonnie, Dale	E	193	6-0	20	Columbus
2	Bonnie, David	FB	195	6-0	20	Columbus
1	*Brugge, Robert	HB	194	6-0	20	Parma
0	Cannavino, M.	HB	168	5-11	21	Cleveland
9	*Crane, Jameson	E	194	5-10	20	Columbus
0	*Csuri, Charles	T	199	6-0	24	Cleveland
4	*Dean, Hal	G	205	5-11	24	Wooster
2	*Dendiu, Traian	E	191	6-0	20	Campbell
8	*DiPierro, Raymond	G	197	5-9	20	Toledo
7	Dixon, Stanley	E	202	6-1	22	Wyoming
4	Doolittle, William	QB	188	5-9	23	Mansfield
2	Duncan, Howard	C	221	6-3	22	Lakewood
2	*Fazio, Charles	T	208	6-3	20	Marion
3	Gaudio, Robert	G	203	5-10	21	Cleveland
0	Hague, James	FB	181	6-0	18	Rocky River
6	*Hamilton, Forrest	T	212	6-3	18	Cleveland
2	*Jabbusch, Robert	G	195	5-10	23	Elyria
6	*James, Thomas	HB	184	5-9	23	Massillon
7	Kirk, Brenton	T	216	6-0	21	New Philadelphia
4	*Krall, Gerald	HB	181	5-10	19	Toledo
9	Krieger, George	G	191	5-11	20	Columbus
5	*McGinnis, Robert	G	200	6-0	20	Wyoming
5	Morrison, Fred	E	206	6-1	19	Columbus
3	Newell, William	HB	172	5-11	18	Columbiana
3	O'Hanlon, Richard	T	214	6-2	18	East Liverpool
	*Oliver, Glenn	FB	192	5-11	20	Columbus
3	Palmer, James	E	180	6-0	22	Springfield
5	*Palmer, Richard	QB	193	5-10	24	Cleveland
3	*Parks, Ernest	E	240	6-4	20	Canton
3	Perini, Pete	FB	214	5-10	18	Washington, NJ
3	Phillips, Thomas	HB	176	5-9	22	Berea
5	*Plank, Ernest	E	205	5-11	22	Columbus
	Quattrone, Joseph	G	202	5-11	21	Steubenville
	*Renner, Charles	C	189	5-11½	20	Akron
	*Schneider, Wilbur	G	178	5-7	23	Gahanna
	*Schnittker, Max	T	223	6-2	19	Sandusky
	Schuster, George	G	180	5-11	22	Canton
	Shannon, Richard	E	211	6-2	20	Akron
	Slager, Richard	QB	185	5-11	18	Columbus
	*Souders, Cecil	E	203	6-1	26	Bucyrus
	Spencer, George	QB	202	5-11	21	Columbus
	*Stackhouse, Ray	T	235	6-2	21	Dayton
	*Stungis, John	QB	192	6-1	21	Powhatan Pt.
	Swinehart, Rodney	HB	177	5-9	20	Wooster
	*Teifke, Howard	C	193	6-0	21	Fremont
	Templeton, David	FB	198	5-11	24	Bedford, IN
	Thomas, James	G	202	5-5½	22	Bellaire
	*Verdova, Alex	HB	182	5-10	18	Lakewood
	Whisler, Joseph	FB	207	5-11	22	Willard
	Wilson, Jack	T	205	6-4	21	Xenia
	Wolfe, Russell	HB	159	5-9	22	Upper Sandusky
	Zeigler, Andrew	T	215	6-2	20	Cleveland

*Indicates letters won

1946

Ohio	13	Missouri	13
Ohio	21	S. California	0
Ohio	7	Wisconsin	20
Ohio	14	Purdue	14
Ohio	39	Minnesota	9
Ohio	39	Northwestern	27
Ohio	20	Pittsburgh	13
Ohio	7	Illinois	16
Ohio	6	Michigan	58

Season Summary

Games Won, 4; Lost, 3; Tied, 2

WARREN AMLING
All-American Tackle

Michigan's "Dream Backfield", L to R; Bump Elliott, wingback; Jack Weisenburger, fullback; Howard Yerges, quarterback; Bob Chappuis, tailback.

Michigan's National Champions lined up as follows, left to right: Lineman: Rifenburg, Pritula, Soboleski, Tomasi White, Hilkene, and Mann. Backs are Elliott, Weisenburger, Yerges and Chappuis.

November 22, 1947

Ann Arbor, Michigan

Michigan Wears Down Ohio State, 21-0

Wolves Held To 7-0 Edge In First Half

The team that had everything, Michigan's mighty Wolverines, completed its nine-game sweep of the season and cleared the track for the Rose Bowl. Held to one touchdown in the first half, the Wolverines slashed forth with all their weapons to conquer battered, crippled but magnificently fighting Ohio State, 21 to 0.

Michigan drove 68 yards for its first touchdown at 11:25 of the first period with Chalmers (Bump) Elliott ripping three yards for the score. The second Michigan touchdown came on an 80-yard drive at 9:10 of the third period with Chappuis' deadly passing accounting for more than half the distance. This time Chappuis darted 3 yards around end for the score.

The final Wolverine scoring march was 35 yards and this time Jack Weisenburger, the industrious Michigan fullback galloped the remaining three yards. Jim Brieske, the Wolverines' almost errorless placekicker, booted all three conversions.

Unlucky to the finish, Ohio's best scoring opportunity came in the last quarter when guard Tom Snyder recovered a Chappuis fumble on the Michigan 10 yard line. On the first try, the ball was fumbled in a plunge at center and Michigan's Ed McNeill of Toledo recovered.

Chappuis had a lot of help from Bob Mann, the amazing left end, McNeill, and Weisenburger as well as Howard Yerges in finally pushing their three touchdowns over. The Michigan line anchored by White at center struggled but overcame the determined but outclassed Buckeyes.

Bump Elliott and Pete Elliott

STATISTICS

	UM	OSU
First Downs	24	9
Rushes-Yards	57-233	37-119
Passing Yardage	217	55
Return Yardage	37	89
Passing	12-33-1	3-17-4
Punts	7-37.8	10-35.7
Fumbles Lost	2	0
Yards Penalized	30	25

1947			
Ohio	13	Missouri	7
Ohio	20	Purdue	24
Ohio	0	S. California	32
Ohio	13	Iowa	13
Ohio	0	Pittsburgh	12
Ohio	0	Indiana	7
Ohio	7	Northwestern	6
Ohio	7	Illinois	28
Ohio	0	Michigan	21

Season Summary

Games Won, 2; Lost, 6; Tied, 1

WESLEY E. FESLER
Ohio State Head Coach
1947-1950

OHIO

No.	Name	Pos.	Wt.	Hgt.	Class	Home Town
10	*Cannavino, M.	RH	168	5-11½	Jr.	Cleveland
11	**Brugge, Robert	LH	195	5-11	Jr.	Parma
12	Clark, James	LH	175	6-0	So.	Columbus
14	*Gordon, George	LH	155	5-8	Jr.	Columbus
15	*Sensanbaugher, D.	RH	195	5-8	Jr.	Uhrichsville
16	**Verdova, Alex	RH	186	5-10½	Jr.	Lakewood
21	*Perini, Pete	QB	218	5-11½	So.	New Village, NJ
22	Slager, Richard	QB	192	6-0	So.	Columbus
24	*Doolittle, William	QB	183	5-9	Jr.	Mansfield
25	Savic, Pandel	QB	188	6-0	So.	Girard
26	**Stungis, John	QB	200	6-1	Jr.	Powhatan Pt.
31	Oliver, Glenn	FB	195	5-11	Jr.	Columbus
33	**Cline, Ollie	FB	202	5-11	Jr.	Fredericktown
34	Henry, Joseph	FB	193	5-11	So.	Columbus
36	*Whisler, Joseph	FB	214	5-11½	Jr.	Willard
40	Wertz, George	LH	167	5-9	So.	Piqua
42	*Swinehart, Rodney	LH	177	5-10	So.	Wooster
47	Demmel, Robert	RH	182	5-10	So.	Fremont
48	Newell, William	RH	175	5-11	So.	Columbiana
52	*Duncan, Howard	C	220	6-3	Sr.	Lakewood
53	*Lininger, Jack	C	199	5-11	So.	Van Wert
54	*Renner, Charles	C	190	6-0½	Jr.	Akron
56	**Teifke, Howard	C	189	6-0	Jr.	Fremont
60	*Toneff, George	LG	190	5-9	So.	Barberton
62	**Jabbusch, Robert	LG	196	5-10½	Sr.	Elyria
63	*O'Hanlon, Richard	RG	235	6-2	So.	East Liverpool
64	Mattey, George	LG	215	5-10	So.	Cleveland
66	*Snyder, Thomas	RG	205	5-10	So.	Upper Sandusky
67	*Templeton, David	RG	215	5-11½	Sr.	Bedford, IN
68	**DiPierro, Ray	LG	197	5-10	Jr.	Toledo
69	Krieger, George	RG	191	5-11	So.	Columbus
70	Moldea, Emil	LT	235	6-2	Sr.	Akron
71	Jennings, Jack	RT	227	6-3	So.	Columbus
72	**Fazio, Charles	RT	212	6-3	Jr.	Marion
73	Prchlik, Richard	RT	201	6-3	So.	Cleveland
74	Fritzsche, James	LT	238	6-5	So.	Bedford
75	Edwards, William	RT	225	6-4	So.	Willoughby
76	**Hamilton, Forrest	LT	212	6-3	Jr.	Cleveland
77	Kirk, Brenton	LT	213	6-2	So.	New Philadelphia
78	Dawson, Jack	RT	203	6-0	So.	Toledo
79	*Wilson, Jack	FB	217	6-4	So.	Xenia
80	Hague, James	RE	190	6-0	So.	Rocky River
81	Shannon, Richard	LE	215	6-1½	So.	Akron
82	Bonnie, Dale	LE	188	6-2	So.	Columbus
83	Dorsey, Robert	RE	190	5-10	Jr.	Houston, TX
84	*Bonnie, David	RE	195	6-0	So.	Columbus
85	*Morrison, Fred	LE	207	6-2	So.	Columbus
86	Palmer, James	RE	180	6-2	Jr.	Springfield
87	Dixon, Stanley	LE	202	6-1	Jr.	Wyoming
88	**Dendiu, Traian	RE	189	6-0	Jr.	Campbell
89	**Crane, Jameson	LE	190	5-10	Sr.	Cleveland

* indicates letters won

MICHIGAN

No.	Name	Pos.	Wt.	Hgt.	Class	Home Town
11	Wistert, Alvin	T	218	6-3	Jr.	Chicago, IL
15	Kuick, Donald O.	HB	178	6-2	So.	Midland
18	*Elliott, C. W.	HB	168	5-10	Jr.	Bloomington, IL
19	*Fonde, Henry	HB	158	5-8	Sr.	Knoxville, TN
23	Ghindia, John	QB	175	5-10	So.	Ecorse
24	***Yerges, Howard	QB	178	5-9	Sr.	Columbus, OH
25	*Kiesel, George	QB	185	5-11	Sr.	Ferndale
33	*Peterson, T. R.	FB	183	5-9	So.	Racine, WI
36	Jackson, N. E.	E	180	6-0	So.	Canton, OH
38	Kempthorn, R. J.	FB	190	6-0	So.	Canton, OH
40	Lentz, C. W., Jr.	HB	160	5-9	So.	Toledo, OH
41	**Derricotte, Gene A.	HB	175	5-11	Jr.	Defiance, OH
42	*Teninga, Walter H.	QB	186	5-10	So.	Chicago, IL
45	**Elliott, Peter R.	QB	187	6-0	Jr.	Bloomington, IL
48	***Weisenburger, J. E.	FB	178	6-1	Sr.	Muskegon Hts.
49	**Chappuis, R. E.	HB	184	6-0	Sr.	Toledo, OH
52	Salucci, Ralph	G	172	5-8	So.	Dearborn
53	Erben, Robert	C	185	5-11	So.	Akron, OH
54	Maturo, John	G	185	5-10	So.	Hamden, CT
55	*White, John T.	C	185	6-3	Sr.	River Rouge
56	**Brieske, James F.	C	195	6-2	Sr.	Harbor Beach
57	Kulpinski, John J.	C	210	6-0	So.	Detroit
58	Nichols, Donald M.	C	190	6-0		Allegan
59	**Dworsky, Daniel	C	208	6-0	Jr.	Sioux Falls, SD
60	*Ballou, Robert	G	200	6-2	Jr.	Chester, VT
61	Heneveld, Lloyd A.	G	190	6-0	So.	Holland
62	**Sickels, Quentin B.	G	195	6-2	Jr.	Benton Harbor
63	Kampe, Kurt	G	180	5-8	Sr.	Detroit
64	Strauss, Richard	G	204	6-1	So.	Lansing
65	**Tomasi, Dominic	G	180	5-10	Jr.	Flint
66	Twining, Robert	G	190	5-11	So.	Ann Arbor
67	McClelland, D. B.	G	190	6-0	So.	Calumet
68	**Wilkins, Stuart F.	G	186	5-10	Jr.	Canton, OH
69	**Soboleski, J. R.	G	193	5-11	Sr.	Grand Rapids
70	Brielmaier, G. E.	T	210	6-1	So.	Detroit
71	Fitch, Alan	G	185	5-10	So.	Detroit
72	**Pritula, William	T	189	5-11	Sr.	Detroit
73	Atchison, James	T	198	6-1	So.	Cleveland, OH
74	Marshall, R. W.	T	200	6-2	So.	North Bay, Ont.
75	***Hilkene, B. L. (C)	T	192	6-2	Sr.	Indianapolis, IN
76	Kohl, Ralph A.	T	223	6-2	So.	Cleveland, OH
77	*Johnson, G. W.	T	188	6-1	Jr.	Columbus, OH
78	Dendrinos, Peter C.	T	210	6-2	So.	Muskegon Hts.
81	**Mann, Robert	E	167	5-11	Sr.	New Bern, NC
82	Hollway, Robert C.	E	195	6-3	So.	Ann Arbor
83	*Hershberger, D. P.	E	185	6-1	Jr.	Freeport, IL
84	Wisniewski, Irvin C.	E	194	6-3	Jr.	Lambertville
85	**McNeill, Edward D.	E	190	6-1	Jr.	Toledo, OH
87	**Ford, Leonard	E	208	6-5	Jr.	Washington, D. C.
88	Anderson, John M.	E	195	6-5	So.	Manistee
89	**Rifenburg, Richard	E	195	6-3	So.	Saginaw

* indicates letters won

1947

Michigan	55	MSU	0
Michigan	49	Stanford	13
Michigan	69	Pittsburgh	0
Michigan	49	Northwestern	21
Michigan	13	Minnesota	6
Michigan	14	Illinois	7
Michigan	35	Indiana	0
Michigan	40	Wisconsin	6
Michigan	21	Ohio State	0

Season Summary

Games Won, 9; Lost, 0; Tied, 0

ROBERT CHAPPUIS
All-American Halfback

CHALMERS "BUMP" ELLIOTT
All-American Halfback

Chappius breaks into an open field.

November 20, 1948

Columbus, Ohio

Wolves Hit By Air To Top Bucks, 13 To 3

Boost Victory String To 23 And Retain Big Nine Title

BENNIE OOSTERBAAN
Michigan Head Coach 1948-58

Ortman (49) and Elliott (45)

Michigan's talented football forces, tremendous on defense and with an air attack like a blast of lightning, completed their second straight perfect season. For the 23rd straight victory in their sensational streak that dates back to midseason of 1946, the brilliant—and fortunate—Wolverines conquered a stubbornly battling Ohio State team, 13-3.

Ohio scored in the first quarter on a Michigan miscue. After an excellent punt by OSU's Joe Whisler went out of bounds on the Michigan 12, a long lateral was fumbled by Michigan's Ortmann and recovered by Jack Lininger on UM's 7-yard line. The Michigan defense stiffened and on fourth down from the 23, OSU's Jimmy Hague with Dick Widdoes holding, booted a 33-yard field goal to give Ohio a 3-0 lead.

In the second quarter Michigan got on track driving 91 yards for a score. Ohio was called for interference on one pass play which was good for 34 yards. Another pass from Elliott to Ortmann was good for 13. From Ohio's 44, Ortmann connected on a long one to Allis who caught it on Ohio's 17 and took it over for the score. Allis then booted the PAT for a 7-3 halftime lead.

Ohio stormed out in the third quarter and moved the ball to the Michigan 20. There a pass by Dick Slager was intercepted by the durable quarterback Elliott, the only man on the team who played both offense and defense. He was downed on the Michigan 16 and Ohio never came that close again.

It was 7-3 going into the fourth quarter. Michigan's second touchdown onslaught started from its 38-yard line. Two passes from Teninga to Koceski moved the ball into Ohio territory. Elliott then hit Allis for a first down on the 11. Two ground plunges made the 3-yard line. On third down a hole was driven in the center of the Ohio line, and Peterson went through for the score. Allis had trouble with the placement so the score remained 13-3.

The game marked Ohio's 75th anniversary and a crowd of 82,754 watched the battle.

STATISTICS

	OSU	UM
First Downs	14	9
Rushes-Yards	51-130	36-54
Passing Yards	73	116
Return Yards	64	127
Passing	7-20-2	7-16-0
Punts-Average	10-36.5	9-42
Fumbles-Lost	3-1	3-2

UM	0	7	0	6	13
OSU	3	0	0	0	3

MICHIGAN

1948			
Michigan	13	MSU	7
Michigan	14	Oregon	0
Michigan	40	Purdue	0
Michigan	28	Northwestern	0
Michigan	27	Minnesota	14
Michigan	28	Illinois	20
Michigan	35	Navy	0
Michigan	54	Indiana	0
Michigan	13	Ohio State	3

Season Summary

Games Won, 9; Lost, 0

PETE ELLIOTT
All-American Quarterback

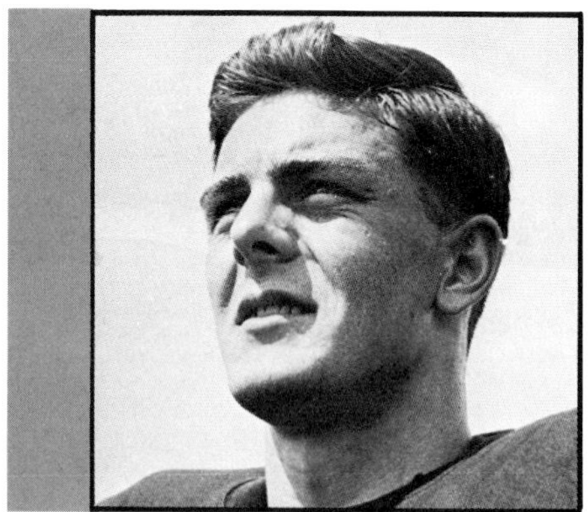

RICHARD RIFENBURG
All-American End

ALVIN WISTERT
All-American Tackle

No.	Name	Pos.	Wt.	Hgt.	Class	Home Town
11	*Wistert, Alvin	T	218	6-3	Jr.	Chicago, IL
16	Van Summern, R.	HB	187	6-0	Jr.	Kenmore, NY
18	Koceski, Leo R.	HB	163	5-10	So.	Canonsburg, PA
19	Souchek, Donald	HB	180	5-9	Jr.	Onekema
22	Raymond, Harold	G	172	5-9	Sr.	Flint
23	Ghindia, John	QB	175	5-10	Jr.	Escorse
24	Small, Irwin	QB	160	5-8	Jr.	Tarrytown, NY
26	Bartlett, William H.	QB	180	5-9	Jr.	Muskegon
28	Palmer, Peter	QB	190	5-11	So.	Indianapolis, IN
30	Dufek, Donald	FB	185	5-11	So.	Evanston, IL
32	Straffon, Ralph A.	FB	185	5-8	So.	Croswell
33	*Peterson, Tom R.	FB	185	5-9	Jr.	Racine, WI
36	Jackson, Norman	FB	185	6-0	Jr.	Canton, OH
38	*Kempthorn, Dick	FB	195	6-0	Jr.	Canton, OH
40	Lentz, Charles W.	HB	162	5-9	Jr.	Toledo, OH
41	*Derricotte, Gene A.	HB	178	5-11	Sr.	Defiance, OH
42	*Teninga, Walter H.	HB	179	5-10	Jr.	Chicago, IL
45	*Elliott, Peter	QB	188	6-0	Sr.	Bloomington, IL
46	Jennings, William	HB	168	5-9	Jr.	Negaunee
49	Ortmann, C. H.	HB	183	6-1	So.	Milwaukee, WI
53	Erben, Robert	C	190	5-11	Jr.	Akron, OH
55	Farrer, Richard	C	195	6-0	So.	Trenton, OH
56	Kreager, Carl	C	216	6-4	So.	Detroit
58	Padgen, John	C	190	5-11	So.	Calumet City, IL
59	*Dworsky, Don	C	210	6-0	Sr.	Sioux Falls, SD
60	Powers, John	G	178	5-9	So.	Tulsa, OH
61	*Heneveld, Lloyd	G	190	6-0	Jr.	Holland, MI
62	*Sickels, Quentin	G	195	6-2	Sr.	Benton Harbor
63	Fitch, Alan	G	185	5-10	Jr.	Detroit
64	Jackson, Allen	G	180	6-0	Jr.	Dearborn
65	*Tomasi, D. (C)	G	180	5-10	Sr.	Flint
66	Wolter, James R.	G	195	6-0	So.	Ypsilanti
67	*McClelland, D. B.	G	190	6-0	Jr.	Calumet
68	*Wilkins, F. Stuart	G	186	5-10	Sr.	Canton, OH
69	*Soboleski, Joseph	T	195	5-11	Sr.	Grand Rapids
70	Eizonas, John	T	238	6-1	Jr.	Detroit
72	*Wahl, Allen	T	210	6-2	So.	Oak Park, IL
73	Atchison, James	T	195	6-1	Jr.	Cleveland, OH
74	McWilliams, R.	T	248	6-3	So.	Cleveland, OH
76	*Kohl, Ralph A.	T	220	6-2	Sr.	Cleveland, OH
77	Ohlenroth, William	T	205	6-3	So.	Chicago, IL
78	*Dendrinos, Peter C.	T	212	6-2	Jr.	Muskegon Hts.
79	Hess, John	E	195	6-2	So.	Grand Rapids
80	Sutherland, G.	E	185	6-0	So.	Montclair, NJ
82	*Hollway, Robert C.	E	200	6-3	Jr.	Ann Arbor
83	*Hershberger, Donn	E	190	6-1	Jr.	Freeport, IL
84	*Wisniewski, Irwin	E	193	6-3	Jr.	Lambertsville
85	*McNeil, Edward	E	194	6-1	Sr.	Toledo, OH
86	Clark, Oswald	E	200	6-2	Jr.	Montclair, NJ
88	Allis, Harry	E	190	6-0	So.	Flint
89	*Rifenburg, Dick	E	197	6-3	Jr.	Saginaw

* indicates letters won

OHIO

Name	Pos.	Wt.	Hgt.	Class	Home Town
Anderson, Thomas	QB	190	6-1	Jr.	St. Marys
Basinger, Edward	E	178	6-1	So.	Lima
Biltz, John	G	210	6-0	So.	Bedford
*Bonnie, Dale	E	188	6-2	Jr.	Columbus
**Bonnie, David	HB	197	6-0	Jr.	Columbus
Brickman, Robert	G	192	6-0	So.	Lima
**Cannavino, Michael	HB	168	5-11½	Sr.	Cleveland
*Clark, James	HB	175	6-0	Jr.	Columbus
Dawson, Jack	T	204	6-1	Jr.	Toledo
*Demmel, Robert	HB	181	5-10	Jr.	Fremont
***DiPierro, Ray	G	196	5-10	Sr.	Toledo
*Dorsey, Robert	E	191	5-10	Sr.	Houston, TX
Edwards, William	T	225	6-4	Jr.	Willoughby
Ellwood, Richard	HB	180	5-10	So.	Dover
Endres, George	G	190	5-10	So.	Cincinnati
***Fazio, Charles	T	212	6-3	Sr.	Marion
*Gandee, Charles	FB	200	5-10	Jr.	Berea
Gandee, Sherwin	E	185	6-0	So.	Akron
Gilbert, Charles	E	185	6-0	Jr.	Columbus
*Hague, James	E	190	6-0	Jr.	Rocky River
Hasselo, Albert	E	197	6-1	So.	Cleveland
Henry, Joseph	FB	194	5-11	Jr.	Columbus
*Jennings, Jack	T	228	6-3	Jr.	Columbus
King, Dale	E	185	6-0	So.	Columbus
*Kirk, Brenton	G	215	6-2	Sr.	New Philadelphia
**Krall, Gerald	HB	181	5-10	Jr.	Toledo
**Lininger, Jack	C	200	5-11	Jr.	Van Wert
Manz, Jerry	G	210	5-10	So.	Toledo
*Marshall, Clyde	FB	190	5-10	So.	Mingo Junction
Mattey, George	G	218	5-10	Jr.	Cleveland
McCleery, Tony	HB	185	6-0	So.	Delaware
McCullough, Robert	C	170	6-1	So.	Uhrichsville
Miller, William	T	195	6-2	So.	Fremont
Momsen, Robert	T	200	6-2	So.	Toledo
**Morrison, Fred	FB	207	6-2	Jr.	Columbus
*Newell, William	HB	175	5-11	Jr.	Columbiana
**O'Hanlon, Richard	T	234	6-2	Jr.	East Liverpool
Palmer, James	E	185	6-2	Sr.	Springfield
**Perini, Peter	QB	220	5-11	Jr.	New Village, NJ
**Renner, Charles	C	190	6-0½	Sr.	Akron
*Savic, Pandel	QB	188	6-0	Jr.	Girard
*Shannon, Richard	T	217	6-1½	Jr.	Akron
*Slager, Richard	HB	193	6-0	Jr.	Columbus
**Snyder, Thomas	G	203	5-10	Jr.	Upper Sandusky
Sturtz, Karl	HB	178	5-11½	So.	Coshocton
**Swinehart, Rodney	HB	178	5-10	Jr.	Wooster
Tabener, Joe	G	220	5-9	So.	Toledo
***Teifke, Howard	C	190	6-0	Sr.	Fremont
**Templeton, David	G	216	5-11½	Sr.	Bedford, IN
Thomas, James	G	195	5-6	So.	Bellaire
*Toneff, George	G	190	5-9	Jr.	Barberton
Trautwein, William	T	235	6-4	So.	Athena
***Verdova, Alex	HB	186	5-10½	Sr.	Lakewood
*Watson, Thomas	E	195	6-2	So.	Urbana
Wertz, George	QB	166	5-9	Jr.	Piqua
**Whisler, Joseph	FB	230	5-11½	Sr.	Willard
Widdoes, Richard	QB	165	5-8	So.	Columbus
**Wilson, Jack	T	217	6-4	Jr.	Xenia
Wolf, Ronald	C	200	6-1	So.	Ludlow, KY

* indicates letters won

1948

Ohio	21	Missouri	7
Ohio	20	S. California	0
Ohio	7	Iowa	14
Ohio	17	Indiana	0
Ohio	34	Wisconsin	32
Ohio	7	Northwestern	21
Ohio	41	Pittsburgh	0
Ohio	34	Illinois	7
Ohio	3	Michigan	13

Season Summary

Games Won, 6; Lost 3

November 19, 1949

Ann Arbor, Michigan

Hague's Second Try For Point Writes Rose Bowl Ticket For Buckeyes

Buckeyes And Wolverines Share Big Nine Title

Everything was roses in Ohio—the Pasadena Rose Bowl variety—because the Buckeyes of Wes Fesler came from behind in the second half to tie the Michigan Wolverines, 7 to 7, before 97,239, thus earning a share of the Western Conference title with Michigan, but more important, winning the right to compete in the Rose Bowl, January 2. Virtually kicked out of the Bowl picture in midseason when they lost to Minnesota, 27 to 0, and underdogs by a touchdown in this Michigan game, the Buckeyes proved to this packed stadium that they deserve all the plaudits that go to a real champion because they came from behind when the chips were down.

In the first half, the Buckeyes, who had been slow starters all season, looked as if they would be lucky to hold the score down. The famed Michigan line outcharged the Buckeyes from the start, and the blocking received by Ohio State backs was nothing to talk about. The boy who sparked the Buckeyes in the second half was Jerry Krall, who, playing with a leg injury, was the first to prove that yardage could be made through the Michigan line, and the rest of the Buckeyes followed to push over their tally.

The Wolverines, best of the Big Nine schools to turn a break into a touchdown, got the break early in the opening quarter. Fred Morrision, the Buckeye punter, fumbled the pass from center and then was run out of bounds on his 45 on fourth down to set up Michigan's touchdown march. Chuck Ortmann tossed a pass to Barry Allis for nine yeards and then ran to the 34 for a first down. Ortmann and Don Dufek then worked the ball to the 11, from where Walt Teninga caught Leo Koceski in the end zone with a jump pass. Allis converted and the Wolverines lead 7 to 0. After several other scoring chances fizzled for Michigan and Ohio State completely incompacitated, the first half ended 7 to 0.

The Buckeyes started the second half as if the first was all a mistake. With Krall, Janowicz, Armstrong, and Hamilton hauling the pigskin, the Buckeyes marched to the Michigan 14, but a pass interception by Michigan's Lentz halted that drive. After an exchange of punts, Michigan appeared on its way to sew up the game in the third quarter. Staring from their own 33, the Wolverines worked the ball to the OSU 16 with an Ortmann to Wisniewski pass climaxing the drive. Then after Koceski picked up four, the attack bogged down and Ohio State took over.

The drive that led to Ohio State's tying touchdown started on the Buckeye 20 with nine minutes to play after the Bucks took a Michigan punt. Morrison ran to the 35 for a first down, and Krall followed with a drive to the 47. A Savic to Hamilton pass took the ball to the 4, from where Morrision went over in two plunges. It was up to Jim Hague's toe to tie the score and keep alive the Buckeye Rose Bowl hopes. His first kick went right of the uprights, but Michigan was offside. Hague made it on his second attempt.

STATISTICS

	OSU	UM
First Downs	14	10
Yards Rushing	147	187
Yards Passing	84	101
Passes Attempted	21	33
Passes Completed	5	9
Passes Intercepted by	1	2
Punting Average	33.1	40.1
Fumbles Lost	1	2
Yards Penalized	15	26

OSU	0	0	0	7	7
UM	7	0	0	0	7

1949

Ohio State Scoring: Touchdown—Morrison.
Conversion—Hague

Michigan Scoring: Touchdown—Koceski. Conversion—Allis.

1949			
Ohio	35	Missouri	34
Ohio	46	Indiana	7
Ohio	13	USC	13
Ohio	0	Minnesota	27
Ohio	21	Wisconsin	0
Ohio	24	Northwestern	7
Ohio	14	Pittsburgh	10
Ohio	30	Illinois	17
Ohio	7	Michigan	7

Season Summary

Games Won, 6; Lost, 1; Tied 2

OHIO

No.	Name	Pos.	Wt.	Hgt.	Class	Age	Home Town
10	Hamilton, Ray	RH	175	5-11	So.	19	Canton
11	Sturtz, Karl	RH	178	6-0	Jr.	21	Coshocton
12	*Clark, James	LH	180	6-0	Sr.	24	Columbus
14	Doyle, Richard	LH	183	6-0	So.	19	Rochester, P
15	Chiappini, Al	LH	167	5-9	So.	21	Jeanette, PA
16	Klevay, Walter	RH	164	5-10	So.	19	Independenc
21	Petersen, Bill	QB	182	6-0	So.	18	Cleveland
23	Arledge, Richard	QB	183	6-0	So.	19	Chillicothe
24	Ellwood, R.	QB	189	5-10	Jr.	20	Dover
25	*Savic, Pandel	QB	194	6-0	Sr.	24	Girard
26	*Wertz, George	QB	174	5-8	Sr.	22	Piqua
28	*Widdoes, R.	QB	174	5-8	Jr.	20	Columbus
30	Wagner, Jack	FB	183	6-1	So.	19	Piqua
31	Janowicz, Victor	FB	185	5-9	So.	19	Elyria
32	*Gandee, Charles	FB	204	5-10	Jr.	22	Berea
33	*Morrison, Fred	FB	214	6-2	Sr.	23	Columbus
36	*Perini, Pete	FB	222	6-0	Sr.	21	New Village,
41	*Newell, William	RH	173	5-11	Sr.	21	Columbiana
42	*Swinehart, Rod	LH	178	5-10	Sr.	23	Wooster
44	*Krall, Gerald	LH	177	5-10	Sr.	22	Toledo
46	Blubaugh, Park	RH	192	6-1	So.	20	Lima
47	Palmer, James	LE	185	6-1	Sr.	25	Springfield
48	Henry, Joseph	RH	186	5-11	Sr.	24	Columbus
52	McCullough, B.	C	188	6-1	Jr.	20	Uhrichsville
53	*Lininger, Jack	C	211	5-11	Sr.	22	Van Wert
54	Heid, Robert	C	181	6-0	So.	19	Fremont
55	Rath, Thomas	C	197	5-10	So.	20	Defiance
57	Marold, John	C	197	5-10	So.	19	Hempstead,
60	*Toneff, George	LG	187	5-8	Sr.	22	Barberton
62	*Mantz, Jerry	LG	215	5-10	Jr.	20	Toledo
63	Endres, George	RG	189	5-10	Jr.	20	Cincinnati
64	*Mattey, George	LG	223	5-10	Sr.	22	Cleveland
65	Smith, Carroll	RG	187	5-11	So.	19	Sebring
66	Biltz, John	RG	208	6-1	Jr.	22	Bedford
67	Wittman, Julius	LT	211	6-1	So.	19	Massillon
68	Faehl, Paul	LG	210	5-11	So.	22	Piqua
69	Thomas, James	RG	206	5-7	Jr.	25	Bellaire
70	*Miller, William	LT	230	6-4	Jr.	22	Fremont
71	*Jennings, Jack	LT	240	6-3	Sr.	22	Columbus
72	Campanella, Joe	RT	226	6-2	So.	19	Cleveland
73	Momsen, Robert	LT	220	6-3	Jr.	20	Toledo
74	*O'Hanlon, R.	LT	215	6-2	Sr.	21	East Liverpo
75	Edwards, Bill	RT	219	6-4	Sr.	23	Willoughby
76	*Trautwein, Bill	RT	237	6-4	Jr.	23	Athens
77	Endres, Robert	LT	202	6-1	So.	18	Cincinnati
78	*Dawson, Jack	RT	232	6-2	Sr.	21	Toledo
79	*Wilson, Jack (C)	RT	214	6-4	Sr.	24	Xenia
80	*Hague, James	RE	200	6-1	Sr.	21	Rocky River
81	Armstrong, R.	LE	187	6-4	So.	19	Cleveland
82	Anderson, R.	RE	184	6-1	So.	19	Portsmouth
83	Behrens, L.	RE	172	6-4	So.	19	Middleton
85	King, Dale	LE	201	6-0	Jr.	20	Columbus
86	Ruzich, Steve	LG	205	6-2	So.	21	Madison
87	Basinger, Ed	RE	184	6-1	Jr.	20	Lima
88	*Watson, Thomas	RE	201	6-2	Jr.	22	Urbana
89	*Gilbert, Charles	LE	194	6-0	Sr.	22	Columbus
90	Logan, Richard	RT	208	6-1	So.	19	Mansfield
91	Bell, Robert	LE	184	6-1	So.	19	Worthingtor
92	Bilkie, Edward	RE	175	6-0	Jr.	21	Detroit

* indicates letters won

MICHIGAN

No.	Name	Pos.	Wt.	Hgt.	Class	Age	Home Town
1	*Wistert, Alvin (C)	T	223	6-3	Sr.	33	Northville
5	Wilcox, John	HB	160	5-8	Sr.	21	Detroit
6	*Van Summern, R.	HB	187	5-11	Sr.	22	Kenmore, NY
7	Ryan, Prentice	HB	164	5-8	Sr.	22	Detroit
8	*Koceski, Leo R.	HB	165	5-10	Jr.	20	Cannonsburg, PA
9	Peterson, Donald	HB	175	5-10	So.	20	Racine, WI
3	*Ghindia, John V.	QB	180	5-10	Sr.	24	Ecorse
4	Putich, William	QB	165	5-9	So.	18	Cleveland, OH
5	Burns, Jerry	HB	155	5-8	Sr.	20	Ann Arbor
6	*Bartlett, William	QB	180	5-9	Sr.	22	Muskegon
8	Palmer, Peter	QB	190	5-11	Jr.	19	Indianapolis, IN
0	*Dufek, Donald	FB	185	5-11	Jr.	20	Evanston, IL
2	Straffon, Ralph	FB	188	5-8	Jr.	22	Croswell
3	*Peterson, Thomas	FB	185	5-9	Sr.	23	Racine, WI
6	Jackson, Norman	FB	185	6-0	Sr.	21	Canton, OH
8	*Kempthorn, R.	FB	195	6-0	Sr.	21	Canton, OH
9	Contino, Amato	FB	190	5-9	So.	20	Port Washington, NY
0	*Lentz, Charles W.	HB	165	5-10	Sr.	20	Toledo, OH
1	Osterman, Russell	HB	170	5-11	Jr.	21	Baraga
2	*Teninga, Walter H.	HB	180	5-10	Sr.	22	Chicago, IL
6	Ely, Roger	QB	175	5-11	So.	18	Montpelier, OH
8	Eldridge, James E.	HB	175	5-10	So.	18	Monroe
9	*Ortmann, Charles	HB	190	6-1	Jr.	20	Milwaukee, WI
0	Robinson, Otho	G	220	5-9	Jr.	23	Covington, KY
1	Beel, Joseph G.	G	190	5-8	So.	18	Detroit
2	Flynn, Leo M.	T	188	6-2	Jr.	21	Chicago, IL
3	*Erben, Robert F.	C	190	5-11	Sr.	22	Akron
4	Smale, Harry	C	195	6-0	Jr.	20	Chicago, IL
5	*Farrer, Richard D.	C	195	6-0	Jr.	21	Trenton
6	Kreager, Carl A.	C	220	6-4	Jr.	20	Detroit
7	Sauls, Reginald	C	184	5-10	Jr.	22	Detroit
8	Padjen, John	G	180	5-9	Jr.	22	Lansing
9	*Momsen, Anton	C	205	6-2	Jr.	21	Toledo, OH
0	Powers, John E.	G	176	5-10	Jr.	21	Tulsa, OK
1	*Heneveld, Lloyd A.	G	190	6-0	Sr.	25	Holland
2	Smith, Gilbert	G	180	5-11	So.	19	Ann Arbor
3	Fitch, Alan	G	185	5-10	Jr.	20	Kensington, MD
4	*Jackson, Allen M.	G	185	6-0	Jr.	21	Detroit
5	Stapp, William	G	178	5-9	Jr.	21	Sausalito, CA
6	Wolter, James	G	190	6-0	So.	22	Ypsilanti
7	*McClelland, Don	G	190	6-0	Sr.	21	Calumet
8	Kinyon, Peter	G	190	5-11	So.	19	Ann Arbor
9	McWilliams, R.	T	248	6-3	Jr.	21	Cleveland, OH
0	Dunne, Arthur L.	T	211	6-4	So.	19	Winnetka, IL
1	Tandjourian, R.	T	180	6-0	Jr.	21	Detroit
2	*Wahl, Robert A.	T	212	6-2	Jr.	21	Oak Park, IL
3	*Atchison, James L.	T	195	6-1	Sr.	22	Cleveland, OH
5	Stribe, Ralph	T	198	6-0	So.	20	Detroit
6	Johnson, Thomas	T	225	6-2	So.	18	Muskegon Hts.
7	*Ohlenroth, William	T	205	6-1	Jr.	20	Chicago, IL
8	*Hinton, Gene	T	225	6-2	So.	21	Drumright, OK
9	Hess, John H.	T	195	6-2	Jr.	20	Grand Rapids
0	Sutherland, G.	E	185	6-0	Jr.	21	Montclair, NJ
1	Dingman, Robert	E	185	6-1	So.	18	Saginaw
2	*Hollway, Robert C.	E	200	6-3	Sr.	21	Ann Arbor
3	Popp, Leslie	E	180	6-1	Jr.	20	Fort Wayne, IN
4	*Wisniewski, Irvin	E	195	6-3	Sr.	23	Lambertville
5	Kelsey, Thomas	E	190	6-2	So.	21	Lakewood, OH
6	*Clark, Oswald V.	E	200	6-1	Sr.	23	Montclair, NJ
7	Skala, James	E	190	6-2	So.	18	Chicago, IL
8	*Allis, Harry D.	E	190	6-0	Jr.	21	Flint
9	Pickard, Fred	E	185	6-0	So.	20	Grand Rapids
1	Ray, David	E	178	5-11	So.	18	El Paso, TX
6	Cerecke, Charles	G	190	5-11	Jr.	19	St. Joseph

indicates letters won

1949

Michigan	7	MSU	3
Michigan	27	Stanford	7
Michigan	7	Army	21
Michigan	20	Northwestern	21
Michigan	14	Minnesota	7
Michigan	13	Illinois	0
Michigan	20	Purdue	12
Michigan	20	Indiana	7
Michigan	7	Ohio State	7

Season Summary

Games Won, 6; Lost, 2; Tied, 1

ALVIN WISTERT
All-American Tackle

ALLEN WAHL
All-American Tackle

November 25, 1950

Columbus, Ohio

Michigan Upsets Ohio State, Captures Big 10 Championship, And Rose Bowl Berth

Tony Momsen Blocks Kick, Covers Ball For Deciding TD In Blizzard

Tony Momsen, Michigan's great linebacker from Toledo, made all this possible by blocking a Vic Janowicz punt in the second quarter and falling on the ball in the end zone for a touchdown before 50,503 pneumonia-defying spectators, each of whom became an individual snowman before the game was five minutes along.

This game, played in a swirling snowstorm, driven by a 27 miles-an-hour wind in 10 degree temperature, was amazing in many ways—most amazing being that it was played at all. With the playing field ideal for a ski meet, Ohio State's famed Janowicz could not even skid for yardage and Michigan's running and passing games were complete flops. The Wolverines failed to make a first down and did not complete a pass in nine attempts. They gained only 27 yards net for the entire game, but despite all this, they are the champions again.

Coaches Oosterbaan of Michigan and Fesler of Ohio State thought that officials of both schools were on the wacky side for not postponing the game. But the Wolverines, who came into the game seven point underdogs and in third place, grabbed their fourth championship in as many years.

All the scoring in the snow-blanketed stadium came as a result of blocked punts, and the lines had ample chances to do blocking, what with the Wolverines booting 24 times and the Buckeyes 21. Ohio State was first to get the breaks and it was another Toledo boy, Bob Momsen, brother of Michigan's Tony, broke through and blocked Chuck Ortmann's punt and fell on it on Michigan's eight yard line. The Wolverine forward wall stiffened and after three running plays, the Buckeyes were back on the 21. Janowicz was called on to try for a field goal with the ball placed on the 31, a tremendous task when you consider that he was kicking the ball into a snow-howling wind. But he kicked it through, the ball travelling 41 yards in all, with something to spare. Ortmann, who had a knack of kicking out of bounds inside the Ohio's 15 a good part of the afternoon, booted the ball on the Buckeye three late in the opening quarter. Janowicz tried to kick out on first down, but Tom Johnson, Michigan's junior tackle from Muskegon Heights, broke through to block it, the ball bounding out of the playing field for an automatic safety. Just before the half Ortmann punted from the OSU 40 into the wind and the ball ended up on OSU 10 yard line. Two running plays kicked up nothing and Janowicz went back to punt on third down with only 20 seconds left in the half. Tony Momsen broke through and the ball bounced off his chest and into the end zone. The big Michigan linebacker made one lunge for the ball and missed, but he reached out while lying on the ground and finally grabbed it for a touchdown.

That was the ball game. The second half was a virtual repetition of the first with running and passing playing second fiddle to punting as both elevens laid back and waited for a break. But the breaks had all come in the first half and the only thing there was more of was snow.

STATISTICS

	UM	OSU
First Downs	0	3
Rushing Yardage	27	16
Passing Yardage	0	25
Passes Attempted	9	18
Passes Completed	0	3
Passes Inter. by	2	0
Punts	24	21
Punting Average	30	32
Fumbles Lost	0	1
Yards Penalized	25	30

UM	2	7	0	0	9
OSU	3	0	0	0	3

1950

1950

Michigan	7	MSU	14
Michigan	27	Dartmouth	7
Michigan	6	Army	27
Michigan	26	Wisconsin	13
Michigan	7	Minnesota	7
Michigan	0	Illinois	7
Michigan	20	Indiana	7
Michigan	34	Northwestern	23
Michigan	9	Ohio State	3

Season Summary

Games Won, 5; Lost, 3; Tied, 1

ALLEN WAHL
All-American Tackle

MICHIGAN

No.	Name	Pos.	Wt.	Hgt.	Class	Age
14	Oldham	B	166	5-8	'53	18
15	Howell	B	160	5-8	'53	18
16	Witherspoon	B	178	5-11	'53	18
18	Koceski	B	165	5-10	'51	21
23	Scarr	B	180	6-2	'53	18
24	Putich	B	165	5-9	'52	19
25	Burns	B	155	5-8	'51	22
26	Billings	B	180	5-11	'53	18
27	Topor	B	215	6-0	'53	19
28	Palmer	B	190	5-11	'51	20
30	Dufek	B	185	5-11	'51	21
32	Straffon	B	188	5-8	'51	23
33	Hurley	B	183	5-10	'53	18
35	Rescorla	B	180	6-0	'53	19
36	Jackson, N.	B	185	6-0	'51	22
37	Tinkham	B	170	5-10	'53	18
39	LeClaire	B	190	6-0	'53	19
40	Nulf	B	174	5-9	'53	18
44	Hill	B	172	6-0	'53	18
46	Peterson	B	175	5-10	'52	21
48	Eldridge	B	175	5-10	'52	19
49	Ortmann	B	190	6-1	'51	21
52	Dingman	E	185	6-1	'52	19
53	Melchiori	C	182	6-0	'53	19
54	Smale	G	195	6-0	'51	21
55	Farrer	C	195	6-0	'51	22
56	Kreager	C	220	6-4	'51	21
58	Padjen	C	180	5-9	'51	23
59	Momsen	C	207	6-2	'51	22
60	Powers	G	175	5-11	'51	22
62	Strozewski	T	200	6-0	'53	19
63	Smith	G	190	5-11	'52	19
64	Jackson, A.	G	185	6-0	'51	22
65	Kelsey	G	190	6-2	'52	22
66	Wolter	G	190	6-0	'52	23
67	Timm	C	185	5-11	'53	18
68	Kinyon	G	190	5-11	'52	19
69	McWilliams	G	248	6-3	'51	22
70	Zatkoff	B	208	6-2	'53	18
71	Tandourjian	T	180	6-0	'51	22
72	Wahl	T	217	6-3	'51	22
73	Bartholomew	T	198	6-3	'53	18
75	Stribe	G	198	6-0	'52	21
76	Johnson	T	225	6-2	'52	19
77	Ohlenroth	T	205	6-1	'51	21
78	Hinton	T	225	6-2	'52	22
79	Hess	T	195	6-2	'51	20
80	Osterman	B	170	5-11	'51	22
81	Aartila	E	175	6-0	'53	18
82	Reeme	E	195	6-2	'53	21
83	Popp	E	180	6-1	'51	21
84	Green	E	175	6-0	'53	18
85	Perry	E	178	6-0	'53	17
86	Clark	E	200	6-1	'51	24
87	Skala	E	190	6-2	'52	19
88	Allis	E	190	6-0	'51	22
89	Pickard	E	180	5-11	'52	22
91	Ray	E	178	5-11	'52	19

OHIO

No.	Name	Pos.	Wt.	Hgt.	Class	Age
10	Hamilton	B	177	6-0	'52	20
11	Sturtz	B	182	5-10	'51	22
12	Bruney	B	159	5-11	'53	18
14	Doyle	B	188	6-0	'52	20
16	Klevay	B	168	5-10	'52	20
23	Arledge	B	183	6-0	'52	20
24	Ellwood	B	189	5-10	'51	21
25	Curcillo	B	188	6-1	'53	19
28	Widdoes	B	174	5-8	'51	21
30	Wagner	B	198	6-1	'52	20
31	Janowicz	B	182	5-9	'52	20
32	C. Gandee	B	210	5-10	'51	23
33	Koepnick	B	183	6-0	'53	19
34	Moritz	B	198	6-1	'53	19
36	Hlay	B	212	6-1	'53	20
42	Gentile	B	182	5-10	'53	21
43	Gambill	B	177	5-11	'53	19
44	Skvarka	B	182	5-9	'53	20
47	Demmel	B	180	5-11	'51	24
48	Beekley	B	181	5-9	'53	19
52	McCullough	C	193	6-1	'51	21
54	Heid	C	194	6-0	'52	20
55	Rath	C	212	5-10	'52	21
56	Geib	C	178	5-11	'53	20
57	Marold	C	205	6-0	'52	21
58	Wolter	G	187	5-11	'53	19
59	Ternent	G	195	6-0	'53	18
60	Ruzich	G	209	6-2	'52	22
61	Fischer	G	198	5-11	'53	20
62	Manz	G	225	5-10	'52	21
63	G. Endres	G	189	5-10	'51	21
64	Ronemus	G	185	5-9	'52	19
65	Smith	G	185	5-11	'52	21
66	Biltz	G	208	6-0	'51	23
67	Wittman	T	223	6-1	'52	20
68	Faehl	G	227	5-11	'52	22
69	Savic	G	186	5-10	'53	19
0	Miller	T	242	6-4	'51	23
1	Logan	T	223	6-1	'52	20
2	Campanella	T	226	6-2	'52	20
3	Momsen	T	218	6-3	'51	21
4	Guthrie	T	207	6-0	'53	18
5	Hietikko	T	220	6-3	'53	19
6	Trautwein	T	237	6-4	'51	24
7	R. Endres	T	200	6-1	'52	20
9	Vavroch	T	210	6-1	'53	19
0	Grimes	E	194	6-1	'53	19
1	Armstrong	E	196	6-4	'52	20
2	Anderson	E	185	6-1	'52	20
4	S. Gandee	E	191	6-0	'52	21
5	Moshier	E	196	6-2	'53	19
6	Hinebaugh	E	178	6-3	'53	19
7	Basinger	E	184	6-1	'52	21
	Watson	E	212	6-2	'51	23
9	Walther	E	187	5-10	'53	21
0	Thomas	E	183	6-1	'53	19
	Manyak	E	188	6-0	'53	20
2	Bilkie	E	187	6-1	'51	22

1950

Ohio	27	S. Methodist	32
Ohio	41	Pittsburgh	7
Ohio	26	Indiana	14
Ohio	48	Minnesota	0
Ohio	83	Iowa	21
Ohio	32	Northwestern	0
Ohio	19	Wisconsin	14
Ohio	7	Illinois	14
Ohio	3	Michigan	9

Season Summary

Games Won, 6; Lost, 3

ROBERT MOMSEN
All-American Guard

ROBERT McCULLOUGH
All-American Center

VICTOR JANOWICZ
All-American Back

BILL PUTICH
Michigan Captain

Team send-off for Rose Bowl Game, in front of the Michigan Union.

November 24, 1951

Ann Arbor, Michigan

Michigan Upsets Bucks

Wolverines Win 7-0; Janowicz Is Stopped

W. W. HAYES
Ohio State Head Coach
1951-1978

The Wolverines snatched a 7-0 victory over the Buckeyes before 95,000 fans in a game in which Ohio State was favored to take its first triumph in Ann Arbor since 1937. There have been bitter defeats in the past, many by lopsided scores, but this, the 48th meeting of the arch-rivals, was one of the most unexpected in the long series. The Wolverines not only upset the dope, which favored the invaders by from one to two touchdowns, but they also stopped cold the great Vic Janowicz, upon whom the Buckeyes were counting most as he rounded out his college career. It was an alert Michigan eleven, which capitalized on pass interceptions and Ohio State fumbles, that thwarted any offensive ambitions the Buckeyes might have had.

Michigan's winning touchdown came with only three minutes and ten seconds left in the second quarter. The drive was set up when Janowicz punted short to his own 49. After Wes Bradford, the Troy, Ohio, scatback, picked up two off tackle, Bill Putich hit Ted Topor with a pass good for a first down on the 34. Witherspoon and Peterson contributed additional yardage to the drive. Putich found Don Zanfagna with a pass on the six yard line where he fumbled, but the officials ruled the ball was blown dead before the fumble. The Buckeyes protested what they believed was a fast whistle both on the field and in the dressing room after the game, but to no avail. Then Peterson, the best rusher of the day with 70 yards in 19 attempts, swept his past the Buckeyes around left end for the touchdown. Russ Rescoria converted to make it 7-0.

The Wolverines were able to upset the Buckeyes because they bottled up Janowicz all afternoon. Vic, playing his last game for Ohio State, gained only 53 yards rushing in 14 carries and completed two of three passes for 22 yards. Janowicz' poorest showing came in the kicking department. He booted nine times for a 27 yard average, far below his average of 42 over the season.

STATISTICS

	UM	OSU
First Downs	14	14
Rushing Yardage	135	120
Passing Yardage	80	102
Passes Attempted	29	26
Passes Completed	12	9
Passes Intercepted	4	2
Punts	10	9
Punting Average	32	27
Fumbles Lost	2	4
Yards Penalized	55	15

UM	0	7	0	0	7
OSU	0	0	0	0	0

Michigan Scoring - Touchdown, Peterson. Conversion, Rescoria.

1951

1951

Ohio	7	S. Methodist	0
Ohio	20	Michigan State	24
Ohio	6	Wisconsin	6
Ohio	10	Indiana	32
Ohio	47	Iowa	21
Ohio	3	Northwestern	0
Ohio	16	Pittsburgh	14
Ohio	0	Illinois	0
Ohio	0	Michigan	7

Season Summary

Games won, 4; Lost, 3; Tied, 2

38 year old Hayes replaces Coach Wes Fesler.

Hayes with his son, Steve, and his wife, Anne.

OHIO

No.	Name	Pos.	Wt.	Hgt.	Class	Home Town
10	*Hamilton, Ray	RE	178	5-11	52	Canton
11	Ernst, Richard	RH	169	5-9	54	Cincinnati
12	*Bruney, Fred	LH	166	5-11	53	Martins Ferry
16	*Klevay, Walter	RH	168	5-9	52	Independence
19	Howell, Carroll	RH	167	5-9	55	Portsmouth
20	Borton, John	LH	195	6-1	55	Alliance
22	Leggett, David	QB	190	6-0	55	New Philadelphia
23	Arledge, Richard	QB	194	6-0	52	Chilicothe
24	Hague, Tom	QB	191	6-0	54	Rocky River
25	*Curcillo, Tony	QB	188	6-1	53	Elyria
28	Wilks, William	QB	182	6-2	53	Hamilton
30	*Wagner, Jack	FB	189	6-1	52	Piqua
31	*Janowicz, Victor	LH	181	5-9	52	Elyria
32	Bechtel, Earl	FB	194	6-2	54	Fredericktown
33	*Koepnick, Robert	FB	193	6-0	53	Dayton
34	Moritz, Roger	FB	200	6-1	53	Columbus
36	*Hlay, John	FB	212	6-1	53	Niles
40	Hoffman, James	FB	184	6-0	55	Marysville
42	Goodsell, Doug	LH	184	6-2	55	Columbus
43	Gambill, David	RH	177	5-11	53	Portsmouth
44	*Skvarka, Bernie	LH	180	5-9	53	Struthers
45	Watkins, Robert	FB	182	5-10	55	New Bedford, MA
47	Rosso, George	RH	170	5-10	54	Pittsburgh, PA
48	Beekley, Marts	LH	181	5-9	53	Sharonville
51	Krisher, Jerry	C	240	6-0	55	Massillon
52	Andrews, Lawrence	C	185	5-11	53	Toledo
53	Merrell, James	C	212	6-3	54	Geneva
54	*Heid, Robert (Capt.)	C	200	6-0	52	Fremont
55	*Rath, Thomas	C	215	5-10	52	Defiance
60	*Ruzich, Steve	RG	216	6-2	52	Madison
61	*Fischer, Louis	RG	191	5-10	53	Charleston, WV
62	Takacs, Michael	LG	202	6-0	54	Massillon
63	Reichenbach, James	G	210	5-10	55	Massillon
64	*Ronemus, Thor	RG	190	5-9	53	Springfield
65	*Smith, Carroll	LG	187	5-11	52	Sebring
66	Roberts, Robert	LG	188	5-11	54	Zanesville
67	*Wittman, Julius	RT	211	6-1	52	Massillon
69	Leo, Thomas	G	191	5-11	55	Canton
71	*Logan, Richard	RT	226	6-2	52	Mansfield
73	Jacoby, George	LT	212	5-10	54	Toledo
74	Guthrie, George	LT	215	6-1	53	Columbus
75	*Hietikko, James	LT	216	6-3	53	Conneaut
77	Endres, Robert	RT	208	6-1	52	Cincinnati
79	Vavroch, William	RT	210	6-1	53	Cleveland
80	*Grimes, Robert	RE	194	6-1	53	Middletown
81	*Armstrong, Ralph	LE	208	6-4	52	Cleveland
84	*Gandee, Sherwin	LE	204	6-0	52	Akron
85	Joslin, Robert	LE	182	6-0	54	Middletown
89	*Walther, Richard	RE	191	5-10	53	Dayton
90	Thomas, Richard	RE	180	6-1	53	Martins Ferry
91	Manyak, John	LE	188	6-1	53	Warren
94	Shelton, John	RE	178	6-2	55	Ironton
96	Schiller, Richard	LT	260	6-2	55	Bellaire

* indicates letters won

MICHIGAN

No.	Name	Pos.	Wt.	Hgt.	Class	Home Town
14	*Oldham, Donald L.	HB	166	5-9	Jr.	Indianapolis, IN
15	*Howell, Frank	HB	160	5-8	Jr.	Muskegon Hts.
16	*Witherspoon, T. W.	HB	177	5-11	Jr.	Detroit
18	Hickey, Ed	RH	160	5-8	Fr.	Anaconda, MT
19	*Bradford, Wesley E.	HB	155	5-6	Jr.	Troy, OH
23	McDonald, Duncan	QB	175	6-0	Fr.	Flint
24	*Putich, William (Capt.)	QB-HB	170	5-9	Sr.	Cleveland, OH
26	Billings, William E.	QB	180	5-11	Jr.	Flint
27	Topor, Ted	B	215	6-1	Jr.	E. Chicago, IN
28	Zanfagna, Don	QB	175	5-10	So.	Providence, RI
33	Hurley, Robert	FB	185	5-10	Jr.	Alamosa, CO
35	Rescorla, Russell G.	FB	180	6-0	Jr.	Grand Haven
37	*Tinkham, David J.	HB	170	5-10	Jr.	E. Grand Rapids
38	Balzhiser, Richard E.	FB	185	6-1	So.	Wheaton, IL
39	*LeClaire, Laurence E.	FB	190	6-0	Jr.	Anaconda, MT
41	Eaddy, Don	LH	165	5-11	Fr.	Grand Rapids
44	Kress, Ted	HB	175	5-11	So.	Detroit
46	*Peterson, Donald W.	HB	175	5-11	Sr.	Racine, WI
49	Evans, Don	LH	187	5-11	Fr.	Chagrin Falls, OH
51	Popp, Leslie	E	188	5-11	Sr.	Fort Wayne, IN
53	O'Shaughnessy, R. E.	C	190	5-11	So.	Seaford, NY
54	Melchiori,Wayne F.	C	185	6-0	Jr.	Stambaugh
55	Morlock, Emil	C	200	6-1	Jr.	Grand Rapids
56	Drake, Donald	T	225	5-10	Fr.	Ypsilanti
57	Ludwig, Dean	C	190	6-2	Fr.	Marion, OH
59	Bowers, Glenn	C	238	6-2	Fr.	Mesa, AZ
60	Wagner, Jim	G	198	5-11	Fr.	Flint
61	Dugger, Donald R.	G	180	5-10	Jr.	Charleston, WV
63	Matheson, Robert	G	188	5-10	Jr.	Detroit
64	Beison, Richard A.	G	200	6-0	So.	Each Chicago, IN
65	*Kelsey, Ray Thomas	G	195	6-2	Sr.	Lakewood, OH
66	Wolter, James	G	190	6-0	Sr.	Ypsilanti
67	*Timm, Robert F.	G	185	5-11	Jr.	Toledo, OH
68	*Kinyon, Peter C.	G	190	5-11	Sr.	Ann Arbor
69	Williams, Ronald M.	G	183	5-9	So.	Massilon, OH
70	*Zatkoff, Roger	C-T	210	6-2	Jr.	Hamtramck
71	Geyer, Ronald	G	225	6-2	Fr.	Toledo, OH
72	Balog, James T.	T	210	6-3	So.	Wheaton, IL
73	Bartholomew, B. A.	T	200	6-3	Jr.	Detroit
75	*Stribe, Ralph C., Jr.	T	200	6-1	Jr.	Detroit
76	*Johnson, Thomas	T	227	6-2	Sr.	Muskegon Hts.
77	Walker, Art	E	198	5-11	Fr.	South Haven
78	Pederson, B. L.	T	215	6-2	Jr.	Marquette
79	Bennett, Donald C.	T	195	6-2	So.	Chicago, IL
80	*Osterman, Russell	E	170	5-11	Sr.	Baraga
81	*Topp, E. Robert	E	185	6-2	So.	Kalamazoo
82	Dingman, Robert W.	E	180	6-0	Sr.	Saginaw
83	Stanford, Tad C.	E	170	6-0	So.	Midland
84	*Green, Merritt II	E	180	6-0	Jr.	Toledo, OH
85	*Perry, Lowell W.	E	178	6-0	Jr.	Ypsilanti
86	Knutson, Eugene P.	E	210	6-4	So.	Beloit, WI
87	Schlicht, Leo	FB	210	6-4	Fr.	Madison, WI
88	Vaselenak, John	E	190	6-2	Fr.	Flint
89	*Pickard, Frederick R.	E	190	6-2	Sr.	Grand Rapids
90	Dutter, George	E	190	6-2	So.	Fort Wayne, IN
91	Ray, Dave	E	180	5-11		El Paso, TX

* indicates letters won

1951

Michigan	0	Michigan State	25
Michigan	13	Stanford	23
Michigan	33	Indiana	14
Michigan	21	Iowa	0
Michigan	54	Minnesota	27
Michigan	0	Illinois	7
Michigan	7	Cornell	20
Michigan	0	Northwestern	6
Michigan	7	Ohio State	0

Season Summary

Games won, 4; Lost, 5; Tied, 0

LOWELL PERRY
All-American End

November 22, 1952

Columbus, Ohio

Ohio State Beats Michigan

Borton-Joslin Combination and Alert Defense Breaks Eight-Year Jinx For Buckeye Eleven

A 27 to 7 triumph scored by the Buckeyes before a jammed stadium of 81,541, kicked Michigan out of the Big Ten title and a trip to the Rose Bowl. It was the passing of John Borton, the catching of Bob Joslin and Bob Grimes, plus the alertness in the secondary by Fred Bruney, who intercepted three Wolverine aerials, which broke the jinx that Ohio State followers throught would never end.

The Wolverine offensive machine was turned aside in the first quarter on two interceptions by Bruney and a fumble recovery by the Buckeyes. Another interception by Bruney and another costly fumble halted Michigan drives in the second quarter. Two more fumbles thwarted the Wolverines in the third, while a pass interception in the fourth by Toledo's George Jacoby spoiled another Michigan march and set up Ohio State's final touchdown.

Meanwhile the Buckeyes, underdogs by seven points, punched over two touchdowns in the second quarter, the first on an eight yard pass from Borton to Joslin and the second on a twenty-eight pass by the same combination. They added another in the third on Borton's three yard quarterback sneak and drilled in another in the fourth on a nineteen yard heave from Borton to Grimes.

Michigan's one touchdown came with less than five minutes to play with an Ohio State holding penalty moving the ball to the six to set up the score. Frank Howell went the last two yards on a sweep of his own left end.

That was the game, and that was enough to start off a wild demonstration in Columbus which began with the Buckeyes tearing down the goalposts and singing the praises of Coach Woody Hayes, who was on the hook a few weeks earlier following losses to Iowa and Pittsburgh.

STATISTICS

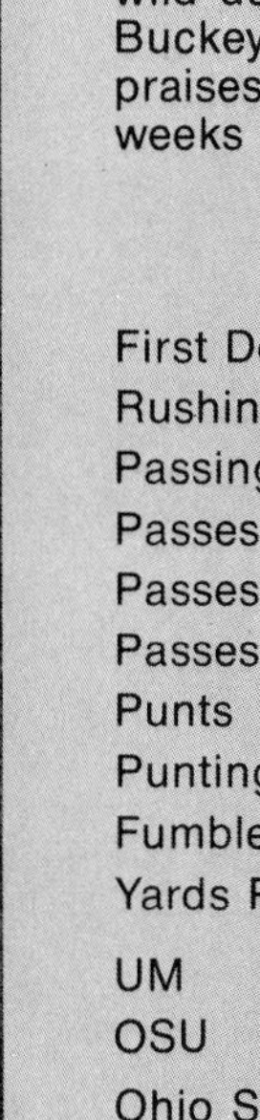

	UM	OSU
First Downs	14	12
Rushing Yardage	188	120
Passing Yardage	134	151
Passes Attempted	19	18
Passes Completed	8	11
Passes Intercepted	0	5
Punts	5	9
Punting Average	39	34
Fumbles Lost	4	2
Yards Penalized	51	65

UM	0	0	0	7	7
OSU	0	14	7	6	27

Ohio Scoring – Touchdowns, Joslin 2, Borton, Grimes. Conversions, Weed 3.

Michigan Scoring – Touchdown, Howell. Conversion, Resocria.

1952			
Michigan	13	Michigan State	27
Michigan	7	Stanford	14
Michigan	28	Indiana	13
Michigan	48	Northwestern	14
Michigan	21	Minnesota	0
Michigan	13	Illinois	22
Michigan	49	Cornell	7
Michigan	21	Purdue	10
Michigan	7	Ohio State	27

Season Summary

Games won, 5; Lost, 4; Tied, 0

MICHIGAN

No.	Name	Pos.	Wt.	Hgt.	Class	Home Town
14	*Oldham, Donald L.	HB	167	5-9	Sr.	Indianapolis, IN
15	*Howell, Frank	HB	165	5-8	Sr.	Muskegon Hts.
16	*Witherspoon, T. W.	HB	185	5-11	Sr.	Detroit
17	Branoff, Tony	HB	180	5-11	Fr.	Flint
18	Hickey, Edward L.	HB	160	5-8	So.	Anaconda
19	Knickerbocker, S.	HB	165	5-10	So.	Chelsea
23	*McDonald, D. B.	QB	175	6-0	So.	Flint
26	*Billings, Bill E.	QB	180	5-11	Sr.	Flint
27	*Topor, Ted P.	QB	212	6-1	Sr.	East Chicago, IN
28	*ZanFagna, Donald M.	QB	180	5-10	Jr.	Providence, RI
30	Baer, Fred N.	FB	180	5-11	So.	LaGrange, IL
32	Gagalis, Peri	FB	190	5-11	So.	Ann Arbor
33	Hurley, Robert	FB	185	5-10	Jr.	Alamosa, CO
35	*Rescorla, Russell G.	FB	180	5-11	Sr.	Grand Haven
37	*Tinkham, David J.	FB	178	5-10	Sr.	E. Grand Rapids
38	Balzhiser, Richard E.	FB	185	6-1	Jr.	Wheaton, IL
39	*LeClaire, Laurence E.	FB	190	6-0	Sr.	Anaconda, MT
42	Kress, E. S. (Ted)	HB	175	5-11	Jr.	Detroit
44	Cline, J. Daniel	HB	168	5-10	So.	Brockport, NY
49	Evans, Donald K.	HB	185	5-11	So.	Chagrin Falls, OH
50	Shomsky, Joseph G.	G	190	5-10	So.	Flint
51	Muellich, George C.	T	185	6-2	So.	Bowling Green, OH
53	*O'Shaughnessy, R. E.	C	190	5-11	Jr.	Seaford, NY
54	Melchiori, Wayne F.	C	185	6-0	Sr.	Stambaugh
55	Wine, Raymond L.	C	195	6-2	Fr.	Port Huron
56	Drake, Donald D.	C	220	5-11	So.	Ypsilanti
58	VanderZeyde, R.	C	190	6-0	Jr.	East Chicago, IN
61	*Dugger, Donald R.	G	178	5-10	Jr.	Charleston, WV
62	*Strozewski, R. J.	T	200	6-0	Sr.	South Bend, IN
63	*Matheson, Robert K.	G	190	5-10	Sr.	Detroit
64	*Beison, Richard A.	G	200	6-0	Jr.	East Chicago, IN
65	Cachey, Theodore J.	G	185	5-11	Jr.	Chicago, IL
66	Chomicz, Casimir A.	G	195	6-1	Fr.	Detroit
67	*Timm, Robert F.	G	185	5-11	Sr.	Toledo, OH
68	Kamhout, C. R., Jr.	T	205	6-2	So.	Grand Haven
69	Williams, Ronald M.	G	185	5-9	Jr.	Massilon, OH
70	*Zatkoff, Roger	T	210	6-2	Sr.	Hamtramck
71	Geyer, H. R.	T	215	6-2	So.	Toledo, OH
72	*Balog, James T.	T	210	6-3	Jr.	Wheaton, IL
73	*Batholomew, B. A.	T	200	6-3	Sr.	Detroit
74	Shields, Kenneth H.	T	215	6-3	Fr.	Detroit
75	*Stribe, Ralph C. Jr.	T	205	6-1	Sr.	Detroit
77	Walker, Arthur D.	T	198	5-11	So.	South Haven
78	*Pederson, B. L.	T	215	6-2	Sr.	Marquette
79	*Bennett, Don	T	195	6-2	Jr.	Chicago, IL
80	Rex, Richard U.	E	185	6-1	Fr.	Pearl Beach
81	Topp, E. Robert	E	190	6-2	Jr.	Kalamazoo
82	*Dingman, Robert W.	E	180	6-0	Sr.	Saginaw
83	*Stanford, Thad C.	E	190	6-2	Jr.	Midland
84	*Green, M., II (Capt.)	E	180	6-0	Sr.	Toledo, OH
85	*Perry, Lowell P.	E	180	6-0	Sr.	Ypsilanti
86	*Knutson, Eugene P.	E	210	6-4	Jr.	Beloit, WI
87	Bowns, Stanley	E	190	6-0	Fr.	Flint
88	Veselenak, John J.	E	190	6-2	So.	Flint
89	Bates, James V.	E	195	6-0	So.	Farmington
90	Dutter, George S.	E	190	6-2	Jr.	Fort Wayne, IN
92	Ritter, Charles A.	T	210	6-0	So.	Cassopolis
93	McIntyre, John	T	190	6-0	Jr.	Monroe
94	Rahrig, Don	G	195	5-11	Jr.	Toledo, OH
96	Pella, G. Roy	T	205	6-2	Sr.	Sudbury, Ont.

* indicates letters won

OHIO

No.	Name	Pos.	Wt.	Hgt.	Class	Home Town
11	Ernst, Richard	RH	168	5-9	Jr.	Cincinnati
12	**Bruney, Fred	LH	172	5-10	Sr.	Martins Ferry
14	*Doyle, Richard	FB	189	6-0	Sr.	Rochester, PA
15	Knecht, Gilbert	LH	180	5-10	So.	Lima
16	Skelly, Jack	RH	170	5-11	So.	Rocky River
17	Bruce, Earle	RH	164	5-8	Jr.	Cumberland, MD
19	Howell, Carroll	LH	167	5-9	So.	Portsmouth
20	*Borton, John	QB	197	6-1	So.	Alliance
21	Petersen, William	QB	200	6-0	Sr.	Cleveland
22	Leggett, David	QB	196	6-0	So.	New Philadelphia
23	Koder, Robert	QB	185	5-10	Jr.	Toledo
24	Weed, Thurlow	QB	128	5-5	So.	Columbus
26	**Curcillo, Tony	RH	192	6-1	Sr.	Elyria
28	*Wilks, Wiliam	QB	182	6-2	Sr.	Hamilton
29	Edwards, Frank	QB	178	6-1	So.	Columbus
30	Ludwig, Paul	FB	212	6-3	Fr.	Marion
32	Bechtel, Earl	FB	192	6-2	Jr.	Fredericktown
33	**Koepnick, Robert	RH	194	6-0	Sr.	Dayton
34	Morse, James	FB	190	6-0	So.	Columbus
36	**Hlay, John	FB	212	6-1	Sr.	Niles
40	Cassady, Howard	LH	168	5-10	Fr.	Columbus
42	*Goodsell, Douglas	FB	192	6-2	So.	Columbus
43	Gambill, David	RH	177	5-9	Sr.	Portsmouth
44	**Skvarka, Bernie	LH	182	5-9	Sr.	Struthers
45	Watkins, Robert	RH	182	5-9	So.	New Bedford, MA
46	Bond, Robert	RH	182	6-1	Fr.	Akron
47	*Rosso, George	RH	174	5-10	Jr.	Pittsburgh, PA
48	*Beekley, Marts	RH	183	5-9	Sr.	Sharonville
50	Ruehl, James	C	210	6-2	So.	Cumberland, MD
51	*Krisher, Jerry	C	227	6-0	So.	Massillon
53	*Merrell, James	C	222	6-3	Jr.	Geneva
55	Thornton, Robert	C	196	6-0	Jr.	Willard
56	Dawdy, Donald	C	200	6-1	Jr.	Cincinnati
58	Mott, William	C	190	6-2	So.	Proctorville
59	Ternent, William	LG	197	6-1	Sr.	Columbus
60	Sidell, Rolo	LG	209	6-0	So.	Oak Harbor
61	**Fischer, Louis	RG	197	5-11	Sr.	Charleston, WV
62	*Takacs, Michael	LG	208	6-0	Jr.	Massillon
63	*Reichenbach, James	RG	203	5-10	So.	Massillon
64	Williams, David	LG	204	5-11	So.	Pittsburgh, PA
65	Hamilton, Walter	RG	192	5-11	So.	Columbus
66	Roberts, Robert	LG	188	5-11	Jr.	Zanesville
68	Riticher, Ray	RG	212	5-10	So.	Toledo
70	Schiller, Richard	RT	228	6-2	So.	Bellaire
71	Myers, Robert	RT	225	6-5	So.	Springfield
72	Schumacher, James	RT	210	6-0	So.	Massillon
73	*Jacoby, George	RT	222	5-11	Jr.	Toledo
74	*Guthrie, George	RT	221	6-1	Sr.	Columbus
75	**Hietikko, James	LT	221	6-3	Sr.	Conneaut
76	Denker, Irv	LT	219	6-1	Jr.	New York, NY
77	Swartz, Donald	LT	230	6-1	So.	Newark
78	Edgington, Harry	LT	209	6-3	Jr.	Toledo
79	Vavroch, William	LT	203	6-1	Sr.	Cleveland
80	**Grimes, Robert	LE	196	6-1	Sr.	Middletown
82	*Anderson, Richard	RE	192	6-1	Sr.	Portsmouth
83	Dugger, Dean	RE	216	6-2	So.	Charleston, WV
84	Croy, Jack	LE	181	6-1	So.	Dayton
85	*Joslin, Robert	RE	187	6-0	Jr.	Middletown
86	Campbell, Jack	RE	185	5-11	So.	New Philadelphia
87	Corbitt, Walter	LE	190	6-1	So.	Portsmouth
88	Hague, Thomas	LE	192	6-0	Jr.	Rocky River
90	*Thomas, Richard	LE	181	6-1	Sr.	Martins Ferry
91	Manyak, John	LE	191	6-1	Sr.	Warren
92	Ashton, William	LE	190	6-1	So.	Piqua
93	Katula, Theodore	RE	182	6-1	Jr.	Campbell

* indicates letters won

1952

Ohio	33	Indiana	13
Ohio	14	Purdue	21
Ohio	23	Wisconsin	14
Ohio	35	Wash. State	7
Ohio	0	Iowa	8
Ohio	24	Northwestern	21
Ohio	14	Pittsburgh	21
Ohio	27	Illinois	7
Ohio	27	Michigan	7

Season Summary

Games won, 6; Lost 3

MIKE TAKACS
All-American Guard

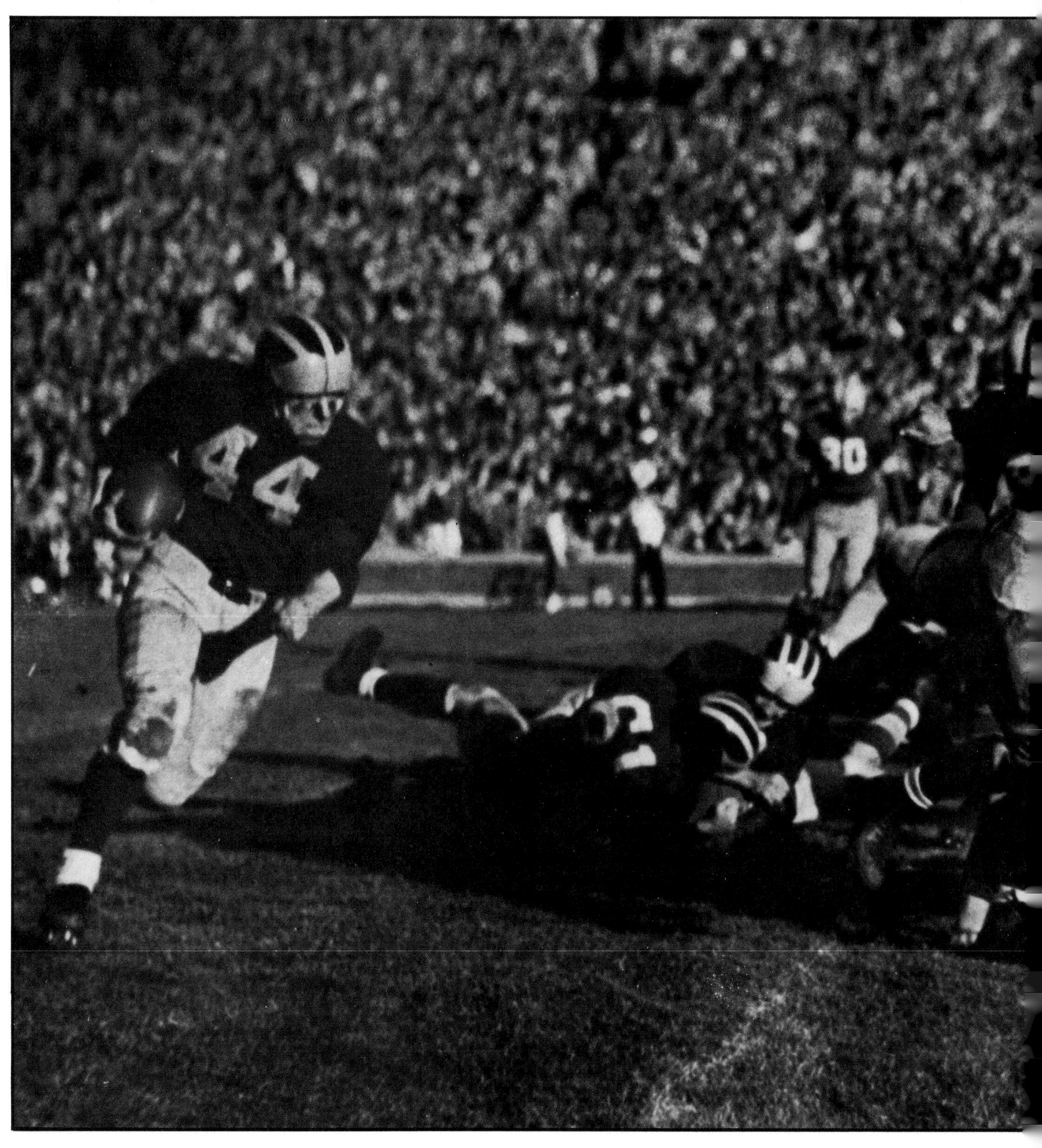

November 21, 1953

Ann Arbor, Michigan

Michigan Crushes Ohio State, 20-0

Wolverines Defeat State At Own Game . . . And Easily

It happened again. The figures favored Ohio State; tradition favored Michigan, and tradition prevailed once more as the Wolverines trounced the Buckeyes 20 to 0 before 90,126 paid customers. It was the day that Ohio State was supposed to break a Michigan Stadium jinx, which has seen the Buckeyes go without victory here since 1937. The running and passing statistics said the Bucks would do it. But the Wolverines did what they usually do for this game. They got good and high.

With Tony Branoff, a Flint, Michigan product, doing most of the running, Michigan marched to a 13-0 halftime lead after a scoreless first period. The lead was increased to 20-0 after three periods. The Bucks only real bid for a score coming on a Michigan fumble on their own 16. But Michigan stiffened and held the Buckeyes out of the end zone.

Dick Balzhiser scored Michigan's first touchdown from a foot out with Lou Baldacci from Akron converting the extra point. After Balzhiser intercepted a Borton pass, Branoff, Hurley, and Cline picked up valuable yardage with Branoff cutting off right tackle for the last six yards to paydirt. Another score resulted from a pass interception by Tad Stanford, Wolverine end, who was finally dropped on the Buckeyes' two yard line. Cline punched over the last touchdown of the day with Balducci once again converting.

The Wolverines beat the Buckeyes at their own game – rushing. They picked up 285 yards in that department to only 95 for Ohio State. Ohio State did better through the air in the way of picking up more yardage than Michigan, completing 10 of 21 for 107 yards, but five interceptions by the Wolverines erased any advantage the Bucks might have gotten in that direction.

The Wolverines knew before the game that they had to stop Watkins to have a chance. Watkins, second best rusher in the nation, picked up net of 71 yards in 19 carries. Tossed for a loss only once previously this season, Watkins was dropped three times for losses by the Michigan forward wall. Cassady, OSU's breakaway runner, didn't get a break at all as he was held to a net of 34 yards in 13 attempts. Branoff of Michigan personally accounted for more rushing yardage than the entire Buckeye backfield, getting 113 yards in 17 tries, thus making up for a poor showing by Ted Kress, the Michigan tailback, who was held to a mere 16.

STATISTICS

	UM	OSU
First Downs	15	10
Rushing Yardage	285	98
Passing Yardage	19	107
Passes Attempted	12	21
Passes Completed	2	10
Passes Intercepted	2	5
Punts	5	5
Punting Average	37	33
Fumbles Lost	1	1
Yards Penalized	74	10

UM	0	13	0	7	20
OSU	0	0	0	0	0

Michigan Scoring – Touchdowns, Balzhiser, Branoff, Cline. Conversions, Baldcucci 2.

1953

1953	
Ohio 36	Indiana 12
Ohio 33	California 19
Ohio 20	Illinois 41
Ohio 12	Pennsylvania .. 6
Ohio 20	Wisconsin 19
Ohio 27	Northwestern .. 13
Ohio 13	Michigan State 28
Ohio 21	Purdue 6
Ohio 0	Michigan 20

Season Summary

Games won, 6; Lost, 3

OHIO

No.	Name	Pos.	Wt.	Hgt.	Class	Home Town
11	Boudrie, James	LH	182	5-11	Jr.	Columbus, OH
12	Auer, John	RH	178	5-8	So.	Mansfield, OH
14	Augenstein, Jack	FB	192	5-10	So.	Loudonville, OH
15	Knecht, Gilbert	FB	187	5-10	Jr.	Lima, OH
19	*Howell, Carroll	LH	171	5-9	Jr.	Portsmouth, OH
20	*Borton, John	QB	198	6-1	Jr.	Alliance, OH
22	*Leggett, David	Q-F	192	6-0	Jr.	New Philadelphia, O
23	Gage, Ralph	QB	177	5-10	So.	Painesville, OH
24	*Weed, Thurlow	PK	146	5-5	Jr.	Columbus, OH
25	Feinthal, Kenneth	QB	188	6-1	So.	Middletown, OH
28	Booth, William	QB	180	6-0	So.	Youngstown, OH
30	Hans, Joseph	LH	165	5-8	So.	Columbus, OH
33	Brilliant, George	FB	189	5-7	So.	Columbus, OH
34	Spears, Thomas	LH	196	6-0	So.	Wheeling, W.Va.
35	Gibbs, Jack	FB	181	5-10	Jr.	Columbus, OH
36	Campbell, Jack	FB	194	6-2	So.	Lima, OH
40	*Cassady, Howard	LH	172	5-10	So.	Columbus, OH
42	Robson, Charles	QB	168	5-10	So.	Columbus, OH
44	Harkrader, Jerry	RH	170	5-9	So.	Middletown, OH
45	*Watkins, Robert	R-F	192	5-9	Jr.	New Bedford, MA
46	*Bond, Robert	FB	183	5-11	So.	Akron, OH
47	*Rosso, George	RH	176	5-10	Sr.	Pittsburgh, PA
48	Shedd, Jan	RH	173	5-10	So.	Columbus, OH
49	Young, Richard	RH	166	5-10	Jr.	Columbus, OH
50	*Ruehl, James	RT	218	6-3	Jr.	Cumberland, MD
51	*Krisher, Jerry	C	221	6-0	Jr.	Massillon, OH
54	Nosky, Richard	LG	200	6-1	Sr.	Lakewood, OH
55	*Thornton, Richard	C	189	6-0	Sr.	Willard, OH
56	Dawdy, Donald	C	218	6-1	Sr.	Cincinnati, OH
57	Nestich, Martin	C	194	5-11	So.	Youngstown, OH
58	Mott, William	C	213	6-4	Jr.	Proctorville, OH
59	Vargo, Kenneth	C	190	6-1	So.	Martins Ferry, OH
60	Weaver, David	RG	190	5-9	So.	Hamilton, OH
61	Ramser, Richard	RG	207	5-10	So.	Shadyside, OH
62	*Takacs, Michael	LG	206	6-0	Sr.	Massillon, OH
63	*Reichenbach, James	RG	203	5-10	Jr.	Massillon, OH
64	Williams, David	LG	195	5-11	Jr.	Pittsburgh, PA
65	Jones, Herbert	LG	182	5-10	So.	Columbus, OH
66	*Roberts, Robert	LG	188	5-11	Sr.	Zanesville, OH
67	Stewart, Roland	LT	208	6-1	So.	Ashland, OH
68	*Riticher, Raymond	RG	195	5-10	Jr.	Toledo, OH
69	Slagle, William	RG	200	5-10	Sr.	Springfield, OH
70	Hilinski, Richard	LT	228	6-2	Jr.	Cleveland, OH
71	Rader, Ted	LT	216	6-3	So.	Wadsworth, OH
72	*Schumacher, James	RT	208	6-0	Jr.	Massillon, OH
73	*Jacoby, George (CC)	RT	210	5-11	Sr.	Toledo, OH
74	Stoeckel, Donald	LT	206	6-0	So.	Hamilton, OH
75	Whetstone, Robert	LT	200	5-11	So.	Barberton, OH
76	Verhoff, Jack	LT	260	6-4	So.	Columbus, OH
77	*Swartz, Donald	LT	224	6-1	Jr.	Newark, OH
78	Ebinger, Elbert	RT	219	6-3	So.	Hamilton, OH
79	Machinsky, Francis	RT	209	6-0	So.	Uniontown, PA
80	Brubaker, Richard	RE	198	6-1	Jr.	Shaker Heights, O
82	*Ludwig, Paul	RE	206	6-3	So.	Marion, OH
83	*Dugger, Dean	LE	204	6-2	Jr.	Columbus, OH
84	Hesler, Robert	RE	193	6-0	So.	Hamilton, OH
85	*Joslin, Robert (CC)	RE	191	6-0	Sr.	Middletown, OH
87	Collmar, William	RE	172	6-2	So.	Martins Ferry, OH
88	*Hague, Thomas	LE	198	6-0	Sr.	Rocky River, OH
89	Guzik, Frank	LE	194	6-3	So.	Cleveland, OH
92	Ashton, William	LE	187	6-2	Jr.	Piqua, OH

* indicates letters won

MICHIGAN

No.	Name	Pos.	Wt.	Hgt.	Class	Home Town
12	Wheeler, Jack C.	FB	187	6-0	So.	Ypsilanti
14	Ames, Robert T.	HB	172	5-10	So.	Algonac
15	Corey, George R.	HB	175	5-10	So.	Baden, PA
16	Rentschler, David F.	HB	183	6-0	So.	Detroit
17	*Branoff, Tony	HB	180	5-11	So.	Flint
18	Hickey, Edward	HB	160	5-8	Sr.	Anaconda, MT
19	*Knickerbocker, S.	HB	165	5-10	Jr.	Chelsea
22	Murray, Douglas	QB	170	5-11	So.	Muskegon
23	*McDonald, Duncan	QB	175	6-0	Jr.	Flint
24	Kenaga, Ray	QB	170	5-11	Jr.	Sterling, IL
27	Baldacci, Louis G.	QB	205	6-0	So.	Akron, OH
28	McKinley, G. William	QB	195	6-1	So.	Norwalk, OH
30	*Baer, Fred	FB	180	5-11	Jr.	LaGrange, IL
32	Gagalis, Peri	FB	190	5-10	Jr.	Ann Arbor
33	*Hurley, Robert	FB	180	5-10	Sr.	Alamosa, CO
35	Johnson, Earl, Jr.	FB	200	5-11	So.	Muskegon Hts.
38	*Balzhiser, Richard	FB	186	6-0	Sr.	Wheaton, IL
40	Cox, Larry G.	HB	175	5-11	So.	Dowagiac
41	*Kress, Ted	HB	175	5-11	Sr.	Detroit
42	Hendricks, T., Jr.	HB	178	5-11	So.	Detroit
43	Krahl, Joseph W.	FB	185	6-0	Jr.	Wheaton, IL
44	*Cline, J. Daniel	HB	168	5-10	Jr.	Brockport, NY
46	*Sriver, Robert	HB	178	5-11	So.	Mishawaka, IN
50	Kamhout, Carl	T	205	6-2	Jr.	Grand Haven
51	Muellich, George	G	195	6-2	Jr.	Bowling Green, OH
52	Bowman, James	C	190	5-11	Jr.	Charlevoix
53	*O'Shaughnessy, D. (C)	C	190	5-11	Sr.	Seaford, NY
55	Morrow, John M., Jr.	C	220	6-2	So.	Ann Arbor
56	Drake, Donald	C	215	5-11	Jr.	Ypsilanti
58	VanderZeyde, Ray	C	192	6-0	Sr.	East Chicago, IN
59	Peckham, John	C	220	6-2	So.	Sioux Falls, SD
60	Marion, Robert	G	178	5-10	So.	Muskegon Hts.
61	*Dugger, Don	G	185	5-10	Sr.	Charleston, WV
62	*Strozewski, Richard	T	205	6-0	Sr.	South Bend, IN
63	Shomsky, Joseph	G	193	5-10	Jr.	Flint
64	*Beison, Richard	G	200	6-0	Sr.	East Chicago, IL
65	*Cachey, Ted	G	185	5-11	Sr.	Chicago, IL
66	*Fox, James W.	G	185	6-0	So.	Saginaw
67	Brown, Wilbur P.	G	180	5-11	So.	Toledo, OH
68	Ritter, Charles	G	210	6-0	Jr.	Cassopolis
69	*Williams, Ronald	G	185	5-9	Sr.	Massillon, OH
70	VorenKamp, Richard	E	190	6-0	So.	Grand Rapids
71	*Geyer, Ronald	T	220	6-2	Jr.	Toledo, OH
72	*Balog, James	T	210	6-3	Sr.	Wheaton, IL
73	Milligan, Robert	T	195	6-1	Jr.	Dearborn
74	Shields, Kenneth	T	215	6-3	So.	Detroit
75	Kolesar, William P.	T	190	6-0	So.	Mentor, OH
76	Meads, G. Edgar	G	190	6-0	So.	Oxford
77	*Walker, Arthur	T	200	5-11	Jr.	South Haven
78	Krahnke, Charles H.	T	205	6-0	So.	Charlevoix
79	*Bennett, Don	T	195	6-2	Sr.	Chicago, IL
80	Kuchka, John M.	E	185	6-0	So.	Berwick, PA
81	*Topp, Robert	E	190	6-2	Sr.	Kalamazoo
82	Gonser, Jerry I.	E	190	6-0	So.	Saline
83	*Stanford, Tad	E	175	6-0	Sr.	Midland
84	Williams, Gerald H.	E	188	6-2	So.	Flint
85	Williams, Dave	E	195	6-4	Fr.	Dearborn
86	*Knutson, Gene	E	210	6-4	Sr.	Beloit, WI
87	*Schlicht, Leo	E	210	6-4	Sr.	Madison, WI
88	Veselenak, John	E	190	6-2	Jr.	Flint
89	*Bates, James V.	C	195	6-0	Jr.	Farmington
90	*Dutter, George	E	190	6-2	Sr.	Fort Wayne, IN
91	Wolgast, Pete	T	185	6-2	Jr.	Petoskey

* indicates letters won

1953

Michigan	50	Washington	0
Michigan	26	Tulane	7
Michigan	14	Iowa	13
Michigan	20	Northwestern	12
Michigan	0	Minnesota	22
Michigan	24	Pennsylvania	14
Michigan	3	Illinois	19
Michigan	6	Michigan State	14
Michigan	20	Ohio State	0

Season Summary

Games won, 6; Lost, 3; Tied, 0

CACHEY, M.
CASSADY, O.
THORNTON, O.
NYREN, M.
LINE OF SCRIMMAGE
CLINE, M.
5

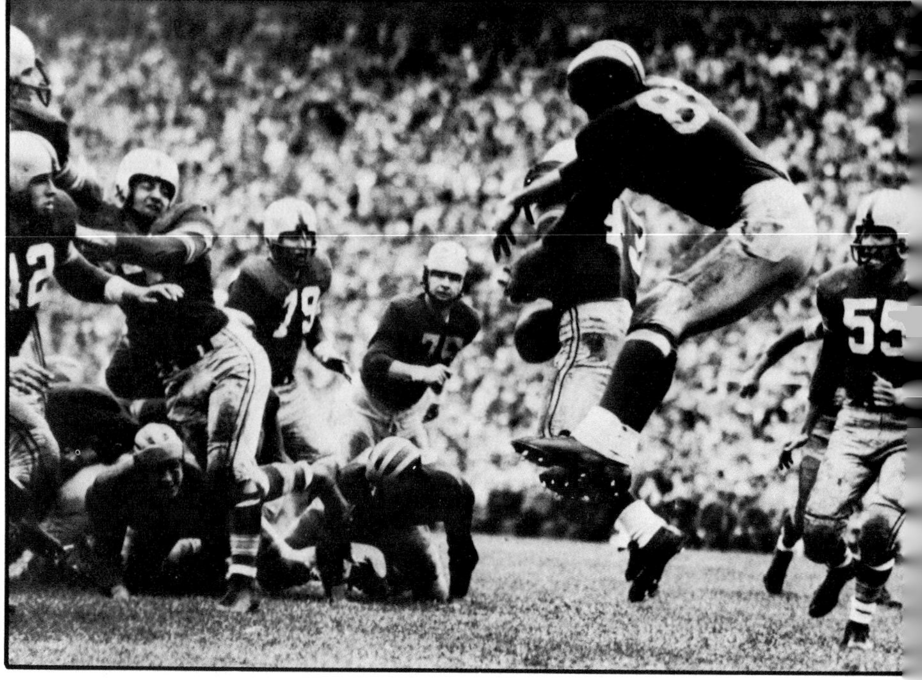

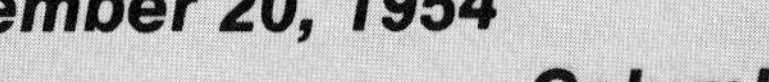

November 20, 1954

Columbus, Ohio

Buckeyes Big Fourth Period Beats Wolverines By 21 To 7 Score

Hayes' Half-Time Talk Spurs Bucks In Rally That Led To Rose Bowl

Fighting desperately and dramatically to overcome a spirited Michigan team, the Buckeyes achieved the three most-prized possessions of intercollegiate football—an unbeaten season, Big Ten Championship, and a trip to the Rose Bowl. The final socre—Ohio State 21, Michigan 7—did not indicate the actual closeness of the play involved.

Using finesse and confidence, Michigan took the opening kickoff and marched 68 yards for a quick and easy touchdown. The fired-up Wolverines smashed the supposedly more powerful Buckeye line in a manner which pointed to the remainder of the 2,500 miles to Pasadena. Then with unexpected and electrifying quickness, Ohio State converted a pass interception into a touchdown to pull even at 7 to 7 at halftime.

In the third period, it was a non-scoring play by one foot when Ohio's Jim Parker saved the day and the entire season with one mighty tackle stopping Michigan's Dave Hill on the one-foot line. Given this reprieve, the Scarlet and Gray came out fighting. Leggett pulled the Buckeyes out of the danger zone with one lightning thrust. Howard "Hopalong" Cassady broke loose for his biggest effort of the day, a 47 yard jaunt. From the 37, Leggett and Bobo alternately bypassed the Michigan line to go to the nine. Leggett then threw a pass into the endzone that Dick Brubaker grasped in spectacular fashion. Tad Weed converted the extra point to make it 14 to 7.

After Michigan's Cline threw a pass which was intercepted by Cassady and returned to the Buckeye's 38, the Ohio scoring machinery started up again. With Bobo contributing a 28 yard gain and consistent short gains by Cassady, Leggett, and Jerry Harkrader, Ohio moved to the Michigan five. A penalty cost Ohio five. From the 10, Leggett hit Harkrader who was knocked out of bounds on the Michigan one. Cassady leaped over in one play and Weed kicked the point as the bells of victory tolled a 21-7 masterpiece.

Michigan was handicapped by the absence of halfback Tony Branoff, who had done the 20 to 0 carving job on Ohio State the previous year. Watkins, Ohio crushing blocker and ball carrier, didn't handle the ball once as he had to retire with leg muscle spasms at halftime. Despite the fierce play, four Buckeyes played the entire 60 minutes. They were center Bob Thorton of Willard, tackle Jim Reichenbach, Leggett, and Cassady.

Hayes was fighting off tears as he complimented individual players and the entire OSU squad in the post-game interview. "There's just one thing I want to say," he yelled. Then he climbed up on a table and leaped off shouting, "Whoopee!"

STATISTICS

	OSU			UM	
First Downs	13			15	
Rushing Yardage	196			229	
Passing Yardage	58			74	
Passes Attempted	9			14	
Passes Completed	4			6	
Passes Intercepted by	3			1	
Punts	5			3	
Punting Average	24			42	
Fumbles Lost	1			2	
Yards Penalized	35			86	
OSU	0	7	0	14	21
UM	7	0	0	0	7

Ohio Scoring: Touchdowns - Kriss, Brubaker, Cassady.
Conversions - Weed 3.
Michigan Scoring: Touchdown- Cline. Conversion - Kramer.

1954			
Michigan	14	Washington	0
Michigan	7	Army	26
Michigan	14	Iowa	13
Michigan	7	Northwestern	0
Michigan	34	Minnesota	0
Michigan	9	Indiana	13
Michigan	14	Illinois	7
Michigan	33	MSU	7
Michigan	7	Ohio State	21

Season Summary

Games Won, 6; Lost, 3; Tied, 0

ARTHUR WALKER
All-American Tackle

Relaxing before the big game are Ron Kramer, Lou Baldacchi and co-ed Linda Landsnals.

MICHIGAN

No.	Name	Pos.	Wt.	Hgt.	Class	Home Town
30	*Baer, Fred	FB	188	5-11	Sr.	LaGrange, IL
27	*Baldacci, Louis G.	QB	196	6-1	Jr.	Akron, OH
28	Baldwin, Paul T.	QB	200	6-0	So.	Escanaba
41	Barr, Terry A.	HB	172	6-1	So.	Grand Rapids
37	Basford, Michael	FB	177	5-11	So.	Birmingham
58	*Bates, James V.	C	198	6-0	Sr.	Farmington
52	Bowman, Jim	C	187	5-11	Sr.	Charlevoix
17	*Branoff, Tony	HB	188	5-11	Jr.	Flint
89	Brooks, Charles E.	E	202	6-1	So.	Marshall
67	Brown, Wilbur P.	G	184	5-11	Jr.	Toledo, OH
65	*Cachey, Ted (C.)	G	178	5-10	Sr.	Chicago, IL
44	*Cline, J. Daniel	HB	175	5-10	Sr.	Brockport, NY
15	Corey, George R.	HB	163	5-10	Jr.	Baden, PA
55	Corona, Clement L.	G	218	6-2	So.	Berwick, PA
74	Crisler, Prescott A.	T	214	6-4	So.	Ann Arbor
73	Davies, James H.	T	209	5-10	So.	Muskegon Hts.
56	Drake, Donald	C	213	5-11	Sr.	Ypsilanti
66	*Fox, James W.	G	190	6-0	Jr.	Saginaw
32	Gagalis, Peri	FB	204	5-11	Sr.	Ann Arbor
71	*Geyer, Ronald	T	225	6-2	Sr.	Toledo, OH
53	Goebel, Jerry P.	C	214	6-3	So.	Grosse Pointe
82	Gonser, Jerry I.	E	187	6-0	Jr.	Saline
25	Greenwood, John C.	HB	172	5-10	So.	Bay City
42	Hendricks, Thomas	HB	181	5-11	Jr.	Detroit
18	*Hickey, Edward	HB	173	5-8	Sr.	Anaconda, MT
45	Hill, David J.	FB	188	6-0	Jr.	Ypsilanti
69	Hill, Richard F.	G	188	5-11	So.	Gary, IN
35	Johnson, Earl	FB	196	5-11	Jr.	Muskegon Hts.
50	Kamhout, Carl	G	203	6-2	Sr.	Grand Haven
24	*Kenaga, Ray	QB	182	5-11	Sr.	Sterling, IL
19	*Knickerbocker, S.	HB	173	5-11	Sr.	Chelsea
75	*Kolesar, William	T	221	6-0	Jr.	Mentor, OH
43	Krahl, Joseph	HB	186	6-0	Sr.	Wheaton, IL
87	Kramer, Ronald J.	E	210	6-3	So.	E. Detroit
62	Kuchka, John M.	G	187	6-0	Jr.	Berwick, PA
26	Maddock, James A.	QB	187	6-0	So.	Chicago, IL
85	Maentz, Thomas S.	E	205	6-2	So.	Holland
60	Marion, Robert L.	G	192	5-10	Jr.	Muskegon Hts.
10	Matulis, Charles F.	HB	165	5-9	So.	E. Chicago, IN
23	*McDonald, Duncan	QB	170	6-0	Sr.	Flint
80	McKoan, Joseph H.	E	189	6-0	So.	Algonac
76	Meads, G. Edgar	T	199	6-0	Jr.	Oxford
78	*Morrow, John M.	T	228	6-2	Jr.	Ann Arbor
64	Nyren, Marvin R.	G	200	6-0	So.	Des Plaines, IL
72	Orwig, James B.	T	191	6-0	So.	Toledo, OH
59	*Peckham, John	C	227	6-2	Jr.	Sioux Falls, S D
79	Preston, James O.	T	200	6-1	So.	Battle Creek
40	Rentschler, David F.	HB	192	6-0	Jr.	Detroit
68	Ritter, Charles	G	195	6-0	Sr.	Cassopolis
81	Rotunno, Michael J.	E	187	6-0	So.	Canton, OH
16	Shannon, Edward J.	HB	172	5-8	So.	River Forest, IL
63	Shomsky, Joseph	G	193	5-11	Sr.	Flint
54	Snider, Eugene	C	195	6-0	So.	Hamtramck
46	Sriver, Robert E.	HB	172	5-11	Jr.	Mishawaka, IN
57	Steele, Dale E.	C	194	5-11	So.	Richmond, IN
61	Steinmeyer, W. B.	G	183	5-11	So.	Toledo, OH
39	Uzis, Alfred R.	FB	192	5-11	So.	E. Chicago, IN
88	*Veselenak, John	E	192	6-2	Sr.	Flint
70	VorenKamp, R. J.	G	200	6-0	Jr.	Grand Rapids
77	*Walker, Arthur	T	218	5-11	Sr.	South Haven
83	Ward, David H.	E	192	6-1	So.	Midland
84	*Williams, Gerry	E	189	6-2	Jr.	Flint

* indicates letters won

Captains:
C. Richard Brubaker
John R. Borton

OHIO

No.	Name	Pos.	Wt.	Hgt.	Class	Home Town
12	Williams, Raymond	HB	182	5-10	So.	Loveland
16	Archer, Jack	HB	174	5-10	So.	Dayton
18	Williams, Lee	FB	170	5-10	So.	Springfield
19	**Howell, Carroll	HB	174	5-9	Sr.	Portsmouth
20	***Barton, John (CC)	QB	207	6-1	Sr.	Alliance
22	**Leggett, David	QB	198	6-1	Sr.	New Philadelphia
23	Gage, Ralph	QB	192	5-11	Jr.	Painesville
24	**Weed, Thurlow	PK	148	5-5	Sr.	Columbus
25	Richards, David	QB	155	5-9	So.	Barnesville
26	Theis, Franklyn	QB	190	5-10	So.	Nyack, NY
27	Lilienthal, Robert	QB	166	6-0	So.	Cambridge
28	*Booth, William	QB	176	6-0	Jr.	Youngstown
29	Robson, Charles	QB	179	5-10	Jr.	Columbus
30	Young, James	FB	195	6-0	So.	Van Wert
33	Vicic, Donald	FB	209	6-1	So.	Euclid
34	Nussbaum, Lee	FB	212	6-1	So.	Massillon
35	Gibbs, Jack	FB	175	5-10	Sr.	Columbus
40	**Cassady, Howard	HB	168	5-10	Jr.	Columbus
42	Bobo, Hubert	FB	192	6-0	So.	Chauncey Dover
43	Roseboro, James	HB	170	5-9	So.	Ashland
44	*Harkrader, Jerry	HB	176	5-9	Jr.	Middletown
45	**Watkins, Robert	HB	191	5-9	Sr.	New Bedford, MA
46	Thompson, Kenneth	HB	190	6-0	So.	Dayton
48	Shedd, Jan	HB	177	5-10	Jr.	Columbus
49	*Young, Richard	HB	164	5-10	Sr.	Columbus
50	Dillman, Thomas	C	191	6-2	So.	Middletown
52	**Bond, Robert	C	183	5-11	Jr.	Akron
53	Slicker, Richard	C	193	6-3	So.	Toledo
54	Sommers, Karl	C	215	6-2	So.	Martins Ferry
55	**Thornton, Robert	C	192	6-0	Sr.	Willard
56	Jobko, William	G	188	6-1	So.	Lansing
58	Quinn, Thomas	G	204	5-10	So.	Portsmouth
59	*Vargo, Kenneth	C	194	6-1	Jr.	Martins Ferry
60	*Weaver, David	G	188	5-8	Jr.	Hamilton
61	Ramser, Richard	G	193	5-11	Jr.	Shadyside
62	Parker, James	G	248	6-3	So.	Toledo
63	***Reichenbach, J.	G	200	5-10	Sr.	Massillon
64	*Williams, David	G	215	6-0	Sr.	Dormont, PA
65	Wassmund, James	G	195	6-0	So.	Toledo
66	Cole, Robert	G	204	5-10	So.	Carey
67	Howley, Edward	G	197	5-11	So.	Girard
69	Frank, Donald	G	198	5-10	So.	Cleveland
70	*Hilinski, Richard	T	231	6-2	Sr.	Cleveland
71	***Krisher, Jerry	T	224	6-0	Sr.	Massillon
73	Cummings, William	T	239	6-2	So.	Toledo
74	*Stoeckel, Donald	T	211	6-0	Jr.	Hamilton
75	Guy, Richard	T	209	6-3	So.	Mansfield
76	Cooper, Kenneth	T	210	6-0	So.	Sylvania
77	**Swartz, Donald	T	238	6-1	Sr.	Newark
78	Ebinger, Elbert	T	241	6-3	Jr.	Hamilton
79	*Machinsky, Francis	T	206	6-0	Jr.	Uniontown, PA
80	*Brubaker, R. (CC)	E	203	6-0	Sr.	Shaker Heights
81	Kriss, Frederick	E	189	5-11	So.	El Paso, TX
82	**Ludwig, Paul	E	208	6-3	Jr.	Marion
83	**Dugger, Dean	E	213	6-2	Sr.	Columbus
84	Trabue, Jerry	E	200	6-3	So.	Columbus
85	Shingledecker, W.	G	182	5-10	So.	Springfield
86	Humbert, Stanley	E	204	6-2	So.	Cincinnati
87	Collmar, William	E	177	6-1	Jr.	Martins Ferry
88	*Spears, Thomas	E	197	6-0	Jr.	Wheeling, WV
89	Michael, William	E	210	6-1	So.	Hamilton
92	Blazeff, Lalo	E	187	6-0	So.	Akron
93	Ellwood, Frank	E	190	5-11	So.	Dover

* indicates letters won

1954

Ohio	28	Indiana	0
Ohio	21	California	13
Ohio	40	Illinois	7
Ohio	20	Iowa	14
Ohio	31	Wisconsin	14
Ohio	14	Northwestern	7
Ohio	26	Pittsburgh	0
Ohio	28	Purdue	6
Ohio	21	Michigan	7

Season Summary

Games Won, 9; Lost, 0

HOWARD CASSADY
All-American Back

DEAN DUGGER
All-American End

Above: Ohio State's linemen and backs grind Michigan to pieces. Buckeye back Sutherin goes for seven yards in this shot.
At right: Rose Bowl Coach Hayes is telling reporters that bands should not have been permitted on the field at halftime because playing conditions then became intolerable.

November 19, 1955

Ann Arbor, Michigan

Terry Barr streaks for more yardage.

Ohio State Trounces Michigan, 17 – 0

Cassady Ends Career In Glory; Parker Is Standout In Line

In an overwhelming demonstration of championship quality, the Buckeyes knocked mighty Michigan out of the title and Rose Bowl. The great frustration and disappointment expressed by the All-Americans symbolized the feelings of the Michigan team and fans. On that day Michigan was not in the same league. Equipped with a great offensive potential, the Wolverines got past midfield only once, and that on a cheap ride through a penalty.

Ohio scored in the second quarter. Playing possession football, advancing it steadily behind the solid thrusts of Cassady and Vicic, quarterback Frank Ellwood and an unheralded substitute—Don Sutherin, the only player to go the full sixty bruising minutes—Ohio got to the Michigan seven. On fourth down Woody Hayes sent in his field goal kicker, Kriss, who angled a three-pointer into the wind from the 14-yard line.

Ohio kept pounding away at the Michigan line. Cassady, Sutherin, Vicic, and Ellwood bored continuously through gaping holes created by Ohio's magnificent inside musclemen—Jim Parker, Ken Vargo, and Moose Machinsky, with some assists from the others, ends Bill Michael and 168-pound Leo Brown and tackles Don Stoeckel and Dave Weaver. They marred Michigan's rating as the Big Ten's No. 1 defensive team.

After a Michigan gamble to make a first down failed, Ohio's human bulldozers took the ball 34 yards for the score. At UM's three-yard line and within 50 seconds after the fourth period opened, Hopalong Cassady plunged into the end zone. Cassady, playing with a sore neck received in an auto collision two days earlier, looked in perfect health as he scored his last collegiate touchdown. The PAT failed.

Michigan attempted a comeback but it nearly collapsed when Maddock tried a feeble pass from his end zone. It went to Barr who was tackled in the end zone by OSU's Thomas for a safety and another two points.

Ron Kramer of Michigan got off a one-yard kick from the 20, which was either accidental or foolish. Ohio was awarded the ball. Here the game broke wide open with more flags on the field than in the United Nations Building. Having seen the budding roses wilt and die, Michigan tried to roughhouse it. Kramer was given a personal foul for slugging Ellwood. When Michigan was penalized to the six, Kramer beefed so loudly and violently that he was promptly dismissed from the field. Al Sigman, a Michigan tackle, also was ordered from the game. These two penalties moved the ball to the 18-inch line, where it was easy for Vicic to score. Sutherin's conversion was wide .

After that nearly every scrimmage brought another round of drop-the-hand-kerchief. Fans came out of the stands to rip down the goal posts. They crowded the sidelines. The rioting, a sad finish to an otherwise glorious season for both teams, reached a comic opera pitch at one point when fans intercepted a pass.

STATISTICS

	OSU	UM
First Downs	20	5
Rushing Yardage	333	95
Passing Yardage	4	14
Passing	1-3-0	3-9-2
Punts-Average	3-35	6-43
Fumbles Lost	2	0
Yards Penalized	50	70

OSU	0	3	0	14	17
UM	0	0	0	0	0

1955			
Ohio	28	Nebraska	20
Ohio	0	Stanford	6
Ohio	27	Illinois	12
Ohio	14	Duke	20
Ohio	26	Wisconsin	16
Ohio	49	Northwestern	0
Ohio	20	Indiana	13
Ohio	20	Iowa	10
Ohio	17	Michigan	0

Season Summary

Games Won, 7; Lost, 2

HOWARD CASSADY
All-American Back

JAMES PARKER
All-American Guard

OHIO

No.	Name	Pos.	Wt.	Hgt.	Class	Home Town
10	Ledman, Kenneth	PK	175	5-11	Jr.	Columbus
14	Beerman, Raymond	HB	177	5-11	So.	Toledo
15	Disher, Larry	E	182	5-11	So.	Waterville
16	Cannavino, Joseph	HB	168	5-11	So.	Cleveland
18	Williams, Lee	FB	171	5-10	Jr.	Springfield
23	Crawford, Thomas	QB	172	5-11	So.	Toledo
24	Ellwood, Franklin	QB	193	5-11	Jr.	Dover
25	Karow, Robert	QB	180	5-11	So.	Columbus
26	Theis, Franklyn	QB	192	5-10	Jr.	Nyack, NY
27	Lilienthal, Robert	QB	178	6-0	Jr.	Cambridge
28	*Booth, William	QB	190	6-0	Sr.	Youngstown
33	*Vicic, Donald	FB	211	6-1	Jr.	Euclid
35	Trivisonno, Joseph	FB	210	5-11	So.	Cleveland
36	Cisco, Galen	FB	209	5-11	So.	St. Marys
40	*Cassady, Howard	HB	181	5-10	Sr.	Columbus
43	*Roseboro, James	HB	174	5-9	Jr.	Ashland
44	*Harkrader, Jerry	HB	189	5-9	Sr.	Middletown
45	Sutherin, Donald	HB	199	5-10	So.	Toronto, OH
46	Thompson, Kenneth	HB	193	6-0	Jr.	Dayton
47	Wable, Robert	HB	167	5-10	So.	Sistersville, WV
48	Shedd, Jan	HB	177	5-10	Sr.	Columbus
49	Richards, David	HB	162	5-9	Jr.	Barnesville
50	*Dillman, Thomas	C	200	6-2	Jr.	Middletown
51	Holdren, Richard	G	198	5-8	So.	West Liberty
52	*Bond, Robert	C	184	5-11	Sr.	Akron
53	Barnes, Ronald	PK	200	6-0	So.	Portsmouth
54	Sommer, Karl	C	224	6-2	Jr.	Martins Ferry
55	Breehl, Edward	C	178	6-0	So.	New Philadelphia
57	Martin, John	T	208	5-11	So.	Waverly
58	Quinn, Thomas	T	190	5-10	Jr.	Portsmouth
59	*Vargo, Kenneth	C	200	6-1	Sr.	Martins Ferry
60	*Weaver, David	G	191	5-8	Sr.	Hamilton
61	*Ramser, Richard	G	198	5-11	Sr.	Shadyside
62	*Parker, James	G	248	6-3	Jr.	Toledo
63	*Jobko, William	G	192	6-1	Jr.	Lansing
64	Thomas, Aurelius	G	200	6-1	So.	Columbus
65	Wassmund, James	G	200	6-0	Jr.	Toledo
66	Cole, Robert	G	200	5-10	Jr.	Carey
67	Baldacci, Thomas	G	201	6-0	So.	Akron
68	Provenza, Russell	G	196	5-10	So.	Lorain
69	Facchine, Richard	G	208	5-9	So.	Vandergrift, PA
70	Nagy, Alex	T	218	6-2	So.	Warren
71	Perry, Charles	T	219	5-11	So.	Columbus
72	*Whetstone, Robert	T	210	5-11	Jr.	Barberton
73	Cummings, William	T	248	6-2	Jr.	Toledo
74	*Stoeckel, Donald	T	206	6-0	Sr.	Hamilton
75	*Guy, Richard	T	218	6-3	Jr.	Mansfield
77	Cook, Ronald	T	205	6-1	So.	Lima
78	Ebinger, Elbert	T	250	6-3	Sr.	Hamilton
79	*Machinsky, Francis	T	224	6-0	Sr.	Uniontown, PA
80	Zawacki, Charles	E	200	6-2	So.	Uniontown, PA
81	*Kriss, Frederick	E	194	5-11	Jr.	El Paso, TX
83	Niederhauser, Don	E	202	6-5	So.	Toledo
85	Brown, Leo	E	168	5-10	So.	Portsmouth
86	Humbert, Stanley	E	207	6-2	Jr.	Cincinnati
87	*Collmar, William	E	173	6-1	Sr.	Martins Ferry
88	*Spears, Thomas	E	199	6-0	Sr.	Wheeling, WV
89	*Michael, William	E	222	6-1	Jr.	Hamilton
91	Trittipo, John	E	168	6-0	So.	Gambier

* indicates letters won

MICHIGAN

No.	Name	Pos.	Wt.	Hgt.	Class	Home Town
27	*Baldacci, Louis G.	FB	196	6-1	Sr.	Akron, OH
28	Baldwin, Paul T.	QB	198	6-0	Sr.	Escanaba
41	*Barr, Terry A.	HB	182	6-0	Jr.	Grand Rapids
37	Basford, Michael	FB	180	5-11	Jr.	Birmingham
58	*Bates, James V.	C	200	6-0	Sr.	Farmington
65	Berger, Thomas E.	G	183	5-11	So.	Detroit
68	Bochnowski, Alex	G	185	5-9	So.	Munster, IN
52	Bowman, James	C	194	5-11	Sr.	Charlevoix
17	*Branoff, Tony D.	HB	190	5-11	Sr.	Flint
89	*Brooks, Charles	E	198	6-1	Jr.	Marshall
15	*Corey, George R.	HB	166	5-10	Sr.	Baden, PA
67	Corona, Clement	G	221	6-2	Jr.	Berwick, PA
73	Davies, James J.	T	214	5-10	Jr.	Muskegon Hts.
22	Dickey, James A.	QB	188	6-0	So.	Miamisburg, OH
57	Eldred, Dale L.	G	199	5-11	Jr.	Minneapolis, MN
86	Faul, Lawrence J.	E	185	6-0	Jr.	Riv. Forest, IL
66	*Fox, James W.	G	191	6-0	Sr.	Saginaw
53	*Goebel, Jerry P.	C	211	6-3	Jr.	Grosse Pointe
82	Gonser, Jerry I.	E	187	6-0	Sr.	Saline
77	Gray, James	T	209	6-0	Fr.	Battle Creek
25	Greenwood, John	QB	170	5-10	Jr.	Bay City
42	*Hendricks, Thomas	HB	188	5-11	Sr.	Detroit
79	Heynen, Richard B.	T	195	6-0	Jr.	Grand Rapids
18	*Hickey, Edward L.	HB	175	5-9	Sr.	Anaconda, MT
45	*Hill, David J.	FB	188	6-0	Sr.	Ypsilanti
69	*Hill, Richard F.	G	194	5-11	Jr.	Gary, IN
12	Janecke, Jerry	HB	171	5-10	So.	Rock Island, IL
35	Johnson, Earl	FB	194	5-11	Sr.	Muskegon Hts.
74	Kamhout, Carl R.	T	212	6-2	Sr.	Grand Haven
83	Ketteman, Dick	E	178	6-1	So.	Toledo, OH
44	Klinge, Walter W.	HB	183	5-11	So.	W. Brooklyn, IL
19	*Knickerbocker, S.	HB	173	5-11	Sr.	Chelsea
75	*Kolesar, William	T	214	6-0	Sr.	Mentor, OH
62	Krahnke, Charles	G	210	6-0	Sr.	Wyandotte
87	*Kramer, Ronald J.	E	222	6-3	Jr.	East Detroit
33	Krueger, Frederick	E	181	5-11	So.	Allen Park
23	Lousman, Jack R.	QB	187	6-0	So.	Ann Arbor
56	MacPhee, William	C	185	6-0	So.	Grand Haven
26	*Maddock, James	QB	189	5-11	Jr.	Chicago, IL
85	*Maentz, Thomas	E	207	6-2	Jr.	Holland
60	*Marion, Robert L.	G	194	5-10	Sr.	Muskegon Hts.
10	Matulis, Charles	HB	171	5-9	Jr.	E. Chicago, IN
80	McKoan, Joseph H.	E	193	6-0	Jr.	Algonac
76	*Meads, G. Edgar (C.)	G	198	6-0	Sr.	Oxford
88	Morrow, Gordon H.	E	220	6-3	So.	Ann Arbor
78	*Morrow, John M.	T	228	6-2	Sr.	Ann Arbor
64	Nyren, Marvin R.	G	204	6-0	Jr.	Des Plaines, IL
72	Orwig, James B.	T	194	6-0	Jr.	Toledo, OH
71	Owen, David G.	T	214	6-0	Jr.	Milwaukee, WI
43	Pace, James E.	HB	185	5-11	So.	Little Rock, AR
63	Paplomatas, James	G	192	5-10	So.	Rochester, PA
59	*Peckham, John	C	227	6-2	Sr.	Sioux Falls, SD
54	Rembiesa, Donald	C	185	5-11	So.	Dearborn
84	Rentschler, David F.	E	190	6-0	Sr.	Detroit
81	*Rotunno, Michael	E	192	6-1	Jr.	Canton, OH
16	*Shannon, Edward	HB	172	5-8	Jr.	Riv. Forest, IL
14	Shatusky, Mike	HB	172	5-10	Jr.	Menominee
70	Sigman, Lionel A.	T	215	5-10	Jr.	Ann Arbor
46	Sriver, Robert E.	HB	178	5-11	Sr.	Mishawaka, IN
61	Steinmeyer, Bill	G	198	5-11	Jr.	Toledo, OH
24	VanPelt, James S.	QB	178	5-11	So.	Evanston, IL
38	Zervas, Stephen J.	FB	193	6-0	Sr.	Hazel Park

* indicates letters won

1955

Michigan	42	Missouri	7
Michigan	14	MSU	7
Michigan	26	Army	2
Michigan	14	Northwestern	2
Michigan	14	Minnesota	13
Michigan	33	Iowa	21
Michigan	6	Illinois	25
Michigan	30	Indiana	0
Michigan	0	OSU	17

Season Summary

Games Won, 7; Lost, 2; Tied, 0

RON KRAMER
All-American End

November 24, 1956

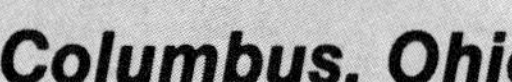

Columbus, Ohio

Wolverines Gain Revenge, No. 2 Spot In Big 10

Two Quick Touchdowns Put Oosterbaan Men On Victory Highway

Michigan exploded and Ohio State stalled. As a result, the inspired, revengeful, and workmanlike Wolverines rolled to an impressive 19 to 0 victory. In the process, Michigan pulled Ohio State off its two year perch atop the Big Ten and sent them unmercifully reeling into a fourth place tie with co favorite, Michigan State. The Wolverines sneaked into second place behind newly crowned Iowa.

So convincing was Michigan's superiority, stimulated on the ground by breakaway Jim Pace and bulldozing John Herrnstein and in the air by quarterbacks Jim Van Pelt, Jim Maddock, and Bob Ptacek, that many of the 82,223 spectators left the cold concrete horseshoe stadium long before the game ended.

Ohio won the coin toss, but co captains Bill Michael and Frank Ellwood chose to defend the south goal to take advantage of a 7 mph wind, which gave Michigan the option of receiving. Ernie Spychalski's kickoff was returned by Pace to the Michigan 22. Mixing a smooth, efficient single wing and T formation, quarterback Van Pelt engineered the successful drive on the dashing feet of Pace and Herrnstein and his own right arm. An 18 yard pass to Pace brought the ball to the Ohio State 21 where Van Pelt shot an angular pass to Barr. Barr roared through four Ohio defenders, nimbly crossing at the corner to score. Ron Kramer's placement made it 7 to 0.

Tom Maentz set up Michigan's second score with a fumble jarring tackle of Ohio's Jimmy Roseboro on his 27 yard line. Van Pelt recovered. Ohio State stiffened and Van Pelt arched a punt out of bounds on Ohio's two yard line. Roseboro fumbled again and Barr recovered for Michigan on the nine yard line. Barr, several plays later, carried the ball to paydirt behind a key block by Herrnstein. Roseboro blocked Kramer's extra point kick. After a field goal attempt which was blocked by the Buckeye's Dick Schafrath, the half ended 13 to 0.

The third period saw Michigan thwart two steady downfield marches by the Buckeyes at times with an 11 man defensive line. Both times the Wolverines took over possession on downs.

Pace set up Michigan's third touchdown with a 46 yard run and by taking a 24 yard pass from Jim Maddox to go to the Ohio four. Herrnstein nudged the ball to the one in two carries, and Maddox carried it over. Kramer missed on a wide placement.

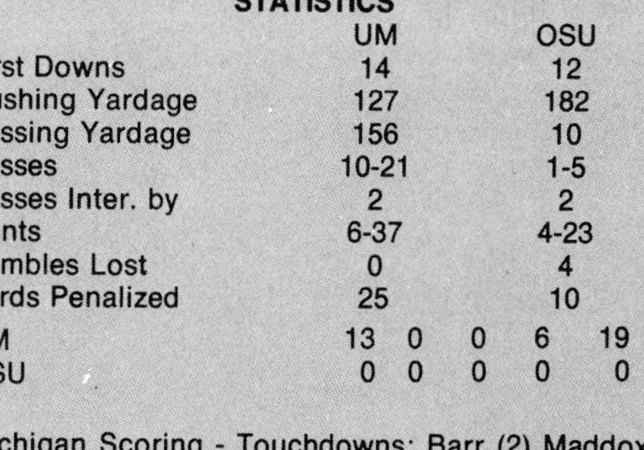

STATISTICS

	UM	OSU
First Downs	14	12
Rushing Yardage	127	182
Passing Yardage	156	10
Passes	10-21	1-5
Passes Inter. by	2	2
Punts	6-37	4-23
Fumbles Lost	0	4
Yards Penalized	25	10

UM	13	0	0	6	19
OSU	0	0	0	0	0

Michigan Scoring - Touchdowns: Barr (2) Maddox: Conversion: Kramer

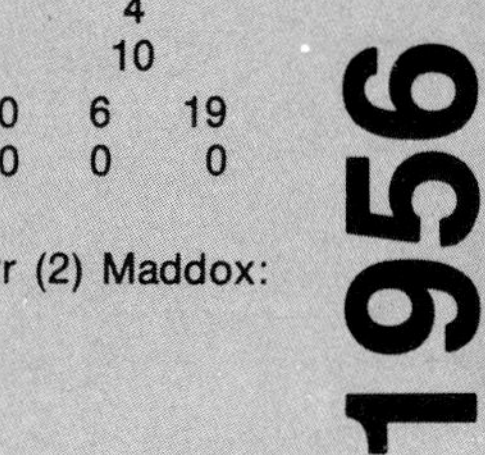

1956	
Michigan 42	U.C.L.A. 13
Michigan 0	MSU 9
Michigan 48	Army 14
Michigan 34	Northwestern 20
Michigan 7	Minnesota ... 20
Michigan 17	Iowa 14
Michigan 17	Illinois 7
Michigan 49	Indiana 26
Michigan 19	OSU 0

Season Summary

Games Won, 7; Lost, 2

RON KRAMER
All-American End

MICHIGAN

No.	Name	Pos.	Wt.	Hgt.	Class	Home Town
10	Stovall, Jack	HB	180	5-9	Jr.	Howell
14	Shatusky, Mike	HB	175	5-11	Sr.	Menominee
15	Batsakes, John	HB	174	5-8	Jr.	Ann Arbor
16	Shannon, Ed	HB	171	5-8	Sr.	River Forest, IL
18	McCoy, Ernie	HB	165	5-10	Jr.	Ann Arbor
22	Spidel, John	QB	174	5-11	So.	Greenville, OH
23	Lousma, Jack	QB	192	6-0	So.	Ann Arbor
24	Van Pelt, Jim	QB	187	5-11	Jr.	Evanston, IL
25	Greenwood, John	HB	175	5-9	Sr.	Bay City
26	Maddock, Jim	QB	187	5-10	Sr.	Chicago, IL
28	Sytek, Jim	QB	185	5-11	So.	Detroit
32	Dickey, Jim	FB	185	6-1	Jr.	Miamisburg, OH
33	Byers, Jim	FB	198	6-0	So.	Evansville, IN
35	Sisinyak, Eugene	FB	195	6-0	So.	Monroe
36	Herrnstein, John	FB	212	6-2	So.	Chillicothe, OH
38	Zervas, Steve	FB	192	5-11	Jr.	Hazel Park
41	Barr, Terry	HB	184	6-0	Sr.	Grand Rapids
42	Zachary, John	HB	168	5-10	So.	Chicago, IL
43	Pace, Jim	HB	192	5-11	Jr.	Little Rock, AR
48	Rentschler, Dave	HB	195	6-1	Jr.	Grosse Pointe
49	Ptacek, Bob	HB	206	6-1	So.	Cleveland, OH
50	Orvis, Douglas	G	180	5-11	So.	Flint
54	Rembiesa, Don	C	190	5-11	Jr.	Dearborn
55	Wine, Ray	C	200	6-2	So.	Port Huron
56	MacPhee, Bill	C	192	6-0	Jr.	Grand Haven
58	Snider, Gene	C	205	6-1	Jr.	Hamtramck
60	Jenks, John	G	202	5-10	So.	Chicago, IL
61	Callahan, Alex	G	190	6-0	So.	Wyandotte
62	Haller, Dave	G	191	6-1	So.	Park Ridge, IL
63	Faul, Larry	G	195	6-0	Jr.	River Forest, IL
64	Nyren, Marvin	G	205	6-0	Jr.	Des Plaines, IL
65	Berger, Tom	G	185	5-11	Jr.	Detroit
66	Boshoven, Robert	G	205	6-0	Jr.	Grand Rapids
67	Corona, Clem	G	221	6-1	Sr.	Berwick, PA
68	Bochonowski, Alex	G	190	5-10	Jr.	E. Chicago, IN
69	Hill, Dick	G	198	5-11	So.	Gary, IN
70	Sigman, Al	T	217	5-11	Sr.	Ann Arbor
71	Kreger, John	T	246	6-6	Jr.	Flat Rock
72	Orwig, Jim	T	196	6-0	Sr.	Toledo, OH
73	Davies, Jim	T	215	5-11	Sr.	Muskegon Hts.
74	Boyden, Joel	G	249	6-6	So.	Muskegon
75	Smith, Willie	T	237	6-2	So.	Little Rock, AR
76	Stetten, Maynard	T	205	6-2	So.	Gibraltar
77	Gray, Jim	T	215	6-3	So.	Battle Creek
78	Marciniak, Jerry	T	220	6-2	So.	Chicago, IL
79	Heynen, Dick	T	198	6-1	Sr.	Grand Rapids
80	Krueger, Fred	E	180	5-11	Jr.	Allen Park
81	Rotunno, Mike	E-C	191	6-1	Sr.	Canton, OH
82	Johnson, Walter	E	211	6-4	So.	Dearborn
83	Ketteman, Richard	E	181	6-1	Jr.	Toledo, OH
84	Bowers, Dave	E	195	6-2	Jr.	Traverse City
85	Maentz, Tom (Capt.)	E	210	6-3	Sr.	Holland
86	Prahst, Gary	E	210	6-4	So.	Berea, OH
87	Kramer, Ron	E-HB	216	6-3	Sr.	E. Detroit
88	Morrow, Gordon	E	208	6-3	So.	Ann Arbor
89	Brooks, Charles	E	202	6-2	Sr.	Marshall

* indicates letters won

OHIO

No.	Name	Pos.	Wt.	Hgt.	Class	Home Town
12	Deshler, Dana	FB	191	5-11	So.	Columbus
14	Beerman, Raymond	HB	185	5-11	Jr.	Toledo
15	Craig, George	HB	197	6-1	So.	Clairton, PA
16	*Cannavino, Joseph	HB	172	5-11	Jr.	Cleveland
17	McMurry, Preston	HB	173	5-9	So.	Pittsburgh, PA
18	Clark, Donald	HB	188	5-11	So.	Akron
19	Lord, James	HB	181	5-10	So.	Columbus
22	Kremblas, Frank	QB	208	6-1	So.	Akron
23	Crawford, Thomas	QB	176	5-11	Jr.	Toledo
24	*Ellwood, Franklin (CC)	QB	188	5-11	Sr.	Dover
26	*Theis, Franklyn	QB	198	5-10	Jr.	Nyack, NY
30	McCarthy, Patrick	FB	181	6-0	So.	Detroit, MI
33	**Vicic, Donald	FB	212	6-1	Sr.	Euclid
34	Lord, John	E	175	5-10	So.	Columbus
35	*Trivisonno, Joseph	FB	214	5-11	Jr.	Cleveland
36	*Cisco, Galen	FB	204	5-11	Jr.	St. Marys
37	Peggs, Carl	HB	182	5-10	Jr.	Fostoria
38	Ballinger, Gary	FB	178	5-10	So.	Marion
41	Curtis, John	HB	170	5-8	So.	Toledo
43	**Roseboro, James	HB	177	5-9	Sr.	Ashland
44	LeBeau, Richard	HB	188	6-0	So.	London
45	*Sutherin, Donald	HB	198	5-11	Jr.	Toronto
46	**Thompson, Kenneth	HB	196	6-0	Sr.	Dayton
47	Wable, Robert	HB	169	5-10	Jr.	Sistersville, WV
48	Robinson, Philip	HB	176	5-9	So.	Columbus
49	Richards, David	HB	154	5-9	Jr.	Maumee
50	**Dillman, Thomas	C	198	6-2	Sr.	Middletown
51	Hammons, Roger	T	229	6-1	So.	Hamilton
52	Provenza, Russell	C	186	5-11	Jr.	Lorain
53	James, Daniel	C	256	6-2	So.	Cincinnati
54	Sommer, Karl	C	219	6-2	Sr.	Martins Ferry
55	Breehl, Edward	C	183	6-0	Jr.	New Philadelphia
56	Walsh, Leo	C	177	6-0	So.	Cleveland
58	Fronk, Daniel	G	185	5-11	Jr.	Dover
59	Jones, Herbert	G	192	5-10	Jr.	Columbus
60	Spychalski, Ernest	G	243	6-2	So.	Toledo
61	Bailey, Ralph	G	195	6-0	So.	Springfield
62	**Parker, James	G	254	6-3	Sr.	Toledo
63	Bowsher, Gerry	G	198	5-10	So.	Toledo
64	*Thomas, Aurelius	G	200	6-1	Jr.	Columbus
65	Wassmund, James	G	194	6-0	Sr.	Toledo
66	Cole, Robert	T	214	5-10	Sr.	Carey
67	*Baldacci, Thomas	G	191	6-0	Jr.	Akron
68	Ballmer, Paul	G	183	5-10	So.	Lancaster
70	Nagy, Alex	T	230	6-2	Jr.	Warren
71	Schafrath, Richard	T	203	6-2	So.	Wooster
72	*Martin, John	T	207	5-11	Jr.	Waverly
73	Cummings, William	T	240	6-2	Sr.	Toledo
74	Humbert, Stanley	T	214	6-2	Sr.	Cincinnati
75	**Guy, Richard	T	214	6-3	Sr.	Mansfield
76	Wilson, Clifford	T	230	6-2	So.	Newcomerstown
77	*Cook, Ronald	T	206	6-1	Jr.	Lima
78	Crawford, Albert	T	220	6-0	So.	Canton
79	**Michael, William (CC)	E	224	6-1	Sr.	Hamilton
80	*Zawacki, Charles	T	211	6-2	Jr.	Uniontown, PA
81	**Kriss, Frederick	E	187	6-11	Sr.	El Paso, TX
82	Disher, Larry	E	182	5-11	Jr.	Waterville
83	Schenking, Fred	E	204	6-4	So.	Coldwater
85	*Brown, Leo	E	168	5-10	Jr.	Portsmouth
86	Trittipo, John	E	174	6-0	Jr.	Gambier
87	Bowermaster, Russell	E	197	6-2	So.	Hamilton
88	Morgan, Thomas	E	196	6-2	So.	Hamilton
89	Katula, Theodore	E	191	6-1	Jr.	Campbell

* indicates letters won

1956

Ohio	34	Nebraska	7
Ohio	32	Stanford	20
Ohio	26	Illinois	6
Ohio	6	Penn State	7
Ohio	21	Wisconsin	0
Ohio	6	Northwestern	2
Ohio	35	Indiana	14
Ohio	0	Iowa	6
Ohio	0	Michigan	19

Season Summary

Games Won, 6; Lost, 3

JAMES PARKER
All-American Guard

At right: Jim Pace is #43.
Below: Practice for the photographers.

Ohio State Team of 1957 being welcomed at Los Angeles by the Rose Queen and her Court.

November 23, 1957

Ann Arbor, Michigan

Ohio State Beats Michigan 31-14

Wolves Crushed By Ground Attack

Ohio State's mighty football team put some frosting on its Big Ten Championship with a crushing 31-14 victory over its principal rival, Michigan. The Buckeye's impressive victory rounded out another perfect unbeaten Big Ten record, their third in the last four years, reconfirmed their New Year's Day reservations to the Rose Bowl, and boosted their chances of being rated the Number 1 collegiate team in the land in the final poll.

As 101,001 watched, the fired up Wolverines, a three point underdog, rode the legs of Jimmy Pace, who earned the individual ground gaining honors by one yard over Ohio's Bob White, to a surprising 14-10 halftime lead. The Ohioans, with faultless ball handling and directed brilliantly by quarterback Frank Kremblas, poured across three touchdowns in the second half. Two of the touchdowns came by taking the ball away from Michigan on a fumble and a pass interception to break open what was otherwise a thriller.

In the first half, Michigan socred touchdowns on the running of Pace and a 25 yard pass play from Van Pelt to Myers with Van Pelt adding the conversion points. Ohio State pushed across one TD in the first quarter on a run by Le Beau as Sutherin added the extra point and a field goal in the second quarter.

Ohio took the second half opening kickoff from its own 42 to score with Le Beau streaking through center for the final eight yards. When Michigan got possession on the kickoff, they moved to the Ohio 31 where Tony Rio, substituting for the injured Johnny Herrnstein, fumbled and White pounced on it in what turned out to be the turning point of the ball game. Kremblas then engineered a drive to score to take a commanding 24-14 lead.

The final score came when Kremblas timed a perfect lateral to Cannavino on an end sweep good for the final 13 yards. On the extra point, a Michigan player committed a personal foul and this set off violent brawling by fans, reminiscent of the "snowball" game of two years previous.

It was the Buckeyes seventh successive Big Ten victory and brought their overall record to eight victories and one defeat at the hands of Texas Christian in the opener. Michigan ended up with three victories, three defeats, and one tie in the conference, its poorest record in five years.

STATISTICS

	OSU				UM
First Downs	19				16
Rushing Yardage	372				270
Passing Yardage	49				107
Passes	3-9				5-12
Passes Inter. by	1				0
Punts	4-30				2-46
Fumbles Lost	0				3
Yards Penalized	12				6
OSU	7	3	14	7	31
UM	7	7	0	0	14

Ohio State Scoring - Touchdowns: Le Beau (2); Kremblas, Cannavino. Fieldgoal - Sutherin (32 yards). Conversions: Sutherin, Kremblas (2).

Michigan Scoring - Touchdowns: Pace, Myers. Conversions: Van Pelt (2)

1957

1957			
Ohio	14	Texas Christian	18
Ohio	35	Washington	7
Ohio	21	Illinois	7
Ohio	56	Indiana	0
Ohio	16	Wisconsin	13
Ohio	47	Northwestern	6
Ohio	20	Purdue	7
Ohio	17	Iowa	13
Ohio	31	Michigan	14

Season Summary
Won, 8; Lost, 1

AURELIUS THOMAS
All-American Guard

OHIO

No.	Name	Pos.	Ht.	Wgt.	Class	Home Town
66	Anders, Richard	LG	5-8	180	So.	Washington, C.H.
68	Arnold, Birtho	RG	6-2	269	So.	So. Columbus
61	Bailey, Ralph	RG	6	198	Jr.	Springfield
67	*Baldacci, Thomas	LG	6	195	Sr.	Akron
41	Ballinger, Jerry	LH	5-10	178	Jr.	Marion
87	*Bowersmaster, Russell	LE	6-2	202	Jr.	Hamilton
55	Breehl, Edward	C	6	192	Sr.	New Philadelphia
85	*Brown, Leo (Co-Capt.)	RE	5-10	165	Sr.	Portsmouth
16	*Cannavino, Joseph	LH	5-11	172	Sr.	Cleveland
43	Carr, Leroy	RH	6-1	178	So.	Portsmouth
36	*Cisco, G. (Co-Capt.)	FB	5-11	203	Sr.	St. Marys
18	*Clark, Donald	LH	5-11	191	Jr.	Akron
77	*Cook, Ronald	RT	6-1	204	Sr.	Lima
62	Cowans, Leroy	RG	5-10	207	So.	Cleveland
78	*Crawford, Al	LT	6	234	Jr.	Canton
23	Crawford, Thomas	QB	5-11	178	Sr.	Toledo
82	Disher, Larry	LE	5-11	182	Sr.	Waterville
46	Dresser, John	LH	6-1	192	So.	Toledo
51	Fields, Jerry	C	6-1	206	So.	Coal Grove
58	Fronk, Daniel	C	5-11	189	Jr.	Dover
30	Gage, Ralph	FB	5-10	174	Jr.	Painesville
84	Houston, James	LE	6-2	216	So.	Massillon
53	*James, Dan	C	6-2	258	Jr.	Cincinnati
65	*Jobko, William	LG	6-1	215	Sr.	Lansing
59	*Jones, Herbert	LG	5-10	192	Sr.	Columbus
19	Kilgore, David	PK	5-9	164	So.	Dayton
22	*Kremblas, Frank	QB	6-1	193	Jr.	Akron
44	*LeBeau, Richard	RH	6	181	Jr.	London
76	Marshall, James	RT	6-3	226	So.	Columbus
72	*Martin, John	RT	5-11	212	Sr.	Waverly
74	Matz, James	RT	6	222	So.	Chillicothe
86	Michael, Richard	LE	6-2	217	So.	Hamilton
88	*Morgan, Thomas	RE	6-2	196	Jr.	Hamilton
70	Nagy, Alex	LT	6-2	230	Sr.	Warren
25	Okulovich, Andy	QB	5-11	184	Jr.	Cleveland
48	*Robinson, Philip	RH	5-9	176	Jr.	Columbus
21	Samuels, James	QB	6	182	So.	Eaton
71	*Schafrath, Richard	LT	6-2	208	Jr.	Wooster
83	Schenking, Fred	RE	6-4	206	Jr.	Coldwater
75	Schram, Bruce	LT	6	206	Jr.	Massillon
60	*Spychalski, Ernest	RG	6-2	234	Jr.	Toledo
45	*Sutherin, Donald	RH	5-11	194	Sr.	Toronto, Can.
64	*Thomas, Aurelius	RG	6-1	204	Sr.	Columbus
35	*Trivisonno, Joseph	FB	5-11	209	Sr.	Cleveland
73	Wagner, David	LT	6-2	230	So.	Portsmouth
15	Wentz, William	RH	5-11	168	So.	Canton
33	White, Robert	FB	6-2	212	So.	Covington, KY
47	Zuhars, David	LH	6-1	178	So.	Columbus

* Letterman

MICHIGAN

No.	Name	Pos.	Ht.	Wgt.	Class	Home Town
15	Batsakes, John	HB	5-8	170	Sr.	Ann Arbor
65	*Berger, Thomas	G	5-11	185	Sr.	Detroit
68	*Bochnowski, Alex	G	5-10	190	Sr.	E. Chicago, IN
81	Boshoven, Robert	E	6	205	Sr.	Grand Rapids
84	*Bowers, David	E	6-2	195	Sr.	Traverse City
97	Boyden, Joel	T	6-6	260	Jr.	Muskegon
26	Brown, David	QB	5-11	185	So.	Battle Creek
74	Bushong, Jared	T	6-2	210	So.	Toledo, OH
33	*Byers, James	FB	6	198	Jr.	Evansville, IN
61	Callahan, Alex	G	6	185	Jr.	Wyandotte
92	Cowan, Keith	T	6	205	So.	Cleveland, OH
94	Crownley, Ermin	T	6-1	226	So.	Detroit
73	*Davies, James	T	5-11	220	Sr.	Muskegon Heights
67	DeMassa, Thomas	G	5-8	188	So.	Detroit
57	*Dickey, James	C	6	188	Sr.	Miamisburg, OH
52	Dupay, Michael	C	6-3	212	So.	Monongahela, PA
63	*Faul, Lawrence	G	6	195	Sr.	River Forest, IL
69	Fillichio, Mike	G	5-10	195	So.	River Forest, IL
70	Genyk, George	T	6	190	So.	Detroit
53	*Goebel, Jerry	C	6-3	214	Sr.	Grosse Pointe
96	Golvach, Duane	C	6	210	So.	Dearborn
77	Gray, James	T	6-3	221	Jr.	Battle Creek
10	Groce, Alvin	HB	5-11	175	So.	Clairton, PA
39	Haller, David	FB	6	185	Jr.	Park Ridge,IL
41	Harper, Darrell	HB	6-1	190	So.	Royal Oak
36	*Herrnstein, John	FB	6-2	212	Jr.	Chillicothe, OH
79	*Heynen, Richard	T	6-1	200	Sr.	Grand Rapids
51	Hoke, Hugh	G	5-9	185	Jr.	Schuykill Haven, PA
89	Johnson, Robert	E	6-1	189	Jr.	Chicago, IL
82	*Johnson, Walter	E	6-2	214	Jr.	Dearborn
16	Julian, Fred	HB	5-9	178	So.	Detroit
91	Keller, Dale	E	6-1	198	So.	Flint
83	Ketteman, Richard	E	6-1	187	Sr.	Toledo, OH
95	Kolcheff, Donald	E	6	183	So.	Dearborn
71	Kreger, John	T	6-6	248	Sr.	Flat Rock
80	Krueger, Frederick	E	5-11	185	Sr.	Allen Park
45	Leith, Jerry	HB	5-9	167	Jr.	Ann Arbor
48	*Lousma, Jack R.	HB	6	192	Jr.	Ann Arbor
56	MacPhee, William	C	6	191	Sr.	Grand Haven
78	*Marciniak, Gerald	G	6-2	220	Jr.	Chicago, IL
18	McCoy, Ernest	HB	5-10	170	Sr.	Ann Arbor
40	McPherson, James	QB	5-10	185	So.	Herrin, IL
17	Myers, Bradley	HB	6	185	So.	Evanston, IL
88	Morrow, Gordon	E	6-3	212	Sr.	Ann Arbor
27	Noskin, Stanton	QB	5-11	180	So.	Chicago, IL
64	*Nyren, Marvin	G	6	205	Sr.	Des Plaines, IL
62	Olm, Fred	G	5-10	210	So.	Niles
60	Oppman, Douglas	G	5-10	195	Jr.	Gary, IN
72	*Orwig, James (Capt.)	T	6	200	Sr.	Toledo, OH
43	*Pace, James	HB	6	195	Sr.	Little Rock, AR
66	Poulos, Paul	G	5-11	190	So.	Freedom, PA
86	*Prahst, Gary	E	6-4	210	Jr.	Berea, OH
49	*Ptacek, Robert	HB	6-1	200	Jr.	Cleveland, OH
32	Renwick, William	FB	6	194	So.	Corunna
37	Rio, Anthony	FB	6	185	Jr.	Chicago, IL
14	*Shatusky, Michael	HB	5-11	175	Sr.	Menominee
35	*Sisinyak, Eugene	FB	6	190	Jr.	Monroe
30	Smith, Gerald	FB	5-10	185	So.	Detroit
75	*Smith, Willie	T	6-2	240	Jr.	Little Rock, AR
58	*Snider, Gene	C	6-1	210	Sr.	Hamtramck
22	*Spidel, John	QB	5-11	178	Jr.	Greenville, OH
76	Stetten, Maynard	T	6-2	205	Jr.	Gibraltar
28	Sytek, James	QB	5-11	195	Jr.	Detroit
85	Teuscher, Charles	E	6-1	197	So.	Aurora, IL
24	*Van Pelt, James	QB	5-11	185	Jr.	Evanston, IL
59	Vavroch, John	G	6	205	Jr.	Cleveland, OH
55	*Wine, Raymond	C	6-2	196	Jr.	Port Huron
42	Zachary, John	HB	5-11	175	Jr.	Chicago, IL
38	Zervas, Stephen	FB	5-11	192	Sr.	Hazel Park

* Lettermen

1957

Michigan	16	S. California	6
Michigan	26	Georgia	0
Michigan	6	Mich. State	35
Michigan	34	Northwestern	14
Michigan	24	Minnesota	7
Michigan	21	Iowa	21
Michigan	19	Illinois	20
Michigan	27	Indiana	13
Michigan	14	Ohio State	31

Season Summary

Games Won, 5; Lost, 3; Tied, 1

JAMES PACE
All-American Halfback

Michigan fumbles at the end of the game.

November 22, 1958

Columbus, Ohio

Ohio State Stops Michigan, 20 To 14

Wolverines Threaten In Last Minutes As Oosterbaan Bows Out Gloriously

Michigan's dramatic last minute bid to upset highly-favored Ohio State, and "win the last one for Bennie," ended in frustrating failure and a 20-14 defeat.

With only a scarce 40 seconds remaining, halfback Brad Myers of UM cracked into the massed Ohio defenders. He was tackled viciously by Dick Schafrath and 10 other Buckeyes. Myers fumbled. A Buckeye sophomore quarterback, Jerry Fields fell on the football on Ohio's 4-yard line to preserve the hard-won Big Ten windup.

Fired high in an effort to present their leader, Bennie Oosterbaan, with a victory as his going-away present, Michigan completely surprised and pressed Ohio State with a record-breaking passing performance. UM's Bob Ptacek's aerial outburst cracked a Western Conference record of 22 completions created only a week earlier by Iowa's Randy Duncan against the same Ohio State team.

Winning the coin toss and choosing the ball, the Wolverines moved confidently and quickly to a touchdown. They went 83 yards in 12 plays. Ptacek, whose short, killing passes scrambled Ohio's defenses, ran and passed to the first TD. The payoff was a 7-yarder to end Gary Prahst in the end zone. The PAT pass failed.

After a Michigan fumble on their own 12, Ohio's Dick LeBeau carried into the end zone for the tying touchdown. Ohio missed the point when Dave Kilgore's kick went wide.

Myers became a workhorse hero as Michigan bounced right back for another TD. The second-string junior halfback caught four passes from Ptacek, totaling 40 yards and carried three times for another 7 yards. The TD was scored on a pass from Ptacek to Prahst covering the last 32 yards. This time Ptacek and Prahst connected for the two extra points.

Ohio scored again before the half when the Michigan secondary ignored Jim Herbstreit. In isolated splendor on the eight-yard line, Herbstreit was a perfect target for quarterback Fields. He caught the ball and raced in to make the score 14-12, UM in the lead. Fields and Herbstreit tried an encore pass for the matching points but failed.

In the second half, the undermanned Wolverines, showing wear and tear, were unable to stop the Buckeyes from putting on at least one old familiar crunch-crunch, all-the-way drive. The Buckeyes moved 80 yards in 11 plays, mostly on short stabs by White and Clark, and one substantial 21-yard pass from Fields to Clark. White got the touchdown honor on a line-busting six-yard gain. Fields picked up the two extra points as he barely slithered across the goal line to give Ohio its final 20-14 margin.

Michigan had one last chance as Gerald Smith, an inexperienced Wolverine sub, intercepted a Fields' aerial putting the ball on Ohio's 34. Using a running, control attack, Michigan moved steadily toward Ohio's goal. Myers plunged into the concrete line of OSU and fumbled which ended the threat and the game.

STATISTICS

	OSU	UM
First Downs	12	24
Rushes - Yardage	31-187	37-118
Passing - Yardage	75	241
Return Yardage	66	73
Passing	5-10-1	25-39-2
Fumbles - Lost	1-1	4-4
Penalties - Yards	1-5	4-40

1958			
Michigan	20	U.S.C.	19
Michigan	12	M.S.U.	12
Michigan	14	Navy	20
Michigan	24	Northwestern	55
Michigan	20	Minnesota	19
Michigan	14	Iowa	37
Michigan	8	Illinois	21
Michigan	6	Indiana	8
Michigan	14	Ohio State	20

Season Summary

Games Won, 2; Lost, 6; Tied, 1

MICHIGAN

No.	Name	Pos.	Ht.	Wgt.	Class	Home Town
10	*Groce, Alvin	HB	5-11	166	Jr.	Clairton, PA
14	McNitt, Gary	HB	5-9	196	So.	Mesick
15	Batsakes, John	HB	5-8	172	Sr.	Ann Arbor
16	*Julian, Fred	HB	5-9	184	Jr.	Detroit
17	*Myers, Bradley	HB	6	196	Jr.	Evanston, IL
18	Raeder, Paul	HB	5-11	187	So.	Lorain, OH
19	Leith, Jerry	HB	5-9	167	Sr.	Ann Arbor
20	Hannah, Donald	QB	6	178	So.	Gary, IN
21	Barger, Phil	QB	5-11	188	So.	Toronto, Can.
22	*Spidel, John	QB	5-11	180	Sr.	Greenville, OH
24	McPherson, James	QB	5-10	175	Jr.	Herrin, IL
27	*Noskin, Stanton	QB	5-11	180	Jr.	Chicago, IL
28	Sytek, James	QB	5-11	194	Sr.	Detroit
32	Fitzgerald, Dennis	FB	5-9	184	So.	Ann Arbor
33	*Byers, James	C	6	198	Sr.	Evansville, IN
35	*Sisinyak, Eugene	FB	6	195	So.	Monroe
36	*Herrnstein, John	FB	6-2	215	Sr.	Chillicothe, OH
37	*Rio, Anthony	FB	6	189	Sr.	Chicago, IL
38	Walker, John	FB	6	195	So.	Milford
39	Stuart, Henry	FB	5-11	191	So.	Detroit
41	*Harper, Darrell	HB	6-1	195	Jr.	Royal Oak
42	Zachary, Jack	HB	5-9	174	Sr.	Chicago, IL
45	Vollmar, James	HB	6	178	So.	Wyandotte
46	Newman, Harry, Jr.	HB	5-9	185	So.	Franklin
48	Bushong, Reid	HB	6-1	179	So.	Toledo, OH
49	*Ptacek, Robert	HB	6-1	204	Sr.	Cleveland, OH
50	Kerr, Thomas	C	6-1	203	So.	Hobart, IN
51	Smith, Gerald	C	5-11	185	Jr.	Detroit
53	Hall, B. Lee	T	6	206	So.	Charlotte
55	Syring, Richard	C	6	189	So.	Bay City
57	*Dickey, James	C	6-1	191	Sr.	Miamisburg, OH
58	*Morrow, Gordon	C	6-3	228	Sr.	Ann Arbor
60	Oppman, Douglas	G	5-10	192	Jr.	Gary, IN
61	*Callahan, Alex	G	6	195	Sr.	Wyandotte
62	Olm, Fred	G	5-11	223	Jr.	Niles
63	Palomaki, David	G	6-1	205	So.	Ishpeming
65	Curtis, Guy	G	6-1	222	So.	South Bend, IN
66	Poulos, Paul	G	5-11	198	Jr.	Freedom, PA
67	DeMassa, Thomas	G	5-8	188	Jr.	Detroit
68	Deskins, Donald	G	6-2	241	So.	Jamaica, NY
69	*Fillichio, Mike	G	5-10	190	Jr.	River Forest, IL
70	*Genyk, George	T	6-1	200	Jr.	Detroit
71	Walls, Grant	T	6	189	So.	Norwalk, OH
72	Dupay, Michael	T	6-2	207	Jr.	Monongahela, PA
73	Swanson, Robert	T	6	212	So.	Benton Harbor
74	*Bushong, Jared	T	6-2	209	Jr.	Toledo, OH
76	Stetten, Maynard	T	6-2	206	Sr.	Gibraltar
77	Gray, James	T	6-3	233	Sr.	Battle Creek
78	*Marciniak, Jerry	T	6-2	236	Sr.	Chicago, IL
79	Stine, William	T	6-1	215	So.	Toledo, OH
81	Halstead, John	E	6-2	205	So.	Bay City
82	*Johnson, Walter	E	6-2	214	Sr.	Dearborn
84	Brefeld, Joseph	E	6-2	212	So.	Cincinnati, OH
86	*Prahst, Gary	E	6-4	220	Sr.	Berea, OH
88	Kane, Gary	E	6-2	215	So.	Elgin, IL
89	Johnson, Robert	E	6-2	199	Sr.	Chicago, IL
90	Cowan, Keith	E	6	205	Jr.	Cleveland, OH
93	Hildebrand, Willard	T	6-2	216	So.	Chillicothe, OH
96	Maki, Wesley	T	5-11	214	So.	Marquette

* Indicates letter

OHIO

No.	Name	Pos.	Ht.	Wgt.	Class	Home Town
10	Selby, David	RH	6-1	183	Jr.	Columbus
15	Wentz, William	RH	5-10	172	Jr.	Canton
17	McMurry, Preston	LH	5-9	167	Sr.	Pittsburgh, PA
18	**Clark, Donald	LH	5-11	187	Sr.	Akron
19	Kilgore, David	QB	5-9	158	Jr.	Dayton
22	**Kremblas, Frank	QB	6-1	193	Sr.	Akron
24	Fields, Jerry	QB	6-1	208	So.	Coal Grove
25	Benis, Mike	QB	6	185	So.	Columbus
26	Adulewicz, Casimir	QB	5-9	178	Jr.	Steubenville
28	Ballmer, Paul	QB	5-10	182	Sr.	Lancaster
30	Gage, Ralph	QB	5-10	190	Sr.	Painesville
32	Lindner, James	FB	5-10	196	So.	Enon Valley, PA
33	*White, Robert	FB	6-2	207	Jr.	Covington, KY
34	Fontes, Leonard	FB	5-8	176	Jr.	Wareham, MA
35	Farrall, John	RG	5-11	212	So.	Canton
36	Emelianchik, Robert	FB	5-11	210	Jr.	Brooklyn, NY
37	Armstrong, Jack	FB	6	204	So.	Huron
41	Matte, Thomas	LH	6	190	So.	East Cleveland
42	*Williams, Lee	LH	5-10	171	Sr.	Springfield
43	German, William	RH	5-10	185	So.	Shaker Heights
44	**LeBeau, Richard	RH	6	182	Sr.	London
45	Herbstreit, James	LH	5-8	158	So.	Reading
46	Dresser, John	FB	6-1	212	Jr.	Toledo
47	Moran, John	RH	5-10	188	Jr.	Columbus
48	**Robinson, Philip	RH	5-9	182	Sr.	Columbus
50	Beam, William	C	6-1	208	Jr.	Moundsville, WV
51	Varner, Thomas	C	5-10	202	So.	Saginaw, MI
52	Bowsher, Jerry	LG	5-10	198	Jr.	Toledo
53	*James, Daniel	C	6-2	248	Sr.	Cincinnati
55	Vogelgesang, Don	C	6	188	So.	Canton
57	Seilkop, Kenneth	LG	5-11	196	Jr.	Columbus
58	*Fronk, Daniel	C	5-11	186	Sr.	Dover
60	**Spychalski, Ernest	RG	6-2	229	Sr.	Toledo
61	Bailey, Ralph	LG	6	198	Sr.	Springfield
62	Young, Don	RG	6	214	So.	Dayton
63	Wright, Ernest	RG	6-3	242	So.	Toledo
64	Elfers, Benjamin	LG	5-10	206	So.	Kelleys Island
65	Hauer, Oscar	LG	6-2	209	So.	Hamilton
66	Anders, Richard	C	5-9	184	Jr.	Washington C.H.
67	Hartman, Gabriel	LG	5-9	209	So.	Troy
68	*Arnold, Birtho	RT	6-2	309	Jr.	Columbus
69	Bryant, Gene	RG	6-2	204	So.	Ironton
71	**Schafrath, Richard	RE	6-2	212	Sr.	Wooster
72	Jentes, Charles	LT	6-2	208	So.	Wooster
73	Wagner, David	RT	6-2	230	Jr.	Portsmouth
74	Matz, James	LT	6-1	221	Jr.	Chillicothe
75	Wilson, Clifford	RT	6-3	255	Sr.	Newcomerstown
76	*Marshall, James	RT	6-3	230	Jr.	Columbus
77	Tyrer, James	LT	6-5	244	So.	Newark
78	**Crawford, Al	LT	6	231	Sr.	Canton
79	Whitaker, Larry	RT	6-1	228	So.	St. Johns
80	Fiers, Alan	RE	6-1	202	So.	Indianapolis, IN
81	Lord, John	RE	5-10	173	Sr.	Columbus
82	Tidmore, Samuel	LE	6	210	So.	Cleveland
83	Walter, David	RE	5-9	189	So.	Columbus
84	*Houston, James	LE	6-2	211	Jr.	Massillon
85	Azok, Frank	LE	6-2	177	So.	Lorain
86	Michael, Richard	LE	6-2	217	Jr.	Hamilton
87	**Bowermaster, R.	RE	6-2	203	Sr.	Hamilton
88	**Morgan, Thomas	RE	6-2	188	Sr.	Hamilton
89	Deyo, Charles	RE	6-2	197	So.	Columbus
90	Herrman, Harvey	RT	6-2	226	Jr.	Cincinnati
91	Langermeier, G.	LE	6	197	So.	Cleveland
92	Rowland, James	LE	6-4	213	Jr.	Beckley, WV
93	Korn, Gary	RE	6	195	Jr.	Columbus
94	Warner, Duane	LE	6	174	So.	Arlington
95	Niesz, Dale	LE	6-2	192	So.	East Sparta

* Indicates letter

1958

Ohio	23	S. Methodist	20
Ohio	12	Washington	7
Ohio	19	Illinois	13
Ohio	49	Indiana	8
Ohio	7	Wisconsin	7
Ohio	0	Northwestern	21
Ohio	14	Purdue	14
Ohio	38	Iowa	28
Ohio	20	Michigan	14

Season Summary

Won, 6; Lost, 1; Tied, 2

JAMES HOUSTON
All-American End

ROBERT WHITE
All-American Back

JAMES MARSHALL
All-American Tackle

CHALMERS "BUMP" ELLIOTT
Michigan Head Coach
1959-1968

November 21, 1959

Ann Arbor, Michigan

Wolverines Win 23-14 Over Bucks

Defeat Terminates Worst OSU Season in Last 12 Years

A shivering crowd of 90,093 watched as the Wolverines, on the way back under young head coach Bump Elliott, passed, ran, and kicked their way to a 23-14 victory over the Buckeyes. It was a hard-fought contest and the tackling and blocking could be heard all over the mammoth Michigan oval.

Ohio State, which finished with a 3-5-1 record, had not lost more than three games since 1947 when under Wes Fesler, they had a 2-6-1 mark. Michigan ended the season with a 4-5 record.

Three seniors accounted for all of the Michigan scoring. Fullback Tony Rio got two TD's, the first on an eight-yard pass and the second on a one-yard buck up the middle. The other Michigan touchdown was scored by quarterback Stan Noskin on a four yard run after he couldn't find a man open while back to pass. Halfback Darrell Harper booted two of three extra points and added a 30-yard field goal in the final period.

Ohio State was playing without its jarring fullback, injured Bob White, but he was hardly missed as sophomore Roger Detrick from Dayton more than picked up the slack. Detrick lugged the ball 33 times for 139 yards. On Ohio's first touchdown drive, Detrick carried 11 of the 13 plays needed. He was used as a decoy on the TD play as quarterback Jerry Fields faked to him and then tossed to end Jim Houston from two yards out. Detrick leaped over from the one for the second and final tally for OSU.

The theme of the game was evident from the opening kickoff. Michigan's Harper booted to Field on the six from where he moved to the Ohio State 26 and was met with a booming tackle by end John Halstead causing a fumble Tom Jolson recovered for Michigan on the Ohio 26. The game was halted at this time for several minutes as Halstead was injured on the play and had to be carried from the field on a stretcher. He was admitted to University Hospital with a neck injury and broken nose.

Ohio State was never able to get the lead but the Bucks did tie the game 14-14 midway in the third period.

STATISTICS

	UM	OSU
First Downs	20	20
Rushing Yardage	198	228
Passing Yardage	108	130
Passes	8-11	11-16
Passes Intercepted By	3	1
Punts	2-34	1-30
Fumbles Lost	2	2
Yards Penalized	10	10

UM	7	7	6	3	23
OSU	6	0	8	0	14

Mich. Scoring — Rio 2 (8 yd. pass from Noskin; 1 yd. run); Noskin (4 yd. run); Harper (2 PAT; 30 yd. FG)

OSU Scoring — Houston (2 yd. pass from Field); Detrick (1 yd. run); Herbstreit (PAT pass from Field)

1959			
Ohio	14	Duke	13
Ohio	0	S. California	17
Ohio	0	Illinois	9
Ohio	15	Purdue	0
Ohio	3	Wisconsin	12
Ohio	30	MSU	24
Ohio	0	Indiana	0
Ohio	7	Iowa	16
Ohio	14	Michigan	23

Season Summary

Won, 3; Lost, 5; Tied, 1

JAMES HOUSTON
All-American End

OHIO

No.	Name	Pos.	Ht.	Wgt.	Class	Home Town
26	Adulewicz, Casimir	QB	5-9	173	Sr.	Steubenville
53	*Anders, Richard	C	5-9	180	Sr.	Washington C.H.
30	Archambeau, Louis	LH	5-10	175	Sr.	Toledo
68	*Arnold, Birtho	RT	6-2	301	Sr.	Columbus
60	Banks, John	RG	5-10	210	So.	Hamilton
50	Beam, William	C	6	216	Sr.	Moundsville, WV
21	Benis, Mike	QB	6-10	185	Jr.	Columbus
52	Bowsher, Jerry	LG	5-11	211	Sr.	Toledo
88	Bryant, Charles	LE	6-1	209	So.	Zanesville
71	Bunnell, Paul	RT	6-2	223	So.	Bradford
93	Clotz, Dennis	RT	6-1	203	So.	Amherst
59	Coburn, Michael	C	6-1	209	So.	Akron
32	Detrick, Roger	FB	5-9	198	So.	Dayton
69	Ehrensberger, Fred	LG	5-9	205	So.	Dayton
36	Emelianchik, Robert	FB	5-10	205	Sr.	Brooklyn, NY
56	Farrall, John	LG	5-10	207	Jr.	Canton
46	Ferguson, Robert	LH	6	217	So.	Troy
24	*Fields, Jerry	QB	6-1	209	Jr.	Coal Grove
80	Fiers, Alan	RE	6-1	209	Jr.	Indianapolis, IN
34	*Fontes, Leonard	FB	5-8	182	Sr.	Wareham, MA
35	German, William	RH	5-10	170	Jr.	Shaker Heights
47	Hansley, Gary	RH	5-9	198	So.	Cleveland
44	Hansley, Terence	LH	6	190	Sr.	Cleveland
18	Hardman, Von Allen	LH	6	177	So.	Spencer, WV
61	Harbin, Jerry	RG	5-10	210	So.	Marion
67	*Hartman, Gabriel	RG	5-9	214	Jr.	Troy
65	*Hauer, Oscar	LG	6-2	211	Jr.	Hamilton
12	Haupt, Richard	RH	5-11	172	So.	Sumner, IA
45	*Herbstreit, James	RH	5-8	159	Jr.	Reading
90	Herrmann, Harvey	LT	6-2	235	Sr.	Cincinnati
14	Hess, Brice	LH	5-11	168	So.	Mt. Vernon
49	Houck, Ronnie	LH	5-10	169	So.	Troy
84	*Houston, James (C)	RE	6-2	216	Sr.	Massillon
64	Ingram, Michael	LG	5-9	212	So.	Bellaire
72	Jentes, Charles	LT	6-2	212	Jr.	Wooster
19	*Kilgore, David	PK	5-9	158	Sr.	Dayton
28	Korn, Gary	LE	6	195	Sr.	Columbus
17	Lambert, Howard	RH	5-7	166	So.	Bellefontaine
54	Lindner, James	C	5-11	200	Jr.	Enon Valley, PA
23	Lister, Robert	QB	6-2	190	So.	Marion
91	Martin, Paul	RE	6-2	184	So.	Canton
41	*Matte, Thomas	QB-LH	6	190	Jr.	East Cleveland
74	*Matz, James	LT	6-1	215	Sr.	Chillicothe
70	*Michael, Richard	RT	6-3	218	Sr.	Hamilton
83	Niesz, Dale	RE	6-2	198	Jr.	East Sparta
87	Perdue, Thomas	LE	5-11	188	So.	Huntington, WV
89	Rice, Richard	C	5-11	195	So.	Parma
75	Roberts, Jack	LT	6	237	So.	Strongsville
92	Rowland, James	LE	6-4	213	Sr.	Beckley, WV
57	Seilkop, Kenneth	LG	5-11	207	Sr.	Columbus
86	Shuster, Robert	RT	5-11	212	So.	Cleveland
25	Spichek, Willie	QB	5-11	176	So.	Elbert, WV
81	Stephens, Larry	RE	6	190	So.	Coshocton
42	Strait, Lynn	LH	5-11	178	So.	Logan
16	Tingley, David	RH	5-9	181	So.	London
78	Tolford, George	RT	6	225	Jr.	Swanton
77	*Tyrer, James	LT	6-5	248	Jr.	Newark
51	Varner, Thomas	C	5-10	202	Jr.	Saginaw, MI
55	Vogelgesang, Don	C	6	190	Jr.	Canton
22	Wallace, Jack	QB	6-3	212	So.	Middletown
94	Warner, Duane	LE	6	175	Jr.	Arlington
58	Watkins, Jene	C	6	197	So.	Smithfield
76	Weldy, Ronald	RT	6-3	251	So.	Piqua
15	Wentz, William	RH	5-10	175	Sr.	Canton
79	Whitaker, Larry	RT	6	225	Jr.	St. Johns
33	*White, Robert	FB	6-2	214	Sr.	Covington, KY
82	Wittmer, George	RE	6-1	187	So.	Cincinnati
63	*Wright, Ernest	LT	6-3	242	Jr.	Toledo
62	*Young, Don	LG	6-1	214	Jr.	Dayton

* Letterman

MICHIGAN

No.	Name	Pos.	Ht.	Wgt.	Class	Home Town
86	Brown, Robert	E	6-3	212	So.	Kalamazoo
74	*Bushong, Jared	T	6-2	204	Sr.	Toledo, OH
48	*Bushong, Reid	HB	6-1	178	Jr.	Toledo, OH
61	*Callahan, Alex	G	6	193	Sr.	Wyandotte
90	Cowan, Keith	E	6-2	205	Jr.	Cleveland, OH
77	Curtis, Guy	T	6-1	215	Jr.	South Bend, IN
67	DeMassa, Thomas	G	5-8	196	Jr.	Detroit
68	*Deskins, Donald	T	6-2	238	Sr.	Jamaica, NY
34	DeStefano, Guy	FB	5-11	185	So.	Gary, IN
97	Doersam, Paul	T	6-4	215	So.	Saginaw
21	Dougall, Bill	QB	6	180	So.	Detroit
95	Dupay, Michael	T	6-2	210	Sr.	Monongahela, PA
69	*Fillichio, Michael	G	5-10	195	Sr.	River Forest, IL
18	Fitzgerald, J. Dennis	HB	5-10	180	Jr.	Ann Arbor
12	Franklin, Wilbert	HB	5-10	182	So.	Chicago, IL
53	Gee, Thomas	G	5-10	196	Jr.	Melvindale
70	*Genyk, George (Capt.)	G	6	196	Sr.	Detroit
59	Grant, Todd	C	6-4	222	So.	Lathrup Village
10	Haley, John	HB	5-11	170	So.	Bethesda, MD
65	*Hall, B. Lee	G	6	212	So.	Charlotte
42	Hallenbeck, John	HB	5-11	175	So.	Rochester, MN
81	*Halstead, John	E	6-2	208	Jr.	Bay City
20	Hannah, Donald	QB	6	180	Jr.	Gary, IN
41	*Harper, Darrell	HB	6-1	194	Sr.	Royal Oak
80	Heiden, Richard	E	6-3	196	So.	Melvindale
75	Herrala, Wallace	G	5-10	220	So.	Muskegon Hts.
93	*Hildebrand, Willard	T	6-2	210	Jr.	Chillicothe, OH
91	Hornbeck, William	E	6-2	180	Jr.	Los Angeles, CA
64	*Jobson, E. Thomas	T	6	210	Jr.	Flint
89	*Johnson, Robert	E	6-2	206	Sr.	Chicago, IL
16	*Julian, Fred	HB	5-9	188	Sr.	Detroit
88	*Kane, Gary	E	6-3	215	Jr.	Elgin, IL
50	Kerr, Thomas	C	6-1	193	Jr.	Hobart, IN
83	Korowin, James	E	6-2	193	So.	Wyandotte
19	Leith, Jerry	HB	5-7	168	Sr.	Ann Arbor
96	Maentz, Scott	E	6-3	206	So.	Grand Rapids
73	Maloney, Frank	C	5-11	194	So.	Chicago, IL
82	Mans, George	E	6-4	202	So.	Trenton
58	Mans, John	C	6-4	229	So.	Trenton
45	McKee, Robert	HB	6	187	So.	North Bay, Ont.
14	*McNitt, Gary	HB	5-10	195	Jr.	Mesick
24	McPherson, James	QB	5-10	175	Sr.	Herrin, IL
43	McRae, Benjamin	HB	6	168	So.	Newport News, VA
17	*Myers, Bradley	HB	6	197	Sr.	Evanston, IL
46	*Newman, Harry	HB	5-10	188	Jr.	Detroit
27	*Noskin, Stanton	QB	5-11	180	Sr.	Chicago, IL
26	Palmer, Paul	QB	5-10	170	So.	Toronto, Ont., Can.
72	Palomaki, Dave	T	6-1	205	Jr.	Ishpeming
52	Pampu, Virgil	C	6	190	So.	Dearborn
60	Pavloff, Louis	G	6	195	So.	Hazel Park
63	Perry, Ronald	T	6	217	So.	Vineland, NJ
66	*Poulos, Paul	G	5-11	196	Jr.	Freedom, PA
54	Raeder, Paul	FB	5-11	193	Sr.	Lorain, OH
37	*Rio, Anthony	FB	6	182	Sr.	Chicago, IL
78	Schmidt, Paul	T	6-4	230	So.	Skokie, IL
76	Schopf, Jon	G	6-2	218	So.	Grand Rapids
56	Slezak, David	G	5-11	178	So.	Ann Arbor
51	*Smith, Gerald	C	5-10	187	Sr.	Detroit
99	Smith, Jeffrey	E	6-3	190	So.	Kohler, WI
15	Spacht, Ronald	HB	5-10	180	So.	Kent, OH
28	Stamos, John	QB	6-1	204	So.	Chicago, IL
94	Stawski, Willard	T	6-3	210	So.	Caledonia
62	Stieler, Stephen	C	5-9	201	So.	Wyandotte
79	*Stine, William	T	6-2	211	Jr.	Toledo, OH
57	Thomas, David	G	6-2	200	So.	Norwalk, OH
36	Tunnicliff, William	FB	6-1	208	So.	Ferndale
39	Tureaud, Kenneth	FB	6-1	198	So.	Detroit
32	Van Dyne, Rudd	HB	6	193	Jr.	Sedalia, MO
71	Walls, Grant Jr.	T	6	200	Jr.	Norwalk, OH
23	Wooding, Pete	HB	5-10	170	So.	Ann Arbor
92	Wynn, Philip	FB	6-1	198	So.	Carlinville, IL
85	Zubkus, E. James	E	6-1	190	So.	Munhall, PA

* Letterman

1959

Michigan	15	Missouri	20
Michigan	8	MSU	34
Michigan	18	Oregon State	7
Michigan	7	Northwestern	20
Michigan	14	Minnesota	6
Michigan	10	Wisconsin	19
Michigan	20	Illinois	15
Michigan	7	Indiana	26
Michigan	23	Ohio State	14

Season Summary

Games Won, 4; Lost, 5

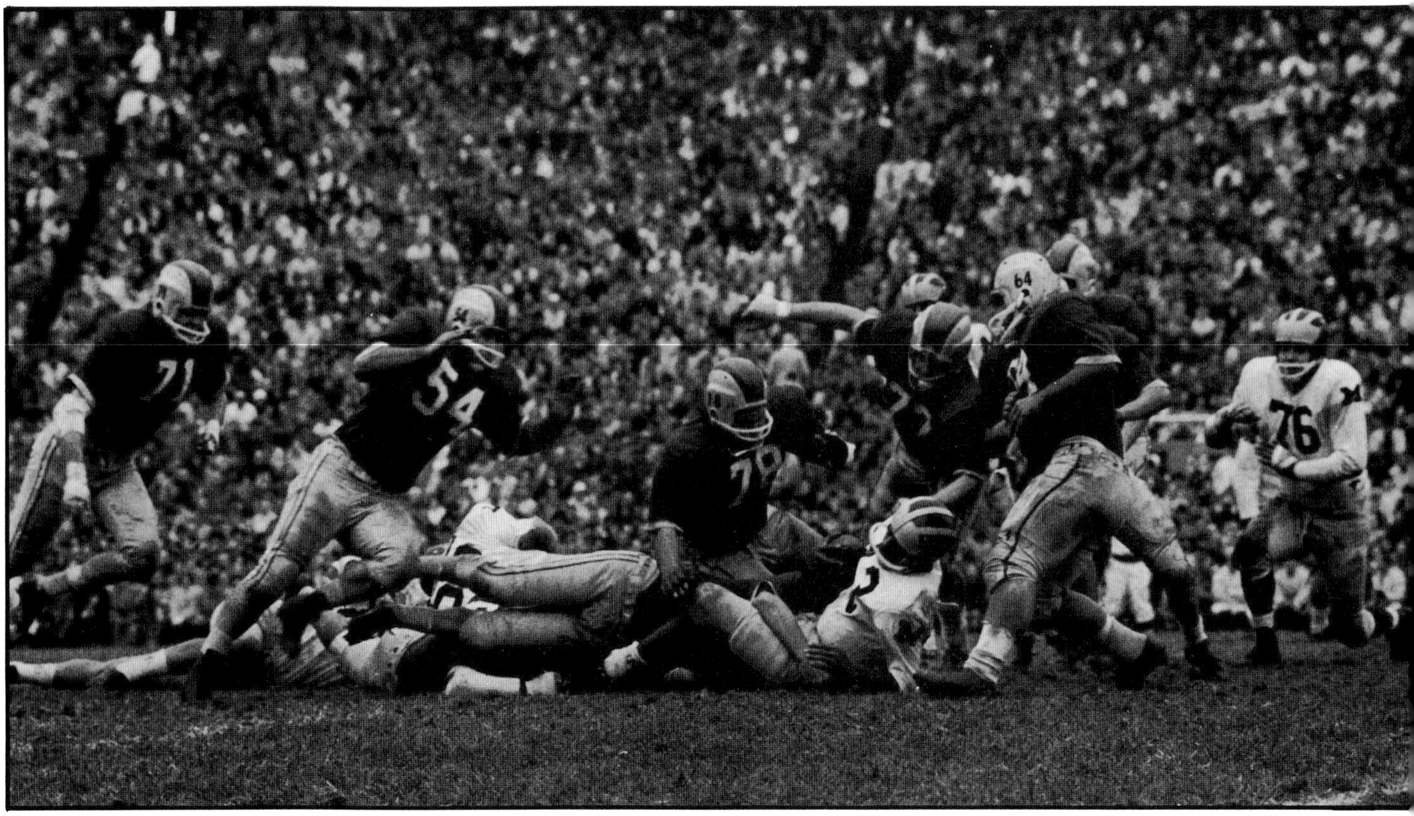

November 19, 1960

Columbus, Ohio

Bucks Squeeze By Stubborn Michigan, 7-0

Ferguson Scores Only TD In Final Quarter

Ohio State's Buckeyes unleashed their vaunted power style of football long enough to fashion a 7-0 triumph over arch-rival Michigan in the 57th meeting of these Big Ten institutions. It was not a spectacular ball game, but it was a real bruiser. The line play was particularly hard-fought all the way.

Each team had excellent scoring opportunities in the first two quarters, but neither made a serious scoring bid in the third period. Ohio moved to the UM 7, but a Ferguson fumble was recovered by John Stamos. Ohio's Tidmore had previously recovered a Michigan fumble to start that drive. The Wolverines advanced to the Buckeye 12 where a field goal was attempted by Bill Freeman with Dave Glinka holding. It was wide to the left.

The Buckeyes' touchdown came with 12:55 remaining in the last period. It was the result of a 58-yard charge which featured the running of fullback Bob Ferguson and quarterback Tom Matte. The drive started on the final play of the third quarter when UM's Reid Bushong punted to Ohio's Bob Klein who returned to the Michigan 42. Relying strictly on powerplays, the Scarlet and Gray required only five plays to cross the goal line for the lone touchdown of the game. The final 17 yards were covered on a burst by hard-charging Bob Ferguson through right guard. The 220-pound junior fullback from Troy, Ohio, simply could not be contained on that brilliant offensive maneuver as it appeared that he was trapped at the line of scrimmage. But he kept twisting and turning while shedding enemy tacklers. The extra point was booted by Ben Jones with Bill Wentz holding.

Dennis Fitzgerald, senior halfback from Ann Arbor, was Michigan's outstanding ground gainer with 63 yards in 17 tries. Ferguson was Ohio's top ball carrier with 80 yards in 16 attempts while the versatile Matte carried 25 times, gained 71, but lost 30 for a net gain of 41 yards.

One of the best plays of the game came in the fourth quarter when Mike Ingram of Ohio intercepted one of Glinka's aerials and lateraled to halfback Jim Herbstreit who sprinted 48 yards to the Michigan 22.

STATISTICS

	OSU	UM
First Downs	9	18
Rushes - Yards	42-128	50-132
Passing Yardage	40	86
Return Yardage	38	37
Passing	7-2-0	18-10-2
Punts	7-31	5-33
Fumbles Lost	1	2
Penalties - Yards	3-13	1-15

1960	
Michigan .. 21	Univ. of Oregon 0
Michigan .. 17	MSU 24
Michigan .. 31	Duke 6
Michigan .. 14	Northwestern .. 7
Michigan .. 0	Minnesota 10
Michigan .. 13	Wisconsin 16
Michigan .. 8	Illinois 7
Michigan .. 29	Indiana 7
Michigan .. 0	Ohio State 7

Season Summary

Games Won, 5; Lost, 4

MICHIGAN

No.	Name	Pos.	Ht.	Wgt.	Class	Home Town
12	Hood, Earl	HB	5-9	175	So.	Chillicothe, OH
14	*McNitt, Gary	FB	5-10	195	Sr.	Mesick
15	Spacht, Ronald	HB	5-10	180	Jr.	Kent, OH
16	Kowalik, John	HB	5-10	180	So.	Detroit
17	Hornbeck, William	HB	6-1	180	Jr.	Royal Oak
18	*Fitzgerald, Dennis	HB	5-10	175	Sr.	Ann Arbor
19	Raimey, David	HB	5-10	190	So.	Dayton, OH
20	Chandler, Robert	QB	6-3	208	So.	LaGrange, IL
22	*Hannah, Don	QB	6	180	Sr.	Gary, IN
24	Glinka, David	QB	6-1	210	So.	Toledo, OH
25	Plesha, Robert	QB	6	178	So.	McCook, IL
28	*Stamos, John	QB	6-1	208	Jr.	Chicago, IL
32	*Van Dyne, Rudd	FB	6	193	Sr.	Sedalia, MO
33	Mcngeau, David	FB	6-3	211	So.	Lincoln Park
34	DeStefano, Guy	FB	5-11	185	Jr.	Gary, IN
35	*Raeder, Paul	HB	5-11	192	Jr.	Kent, OH
36	*Tunicliff, William	FB	6-1	210	Jr.	Ferndale
39	*Tureaud, Kenneth	HB	6-1	198	Jr.	Detroit
40	McKee, Robert	HB	6	187	Jr.	North Bay, Ont., CAN.
42	Strobel, Jack	HB	5-10	182	So.	Maywood, IL
43	*McRae, Benjamin	HB	6	170	Jr.	Newport News, VA
45	Ward, James	HB	6-1	195	So.	Imlay City
46	Agee, Michael	HB	6	175	So.	Farmington
48	*Bushong, Reid	HB	6-1	180	Sr.	Toledo, OH
50	Kerr, Thomas	C	6-1	193	Sr.	Hobart, IN
51	*Smith, Gerald	C	5-11	194	Sr.	Detroit
52	Pampu, Virgil	C	6	190	Jr.	Dearborn
53	Gee, Thomas	G	6	200	Jr.	Melvindale
54	*Walker, John	C	6	205	Sr.	Walled Lake
55	*Syring, Richard	G	6	192	Sr.	Bay City
56	Maloney, Frank	G	5-11	193	Jr.	Chicago, IL
57	Houtman, John	C	6-4	230	So.	Adrian
58	Kriska, Nicholas	G	6	185	So.	Akron, OH
59	*Grant, Todd	C	6-4	230	Jr.	Lathrup Village
60	*Pavloff, Louis	G	6	205	Jr.	Hazel Park
61	Walls, Grant	T	6	205	Sr.	Norwalk, OH
62	Minko, John	G	6-1	215	So.	Connellsville, PA
63	Kocan, Ronald	E	5-11	205	So.	Sharpsville, PA
64	*Jobson, Thomas	T	6	210	Sr.	Flint
65	*Hall, Lee	G	6	220	Jr.	Charlotte
66	*Poulos, Paul	G	5-11	205	Sr.	Freedom, PA
67	Clappison, Frank	G	6-1	200	So.	Farmington
69	O'Donnell, Joseph	FB	6-2	210	So.	Milan
70	Bryce, Gary	T	6-3	225	So.	Royal Oak
72	Conklin, Jon	T	6-2	255	So.	Midland
73	Atchison, John	G	6	195	So.	Centralia, IL
74	Lehr, John	T	6	230	So.	Cincinnati, OH
75	Herrala, Wallace	G	5-10	220	Jr.	Muskegon Hgts.
76	*Schopf, Jon	T	6-2	218	Jr.	Grand Rapids
77	*Curtis, Guy	T	6	215	Sr.	South Bend, IN
78	Schmidt, Paul	T	6-4	235	Jr.	Skokie, IL
79	*Stine, William	T	6-2	235	Sr.	Toledo, OH
80	Filar, Robert	E	6-4	205	So.	Southfield
81	*Halstead, John	E	6-2	215	Sr.	Bay City
82	*Mans, George	E	6-4	208	Jr.	Trenton
83	*Korowin, James	E	6-2	195	Jr.	Wyandotte
85	Zubkus, James	E	6-1	205	Jr.	Munhall, PA
86	Brown, Robert	E	6-5	225	Jr.	Kalamazoo
88	Freehan, William	E	6-3	202	So.	Royal Oak
89	*Johnson, Robert	E	6-2	206	Sr.	Chicago, IL
90	*Cowan, Keith	E	6-2	210	Sr.	Cleveland, OH
93	*Hildebrand, Willard	T	6-2	215	Sr.	Chillicothe, OH
94	Stawski, Willard	T	6-3	215	Jr.	Caledonia
96	*Maentz, Scott	E	6-3	206	Jr.	Grand Rapids
99	Smith, Jeffrey	E	6-3	190	Jr.	Kohler, WI

* Indicates letter

OHIO

No.	Name	Pos.	Ht.	Wgt.	Class	Home Town
12	Haupt, Richard	HB	5-11	168	Jr.	Sumner, IA
15	*Wentz, William	HB	5-10	172	Sr.	Canton
16	Johnson, Kenneth	HB	5-9	162	So.	New Concord
17	Lambert, Howard	FB	5-7	177	Jr.	Bellefontaine
18	Hardman, Von Allen	HB	6	167	Jr.	Spencer, WV
19	Klein, Robert	HB	5-8	168	So.	Athens, MI
20	Jones, Ben	PK	5-11	173	So.	Salem
21	Benis, Michael	QB	6	192	Sr.	Columbus
22	Wallace, Jack	QB	6-3	205	Jr.	Middletown
23	Lister, Robert	QB	6-2	188	Jr.	Marion
25	Mummey, John	LH	6	190	So.	Painesville
26	Mrukowski, William	QB	6-3	190	So.	Elyria
28	Hess, William	HB	5-10	162	So.	Springfield
30	Katterhenrich, David	FB	6-1	212	So.	Bucyrus
32	*Detrick, Roger	FB	5-9	202	Jr.	Vandalia
33	Francis, David	FB	6	202	So.	Columbus
34	Moore, David	E	6-2	198	So.	Fostoria
35	*German, William	HB	5-10	171	Sr.	Shaker Heights
37	Lundstrom, Al	G	6	202	Jr.	Ashtabula
41	**Matte, Thomas	QB	6	192	Sr.	East Cleveland
43	Mangiamelle, R.	HB	6-1	161	So.	Crafton, PA
44	Ulmer, Ed	HB	6-2	177	So.	Brookfield
45	**Herbstreit, James	HB	5-8	168	Sr.	Reading
46	*Ferguson, Robert	FB	6	220	Jr.	Troy
47	Hansley, Gary	HB	5-9	195	Jr.	Cleveland
48	Kumler, Karl	HB	6	190	So.	Columbus
49	*Houck, Ronald	HB	5-10	174	Jr.	Troy
50	Vanscoy, Jerry	C	5-11	200	So.	Harrisville
51	Varner, Thomas	C	5-10	202	Sr.	Saginaw, MI
52	Butts, Robert	G	6-1	225	So.	Benwood, WV
53	Armstrong, William	C	5-11	187	So.	Huron
54	*Lindner, James	C	5-11	202	Sr.	Enon Valley, PA
55	Vogelgesang, Don	G	6	195	Sr.	Canton
56	Farrall, John	G	5-10	207	Sr.	Canton
58	*Watkins, Jene	C	6	196	Jr.	Smithfield
61	Krstolic, Raymond	T	6-1	204	So.	Mentor
62	**Young, Don	G	6-1	228	Sr.	Dayton
64	*Ingram, Michael	G	5-9	219	Jr.	Bellaire
65	**Hauer, Oscar	G	6-2	210	Sr.	Hamilton
66	Foreman, Charles	G	5-9	185	Jr.	Dayton
67	**Hartman, Gabriel	G	5-9	214	Sr.	Troy
68	Moeller, Gary	G	6-1	205	So.	Lima
69	Foster, Rodney	G	6	220	So.	Cleveland
70	Laskoski, Richard	T	6-4	230	So.	Shamokin, PA
71	*Fiers, Alan	T	6-1	193	Jr.	Indianapolis, IN
72	Jentes, Charles	T	6-2	209	Jr.	Wooster
73	Vogel, Robert	T	6-5	222	So.	Massillon
74	**Matz, James	T	6-1	215	Sr.	Chillicothe
75	Roberts, Jack	T	6	237	Jr.	Strongsville
76	Sanders, Daryl	T	6-4	220	So.	Mayfield Heights
77	**Tyrer, James	T	6-5	245	Sr.	Newark
78	*Tolford, George	T	6	215	Sr.	Swanton
80	Middleton, Robert	E	6-3	207	So.	Marion
81	*Stephens, Larry	E	6	192	Jr.	Coshocton
82	*Wittmer, George	E	6-1	188	Jr.	Cincinnati
83	Niesz, Dale	E	6-2	198	Sr.	East Sparta
85	Tidmore, Sam	E	6	210	Jr.	Cleveland
86	Mooney, Charles	T	5-11	208	So.	Marietta
87	*Perdue, Thomas	E	5-11	180	Jr.	Huntington, WV
88	*Bryant, Charles	E	6-2	211	Jr.	Zanesville
89	Rayford, Elwood	E	5-10	175	So.	Toledo
90	Connor, Don	E	6	190	So.	Dayton
91	*Martin, Paul	E	6-2	186	Jr.	Canton
92	Korn, Gary	E	6	195	Sr.	Delphos
93	Clotz, Dennis	T	6-1	200	Jr.	Amherst
94	Warner, Duane	E	6	210	Sr.	Arlington
95	Betz, Wayne	G	6-1	198	So.	Cuyahoga Falls

* Indicates letter

1960

Ohio	24	S. Methodist	0
Ohio	20	S. California	0
Ohio	34	Illinois	7
Ohio	21	Purdue	24
Ohio	34	Wisconsin	7
Ohio	21	Mich. State	10
Ohio	36	Indiana	7
Ohio	12	Iowa	35
Ohio	7	Michigan	0

Season Summary

Won, 7; Lost, 2

ROBERT FERGUSON
All-American Back

Bob Ferguson scores his last touchdown for Ohio State

November 25, 1961

Ann Arbor, Michigan

Ohio State Trounces Michigan 50 To 20

Bucks Explode In Final Half To Wallop UM

Raimey - Fonde - McRae

Ohio State University completed a glorious and undefeated football season by routing traditional rival, the University of Michigan, 50 to 20. The Buckeyes, sparked by the powerhouse running of Bob Ferguson and the lightning-like thrusts of Paul Warfield, were in command throughout the game as they won their sixth straight in the Western Conference.

In the first period of play a pass intercepted by Ohio's Tidmore on Michigan's 35 led to the Bucks' first touchdown. In five plays Ferguson and Mummey moved the ball to the 19. Ferguson boomed through the last 19 for the tally and Van Raaphorst added the PAT from placement.

After a Michigan fumble to start the second quarter, Ohio moved from its own 45 to score in seven plays, Ferguson carrying all but one which was a 29-yard pass from Sparma to Ricketts. Ferguson bulled over from the 1½-yard line and Van Raaphorst again added the extra point.

On the ensuing kickoff Michigan's Raimey electrified the crowd with a 90-yard kickoff return for Michigan's first touchdown. Glinka's try for two points was incomplete. Ohio led 14-6.

On the very next series of downs the Bucks started from their 20-yard line. They made a first down on the 31 from which point Warfield swept right on a counter play and ran 69 yards for the score. Van Raaphorst was good again for a 21-6 lead.

Michigan received the second half kickoff and marched 78 yards in 15 plays for the score. Tunnicliff picked up most of the yardage and McLenna drove over from the one for the score. Glinka's PAT pass was incomplete.

The fourth period opened with OSU on Michigan's one-yard line. The second play of the quarter Ferguson banged off his own right guard from one foot out. Van Raaphorst's kick was good and Ohio led 28-12. After OSU's Ron Houck picked off a Glinka pass, Joe Sparma passed to halfback Bob Klein who raced up the sidelines for an 80-yard touchdown. Van Raaphorst did it again to make the score 35-12. The next time Ohio got the ball Ferguson put on a one-man show with gains of 11, 24, and 14 yards before going over from the one for his fourth TD of the game. Van Raaphorst booted the PAT making it 42-12.

Michigan then marched 55 yards in 10 plays for its third touchdown. Fullback Jack Ward cracked left guard for the TD with just 33 seconds remaining. Ward also ran for the two point conversion.

A spectacular pass from Sparma to Warfield set up the final Ohio touchdown. Sparma passed from his own 20 to Warfield on the Michigan 48 and the sophomore speedster raced to the Michigan 10. Three plays later Sparma passed to Tidmore for the TD. Sparma also passed for the final two points.

STATISTICS

	OSU	UM
First Downs	22	16
Rushing Yardage	312	162
Passing Yardage	200	109
Passes	7-10-1	10-17-2
Punts	1-40	2-36
Fumbles Lost	0	1
Yards Penalized	20	40

1961			
Ohio	7	Texas Christian	7
Ohio	13	UCLA	3
Ohio	44	Illinois	0
Ohio	10	Northwestern	0
Ohio	30	Wisconsin	21
Ohio	29	Iowa	13
Ohio	16	Indiana	7
Ohio	22	Oregon	12
Ohio	50	Michigan	20

Season Summary

Games won, 8; Lost, 0; Tied, 1

ROBERT FERGUSON
All-American Back

OHIO

No.	Name	Pos.	Wt.	Hgt.	Class	Home Town
53	*Armstrong, William	C	187	5-11	Jr.	Huron
18	Baffer, Stewart	PK	215	6-4	So.	Painesville
71	Bearss, James	RG	212	6-3	So.	Toledo
55	Betz, Wayne	RG	203	6-1	Jr.	Cuyahoga Falls
12	Bruney, Robert	RH	164	5-9	So.	Martins Ferry
88	*Bryant, Charles	LE	211	6-2	Sr.	Zanesville
34	*Butts, Robert	FB	217	6-1	Jr.	Benwood, WV
54	Carter, Dennis	C	214	6-2	So.	Springfield
57	Carter, Ronald	LG	194	6-1	So.	Washington CH
93	Clotz, Dennis	RT	209	6-1	Sr.	Amherst
77	Connor, Dan	RT	204	6-3	Jr.	Columbus
56	Fair, Robert	RG	186	5-11	So.	Cincinnati
46	*Ferguson, Robert	FB	227	6-0	Sr.	Troy
11	Fortney, Douglas	QB	162	5-9	So.	West Liberty
69	Foster, Rodney	RG	222	6-0	Jr.	Cleveland
33	*Francis, David	FB	200	6-0	Jr.	Columbus
58	Frank, Dean	C	201	6-1	So.	Dover
35	Hall, William	FB	191	6-1	So.	Ironton
15	Hardman, Von Allen	LH	180	6-0	Sr.	Spencer, WV
14	Haupt, Richard	RH	167	5-11	Sr.	Sumner, IA
28	*Hess, William	LH	168	5-10	Jr.	Springfield
49	*Houck, Ronald	RH	174	5-10	Sr.	Troy
62	Hullinger, Dennis	RT	200	6-3	So.	Lima
64	*Ingram, Michael	LG	215	5-9	Sr.	Bellaire
65	Jenkins, Thomas	LG	228	6-1	So.	Dayton
21	*Johnson, Kenneth	LH	155	5-9	Jr.	New Concord
20	*Jones, Ben	PK	170	5-11	Jr.	Salem
45	Jones, William	RH	182	5-11	So.	Warren
30	*Katterhenrich, David	FB	210	6-1	Jr.	Bucyrus
19	*Klein, Robert	RH	174	5-8	Jr.	Athens, MI
61	Krstolic, Raymond	LT	216	6-1	Jr.	Mentor
48	Kumler, Karl	LH	196	6-0	Jr.	Columbus
17	Lambert, Howard	FB	184	5-7	Sr.	Bellefontaine
70	Laskoski, Richard	LT	220	6-4	Jr.	Shamokin, PA
23	Lister, Robert	QB	186	6-2	Sr.	Marion
36	Lyons, Douglas	FB	200	6-1	So.	Parma
79	Mamula, Charles	RT	230	6-3	So.	Martins Ferry
43	Mangiamelle, R.	LH	163	5-11	Jr.	Crafton, PA
91	*Martin, Paul	RE	192	6-2	Sr.	Canton
80	*Middleton, Robert	RE	214	6-3	Jr.	Marion
60	Mirick, Wesley	RG	217	6-0	So.	Columbus
68	*Moeller, Gary	C	212	6-1	Jr.	Lima
26	*Mrukowski, William	QB	200	6-3	Jr.	Elyria
25	*Mummey, John	QB	197	6-0	Jr.	Painesville
63	Parker, Albert	LG	217	6-1	So.	Dover
87	*Perdue, Thomas	LE	192	6-0	Sr.	Wellston
89	Rayford, Elwood	LE	171	5-10	Jr.	Toledo
83	Ricketts, Ormonde	RE	194	6-1	So.	Springfield
75	Roberts, Jack	LT	236	6-0	Sr.	Strongsville
76	*Sanders, Daryl	RT	227	6-5	Jr.	Mayfield Heights
84	Smith, Keith	RT	214	6-3	So.	Dayton
41	Snell, Matthew	RH	203	6-2	So.	Locust Valley, NY
24	Sparma, Joseph	QB	190	6-2	So.	Massillon
72	Stanley, Bernie	RT	230	6-0	So.	Proctorville
67	*Stephens, Larry	RG	204	6-0	Sr.	Coshocton
66	Sunderhaus, Dale	RT	219	6-1	So.	Cincinnati
85	*Tidmore, Samuel	RE	215	6-0	Sr.	Cleveland
16	*Tingley, David	FB	183	5-9	Sr.	London
78	*Tolford, George	LT	218	6-0	Sr.	Swanton
44	*Ulmer, Ed	LG	186	6-2	Jr.	Brookfield
74	Unger, William	LT	229	6-0	So.	Mt. Morris, IL
86	VanRaaphorst, R.	RE	205	6-1	So.	Ligonier, PA
73	*Vogel, Robert	LT	230	6-5	Jr.	Massillon
22	*Wallace, Jack	QB	221	6-3	Sr.	Middletown
42	Warfield, Paul	LH	188	6-0	So.	Warren
82	*Wittmer, George	LE	194	6-1	Sr.	Cincinnati
51	Zima, Albert	C	198	6-0	Jr.	Youngstown

* indicates letters won

MICHIGAN

No.	Name	Pos.	Wt.	Hgt.	Class	Home Town
25	Alix, Denis	QB	170	6-0	So.	Bloomfield
67	Baty, Donald	G	204	6-1	So.	Hastings
88	Bickle, Douglas G.	E	210	6-3	So.	Traverse City
70	Blanchard, Donald	T	230	6-3	So.	White Pigeon
86	Brown, Robert	E	225	6-4	Sr.	Kalamazoo
20	Chandler, Robert	QB	210	6-3	Jr.	LaGrange, IL
46	Chapman, Harvey, Jr.	HB	175	5-11	So.	Farmington
68	Collins, Chuck	G	215	6-0	Jr.	Grand Rapids
50	Cowan, Jerry	G	185	5-11	Jr.	LaSalle
77	*Curtis, Guy	T	215	6-0	Sr.	South Bend, IN
38	Dodd, William	FB	200	5-10	So.	Virden, IL
22	Dougall, William	QB	178	6-2	Sr.	Detroit
80	Filar, Robert	E	205	6-4	Jr.	Southfield
24	*Glinka, David	QB	195	5-11	Jr.	Toledo, OH
59	*Grant, Todd	C	230	6-4	Sr.	Lathrup Village
65	*Hall, B. Lee	G	210	6-0	Sr.	Charlotte
12	Hood, Edward	HB	175	5-9	Jr.	Detroit
17	Hornbeck, William	HB	185	6-1	Sr.	Royal Oak
57	*Houtman, John	T	235	6-4	Jr.	Adrian
79	Keating, Tom	T	220	6-3	So.	Chicago, IL
48	Kornowa, Donald	HB	195	6-0	So.	Toledo, OH
83	*Korowin, James	E	195	6-2	Sr.	Wyandotte
16	Kowalik, John	HB	176	5-10	Jr.	Detroit
63	Kurtz, David W.	G	201	6-0	So.	Toledo, OH
74	Lehr, John	T	225	6-0	Jr.	Cincinnati, OH
52	Lovell, Robert	T	216	6-2	So.	Birmingham
96	*Maentz, Scott	E	230	6-3	Sr.	East Grand Rapids
56	Maloney, Frank	C	195	5-11	Sr.	Chicago, IL
32	*Mans, George (Capt.)	E	212	6-4	Sr.	Trenton
18	McLenna, Bruce	HB	218	6-3	So.	Fenton
43	*McRae, Bennie	HB	172	6-0	Sr.	Newport News, VA
62	*Minko, John	T	222	6-1	Jr.	Connellsville, PA
84	Mongeau, David	E	208	6-2	Jr.	Lincoln Park
58	Muir, William	C	205	6-0	So.	Cuyahoga Falls, OH
66	Nolan, Delbert	G	205	5-11	So.	Clare
69	*O'Donnell, Joseph	G	220	6-2	Jr.	Milan
60	*Pavloff, Louis	G	204	6-0	Sr.	Hazel Park
21	Prichard, Thomas	QB	198	5-10	So.	Marion, OH
35	*Raeder, J. Paul	FB	190	5-11	Sr.	Kent, OH
19	*Raimey, David	HB	195	5-10	Jr.	Dayton, OH
78	Schmidt, Paul	T	245	6-4	Sr.	Skokie, IL
61	Schmitt, Roger	G	196	5-11	So.	Buffalo, NY
76	*Schopf, Jon	T	230	6-2	Sr.	Kenilworth, IL
73	Schram, Richard	T	210	6-1	So.	Jackson
51	Slezak, David	C	185	5-11	Jr.	Ann Arbor
99	Smith, Jeffrey	E	200	6-3	Sr.	Kohler, WI
5	Spacht, Ronald	HB	180	5-10	Sr.	Kent, OH
33	Sparkman, R. Wayne	FB	185	5-11	So.	Plymouth
8	*Stamos, John	QB	208	6-1	Sr.	Chicago, IL
64	Stawski, Willard	T	215	6-3	Jr.	Caledonia
75	Striegel, Daniel	T	230	6-3	So.	Arlington Hts., IL
2	*Strobel, Jack	HB	175	5-10	Jr.	Maywood, IL
4	Szymanski, Richard	G	185	5-10	Jr.	Toledo, OH
9	Tageson, William	E	197	6-3	So.	Bad Axe
6	*Tunnicliff, Bill	FB	230	6-0	Sr.	Ferndale
9	*Tureaud, Kenneth	FB	194	6-0	Sr.	Detroit
4	Vuocolo, Michael	HB	180	5-10	So.	Lock Haven, PA
4	*Walker, John	C	205	6-0	Sr.	Milford
5	*Ward, James	HB	195	6-1	Jr.	Imlay City
4	Watters, Thomas	RH	197	5-10	So.	Wilkensburg, PA
2	Wiley, James	T	225	6-1	So.	Portland, OR
1	Yanz, John	E	195	6-3	So.	Chicago, IL
5	*Zubkus, E. James	E	205	6-1	Sr.	Munhall, PA

indicates letters won

1961

Michigan	29	UCLA	6
Michigan	38	Army	8
Michigan	0	Michigan State	28
Michigan	16	Purdue	14
Michigan	20	Minnesota	23
Michigan	28	Duke	14
Michigan	38	Illinois	6
Michigan	23	Iowa	14
Michigan	20	Ohio State	50

Season Summary

Games won, 6; Lost, 3; Tied, 0

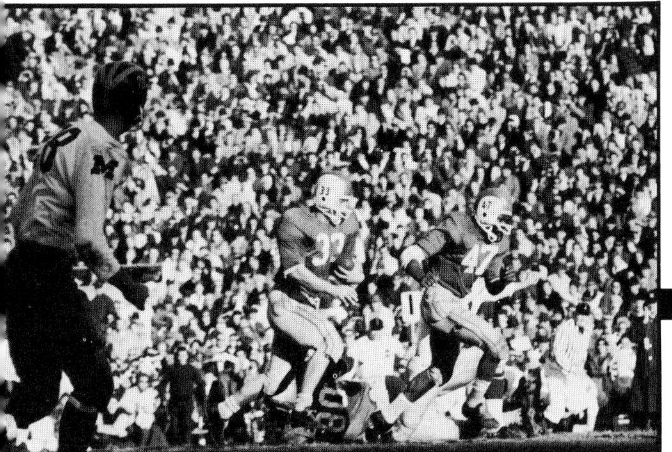

November 24, 1962

Columbus, Ohio

Bucks Grind It Out Over Wolverines, 28 To 0

Michigan Never Out Of Trouble As OSU's Fullbacks Score

An Ohio Stadium crowd of 82,349 saw fullback Dave Francis crunch out 186 yards and score two touchdowns. His reliefmen, senior classmates Bob Butts and Dave Katterhenrich, had fewer opportunities but each drove for a touchdown as well. OSU's tackles Bob Vogel and Daryl Sanders and center Billy Joe Armstrong were particularly effective clearing the way for the big backs.

The second time Ohio State gained possession in the first quarter, the ball was given to Dave Francis on eight straight plays. He gained 42 yards and a 10-yard penalty down deep — only yardage stepped off for the entire game — helped. Francis completed the do-it-yourself job by going over the left side for the touchdown from inside the one. Mamula added the PAT making it 7-0. Ohio State tried a 27-yard field goal before the half ended but it was wide.

In the third period Francis went to work again. From their own 35 the Buckeyes drove to the three of Michigan. Francis bulled over and Mamula added the PAT to make it 14-0.

OSU began another drive which carried through into the final period. Francis was replaced by Butts. On his first carry he churned 24 yards on a trap to Michigan's three-yard line. Two more carries by Butts and Mamula's kick made it 21-0.

After a passing attack by Michigan stalled on Ohio's 32, the Bucks came bombing back again. Francis broke a 52-yarder up the middle. He finally was downed on the Wolverines' six-yard line. Katterhenrich replaced Francis and on the next play scored the final touchdown. Again Mamula converted for the final score, 28 to 0.

STATISTICS

	UM	OSU
First Downs	9	19
Rushing Yardage	71	338
Passing Yardage	68	7
Passing	5-11-1	3-6-0
Punts - Average	6-33	3-33
Yards Penalized	10	0

1962

1962		
Michigan .. 13	Nebraska	25
Michigan .. 17	Army	7
Michigan .. 0	Mich. State	28
Michigan .. 0	Purdue	37
Michigan .. 0	Minnesota	17
Michigan .. 12	Wisconsin	34
Michigan .. 14	Illinois	10
Michigan .. 14	Iowa	28
Michigan .. 0	Ohio State	28

Season Summary

Games Won, 2; Lost, 7; Tied, 0

MICHIGAN

No.	Name	Pos.	Ht.	Wgt.	Class	Home Town
12	Hood, Ed	HB	5-9	175	Sr.	Detroit
16	Kowalik, John, Jr.	HB	5-10	181	Sr.	Detroit
17	Rindfuss, Dick	HB	6-1	188	So.	Niles, OH
19	Raimey, David	HB	5-10	195	Sr.	Dayton, OH
20	Chandler, Bob	QB	6-3	199	Jr.	LaGrange, IL
21	Prichard, Tom	HB	5-10	180	Jr.	Marion, OH
23	Bay, Richard	QB	5-10	168	So.	Waukegan, IL
26	Evashevski, Forest	QB	6	182	Jr.	Iowa City, IA
28	Timberlake, Bob	QB	6-4	200	So.	Franklin, OH
33	Sparkman, Wayne	FB	5-11	189	Jr.	Plymouth
37	Anthony, Mel	FB	5-11	195	So.	Cincinnati, OH
38	Dodd, Bill	FB	5-11	203	Jr.	Virden, IL
41	Jones, Dennis	HB	6-2	191	So.	Worthington, OH
42	Strobel, Jack	HB	5-9	175	Jr.	Maywood, IL
45	Ward, Jim	E	6-1	196	Sr.	Imlay City
46	Chapman, Harvey, Jr.	HB	5-11	180	Jr.	Farmington
50	Kovacevich, Dave	G	5-10	203	Jr.	Chicago, IL
51	Patchen, Brian	C	5-11	207	So.	Steubenville, OH
55	Green, Jim	C	6-1	212	So.	Trenton
56	Seamon, David	C	6-3	223	So.	Grand Rapids
58	Muir, Bill	C	6	200	Jr.	Cuyahoga Falls, OH
59	Blanchard, Don	C	6-3	233	Jr.	Sturgis
60	Pavloff, Louis	G	6	210	Sr.	Hazel Park
61	Marcum, John	G	6	205	Jr.	Monroe
62	Minko, John	G	6-1	226	Sr.	Connellsville, PA
63	Kurtz, Dave	G	6	204	Jr.	Toledo, OH
64	Szymanski, Dick	G	5-10	187	Sr.	Toledo, OH
65	Hahn, Dick	G	6	195	So.	Norton, OH
69	O'Donnell, Joe	T	6-2	219	Sr.	Milan
70	Simkus, Arnold	T	6-4	225	So.	Detroit
71	Frontczak, John	T	6-3	230	So.	Dowagiac
73	Schram, Dick	T	6-1	220	Sr.	Jackson
76	Lauterbach, Ronald	T	6-3	232	Sr.	Dayton, OH
77	Butler, Dave	G	6-1	220	So.	Detroit
79	Keating, Tom	T	6-3	206	Jr.	Chicago, IL
80	Farabee, Ben	E	6-2	201	So.	Holland
81	Yanz, John	E	6-2	201	Jr.	Chicago, IL
82	Conley, Jim	E	6-3	193	So.	Springdale, PA
83	Laskey, Bill	E	6-1	206	So.	Milan
85	Lambert, Fred	E	6-3	215	So.	Millburn, NJ
86	Brown, Bob	E	6-5	226	Sr.	Kalamazoo
88	Kocan, Ron	E	5-11	203	Sr.	Sharpsville, PA
89	Tageson, Bill	E	6-3	195	Jr.	Bad Axe
91	Franzen, Raymond	T	6	218	So.	Centerline
92	McAleer, Pat	E	6-4	222	So.	Kenosha, WI
93	Mayer, Richard	E	6-2	187	So.	Evanston, IL
94	Mader, Gerald	T	6-3	217	So.	Chicago, IL
95	McLeese, Ronald	T	6-4	250	So.	Roseville
97	Frontczak, Nick	G	5-10	210	So.	Detroit
99	Woodward, Paul	T	6-2	221	Jr.	Cincinnati, OH

OHIO

No.	Name	Pos.	Ht.	Wgt.	Class	Home Town
11	Fortney, Douglas	LH	5-9	162	Jr.	West Liberty
12	Bruney, Robert	RH	5-9	168	Jr.	Martins Ferry
14	Barnett, Tyrone	LH	5-8	166	So.	Orrville
16	Bodenbender, George	RH	6	177	So.	Bellefontaine
18	Scott, Robert	LH	6-2	203	So.	Connellsville, PA
19	**Klein, Robert	RH	5-8	170	Sr.	Athens, MI
20	Price, Charles	QB	6	193	So.	Middletown
22	Yonclas, Nicholas	QB	5-10	177	So.	Delhi, NY
23	Chonko, Arnold	QB	6-2	194	So.	Parma
24	*Sparma, Joseph	QB	6-1	193	Jr.	Massillon
25	**Mummey, John	QB	6	198	Sr.	Painesville
26	**Mrukowski, William	QB	6-3	196	Sr.	Elyria
27	Kaylor, Ronald	QB	6-3	180	So.	Canton
28	**Hess, William	RH	5-10	170	Sr.	Springfield
30	**Katterhenrich, David	FB	6-1	222	Sr.	Bucyrus
32	Drenik, Douglas	FB	6-1	188	So.	Wickliffe
33	*Francis, David	FB	6	209	Sr.	Columbus
34	*Butts, Robert	FB	6-1	225	Sr.	Benwood, WV
35	Hall, William	LE	6-1	201	Jr.	Ironton
36	Lyons, Douglas	FB	6-2	203	Jr.	Parma
38	Hartley, Robert	FB	5-11	202	So.	Covington
41	*Snell, Matthew	LE	6-2	212	Jr.	Locust Valley, NY
42	*Warfield, Paul	LH	6	182	Jr.	Warren
43	Mangiamelle, Richard	RH	5-11	171	Sr.	Crafton, PA
44	Allman, David	RH	5-9	180	So.	Coshocton
45	Truster, Jerry	LG	6	198	So.	Columbus
46	Harkins, Don	LH	6-1	188	So.	Urbana
47	Espy, Bennie	RH	6	177	So.	Sandusky
48	Kumler, Karl	LH	6	190	Sr.	Columbus
49	Lindsey, Leon	LH	5-10	180	So.	Steubenville
50	Federle, Thomas	C	5-11	203	So.	Cincinnati
51	Zima, Albert	C	6	196	Sr.	Youngstown
52	Fitz, Thomas	RG	6-2	208	So.	Cuyahoga Falls
53	**Armstrong, William	C	5-11	189	Sr.	Huron
54	Coleman, Paul	C	6-2	220	So.	Columbus
55	*Betz, Wayne	RG	6-1	207	Sr.	Cuyahoga Falls
56	Goering, William	RG	5-11	203	So.	Cleveland
57	Stanley, Bernie	RT	6	230	So.	Proctorville
58	Dreffer, Stephan	C	5-9	197	So.	Montpelier
59	Cummins, Thomas	C	5-10	188	So.	London
60	*Mirick, Wesley	LG	6	220	Jr.	Columbus
61	*Krstolic, Raymond	RG	6-1	213	Sr.	Mentor
62	Hullinger, Dennis	LT	6-3	215	Jr.	Lima
63	Parker, Albert	LG	6-1	212	Jr.	Dover
64	Snyder, Larry	LG	6-2	203	So.	Wooster
65	*Jenkins, Thomas	LG	6-1	226	Jr.	Dayton
66	Sunderhaus, Dale	RT	6-1	218	Jr.	Cincinnati
67	Bearss, James	LG	6-3	211	So.	Toledo
68	**Moeller, Gary	C	6-1	214	Sr.	Lima
69	*Foster, Rodney	RG	6	230	Sr.	Cleveland
70	*Laskowski, Richard	LT	6-4	222	Sr.	Shamokin, PA
71	Kasunic, Gerald	RT	6-1	212	So.	Cleveland
73	**Vogel, Robert	LT	6-5	230	Sr.	Massillon
74	Unger, William	RT	6	229	Jr.	Mt. Morris, IL
75	Kohut, William	RT	6-4	233	So.	Youngstown
76	**Sanders, Daryl	RT	6-5	226	Sr.	Mayfield Heights
77	Orazen, Ed	LT	6	218	So.	Euclid
78	Porretta, Daniel	RT	6	218	So.	Clairton, PA
79	Mamula, Charles	LT	6-3	220	Jr.	Martins Ferry
80	**Middleton, Robert	RE	6-3	218	Sr.	Marion
81	Meyer, Terry	LE	6-4	212	So.	Dayton
82	Spahr, William	RE	6-2	180	So.	Columbus
83	*Ricketts, Ormonde	LE	6-1	200	Jr.	Springfield
84	Housteau, Joseph	RE	6-2	205	So.	Girard
85	Davidson, James	RE	6-4	208	So.	Alliance
86	*Van Raaphorst, Richard	LE	6-1	206	Jr.	Ligonier, PA
87	Jones, David	LE	6-3	198	So.	Euclid
88	Kiehfuss, Thomas	RE	6-3	198	So.	Cincinnati
89	Anderson, Thomas	RE	6-1	195	So.	Orrville
90	Ladwig, Eric	LE	6	210	So.	Cleveland
91	Mobley, Ben	LE	6-2	195	So.	Montclair, NJ
92	Howman, Dennis	FB	6-1	205	So.	Wooster
94	Longer, Robert	RT	6-2	220	So.	Cleveland
95	Rector, Robert	C	5-10	185	So.	Toronto, Can.
96	Walters, Niles	RG	6-2	210	So.	Clairton, PA
97	Wortman, Robert	LT	6-2	226	So.	Cincinnati
98	Fair, Robert	RG	5-11	186	Jr.	Cincinnati

1962

Ohio	41	North Carolina	7
Ohio	7	U.C.L.A.	9
Ohio	51	Illinois	15
Ohio	14	Northwestern	18
Ohio	14	Wisconsin	7
Ohio	14	Iowa	28
Ohio	10	Indiana	7
Ohio	26	Oregon	7
Ohio	28	Michigan	0

Season Summary
Won, 6; Lost, 3

November 30, 1963

Ann Arbor, Michigan

Bucks Rally To Whip Michigan, 14 To 10

Unverferth Passes, Runs For TDs To Wipe Out Lead

The ultra-conservative football forces from Ohio State University, long regarded as 99 percent infantry and one percent aerial revised the script and bombed Michigan, 14-10, in the final game of the season for the aged and honorable rivals.

On the second play of the game, OSU's Matt Snell gained five yards but fumbled and UM's Jack Clancy recovered on the Ohio 27. The Wolverines were stopped on the 10 and Timberlake kicked a 28-yard field goal.

Later in the half Michigan drove 63 yards in 11 plays for their first touchdown. Dick Rindfuss blasted over Ohio State's right tackle for the two remaining yards. Timberlake converted the PAT to increase Michigan's lead to 10-0.

Before the half could end, Unverferth passed to Warfield in the end zone, behind Clancy and Rindfuss, for a 35-yard touchdown play. Dick Van Raaphorst kicked the point, and it was 10-7, Michigan, at the half.

In the second half it remained even until Unverferth skirted Michigan's right end for five yards and the score. Van Raaphorst added the conversion for the final score, Ohio winning 14-10.

Unverferth passed 14 times, completed 7, for 105 yards, and Warfield caught five of them for 76 yards. The Buckeye quarterback also ran the ball 10 times for 52 yards, with Snell and Tom Barrington complementing his run-pass strategy. Warfield, an All-American performer in the opinion of many experts was all-everything, principally in his role as decoy. On at least a half-dozen plays, his maneuvers as a decoy set up runs for Unverferth or the others.

Timberlake, with excellent support from fullback Mel Anthony, accounted for 80 yards running and 35 yards passing, and the small assembly of blanketed spectators, 36,424, clamored for more passing and less running. But Timberlake, with a 10-0 lead, remained on the ground. Eight of his 15 passes were thrown in the Wolverines' final two series, but, then, it was too late.

STATISTICS

	OSU	UM
First Downs	17	14
Rushing Yardage	192	188
Passing Yardage	105	35
Passes	7-14	5-13
Passes Inter. by	1	1
Punts	5-35	5-32
Fumbles Lost	1	0
Yards Penalized	29	30

1963			
Ohio	17	Texas A. & M.	0
Ohio	21	Indiana	0
Ohio	20	Illinois	20
Ohio	3	USC	32
Ohio	13	Wisconsin	10
Ohio	7	Iowa	3
Ohio	7	Penn State	10
Ohio	8	Northwestern	17
Ohio	14	Michigan	10

Season Summary

Games won, 5; Lost, 3; Tied, 1

OHIO

No.	Name	Pos.	Wt.	Hgt.	Class	Home Town
72	Anderson, Richard	T	232	6-5	So.	Medina
61	Andrick, Theodore	G	208	5-11	So.	Cuyahoga Falls
14	*Barnett, Tyrone	HB	166	5-8	Jr.	Orrville
67	Bearss, James	G	211	6-3	Jr.	Toledo
12	*Bruney, Robert	HB	168	5-9	Sr.	Martins Ferry
66	Bugel, Thomas	G	200	6-0	So.	W. Homestead, PA
23	*Chonko, Arnold	QB	194	6-2	Jr.	Parma
51	Cochran, Terrence	C	186	5-9	So.	Richwood
59	Cummins, Thomas	C	190	5-10	Jr.	London
73	Davidson, James	T	215	6-4	Jr.	Alliance
30	*Dreffer, Stephan	FB	197	5-9	Jr.	Montpelier
32	*Drenik, Douglas	HB	186	6-1	Jr.	Wickliffe
47	*Espy, Bennie	HB	177	6-0	Jr.	Sandusky
50	Federle, Thomas	C	200	5-11	Jr.	Cincinnati
52	Fitz, Thomas	C	208	6-2	Jr.	Cuyahoga Falls
62	Funk, Robert	G	224	6-1	So.	Lakewood
46	*Harkins, Donald	HB	188	6-1	Jr.	Urbana
38	Hartley, Robert	FB	200	5-11	So.	Covington
65	*Jenkins, Thomas	G	226	6-1	Sr.	Dayton
71	Kasunic, Gerald	T	210	6-1	Jr.	Cleveland
27	Kaylor, Ronald	QB	185	6-3	Jr.	Canton
53	Kelley, Dwight	C	212	5-11	So.	Bremen
88	*Kiehfuss, Thomas	E	205	6-3	Jr.	Cincinnati
87	Lashutka, Gregory	E	214	6-5	So.	Cleveland
49	Lindsey, Leon	HB	180	5-10	Jr.	Steubenville
48	Lykes, Robert	HB	180	6-1	So.	Akron
79	*Mamula, Charles	T	220	6-3	Sr.	Martins Ferry
58	Miller, Gary	G	200	6-0	So.	Bellevue
60	*Mirick, Wesley	G	220	6-0	Sr.	Columbus
91	Mobley, Ben	E	196	6-2	Jr.	Montclair, NJ
77	*Orazen, Ed	T	218	6-0	Jr.	Euclid
76	Palmer, John	T	212	6-1	So.	Kettering
63	*Parker, Albert	G	212	6-1	Sr.	Dover
78	*Porretta, Daniel	G	218	6-0	Jr.	Clairton, PA
20	Price, Charles	QB	193	6-0	Jr.	Middletown
83	*Ricketts, Ormonde	E	200	6-1	Sr.	Springfield
69	Ridder, William	G	217	5-9	So.	Springfield
33	Sander, Willard	FB	210	6-2	So.	Cincinnati
41	*Snell, Matthew	FB	214	6-2	Sr.	Locust Valley, NY
82	*Spahr, William	E	182	6-2	Jr.	Columbus
57	Stanley, Bernie	T	230	6-0	Jr.	Proctorville
80	Stock, Robert	E	197	6-1	So.	Washington, PA
26	Unverferth, Donald	QB	205	6-3	So.	Dayton
68	VanHorn, Douglas	T	226	6-2	So.	Columbus
86	*VanRaaphorst, R.	E	210	6-1	Sr.	Ligonier, PA
42	*Warfield, Paul	HB	182	6-0	Sr.	Warren
22	Yonclas, Nicholas	QB	177	5-10	Jr.	Delhi, NY

* indicates letters won

MICHIGAN

No.	Name	Pos.	Wt.	Hgt.	Class	Home Town
25	Alix, Denis	QB	185	6-0	Sr.	West Bloomfield
36	Allison, Bruce	FB	205	6-0	So.	Ypsilanti
60	Ancona, Perry	G	206	6-0	So.	Madeira, OH
37	*Anthony, Melvin	FB	202	6-0	Jr.	Cincinnati, OH
23	Bay, Richard	QB	170	5-10	Jr.	Waukegan, IL
59	*Blanchard, Don	T	226	6-3	Sr.	Sturgis
16	Brigstock, Thomas	HB	186	6-0	So.	Battle Creek
77	Butler, David	G	218	6-1	Jr.	Detroit
53	Cecchini, Thomas	C	195	6-0	So.	Detroit
20	*Chandler, Robert	QB	208	6-3	Sr.	LaGrange, IL
46	*Chapman, Harvey	HB	177	5-11	Sr.	Farmington
24	Clancy, Jack	HB	196	6-1	So.	Detroit
82	*Conley, James	E	191	6-3	Jr.	Springdale, PA
56	Day, Floyd	G	202	6-2	So.	Flushing
31	Dehlin, Charles	FB	198	5-11	So.	Flushing
38	*Dodd, William	HB	204	6-0	Sr.	Virden, IL
71	England, Robert	T	245	6-3	So.	Ypsilanti
26	*Evashevski, Forest	QB	185	6-0	Sr.	Iowa City, IA
80	*Farabee, Ben	E	206	6-3	Jr.	Holland
92	Fette, Thomas	E	190	6-2	So.	St. Joseph
97	Frontczak, Stanley	G	208	5-11	Jr.	Detroit
10	Gorte, Michael	HB	185	5-10	So.	Owosso
55	*Green, James	C	210	6-1	Jr.	Trenton
89	Greene, Edward	E	190	5-11	So.	Flat Rock
65	*Hahn, Richard	G	206	6-0	Jr.	Norton, OH
74	Haverstock, Thomas	T	219	6-3	So.	Harrisburg, PA
81	Henderson, John	E	185	6-3	Jr.	Dayton, OH
22	Hollis, Peter	QB	195	6-1	So.	Detroit
57	*Houtman, John	G	244	6-4	Sr.	Adrian
88	Hoyne, Jeffrey	E	197	6-1	So.	Chicago, IL
41	*Jones, Dennis	HB	185	6-2	Jr.	Worthington, OH
79	*Keating, Thomas	T	240	6-3	Sr.	Chicago, IL
68	Keating, William	G	221	6-1	So.	Chicago, IL
78	Kines, Charles	T	228	6-1	So.	Niles, OH
84	Kirby, Craig	E	179	6-1	So.	Royal Oak
50	*Kovacevich, David	G	215	5-10	Sr.	Chicago, IL
63	*Kurtz, David	G	214	6-0	Sr.	Toledo, OH
83	*Laskey, William	E	211	6-1	Jr.	Milan
40	Legacki, Norman	E	172	6-0	So.	Philadelphia, PA
96	Mack, Thomas	E	216	6-3	So.	Bucyrus, OH
94	*Mader, Gerald	T	220	6-3	Jr.	Chicago, IL
61	*Marcum, John	G	208	6-0	Jr.	Monroe
73	McAleer, Patrick	T	215	6-4	Jr.	Kenosha, WI
90	McDonald, Kenneth	E	198	6-1	So.	Detroit
58	*Muir, William	C	210	6-0	Sr.	Cuyahoga Falls, OH
69	*O'Donnell, J. (Capt.)	G	238	6-2	Sr.	Milan
14	Ott, Richard	HB	162	5-11	So.	Mansfield, OH
93	Parkhill, Thomas	T	195	6-1	So.	Ada, OH
54	Pasch, John	G	210	6-2	Sr.	Toledo, OH
51	Patchen, Brian	C	210	5-11	Jr.	Steubenville, OH
21	*Prichard, Thomas	QB	180	5-10	Sr.	Marion, OH
18	Quist, Robert	HB	194	5-11	So.	Grand Rapids
12	Reid, Dorie	HB	165	5-7	So.	Ferndale
62	Ries, Richard	G	225	6-2	So.	Royal Oak
17	*Rindfuss, Richard	HB	192	6-0	Jr.	Niles, OH
43	Rowser, John	HB	175	6-0	So.	Detroit
76	Ruzicka, Charles	T	239	6-1	So.	Skokie, IL
91	Sarnacke, Phil	E	193	6-1	Jr.	Detroit
49	Scharl, James	HB	202	6-0	So.	Detroit
39	Schick, Gary	FB	205	6-2	So.	Grosse Pointe
66	Schmidt, Robert	T	230	5-10	So.	Cincinnati, OH
70	*Simkus, Arnold	T	237	6-4	Jr.	Detroit
86	Smith, Stephen	E	228	6-5	So.	Park Ridge, IL
33	*Sparkman, Wayne	FB	186	5-11	Sr.	Plymouth
67	Stagg, Frank	G	225	6-2	So.	Hazel Park
64	*Szymanski, Richard	C	185	5-10	Sr.	Toledo, OH
45	Tennant, Byron	C	205	6-0	So.	Worthington, OH
28	*Timberlake, Robert	QB	211	6-4	Jr.	Franklin, OH
95	Van Blaricom, Kirk	T	235	6-3	So.	Kalamazoo
42	Wells, Richard	HB	172	5-9	So.	Grand Rapids
99	Woodward, Paul	G	216	6-2	Jr.	Cincinnati, OH
52	Wright, Kenneth	C	207	6-1	So.	Bay City
75	Yearby, William	T	223	6-3	So.	Detroit

* indicates letters won

1963

Michigan	27	S. Methodist	16
Michigan	13	Navy	26
Michigan	7	Michigan State	7
Michigan	12	Purdue	23
Michigan	0	Minnesota	6
Michigan	27	Northwestern	6
Michigan	14	Illinois	8
Michigan	21	Iowa	21
Michigan	10	Ohio State	14

Season Summary

Games won, 3; Lost, 4; Tied, 2

November 21, 1964

Columbus, Ohio

Michigan Defense Drops OSU, 10-0

84,685 See Wolverines Cop Title, Rose Bowl Trip

Jim Detwiler, a sophomore halfback with Michigan's thirdstring unit before the season opened, put the Wolverines in the Rose Bowl by a mere margin of 24 percentage points when he scored the only touchdown in a 10-0 victory over Ohio State for the Big Ten championship.

With the Wolverines on Ohio State's 18-yard line in the second period of the game, Detwiler cut a pass pattern that enabled Bob Timberlake to complete a 17-yard scoring play for the only touchdown of the day. Timberlake shoved the lead to 7-0 when he kicked his 20th successive extra point without a miss that season. He put the game out of reach in the opening minutes of the fourth quarter when he kicked a 27-yard field goal.

It was only Ohio State's second defeat in its nine game season, but the Buckeyes went into the game in 23-degree weather unbeaten in the Big Ten and needed a tie or a victory to take its fifth title in Coach Woody Hayes' 14 years as guardian of the Bucks.

Michigan's rushing attack, the best in all college football with a 253-yard average for eight games, failed to get the Wolverines within scoring range until Timberlake's field goal. But it was sophomore Stan Kemp's 50-yard punt, aided by an 18 mile-an-hour wind, that set up Detwiler's touchdown. UM's John Henderson, charging in under the punt, recovered the ball as it bounced behind Rein. It put the Wolverines 20 yards short of Ohio's goal line. A scramble by Timberlake to the 17 preceded the TD pass to Detwiler.

Fighting back in the fourth quarter, the Buckeyes opened up their air attack with quarterback Don Unverferth going for the long play. But Michigan's Rick Volk, a sophomore from Wauseon, Ohio, repeatedly grounded the attack, twice intercepting passes and finally batting away the last pass Underferth threw that season. A 27-yard punt return by Volk had set up the field goal by Timberlake.

The "hot game" thawed out the crowd which was the second largest in the history of Ohio Stadium.

STATISTICS

	UM	OSU
First Downs	9	10
Rushing Yardage	115	103
Passing Yardage	45	77
Passing	3-9-0	7-21-2
Punts-Average	3-39	6-30
Fumbles Lost	2	2
Yards Penalized	36	25

1964			
Michigan	24	Air Force	7
Michigan	21	Navy	0
Michigan	17	Mich. State	10
Michigan	20	Purdue	21
Michigan	19	Minnesota	12
Michigan	35	Northwestern	0
Michigan	21	Illinois	6
Michigan	34	Iowa	20
Michigan	10	Ohio State	0

Season Summary

Games Won, 8; Lost, 1; Tied, 0

ROBERT TIMBERLAKE
All-American Quarterback

WILLIAM YEARBY
All-American Tackle

MICHIGAN

No.	Name	Pos.	Ht.	Wgt.	Class	Home Town
15	Bass, Michael	HB	6	175	So.	Ypsilanti
17	*Rindfuss, Richard	HB	6	192	Sr.	Niles, OH
18	Sygar, Richard	HB	5-11	184	So.	Niles, OH
19	Ward, Carl	HB	5-9	178	So.	Cincinnati, OH
24	Clancy, Jack	HB	6-1	193	Jr.	Detroit
26	*Evashevski, Forest	QB	6	185	Sr.	Iowa City, IA
28	*Timberlake, Robert	QB	6-4	210	Sr.	Franklin, OH
29	Gabler, Wallace	QB	6-2	186	Jr.	Royal Oak
30	Kemp, Stanley	E	6-1	185	So.	Greenville
31	*Dehlin, Barry	FB	5-11	204	Jr.	Flushing
32	Radigan, Timothy	FB	5-11	200	So.	Lansing
33	Fisher, David	FB	5-10	210	So.	Kettering, OH
37	*Anthony, Melvin	FB	6	201	Sr.	Cincinnati, OH
38	Greene, Edward	E	5-11	190	Jr.	Flat Rock
39	Schick, Gary	FB	6-2	210	Jr.	Grosse, Pte.
41	Lee, Louis	HB	6-2	190	So.	Willow Grove, PA
42	*Wells, Richard	HB	5-9	172	Jr.	Grand Rapids
48	Detwiler, James	HB	6-3	209	So.	Toledo, OH
49	Volk, Richard	QB	6-3	195	So.	Wauseon, OH
51	*Patchen, Brian	C	5-11	205	Jr.	Steubenville, OH
52	Wright, Kenneth	C	6-1	215	So.	Bay City
53	*Cecchini, Thomas	C	6	195	Jr.	Detroit
55	Bailey, Donald	G	5-11	190	So.	Greensburg, PA
58	*Muir, William	C	6	200	Sr.	Cuyahoga Falls, OH
59	Nunley, Frank	C	6-2	210	So.	Belleville
61	*Marcum, John	G	6	210	Sr.	Monroe
63	Mielke, Robert	G	6-1	210	So.	Chicago, IL
64	Flanagan, Dennis	G	6-2	210	Jr.	Niles, OH
68	Keating, William	G	6-2	226	Jr.	Chicago, IL
70	*Simkus, Arnold	T	6-4	230	Sr.	Detroit
74	Haverstock, Thomas	T	6-3	218	Jr.	Harrisburg, PA
75	*Yearby, William	T	6-3	222	Jr.	Detroit
76	*Ruzicka, Charles	T	6-1	235	Jr.	Skokie, IL
77	Butler, David	G	6-1	215	Sr.	Detroit
78	Kines, Charles	T	6	230	Jr.	Niles, OH
80	*Farabee, Ben	E	6-3	205	Sr.	Holland
81	*Henderson, John	E	6-3	187	Sr.	Dayton, OH
82	*Conley, James	E	6-3	198	Sr.	Springdale, PA
83	*Laskey, William	E	6-2	217	Sr.	Milan
84	*Kirby, Craig	E	6-2	190	Jr.	Royal Oak
85	Wilhite, Clayton	E	6-4	200	So.	Bay City
86	*Smith, Stephen	E	6-5	230	Jr.	Park Ridge, IL
88	*Hoyne, Jeffrey	E	6-1	186	Jr.	Chicago, IL
93	Parkhill, Thomas	E	6-2	202	Jr.	Ada, OH
94	*Mader, Gerald	T	6-3	230	Sr.	Chicago, IL
96	Mack, Thomas	T	6-3	220	Jr.	Bucyrus, OH

* Denotes letterman

OHIO

No.	Name	Pos.	Ht.	Wgt.	Class	Home Town
11	Thomas, Will	RH	6	174	So.	Lima
12	McCoy, John	RH	5-10	188	So.	Wooster
14	**Barnett, Tyrone	RH	5-8	172	Sr.	Orrville
15	Fill, John	LH	5-9	177	So.	Cuyahoga Heights
16	Bodenbender, George	RH	6	184	Sr.	Bellefontaine
17	Meinerding, Wesley	RH	6	209	So.	Canton
19	Adderley, Nelson	LH	5-11	183	Jr.	Philadelphia, PA
20	Newcomer, Mark	QB	5-11	175	So.	Gibsonburg
21	Allen, Richard	QB	6-1	177	Jr.	Sidney
22	*Yonclas, Nicholas	QB	5-10	180	Sr.	Delhi, NY
23	**Chonko, Arnold	QB	6-2	209	Sr.	Parma
25	*Barrington, Thomas	LH	6-1	216	Jr.	Lima
26	*Unverferth, Donald	QB	6-3	208	Jr.	Dayton
27	Kaylor, Ronald	QB	6-3	200	Sr.	Canton
28	VanFossen, Jesse	RH	5-10	156	Jr.	Centerburg
30	**Dreffer, Stephan	FB	5-9	204	Sr.	Montpelier
32	**Drenik, Douglas	FB	6-1	190	Sr.	Wickliffe
33	*Sander, Willard	FB	6-2	215	Jr.	Cincinnati
34	Farbizo, Thomas	FB	5-11	194	So.	New Philadelphia
35	Baas, James	FB	6-1	205	So.	Columbus
36	Hudson, Paul	FB	5-11	205	So.	Coatesville, PA
37	Wallenhurst, Douglas	QB	5-10	187	So.	Massillon
38	Reed, Samuel	RE	5-8	183	So.	Garrettsville
44	Richley, Richard	LH	5-9	183	Jr.	Cincinnati
45	Rein, Robert	RH	5-11	182	So.	Niles
46	**Harkins, Donald	RH	6-1	200	Sr.	Urbana
47	**Espy, Bennie	LH	6	178	Sr.	Sandusky
48	Lykes, Robert	LH	6-1	185	Jr.	Akron
49	Lindsey, Leon	LH	5-10	180	Sr.	Steubenville
50	*Federle, Thomas	C	5-11	197	Sr.	Cincinnati
51	Cochran, Terrence	C	5-9	198	Jr.	Richwood
52	Fitz, Thomas	LG	6-2	219	Sr.	Cuyahoga Falls
53	*Kelley, Dwight	C	5-11	216	Jr.	Bremen
54	Truster, Jerry	LG	6	208	Sr.	Columbus
55	Rutherford, William	C	5-10	188	So.	Columbus
56	Oates, James	C	6	229	Jr.	Dunkirk
57	Anderson, Kim	C	6	194	So.	Orrville
58	Miller, Gary	RG	6	213	So.	Bellevue
59	Cummins, Thomas	C	5-10	190	Sr.	London
60	Phelan, Robin	LG	6	194	So.	Columbus
61	Andrick, Theodore	LG	5-11	208	Jr.	Cuyahoga Falls
62	Funk, Robert	RG	6-1	236	Jr.	Lakewood
63	Eachus, William	RG	6	209	So.	Gallipolis
64	Snyder, Larry	RG	6-2	198	Sr.	Wooster
65	Pryor, Ray	LG	6	220	So.	Hamilton
66	*Bugel, Thomas	LG	6	203	Jr.	W. Homestead, PA
67	Windle, Gary	LG	5-11	214	So.	Warren
68	*Van Horn, Douglas	RT	6-2	236	Jr.	Columbus
69	*Ridder, William	RG	5-10	212	Jr.	Springfield
70	Green, Mark	RT	6-4	250	So.	Groveport
71	*Kasunic, Gerald	RT	6-1	228	Sr.	Cleveland
72	Anderson, Richard	RT	6-5	238	Jr.	Lodi
73	*Davidson, James	LT	6-4	231	Sr.	Alliance
74	Current, Michael	LT	6-4	230	So.	Lima
75	Kohut, William	LT	6-4	251	Sr.	Youngstown
76	Burgin, Asbury	RT	6-2	232	So.	Euclid
77	*Orazen, Edward	LT	6	232	Sr.	Euclid
78	**Porretta, Daniel	RG	6-1	230	Sr.	Clairton, PA
79	Hill, Joseph	LT	6-1	239	So.	Columbus
80	Stock, Robert	LE	6-1	193	Jr.	Washington, PA
81	Anders, Billy	LE	6-2	191	So.	Sabina
82	**Spahr, William	LE	6-2	192	Sr.	Columbus
83	Walden, Robert	LE	6	176	So.	Middletown
84	Housteau, Joseph	RE	6-2	213	Jr.	Girard
85	Nein, James	LH	6-2	193	So.	Middletown
86	Palmer, John	RE	6-1	208	Jr.	Kettering
87	*Lashutka, Gregory	RE	6-5	219	Jr.	Cleveland
88	**Kiehfuss, Thomas	RE	6-3	205	Sr.	Cincinnati
89	Anderson, Thomas	LE	6-1	200	Sr.	Orrville
90	Cairns, Gary	RG	6-1	238	So.	Canton
91	Mobley, Ben	LE	6-2	208	Sr.	Montclair, NJ
92	Howman, Dennis	FB	6-1	208	Sr.	Wooster
93	Orazen, Michael	RE	6	203	So.	Euclid
94	Longer, Robert	RT	6-2	192	Sr.	Cleveland
95	George, August	RG	6	222	So.	Kettering
96	Smith, Larry	RT	5-10	209	Jr.	Amsterdam
97	Wortman, Robert	LT	6-2	238	Sr.	Cincinnati
98	Vargo, Thomas	LG	5-10	190	So.	Columbus

* Denotes letters won

1964

Ohio	27	S. Methodist	8
Ohio	17	Indiana	9
Ohio	26	Illinois	0
Ohio	17	S. California	0
Ohio	28	Wisconsin	3
Ohio	21	Iowa	19
Ohio	0	Penn State	27
Ohio	10	Northwestern	0
Ohio	0	Michigan	10

Season Summary

Won, 7; Lost, 2

ARNOLD CHONKO
All-American Back

JAMES DAVIDSON
All-American Tackle

DWIGHT KELLEY
All-American Linebacker

Very few fans leave their seats during the great halftime shows. No doubt, these **are** the **two** "Best Damn Bands In The Land"

November 20, 1965

Ann Arbor, Michigan

Buckeyes Jolt Wolves, 9-7, On Funk's Field Goal

Michigan Has Last Chance On 49-Yard FG Attempt

Ohio State got life by a pass, almost died with a pass, then was resurrected by a kick to defeat the University of Michigan, 9-7. Buckeye senior Bob Funk couldn't kick an extra point, but it was his field goal with 1:15 left in the game that booted the Buckeyes to victory over their traditional rivals. He had missed one earlier.

After being stymied in their first drive, the Buckeyes' quarterback Don Unverferth moved his team 76 yards in 15 plays for its first score. He completed six passes for 51 yards in the drive, five of them to Anders and another to Bo Rein for 13 yards. Anders was all over the field to pull down Buckeye bombs. He ranged to both sidelines for short hooks, took one down the middle for a first down on the Wolverines' six, then went straight down from left end on the TD toss and picked the ball off between Wolverine defenders Rick Volk and Frank Nunley. Funk's PAT attempt failed.

In the second quarter Ohio was beginning to move again when an Unverferth pass meant for Anders was picked off by Mike Bass who was downed on OSU's 15-yard line. Dave Fisher, who carried the ball 24 times for 96 yards from his fullback spot for the Wolverines, was then called upon four straight times, and on his fourth attempt he sliced across right end and through the hands of would-be OSU tackler Bob Walden for the touchdown. Dick Sygar converted the extra point giving Michigan a 7-6 halftime lead.

In the third quarter Michigan's Sygar missed two field goal attempts on a 13-yarder and the other a 25-yarder. Ward provided some excitement with a 55-yard run to the Ohio State 17 from where the Wolves drove to OSU's five before Sygar's first FG attempt. On their next series the Wolverines marched 64 yards with Sygar missing his second FG attempt.

Ohio State's second series of the fourth quarter began on its own nine with 7:25 to go in the game. Unverferth completed one pass to Rein. Then the runners took over. Rein and Sander moved the ball to Michigan's 16. It was fourth and five with 1:15 to go when Funk came on the field, and with Arnold Fontess holding the ball, sent a high, end-over-end kick floating through the uprights from a slight angle to the right.

Gabler came in to provide the Wolverines with one last brilliant effort, but time ran out on him. His passes took Michigan from its own 27 to Ohio's 33 where with 12 seconds left, De'Eramo's kick fell short.

STATISTICS

	OSU	UM
First Downs	19	18
Rushing Yardage	138	249
Passing Yardage	123	86
Passing	15-29-2	7-16-0
Punts	3-46	4-42
Fumbles Lost	1	0
Yards Penalized	10	35

1965

Ohio	3	North Carolina	14
Ohio	23	Washington ...	21
Ohio	28	Illinois	14
Ohio	7	Michigan State	32
Ohio	20	Wisconsin	10
Ohio	11	Minnesota	10
Ohio	17	Indiana	10
Ohio	38	Iowa	0
Ohio	9	Michigan	7

Season Summary

Games won, 7; Lost, 2

DOUGLAS VANHORN
All-American Tackle

DWIGHT KELLEY
All-American Linebacker

OHIO

No.	Name	Pos.	Wt.	Hgt.	Class	Home Town
75	Adams, Thomas	RT	210	6-3	So.	Fairport
19	Adderley, Nelson	RH	183	5-11	Sr.	Philadelphia, PA
21	Allen, Richard	QB	177	6-1	Sr.	Sidney
18	Amlin, George	LH	165	5-10	So.	Tiffin
81	Anders, Billy	LE	191	6-2	Jr.	Sabina
57	*Anderson, Kim	LE	190	6-0	Jr.	Orrville
72	*Anderson, Richard	LT	238	6-5	Sr.	Lodi
61	*Andrick, Theodore	LG	212	5-11	Sr.	Cuyahoga Falls
25	*Barrington, Thomas	FB	202	6-1	Sr.	Lima
66	*Bugel, Thomas	LG	208	6-0	Sr.	W. Homestead,
76	Burgin, Asbury	LT	232	6-2	Jr.	Euclid
51	Cochran, Terrence	C	198	5-9	Sr.	Richwood
74	Current, Michael	RT	237	6-4	Jr.	Lima
78	Dwyer, Donald	RT	218	6-2	So.	Lima
63	Eachus, William	LG	211	6-0	Jr.	Gallipolis
34	Farbizo, Thomas	FB	194	5-11	Jr.	New Philadelph
73	Fender, Paul	LT	228	6-3	So.	Warren
15	*Fill, John	LH	177	5-9	Jr.	Cuyahoga Heig
23	Fontes, Arnold	QB	184	5-11	So.	Canton
62	*Funk, Robert	PK	222	6-1	Sr.	Lakewood
95	George, August	RG	222	6-0	Jr.	Kettering
41	Hubbard, Rudy	LH	192	6-0	So.	Hubbard
36	*Hudson, Paul	FB	207	6-0	Jr.	Coatesville, PA
80	Johnson, Robert	LE	210	6-1	So.	Logan
53	*Kelley, Dwight	C	216	5-11	Sr.	Bremen
77	Kelly, John	LT	215	6-0	So.	Englewood
87	*Lashufka, Gregory	RE	219	6-5	Sr.	Cleveland
48	Lykes, Robert	LH	185	6-1	Sr.	Akron
12	*McCoy, John	FB	188	5-10	Jr.	Wooster
17	Meinerding, Wesley	RH	203	6-0	Jr.	Canton
58	*Miller, Gary	LT	216	6-0	Jr.	Bellevue
85	*Nein, James	RH	193	6-2	Jr.	Middletown
20	Newcomer, Mark	QB	175	5-11	Jr.	Gibsonburg
56	Oates, James	C	229	6-0	Sr.	Dunkirk
93	Orazen, Michael	RE	203	6-0	Jr.	Euclid
86	*Palmer, John	RE	208	6-1	Sr.	Kettering
30	Portsmouth, Thomas	RH	175	5-10	So.	Middletown
65	*Pryor, Ray	C	220	6-0	Jr.	Hamilton
38	Reed, Samuel	LE	183	5-8	Jr.	Garrettsville
45	*Rein, Robert	LH	182	5-11	Jr.	Niles
44	Richley, Richard	LH	183	5-9	Sr.	Cincinnati
69	*Ridder, William	RG	212	5-10	Sr.	Springfield
55	Rutherford, William	C	188	5-10	Jr.	Columbus
33	*Sander, Willard	FB	215	6-2	Sr.	Cincinnati
96	Smith, Larry	RT	209	5-10	Sr.	Amsterdam
64	Snyder, Larry	RG	198	6-2	Sr.	Wooster
11	Thomas, Will	RH	174	6-0	Jr.	Lima
26	*Unverferth, Donald	QB	208	6-3	Sr.	Dayton
68	*Van Horn, Douglas	RG	236	6-2	Sr.	Columbus
98	Vargo, Thomas	LG	190	5-10	Jr.	Columbus
83	*Walden, Robert	LE	180	6-0	Jr.	Middletown

* indicates letters won

MICHIGAN

Name	Pos.	Wt.	Hgt.	Class	Home Town
Allison, Bruce	FB	210	6-0	Sr.	Ypsilanti
Ancona, Perry	G	215	6-0	Sr.	Madeira, OH
*Bailey, Donald	G	198	5-11	Jr.	Greensburg, PA
*Bass, Michael	HB	182	6-0	Jr.	Ypsilanti
Berline, James	E	195	6-0	So.	Niles, OH
Brigstock, Thomas	HB	197	6-1	Sr.	Battle Creek
Broadnax, Stanley	G	217	6-0	So.	Cincinnati, OH
Buzynski, John	C	215	6-4	Jr.	Detroit
Byers, David	T	221	6-2	So.	Warren
Cartwright, Henry	T	235	6-3	Jr.	Detroit
*Cecchini, T. (Capt.)	C	194	6-0	Sr.	Detroit
*Clancy, Jack	E	195	6-1	Jr.	Detroit
Danhof, Jerome	C	228	6-3	Jr.	Detroit
Day, Floyd	G	202	6-2	Sr.	Canton, OH
Dayton, Joseph	C	218	6-2	So.	Detroit
*Dehlin, Barry	G	215	5-11	Sr.	Flushing
D'Eramo, Paul	C	212	5-10	So.	Youngstown, OH
*Detwiler, James	HB	215	6-3	Jr.	Toledo, OH
Doty, Alfred	FB	205	5-10	So.	Mount Morris
*Fisher, David	FB	215	5-10	Jr.	Kettering, OH
Flanagan, Dennis	G	215	6-2	Sr.	Niles, OH
Goss, Thomas	T	217	6-2	So.	Knoxville, TN
Gabler, Wallace	QB	195	6-2	Sr.	Royal Oak
Greene, Edward	E	200	5-11	Sr.	Flat Rock
Hanna, Henry	G	220	6-0	Jr.	Youngstown, OH
Hardy, William	T	225	6-1	Jr.	Detroit
Heffelfinger, Jon	E	201	6-2	So.	Battle Creek
Hollis, Peter	QB	190	6-0	Sr.	Detroit
*Hoyne, Jeffrey	E	190	6-1	Sr.	Chicago, IL
Hribal, James	T	225	6-0	Jr.	Dearborn
Humphries, Derrick	E	192	6-2	So.	Detroit
Irwin, John	HB	175	5-11	So.	Allegan
Johnson, Paul	T	226	6-0	So.	Bay City
*Keating, William	G	226	6-2	Sr.	Chicago, IL
*Kemp, Stanley	E	185	6-1	Jr.	Greenville
*Kines, Charles	T	238	6-1	Sr.	Niles, OH
*Kirby, Craig	E	185	6-2	Sr.	Royal Oak
Knapp, George	G	225	6-1	Jr.	Bay City
Lancaster, George	C	190	6-1	So.	Struthers, OH
*Lee, Louis	HB	192	6-2	Jr.	Willow Grove, PA
Legacki, Norman	HB	188	6-1	Sr.	Philadelphia, PA
Leslie, Kent	FB	198	6-0	So.	Ann Arbor
*Mack, Thomas	T	235	6-3	Sr.	Bucyrus, OH
England, Robert	T	240	6-2	Sr.	Ypsilanti
McLaughlin, Donald	E	205	6-0	Jr.	Chelsea
*Mielke, Robert	G	218	6-1	Jr.	Chicago, IL
Morgan, Dennis	FB	222	5-11	So.	Phoenixville, PA
Nelson, Douglas	HB	180	6-0	So.	Adrian
*Nunley, Frank	C	222	6-2	Jr.	Belleville
O'Donnell, Raymond	T	208	6-1	Jr.	Milan
Parkhill, Thomas	E	205	6-2	Sr.	Ada, OH
Phillips, Raymond	T	222	6-3	So.	Evanston, IL
Pitlosh, Max	G	250	6-1	Jr.	Detroit
Porter, David	G	221	6-3	So.	Lansing
Pullen, Thomas	E	190	6-4	So.	Ottawa, Canada
Radigan, Timothy	FB	206	5-11	Jr.	Lansing
Rosema, Roger	E	208	6-3	So.	Grand Rapids
*Rowser, John	HB	182	6-0	Jr.	Detroit
*Ruzicka, Charles	T	238	6-1	Sr.	Skokie, IL
Salmi, Terry	E	205	6-1	So.	Wakefield
Schick, Gary	FB	215	6-2	Sr.	Grosse Pointe
Seiber, James	QB	180	5-10	Jr.	Niles, OH
Sharpe, Ernest	HB	190	5-11	So.	Palos Hts., IL
*Smith, Stephen	E	229	6-5	Sr.	Park Ridge, IL
Spencer, Royce	E	205	6-1	So.	Chicago, IL
*Sygar, Richard	HB	180	5-11	Jr.	Niles, OH
Tennant, Byran	C	212	6-0	Sr.	Worthington, OH
VanBlaricom, Paul	T	241	6-3	Sr.	Kalamazoo
Vidmer, Richard	QB	184	6-0	So.	Greensburg, PA
*Volk, Richard	HB	190	6-3	Jr.	Wauseon, OH
*Ward, Carl	HB	177	5-9	Jr.	Cincinnati, OH
*Wells, Richard	HB	178	5-9	Sr.	Grand Rapids
*Wilhite, Clayton	E	204	6-4	Jr.	Bay City
Wright, Kenneth	G	215	6-1	Jr.	Bay City
Yanz, Richard	G	204	6-2	So.	Chicago, IL
*Yearby, William	T	230	6-3	Sr.	Detroit
Yedinak, Martin	HB	175	5-8	So.	Alpena

dicates letters won

1965

Michigan	31	North Carolina	24
Michigan	10	California	7
Michigan	7	Georgia	15
Michigan	7	Michigan State	24
Michigan	15	Purdue	17
Michigan	13	Minnesota	14
Michigan	50	Wisconsin	14
Michigan	23	Illinois	3
Michigan	22	Northwestern	34
Michigan	7	Ohio State	9

Season Summary

Games won, 4; Lost, 6; Tied, 0

WILLIAM YEARBY
All-American Tackle

18

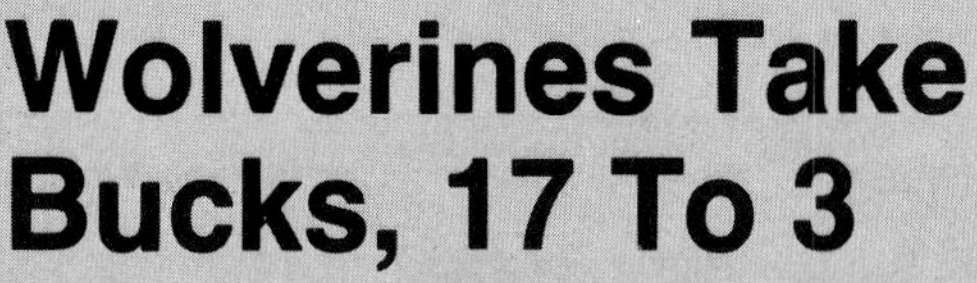

November 19, 1966

Columbus, Ohio

Wolverines Take Bucks, 17 To 3

Backs From Ohio Shine For Michigan

Michigan captured the 63rd battle between the two archrivals behind the slashing running of three Ohio-born backs, Jim Detwiler of Toledo, Dave Fisher of Kettering, and Carl Ward of Cincinnati. That trio gained 239 yards, 93 more than the entire Buckeye team and Ohio State slipped into the Big Ten's second division with Hayes' first losing mark (4-5) since 1959.

The scoring started with goals by each team. Michigan's came first on a 24-yarder by Dick Sygar at 12:03 of the opening quarter. Then Ohio's Gary Cairns delivered a 3-pointer from the 16 with 3:50 left in the first half.

The actual turning point of the grim duel came with just 1:16 left in the first half. That was when the nation's No. 1 pass receiver, Jack Clancy, made a circus catch to put the Wolverines in position to break the 3-all deadlock. An offensive pass interference penalty had just set Michigan back to the Ohio 41 with a third-and-25 situation. Vidmer retreated and fired a shot over the middle where Clancy leaped high for the ball at the 12 and tumbled to the turf at the seven. On the next play Detwiler burst through right tackle to break the tie and set the stage for victory.

In the third quarter after a 15-yard clipping penalty, OSU gave up the ball. Michigan started a 56-yard drive that resulted in the clinching touchdown. It was scored on a 28-yard pass from quarterback Dick Vidmer to Clayton Wilhite. Sygar, as he did after the first TD, converted the PAT.

In the fourth period Ohio penetrated to the 6 with 10:40 left to play after Ohio's Bob Walden intercepted a Michigan pass at UM's 21. Ohio got two more chances; but couldn't penetrate deeper than the Michigan 19 and the game ended moments after Bo Rein fumbled to end the last march. John Rowser recovered for Michigan.

STATISTICS

	UM	OSU
First Downs	21	20
Rushing Yardage	272	146
Passing Yardage	220	122
Passes	5-16-1	11-29-2
Punts	3-43	4-31
Fumbles Lost	1	1
Yards Penalized	89	38

1966

1966

Michigan	. . 41	Oregon State . .	0
Michigan	. . 17	California	7
Michigan	. . 7	North Carolina	21
Michigan	. . 7	Michigan State	20
Michigan	. . 21	Purdue	22
Michigan	. . 49	Minnesota	0
Michigan	. . 28	Wisconsin	17
Michigan	. . 21	Illinois	28
Michigan	. . 28	Northwestern . .	20
Michigan	. . 17	Ohio State	3

Season Summary

Games won, 6; Lost, 4; Tied, 0

JOHN CLANCY
All-American End

RICHARD VOLK
All-American Halfback

MICHIGAN

No.	Name	Pos.	Wt.	Hgt.	Class	Home Town
12	Hoey, George	HB	170	5-10	So.	Flint
14	Jobe, Theodore	HB	178	6-0	So.	Toledo, OH
15	*Bass, Mike	RH	180	6-0	Sr.	Ypsilanti
16	Wedge, Robert	HB	193	6-2	So.	Port Huron
17	*Sharpe, Ernest	LH	191	5-11	Jr.	Palos Heights, I
18	*Sygar, Richard	S	185	5-11	Sr.	Niles, OH
19	*Ward, Carl	RH	178	5-9	Sr.	Cincinnati, OH
20	Thomas, John	QB	192	6-1	Jr.	Walled Lake
21	Kieta, Robert	QB	181	6-0	So.	Chicago, IL
22	Brown, Dennis	QB	178	5-10	So.	Lincoln Park
24	*Clancy, Jack	RE	192	6-1	Sr.	Detroit
26	Hartman, Jerald	HB	168	6-1	So.	Ann Arbor
27	*Vidmer, Richard	QB	185	6-1	Jr.	Greensburg, PA
30	Doty, Alfred	HB	195	5-10	Jr.	Mt. Morris
32	*Radigan, Timothy	FB	206	5-11	Sr.	Lansing
33	*Fisher, David	FB	210	5-10	Sr.	Kettering, OH
34	*Morgan, Dennis	LB	230	5-11	Jr.	Phoenix, PA
35	Reynolds, John	FB	218	5-10	So.	Grosse Pts. Wo
36	Washington, Martin	RG	194	5-10	So.	Ecorse
38	Beier, Michael	HB	191	5-11	So.	Fremont, OH
39	Doane, Thomas	HB	207	5-10	So.	Wauseon, OH
40	Johnson, Ronald	HB	192	6-1	So.	Detroit
41	*Lee, Louis	HB	195	6-2	Sr.	Willow Grove, P
43	*Rowser, John	LH	183	6-0	Sr.	Detroit
44	Nelson, Douglas	HB	186	6-0	Jr.	Adrian
45	Spencer, Royce	RE	208	6-1	Jr.	Chicago, IL
48	*Detwiler, James	LH	215	6-3	Sr.	Toledo, OH
49	*Volk, Richard	S	192	6-3	Sr.	Wauseon, OH
50	*Dehlin, Barry	LB	205	5-11	Sr.	Flushing
51	*D'Eramo, Paul	LB	208	5-10	Jr.	Youngstown, O
52	*Wright, Kenneth	RT	230	6-1	Sr.	Bay City
55	*Bailey, Donald	RG	225	6-0	Sr.	Greensburg, PA
57	Danhof, Jerry	C	228	6-3	Sr.	Detroit
58	*Dayton, Joseph	C	229	6-2	Jr.	Detroit
59	*Nunley, Frank	LB	218	6-2	Sr.	Belleville
60	Baumgartner, Robert	LG	215	6-0	So.	Chicago, IL
61	Broadnax, Stanley	RT	230	6-0	Jr.	Cincinnati, OH
62	*Johnson, Paul	LT	231	6-0	Jr.	Bay City
63	*Mielke, Robert	MG	223	6-1	Sr.	Chicago, IL
64	*Hanna, Henry	LG	220	6-0	Sr.	Youngstown, O
65	Goss, Thomas	MG	225	6-2	Jr.	Knoxville, TN
66	*Hardy, William	LT	229	6-1	Sr.	Detroit
67	Yanz, Richard	LG	212	6-1	So.	Chicago, IL
69	Landsittel, Thomas	RG	198	5-10	Sr.	Delaware, OH
70	Porter, David	RT	237	6-3	Jr.	Lansing
71	Hribal, James	RT	220	6-0	Sr.	Dearborn
72	*Phillips, Raymond	LT	228	6-3	Jr.	Evanston, IL
73	Mair, Peter	LT	233	6-4	Sr.	Allentown, PA
74	Monthei, Dennis	MG	198	6-2	Jr.	Detroit
75	Williamson, Richard	LT	225	6-4	Jr.	East Detroit
76	Penksa, Robert	RT	228	6-1	So.	Niles, OH
77	Byers, David	LT	235	6-3	Jr.	Warren
80	*Kemp, Stanley	LE	185	6-1	Sr.	Greenville
81	*Pullen, Thomas	RE	195	6-3	Jr.	Ottawa, Canad
83	*Rosema, Roger	LE	214	6-2	Jr.	Grand Rapids
84	Kramer, Jon	LE	213	6-3	So.	Toledo, OH
85	*Wilhite, Clayton	LE	210	6-4	Sr.	Bay City
86	Humphries, Derrick	RE	190	6-2	Jr.	Detroit
88	Sipp, Warren	LE	216	6-1	So.	Akron, OH
89	Salmi, Terry	RE	208	6-1	Jr.	Wakefield
90	Stincic, Thomas	RE	217	6-3	So.	Cleveland, OH
97	Berline, James	RE	188	6-0	Jr.	Niles, OH

* indicates letters won

OHIO

No.	Name	Pos.	Wt.	Hgt.	Class	Home Town
11	*Thomas, Will	LH	185	6-0	Sr.	Lima
12	**McCoy, John	LB	191	5-10	Sr.	Wooster
14	*Elliott, Samuel	QB	188	6-0	Jr.	Torrence, CA
15	**Fill, John	LH	175	5-9	Sr.	Cuyahoga Hts.
16	Peyton, Leroy	RH	170	5-8	So.	Lorain
17	*Meinerding, Wesley	FB	203	6-0	Sr.	Canton
18	Amlin, George	S	167	5-10	Jr.	Tiffin
19	Bender, Edward	RH	175	6-0	So.	Akron
20	Powers, William	PK	170	6-1	So.	Bay Village
23	*Fontes, Arnold	RH	180	5-11	Jr.	Canton
24	Long, William	QB	170	6-1	So.	Dayton
28	Ehrsam, Gerald	QB	190	6-0	So.	Toledo
30	*Portsmouth, Thomas	S	175	5-10	Jr.	Middletown
32	Smith, Rudy	FB	207	6-0	So.	Cincinnati
33	Bartley, Thomas	LB	188	5-11	So.	Springfield
35	*Baas, James	LE	200	6-1	Sr.	Columbus
36	*Hudson, Paul	FB	210	6-0	Sr.	Coatesville, PA
41	*Hubbard, Rudy	LH	188	6-0	Jr.	Hubbard
42	Reynolds, David	LH	193	5-11	Jr.	Lima
45	**Rein, Robert	RH	180	5-11	Sr.	Niles
46	*Hamlin, Stanley	RH	183	6-1	Jr.	Monessen, PA
47	Hodge, Glenn	LH	175	6-2	So.	Oberlin
48	Bombach, Jaren	RH	192	6-1	So.	Dayton
52	Roman, James	C	212	6-0	So.	Canton
53	Muhlbach, John	C	187	5-10	So.	Massillon
54	Stier, Mark	LB	200	6-1	So.	Louisville
55	Rutherford, William	C	185	5-10	Sr.	Columbus
56	Worden, Dirk	LB	195	6-0	So.	Lorain
57	**Anderson, Kim	LB	190	6-0	Sr.	Orrville
58	**Miller, Gary	LT	223	6-0	Sr.	Bellevue
59	Roush, Gary	LT	196	6-4	So.	Springfield
62	Kelley, John	RG	219	6-0	Jr.	Englewood
63	*Eachus, William	LG	218	6-0	Sr.	Gallipolis
64	Kafury, Michael	MG	218	6-1	So.	Cambridge
65	**Pryor, Ray	C	2$8	6-0	Sr.	Hamilton
66	DiFederico, Jules	RT	222	6-1	So.	Steubenville
67	Ford, John	RT	220	6-1	So.	Springfield
68	**Palmer, John	LG	208	6-1	Sr.	Kettering
69	Stottlemyer, Victor	MG	205	6-0	So.	Chillicothe
70	Foley, David	RT	248	6-5	So.	Cincinnati
71	*Himes, Richard	RG	250	6-4	Jr.	Canton
73	Fender, Paul	RT	232	6-3	Jr.	Warren
74	*Current, Michael	LT	246	6-4	Sr.	Lima
75	Ervin, Terry	RT	226	6-2	So.	Wellston
76	*Burgin, Asbury	RG	225	6-2	Sr.	Euclid
78	*Dwyer, Donald	RT	221	6-2	Jr.	Lima
79	Urbanik, William	LT	229	6-3	So.	Donora, PA
0	*Johnson, Robert	LB	208	6-1	Jr.	Logan
1	*Anders, Billy	LE	190	6-2	Jr.	Sabina
2	Mayes, Rufus	RE	228	6-5	So.	Toledo
3	**Walden, Robert	LE	185	6-0	Sr.	Middletown
4	Jenkins, Joseph	RE	195	6-2	So.	East Cleveland
5	*Nein, James	RH	192	6-2	Jr.	Middletown
7	Smith, Robert	RE	225	6-4	So.	Lakewood
8	Dillon, Dan	LE	192	6-0	Sr.	Springfield
9	Roman, Nicholas	LE	210	6-4	So.	Canton
0	Cairns, Gary	PK	230	6-1	Jr.	Canton
1	Sobolewski, John	RE	190	6-1	So.	Steubenville
2	Stowe, John	LE	220	6-2	So.	Columbus
3	Orazen, Michael	RE	217	6-0	Jr.	Euclid
4	Tabacca, Jerome	RE	213	6-2	So.	Warren
6	Timko, Richard	LE	171	6-0	So.	Pataskala

indicates letters won

1966

Ohio	14	Texas Christian	7
Ohio	22	Washington	38
Ohio	9	Illinois	10
Ohio	8	Michigan State	11
Ohio	24	Wisconsin	13
Ohio	7	Minnesota	17
Ohio	7	Indiana	0
Ohio	14	Iowa	10
Ohio	3	Michigan	17

Season Summary

Games won, 4; Lost, 5

RAY PRYOR
All-American Center

November 25, 1967

Ann Arbor, Michigan

Ohio Stems Michigan Rally For 24-14 Victory

Schmidlin, Worden, Defensive Stars For OSU

Anyone who wanted to know what Ohio State football is all about had only to watch the first half of the traditional OSU-Michigan battle. The crisp-blocking Buckeyes sat Michigan defenders on their seats of their pants as they rolled up 238 yards and 21 points before the Wolverines could retaliate.

Ohio State scored the first two times it had the ball in the first half, was stymied the third time, but then scored on its next series. A missed field goal by OSU's Gary Cairns seemed to spark the Michigan offense which had only 3:10 left in the first half. Dennis Brown mixed up his passes with Ron Johnson's running for the 80-yard scoring drive. Brown passed to Jim Berline for the TD, but Johnson gained 31 yards with his rushes. His season total of 1005 yards breaks a Big Ten record.

Johnson, however, had to take a back seat to two Buckeye rushers, Jim Otis who gained 114 yards, and Rudy Hubbard who added 103. Hubbard, a little used senior, scored two of Ohio's three touchdowns. Ohio State went 79 yards in 10 plays with Hubbard scampering the last 22 yards for the tally. Cairns' conversion kick was good. The second drive consumed 64 yards in seven plays. Hubbard went the last 12 yards and again Cairns was accurate for a 14-0 lead. The third touchdown went 53 yards in seven plays. Bill Long, the sometimes-maligned OSU quarterback plunged over from the one for Ohio's final touchdown. Cairns was good for the PAT.

The third period was scoreless with several scoring threats which could not produce. In the fourth quarter, action continued as OSU's Tom Portsmouth intercepted a Wolverine pass on the Buckeyes' one-yard line. The Buckeye punter, Portsmouth, boomed the ball out of his own end zone to the Ohio 47, but the Wolves were not to be denied. They scored in six plays with Brown hitting John Gabler with a simple cut-in pass for the 13-yard touchdown. Titas again converted the PAT making the score 21-14, Ohio winning.

An onside kick by Michigan failed as OSU's Dave Foley covered the ball. Ohio moved down to the 19 and Cairns came in to kick from the 27 for the big three points, and Michigan's threatening gestures were finished for the day.

STATISTICS

	OSU	UM
First Downs	17	18
Rushing Yardage	283	128
Passing Yardage	45	179
Return Yardage	75	107
Passes	5-6-0	17-24-1
Punts	5-38	5-34
Fumbles Lost	0	3
Yards Penalized	8	34

1967

1967			
Ohio	7	Arizona	14
Ohio	30	Oregon	0
Ohio	6	Purdue	41
Ohio	6	Northwestern	2
Ohio	13	Illinois	17
Ohio	21	Michigan State	7
Ohio	17	Wisconsin	15
Ohio	21	Iowa	10
Ohio	24	Michigan	14

Season Summary

Games won, 6; Lost, 3

OHIO

No.	Name	Pos.	Wt.	Hgt.	Class	Home Town
81	**Anders, Billy	LE	194	6-2	Sr.	Sabina
16	Armstrong, Michael	RH	192	5-11	So.	Springfield
33	Bartley, Thomas	LB	191	5-11	Jr.	Springfield
19	Bender, Edward	RH	172	6-0	Jr.	Akron
48	Bombach, Jaren	LH	198	6-1	Jr.	Dayton
12	Brungard, David	LH	186	5-10	So.	Youngstown
90	*Cairns, Gary	PK	212	6-1	Sr.	Canton
78	**Dwyer, Donald	LT	241	6-2	Sr.	Lima
28	*Ehrsam, Gerald	QB	194	6-0	Jr.	Toledo
14	**Elliott, Samuel	QB	183	6-0	Sr.	Torrance, CA
75	*Ervin, Terry	RT	232	6-2	Jr.	Wellston
58	Fertig, Dwight	LB	228	6-1	So.	Ravenna
70	*Foley, David	RT	246	6-5	Jr.	Cincinnati
11	Gillian, Ray	LH	182	5-11	So.	Uniontown, PA
51	Hackett, William	LB	204	6-0	So.	London
65	Hart, Randy	RG	220	6-1	So.	Willoughby
71	**Himes, Richard	LT	243	6-4	Sr.	Canton
41	**Hubbard, Rudolph	RH	196	6-0	Sr.	Hubbard
34	Huff, Paul	FB	217	6-3	So.	Dover
72	Hutchison, Charles	RT	242	6-3	So.	Carrollton
61	Jack, Alan	RG	215	6-0	So.	Wintersville
42	Jenkins, Joseph	RE	198	6-2	Jr.	East Cleveland
62	*Kelley, John	LG	225	6-0	Sr.	Englewood
24	*Long, William	QB	180	6-1	Jr.	Dayton
82	*Mayes, Rufus	RE	230	6-5	Jr.	Toledo
53	*Muhlbach, John	C	190	5-10	Jr.	Massillon
9	**Nein, James	LB	208	6-2	Sr.	Middletown
77	Nielsen, Brad	RT	222	6-3	So.	Columbus
35	Otis, James	FB	208	6-0	So.	Celina
15	Polaski, Michael	RH	166	5-10	So.	Columbus
85	Pollitt, William	RT	215	6-2	So.	Dayton
30	**Portsmouth, Thomas	S	181	5-10	Sr.	Middletown
20	Powers, William	PK	172	6-1	Jr.	Bay Village
46	Provost, Ted	LH	180	6-2	So.	Navarre
55	Radtke, Michael	LB	200	6-1	So.	Wayne, NJ
52	*Roman, James	C	210	6-0	Jr.	Canton
89	*Roman, Nicholas	RE	219	6-4	Jr.	Canton
59	Roush, Gary	RT	198	6-4	Jr.	Springfield
23	Rusnak, Kevin	QB	190	6-1	So.	Garfield, NJ
74	Schmidlin, Paul	LT	221	6-1	So.	Toledo
95	Shannon, James	C	200	6-0	So.	Columbus
50	Smith, Butch	LB	224	6-1	So.	Hamilton
87	Smith, Robert	RE	221	6-4	Jr.	Lakewood
32	*Smith, Rudy	FB	203	6-0	Jr.	Cincinnati
91	*Sobolewski, John	RE	190	6-1	Jr.	Steubenville
54	*Stier, Mark	LB	208	6-1	Jr.	Louisville
69	*Stottlemyer, Victor	MG	200	6-0	Jr.	Chillicothe
92	Stowe, John	LE	203	6-2	Jr.	Columbus
60	Tabacca, Jerome	LG	222	6-2	Jr.	Warren
79	Urbanik, William	LT	238	6-3	Jr.	Donora, PA
88	Whitfield, David	LE	182	6-0	So.	Massillon
56	*Worden, Dirk	LB	197	6-0	Jr.	Lorain

* indicates letters won

MICHIGAN

No.	Name	Pos.	Wt.	Hgt.	Class	Home Town
95	Banar, James	OT	218	6-0	Jr.	Detroit
60	Baumgartner, Bob	OG	219	6-0	Jr.	Chicago, IL
97	Berline, Jim	OE	185	6-0	Sr.	Niles, OH
61	Broadnax, Stan	OT	226	6-0	Sr.	Cincinnati, OH
22	Brown, Dennis	QB	175	5-10	Jr.	Lincoln Park
66	Brown, Richard	OT	215	6-1	So.	Auburn
56	Caldarazzo, Dick	OG	210	5-10	So.	Melrose Park, IL
48	Craw, Garvie	OB	211	6-2	So.	Montclair, NJ
25	Curtis, Tom	DHB	184	6-1	So.	Aurora, OH
58	*Dayton, Joe (Capt.)	C	225	6-2	Sr.	Detroit
52	Denzin, David	C	220	6-2	Jr.	Xenia, OH
51	*D'Eramo, Paul	C	214	5-10	Sr.	Youngstown, OH
30	Doty, Alfred	SB	187	5-10	Sr.	Mt. Morris
50	Drehmann, Peter	OT	206	6-1	So.	Abington, PA
79	Duffy, James	OG	215	6-1	Sr.	Winchester, MA
93	Falkenhagen, Curt	DE	198	6-2	So.	Bridgeport
23	Farabee, David	OHB	185	6-0	Jr.	Holland
37	Federico, Eric	FB	197	5-11	So.	Trenton
64	Francis, Alan	MG	190	5-10	So.	Euclid, OH
54	Frysinger, Terry	DT	212	6-2	Jr.	Ecorse
18	Gabler, John	OHB	208	6-2	So.	Royal Oak
65	*Goss, Tom	DT	225	6-2	Sr.	Knoxville, TN
77	Hall, Werner	OT	226	6-0	So.	Sandusky, OH
57	Hankwitz, Mike	LB	194	6-1	So.	Scottville
80	Harris, William	OE	184	6-1	So.	Mt. Clemens
26	*Hartman, Gerald	SB	170	6-1	Jr.	Ann Arbor
24	Healy, Brian	DHB	170	6-1	So.	Sandusky, OH
32	Heffelfinger, Jon	DE	205	6-2	Sr.	Battle Creek
12	Hoey, George	DHB	169	5-10	Jr.	Flint
36	*Humphries, Derrick	OE	192	6-2	Sr.	Detroit
62	*Johnson, Paul	OT	231	6-0	Sr.	Bay City
40	*Johnson, Ronald	OHB	196	6-1	Jr.	Detroit
21	Kieta, Robert	SB	181	6-0	Jr.	Chicago, IL
34	*Kramer, Jon	MG	215	6-3	Jr.	Toledo, OH
68	Kunsa, Joseph	OG	207	6-0	Jr.	W. Braddock, PA
28	Lynch, John	DHB	175	5-10	Jr.	Chicago, IL
73	*Mair, Peter	OT	228	6-4	Sr.	Allentown, PA
38	Mandich, James	OE	215	6-3	So.	Solon, OH
94	*Miklos, Gerald	DT	227	6-3	Jr.	Chicago, IL
74	Monthei, Dennis	MG	201	6-2	Sr.	Detroit
34	*Morgan, Dennis	LB	215	5-11	Sr.	Phoenixville, PA
71	Mouch, William	OT	260	6-5	So.	Cincinnati, OH
44	Nelson, Douglas	SB	181	6-0	Sr.	Adrian
76	Penksa, Robert	OT	225	6-1	Jr.	Niles, OH
72	*Phillips, Ray	OG	229	6-3	Sr.	Evanston, IL
29	Pierson, Barry	DHB	173	6-0	So.	St. Ignace
70	*Porter, Dave	DT	231	6-3	Sr.	Lansing
5	Pryor, Cecil	LB	218	6-4	So.	Corpus Christi, TX
1	*Pullen, Tom	OE	198	6-3	Sr.	Ottawa, Can.
9	Ritley, Robert	OT	228	6-0	So.	Garfield Hgts., OH
3	*Rosema, Roger	DE	225	6-2	Sr.	Grand Rapids
6	Sansom, Elijah	DHB	191	6-1	Jr.	Detroit
9	Sarantos, Peter	C	207	6-0	So.	Elkhart, IN
1	Seymour, Philip	DE	195	6-4	So.	Berkley
7	*Sharpe, Ernest	OHB	191	5-11	Sr.	Palos Hts., IL
3	*Sipp, Warren	FB	209	6-1	Jr.	Akron, OH
2	Sirosky, Dennis	LB	221	6-0	Jr.	Ecorse
9	Sorenson, Eric	OE	188	6-0	So.	Royal Oak
5	Spencer, Royce	OE	208	6-1	Sr.	Chicago, IL
0	*Stincic, Tom	DE	217	6-3	Jr.	Cleveland, OH
0	Thomas, John	QB	198	6-1	Sr.	Walled Lake
1	Titas, Frank	FB	205	6-2	So.	Cleveland, OH
7	*Vidmer, Richard	QB	183	6-1	Sr.	Greensburg, PA
1	Wadhams, Timothy	DHB	178	6-1	So.	Ann Arbor
6	Washington, Martin	OG	194	5-10	Jr.	Ecorse
0	Wall, Kenneth	DHB	180	6-2	So.	LaGrange, IL
3	*Wedge, Robert	LB	201	6-2	Jr.	Port Huron
5	Weinmann, Tom	OE	214	6-2	So.	Ann Arbor
9	Werner, Mark	DHB	188	6-2	So.	Cincinnati, OH
3	White, Robert	OHB	190	6-2	So.	Middleville
2	Wilhite, James	MG	204	6-3	Jr.	Bay City
5	*Williamson, Dick	DT	227	6-4	Sr.	East Detroit
6	Woolley, Edwin	DE	218	6-1	So.	Pitman, NJ
7	Yanz, Richard	OG	217	6-1	Jr.	Chicago, IL

indicates letters won

1967

Michigan	10	Duke	7
Michigan	9	California	10
Michigan	21	Navy	26
Michigan	0	Michigan State	34
Michigan	20	Indiana	27
Michigan	15	Minnesota	20
Michigan	7	Northwestern	3
Michigan	21	Illinois	14
Michigan	27	Wisconsin	14
Michigan	14	Ohio State	24

Season Summary

Games won, 4; Lost, 6 Tied, 0.

#10 Rex Kern

.#27 Don Moorhead, #22 Denny Brown

Bill Harris (in earlier game of the season)

Michigan's thirteenth football coach, Bo Schembechler (left) and the man he succeeded at the end of the 1968 season, Bump Elliott. Elliott was named as associate athletic director at this same news conference.

(from an earlier game during the season)

November 23, 1968

Columbus, Ohio

Bowl-Bound Buckeyes Bomb Michigan, 50-14

Otis Scores Four Times In Big Ten Clincher

Buckeye fans watched in awe as their sophomore-dominated team completely swamped a mighty Michigan team in the second half to win the Big Ten championship and a Rose Bowl date with Southern California on January 1. OSU's junior fullback, Jim Otis of Celina, Ohio, scored four touchdowns and outran Michigan's marvelous tailback, Ron Johnson, 143 yards to 91.

The Buckeye sophomores, led by versatile quarterback Rex Kern, played like veterans. Kern scored two touchdowns, netted 96 of OSU's 421 yards rushing, and, throwing only when he had to, hit on 5 of 8 passes for 41 yards.

The first quarter action resulted in each team scoring a touchdown. Michigan scored on a one-yard plunge by Ron Johnson with Killian providing the PAT. Ohio's Otis crossed the goal line from 5 yards out to knot the score after Roman's kick for the extra point.

Kern from 5 yards out and Otis from 2 gave Ohio State two TDs in the second quarter. Roman added both extra points. Michigan's Johnson scored from the one-yard line and Killian booted the extra point. The score at halftime was 21-14 in favor of Ohio.

Ohio State took the second half kickoff and drove 72 yards in 11 plays, Otis doing most of the brutal work and Larry Zelina going six yards through a big hole for the touchdown.

The fourth quarter was when Michigan was buried. Roman kicked a 32-yard field goal. Kern scored on a three-yard run and Otis scored two touchdowns from two yards out and one yard out. Roman kicked two extra points. A pass for the third failed.

John Tatum, Dave Whitfield, and Jim Stillwagon were the defensive stars for OSU while offensive tackles Rufus Mayes and Dave Foley chopped huge gaps in Michigan's defensive line.

Michigan's fine senior quarterback Dennis Brown hit his targets 14 times for 171 yards, Jim Mandich grabbing seven of the throws.

STATISTICS

	OSU	UM
First Downs	28	17
Rushing Yardage	421	140
Passing Yardage	146	171
Return Yardage	62	15
Passes	6-9-1	14-24-3
Punts	2-30	5-40
Fumbles Lost	2	1
Yards Penalized	37	43

1968			
Michigan	7	California	21
Michigan	31	Duke	10
Michigan	32	Navy	9
Michigan	28	Mich. State	14
Michigan	27	Indiana	22
Michigan	33	Minnesota	20
Michigan	35	Northwestern	0
Michigan	36	Illinois	0
Michigan	34	Wisconsin	9
Michigan	14	Ohio State	50

Season Summary

Games won, 8; Lost, 2; Tied, 0.

RON JOHNSON
All-American Halfback

MICHIGAN

No.	Name	Pos.	Wt.	Hgt.	Class	Home Town
10	Wall, Kenneth	DHB	180	6-2	So.	LaGrange, Ill.
12	*Hoey, George	DHB	168	5-10	Sr.	Flint
18	*Gabler, John	HB	208	6-2	Jr.	Royal Oak
20	Thomas, John	QB	198	6-1	Sr.	Walled Lake
21	Kieta, Robert	OHB	181	6-0	Sr.	Chicago, Ill.
22	*Brown, Denny	QB	175	5-10	Sr.	Lincoln Park
23	Betts, Jim	QB	180	6-4	So.	Cleveland, O.
24	*Healy, Brian	DHB	170	6-1	Jr.	Sandusky, O.
25	*Curtis, Tom	DHB	184	6-1	Jr.	Aurora, O.
26	*Hartman, Jerry	DHB	170	6-1	Sr.	Ann Arbor
27	Moorhead, Don	QB	197	6-3	So.	Southaven
29	*Pierson, Barry	DHB	173	6-0	Jr.	St. Ignace
30	Staroba, Paul	E	195	6-3	So.	Flint
31	Francis, Al	MG	190	5-10	Jr.	Euclid, O.
32	Sirosky, Dennis	LB	197	6-0	Sr.	Ecorse
33	**Sipp, Warren	FB	209	6-1	Sr.	Akron, O.
35	Killian, Tim	LB	220	6-4	So.	Lincoln Park
36	Washington, Martin	G	194	5-10	Jr.	Ecorse
37	Federico, Eric	FB	197	5-11	Jr.	Trenton
39	Hill, Henry	MG	200	5-10	So.	Detroit
40	**Johnson, Ron	HB	196	6-1	Sr.	Detroit
43	White, Bob	DHB	190	6-2	Jr.	Middleville
45	Scheffler, Lance	HB	190	6-0	So.	Trenton
46	Sansom, Elijah	DE	188	6-1	Sr.	Detroit
48	*Craw, Garvie	FB	211	6-2	Jr.	Montclair, N.J.
49	Werner, Mark	DHB	185	6-2	Jr.	Cincinnati, O.
50	*Drehmann, Pete	T	206	6-1	Jr.	Abington, Pa.
51	Sample, Fred	C	225	6-0	So.	Pittsburgh, Pa.
52	Denzin, Dave	C	220	6-2	Sr.	Xenia, O.
53	**Wedge, Bob	LB	193	6-2	Sr.	Port Huron
55	Pryor, Cecil	LB	218	6-4	Jr.	Corpus Christi, Tex.
56	Caldarazzo, Richard	G	210	5-10	Jr.	Melrose Park, Ill.
57	*Hankwitz, Mike	LB	190	6-2	Jr.	Scottsville
59	Sarantos, Pete	C	200	6-0	Jr.	Elkhart, Ind.
61	*Broadnax, Stan	G	226	6-0	Sr.	Cincinnati, O.
62	Baldwin, Ed	G	220	6-1	So.	Hamilton, O.
63	Jones, Joe	G	195	6-0	Jr.	Evanston, Ill.
64	*Titas, Frank	G	205	6-2	Jr.	Cleveland, O.
65	**Goss, Tom	DT	225	6-2	Sr.	Knoxville, Tenn.
66	Wolff, John	G	220	6-1	So.	Delmont, Pa.
70	Huff, Marty	LB	220	6-2	So.	Toledo, O.
71	Harpring, Jack	T	216	6-4	So.	Cincinnati, O.
72	Dierdorf, Dan	T	255	6-3	So.	Canton, O.
73	Abrahams, Moris	DT	225	6-2	Jr.	Ann Arbor
74	Parks, Dan	DT	235	6-5	So.	Birmingham
75	Hall, Werner	T	225	6-0	Jr.	Sandusky, O.
76	*Penksa, Bob	T	225	6-1	Sr.	Niles, O.
77	Catallo, Guido	DT	260	6-4	So.	East Detroit
78	McCoy, Richard	DT	230	6-4	So.	Alliance, O.
79	Duffy, Jim	G	215	6-1	Sr.	Winchester, Mass.
80	Harris, Bill	E	195	6-1	Jr.	Mt. Clemens
81	Flanagan, Steve	DE	193	6-2	So.	Oak Park, Ill.
82	Newell, Pete	DE	218	6-4	So.	Park Ridge, Ill.
84	*Kramer, Jon	DE	215	6-3	Sr.	Toledo, O.
85	*Weinmann, Tom	E	214	6-2	Jr.	Ann Arbor
86	Imsland, Jerry	E	210	6-2	Jr.	Northville
88	*Mandich, Jim	E	215	6-3	Jr.	Solon, O.
89	McCaffrey, Tom	E	185	6-2	So.	Silver Springs, Md.
90	*Stincic, Tom	LB	217	6-3	Sr.	Cleveland, O.
91	*Seymour, Phil	DE	193	6-4	Jr.	Berkley
92	*Wilhite, Jim	T	204	6-3	Jr.	Bay City
93	Flanagan, Stephen	DE	193	6-2	So.	Oak Park, Ill.
94	*Miklos, Jerry	MG	227	6-3	Sr.	Chicago, Ill.
96	Woolley, Ed	DE	218	6-1	Jr.	Pitman, N.J.
97	Moore, Ed	DE	200	6-1	So.	Youngstown, O.

* indicates letters won

OHIO

No.	Name	Pos.	Wt.	Hgt.	Class	Home Town
	Sensibaugh, Michael	S	188	6-0	So.	Cincinnati
	Kern, Rex	QB	180	6-0	So.	Lancaster
	*Gillian, Ray	OLH	194	5-11	Jr.	Uniontown, Pa.
	*Brungard, David	OLH	184	5-10	Jr.	Youngstown
	Smith, Bruce	S	150	5-10	So.	Gallipolis
	*Polaski, Michael	DRH	168	5-10	Jr.	Columbus
	Zelina, Lawrence	ORH	195	6-0	So.	Cleveland
	Trapuzzano, Robert	LB	192	6-0	Jr.	McKees Rocks, Pa.
	Maciejowski, Ronald	QB	186	6-2	So.	Bedford
	Bender, Edward	ORH	172	6-0	Sr.	Akron
	Burton, Arthur	DLH	194	6-1	Jr.	Fostoria
	Hayden, Leophus	OLH	206	6-2	So.	Dayton
	*Rusnak, Kevin	ORE	180	6-1	Jr.	Garfield
	**Long, William	QB	182	6-1	Sr.	Dayton
	Page, Steven	S	176	5-10	So.	Columbia Station
	Anderson, Tim	DRH	194	6-0	So.	Follansbee, W. Va.
	**Ehrsam, Gerald	S	191	6-0	Sr.	Toledo
	Merryman, Dick	K	175	5-8	Jr.	Hannibal
	Tatum, John	LB	202	6-0	So.	Passaic, N.J.
	*Bartley, Thomas	LB	200	5-11	Sr.	Springfield
	*Huff, Paul	FB	222	6-3	Jr.	Dover
	*Otis, James	FB	208	6-0	Jr.	Celina
	Akers, Carl	K	200	6-2	So.	S.Charleston, W.Va.
	Suber, Vince	LB	186	6-1	So.	Struthers
	Gentile, James	LB	218	6-2	Jr.	Poland
	Brockington, John	ORH	216	6-1	So.	Brooklyn, N.Y.
	Greene, Horatius	OLH	176	5-11	Jr.	Jersey City, N.J.
	King, Gerald	DLE	208	6-3	So.	Columbus
	*Provost, Ted	DLH	182	6-3	Jr.	Navarre
	Coburn, James	FB	190	5-11	So.	Maumee
	Marsh, Jack	DRE	208	6-2	So.	Elyria
	*Smith, Butch	DRT	222	6-2	Jr.	Hamilton
	Hackett, William	MG	202	6-1	Jr.	London
	**Roman, James	C	205	6-0	Sr.	Canton
	**Muhlbach, John	C	192	5-10	Sr.	Massillon
	**Stier, Mark	LB	204	6-1	Sr.	Louisville
	*Radtke, Michael	LB	200	6-1	Jr.	Wayne, N.J.
	**Worden, Dirk	LB	198	6-0	Sr.	Lorain
	*Backhus, Thomas	OLG	207	5-11	Jr.	Cincinnati
	Qualls, Larry	C	190	6-0	So.	Dayton
	Roush, Gary	ORT	195	6-4	Sr.	Springfield
	*Jack, Alan	ORG	215	6-0	Jr.	Wintersville
	Strickland, Phillip	ORG	213	6-1	So.	Cincinnati
	Adams, Douglas	LB	214	6-0	So.	Xenia
	Kurz, Ted	ORG	222	6-2	So.	Struthers
	Hart, Randy	OLT	224	6-2	Jr.	Willoughby
	Donovan, Brian	OLG	202	6-3	So.	Columbus
	Holloway, Ralph	DRT	227	6-1	So.	Oberlin
	Stillwagon, James	MG	216	6-0	So.	Mt. Vernon
	**Stottlemyer, Victor	MG	203	6-0	Sr.	Chillicothe
	**Foley, David	OLT	255	6-5	Sr.	Cincinnati
	Troha, Richard	OLT	232	6-3	So.	Cleveland
	*Hutchison, Charles	ORT	242	6-3	Jr.	Carrollton
	**Mayes, Rufus	ORT	245	6-5	Sr.	Toledo
	*Schmidlin, Paul	DLT	224	6-1	Jr.	Toledo
	Cheney, David	OLG	227	6-3	So.	Lima
	Oppermann, James	OLT	228	6-4	So.	Bluffton
	*Nielsen, Brad	DRT	222	6-3	Jr.	Columbus
	*Urbanik, William	DLT	231	6-3	Jr.	Donora, Pa.
	White, Jan	ORE	216	6-2	So.	Harrisburg, Pa.
	Kuhn, Richard	OLE	205	6-2	So.	Louisville
	Jankowski, Bruce	ORE	192	5-11	So.	Fair Lawn, N.J.
	Debevc, Mark	DRE	206	6-1	So.	Geneva
	Lapuh, Edward	DLE	198	6-1	So.	Cleveland
	Aston, Daniel	DRE	208	6-2	Jr.	Cincinnati
	Smith, Robert	OLE	221	6-4	Sr.	Lakewood
	*Whitfield, David	DLE	185	6-0	Jr.	Massillon
	Ecrement, Thomas	DLE	192	6-0	So.	Canton
	*Sobolewski, John	DRE	195	6-1	Sr.	Steubenville
	Stowe, John	OLE	200	6-2	Sr.	Columbus
	Crapser, Steven	DLT	216	6-1	Jr.	Columbus
	Conroy, James	ORG	208	6-2	So.	Bay Village
	Pollitt, William	LB	212	6-2	Jr.	Dayton
	Waugh, Charles	OLG	180	6-0	So.	Clinton

dicates letters won

1968

Ohio	35	S.M.U.	14
Ohio	21	Oregon	6
Ohio	13	Purdue	0
Ohio	45	Northwestern	21
Ohio	31	Illinois	24
Ohio	25	Mich. State	20
Ohio	43	Wisconsin	8
Ohio	33	Iowa	27
Ohio	50	Michigan	14

Season Summary

Games Won, 9; Lost, 0

DAVID FOLEY
All-American Tackle

RUFUS MAYES
All-American Tackle

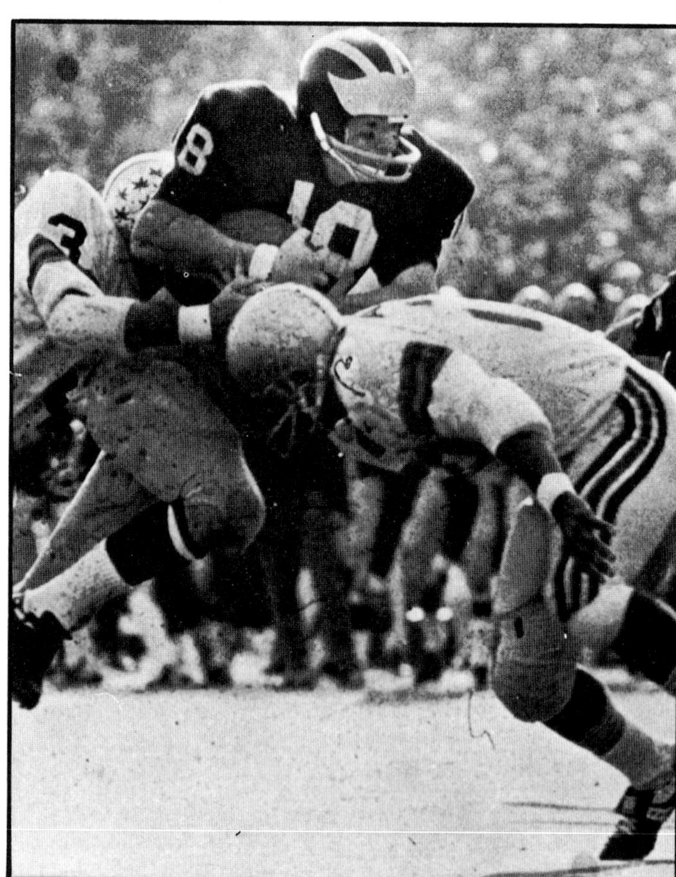

November 22, 1969

Ann Arbor, Michigan

Michigan Demolishes Ohio State, 24 to 12

First Half Provides All Of The Scoring

Bo Schembechler's Wolverines outhustled, outmaneuvered, and outmuscled the nation's topranked team for a 24-12 victory that forever will be etched in the record books as one of the collegiate game's stunning upsets. For Michigan it meant a share of the Big Ten championship with the Buckeyes and a trip to the Rose Bowl. Ohio State, a 17-point favorite, saw a 22-game winning streak go down the drain along with hopes of establishing itself as one of the most outstanding teams of all time.

At the beginning it seemed as if OSU was going to get its customary fast start as Larry Zelina returned a punt 32 yards to the UM 16-yard line and five plays later Otis punched over from the one-yard line. The PAT by Stan White failed.

Quarterback Don Moorhead then went to work for Michigan sending backs Billy Taylor and Garvie Craw through the line, and mixing in a couple of short-range passes. The Wolverines drove 55 yards in 10 plays and Craw went over from the three. Frank Titas kicked the extra point giving Michigan a 7-6 lead.

Early in the second period the Buckeyes steamed 73 yards in 10 plays, three of them pass completions by Kern who hit tight end Jan White for a 22-yard touchdown toss. Stan White's kick was good that time, but when Michigan was offside on the play, Hayes elected to take the penalty and try to run for two points. Kern ate the ball and the score stayed 12-7. That was to be the last score Ohio could muster.

Michigan then assumed control of the contest. Taylor and Moorhead did most of the work on UM's go-ahead touchdown drive of 67 yards. Moorhead connected on short passes to Bill Harris and Jim Mandich along the way and Taylor broke three tackles in a dazzling 27-yard dash to the six-yard line. Craw carried to the one, then into the end zone. A few moments later Barry Pierson, who intercepted three Buckeye passes, got away on a 60-yard punt return to the Ohio State three-yard line. Craw made a yard and Moorhead scored from the two. Titas' kick made it 21-12. The next time Michigan got the ball it moved again only to have a Moorhead to Mandich TD pass called back on a penalty. So Tim Killian trotted onto the field and booted a 25-yard field goal.

There was no further scoring although the Wolverines had chances galore in the second half.

STATISTICS

	UM	OSU
First Downs	21	20
Rushing Yardage	266	222
Passing Yardage	108	155
Return Yardage	143	64
Passes	10-20-1	10-28-6
Punts	3-42	3-27
Fumbles Lost	0	2
Yards Penalized	36	5

1969

1969

Ohio	62	Texas Christian	0
Ohio	41	Washington	14
Ohio	54	Mich. State	21
Ohio	34	Minnesota	7
Ohio	41	Illinois	0
Ohio	35	Northwestern	6
Ohio	62	Wisconsin	7
Ohio	42	Purdue	14
Ohio	12	Michigan	24

Season Summary

Won, 8; Lost, 1

REX KERN
All-American Back

JIM OTIS
All-American Back

OHIO

No.	Name	Pos.	Ht.	Wgt.	Class	Home Town
63	Adams, Douglas	LB	6	214	Jr.	Xenia
26	Anderson, Tim	DB	6	194	Jr.	Follansbee, WV
86	Aston, Daniel	DE	6-2	206	Sr.	Cincinnati
57	Backhus, Thomas	ORG	5-11	212	Sr.	Cincinnati
66	Betz, Steve	OLG	6-2	222	So.	Minerva
42	Brockington, John	FB	6-1	216	Jr.	Brooklyn, NY
21	Burton, Arthur	RB	6-1	194	Sr.	Fostoria
24	Campana, Thomas	OB	5-11	185	So.	Kent
75	Cheney, David	OT	6-3	224	Jr.	Lima
47	Coburn, James	FB	5-11	190	Jr.	Maumee
54	Conroy, James	C	6-2	214	Jr.	Bay Village
94	Crapser, Steven	DT	6-1	216	Sr.	Columbus
83	Debevc, Mark	DG	6-1	214	Jr.	Geneva
52	DeLeone, Thomas	C	6-2	214	So.	Kent
53	Donovan, Brian	C	6-3	202	Jr.	Columbus
70	Gentile, James	LB	6-2	218	Sr.	Poland
11	Gillian, Ray	OHB	5-11	198	Sr.	Uniontown, PA
51	Hackett, William	LB	6-1	202	Sr.	London
85	Harris, Jimmie	OE	5-11	182	So.	Dayton
65	Hart, Randall	OT	6-2	234	Sr.	Willoughby
22	Hayden, Leophus	OB	6-2	206	Jr.	Dayton
67	Holloway, Ralph	DT	6-1	227	Jr.	Oberlin
59	Houser, Thomas	MG	6-2	220	So.	Massillon
28	Howard, Harry	DB	6	190	So.	Cincinnati
78	Huff, Paul	OT	6-3	250	Sr.	Dover
72	Hutchison, Charles	OT	6-3	232	Sr.	Carrollton
61	Jack, Alan	OG	6	218	Sr.	Wintersville
82	Jankowski, Bruce	OE	5-11	192	Jr.	Fair Lawn, NJ
10	Kern, Rex	QB	6	186	Jr.	Lancaster
81	Kuhn, Richard	OE	6-2	211	Jr.	Louisville
64	Kurz, Ted	OG	6-2	222	Sr.	Struthers
19	Lamka, Donald	QB	5-11	190	So.	Cleveland
87	Luttner, Kenneth	DE	6-2	208	So.	Medina
18	Maciejowski, Ronald	QB	6-2	190	Jr.	Bedford
69	Mason, Glen	LB	6-2	205	So.	Colonia, NJ
77	Nielsen, Brad	DT	6-3	217	Sr.	Columbus
76	Oppermann, James	OT	6-4	228	Jr.	Bluffton
35	Otis, James	FB	6	214	Sr.	Celina
15	Polaski, Michael	DB	5-10	168	Sr.	Columbus
97	Pollitt, William	LB	6-2	218	Sr.	Dayton
46	Provost, Ted	DB	6-3	187	Sr.	Navarre
55	Radtke, Michael	LB	6-1	198	Sr.	Wayne, NJ
89	Roman, Nicholas	DE	6-4	226	Sr.	Canton
23	Rusnak, Kevin	OE	6-1	188	Sr.	Garfield, NJ
74	Schmidlin, Paul	DT	6-1	224	Sr.	Toledo
3	Sensibaugh, Michael	S	6	190	Jr.	Cincinnati
20	Sharp, William	S	5-10	170	So.	Lima
73	Simon, Richard	OT	6-2	225	So.	Parma
14	Smith, Bruce	S	5-10	160	Jr.	Gallipolis
50	Smith, Robert	DT	6-2	222	Sr.	Hamilton
68	Stillwagon, James	MG	6	216	Jr.	Mt. Vernon
62	Strickland, Phillip	LB	6-1	210	Jr.	Cincinnati
32	Tatum, Jack	DB	6	204	Jr.	Passaic, NJ
17	Trapuzzano, Robert	DB	6	192	Sr.	McKees Rocks, PA
71	Troha, Richard	OT	6-3	232	Jr.	Cleveland
79	Urbanik, William	DT	6-3	231	Sr.	Donora, PA
60	Vecanski, Milan	MG	6-1	227	So.	Harrisburg, PA
91	Wakefield, Richard	OE	6-4	195	So.	Avon Lake
80	White, Jan	OE	6-2	207	Jr.	Harrisburg, PA
56	White, Stanley	LB	6-1	210	So.	Kent
88	Whitfield, David	DE	6	185	Sr.	Massillon
16	Zelina, Larry	OB	6	196	Jr.	Cleveland

TED PROVOST
All-American Back

JAMES STILLWAGON
All-American Guard

JACK TATUM
All-American Linebacker

MICHIGAN

No.	Name	Pos.	Ht.	Wgt.	Class	Home Town
73	Abrahams, Morris	OT	6-3	230	Sr.	Ann Arbor
54	Alexander, Joe	DB	5-8	200	So.	Detroit
62	Baldwin, Ed	OG	6	207	Jr.	Hamilton, OH
60	**Baumgartner, Bob	OG	6	215	Sr.	Chicago, IL
99	Beckman, Tom	DT	6-7	230	So.	Chesaning
28	Berutti, William	QB	6-2	194	Jr.	Franklin, OH
23	*Betts, Jim	QB	6-3½	185	Jr.	Cleveland, OH
76	Brandstatter, Jim	OT	6-3	235	So.	East Lansing
34	Brown, Richard	MG	6-2	212	Sr.	Bay City
56	Caldarazzo, Dick	OG	5-11	215	Sr.	Melrose Park, IL
94	Carpenter, Al	DE	6-2	210	So.	Flint
36	Coin, Dana	DE	6-2	213	So.	Pontiac
20	Connell, Dennis	QB	6-2	178	So.	Chicago, IL
48	**Craw, Garvie	FB	6-2	218	Sr.	Montclair, NJ
25	**Curtis, Tom	DB	6-1	188	Sr.	Aurora, OH
35	Darden, Tom	DB	6-1½	186	So.	Sandusky, OH
72	*Dierdorf, Dan	OT	6-4	243	Jr.	Canton, OH
22	Doughty, Glenn	TB	6-2	195	So.	Detroit
46	Dutcher, Gerald	DB	6-2	180	Jr.	Carunna
21	Elliott, Bruce	DB	6	172	So.	Indianapolis, IN
37	*Federico, Eric	FB	5-11	200	Sr.	Trenton
31	*Francis, Al	MG	5-10	195	Sr.	Euclid, OH
18	**Gabler, John	WB	6-2	203	Sr.	Royal Oak
92	Grambau, Fred	DT	6-4	227	So.	Ossineke
14	Gusich, Frank	DB	6	187	So.	Garfield Heights, OH
75	*Hall, Werner	OT	6	219	Sr.	Sandusky, OH
81	**Hankwitz, Mike	TE	6-1	203	Sr.	Scottsville
71	*Harpring, Jack	OT	6-4	218	Jr.	Cincinnati, OH
80	*Harris, William	SE	6-1	189	Jr.	Mt. Clemens
17	Harrison, Gregory	FB	5-11	188	Jr.	Jackson
24	**Healy, Brian	DB	6-1	167	Sr.	Sandusky, OH
44	Henry, Preston	TB	6	185	So.	Flint
39	*Hill, Henry	MG	5-11	224	Jr.	Detroit
70	*Huff, Marty	LB	6-2	228	Jr.	Toledo, OH
89	Huiskens, Tom	TE	6-2	200	So.	Bay City
52	Hulke, Scott	C	6-5	207	So.	Elgin, IL
86	*Imsland, Jerry	SE	6-2	203	Sr.	Northville
63	Jones, Joseph	LB	6	191	Sr.	Evanston, IL
90	Keller, Mike	DE	6-3	205	So.	Grand Rapids
57	*Killian, Tim	C	6-4	215	Jr.	Lincoln Park
38	Lindenfeld, Dick	DB	6-1	185	So.	St. Joseph
67	Lukz, Joseph	OG	6-2	202	Sr.	Niles, OH
88	**Mandich, Jim	TE	6-3	217	Sr.	Solon, OH
97	*Moore, Ed	LB	6-1	210	Jr.	Youngstown, OH
27	*Moorhead, Don	QB	6-3	193	Jr.	South Haven
53	Murdock, Guy	C	6-2	210	So.	Barrington, IL
78	*McCoy, Dick	DT	6-4	240	Jr.	Alliance, OH
65	McKenzie, Reggie	OG	6-3	236	So.	Highland Park
82	*Newell, Pete	DT	6-4	226	Jr.	Park Ridge, IL
83	Nieman, Tom	TE	6-1	205	Jr.	Evanston, IL
84	Oldham, Mike	SE	6-3	195	So.	Cincinnati, OH
74	*Parks, Dan	DT	6-5	234	Jr.	Birmingham
29	**Pierson, Barry	DB	6	175	Sr.	St. Ignace
55	*Pryor, Cecil	DE	6-5	240	Sr.	Corpus Christi, TX
69	Ritley, Robert	OT	6	218	Sr.	Garfield Heights, OH
95	Rosema, Bob	DE	6-4	197	So.	Grand Rapids
26	Ross, William	QB	6-3	203	So.	Beaver Falls, PA
59	Sarantos, Pete	C	6	205	Sr.	Elkhart, IN
45	*Scheffler, Lance	TB	6	193	Jr.	Trenton
12	Schmitz, Jim	WB	6	167	So.	Park Ridge, IL
32	Seyferth, John	FB	6-3	198	So.	Darien, CT
35	Seymour, Paul	SE	6-5	235	So.	Berkley
91	**Seymour, Phil	DE	6-4	200	Sr.	Berkley
61	Shaw, Donald	OG	6-1	200	So.	Ithaca
50	Smith, Mike	C	6-4	218	So.	Rockford
30	*Staroba, Paul	WB	6-3	201	Jr.	Flint
43	Takach, Thomas	DE	6-1	215	Sr.	Detroit
42	Taylor, Bill	TB	5-10	195	So.	Barberton, OH
33	Taylor, Mike	LB	6-1½	210	So.	Detroit
64	**Titas, Frank	OG	6-2	215	Sr.	Cleveland, OH
41	Wadhams, Tim	DB	6-1	185	Sr.	Ann Arbor
49	*Werner, Mark	DB	6-2	191	Sr.	Cincinnati, OH
43	White, Robert	DB	6-2	189	Sr.	Middleville
66	Wolff, John	OG	6-1	220	Jr.	Delmont, PA
6	Zuccarelli, David	DB	6	183	So.	Chicago, IL
8	Zuganellis, George	LB	6	200	Sr.	Chicago, IL

Letters won

1969

Michigan	42	Vanderbilt	14
Michigan	45	Washington	7
Michigan	17	Missouri	40
Michigan	31	Purdue	20
Michigan	12	Mich. State	23
Michigan	35	Minnesota	9
Michigan	35	Wisconsin	7
Michigan	57	Illinois	0
Michigan	51	Iowa	6
Michigan	24	Ohio State	12

Season Summary

Games Won, 8; Lost, 2

TOM CURTIS
All-American Halfback

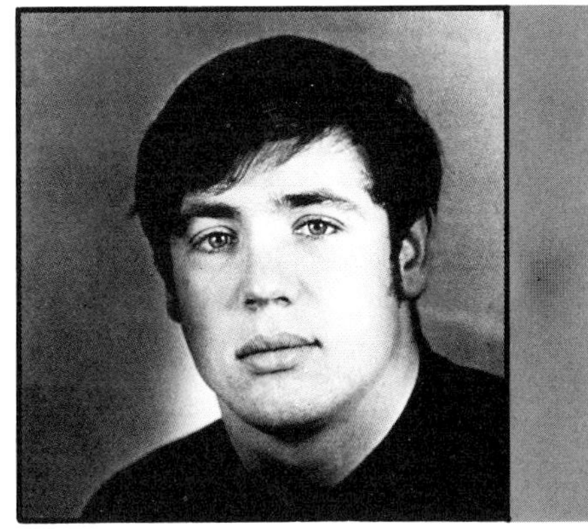

JIM MANDICH
All-American End

November 21, 1970

Columbus, Ohio

Buckeyes Rise To Challenge, Strangle UM, 20-9

Ohio's Defense Stops Michigan's Ground Game

Figures sometimes lie, but one distinct set told the story of Ohio State's revenge. Extremely proud of its rushing game, Michigan was limited to a net of only 37 yards rushing. Never has unbeaten Ohio State's defense been better.

Michigan opened the game with a mistake when Lance Scheffler fumbled the opening kickoff and Harry Howard recovered for Ohio State at the Wolverines' 25-yard line. Schram booted a 28-yard field goal and Ohio State quickly led 3-0. Michigan got that back when safety Jim Betts picked off a Kern pass at the Ohio 44 and returned it 25 yards to the Ohio 18. Coin kicked a 31-yard field goal on the first play of the second quarter to pull Michigan even, 3-3.

Kern made amends by beating a Michigan blitz and hitting split-end Bruce Jankowski on a perfect post pattern for a 26-yard touchdown. After Schram converted the extra point, the Bucks had a 10-3 and that ended the scoring in the first half.

Michigan marched 50 yards in the third quarter with Don Moorhead passing 13 yards to wide receiver Paul Staroba for the touchdown. With Dana Coin poised for the placement kick, it looked like a new game with Michigan owning the momentum, but a West Virginian named Tim Anderson put in a bid for hero honors when he blasted through to block the kick and that was as close as Michigan ever got.

Little Fred Schram kicked a field goal of 27 yards with 10:58 remaining to cap a 63-yard drive and widen Ohio State's lead to 13-9.

At this point OSU linebacker Stan White buried the Wolverines. Two plays following the kickoff, White leaped high to intercept a Moorhead pass and returned it 15 yards to Michigan's 9-yard line. Three plays later tailback Leo Hayden, who gained 117 yards in 28 carries, practically walked the final four yards into the end zone after a perfect option play by Rex Kern. Schram was perfect for the PAT. The final score, Ohio State 20, Michigan 9.

STATISTICS

	OSU	UM
First Downs	18	10
Rushing Yardage	242	37
Passing Yardage	87	118
Return Yardage	54	25
Passes	8-12-1	12-26-1
Punts	6-28	7-41
Fumbles Lost	1	2
Yards Penalized	31	48

MICHIGAN

1970		
Michigan	..20	Arizona 9
Michigan	..17	Washington ... 3
Michigan	..14	Texas A. & M. . 10
Michigan	..29	Purdue 0
Michigan	..34	Mich. State 20
Michigan	..39	Minnesota 13
Michigan	..29	Wisconsin 15
Michigan	..42	Illinois 0
Michigan	..55	Iowa 0
Michigan	.. 9	Ohio State 20

Season Summary
Games Won, 9; Lost, 1; Tied, 0

MARTY HUFF
All-American Linebacker

DAN DIERDORF
All-American Tackle

HENRY HILL
All-American Guard

No.	Name	Pos.	Ht.	Wgt.	Class	Home Town
14	*Gusich, Frank	LB	6-1	187	Jr.	Garfield Hts., OH
15	Rather, Bo	DB	6-1	175	So.	Sandusky, OH
16	Zuccarelli, Dave	DB	5-11	185	Jr.	Chicago, IL
17	Harrison, Greg	DB	5-11	190	Sr.	Jackson
19	Daniels, John	DB	6-4½	192	So.	Newark, OH
21	*Elliott, Bruce	DB	6	170	Jr.	Indianapolis, IN
22	*Doughty, Glenn	TB	6-1	196	Jr.	Detroit
23	**Betts, Jim	S	6-4	194	Sr.	Cleveland, OH
25	McBride, Jack	QB	6-2½	190	So.	Chicago, IL
26	Ross, Bill	QB	6-3	210	Jr.	Beaver Falls, PA
27	**Moorhead, Don	QB	6-3½	199	Sr.	South Haven
28	*Berutti, Bill	WB	6-1	191	Sr.	Franklin, OH
29	Pighee, John	SE	6-1½	190	So.	Cleveland, OH
30	**Staroba, Paul	SE	6-3½	205	Sr.	Flint
32	*Seyferth, Fritz	FB	6-3	211	Jr.	Darien, CT
33	*Taylor, Mike	LB	6-2½	212	Jr.	Detroit
35	*Darden, Tom	DB	6-1	191	Jr.	Sandusky, OH
36	*Coin, Dana	K	6-1½	211	Jr.	Pontiac
37	Kee, Tom	LB	6	204	So.	Wheaton, IL
39	**Hill, Henry	MG	5-11	217	Sr.	Detroit
40	Coakley, Gary	SE	6-2½	201	So.	Detroit
41	Logan, Randy	WB	6-½	200	So.	Detroit
42	*Taylor, Bill	FB	5-11	202	Jr.	Barberton, OH
43	Haslett, Bill	SE	5-10	170	So.	Niles
44	*Henry, Preston	TB	6	185	Jr.	Flint
45	**Scheffler, Lance	TB	5-11	201	Sr.	Trenton
46	Dutcher, Jerry	DB	6-1	177	Sr.	Corunna
50	Smith, Mike	C	6-3	233	Jr.	Rockford
52	Hulke, Scott	C	6-5	215	Jr.	Elgin, IL
53	*Murdock, Guy	C	6-2½	209	Jr.	Barrington, IL
55	Swan, Bob	LB	6-4	218	So.	Detroit
56	Hart, Bill	C	6-4½	215	So.	Rockford
57	**Killian, Tim	OG	6-3	226	Sr.	Lincoln Park
59	Duffy, Mark	C	5-11	211	Sr.	Chicago, IL
60	Coyle, Tom	OG	6-½	223	So.	Chicago, IL
64	Moran, Bill	LB	6-½	193	So.	Chicago, IL
65	*McKenzie, Reggie	OG	6-4	225	Jr.	Highland Park
66	Wolff, John	OG	6-1	209	Sr.	Delmont, PA
68	Ellis, Greg	MG	6-2	212	So.	Connorsville, IN
70	**Huff, Marty	LB	6-3	224	Sr.	Toledo, OH
71	**Harpring, Jack	OT	6-4	217	Sr.	Cincinnati, OH
72	**Dierdorf, Dan	OT	6-3	241	Sr.	Canton, OH
73	Coode, Jim	OT	6-4	221	So.	Mayfield, OH
74	Smith, Tony	DT	6-5	224	So.	Detroit
75	**Hall, Werner	OG	6	207	Sr.	Sandusky, OH
76	*Brandstatter, Jim	OT	6-2	256	Jr.	East Lansing
77	Ferchau, Tom	OT	6-1	220	So.	Bay Village, OH
78	**McCoy, Dick	DT	6-3	229	Sr.	Alliance, OH
79	Poplawski, Tom	OT	6-4	230	So.	Warren
80	**Harris, Bill	SE	6-1½	191	Sr.	Mt. Clemens
81	Schumacher, Jerry	TE	6-½	217	So.	Chicago, IL
82	**Newell, Pete	DT	6-4	227	Sr.	Park Ridge, IL
83	Nieman, Tom	TE	6-1	196	Sr.	Evanston, IL
84	*Oldham, Mike	SE	6-2½	191	Jr.	Cincinnati, OH
85	Seymour, Paul	TE	6-5	239	Jr.	Berkley
86	Eaton, Don	DB	6-5	189	So.	Lancaster, OH
89	Huiskens, Tom	TE	6-2	206	Jr.	Bay City
90	*Keller, Mike	DE	6-3	213	Jr.	Grand Rapids
91	**Seymour, Phil	DE	6-3	210	Sr.	Berkley
92	*Grambau, Fred	DT	6-2	233	Jr.	Ossineke
94	*Carpenter, Al	DE	6-2	211	Jr.	Flint
95	Rosema, Bob	DE	6-3	199	Jr.	Grand Rapids
96	Spearman, Clint	DE	6-3	220	So.	Hamilton, OH
97	**Moore, Ed	LB	6-1	200	Sr.	Youngstown, OH
99	*Beckman, Tom	DT	6-6	238	Jr.	Chesaning

* Denotes letter

OHIO

No.	Name	Pos.	Ht.	Wgt.	Class	Home Town
1	Schram, Fred	PK	5-10	174	Jr.	Massillon
2	Johnston, Paul	PK	5-10	172	Jr.	Cleveland
3	**Sensibaugh, Michael	S	6	182	Sr.	Cincinnati
4	Rice, Elliott	PK	6	164	So.	Jefferson
5	Sivinski, Daniel	S	5-11	178	So.	Columbus
6	Dale, Michael	DCB	5-10	182	Sr.	Erie, PA
7	Zeune, Roger	DRH	5-8	146	So.	Pataskala
8	Cunningham, Dan	DLH	5-7	145	Jr.	Columbus
9	Conroy, Robert	C	5-11	205	So.	Youngstown
10	**Kern, Rex	QB	6	184	Sr.	Lancaster
11	Cowman, Randall	DCB	6	188	So.	Dayton
12	Moore, Ross	QB	5-11	190	So.	Allentown, PA
14	Smith, Bruce	S	5-10	154	Sr.	Gallipolis
15	Zetts, Gary	QB	6-3	194	So.	Struthers
16	**Zelina, Larry	ORH	6	193	Sr.	Cleveland
17	Lucki, Martin	DLH	6-2	173	So.	Bridgeport
18	**Maciejowski, Ronald	QB	6-2	197	Sr.	Bedford
19	*Lamka, Donald	DCB	5-11	196	Jr.	Cleveland
20	Kinsey, Marvin	DRH	6-2	188	So.	East Liverpool
22	**Hayden, Leophus	OLH	6-2	214	Sr.	Dayton
23	Battista, Thomas	DRH	6-3	182	So.	Weirton, WV
24	*Campana, Thomas	ORH	5-11	188	Jr.	Kent
25	Sloan, Gary	ORH	6-1	192	So.	Napoleon
26	**Anderson, Tim	DRH	6	200	Sr.	Colliers, WV
27	Wright, David	OLH	6	198	Sr.	Chagrin Falls
28	*Howard, Harry	DLH	6-1	192	Jr.	Cincinnati
30	Beecroft, Charles	DLT	6-3	221	So.	Dayton
32	**Tatum, Jack	DCB	6	204	Sr.	Passaic, NJ
33	Galbos, Richard	OLH	6	200	So.	Mentor
34	Bledsoe, John	FB	6-1	210	So.	Westlake
35	Scannell, Michael	LB	6-2	208	So.	Sylvania
39	Ferko, Richard	LB	5-11	200	So.	Pittsburgh, PA
41	Seifert, Richard	S	6-1	188	So.	Cuyahoga Falls
42	**Brockington, John	FB	6-1	222	Sr.	Brooklyn, NY
44	Hughes, John	DLH	6-1	196	So.	Duquesne, PA
45	King, Jerry	DLE	6-3	213	Sr.	Columbus
46	Breuleux, Jon	ORT	6-5	248	So.	Alexandria, VA
47	Coburn, James	FB	5-11	203	Sr.	Maumee
50	Pitstick, Anthony	OLG	6-3	215	So.	Xenia
51	Dixon, Kenneth	LB	6-3	205	So.	Wintersville
52	*DeLeone, Thomas	C	6-2	221	Jr.	Kent
53	**Donovan, Brian	OLG	6-3	206	Sr.	Columbus
54	*Conroy, James	C	6-2	217	Sr.	Bay Village
55	Fletcher, Kevin	MG	6-1	221	So.	East Orange, NJ
56	Nixon, Thomas	C	6-2	214	So.	Mansfield
57	**Kuhn, Richard	OLG	6-2	221	Sr.	Louisville
58	Bonica, Charles	ORT	6-3	242	So.	Waltham, MA
59	Pisanelli, Fred	LB	6-2	212	So.	Warren
60	Vecanski, Milan	ORG	6-1	224	Jr.	Harrisburg, PA
61	**Gentile, James	ORG	6-2	222	Sr.	Poland
62	**Strickland, Phillip	LB	6-1	225	Sr.	Cincinnati
63	**Adams, Douglas	LB	6	220	Sr.	Xenia
64	Waugh, Charles	ORG	6	184	Sr.	Clinton
65	Hicks, John	ORT	6-3	247	So.	Cleveland
66	Lago, Gary	ORG	6-2	224	So.	Ashtabula
67	**Holloway, Ralph	DRT	6-1	230	Sr.	Oberlin
68	**Stillwagon, James	MG	6	225	Sr.	Mt. Vernon
69	Mason, Glen	MG	6-2	216	Jr.	Colonia, NJ
70	Hasenohrl, George	DLT	6-1	245	So.	Garfield Heights
71	Belgrave, Earl	DRT	6-5	244	So.	Brooklyn, NY
72	Conley, William	OLG	5-10	202	Jr.	Columbus
73	*Simon, Richard	ORT	6-2	228	Jr.	Parma
74	Long, David	OLT	6-1	223	Jr.	Delphos
75	**Cheney, David	OLT	6-3	227	Sr.	Lima
76	Oppermann, James	DLT	6-4	236	Sr.	Bluffton
77	Stoudenmire, Malory	DLT	6-3	225	So.	Cleveland
78	Wersel, Timothy	ORG	6-2	219	So.	Cincinnati
79	Williams, Shad	DRT	6-3	229	So.	Portsmouth
80	**White, Jan	OLE	6-2	209	Sr.	Harrisburg, PA
82	**Jankowski, Bruce	ORE	5-11	188	Sr.	Fair Lawn, NJ
83	**Debevc, Mark	DLE	6-1	220	Sr.	Geneva
84	Marsh, Jack	DRE	6-2	210	Sr.	Elyria
85	*Harris, Jimmie	ORE	5-11	176	Jr.	Dayton
86	*Cappell, Richard	DRE	6	198	Jr.	Dover
87	*Luttner, Kenneth	DRE	6-2	209	Jr.	Medina
88	*White, Stanley	LB	6-1	222	Jr.	Kent
89	Mountz, Gregory	OLE	6-3	208	Jr.	Hummelstown, PA
90	Teague, Mervin	DLE	6-5	210	So.	Youngstown
91	*Wakefield, Richard	OLE	6-4	201	Jr.	Avon Lake
92	Burrows, Roger	OLE	6-2	207	Sr.	Brunswick
94	Strong, Terry	DLE	6-3	188	So.	Weirton, WV

1970

Ohio	56	Texas A. & M.	13
Ohio	34	Duke	10
Ohio	29	Mich. State	0
Ohio	28	Minnesota	8
Ohio	48	Illinois	29
Ohio	24	Northwestern	10
Ohio	24	Wisconsin	7
Ohio	10	Purdue	7
Ohio	20	Michigan	9

Season Summary

Won, 9; Lost, 0

TIM ANDERSON
All-American Back

MIKE SENSIBAUGH
All-American Back

JAN WHITE
All-American End

JACK TATUM
All-American Linebacker

JAMES STILLWAGON
All-American Guard

JOHN BROCKINGTON
All-American Back

The Winning Touchdown

A Taylor Dance Step

A Darden Interception

November 20, 1971

Ann Arbor, Michigan

Michigan Stops Buckeyes On Late Touchdown, 10-7

Ohio State Coach Woody Hayes Visibly Upset With Officials

Coach Bo Schembechler's undefeated, untied Michigan conservatives stuck largely with their old grind-it-out attack and made it pay off with a 10-7 come-from-behind victory over Ohio State before a record crowd in Michigan Stadium of 104,016.

After Michigan's touchdown which made the score 10-7, the limelight belonged to Woody Hayes who raced on the field complaining that pass interference should have been called on an interception by Michigan's Tom Darden. Hayes' players finally restrained him and escorted him back toward the bench, but a few moments later after a penalty against OSU, he pulled two yard-marker sticks from the hands of officials and threw them on the field. This act typified the frustration of all Ohio State adherents who saw their underdog heroes' tremendously gutsy performance go down the drain.

In the first half the only scoring came in the second quarter on a 32-yard field goal by Michigan's Dana Coin. The Bucks came back in the third period thanks to a blazing 85-yard TD punt return by Tom Campana. Schram added the PAT conversion to give the Buckeyes a 7-3 lead and it looked for a while like that might be enough to win the game.

Michigan got the football with 7:08 to play on its own 29-yard line. Billy Taylor, who gained 118 yards during the rainy, cold afternoon, started moving it. While moving the ball downfield, junior quarterback Larry Cipa hit split-end Bo Rather for 28 yards on a pass play. Cipa, replacing starter Tom Slade who suffered a hip injury in the first quarter, went back to the ground game. Fullback Fritz Seyferth, playing because Ed Shuttlesworth had suffered a knee injury, made a first down for the Wolverines on the Ohio 21. Then Cipa went down the line on the option, drew two defenders toward him, and deftly pitched out to Taylor going around right end. Rather made a good crackback block on a linebacker and Seyferth, leading the play, completely wiped out defensive back Campana with a crashing block. Taylor went all the way untouched for the TD. Coin added the PAT. That ended the scoring as Michigan won, 10-7.

STATISTICS

	UM	OSU
First Downs	20	7
Russes-Yards	71-289	41-78
Passing Yardage	46	60
Return Yardage	25	166
Passes	2-10-0	5-10-2
Punts	8-44	8-35
Fumbles Lost	2	1
Yards Penalized	49	64

1971			
Ohio	52	Iowa	21
Ohio	14	Colorado	20
Ohio	35	California	3
Ohio	24	Illinois	10
Ohio	27	Indiana	7
Ohio	31	Wisconsin	6
Ohio	14	Minnesota	12
Ohio	10	Michigan State	17
Ohio	10	Northwestern	14
Ohio	7	Michigan	10

Season Summary

Games won, 6; Lost, 4

TOM DeLEONE
All-American Center

1971			
Michigan	21	Northwestern	6
Michigan	56	Virginia	0
Michigan	38	UCLA	0
Michigan	46	Navy	0
Michigan	24	Michigan State	13
Michigan	35	Illinois	6
Michigan	35	Minnesota	7
Michigan	61	Indiana	7
Michigan	63	Iowa	7
Michigan	20	Purdue	17
Michigan	10	Ohio State	7

Season Summary

Games won, 11; Lost, 0; Tied 0.

OHIO

No.	Name	Pos.	Wt.	Hgt.	Class	Home Town
23	Battista, Tom	OE	182	6-3	Jr.	Weirton, W.Va.
99	Baxa, Tom	DT	238	6-5	Jr.	St. Clairsville
78	Beecroft, Charles	OT	221	6-3	Jr.	Dayton
77	Belgrave, Earl	OT	244	6-5	Jr.	Brooklyn, N.Y.
58	*Bonica, Charles	OG	248	6-3	Jr.	Waltham, Mass.
15	Boyle, Bill	QB	178	6-0	So.	Columbus
25	Bradshaw, Morris	HB	194	6-2	So.	Edwardsville, Ill.
93	Brown, Jeff	DE	198	6-4	Jr.	Chambersburg, Pa.
24	**Campana, Tom	HB	190	5-11	Sr.	Kent
86	**Cappell, Rich	DE	204	6-0	Sr.	Dover
64	*Conley, Bill	OG	204	5-10	Sr.	Columbus
11	Cowman, Randy	DHB	194	6-0	Jr.	Dayton
45	Cummings, John	OT	260	6-2	Jr.	Cincinnati
8	Cunningham, Dan	DHB	154	5-7	Sr.	Columbus
67	Cutillo, Dan	DT	230	6-1	So.	Amityville, N.Y.
16	Davis, Jeff	DHB	182	5-10	So.	Erie, Pa.
52	**DeLeone, Tom	C	227	6-2	Sr.	Kent
51	*Dixon, Ken	LB	206	6-3	Jr.	Wintersville
37	Eggers, Pat	FB	215	6-3	So.	Toledo
39	*Ferko, Rick	LB	198	5-11	Jr.	Pittsburgh, Pa.
46	Gaffney, Mike	HB	203	6-2	So.	Euclid
33	*Galbos, Rick	HB	200	6-0	Jr.	Mentor
22	Gales, Rick	HB	176	5-9	So.	Niles
53	Gradishar, Randy	LB	218	6-3	So.	Warren
18	Hare, Greg	QB	198	6-3	So.	Cumberland, Md.
85	**Harris, Jimmie	OE	176	5-11	Sr.	Dayton
70	*Hasenohrl, George	DT	244	6-1	Jr.	Garfield Heights
28	**Howard, Harry	DHB	192	6-1	Sr.	Cincinnati
2	Johnston, Paul	PK	176	5-10	Sr.	Cleveland
84	Jones, Scott	OE	206	6-3	So.	Parma
38	Keith, Randy	FB	212	5-11	So.	Cincinnati
14	Kelly, Bob	DBH	194	6-1	So.	Butler, Pa.
62	Koegel, Vic	LB	200	6-1	So.	Cincinnati
63	Kregel, Jim	OG	227	6-2	So.	Toledo
92	*Lago, Gary	P	222	6-2	Jr.	Ashtabula
19	**Lamka, Don	QB	191	5-11	Sr.	Cleveland
47	Lippert, Elmer	HB	177	5-7	So.	Sandusky
87	**Luttner, Ken	DE	206	6-2	Sr.	Medina
81	Marendt, Tom	DE	206	6-1	So.	Indianapolis, Ind.
30	Mathis, Lou	DHB	206	6-0	So.	Patterson, N.J.
32	Middleton, Rick	MG	211	6-3	So.	Delaware
12	Moore, Ross	QB	188	5-11	Jr.	Allentown, Pa.
56	*Nixon, Tom	C	220	6-2	Jr.	Mansfield
80	Pagac, Fred	OE	205	6-1	So.	Richeyville, Pa.
59	Pisanelli, Fred	LB	200	6-2	Jr.	Warren
50	Pitstick, Anthony	OG	212	6-3	Jr.	Xenia
35	Rich, Rocco	MG	218	5-11	So.	Canton
83	Scannell, Mike	DE	204	6-2	Jr.	Sylvania
1	*Schram, Fred	PK	185	5-10	Sr.	Massillon
76	Scott, Dan	OT	250	6-3	So.	Amityville, N.Y.
41	*Seifert, Rick	S	188	6-1	Jr.	Cuyahoga Falls
73	**Simon, Rick	OT	228	6-2	Sr.	Parma
96	Smurda, John	OE	194	6-1	So.	Allentown, Pa.
94	*Strong, Terry	DE	198	6-3	Jr.	Weirton, W.Va.
36	Szabo, Tom	DT	227	6-1	So.	Elyria
60	*Vecanski, Milan	OG	222	6-1	Sr.	Harrisburg, Pa.
91	**Wakefield, Dick	OE	202	6-4	Sr.	Avon Lake
88	**White, Stan	LB	224	6-1	Sr.	Kent

* indicates letters won

MICHIGAN

No.	Name	Pos.	Wt.	Hgt.	Class	Home Town
20	Banks, Harry	TB	177	5-10	So.	Cleveland
99	**Beckman, Thomas C.	DT	246	6-5	Sr.	Chesaning
24	Brandon, David A.	Wolf	202	6-3	So.	Plymouth
76	**Brandstatter, James P.	OT	245	6-4	Sr.	East Lansing
80	Calin, Peter J.	SE	177	6-3	So.	Willingboro, NJ
94	**Carpenter, A. J. (Butch)	DE	215	6-2	Sr.	Flint
12	Casey, Kevin	QB	175	6-2	So.	Grand Rapids
19	Cederberg, Jon C.	TB	177	5-10	So.	Plymouth
70	Cherry, John A.	OT	230	6-5	So.	Willard, OH
13	Cipa, Lawrence A.	QB	203	6-3	Jr.	Cincinnati, OH
40	Coakley, Gary R.	SE	197	6-2	Jr.	Detroit
36	**Coin, Dana S.	K-LB	229	6-1	Sr.	Pontiac
39	Coleman, Don	FB	210	6-2	So.	Toledo, OH
73	Coode, James E.	OT	235	6-3½	Jr.	Mayfield, OH
60	*Coyle, Thomas J.	OG	233	6-0	Jr.	Chicago, IL
35	**Darden, Thomas W.	DB	195	6-2	Sr.	Sandusky, OH
57	Day, Michael J.	LB	201	6-1	So.	Livonia
25	Dotzauer, Barry S.	DB	162	6-1	So.	Cincinnati, OH
22	**Doughty, Glenn M.	WB	204	6-2	Sr.	Detroit
28	Drake, Thomas E.	DB	175	5-11	So.	Midland
59	Duffy, Mark F.	C	224	5-11	Sr.	Chicago, IL
86	*Eaton, Donald R.	DE	194	6-4	Jr.	Lancaster, OH
21	**Elliott, Bruce N.	DB	175	6-0	Sr.	Indianapolis
45	Elliott, David L.	DB	170	6-2	So.	Indianapolis
68	*Ellis, Gregory A.	MG	223	6-2	Jr.	Cornersville, IN
89	Fediuk, Arthur W.	TE	212	6-2	So.	Livonia
71	Gallagher, David D.	DT	225	6-4	So.	Piqua, OH
92	*Grambau, Fredrick E.	DT	234	6-2½	Jr.	Ossineke
14	**Gusich, Frank J.	Wolf	188	6-0	Sr.	Garfield Hts., OH
48	Gustafson, Lawrence J.	WB	176	5-11	So.	Mays Landing, NJ
69	Hainrihar, Gary	OG	220	6-2	So.	Cicero, IL
56	*Hart, William J.	C	227	6-4	Jr.	Rockford
43	Haslerig, Clinton E.	WB	182	6-1	So.	Cincinnati, OH
61	Hoban, Michael A.	OG	232	6-2	So.	Chicago, IL
52	Hulke, Scott E.	OT	224	6-5	Sr.	Elgin, IL
82	Johnson, Larry L.	DE	203	6-1	So.	Munster, IN
27	Johnston, James D.	Wolf	175	5-11	So.	Dallas, TX
37	*Kee, Thomas G.	LB	210	5-11	Jr.	Wheaton, IL
90	**Keller, Michael F.	DE	215	6-3	Sr.	Grand Rapids
10	Koss, Gregory	QB	180	6-5	So.	Cuyahoga Falls, OH
41	Logan, Randolph	DB	192	6-2	Jr.	Detroit
72	Lyall, James M.	DT	224	6-5	So.	N. Olmstead, OH
18	*McBride, John R.	QB	191	6-2½	Jr.	Chicago, IL
65	**McKenzie, Reginald	OG	232	6-4	Sr.	Highland Park
62	Masterson, Kevin J.	OG	227	6-0	So.	Cleveland, OH
93	Middlebrook, John P.	LB	210	6-0	Sr.	Jackson
53	**Murdock, Guy B.	C	210	6-2	Sr.	Barrington, IL
34	Mutch, Craig A.	LB	203	6-1	So.	Detroit
84	**Oldham, Michael	SE	198	6-3	Sr.	Cincinnati, OH
79	Poplawski, Thomas	OT	225	6-4	Jr.	Warren
15	*Rather, David E. (Bo)	SE	180	6-1	Jr.	Sandusky, OH
95	Rosema, Robert J.	DE	193	6-3	Sr.	Grand Rapids
63	*Schumacher, Gerald F.	OG	224	6-2	Jr.	Chicago, IL
83	Seal, Paul N.	TE	213	6-6	So.	Detroit
55	Sexton, Walter E.	MG	200	5-11	So.	Massapequa, NY
32	**Seyferth, John F. (Fritz)	FB	218	6-3	Sr.	Darien, CT
85	*Seymour, Paul C.	TE	231	6-5	Jr.	Royal Oak
31	Shuttlesworth, E. Ed.	FB	235	6-2	So.	Cincinnati, OH
17	Slade, Thomas A.	QB	198	6-1	So.	Saginaw
74	*Smith, Tony L.	DT	230	6-5	Jr.	Detroit
96	*Spearman, Clinton	DE	223	6-3	Jr.	Hamilton, OH
64	Staveren, Howard M.	DT	278	6-7	So.	Los Angeles, CA
38	Steger, Geoffrey C.	Wolf	188	6-0	So.	Winnetka, IL
23	Szydlowski, Ron E.	WB	160	5-9	So.	Wyandotte
44	Taylor, Lonnie	DB	180	5-10	So.	Ypsilanti
33	**Taylor, Michael	LB	224	6-1½	Sr.	Detroit
42	**Taylor, William L.	TB	195	5-11	Sr.	Barberton, OH
66	Thomas, John E.	C	215	6-3	So.	Detroit
30	Thornbladh, Robt.	FB	224	6-2	So.	Plymouth
75	Troszak, Douglas	DT	241	6-3	So.	Warren
78	Tucker, Curtis J.	OT	243	6-1	So.	Cleveland, OH
46	Vercel, Jovan	MG	214	6-0	So.	Highland, IN
49	Walker, Alan (Cowboy)	TB	202	6-1½	Jr.	Cincinnati, OH
54	Warner, Donald R.	MG	197	5-11	So.	Dearborn
67	West, Alfred L.	DT	223	6-3	Jr.	Baton Rouge, LA
91	Williamson, Walter L.	DE	224	6-4	So.	Detroit
16	Zuccarelli, David C.	WB	196	6-0	Jr.	Chicago, IL

* indicates letters won

TOM DARDEN
All-American Halfback

REGGIE McKENZIE
All-American Guard

BILLY TAYLOR
All-American Halfback

MIKE TAYLOR
All-American Linebacker

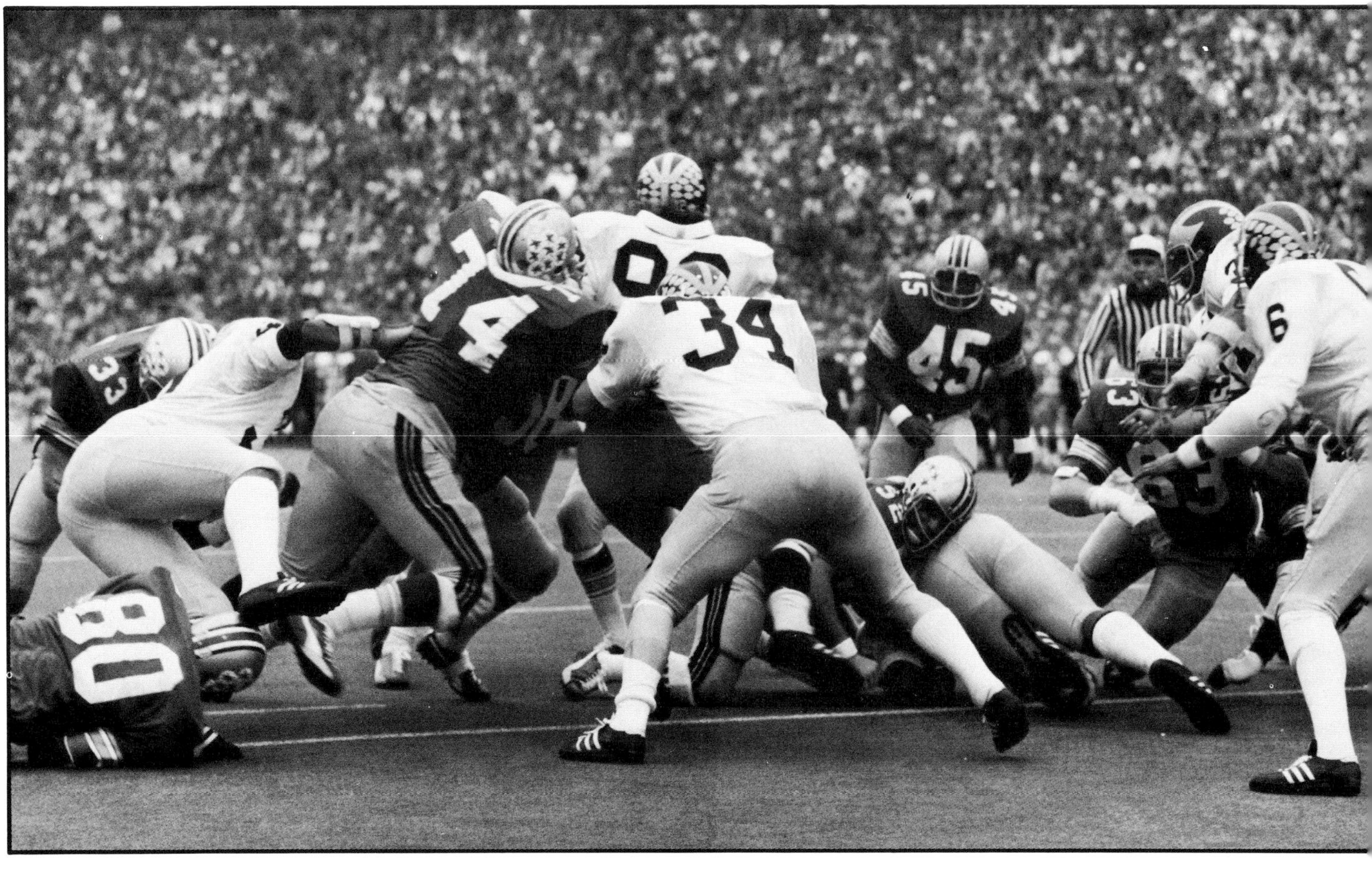

November 25, 1972

Columbus, Ohio

Goal-Line Stands Carry Bucks Over Wolverines, 14-11

Buckeye Defense Stymies Powerful Michigan Offense

Thanks to two magnificent goal-line stands by Ohio State's defensive unit, the Buckeyes upset Michigan, 14-11, before 87,040 in Ohio Stadium. With one of the powerful running games in collegiate football, Michigan twice failed to get into the end zone from inside the 1-yard line. A field goal on either occasion would have made Michigan undisputed Big Ten champion, but after defeat, they shared it with Ohio State.

Michigan took a 3-0 lead early in the second quarter when Mike Lantry kicked a 35-yard field goal. Ohio State came right back driving 46 yards in seven plays as fullback Harold (Champ) Henson scored his 20th touchdown of the season on a 1-foot lunge for a 7-3 lead when Conway converted the PAT.

Ohio State put Michigan in deep trouble with a perfectly executed 78-yard touchdown drive following the second-half kickoff. Archie Griffin capped the five-play drive by breaking up the middle for 30 yards and the touchdown that put the Buckeyes ahead 14-3. Once again Conway converted the point after touchdown.

Chuck Heater from Tiffin, Ohio, put Michigan right back in the game when he returned the kickoff 40 yards to the Michigan 42. The Wolverines promptly marched 58 yards in 13 plays. Shuttlesworth stormed over right tackle from the 1-yard line on fourth down, and Franklin converted for a 2-point PAT on a pass to Haslerig making the score 14-11 with 4:48 remaining in the third quarter. The Ohio State defense made those three points stand up.

STATISTICS

	OSU	UM
First Downs	10	21
Rushes-Yards	41-175	60-184
Passing Yards	17	160
Return Yards	8	12
Passes	1-3-1	13-23-0
Punts	5-38	2-37
Fumbles-Lost	0-0	1-0
Penalties-Yards	3-35	6-40

Ohio State	0	7	7	0	14
Michigan	0	3	8	0	11

1972			
Michigan	7	Northwestern	0
Michigan	26	UCLA	9
Michigan	41	Tulane	7
Michigan	35	Navy	7
Michigan	10	Michigan State	0
Michigan	31	Illinois	7
Michigan	42	Minnesota	0
Michigan	21	Indiana	7
Michigan	31	Iowa	0
Michigan	9	Purdue	6
Michigan	11	Ohio State	14

Season Summary

Games won, 10; Lost, 1

RANDY LOGAN
All-American Halfback

PAUL SEYMOUR
All-American Tackle

MICHIGAN

No.	Name	Pos.	Wt.	Hgt.	Class	Home Town
58	Armour, Jim	OG	220	6-4	Jr.	Detroit
20	*Banks, Harry	TB	177	5-10	Jr.	Cleveland
32	Banks, Larry	MG	210	6-2	Jr.	Cleveland
85	Brandon, Dave	DE	202	6-3	Jr.	Plymouth
6	Brown, Dave	S	185	6-1	So.	Akron, OH
8	Burks, Roy	DB	185	6-2	So.	Midland
46	Carpenter, John	TB	175	5-11	So.	Detroit
12	*Casey, Kevin	QB	175	6-2	Jr.	Grand Rapids
19	*Cederberg, Jon	TB	177	5-10	Jr,	Plymouth
24	Chapman, Gil	WB	185	5-9	So.	Elizabeth, NJ
70	Cherry, John	OT	230	6-5	Jr.	Willard, OH
13	*Cipa, Larry	QB	203	6-3	Jr.	Cincinnati, OH
40	*Coakley, Gary	SE	197	6-2	Sr.	Detroit
39	Coleman, Don	DE	210	6-2	Jr.	Toledo, OH
73	Coode, Jim	OT	235	6-4	Jr.	Mayfield, OH
60	*Coyle, Tom	OG	233	6-0	Sr.	Chicago, IL
80	*Daniels, John	SE	199	6-4	Sr.	Newark, OH
57	Day, Mike	LB	201	6-1	Jr.	Livonia
84	DenBoer, Greg	TE	233	6-6	So.	Kentwood
25	*Dotzauer, Barry	DB	162	6-1	Jr.	Cincinnati, OH
28	*Drake, Tom	DB	175	6-1	Jr.	Midland
86	**Eaton, Don	DE	194	6-4	Sr.	Lancaster, OH
45	*Elliott, Dave	DB	170	6-2	Jr.	Coral Gables, FL
68	**Ellis, Greg	MG	223	6-2	Sr.	Connersville, IN
89	Fediuk, Art	TE	212	6-2	Jr.	Livonia
9	Franklin, Dennis	QB	185	6-1	So.	Massillon, OH
42	Franklin, Glenn	WB	185	5-10	So.	Warren, OH
50	Franks, Dennis	C	218	6-1	So.	Bethel Park, PA
71	*Gallagher, Dave	DT	225	6-4	Jr.	Piqua, OH
92	**Grambau, Fred	DT	234	6-2	Sr.	Ossineke
48	*Gustafson, Larry	WB	176	5-11	Jr.	Mays Landing, NJ
69	Hainrihar, Gary	C	220	6-2	Jr.	Cicero, IL
22	Harden, Linwood	DB	185	6-1	So.	Detroit
56	**Hart, Bill	C	227	6-4	Sr.	Rockford
43	*Haslerig, Clint	WB	182	6-1	Jr.	Cincinnati, OH
44	Heater, Chuck	TB	205	6-0	So.	Tiffin, OH
61	*Hoban, Mike	OG	232	6-2	Jr.	Chicago, IL
93	Hoban, Bill	DE	210	6-3	So.	Chicago, IL
7	Jacoby, Mark	DE	190	6-1	So.	Toledo, OH
35	Jekel, Rich	FB	195	5-9	So.	Clio
82	Johnson, Larry	DE	203	6-1	Jr.	Munster, IN
27	Johnston, Jim	Wolf	175	5-11	Jr.	Dallas, TX
21	Kampe, Kurt	DB	165	5-10	So.	Defiance, OH
37	**Kee, Tom	LB	210	5-11	Sr.	Wheaton, IL
67	King, Steve	OT	225	6-5	So.	Tiffin, OH
10	Koss, Greg	5	180	6-5	Jr.	Cuyahoga Falls, OH
88	Kupec, C. J.	TE	235	6-8	So.	Oak Lawn, IL
36	Lantry, Mike	PK	220	6-2	So.	Oxford
41	*Logan, Randy	Wolf	192	6-2	Sr.	Detroit
95	Long, Norm	MG	230	6-3	So.	Trenton
72	Lyall, Jim	DT	224	6-5	Jr.	N. Olmstead, OH
26	MacKenzie, Doug	S	175	6-3	So.	Warren
76	McClain, Mark	OT	225	6-3	So.	Thornridge, IL
62	Masterson, Kevin	MG	227	6-0	Jr.	Cleveland, OH
65	Metz, Dave	OG	225	6-2	So.	Harrison, OH
34	Mutch, Craig	LB	203	6-1	Jr.	Detroit
97	Perlinger, Jeff	DT	225	6-3	So.	Crystal, MN
29	Pighee, John	S	194	6-3	Sr.	Cleveland, OH
90	Pollister, Ed	DE	195	6-3	So.	Elk Rapids
79	*Poplawski, Tom	OT	225	6-4	Jr.	Warren
15	**Rather, Bo	SE	180	6-1	Sr.	Sandusky, OH
33	Russ, Carl	LB	215	6-2	So.	Muskegon Heights
63	**Schumacher, Jerry	OG	224	6-2	Sr.	Chicago, IL
83	*Seal, Paul	TE	213	6-6	Jr.	Detroit
55	*Sexton, Walt	MG	200	5-11	Jr.	Massapequa, NY
77	**Seymour, Paul	OT	250	6-5	Sr.	Berkley
31	*Shuttlesworth, Ed	FB	227	6-2	Jr.	Cincinnati, OH
17	*Slade, Tom	QB	198	6-1	Jr.	Saginaw
74	**Smith, Tony	DT	230	6-5	Sr.	Detroit
14	Spahn, Jeff	QB	170	5-11	So.	Steubenville, OH
96	**Spearman, Clint	DE	223	6-3	Sr.	Hamilton, OH
59	Strinko, Steve	LB	235	6-3	So.	Middletown, OH
23	Szydlowski, Ron	WB	160	5-9	Jr.	Wyandotte
66	Thomas, John	C	215	6-3	Jr.	Detroit
30	*Thornbladh, Bob	FB	224	6-2	Jr.	Plymouth
75	*Troszak, Doug	DT	241	6-3	Jr.	Warren
78	*Tucker, Curtis	OG	239	6-1	Jr.	Cleveland, OH
64	Tumpane, Pat	OT	240	6-4	So.	Midlothian, IL
94	VanTongeren, Rick	DE	196	6-1	So.	Holland
52	Vercel, Jovan	LB	214	6-0	Jr.	Highland, IN
54	Warner, Don	MG	197	5-11	Jr.	Dearborn
91	Williamson, Walt	DE	224	6-4	Jr.	Detroit
53	Wojtys, Ed	LB	210	5-2	So.	Detroit
16	*Zuccarelli, Dave	Wolf	196	6-0	Sr.	Chicago, IL

* indicates letters won

OHIO

Name	Pos.	Wt.	Hgt.	Class	Home Town
Wilkins, Dwight	LB	228	5-10	So.	Cincinnati
Conway, Blair	PK	155	5-7	Jr.	Middleburg Hts.
Keith, Randall	FB	210	5-11	Jr.	Cincinnati
McBrayer, Tom	PK	185	6-0	So.	Hilliard
Thompson, Monty	CB	185	6-1	Jr.	Portsmouth
Ezzo, Billy	SE	146	5-8	So.	Conastota, NY
Murphy, Robert	SE	197	6-2	Sr.	Seattle, WA
Cowman, Randall	CB	191	6-0	Sr.	Dayton
Boyle, William	QB	180	6-0	Jr.	Columbus
Davis, Jeff	DLH	185	5-10	Jr.	Erie, PA
Morrison, Steve	QB	204	6-3	So.	Huntington, WV
Hare, Gregory	QB	198	6-3	Jr.	Cumberland, MD
Purdy, David	QB	188	6-3	So.	Swanton
Colzie, Cornelius	DHL	194	6-0	So.	Coral Gables, FL
Kern, Carl	DRH	190	6-0	Jr.	Dallas, PA
Battista, Thomas	ORE	183	6-3	Sr.	Weirton, WV
Parsons, Richard	S	184	5-11	So.	Cuyahoga Falls
Bradshaw, Morris	ORH	200	6-2	Jr.	Edwardsville, IL
DeFillippo, Joe	OLH	198	6-3	So.	Lancaster
Holycross, Timothy	OLH	188	5-11	So.	Bedford Heights
Plank, Douglas	DRH	185	5-11	So.	North Irwin, PA
Mathis, Lou	CB	207	6-0	Jr.	Paterson, NJ
Middleton, Rick	LB	214	6-3	Jr.	Delaware
Galbos, Richard	ORH	211	6-0	Sr.	Mentor
Bledsoe, John	FB	212	6-1	Sr.	Westlake
Rich, Rocco	LB	222	5-11	Jr.	Canton
Bowers, Brian	LB	219	6-0	So.	Uniontown
Henson, Harold	FB	225	6-4	So.	Ashville
Ferko, Richard	LB	204	5-11	Sr.	Pittsburgh, PA
Seifert, Richard	S	186	6-1	Sr.	Cuyahoga Falls
Jones, Arnold	LB	222	5-11	So.	Dayton
Hughes, John	CB	194	6-1	Jr.	Duquesne, PA
Geffney, Mike	ORH	203	6-2	Jr.	South Euclid
Lippert, Elmer	ORH	183	5-7	Jr.	Sandusky
Pitstick, Anthony	ORG	223	6-3	Sr.	Xenia
Myers, Steven	C	234	6-2	So.	Kent
Gradishar, Randy	LB	238	6-3	Jr.	Champion
Fletcher, Kevin	LB	221	6-1	Sr.	East Orange, NJ
Nixon, Thomas	C	221	6-1	Sr.	Mansfield
Luke, Steven	C	195	6-2	So.	Massillon
Bonica, Charles	OG	256	6-3	Sr.	Waltham, MA
Belgrave, Earl	ORT	257	6-5	Sr.	Brooklyn, NY
Trepanier, Edwin	DT	250	6-4	Jr.	Rocky River
Husband, John	ORG	212	6-2	Jr.	Elyria
Koegel, Victor	LB	216	6-1	Jr.	Cincinnati
Kregel, James	ORG	234	6-2	Jr.	Toledo
Wiggins, Lawrence	OLG	229	6-0	So.	Columbus
Wersel, Timothy	OLG	215	6-2	Sr.	Cincinnati
Cutillo, Daniel	DRT	231	6-1	Jr.	Amityville, NY
Cummings, John	OLT	254	6-2	Sr.	Cincinnati
Mack, Richard	OLG	215	6-0	So.	Bucyrus
Hasenohrl, George	DLT	262	6-1	Sr.	Garfield Heights
Cusick, Peter	DRT	242	6-2	So.	Lakewood
Schumacher, Kurt	ORT	244	6-4	So.	Lorain
Dannelley, Scott	ORT	229	6-3	So.	Williamsport, PA
Hicks, John	ORT	254	6-3	Jr.	Cleveland
Teague, Mervin	OLT	221	6-5	Sr.	Youngstown
Scott, Daniel	ORT	260	6-3	Jr.	Amityville, NY
France, Doug	OLT	265	6-6	So.	Dayton
Beecroft, Charles	DLT	224	6-3	Sr.	Dayton
Williams, Shad	DRT	238	6-3	Sr.	Portsmouth
Pagac, Fred	OLE	208	6-1	Jr.	Richeyville, PA
Marendt, Thomas	DLT	220	6-1	Jr.	Indianapolis, IN
Hazel, David	DLT	188	6-1	Jr.	Xenia
Scannell, Michael	DLE	207	6-2	Sr.	Sylvania
Jones, Scott	SE	209	6-3	Jr.	Parma Heights
Smurda, John	TE	214	6-1	Jr.	Allentown, PA
Donovan, Brenden	DLE	180	5-10	So.	Columbus
Bartoszek, Michael	TE	206	6-4	So.	Eire, PA
DeCree, Van	DRE	216	6-1	So.	Warren
Powell, Theodore	TE	225	6-2	Jr.	Hampton, VA
Straka, Mark	TE	220	6-5	Jr.	Elyria
Cope, James	DRE	205	6-2	So.	McKeesport, PA
Lago, Gary	P	229	6-2	Sr.	Ashtabula
Baxter, Charles	TE	222	6-2	Jr.	Painesville
Lillvis, Gary	DLT	230	6-2	So.	Ashtabula
Pisanelli, Fred	DLT	208	6-2	Sr.	Warren
O'Rourke, Larry	DT	230	6-0	So.	Yardley, PA

1972

Ohio	21	Iowa	0
Ohio	29	North Carolina	14
Ohio	35	California	18
Ohio	26	Illinois	7
Ohio	44	Indiana	7
Ohio	28	Wisconsin	20
Ohio	27	Minnesota	19
Ohio	12	Michigan State	19
Ohio	27	Northwestern	14
Ohio	14	Michigan	11

Season Summary

Games Won, 8; Lost, 2

JOHN HICKS
All-American Tackle

RANDY GRADISHAR
All-American Linebacker

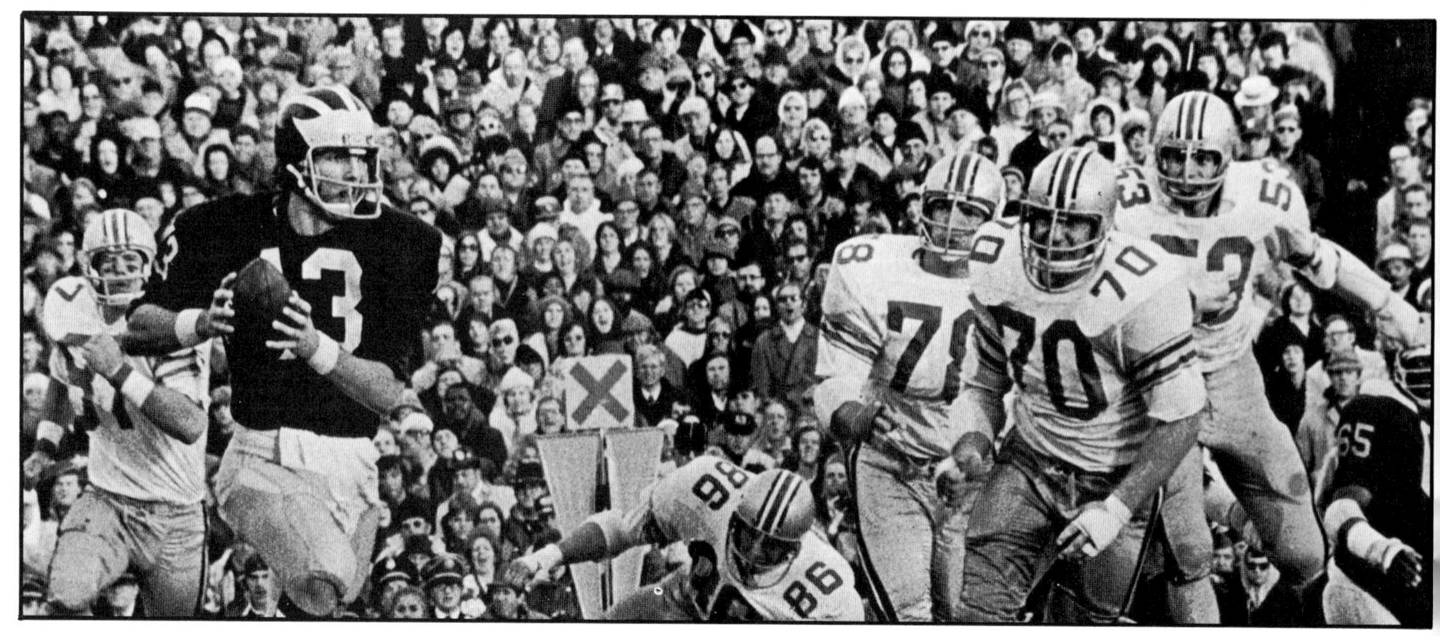

November 24, 1973

Ann Arbor, Michigan

Michigan, Ohio State Football Equals, 10-10

Wolverines Gain Title Tie With Second-Half Rally

Before a crowd of 105,223 the Buckeyes and Wolverines battled to a standoff on the rain-slicked artificial turf in Michigan Stadium. They tied for the Big Ten championship with identical 7-0-1 records. But this tie, a rugged, thumping football game played mostly on the ground, cost both dearly in the beloved poll game where the Bucks were No. 1 and Michigan No. 4.

OSU's little Blair Conway kicked a 31-yard field goal when the Bucks stalled out on the ground with 3:56 gone in the second period. Then after an exchange of punts, the Bucks roared to a touchdown with freshman Pete Johnson bulling ovver from the five with only 53 seconds left in the half. Conway converted the PAT to give the Bucks a 10-0 half time lead.

In the third quarter came the turning point of the game. On fourth down and less than two at the Michigan 34, Ohio elected to go for the yardage. Sophomore Cornelius Greene attempted a quarterback sneak, but was nailed by Michigan's Jeff Perlinger. From there it was a Michigan takeover. With burly Ed Shuttlesworth doing the leg work, Michigan waded to the Ohio State 13-yard from where Lantry kicked a 30-yard field goal on the second play of the fourth quarter.

After an Ohio punt Michigan moved again toward the OSU goal line. A 27-yard pass from Franklin to Paul Seal helped move the ball to the Ohio State 10 when the Wolverines were faced with a fourth and one situation. Franklin made a great fake to Shuttlesworth who charged into a cluster of waiting Ohio State arms, and then slid around the right side and crossed the goal line standing up. Lantry converted the PAT to tie the score at 10-10 with 9:32 left in the game.

Michigan attempted a 58-yard field goal with 1:01 left in the game. It was long enough but was wide to the left. After a last minute interception by Michigan's Tom Drake, Lantry attempted another field goal which was wide to the right. So the score remained 10-10.

STATISTICS

	OSU	UM
First Downs	9	16
Rushes-Yards	49-234	56-204
Passing Yards	0	99
Return Yards	33	16
Passes	0-4-1	7-12-1
Punts	7-31	5-40
Fumbles-Lost	1-0	1-1
Penalties-Yards	0-0	4-37

OSU	0	10	0	0	10
UM	0	0	0	10	10

1973			
Ohio	56	Minnesota	7
Ohio	37	Texas Christian	3
Ohio	27	Washington State	3
Ohio	24	Wisconsin	0
Ohio	37	Indiana	7
Ohio	60	Northwestern	0
Ohio	30	Illinois	0
Ohio	35	Michigan State	0
Ohio	55	Iowa	13
Ohio	10	Michigan	10

Season Summary

Games Won, 9; Lost, 0; Tied, 1

ARCHIE GRIFFIN
All-American Back

JOHN HICKS
All-American Tackle

VAN DeCREE
All-American End

OHIO

No.	Name	Pos.	Wt.	Hgt.	Class	Home Town
95	Applegate, Richard	DLT	252	6-3	Fr.	Cincinnati
93	Ayers, Ronald	ORG	227	6-4	Fr.	Columbus
87	*Bartoszek, Michael	SE	210	6-4	Jr.	Erie, PA
48	*Baschnagel, Brian	ORH	192	6-0	So.	Pittsburgh, PA
92	Battle, Marvin	DRT	247	6-4	Fr.	Brooklyn, NY
34	Bembry, Dan	FB	198	6-1	Fr.	Utica, NY
37	Bowers, Brian	LB	219	6-0	Jr.	Uniontown
13	**Bradshaw, M.	ORH	206	6-2	Sr.	Edwardsville, IL
84	Brudzinski, Robert	DLE	210	6-4	Fr.	Fremont
75	Buonamici, Nicholas	DLT	250	6-3	Fr.	Brentwood, NY
23	Cassady, Craig	DLH	170	6-0	So.	Columbus
20	*Colzie, Neal	DLH	196	6-2	Jr.	Coral Gables, FL
3	*Conway, Blair	PK	157	5-7	Sr.	Middleburg Heig
91	*Cope, James	DRE	222	6-2	Jr.	McKeesport, PA
90	Curto, Patrick	DRE	209	6-2	So.	Groveport
71	*Cusick, Peter	DRT	244	6-2	Jr.	Lakewood
67	**Cutillo, Dan	DLT	232	6-1	Sr.	Amityville, NY
73	*Dannelley, Scott	DLT	246	6-3	Jr.	Williamsport, PA
50	Datish, Michael	C	221	6-3	Fr.	Warren
16	**Davis, Jeff	DRH	182	5-10	Sr.	Erie, PA
29	Davis, Jerome	DLH	185	6-1	Fr.	Middletown
88	*DeCree, Van	DLE	215	6-1	Jr.	Warren
36	*Elia, Bruce	LB	212	6-1	Jr.	Cliffside Park, N
8	*Ezzo, Bill	SE	154	5-7	Jr.	Canastota, NY
12	*Fox, Tim	S	188	6-0	So.	Canton
77	*France, Douglas	OLT	258	6-6	Jr.	Dayton
53	**Gradishar, Randy	LB	236	6-3	Sr.	Champion
66	Graf, Larry	OLG	219	6-1	Sr.	Akron
7	Greene, Cornelius	OB	168	6-0	So.	Washington, D.C
45	*Griffin, Archie	OLH	184	5-9	So.	Columbus
18	**Hare, Greg	QB	202	6-3	Sr.	Cumberland, MD
82	*Hazel, David	SE	188	6-1	Sr.	Xenia
74	**Hicks, John	ORT	258	6-3	Sr.	Cleveland
27	*Holycross, Tim	ORH	190	6-0	Jr.	Bedford Heights
44	**Hughes, John	FB	196	6-1	Sr.	Duquesne, PA
61	Husband, John	ORG	220	6-2	Sr.	Elyria
33	Johnson, Pete	FB	227	6-1	Fr.	Long Beach, NY
42	*Jones, Arnold	LB	228	6-0	Jr.	Dayton
49	Kain, Larry	DLE	212	6-2	Jr.	Dayton
4	**Keith, Randal	FB	214	5-11	Sr.	Cincinnati
21	*Kern, Carl	S	190	6-0	Sr.	Dallas, Pa.
62	**Koegel, Victor	LB	214	6-1	Sr.	Cincinnati
63	**Kregel, James	OLG	234	6-2	Sr.	Toledo
54	*Kuhn, Kenneth	LB	227	6-2	So.	Louisville
51	Lillvis, Gary	OLG	232	6-2	Jr.	Ashtabula
47	**Lippert, Elmer	OLH	180	5-7	Sr.	Sandusky
46	*Luke, Steve	DRH	194	6-2	Jr.	Massillon
64	Lukens, William	ORG	218	6-1	Fr.	Cincinnati
69	*Mack, Richard	ORG	218	5-11	Jr.	Bucyrus
81	**Marenot, Thomas	DRE	218	6-1	Sr.	Indianapolis, IN
30	**Mathis, Louis	DCB	204	6-0	Sr.	Patterson, NJ
32	**Middleton, Richard	LB	222	6-3	Sr.	Delaware
17	*Morrison, Steven	QB	202	6-3	Jr.	Huntington, WV
52	*Myers, Steven	C	240	6-2	Jr.	Kent
80	**Pagac, Fred	TE	210	6-1	Sr.	Richeyville, PA
24	*Parsons, Richard	S	190	5-11	Jr.	Cuyahoga Falls
28	*Plank, Douglas	DCB	197	5-11	Jr.	North Irwin, PA
89	*Powell, Ted	TE	226	6-2	Sr.	Hampton, VA
19	*Purdy, David	QB	188	6-2	Jr.	Swanton
65	Renard, Barney	OLG	219	6-3	Fr.	Maumee
35	**Rich, Tocco	LB	230	5-11	Sr.	Canton
41	Roach, Woodrow	OLH	180	5-9	So.	Washington, D.C
43	Ruhl, Bruce	S	188	6-1	Fr.	Southfield, MI
72	*Schumacher, Kurt	OLT	248	6-4	Jr.	Lorain
76	*Scott, Dan	ORG	258	6-3	Sr.	Amityville, NY
1	Skladany, Thomas	P-PK	185	6-0	Fr.	Bethal Park, PA
97	Smith, Ted	LB	220	6-1	So.	Gibsonburg
85	**Smurda, John	TE	212	6-1	Sr.	Allentown, PA
57	Straka, Mark	C	210	6-4	Sr.	Elyria
94	Szabo, Thomas	DRT	227	6-1	Sr.	Elyria
58	Weiland, Jeffery	LB	214	6-2	So.	Englewood
70	Willard, Robert	ORT	240	6-2	Sr.	Chagrin Falls
83	Williott, Louis	DLE	212	6-1	So.	Youngstown

MICHIGAN

No.	Name	Pos.	Wt.	Hgt.	Class	Home Town
58	Armour, Jim	OG	230	6-3	Sr.	Detroit
32	Banks, Larry	DE	200	6-2	Sr.	Cleveland, OH
5	Bell, Gordon	TB	175	5-9	So.	Troy, OH
85	Brandon, Dave	DE	210	6-3	Sr.	Plymouth
6	*Brown, Dave	S	188	6-1	Jr.	Akron, OH
8	*Burks, Roy	DB	190	6-2	Jr.	Midland
88	Caputo, Matt	DE	210	6-3	So.	Toledo, OH
12	*Casey, Kevin	QB	180	6-2	Sr.	Grand Rapids
19	Cederberg, Jon	TB	185	5-10	Sr.	Plymouth
24	*Chapman, Gil	TB	180	5-9	Jr.	Elizabeth, NJ
70	Cherry, John	OT	235	6-6	Sr.	Willard, OH
13	**Cipa, Larry	QB	210	6-4	Sr.	Cincinnati, OH
39	*Coleman, Don	DE	217	6-2½	Sr.	Daly City, CA
29	Collins, Jerry	SE	185	6-2	So.	Ann Arbor
73	**Coode, Jim	OT	245	6-4	Sr.	Mayfield, OH
99	Coyne, Mike	DT	250	6-3	So.	Chicago, IL
52	Czirr, Jim	C	220	6-3	So.	St. Joseph
56	Davis, Tim	MG	200	5-10	So.	Warren, OH
57	Day, Mike	LB	210	6-1	Sr.	Livonia
84	*Denboer, Greg	TE	233	6-6	Jr.	Kentwood
55	Devich, Dave	LB	210	6-2	So.	Highland, IN
25	**Dotzauer, Barry	DB	162	6-1	Sr.	Cincinnati, OH
28	*Drake, Tom	DB	175	5-11	Jr.	Midland
35	Dufek, Don	Wolf	195	6-0	So.	Ann Arbor
86	**Eaton, Don	DE	194	6-4	Sr.	Lancaster, OH
45	*Elliott, Dave	DB	170	6-1	Jr.	Coral Gables, FL
16	Elzinga, Mark	QB	195	6-3	So.	Bay City
41	Fairbanks, Jack	DB	185	6-0	So.	Hawks
89	Fediuk, Art	TE	212	6-2	Sr.	Livonia
9	*Franklin, Dennis	QB	180	6-1	Jr.	Massillon, OH
42	Franklin, Glenn	WB	185	5-10	Jr.	Warren, OH
50	*Franks, Dennis	C	223	6-1	Jr.	Bethel Park, PA
71	**Gallagher, Dave	DT	245	6-4	Sr.	Piqua, OH
15	Gonzalez, Eduardo	TB	190	5-11	So.	Los Angeles, CA
48	**Gustafson, Larry	WB	180	5-11	Sr.	Mays Landing, NJ
69	*Hainrihar, Gary	OG	223	6-2	Sr.	Cicero, IL
43	**Haslerig, Clint	WB	194	6-1	Sr.	Cincinnati, OH
44	*Heater, Chuck	TB	200	6-0	Jr.	Tiffin, OH
93	*Hoban, Bill	DT	223	6-3	Jr.	Chicago, IL
61	**Hoban, Mike	OG	235	6-2	Sr.	Chicago, IL
40	Holmes, Mike	Wolf	195	6-3	So.	Akron, OH
7	Jacoby, Mark	Wolf	195	6-1	Jr.	Toledo, OH
51	Jensen, Tom	C	220	6-3	Jr.	Springfield, IL
81	Jilek, Dan	DE	205	6-3	So.	Sterling Heights
27	Johnson, Keith	SE	170	6-0	So.	Munster, IN
82	Johnson, Larry	DE	200	6-1	Sr.	Munster, IN
21	Kampe, Kurt	DB	182	5-11	Jr.	Defiance, OH
67	King, Steve	OT	245	6-5	Jr.	Tiffin, OH
92	Koschalk, Rich	MG	205	6-2	So.	Toledo, OH
10	*Koss, Greg	S	190	6-5	Sr.	Cuyahoga Falls, OH
36	*Lantry, Mike	PK	210	6-2	Jr.	Oxford
74	Lewis, Kirk	OT	220	6-3	So.	Garden City
72	Lyall, Jim	DT	224	6-6	Sr.	North Olmstead, OH
26	MacKenzie, Doug	SE	185	6-2	Jr.	Warren
65	*Metz, Dave	OG	235	6-2	Jr.	Harrison, OH
63	Miles, Les	OG	220	6-1	So.	Elyria, OH
68	Moore, Frank	OG	220	5-11	So.	Detroit
77	Morton, Greg	DT	230	6-3	So.	Akron, OH
34	*Mutch, Craig	LB	210	6-1	Sr.	Detroit
96	O'Neal, Calvin	LB	222	6-2	So.	Saginaw
97	Perlinger, Jeff	DT	235	6-3	Jr.	Crystal, MN
80	Przygodski, George	TE	215	6-3	So.	Grand Rapids
76	Randolph, Chuck	DT	230	6-3	So.	Amelia, OH
33	*Russ, Carl	LB	215	6-2	Jr.	Muskegon Heights
83	**Seal, Paul	TE	215	6-6	Sr.	Detroit
31	**Shuttlesworth, Ed	FB	225	6-2	Sr.	Cincinnati, OH
17	**Slade, Tom	QB	195	6-0	Sr.	Saginaw
14	Spahn, Jeff	QB	175	5-11	Jr.	Steubenville, OH
38	*Steger, Geoff	Wolf	195	6-0	Jr.	Winnetka, IL
49	Strabley, Mike	LB	218	6-1	So.	Massillon, OH
94	Strinko, Greg	DE	213	6-3	So.	Middletown, OH
59	*Strinko, Steve	LB	230	6-3	Jr.	Middletown, OH
23	Szydlowski, Ron	WB	175	5-9	Sr.	Wyandotte
66	Thomas, John	C	220	6-2	Sr.	Detroit
30	**Thornbladh, Bob	FB	220	6-2	Sr.	Binghamton, NY
75	**Troszak, Doug	DT	240	6-4	Sr.	Warren
73	**Tucker, Curtis	OT	230	6-2	Sr.	Cleveland, OH
64	Tumpane, Pat	OT	235	6-4	Jr.	Midlothian, IL
46	Vercel, Jovan	LB	214	6-0	Sr.	Highland, IN
54	Warner, Don	MG	195	5-11	Sr.	Dearborn
79	Wheeler, Alan	OT	235	6-5	So.	Cincinnati, OH
91	*Williamson, Walt	DE	224	6-4	Sr.	Detroit

* indicates letters won

1973

Michigan	31	Iowa	7
Michigan	47	Stanford	10
Michigan	14	Navy	0
Michigan	24	Oregon	0
Michigan	31	Michigan State	0
Michigan	35	Wisconsin	6
Michigan	34	Minnesota	7
Michigan	49	Indiana	13
Michigan	21	Illinois	6
Michigan	34	Purdue	9
Michigan	10	Ohio State	10

Season Summary

Games won, 10; Lost, 0; Tied, 1

DAVE BROWN
All-American Halfback

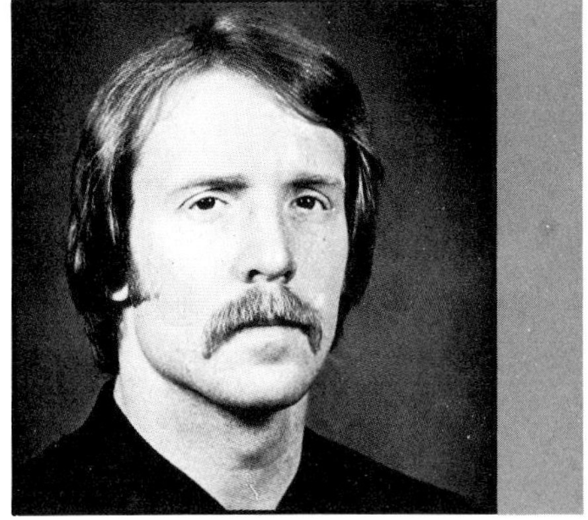

DAVE GALLAGHER
All-American Tackle

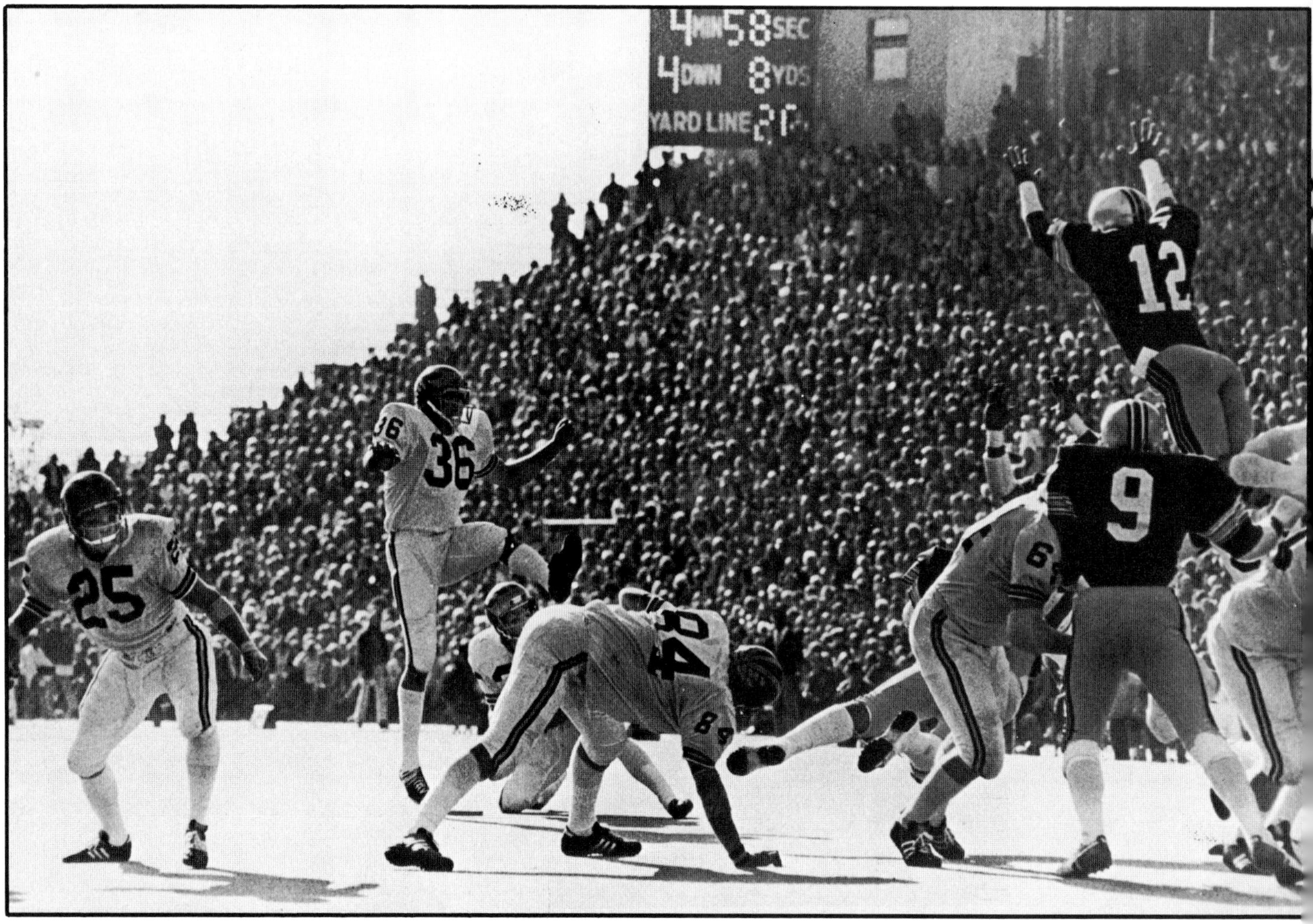
4 MIN 58 SEC
4 DWN 8 YDS
YARD LINE

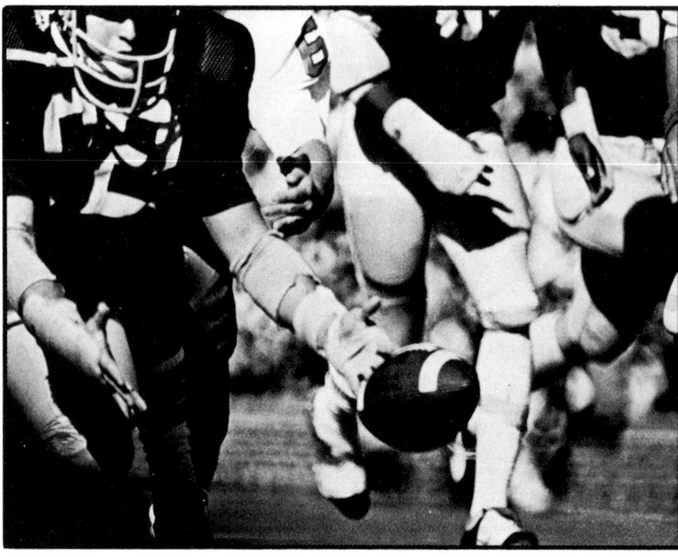

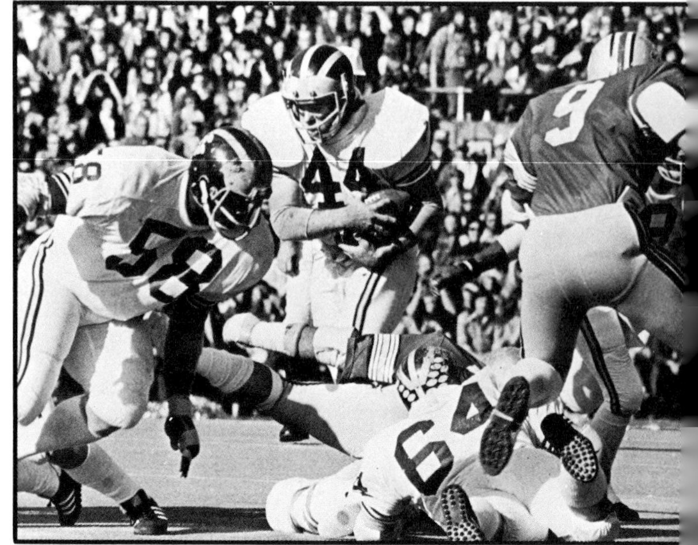

November 23, 1974

Columbus, Ohio

Field Goals Provide Margin Of Victory For Buckeyes, 12-10

Michigan Gets Early Lead But Can't Hold On

With a howling crowd of 88,243 watching in Ohio Stadium, Tom Klaban, a Czechoslovakian refugee, connected on four field goals of 47, 25, 43, 45 yards as favored Ohio State wiped out an early 10-0 Michigan lead.

Klaban, a "walk-on" at Ohio State, wasn't even on a full scholarship until that spectacular show. And while delirium tumbled around Klaban, bitter disappointment struck another kicker, Michigan's Mike Lantry. For the second straight year in an Ohio State game, Michigan died with its boots off as the Wolverines' kicker missed a 33 yard attempt with only 18 seconds left in the game.

Michigan jammed Ohio State on the game's first series and then scored quickly. After running for a first down in three plays, quarterback Dennis Franklin stung the Bucks with a 42-yard touchdown pass to Gil Chapman over the middle and Lantry's PAT made it 7-0.

After a Greene fumble at the Michigan 29, the Wolverines were off again. Hammering out four first downs on the ground with little Gordon Bell carrying on six of the nine plays, the Wolverines finally stalled, and Lantry kicked a 37-yarder for a 10-0 lead. But from that point on, UM's lead began to melt.

Klaban delivered a 47-yarder on the first play of the second quarter, then added two more before the half. An intercepted pass by Bruce Elia set up one of them and the Bucks drove for the other with only two seconds left in the half.

After getting excellent field position at the Michigan 48-yard line on their first possession after the kickoff, Archie Griffin, who gained 111 yards, led the march to the winning score. When OSU ground to a halt at the UM 28, Klaban dropped back and drilled a tall floater between the poles for a 45-yard field goal. From then on defenses took charge until Michigan gained possession at the Wolverine 47 with 57 seconds left to play. With Franklin passing and Rob Lytle running, Michigan moved to the OSU 16 but Lantry's field goal attempt drifted to the left spelling defeat for the Wolverines.

STATISTICS

	UM	OSU
First Downs	14	18
Rushes-Yards	54-195	57-195
Passing Yards	96	58
Return Yards	13	20
Passes	5-14-2	3-6-0
Fumbles-Lost	1-0	2-2
Penalties-Yards	1-15	3-45

OSU	0	9	3	0	12
UM	10	0	0	0	10

1974

1974

Michigan	24	Iowa	7
Michigan	31	Colorado	0
Michigan	52	Navy	0
Michigan	27	Stanford	16
Michigan	21	MSU	7
Michigan	24	Wisconsin	20
Michigan	49	Minnesota	0
Michigan	21	Indiana	7
Michigan	14	Illinois	6
Michigan	51	Purdue	0
Michigan	10	Ohio State	12

Season Summary

Games Won, 10; Lost, 1; Tied, 0

MICHIGAN

No.	Name	Pos.	Wt.	Hgt.	Home
1	Whiteford, Dave	DB	185	6-1	Traverse City
3	Wood, Bob	PK	170	5-9	London, OH
4	Brumbaugh, Phil	DB	160	5-9	Greenville, OH
5	*Bell, Gordon	TB	175	5-9	Troy, OH
6	*Brown, Dave	S	188	6-1	Akron, OH
7	Jacoby, Mark	Wolf	195	6-1	Toledo, OH
8	Zuver, Jerry	S	187	6-3	Archbold, OH
9	*Franklin, Dennis	QB	180	6-1	Massillon, OH
10	Howard, Derek	DB	190	6-3	Hamilton, OH
13	Ceddia, John	QB	190	6-1	Cincinnati, OH
14	Spahn, Jeff	QB	175	5-11	Steubenville, OH
16	Elzinga, Mark	QB	195	6-3	Bay City
17	Hicks, Dwight	S	185	6-3	Pennsauken, NJ
18	Pickens, Jim	DB	188	6-2	Sylvania, OH
19	Truitt, Darrell	Wolf	190	6-1	Cincinnati, OH
20	*Banks, Harry	DB	185	5-10	Cleveland, OH
21	Kampe, Kurt	DB	182	5-11	Defiance, OH
22	Bolden, Jim	DB	180	5-10	Akron, OH
24	*Chapman, Gil	WB	180	5-9	Elizabeth, NJ
25	Lytle, Rob	TB	190	6-1	Fremont, OH
26	Richardson, Dennis	WR	190	6-0	Lima, OH
27	*Johnson, Keith	SE	170	6-3	Munster, IN
28	*Drake, Tom	DB	175	5-11	Midland
29	Collins, Jerry	SE	185	6-2	Ann Arbor
30	Brown, Phil	DB	170	6-0	Detroit
31	Andrews, Phil	FB	225	6-2	Brooklyn, NY
32	Banks, Larry	DE	210	6-2	Cleveland, OH
33	*Russ, Carl	LB	215	6-2	Mskgn. Hts.
34	Corbin, Scott	FB	225	6-1	Cincinnati, OH
35	*Dufek, Don	Wolf	195	6-0	Gr. Rapids
36	Lantry, Mike	PK	210	6-2	Oxford
37	*Smith, Jim	SE	200	6-3	Blue Isl., IL
38	*Steger, Geoff	Wolf	195	6-0	Winnetka, IL
39	Vogele, Jerry	FB	235	6-3	Cincinnati, OH
40	Holmes, Mike	DE	200	6-3	Akron, OH
41	Fairbanks, Jack	DB	185	6-0	Hawks
43	Richardson, Max	TB	200	6-2	Ft. Wayne, IN
44	*Heater, Chuck	FB	205	6-0	Tiffin, OH
45	*Elliott, Dave	DB	170	6-1	Coral Gbls., FL
46	Heneveld, Bill	DB	180	5-10	Alto
48	King, Kevin	FB	215	6-2	Oak Lawn, IL
49	Strabley, Mike	LB	218	6-1	Massillon, OH
50	*Franks, Dennis	C	223	6-1	Bethel Park, PA
51	*Jensen, Tom	C	220	6-3	Springfield, IL
52	*Czirr, Jim	C	220	6-3	St. Joseph
53	Hackett, Jim	LB	220	6-2	London, OH
54	Graves, Steve	MG	220	6-2	Cleveland, OH
55	Devich, Dave	LB	210	6-2	Highland, IN
56	*Davis, Tim	MG	220	5-10	Warren, OH
57	Szafranski, Roger	MG	225	5-11	Bay City
58	Armour, James	OG	230	6-3	Detroit
59	*Strinko, Steve	LB	235	6-3	Middletown, OH
62	Lang, Bob	DT	240	6-2	Chicago, IL
63	Miles, Les	OG	220	6-1	Elyria, OH
64	*Tumpane, Pat	OT	235	6-4	Midlothian, IL
65	*Metz, Dave	OG	235	6-2	Harrison, OH
66	Anderson, Steve	LB	220	6-2	Toledo, OH
67	*King, Steve	OT	245	6-5	Tiffin, OH
68	Moore, Frank	OG	220	5-11	Detroit
69	Szara, Gerry	OG	240	6-3	Oak Lawn, IL
70	Hall, Jim	OT	235	6-4	Ypsilanti
71	Hennessy, John	DT	235	6-4	Chicago, IL
73	Dufek, Bill	T	265	6-4	Gr. Rapids
74	*Lewis, Kirk	OG	220	6-3	Gdn. City
75	Coyne, Mike	DT	250	6-3	Chicago, IL
76	Randolph, Chuck	DT	230	6-3	Amelia, OH
77	Morton, Greg	DT	230	6-3	Akron, OH
80	*Przygodski, George	TE	215	6-3	Gr. Rapids
81	*Jilek, Dan	DE	210	6-3	String Hts.
82	*Johnson, Larry	DE	200	6-1	Munster, IN
84	*DenBoer, Greg	TE	233	6-6	Kentwood
85	Stephenson, Curt	SE	170	5-11	Del Mar, CA
86	Anderson, John	TE	208	6-3	Waukesha, WI
89	Traber, Pete	TE	220	6-3	Columbia, MD
90	Phelps, Eric	DE	200	6-1	Salem, NH
92	Koschalk, Rick	MG	205	6-2	Toledo, OH
93	*Hoban, Bill	DT	223	6-3	Chicago, IL
94	Strinko, Greg	DE	213	6-3	Middletown, OH
95	Heffernan, Jack	DT	250	6-2	Staten Island, NY
96	O'Neal, Calvin	LB	222	6-2	Saginaw
97	*Perlinger, Jeff	DT	235	6-3	Crystal, MN

* indicates letters won

DAVE BROWN
All-American Halfback

VAN DECREE
All-American End

ARCHIE GRIFFIN
All-American Back

OHIO

No.	Name	Pos.	Wt.	Hgt.	Home
94	David Adkins	LB	197	6-2	Xenia
22	Joseph Allegro	DHB	174	5-11	W. Pitsbgh., PA
61	Richard Applegate	OG	252	6-3	Cincinnati
59	Ronald Ayers	OG	229	6-4	Columbus
62	Scott Baker	OG	220	6-1	Willoughby
95	Douglas Bargerstock	DT	246	6-2	Taylor, MI
87	*Michael Bartoszek	TE	218	6-4	Erie, PA
48	*Brian Baschnagel	WB	190	6-0	Pitsbgh., PA
67	Eddie Beamon	DT	245	6-2	Cincinnati
37	*Brian Bowers	LB	232	6-0	Uniontown
55	Aaron Brown	LB	222	6-2	Warren
84	*Robert Brudzinski	DE	218	6-4	Fremont
75	*Nicholas Buonamici	DT	238	6-3	Brentwood, NY
23	*Craig Cassady	DHB	174	6-0	Columbus
20	*Neal Colzie	DHB	202	6-2	Miami, FL
91	*James Cope	DE	235	6-2	McKeesport, PA
78	Garth Cox	OT	242	6-5	Wshngtn. Ct. Hs.
90	*Pat Curto	DE	225	6-2	Groveport
96	Martin Cusick	DE	211	6-2	Lakewood
71	*Pete Cusick	DT	250	6-2	Lakewood
39	John D'Amato	LB	218	6-3	Staten Isl., NY
73	*Scott Dannelley	OT	240	6-3	Williamsport, PA
50	Michael Datish	C	240	6-3	Warren
29	*Jerome Davis	S	184	6-1	Middletown
88	*Van DeCree	DE	218	6-1	Warren
86	Joseph Dixon	DE	209	6-3	Trenton, MI
36	*Bruce Elia	LB	219	6-1	Cliffside Pk., NJ
8	*Bill Ezzo	SE	150	5-7	Canastota, NY
58	Jeff Ferrelli	DHB	184	5-10	Columbus
12	*Tim Fox	S	186	6-0	Canton
80	*Douglas France	TE	260	6-6	Dayton
25	Robert Gentry	DHB	200	6-3	Sandusky
7	*Cornelius Greene	QB	170	6-0	Washington, D.C.
45	*Archie Griffin	TB	182	5-9	Columbus
44	Raymond Griffin	WB	174	5-9	Columbus
11	James Harrell	WB	191	5-10	Curtice
66	Tyrone Harris	DT	242	6-3	Columbus
82	*David Hazel	SE	192	6-1	Xenia
38	*Harold Henson	FB	231	6-4	Ashville
27	*Tim Holycross	WB	190	6-0	Bedford Hgts.
35	Robert Hyatt	WB	178	5-10	Lagrange
13	Barry Johnson	TB	187	6-0	Columbus
33	*Pete Johnson	FB	250	6-1	Long Bch., NY
42	*Arnold Jones	LB	240	6-0	Dayton
49	Herman Jones	WB	196	6-3	Miami, FL
98	Paul Jones	DE	206	6-2	Dayton
92	Jeffrey Jurin	DE	197	6-0	Newcomerstown
85	*Larry Kain	TE	221	6-2	Dayton
3	Michael Keeton	P	172	6-0	Caldwell
6	Thomas Klaban	PK	182	6-1	Cincinnati
70	Steve Koegel	OT	217	6-3	Cincinnati
54	*Kenneth Kuhn	LB	230	6-2	Louisville
10	Mark Lang	LB	209	6-1	Cincinnati
81	Robert Lille	TE	222	6-3	Dayton
51	Gary Lillvis	OG	230	6-2	Ashtabula
34	Jeff Logan	TB	182	5-10	North Canton
46	*Steve Luke	DHB	200	6-2	Massillon
64	William Lukens	OG	226	6-1	Cincinnati
69	*Richard Mack	OG	212	5-11	Bucyrus
32	David Mazeroski	FB	209	6-1	Cadiz
5	Tom McBrayer	PK	175	5-11	Hilliard
14	Gary McCutcheon	SE	188	6-0	Berwick, PA
21	Max Midlam	S	194	5-10	Marion
2	Larry Molls	TB	184	6-0	Parma Hgts.
17	*Steven Morrison	QB	188	6-3	Huntington, WV
52	*Steve Myers	C	243	6-0	Kent
68	James O'Rourke	DT	252	6-3	Brooklyn, NY
99	Larry O'Rourke	DT	252	6-2	Yardley, PA
15	James Pacenta	QB	190	6-3	Akron
24	*Richard Parsons	S	192	6-0	Cuyahoga Falls
83	Clarence Perry	DE	219	6-0	Columbus
74	Louis Pietrini	OT	242	6-3	Milford, CT
28	*Douglas Plank	DHB	197	5-11	N. Irwin, PA
53	Douglas Porter	C	216	6-2	Youngstown
18	Pete Prather	QB	182	6-1	Glen Rock, NJ
19	*David Purdy	QB	186	6-2	Swanton
65	Barney Renard	C	228	6-3	Maumee
41	*Woodrow Roach	TB	180	5-9	Wshngtn., D.C.
47	Bob Robertson	TB	205	6-0	Barberton
26	Tom Roche	DHB	180	6-3	Staten Isl., NJ
16	Tony Ross	QB	190	5-10	Ptsbh., PA
43	*Bruce Ruhl	S	186	6-1	Southfield, MI
97	Michael Sapp	LB	210	6-2	Columbus
57	James Savoca	LB	226	6-2	Solon
72	*Kurt Schumacher	OT	254	6-4	Lorain
30	Charles Simon	LB	219	6-2	Dublin
1	*Thomas Skladany	P-PK	194	6-0	Bethel Park, PA
60	*Ted Smith	OG	236	6-1	Gibsonburg
77	Gregory Storer	OT	217	6-5	Cincinnati
76	Thomas Swank	OT	242	6-2	Sandusky
9	Kenneth Thompson	LB	227	6-1	Waverly
79	Christopher Ward	OT	268	6-4	Dayton
63	Darryl Weston	OG	219	6-2	Ptsbh., PA
4	Louis Williott	FB	217	6-1	Youngstown
89	Leonard Willis	SE	182	6-0	Wshgtn., D.C.
25	Scott Wolery	DHB	165	5-8	Delphos

* indicates letters won

1974

Ohio	34	Minnesota	19
Ohio	51	Oregon State	10
Ohio	28	S. Methodist	9
Ohio	42	Wash. State	7
Ohio	52	Wisconsin	7
Ohio	49	Indiana	9
Ohio	55	Northwestern	7
Ohio	49	Illinois	7
Ohio	13	MSU	16
Ohio	35	Iowa	10
Ohio	12	Michigan	10

Season Summary

Games Won, 10; Lost, 1

TOM SKLADANY
All-American Punter

NEAL COLZIE
All-American Back

KURT SCHUMACHER
All-American Tackle

PETE CUSICK
All-American Tackle

STEVE MEYERS
All-American Center

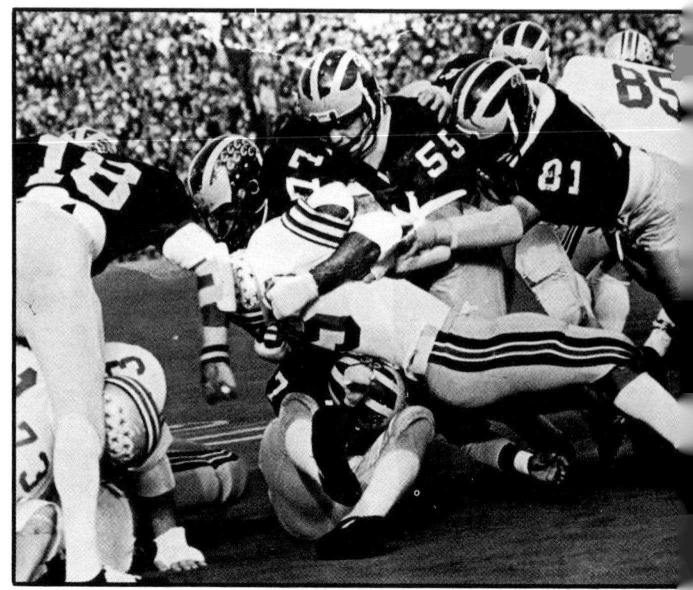

November 22, 1975

Ann Arbor, Michigan

Buckeyes Defeat Michigan, 21 To 14

Greene Is Key For Bucks

For OSU's Archie Griffin, it must have seemed as if he were being pursued by 11 demons in blue shirts. Disappearing under the swarm time after time, Archie was held to 46 yards rushing, ending his streak of 31 straight 100-yard games.

The entire Ohio state running attack was snuffed out by a brilliant Michigan defense, so coach Woody Hayes, proving he was more flexible than many thought, turned to the pass to lift OSU to its 11th straight victory and send the Wolverines down to their first defeat after eight wins and two ties.

In the first quarter, Ohio State, playing typical bruising football, drove from its 37-yard line for a touchdown, scoring on a pass from Greene to Johnson. Klaban converted the PAT for a 7-0 lead.

Michigan, with Bell gaining more than 100 yards in the first half, moved, but stalled, fumbles and interceptions hurting. But the Wolverines tied the score just before halftime, marching on Ohio State, and finally scoring on a halfback pass, a rarely used weapon, Bell to Jim Smith. Michigan's Wood converted the extra point and after a Griffin fumble missed a 37-yard field goal attempt leaving the score 7-7 at halftime.

The battle stalemated in the third quarter, but Michigan finally broke through early in the fourth period with Gordon Bell and Rob Lytle gaining the tough yards and a pair of passes from Leach to Jim Smith moving the ball 39 yards to the Ohio State four. Two cracks by Leach delivered the touchdown, and Bob Wood kicked the extra point for 14-7 advantage.

Greene then began an aerial display that marked one of the greatest comebacks ever by a Buckeye team. Passes from Greene went to Baschnagel for 17 yards, to Len Willis for 14 and then 17, two runs by Griffin of 11 and 12 yards, and Greene brought Ohio storming down the field to the UM 8-yard line. Now it was time for the 240-pound Johnson. He lunged for five, then for two, and then was stopped for no gain. On fourth down he sliced through the right side for the score and the Buckeyes had a tie at 14-14 when Tom Klaban kicked the point with 3:18 to play.

Michigan then came out gambling for the win for a tie would send OSU to the Rose Bowl anyway. Leach was spilled for a 9-yard loss after the kickoff, then hurled an incomplete pass. On third down his pass toward the sideline hung in the air as Ray Griffin swooped in to intercept and race to the Michigan three where Leach knocked him out of bounds. Johnson, scoring his 25th touchdown of the season, waded into the pack to score with 2:23 to play. Klaban added the PAT. The result and final score was 21-14, an astounding OSU victory.

STATISTICS

	OSU	UM
First Downs	12	19
Rushes-Yards	45-124	56-248
Passing Yards	84	113
Return Yards	56	20
Passes	7-16-2	8-21-3
Punts	8-45	6-30
Fumbles-Lost	1-1	2-2
Penalties-Yards	2-10	1-15

OSU	7	0	0	14	21
UM	0	7	0	7	14

1975

1975		
Ohio 21	Michigan State	0
Ohio 17	Penn State	9
Ohio 32	North Carolina	7
Ohio 41	U.C.L.A.	20
Ohio 49	Iowa	0
Ohio 56	Wisconsin	0
Ohio 35	Purdue	6
Ohio 24	Indiana	14
Ohio 40	Illinois	3
Ohio 38	Minnesota	6
Ohio 21	Michigan	14

Season Summary

Games Won, 11; Lost, 0

OHIO

No.	Name	Pos.	Wt.	Hgt.	Class	Home Town
94	*Adkins, Dave	LB	209	6-2	So.	Xenia
22	Allegro, Joe	S	177	5-11	So.	West Pittsburgh, PA
69	Andria, Ernie	OG	238	6-3	Fr.	Wintersville
61	*Applegate, Rick	C	250	6-3	Jr.	Cincinnati
59	*Ayers, Ron	OG	236	6-4	Jr.	Columbus
95	*Bargerstock, Doug	FB	244	6-2	So.	Taylor, MI
48	***Baschnagel, Brian	WB	192	6-0	Sr.	Pittsburgh, PA
67	*Beamon, Eddie	DT	246	6-2	So.	Cincinnati
92	Belko, Greg	LB	217	6-2	Fr.	Lakewood
81	Bell, Farley	DE	222	6-4	Fr.	Toledo
55	*Brown, Aaron	MG	224	6-2	So.	Warren
27	Brown, Richard	LB	208	6-2	Fr.	Columbus
84	*Brudzinski, Bob	DE	228	6-4	Jr.	Fremont
17	Bryant, Robin	DHB	170	6-0	Fr.	Columbus
75	**Buonamici, Nick	DT	242	6-3	Jr.	Brentwood, NY
76	Burke, Tim	OT	252	6-4	Fr.	Wapakoneta
23	**Cassady, Craig	DHB	176	6-0	Sr.	Columbus
71	Cato, Byron	DT	248	6-2	Fr.	Lorain
93	Coburn, Don	DE	195	6-1	Jr.	Wickliffe
36	Cousineau, Tom	LB	220	6-3	Fr.	Fairview Park
78	Cox, Garth	OT	238	6-5	So.	Wash. Court House
90	**Curto, Pat	DE	227	6-2	Sr.	Groveport
39	D'Amato, John	LB	219	6-3	So.	Staten Island, NY
73	***Dannelley, Scott	OT	252	6-3	Sr.	Williamsport, PA
37	Dansler, Kelton	DE	208	6-2	Fr.	Warren
50	Datish, Mike	C	235	6-3	Jr.	Warren
86	Dixon, Joe	DE	221	6-3	So.	Trenton, MI
52	Fisher, John	MG	211	6-2	Fr.	Dayton
12	***Fox, Tim	S	186	6-0	Sr.	Canton
28	Garcia, Joe	LB	222	6-0	Fr.	LaPalma, CA
32	Gentry, Bob	DHB	200	6-3	Jr.	Sandusky
8	Gerald, Rod	QB	174	6-1	Fr.	Dallas, TX
7	**Greene, Cornelius	QB	172	6-0	Sr.	Washington, D.C.
45	***Griffin, Archie	TB	182	5-9	Sr.	Columbus
46	Griffin, Duncan	DHB	184	5-11	Fr.	Columbus
44	*Griffin, Ray	S	177	5-9	So.	Columbus
18	Groom, Jeff	S	198	6-2	So.	Columbus
11	Harrell, Jim	WB	190	5-10	Jr.	Curtice
66	*Harris, Tyrone	DT	242	6-3	So.	Columbus
83	Hornik, Joe	DE	221	6-3	Fr.	North Olmsted
35	*Hyatt, Bob	WB	185	5-10	Jr.	Lagrange
13	Johnson, Barry	TB	181	6-0	Jr.	Columbus
33	**Johnson, Pete	FB	248	6-1	Jr.	Long Beach, NY
49	Jones, Herman	SE	200	6-3	So.	Miami, FL
90	Jones, Larry	LB	220	6-0	Jr.	Dayton
98	Jones, Paul	DE	200	6-2	So.	Dayton
85	**Kain, Larry	TE	232	6-2	Sr.	Dayton
6	*Klaban, Tom	PK	184	6-1	Sr.	Cincinnati
54	***Kuhn, Ken	LB	231	6-2	Sr.	Louisville
10	*Lang, Mark	MG	218	6-1	So.	Cincinnati
34	*Logan, Jeff	TB	184	5-10	So.	North Canton
64	*Lukens, Bill	OG	231	6-1	Jr.	Cincinnati
62	McEndree, Randy	C	230	5-11	Sr.	Cadiz
21	*Midlam, Max	DHB	190	5-10	Jr.	Marion
20	Mills, Leonard	DHB	182	6-3	Fr.	Miami, FL
68	O'Rourke, James	DT	243	6-3	So.	Brooklyn, NY
15	Pacenta, James	QB	190	6-3	Jr.	Akron
74	*Pietrini, Lou	OT	244	6-3	Sr.	Milford, CT
53	*Porter, Doug	C	228	6-2	So.	Youngstown
77	Rice, Dan	OT	223	6-3	Fr.	Cincinnati
41	**Roach, Woodrow	TB	182	5-9	Sr.	Washington, D.C.
26	*Roche, Tom	DHB	182	6-2	So.	Staten Island, NY
43	**Ruhl, Bruce	DHB	188	6-1	Jr.	Southfield, MI
57	*Savoca, Jim	OG	228	6-2	So.	Solon
1	**Skladany, Tom	PT	190	6-0	Jr.	Bethel Park, PA
60	**Smith, Ted	OG	242	6-1	Sr.	Gibsonburg
80	Storer, Greg	TE	218	6-5	So.	Cincinnati
72	Sullivan, Mark	DT	242	6-4	Fr.	New Bedford, MA
9	*Thompson, Ed	LB	220	6-1	Jr.	Waverly
38	Vogler, Tim	TE	212	6-3	Fr.	Covington
79	*Ward, Chris	OT	270	6-4	So.	Dayton
88	Weiland, Jeff	LB	230	6-0	Sr.	Englewood
4	*Williott, Lou	FB	225	6-1	Sr.	Youngstown
89	*Willis, Leonard	SE	184	6-0	Sr.	Washington, D.C.

* indicates letters won

ARCHIE GRIFFIN
All-American Back

TOM SKLADANY
All-American Punter

TIM FOX
All-American Back

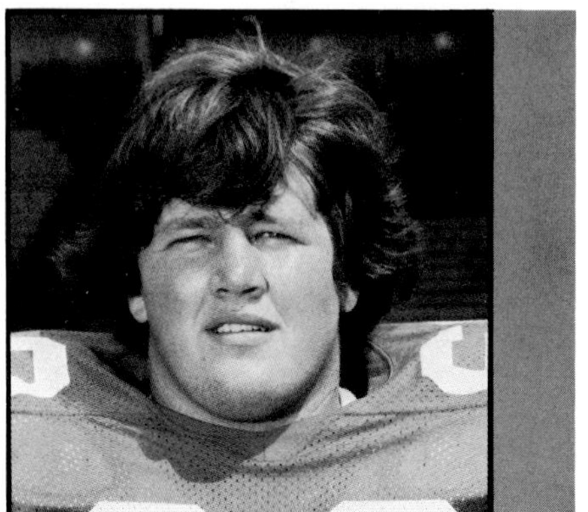

TED SMITH
All-American Guard

MICHIGAN

No.	Name	Pos.	Wt.	Hgt.	Class	Home Town
86	*Anderson, John	DE	215	6-3	So.	Waukesha, WI
66	Anderson, Steve	DT	230	6-2	So.	Toledo, OH
31	Andrews, Phil	FB	217	6-1	So.	Brooklyn, NY
61	Bartnick, Greg	OG	225	6-3	So.	Detroit
5	**Bell, Gordon	TB	178	5-9	Sr.	Troy, OH
12	Bettis, Roger	QB	185	6-3	So.	Minerva, OH
22	*Bolden, Jim	DB	177	6-1	Jr.	Akron, OH
45	Brown, Woody	S	175	5-11	So.	East Detroit
4	Brumbaugh, Phil	DB	160	5-9	Sr.	Greenville, OH
15	Bush, Ken	Wolf	200	5-11	So.	Canton, OH
14	Carian, Rob	QB	195	6-1	Jr.	Indio, CA
29	Collins, Jerry	SE	185	6-2	Sr.	Ann Arbor
34	*Corbin, Scott	FB	220	6-1	So.	Cincinnati, OH
52	**Czirr, Jim	C	225	6-3½	Sr.	St. Joseph
56	**Davis, Tim	MG	201	5-10	Sr.	Warren, OH
55	*Devich, Dave	LB	210	6-1	Sr.	Highland, IN
60	Donahue, Mark	OG	237	6-3½	So.	Oak Lawn, IL
72	Downing, Walt	OG	232	6-4	So.	Coatesville, PA
73	*Dufek, Bill	OT	255	6-4	So.	E. Grand Rapids
35	**Dufek, Don	Wolf	195	6-0	Sr.	E. Grand Rapids
16	*Elzinga, Mark	QB	190	6-2½	Jr.	Bay City
54	Graves, Steve	MG	217	6-1	So.	Cleveland, OH
53	Hackett, Jim	C	220	6-1	Jr.	London, OH
70	*Hall, Jim	OT	235	6-4	Jr.	Ypsilanti
83	Harding, Dave	TE	223	6-4	So.	Northville
71	*Hennessy, John	DT	235	6-4	Jr.	Chicago, IL
17	*Hicks, Dwight	S	180	6-2	So.	Pennsauken, NJ
93	**Hoban, Bill	DT	238	6-4	Sr.	Chicago, IL
40	*Holmes, Mike	DE	210	6-3	Sr.	Akron, OH
10	*Howard, Derek	DB	187	6-2	So.	Hamilton, OH
7	Jackson, Andy	DB	170	6-0	So.	Bowling Green, OH
51	**Jensen, Tom	OG	225	6-3	Sr.	Springfield, IL
81	**Jilek, Dan	DE	212	6-2	Sr.	Sterling Heights
27	**Johnson, Keith	SE	175	6-0	Sr.	Munster, IN
20	Johnson, Ray	S	177	6-0	So.	Gary, IN
21	*Kampe, Kurt	DB	182	5-11	Sr.	Defiance, OH
78	Kenn, Mike	OT	243	6-6½	So.	Evanston, IL
36	King, Kevin	FB	215	6-2	So.	Oak Lawn, IL
67	**King, Steve	OT	245	6-5	Sr.	Tiffin, OH
99	Knickerbocker, Steve	PK	180	6-1	So.	Chelsea
92	*Koschalk, Rick	MG	193	6-2	Sr.	Toledo, OH
62	*Lang, Bob	DT	230	6-1	Jr.	Chicago, IL
74	**Lewis, Kirk	OG	240	6-3½	Sr.	Garden City
41	*Lytle, Rob	FB	190	6-1	Jr.	Fremont, OH
49	Mackall, Rex	LB	215	6-4	So.	Berea, OH
49	Mandich, John	DB	184	6-1	So.	Grosse Pointe
63	Miles, Les	OG	225	6-1	Sr.	Elyria, OH
77	*Morton, Greg	DT	225	6-2	Jr.	Akron, OH
50	Nauta, Steve	C	227	6-2	So.	Norristown, PA
96	*O'Neal, Calvin	LB	230	6-2	Jr.	Saginaw
97	**Perlinger, Jeff	DT	242	6-4	Sr.	Crystal, MN
90	Phelps, Eric	DE	208	6-1	So.	Salem, NH
18	Pickens, Jim	S	188	6-2	So.	Sylvania, OH
80	**Przygodski, George	TE	215	6-3	Sr.	Grand Rapids
76	Randolph, Chuck	DT	227	6-3	Sr.	Amelia, OH
26	Richardson, Dennis	TB	182	5-11	So.	Lima, OH
43	*Richardson, Max	WB	187	6-1	So.	Ft. Wayne, IN
37	**Smith, Jim	WB	198	6-3½	Jr.	Blue Island, IL
44	Smith, Mike	TB	175	5-8	So.	Kalamazoo
58	Stefan, Terry	C	210	6-0	Jr.	Parma, OH
85	Stephenson, Curt	SE	170	6-1	Jr.	LaJolia, CA
42	Strabley, Mike	LB	218	6-0	Jr.	Massillon, OH
94	Strinko, Greg	DE	213	6-3	Sr.	Middletown, OH
57	Szafranski, Roger	MG	193	5-11	Jr.	Bay City
69	Szara, Gerry	OG	250	6-2	So.	Oak Lawn, IL
99	Tedesco, Dominic	DE	210	6-4	So.	Riverside, IL
19	Truitt, Darrell	WB	190	6-0	Jr.	Cincinnati, OH
39	*Vogele, Jerry	LB	235	6-3	Jr.	Cincinnati, OH
84	White, Rick	SE	195	6-5	Jr.	Cincinnati, OH
1	Whiteford, Dave	S	185	6-1	Jr.	Traverse City
3	Wood, Bob	PK	170	5-8	Jr.	London, OH
8	*Zuver, Jerry	Wolf	195	6-2	Jr.	Archbold, OH

* indicates letters won

1975

Michigan	23	Wisconsin	6
Michigan	19	Stanford	19
Michigan	14	Baylor	14
Michigan	31	Missouri	7
Michigan	16	Michigan State	6
Michigan	69	Northwestern	0
Michigan	55	Indiana	7
Michigan	28	Minnesota	21
Michigan	28	Purdue	0
Michigan	21	Illinois	15
Michigan	14	Ohio State	21

Season Summary

Games won, 8; Lost, 1; Tied, 2

DON DUFEK
All-American Back

GO
M CLUB S

November 20, 1976

Columbus, Ohio

Michigan Pounds Ohio State, 22 To 0

Second-Half Uprising Gives UM Big Ten Title, Trip To Rose Bowl

The Wolverines claimed a share of the Big Ten title with the Buckeyes, earned the right to make their first trip to the Rose Bowl in five years, kept OSU from setting a conference record for consecutive wins, and in no small measure found vindication for the near-misses which seemed to haunt this team's visits to Ohio Stadium.

A record Ohio State crowd of 88,250 squirmed as the best in the midwest counterpunched through their kicking games during a 0-0 first half. The Wolverines came out storming after the half and marched 80 yards for the game's first touchdown, running the ball on every play. Davis made the final three yards and Wood kicked for a 7-0 lead. Michigan smothered Ohio's drive and then drove down the field to score again with Davis again doing the honors with a three yard plunge. Jerry Zuver – the nominal holder – scurried in for two extra points on a fake conversion and a 15-0 advantage for UM.

What was to be Ohio State's last bid to avoid its first shutout in Columbus since 1964 ended when Jeff Logan fumbled a pitchout which was recovered at the Michigan 42 by the Wolverines' Steve Graves. After an exchange of interceptions, one by OSU's Tom Roche and the other by Michigan's Jerry Zuver, the Wolverines crunched their way for another TD with Lytle nosediving his way in for the score. Bob Wood's kick made it 22-0 with 8:13 to play. However, for all practical purposes the game was over.

STATISTICS

	UM	OSU
First Downs	23	10
Rushes-Yards	71-366	37-104
Passing Yards	0	69
Return Yards	104	18
Passes	0-6-1	5-14-2
Punts	5-41	8-52
Fumbles-Lost	1-0	1-1
Penalties-Yards	2-10	2-9

Michigan	0	0	15	7	22
Ohio State	0	0	0	0	0

1976

1976

Michigan	40	Wisconsin	27
Michigan	51	Stanford	0
Michigan	70	Navy	14
Michigan	31	Wake Forest	0
Michigan	42	MSU	10
Michigan	38	Northwestern	7
Michigan	35	Indiana	0
Michigan	45	Minnesota	0
Michigan	14	Purdue	16
Michigan	38	Illinois	7
Michigan	22	Ohio State	0

Season Summary

Games Won, 10; Lost, 1

ROB LYTLE
All-American Halfback

MARK DONAHUE
All-American Guard

CALVIN O'NEAL
All-American Linebacker

MICHIGAN

No.	Name	Pos.	Wt.	Hgt.	Class
86	**Anderson, John	E	208	6-3	Jr.
66	Anderson, Steve	G	225	6-2	Jr.
31	Andrews, Phil	FB	217	6-1	Jr.
64	Arbeznik, John	G	230	6-4	So.
61	Bartnick, Greg	G	235	6-3	Jr.
12	Bettis, Roger	QB	185	6-3	Jr.
22	**Bolden, Jim	B	177	6-1	Sr.
28	Braman, Mark	B	190	6-2	So.
45	Brown, Woody	S	175	5-11	Jr.
13	Ceddia, John	QB	185	6-0	Jr.
33	*Davis, Russell	FB	215	6-2	So.
92	DeSantis, Mark	E	212	6-4	So.
60	*Donahue, Mark	G	245	6-3½	Jr.
72	*Downing, Walt	C	250	6-4	Jr.
73	**Dufek, Bill	T	250	6-4	Jr.
68	Giesler, Jon	E	265	6-4	So.
54	Graves, Steve	G	217	6-1	So.
95	Greer, Curtis	T	220	6-4	So.
2	Grieves, Chris	PK	155	6-0	So.
53	Hackett, Jim	C	220	6-1	Sr.
83	Harding, Dave	E	223	6-4	Jr.
71	**Hennessy, John	T	235	6-4	Sr.
17	**Hicks, Dwight	S	180	6-2	Jr.
94	Hollway, Bob	E	200	6-3	So.
10	**Howard, Derek	Wolf	187	6-2	Jr.
25	*Huckleby, Harlan	B	195	6-1½	So.
93	Jackson, William	T	230	6-4	So.
88	*Johnson, Gene	E	220	6-4	So.
20	Johnson, Ray	S	177	6-0	Jr.
9	Johnson, Stacy	QB	185	6-2	So.
51	Kadela, Dave	T	235	6-2	So.
55	Keitz, Dale	G	230	6-2	So.
78	*Kenn, Mike	T	245	6-6½	Jr.
36	King, Kevin	FB	215	6-2	Jr.
19	Labun, Nick	PK	172	5-11	Jr.
62	**Lang, Bob	G	230	6-1	Sr.
7	*Leach, Rick	QB	180	6-1	So.
74	**Lewis, Kirk	G	235	6-3½	Sr.
63	Lindsay, Rock	G	230	6-1	So.
41	**Lytle, Rob	B	195	6-1	Sr.
49	*Mackall, Rex	B	215	6-4	Jr.
45	Malinak, Tim	B	215	6-1	So.
38	Melita, Tom	G	211	6-1½	So.
46	Meter, Jerry	B	205	6-3	So.
77	**Morton, Greg	T	225	6-2	Sr.
50	*Nauta, Steve	C	227	6-2	Jr.
96	**O'Neal, Calvin	B	230	6-2	Sr.
24	Patek, Bob	Wolf	190	6-2	So.
89	Pederson, Chip	E	222	6-5½	So.
90	*Phelps, Eric	E	208	6-1	Jr.
18	*Pickens, Jim	B	188	6-2	Jr.
43	**Richardson, Max	B	187	6-1	Jr.
82	*Schmerge, Mark	E	235	6-3	So.
91	*Seabron, Tom	E	212	6-3½	So.
37	***Smith, Jim	B	195	6-3	Sr.
99	Smith, Lewis	T	235	6-4	So.
44	Smith, Mike	B	175	5-8	Jr.
85	*Stephenson, Curt	E	175	6-1	Jr.
57	Szafranski, Roger	G	210	5-11	Sr.
69	*Szara, Gerry	G	240	6-2	Jr.
99	Tedesco, Dom	E	210	6-4	Jr.
79	Torzy, Mark	T	240	6-4	So.
39	**Vogele, Jerry	B	235	6-3	Sr.
84	White, Rick	E	205	6-5	Jr.
65	Williams, Kyron	G	205	6-1	So.
1	Willner, Gregg	PK	145	5-10	So.
3	*Wood, Bob	PK	170	5-8	Sr.
21	Woodford, Tony	B	170	5-9	So.
8	**Zuver, Jerry	Wolf	195	6-2	Sr.

* indicates letters won

JIM SMITH
All-American End

OHIO

No.	Name	Pos.	Wt.	Hgt.	Class	Home Town
94	*Adkins, D.	B	214	6-2	Jr.	Xenia
22	*Allegro, J.	S	176	5-11	Jr.	W. Pittsburgh, PA
69	*Andria, E.	G	240	6-3	So.	Wintersville
19	Archer, S.	B	191	6-0	So.	Toledo
59	*Ayers, R.	C	234	6-4	Sr.	Columbus
82	Barwig, R.	E	238	6-8	Fr.	Willoughby Hills
67	*Beamon, E.	T	254	6-2	Jr.	Cincinnati
81	*Bell, F.	E	228	6-4	So.	Toledo
29	Blinco, T.	B	225	6-2	Fr.	Lewiston, NY
55	*Brown, A.	G	228	6-2	Jr.	Warren
27	Brown, R.	B	205	6-2	So.	Columbus
84	*Brudzinski, R.	E	224	6-4	Sr.	Fremont
3	Budd, D.	P	172	6-1	Fr.	Chester, NJ
75	*Buonamici, N.	T	242	6-3	Sr.	Brentwood, NY
76	Burke, T.	T	252	6-4	So.	Wapakoneta
63	Burris, S.	T	244	6-3	Fr.	Point Pleasant, WV
38	Campbell, P.	FB	218	6-1	Fr.	Ravenna
41	Caruso, J.	HB	196	6-0	Fr.	Wappingers Falls, NY
7	Castignola, G.	QB	181	6-2	Fr.	Trenton, MI
71	*Cato, B.	G	234	6-2	So.	Lorain
93	Coburn, D.	G	195	6-1	Sr.	Wickliffe
36	*Cousineau, T.	B	224	6-3	So.	Fairview Park
78	Cox, G	T	248	6-4	Jr.	Washington Court House
88	Cox,M.	E	192	6-0	Fr.	London
96	Cusick, M.	E	214	6-2	Jr.	Lakewood
93	Dailey, J.	PK	190	5-9	Jr.	Waverly
32	*Dansler, K.	E	205	6-2	So.	Warren
50	Datish, M.	C	235	6-3	Sr.	Warren
85	Diefenthaler, D.	T	255	6-2	Fr.	Curtice
86	*Dixon, J.	E	221	6-3	Jr.	Trenton, MI
60	Dulin, G.	G	250	6-5	Fr.	Madisonville, KY
28	Durtschi, H.	HB	190	5-9	Jr.	Galion
89	Ferguson, B.	E	172	6-0	Fr.	Troy
4	Ferrelli, J.	HB	181	5-10	Jr.	Columbus
56	Fritz, K.	G	232	6-3	Fr.	Ironton
8	*Gerald, R.	QB	173	6-1	So.	Dallas, TX
42	Gordon, L.	B	192	6-1	So.	New Rochelle, NY
46	*Griffin, D.	S	186	5-11	So.	Columbus
44	*Griffin, R.	S	179	5-9	Jr.	Columbus
12	Guess, M.	S	173	5-11	Fr.	Columbus
54	Hall, D.	G	230	6-3	Fr.	Uniontown, PA
77	Hamilton, W.	G	242	6-2	Fr.	Massillon
11	*Harrell, J.	B	186	5-10	Sr.	Curtice
66	*Harris, T.	T	246	6-3	Jr.	Columbus
95	Heilman, P.	E	218	6-2	Sr.	Defiance
83	*Hornik, J.	E	219	6-3	S.	N. Olmsted
24	Hunter, C.	FB	212	6-2	Fr.	Newark, DE
35	*Hyatt, R.	E	175	5-10	Sr.	Lagrange
87	Jaco, W.	E	247	6-5	So.	Toledo
33	*Johnson, P.	FB	247	6-1	Sr.	Long Beach, NY
48	Johnson, R.	B	194	6-0	Fr.	Santa Maria, CA
49	*Jones, H.	E	200	6-3	Jr.	Miami, FL
98	Kellum, W.	T	212	5-8	So.	Columbus
51	*Lang, M.	C	220	6-1	Jr.	Cincinnati
92	Laser, J.	G	232	6-2	So.	Akron
5	Laughlin, J.	FB	208	6-2	Fr.	Lyndhurst
91	Lillie, R.	E	223	6-3	Jr.	Dayton
34	*Logan, J.	B	182	5-10	Jr.	North Canton
64	*Lukens, W.	G	233	6-1	Sr.	Cincinnati
73	Mackie, D.	T	250	6-4	Fr.	Saugus, MA
21	*Midlam, M.	HB	192	5-10	Sr.	Marion
62	Mills, E.	T	250	6-7	Fr.	Columbus
20	*Mills, L.	HB	190	6-3	So.	Miami, FL
2	Mollis, L.	FB	186	6-0	Sr.	Parma Heights
99	*Moore, J.	E	258	6-5	So.	Tempe, AZ
15	*Pacenta, J.	QB	190	6-3	Sr.	Akron
74	*Pietrini, L.	T	248	6-3	Sr.	Milford, CT
53	*Porter, D.	C	232	6-2	Jr.	Youngstown
65	Renard, B.	G	218	6-3	Sr.	Maumee
90	Robinson, J.	E	225	6-5	So.	Paulding
26	*Roche, T.	HB	190	6-2	Jr.	Staten Island, NY
16	Ross, P.	B	224	6-1	So.	Fort Valley, GA
43	Ruhl, B.	HB	187	6-1	Sr.	Southfield, MI
10	Saunders, J.	HB	185	6-0	Jr.	New Brighton, PA
57	*Savoca, J.	G	228	6-2	Jr.	Solon
68	Sawicki, T.	G	206	6-0	Fr.	Mayfield
37	Schneider, M.	FB	205	6-2	Fr.	Cincinnati
14	Schwartz, B.	HB	188	6-1	Fr.	Simi Valley, CA
17	Scudder, A.	B	190	5-11	So.	Dayton
30	*Simon, C.	B	222	6-2	Jr.	Dublin
1	*Skladany, T.	P	192	6-0	Sr.	Bethel Park, LA
23	Springs, R.	B	196	6-2	So.	Williamsburg, VA
80	*Storer, G	E	224	6-5	Jr.	Cincinnati
39	Stover, A.	HB	190	6-2	So.	Cleveland Heights
6	Strahine, M.	QB	186	6-0	Fr.	Lakewood
72	*Sullivan, M.	T	245	6-4	So.	New Bedford, MA
9	*Thompson, E.	B	221	6-1	Sr.	Waverly
97	Vogler, T.	E	207	6-2	So.	Covington
85	Vogler, T	E	232	6-3	So.	Covington
18	Volley, R.	B	210	6-0	Fr.	Lynchburg, VA
79	*Ward, C.	T	278	6-4	Jr.	Dayton
58	Waugh, T.	G	242	6-1	So.	Norwalk
25	Wolorey, S.	S	170	5-10	Sr.	Delphos
13	Wolfe, C.	B	200	5-10	Sr.	Junction City
61	Wymer, D.	T	240	6-3	Fr.	Findlay
47	Jackson, M.	B	210	6-3	Fr.	Fort Valley, GA

* indicates letters won

1976

Ohio	49	MSU	21
Ohio	12	Penn State	7
Ohio	21	Missouri	22
Ohio	10	U.C.L.A.	10
Ohio	34	Iowa	14
Ohio	30	Wisconsin	20
Ohio	24	Purdue	3
Ohio	47	Indiana	7
Ohio	42	Illinois	10
Ohio	9	Minnesota	3
Ohio	0	Michigan	22

Season Summary

Games Won, 8; Lost, 2; Tied, 1

BOB BRUDZINSKI
All-American End

CHRIS WARD
All-American Tackle

TOM SKLADANY
All-American Punter

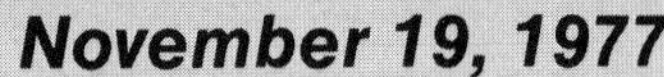

November 19, 1977

Ann Arbor, Michigan

Michigan Beats Ohio State 14-6 For Trip To Rose Bowl

Bucks Win Statistics Battle But Lose Game

A national TV audience enjoyed the annual raucous battle between the Wolverines of the University of Michigan and the Buckeyes of Ohio State University. Bo Schembechler in his ninth matchup with OSU commented, "I've been down there (Columbus) when we got all the statistics and they got all the points. Now this one time, we got the points. That's what this game is all about." Woody Hayes said afterwards, "This was by far the best game we ever played and lost."

Seven times the Buckeyes drove deeply towards the Michigan goal line—five times inside the 15—and each time the Wolverine defense stiffened and stopped them cold.

Ohio State marched the opening kickoff to the UM 12 where the Michigan defense held. Vlade Janakievski came on to boot a 29-yard field goal to give the Bucks a 3-0 advantage. After stopping the Michigan offense on their first series, OSU moved the ball to the Michigan 8 where junior quarterback Rod Gerald was sacked for nine-yard loss. Later Janakievski attempted a 42-yard field goal but misssed.

If the first quarter belonged to the Buckeyes, the second quarter should have been colored Maize and Blue as Michigan dominated. Michigan drove to the OSU 30 in the second quarter, missed a field goal, then came back to march 46 yards for a TD. Rick Leach's third-down-and-eleven pass to Ralph Clayton for 22 yards was the key play. Roosevelt Smith scored from the one and Willner added the PAT to give Michigan the half time lead 7-3.

The Wolverine's inital second half drive fizzled and the Buckeyes took the punt on their own 16. On the next play junior tailback Rod Springs fumbled on the OSU 20 and Michigan's Ron Simpkins recovered. Four plays later UM's quarterback Rick Leach dove in from the three. Again Willner converted the PAT and Michigan led 14-3.

OSU came right back and had a first down on the Michigan 11, but Mike Jolly hit Jeff Logan for a yard loss, Simpkins sacked Gerald for 13, and Janakievski booted a 44-yard field goal resulting in a 14-6 score.

The fourth quarter saw OSU make several drives to score but each time Michigan rose to the occasion and would not let the Buckeyes score. With little time remaining OSU moved to the UM 8. Then on first and goal, Gerald fumbled and the Wolverines recovered. The fumble visibly shook Woody Hayes and he vented this frustration by swinging at an ABC-TV cameraman photographing him.

STATISTICS

	UM	OSU
First Downs	10	23
Net Yards Rushing	152	258
Net Yards Passing	55	144
Att-Com-Inter	13-9-0	16-13-0
Total Net Yards	207	402
Punts-Yards-Blocked	6-40-0	2-39-0
Fumbles-Lost	1-1	4-2
Penalties-Yards	1-5	1-5

UM	0	7	7	0	14
OSU	3	0	3	0	6

1977			
Ohio	10	Miami (FL)	0
Ohio	38	Minnesota	7
Ohio	28	Oklahoma	29
Ohio	35	S. Methodist	7
Ohio	46	Purdue	0
Ohio	27	Iowa	6
Ohio	35	Northwestern	15
Ohio	42	Wisconsin	0
Ohio	35	Illinois	0
Ohio	35	Indiana	7
Ohio	6	Michigan	14

Season Summary

Games Won, 9; Lost, 2

OHIO

No.	Name	Pos.	Wt.	Hgt.	Class	Home Town
94	***Adkins, David	B	213	6-2	Sr.	Xenia
22	**Allegro, Joseph	S	182	5-11	Sr.	West Pittsburgh, PA
69	*Andria, Ernest	G	238	6-3	Jr.	Wintersville
93	Bach, Terry	G	205	5-11	Fr.	Centerville
82	Barwig, Ronald	E	242	6-8	So.	Willoughby Hills
67	***Beamon, Eddie	T	265	6-2	Sr.	Cincinnati
25	Bell, Todd	B	194	6-0	Fr.	Middletown
29	*Blinco, Thomas	B	219	6-2	So.	Lewiston, NY
55	***Brown, Aaron	G	232	6-2	Sr.	Warren
76	Burke, Tim	T	245	6-4	Jr.	Wapakoneta
38	*Campbell, Paul	FB	212	6-1	So.	Ravenna
71	**Cato, Byron	T	238	6-2	Jr.	Lorain
36	**Cousineau, Thomas	B	227	6-3	Jr.	Fairview Park
78	*Cox, Garth	T	246	6-4	Sr.	Washington Ct. House
32	**Dansler, Kelton	E	208	6-2	Jr.	Warren
50	DeLeone, James	C	217	5-11	Fr.	Kent
86	**Dixon, Joseph	E	224	6-3	Sr.	Trenton, MI
47	Donley, Douglas	L	170	6-1	Fr.	Cambridge
60	*Dulin, Gary	T	254	6-4	So.	Madisonville, KY
27	Ellis, Ray	B	192	6-2	Fr.	Canton
39	Ellison, Leon	B	200	6-2	Fr.	Washington, DC
59	Epitropoulos, Ernest	G	212	6-2	Fr.	Warren
33	Epitropoulos, John	B	212	6-1	Fr.	Warren
65	Ferguson, Keith	T	232	6-5	Fr.	Miami, FL
56	*Fritz, Kenneth	G	234	6-3	So.	Ironton
8	**Gerald, Roderic	QB	174	6-1	Jr.	Dallas, TX
46	**Griffin, Duncan	S	188	5-11	Jr.	Columbus
44	***Griffin, Raymond	S	182	5-9	Jr.	Columbus
12	*Guess, Michael	B	175	5-11	So.	Columbus
11	**Harrell, James	B	166	5-10	Sr.	Curtice
66	**Harris, Tyrone	T	244	6-3	Sr.	Columbus
54	Henson, Luther	T	238	6-2	Fr.	Sandusky
83	**Hornik, Joseph	E	226	6-3	Jr.	North Olmsted
89	Hunter, Charles	E	217	6-2	So.	Newark, DE
87	*Jaco, William	E	248	6-5	Jr.	Toledo
13	Janakievski, Vlade	PK	151	5-8	So.	Columbus
21	Johnson, Ricky	B	188	6-0	So.	Santa Maria, CA
49	**Jones, Herman	L	209	6-3	Sr.	Miami, FL
51	***Lang, Mark	G	220	6-1	Sr.	Cincinnati
5	Laughlin, James	E	210	6-2	So.	Lyndhurst
35	Lee, Felix	FB	227	6-1	Fr.	Highland Park, NJ
34	***Logan, Jeff	B	184	5-10	Sr.	North Canton
73	*Mackie, Douglas	T	250	6-4	So.	Saugus, MA
1	McKee, David	P	180	6-2	Jr.	Columbus
61	Medich, David	G	232	6-2	Fr.	Steubenville
90	Megaro, Anthony	B	224	6-2	Fr.	Chicago, IL
64	Miller, Nicholas	G	224	6-3	Fr.	Upland, PA
91	Miller, Ronald	E	210	6-3	Fr.	Auburn, NY
62	Mills, Ed	T	268	6-7	So.	Columbus
20	**Mills, Leonard	B	186	6-3	Jr.	Miami, FL
99	**Moore, Jimmy	E	248	6-5	Jr.	Tempe, AZ
28	Murphy, Robert	B	188	6-1	Fr.	Santa Ynez, CA
43	Murray, Calvin	B	175	5-11	Fr.	Woodbine, NJ
19	Orosz, Thomas	PK	203	6-1	Fr.	Fairport Harbor
30	Payton, Joel	FB	222	6-2	Fr.	Mentor
53	***Porter, Douglas	C	228	6-2	Sr.	Youngstown
70	*Robinson, Joseph	T	256	6-5	Jr.	Paulding
26	Roche, Tom	B	190	6-2	Sr.	Staten Island, NY
16	*Ross, Paul	E	232	6-1	Jr.	Fort Valley, GA
57	***Savoca, James	G	233	6-2	Sr.	Solon
37	Schneider, Michael	FB	210	6-2	So.	Cincinnati
14	*Schwartz, Brian	S	190	6-1	So.	Simi Valley, CA
48	Skillings, Vincent	B	168	6-0	Fr.	Brenizer, PA
23	*Springs, Ronald	B	196	6-2	Jr.	Williamsburg, VA
80	**Storer, Gregory	E	208	6-5	Sr.	Cincinnati
6	Strahine, Michael	QB	192	6-0	So.	Lakewood
72	**Sullivan, Mark	T	234	6-4	Jr.	New Bedford, MA
9	Taylor, Alvin	QB	177	6-0	So.	Newport News, VA
97	Vogler, Terry	B	214	6-2	Jr.	Covington
52	*Vogler, Tim	C	228	6-3	Jr.	Covington
18	Volley, Ricardo	B	206	6-0	So.	Lynchburg, VA
79	***Ward, Christopher	T	272	6-4	Sr.	Dayton
15	Washington, Alvin	B	232	6-3	Fr.	Cleveland
58	Waugh, Thomas	G	242	6-1	Jr.	Norwalk

* indicates letters won

CHRIS WARD
All-American Tackle

AARON BROWN
All-American Guard

TOM COUSINEAU
All-American Linebacker

RAY GRIFFIN
All-American Back

MICHIGAN

No.	Name	Pos.	Wt.	Hgt.	Class	Home Town
21	Allen, Jay	FB	202	6-0	So.	McDonald, PA
86	***Anderson, John	B	219	6-3	Sr.	Waukesha, WI
58	Angood, David	C	229	6-5	So.	Battle Creek
64	Arbeznik, John	G	237	6-3	Jr.	University Heights, OH
61	*Bartnick, Greg	G	233	6-2	Jr.	Detroit
48	Bednarek, Jeff	B	237	6-4	So.	Trenton
42	Bell, Gene	Wolf	196	6-2	So.	East Liverpool, OH
12	Bettis, Roger	QB	190	6-2	Sr.	Minerva, OH
28	Braman, Mark	HB	192	6-1	Jr.	Midland
45	Brown, Woody	S	175	5-10	Sr.	East Detroit
22	Clayton, Ralph	B	211	6-3	So.	Detroit
35	Davis, Michael	FB	226	6-1	So.	Woodbridge, VA
33	**Davis, Russell	FB	220	6-1	Jr.	Woodbridge, VA
92	*DeSantis, Mark	B	215	6-3	Jr.	Harper Woods
29	Diggs, Gerald	B	186	6-0	So.	Chicago, IL
60	Donahue, Mark	G	245	6-3	Sr.	Oak Lawn, IL
72	**Downing, Walt	C	254	6-4	Sr.	Coatesville, PA
14	Gaudette, Roger	HB	186	5-11	So.	Riverview
51	Gilmore, Keith	B	204	6-1	So.	Highland Park
90	Godfrey, Chris	T	239	6-4	So.	Miami Lakes, FL
54	*Graves, Steve	G	218	6-1	Sr.	Cleveland, OH
95	*Greer, Curtis	T	237	6-4	Jr.	Detroit
4	Harden, Michael	HB	179	6-1	So.	Detroit
83	Harding, Dave	B	226	6-3	Sr.	Northville
17	***Hicks, Dwight	Wolf	180	6-1	Sr.	Pennsauken, NJ
94	Hollway, Bob	B	214	6-3	Jr.	W. Bloomfield
10	***Howard, Derek	Wolf	193	6-1	Sr.	Hamilton, OH
25	**Huckleby, Harlan	B	199	6-1½	Jr.	Detroit
93	*Jackson, William	T	226	6-3	Jr.	Richmond, VA
88	**Johnson, Gene	E	227	6-3	Jr.	Flint
15	Johnson, Irvin	B	200	6-2	So.	Warren, OH
9	*Johnson, Stacy	QB	186	6-1	Jr.	Camden, NJ
16	*Jolly, Michael	HB	178	6-3	So.	Melvindale
96	Jones, Larry	G	205	5-10	So.	Port Huron
51	Kadela, Dave	T	236	6-2	Jr.	Dearborn
81	Kasparek, Ed	WR	180	6-1	Jr.	Dearborn
55	Keitz, Dale	T	240	6-1	Jr.	Columbus, OH
94	Keller, Tom	B	203	6-2	So.	Grand Rapids
78	**Kenn, Mike	T	244	6-6½	Sr.	Evanston, IL
36	*King, Kevin	FB	212	6-2	Sr.	Oak Lawn, IL
6	Kozlowski, Jim	HB	180	5-11	So.	Detroit
3	Labun, Nick	PK	172	5-11	Sr.	Rockford, IL
7	**Leach, Rick	QB	192	6-1	Jr.	Flint
78	Leoni, Mike	T	255	6-3	So.	Flint
34	Leoni, Tony	Wolf	194	5-10	So.	Flint
59	Lilja, George	C	239	6-4	So.	Palos Park, IL
63	Lindsay, Rock	T	235	6-2	Jr.	Lapeer
45	Malinak, Tim	B	222	6-1	Jr.	Flemington, PA
80	Marsh, Doug	E	229	6-3	So.	Akron, OH
38	Melita, Tom	G	224	6-1	Jr.	Penns Grove, NJ
46	*Meter, Jerry	B	206	6-3	Jr.	Birmingham
27	Murray, Dan	Wolf	194	6-0	So.	Ann Arbor
56	Novak, Richard	T	244	6-5	So.	Calumet City, IL
53	Owens, Mel	B	222	6-2	So.	DeKalb, IL
31	Page, Craig	B	191	6-1	Jr.	Saginaw
93	Payne, David	B	196	6-1	So.	Detroit
18	**Pickens, Jim	HB	182	6-0	Sr.	Sylvania, OH
67	Powers, John	T	261	6-3	So.	Oak Park, IL
57	Pratl, Ron	B	206	6-3	So.	Oak Lawn, IL
70	Quinn, Gary	T	242	6-3	So.	Quincy, MA
23	Reid, Lawrence	FB	206	6-1	So.	Philadelphia, PA
43	***Richardson, Max	B	187	6-0	Sr.	Fort Wayne, IN
82	*Schmerge, Mark	E	229	6-3	Jr.	Cincinnati, OH
91	**Seabron, Tom	B	208	6-3	Jr.	Detroit
40	*Simpkins, Ron	B	221	6-1	So.	Detroit
44	Smith, Mike	B	170	5-10	Sr.	Kalamazoo
26	Smith, Roosevelt	B	198	5-10	So.	Detroit
85	**Stephenson, Curt	WR	177	6-1	Sr.	LaJolla, CA
69	**Szara, Gerry	G	240	6-1	Sr.	Oak Lawn, IL
99	*Tedesco, Dominic	B	212	6-4	Sr.	Riverside, IL
79	Torzy, Mark	T	241	6-4	Jr.	Warren
5	Wangler, John	QB	189	6-2	So.	Royal Oak
62	Weber, Gary	T	241	6-2	So.	Matawan, NJ
84	*White, Rick	WR	200	6-4	Sr.	Cincinnati, OH
3	Williams, Derek	HB	156	6-0	So.	Detroit
19	Williams, Virgil	B	185	5-10	So.	Lorain, OH
1	Willner, Gregg	PK	156	5-10	Jr.	Miami Beach, FL

* indicates letters won

1977

Michigan	37	Illinois	9
Michigan	21	Duke	9
Michigan	14	Navy	7
Michigan	41	Texas A & M	3
Michigan	24	MSU	14
Michigan	56	Wisconsin	0
Michigan	0	Minnesota	16
Michigan	23	Iowa	6
Michigan	63	Northwestern	20
Michigan	40	Purdue	7
Michigan	14	Ohio State	6

Season Summary

Games Won, 10; Lost, 1

WALT DOWNING
All-American Center

JOHN ANDERSON
All-American Linebacker

November 25, 1978

Columbus, Ohio

University Of Michigan Whips Ohio State, 14-3

Rick Leach Leads Wolves To Third Straight Win Over Bucks

The 75th game in the rivalry between Ohio State and Michigan again determined who would represent the Big Ten Conference in the Rose Bowl against the Trojans of USC. Both teams came into the game with one conference defeat, Michigan lost to Michigan State and Ohio State was defeated by Purdue. The Wolverines were favored mainly because of the stellar abilities of quarterback Rick Leach. The left-handed thrower was slowed throughout the game by a leg injury, but his passing made all the difference as he threw two touchdown passes and barely missed a third. The 88,358 fans had to be impressed with the leadership of perhaps the greatest quarterback Michigan has ever had.

Michigan won the toss and elected to receive. After moving for one first down, the Wolverines punted to Ohio State who started from their own 25 yard line. OSU used an effective ground attack which finally stalled out on the Michigan 21 where Bob Atha attempted a 38-yard field goal. It was wide left. OSU then held Michigan to nine yards in three attempts. The Bucks returned the ball to the UM 49. In five plays OSU had advanced the ball to Michigan's 19 where the drive was halted as much by the slippery turf as it was by the Michigan defense. Once again Bob Atha attempted a field goal which was good for the only points Ohio State would be able to muster for the entire afternoon.

After the ensuing kickoff Michign's Leach went to work through the air. A 26-yard pass from Leach to Marsh started things off. He then hit Woolfolk for 14, and finally crossed the goal line on a 30-yard strike to Feaster. With 9 seconds left in the first quarter, Michigan led 7-3.

The second quarter resulted in five punts and two fumbles, one by each team. Just before the half Michigan threatened. Starting from their own 32, the Wolverines drove relentlessly downfield. With time running out Leach drilled tight end Gene Johnson at the two-yard line. He was stripped of the ball by OSU's Vince Skillings who recovered the ball for Ohio State in the end zone to end the threat. The half time score was 7-3, Michigan.

In the third period Michigan tuned its ground game without the use of Leach on the option play because of his leg injury. Short gains up the middle plus two key passes, one to Marsh for 13 and the other to fullback Lawrence Reid for 11 yards, brought UM to Ohio State's 11 yard line. Leach then rolled left, spotted R. Smith in the clear at the five, and lobbed the ball to him for the score. Willner added the PAT as he had done after the first touchdown and the Wolverines led 14 to 3.

The rest of the game belonged to the Michigan defense which held the Buckeyes to only 34 yards on the ground in the second half. OSU's star freshman quarterback Art Schlichter could not mount anything through the air. Rod Gerald was sent in as quarterback late in the game, but the Michigan defense had the Buckeyes bottled-up deep in their own territory. The game ended with Michigan the winner, 14-3.

STATISTICS

	UM	OSU
First Downs	21	11
Rushes-Yards	58-198	51-168
Passing Yards	166	48
Return Yards	12	29
Passes	11-22-0	5-10-1
Punts	7-35	6-43
Fumbles-Lost	1-1	1-1
Penalties-Yards	3-16	5-35

1978

MICHIGAN

1978

Michigan	31	Illinois	0
Michigan	28	Notre Dame	14
Michigan	52	Duke	0
Michigan	21	Arizona	17
Michigan	15	MSU	24
Michigan	42	Wisconsin	0
Michigan	42	Minnesota	10
Michigan	34	Iowa	0
Michigan	59	Northwestern	14
Michigan	24	Purdue	6
Michigan	14	Ohio State	3

Season Summary

Games Won, 10; Lost, 1

RICK LEACH
All-American Quarterback

No.	Name	Pos.	Wt.	Hgt.	Home Town
64	*Arbeznik, John	OG-C	237	6-3	University Heights, OH
61	**Bartnick, Greg	OG	238	6-2	Detroit
65	Becker, Kurt	OG	230	6-5	Aurora, IL
28	*Braman, Mark	DHB	195	6-1	Midland
8	Breaugh, Jim	QB	188	6-2	West Bloomfield
41	Cannavino, Andy	ILB	205	6-1	Cleveland, OH
85	Christian, Chuck	TE	203	6-3½	Detroit
22	*Clayton, Ralph	WB	211	6-3	Detroit
35	Davis, Michael	FB	226	6-1	Woodbridge, VA
33	***Davis, Russell	FB	215	6-1	Woodbridge, VA
92	**DeSantis, Mark	OLB	215	6-3½	Harper Woods
10	*Dickey, B. J.	QB	185	6-0	Ottawa, OH
29	Diggs, Gerald	DB	186	6-0	Chicago, IL
73	***Dufek, Bill	OT	263	6-4	East Grand Rapids
32	*Edwards, Stanley	TB	191	6-0	Detroit
18	Feaster, Rodney	WR	182	6-1	Flint
14	Gaudette, Roger	DHB	186	5-11	Riverview
68	**Giesler, Jon	OT	253	6-4½	Woodville, OH
90	*Godfrey, Chris	DT	242	6-4	Lathrup Village
95	**Greer, Curtis	DT	222	6-4	Detroit
4	*Harden, Michael	DHB	179	6-1	Detroit
31	Harris, Stuart	DB	184	6-2	Chagrin Falls, OH
75	Hetts, Chuck	OG	246	6-4	Taylor
94	Hollway, Bob	OLB	208	6-2	West Bloomfield
25	***Huckleby, Harlan	TB	199	6-1½	Detroit
97	Jackson, Jeff	OLB	228	6-7½	Toledo, OH
93	*Jackson, William	DT	222	6-3	Richmond, VA
88	***Johnson, Gene	TE	231	6-3	Flint
15	Johnson, Irvin	OLB	205	6-2	Warren, OH
81	Johnson, Oliver	OLB	201	6-3	Detroit
16	**Jolly, Michael	DHB	178	6-3	Melvindale
44	Jones, Rick	ILB	210	6-3	Detroit
81	Kasparek, Ed	WR	180	6-0	Dearborn
55	*Keitz, Dale	MG-DT	233	6-1	Columbus, OH
57	Keough, Kelly	DT	230	6-3	Merrillville, IN
39	Kligis, Mike	DHB	195	6-3	Lombard, IL
6	Kozlowski, Jim	DB	180	5-11	Detroit
69	Kwiatkowski, Dan	OT	235	6-4½	Detroit
7	***Leach, Rick	QB	192	6-1	Flint
76	Leoni, Mike	OT	255	6-3	Flint
34	Leoni, Tony	TB	194	5-10	Flint
59	*Lilja, George	C	245	6-4	Palos Park, IL
63	Lindsay, Rock	OG	235	6-2	Lapeer
45	Malinak, Tim	ILB	217	6-1	Flemington, PA
80	*Marsh, Doug	TE	229	6-3	Akron, OH
38	*Melita, Tom	MG	224	6-1	Penns Grove, NJ
46	**Meter, Jerry	ILB	206	6-2½	Bloomfield Hills
30	Mitchell, Alan	WR	176	6-1	Detroit
52	Motley, Fred	MG	215	6-2½	Dayton, OH
50	**Nauta, Steve	C	229	6-2	Norristown, PA
83	Needham, Ben	OLB	215	6-4	Groveport, OH
96	Nicolau, Dave	DT	235	6-4½	Elk Grove Village
56	Novak, Richard	OT	237	6-5	Calumet City, IL
78	Osbun, Tony	DT	240	6-5	Kenton, OH
53	*Owens, Mel	ILB	227	6-2	DeKalb, IL
89	Pederson, Chip	TE	230	6-5	Bay City
67	*Powers, John	OG	254	6-3	Oak Park, IL
71	Prepolec, John	OG	240	6-4	Bloomfield Hills
70	Quinn, Gary	OG	246	6-3	Quincy, MA
23	Reid, Lawrence	FB	206	6-1	Philadelphia, PA
82	***Schmerge, Mark	TE	229	6-3½	Cincinnati, OH
91	***Seabron, Tom	OLB	208	6-3	Detroit
40	**Simpkins, Ron	ILB	215	6-1	Detroit
26	*Smith, Roosevelt	TB	198	5-10	Detroit
79	Torzy, Mark	OT	250	6-4	Warren
77	*Trgovac, Mike	MG	220	6-2	Austintown, OH
66	Wandersleben, Tom	OG	240	6-3	Euclid, OH
5	Wangler, John	QB	189	6-2	Royal Oak
62	Weber, Gary	DT	234	6-2	Matawan, NJ
19	Williams, Virgil	WB	185	5-10	Lorain, OH
1	*Willner, Gregg	P-PK	156	5-10	Miami Beach, FL
56	Wunderli, Greg	C	225	6-5	St. Louis, MO

* indicates letters won

OHIO

No.	Name	Pos.	Wt.	Hgt.	Home Town
79	Atkins, Kevin	OT	254	6-5	Webster, NY
88	Allen, David	OLB	216	6-2	Warren
69	**Andria, Ernest	OG	238	6-3	Wintersville
93	*Bach, Terry	OLB	210	5-11	Centerville
82	*Barwig, Ronald	TE	250	6-8	Willoughby Hills
25	*Bell, Todd	CB	202	6-1	Middletown
17	Belmer, Clifford	FB	203	6-1	Mansfield
94	Berner, Joseph	ILB	215	6-3	Avon Lake
29	**Blinco, Thomas	ILB	221	6-2	Lewiston, NY
44	Brown, Harold	TB	197	6-2	Kent
74	Brown, Timothy	OT	272	6-6	Warren
76	Burke, Timothy	OT	252	6-5	Wapakoneta
63	Burris, Scott	OG	236	6-3	Point Pleasant, WV
4	Burrows, Norman	QB	176	5-11	Portsmouth
38	**Campbell, Paul	FB	217	6-1	Ravenna
7	*Castignola, Gregory	QB	180	6-2	Trenton, MI
71	***Cato, Byron	DT	241	6-2	Lorain
36	***Cousineau, Thomas	ILB	227	6-3	Fairview Park
96	D'Andrea, Michael	OLB	218	6-4	Akron
32	***Dansler, Kelton	OLB	208	6-1	Warren
50	DeLeone, James	C	217	5-11	Kent
47	*Donley, Douglas	FL	180	6-1	Cambridge
60	**Dulin, Gary	DT	258	6-4	Madisonville, KY
41	Eberts, Mark	SE	187	5-11	Canton
27	*Ellis, Ray	DB	194	6-2	Canton
39	Ellison, Leon	OLB	211	6-2	Washington, D.C.
59	Epitropoulos, Ernest	OG	225	6-2	Warren
33	Epitropoulos, John	ILB	225	6-2	Warren
65	Ferguson, Keith	OT	232	6-5	Miami, FL
55	Foster, Jerome	DT	240	6-4	Detroit, MI
56	**Fritz, Kenneth	OG	238	6-3	Ironton
51	Gatewood, Russell	ILB	225	6-3	Orlando, FL
26	Gayle, James	TB	190	5-10	Hampton, VA
8	***Gerald, Roderic	QB	177	6-1	Dallas, TX
34	Greene, Anthony	FB	240	6-0	Detroit, MI
46	***Griffin, Duncan	CB	188	5-11	Columbus
12	**Guess, Michael	S	176	5-11	Columbus
3	Hall, Ted	DB	212	6-2	Gahanna
54	*Henson, Luther	DT	241	6-2	Sandusky
37	Hicks, Tyrone	SE	180	5-11	Warren
83	***Hornik, Joseph	DT	234	6-3	North Olmsted
80	Houston, James	TE	218	6-3	Akron
89	*Hunter, Charles	TE	203	6-2	Newark, DE
75	Hutchings, John	C	215	6-0	Fremont
87	**Jaco, William	TE	248	6-5	Toledo
13	*Janakievski, Vlade	PK	157	5-8	Columbus
21	*Johnson, Ricky	TB	192	6-0	Santa Maria, CA
24	Lamb, Steven	DB	190	6-0	Findlay
92	Laser, Joel	OT	234	6-2	Akron
5	*Laughlin, James	OLB	214	6-2	Lyndhurst
86	Lee, Ben	OLB	196	6-0	Canton
78	Levenick, Thomas	OG	234	6-4	Washington, IL
81	Light, James	DT	220	6-3	Toledo
73	**Mackey, Douglas	OT	250	6-4	Saugus, MA
1	*McKee, David	P	182	6-2	Columbus
85	Meade, John	TE	237	6-5	Mokena, IL
61	Medich, David	OG	237	6-2	Steubenville
90	*Megaro, Anthony	ILB	227	6-2	Chicago, IL
64	Miller, Nicholas	DT	226	6-3	Upland, PA
91	Miller, Ronald	OLB	216	6-3	Auburn, NY
20	***Mills, Leonard	DB	184	6-3	Miami, FL
99	***Moore, Jimmy	TE	242	6-5	Tempe, AZ
28	Murphy, Robert	DB	193	6-1	Santa Ynez, CA
43	*Murray, Calvin	TB	185	5-11	Woodbine, NJ
18	O'Cain, Timothy	FL	170	5-10	Gahanna
19	*Orosz, Thomas	P-PK	207	6-1	Fairport Harbor
53	Pack, Craig	ILB	218	6-2	Orrville
66	Palahnuk, Michael	OG	235	6-2	Hicksville, NY
84	Pauley, Douglas	SE	180	6-1	Carpinteria, CA
30	*Payton, Joel	FB	221	6-2	Mentor
77	Phillips, David	C	221	6-5	Vienna, WV
95	Phillips, Larry	DT	230	6-3	Vienna, WV
70	**Robinson, Joseph	OT	254	6-5	Paulding
16	**Ross, Paul	OLB	232	6-1	Fort Valley, GA
57	***Savoca, James	OG	228	6-2	Solon
68	*Sawicki, Timothy	MG	217	6-0	Mayfield
10	Schlichter, Arthur	QB	190	6-3	Bloomingburg
14	**Schwartz, Brian	S	190	6-1	Simi Valley, CA
48	*Skillings, Vincent	DB	172	6-0	Brenizer, PA
67	Smith, Joseph	DT	242	6-3	Cincinnati
23	**Springs, Ronald	TB	198	6-2	Williamsburg, VA
6	*Strahine, Michael	QB	194	6-0	Lakewood
72	***Sullivan, Mark	MG	238	6-4	New Bedford, MA
9	Taylor, Alvin	FL	182	6-0	Newport News, VA
97	*Vogler, Terry	ILB	221	6-2	Covington
52	**Vogler, Timothy	C	228	6-3	Covington
22	*Volley, Ricardo	FB	208	6-0	Lynchburg, VA
15	*Washington, Alvin	ILB	222	6-3	Cleveland
11	Watson, Otha	DB	200	6-0	Dayton
58	**Waugh, Thomas	C	242	6-1	Norwalk
49	Williams, Gary	DB	197	6-2	Wilmington

* indicates letters won

1978

Ohio	0	Penn State	19
Ohio	27	Minnesota	10
Ohio	34	Baylor	28
Ohio	35	S. Methodist	35
Ohio	16	Purdue	27
Ohio	31	Iowa	7
Ohio	63	Northwestern	20
Ohio	49	Wisconsin	14
Ohio	45	Illinois	7
Ohio	21	Indiana	18
Ohio	3	Michigan	14

Season Summary

Games Won, 7; Lost, 3; Tied, 1

TOM COUSINEAU
All-American Linebacker

photo by Chance Brockway

November 17, 1979

Ann Arbor, Michigan

Buckeyes Edge Wolverines 18-15 For Rose Bowl Berth

Blocked Punt Decides Outcome

In the first meeting between new Ohio State Coach Earle Bruce and Michigan's Bo Schembechler, the Buckeyes capped a perfect 11-0 regular season with an 18-15 come from behind victory over the host Wolverines. The victory gave the Buckeyes the Big Ten title and a berth in the Rose Bowl.

Ohio State linebacker Jim Laughlin provided the heroics by blocking a Michigan punt late in the fourth quarter. With the Buckeyes trailing 15-12, Ohio State's rush overwhelmed Michigan punter Bryan Virgil as he tried to get off a kick at his 23 yard line. Laughlin knocked the ball down and Todd Bell scooped up the bounding ball and sprinted to the end zone 18 yards away.

Ohio State had gathered 10 men at the line of scrimmage to block the punt, a gamble that proved successful for Coach Bruce. His bold move marked a departure from the conservative Hayes-Schembechler showdowns of previous years.

Still, the solid defense that characterized past battles remained intact. Case in point was a gallant goal line stand by Ohio State in the first period. Michigan drove to a first down on the 11 after Mike Hardin had intercepted a pass by OSU quarterback Art Schlichter, but the Buckeyes held on to stop Michigan at the two on downs. Ohio State linebacker Al Washington dumped Michigan's freshman quarterback Rich Hewlett for a loss on fourth down.

Hewlett was actually a surprise starter for Michigan, considering he had only four plays to his credit all season. Hewlett, however, was injured in the second quarter and replaced by the experienced John Wangler.

Wangler was inserted as the Wolverines trailed 3-0 on a 23-yard field goal by Ohio State's Vlade Janakievski.. Wangler needed just six plays to rally his team with a 39-yard touchdown bomb to Anthony Carter to give Michigan a 7-3 lead with 1 :30 left in the half.

Schlichter responded with a passing display of his own, completing four aerials to move Ohio State from their own 20 to the Michigan 8. Facing a third down and only 11 seconds to go, Coach Bruce played it safe and called on Janakievski for a 25-yard field goal to make it 7-6 Michigan at the half.

The third quarter began with a flurry as Ohio State drove from their 49 to the Michigan 4. A holding penalty on the next play pushed the ball back to the 18 where the Buckeyes faced a third down. Schlichter threw to the corner of the end zone, the ball was tipped by Michigan's Mike Jolley but Ohio State's Chuck Hunter, behind the defender, made the reception for OSU's first touchdown against Michigan in four seasons.

Jolley made up for his misfortune by intercepting a Schlichter pass on Ohio State's ensuing two-point conversion try. The score stood 12-7 at that point.

Michigan bounced back quickly, thanks mainly to a 66-yard pass play from Wangler to Carter to land Michigan on Ohio State's 3. The Buckeyes were then whistled twice for making contact before the center snap. Bruce protested because he claimed Wangler was drawing the Buckeyes offsides by bobbing up and down on his cadence. Still, the penalties left Michigan only inches from paydirt, and Roosevelt Smith plunged in on the next play to put the Wolverines in front 13-12. Schembechler successfully gambled on a two-point conversion as Smith carried for the necessary three yards and a 15-12 lead with 3:50 left in the third quarter.

Schlichter went to work immediately to bring Ohio State back, driving his team to the Michigan 10 on a 43-yard pass play to Doug Donley just before the third period ended. The drive soon ended, however, when Jim Gayle fumbled the ball away at the nine.

Laughlin came up with his big punt block on the next Michigan series to put Ohio State ahead for good. The Ohio State defense stopped Michigan on its next drive, and then the OSU offense used almost all of the last 11 minutes of the game with a well-executed drive to the Michigan 25 to ensure the victory.

Schlichter finished with 196 passing yards on 12 completions in 22 attempts. Gayle led the ground game with 72 yards in just nine carries.

Wangler's two long passes gave him 133 yards on four completions out of nine attempts. Butch Woolfolk, Michigan's highly regarded tailback, was held to 68 yards in 18 carries.

STATISTICS

	OSU	UM
First Downs	20	13
Rushes-Yards	55-236	46-151
Passing Yards	196	147
Passes	12-22-1	5-14-2
Punts/Avg.	4-41	6-32
Fumbles-Lost	1-1	2-0
Penalties-Yards	5-27	1-5

SCORING

Ohio State	0	6	6	6	- 18
Michigan	0	7	8	0	- 15

1979

Great Trio - Woody Hayes chats with two of his former ssistants, Bo Schembechler and Earle Bruce at a special inner honoring Hayes in March of 1979. The event was aged and attended by more than 500 of his former play-rs and associates.

1979

Ohio State	31	Syracuse	8
Ohio State	21	Minnesota	17
Ohio State	45	Washington State	29
Ohio State	17	U.C.L.A.	13
Ohio State	16	Northwestern	7
Ohio State	47	Indiana	6
Ohio State	59	Wisconsin	0
Ohio State	42	Michigan State	0
Ohio State	44	Illinois	7
Ohio State	34	Iowa	7
Ohio State	18	Michigan	15

Season Summary
Games won,11; Lost, 0

KEN FRITZ
All-American Guard

ART SCHLICHTER
All-American Quarterback

OHIO STATE

No.	Name	Pos.	Wt.	Hgt.	Home Town
69	Andria, Ernie	OG	246	6-3	Wintersville, OH
1	Atha, Bob	QB	170	5-11	Worthington, OH
82	Barwig, Ron	TE	242	6-8	Willoughby Hills, OH
25	Bell, Tom	LB	200	6-1	Middletown, OH
34	Belmer, Cliff	FB	205	6-1	Mansfield, OH
29	Blinco, Tom	LB	225	6-2	Lewiston, NY
52	Brown, Bernard	C	218	6-1	Marietta, OH
74	Brown, Tim	OT	268	6-6	Warren, OH
76	Burke, Tim	OT	256	6-5	Wapakoneta, OH
63	Burris, Scott	OG	244	6-3	Point Pleasant, WV
4	Burrows, Norman	CB	181	5-11	Portsmouth, OH
38	Campbell, Paul	FB	218	6-1	Ravenna, OH
7	Castignola, Greg	QB	188	6-2	Trenton, MI
35	Cobb, Glen	LB	208	6-3	Wash. Court House, OH
96	D'Angela, Mike	OLB	206	6-4	Akron, OH
50	DeLeone, Jim	C	212	5-11	Kent, OH
47	Donley, Doug	FL	170	6-1	Cambridge, OH
60	Dunlin, Gary	DT	250	6-4	Madisonville, KY
81	Dwelle, Brad	TE	210	6-4	Sandusky, OH
73	Echols, Reggie	DT	230	6-1	Chardon, OH
27	Ellis, Ray	CB	194	6-2	Canton, OH
39	Ellison, Leon	OLB	210	6-2	Washington, DC
59	Epitropoulos, Ernie	OG	227	6-2	Warren, OH
33	Epitropoulos, John	LB	222	6-2	Warren, OH
65	Ferguson, Keith	OLB	224	6-5	Miami, FL
55	Foster, Jerome	DT	242	6-4	Detroit, MI
56	Fritz, Ken	OG	242	6-3	Ironton, OH
17	Galloway, Tim	S	186	6-2	Columbus, OH
26	Gayle, Jim	TB	194	5-10	Hampton, VA
16	Gorley, Rod	CB	185	6-1	Cincinati, OH
12	Guess, Mike	CB	174	5-11	Columbus, OH
3	Hall, Ted	LB	223	6-2	Gahanna, OH
54	Henson, Luther	DT	254	6-2	Sandusky, OH
37	Hicks, Tyrone	SE	174	5-11	Warren, OH
80	Houston, James	TE	222	6-3	Akron, OH
89	Hunter, Chuck	SE	211	6-2	Newark, DE
57	Hutchings, John	C	202	6-0	Fremont, OH
87	Jaco, Bill	TE	265	6-5	Toledo, OH
13	Janakievski, Vlade	PL	161	5-8	Columbus, OH
21	Johnson, Ricky	TB	186	6-0	Santa Maria, CA
5	Laughlin, Jim	OLB	219	6-2	Lyndhurst, OH
86	Lee, Ben	OLB	212	6-0	Canton, OH
78	Levenick, Tom	OT	248	6-4	Washington, IL
23	Lewis, Doyle	CB	176	6-0	Canton, OH
20	Lindsay, Kelvin	FL	180	6-0	Sandusky, OH
72	Lukens, Joe	OT	250	6-4	Cincinnati, OH
36	Marek, Marcus	LB	210	6-2	Masury, OH
85	Meade, John	TE	225	6-4	Mokenam, IL
90	Megaro, Tony	LB	227	6-2	Chicago, IL
99	Miller, Nick	DT	227	6-3	Upland, PA
91	Miller, Ron	DT	230	6-3	Auburn, NY
28	Murphy, Bob	S	191	6-1	Santa Ynez, CA
43	Murray, Calvin	TB	180	5-11	Woodbine, NJ
19	Orosz, Tom	PT	195	6-1	Fairport Harbor, OH
30	Payton, Joel	FB	226	6-2	Mentor, OH
93	Riehm, Chris	DT	233	6-7	Wadsworth, OH
68	Sawicki, Tim	MG	218	6-0	Mayfield, OH
10	Schlichter, Art	QB	200	6-2	Bloomingburg, OH
14	Schwartz, Brian	LB	196	6-1	Simi Valley, CA
48	Skillings, Vince	S	176	6-0	Brenizer, PA
67	Smith, Joe	C	242	6-3	Cincinnati, OH
46	Spencer, Tim	TB	200	6-1	St. Clairsville, OH
6	Strahine, Mik	QB	195	6-0	Lakewood, OH
97	Sullivan, Mark	MG	212	5-9	Timberlake, OH
9	Taylor, Alvin	FL	180	6-0	Newport News, VA
22	Volley, Ric	FB	208	6-0	Lynchburg, VA
15	Washington, Alvin	LB	230	6-3	Cleveland, OH
11	Watson, Otha	LB	202	6-0	Dayton, OH
58	Waugh, Tom	C	217	6-1	Norwalk, OH
44	Williams, Gary	SE	200	6-2	Wilmington, OH

MICHIGAN

No.	Name	Pos.	Wt.	Hgt.	Home Town
35	Agnew, Doug	OLB	195	6-2	Plymouth, MI
64	Arbeznik, John	OG	243	6-3.5	University Hts., OH
12	Bates, Brad	DB	193	6-1	Port Huron, MI
65	Becker, Kurt	OF	243	6-6	Aurora, IL
82	Betts, Norm	TE	216	6-5	Midland, MI
3	Body, Marion	DB	182	5-10	Detroit, MI
28	Braman, Mark	DB	197	5-1.5	Midland, MI
8	Breaugh, Jim	QB	194	6-2	West Bloomfield, MI
25	Brockington, Fred	WR	200	6-4	Detroit, MI
41	Cannavino, Andy	OLB	220	6-1	Cleveland, OH
9	Carpenter, Brian	DB	160	5-11	Flint, MI
85	Christian, Chuck	TE	219	6-3	Detroit, MI
22	Clayton, Ralph	WB	225	6-3.5	Detroit, MI
92	Coles, Cedric	DT	241	6-2	Detroit, MI
36	Czarnota, Mike	OLB	212	6-2	Detroit, MI
10	Dickey, B.J.	QB	188	6-0	Ottawa, OH
29	Diggs, Gerald	DB	187	6-0	Chicago, IL
32	Edwards, Stan	TB	205	6-1	Detroit, MI
18	Feaster, Rodney	WR	191	6-1	Flint, MI
51	Felten, Jeff	C	227	6-2	Centerville, OH
20	Fischer, Brad	DB	201	6-0	Ortonville, MI
54	Garrity, Tom	C	245	6-4	Grafton, WI
90	Godfrey, Chris	DT	234	6-4	Lathrup Village, MI
95	Greer, Curtis	DT	250	6-5	Detroit, MI
4	Harden, Mike	DB	189	6-.5	Detroit, MI
31	Harris, Stu	WOLF	196	6-2	Chagrin Falls, Oh
73	Hetts, Chuck	OG	246	6-5	Taylor, MI
58	Humphries, Jame	MG	218	5-10.5	Detroit, MI
21	Jackson, Tony	WE	173	5-11	Cleveland, OH
48	Jacoby, Bill	FB	212	6-1	Toledo, Oh
15	Johnson, Irvin	ILB	208	6-3	Warren, OH
81	Johnson, Oliver	OLB	194	6-3.5	Detroit, MI
16	Jolly, Mike	DB	186	6-3	Melvindale, MI
55	Keitz, Dale	DT	233	6-1.5	Columbus, OH
99	Keller, Tom	OLB	210	6-2.5	Grand Rapids, MI
97	Kelsie, Tony	MG	211	5-11.25	Dover, DE
57	Keough, Kelly	C	237	6-3	Merrillville, IN
39	Kligis, Mike	WOLF	190	6-3	Lombard, IL
69	Kwiatkowski, Dan	OT	240	6-4.5	Detroit, MI
93	Lemirande, Mike	OLB	219	6-4.5	Grafton, WI
76	Leoni, Mike	OT	256	6-2.5	Flint, MI
34	Leoni, Tony	TB	192	5-11	Flint, MI
59	Lilja, George	C	247	6-4.5	Palos Park, IL
80	Marsh, Doug	TE	235	6-3	Akron, OH
30	Mitchell, Alan	WR	185	6-1.5	Detroit, MI
54	Moss, Tom	MG	204	5-8	Detroit, MI
52	Motley, Fred	MG	227	6-2	Dayton, OH
72	Muransky, Ed	OT	266	6-2.5	Youngstown, OH
27	Murray, Dan	WOLF	204	6-1	Ann Arbor, MI
79	Neal, Tom	QT	257	6-5.5	Orlando, FL
83	Needham, Ben	OLB	211	6-4	Groveport, OH
96	Nicolau, Dave	DT	232	6-5	Elk Grove Vilg., IL
78	Osbun, Tony	OT	247	6-5	Kenton, OH
53	Owens, Mel	OLB	236	6-2	DeKalb, IL
12	Paciorek, Jim	TE	217	6-3	Orchard Lake, MI
75	Paris, Bubba	OT	273	6-6	Louisville, KY
89	Payne, David	ILB	206	6-1	Detroit, MI
67	Powers, John	LG	270	6-4	Oak Park, IL
70	Quinn, Gary	OG	248	6-3	Quincy, MA
43	Reeves, Jeff	DB	192	6-1	Columbus, OH
23	Reid, Lawrence	FB	223	6-1	Philidelphia, PA
94	Shaw, Vincent	TE	210	6-2	Wheaton, IL
40	Simpkins, Ron	ILB	228	6-.5	Detroit, MI
6	Smith, Kevin	DB	191	6-2.5	Dallas, TX
26	Smith, Roosevelt	TB	202	5-10.5	Detroit, MI
68	Strenger, Rich	OT	241	6-7	Grafton, WI
14	Tech, Karl	PK,P	179	6-0	Grosse Pt. Shores, MI
99	Thompson, Robert	OLB	215	6-3	Blue Island, IL
77	Trgovac, Mike	MG	235	6-2	Austintown, OH
2	Virgil, Bryan	PK	194	5-10	Buchanan, MI
37	Wallace, Zeke	WR	184	6-4	Popano Beach, FL
66	Wanderson, Tom	OG	250	6-2	Euclid, Oh
5	Wangler, John	QB	192	6-3	Royal Oak, MI
60	Warth, Mark	OG	248	6-5.5	Zanesville, OH
49	Washington, Sanford	ILB	214	6-2	Youngstwon, OH
62	Weber, Gary	DT	243	6-2.5	Matawan, NJ
24	Woolfolk, Butch	TB	207	6-1	Westfield, NJ
56	Wunderli, Greg	OG	227	6-6	St. Louis, MO

1979

Michigan	49	Northwestern	7
Michigan	10	Notre Dame	12
Michigan	28	Kansas	7
Michigan	14	California	10
Michigan	21	Michigan State	7
Michigan	31	Minnesota	21
Michigan	27	Illinois	7
Michigan	27	Indiana	21
Michigan	54	Wisconsin	0
Michigan	21	Purdue	24
Michigan	15	Ohio State	18

Season Summary

Games won, 8; Lost, 3

CURTIS GREER
All American Tackle

RON SIMPKINS
All American Linebacker

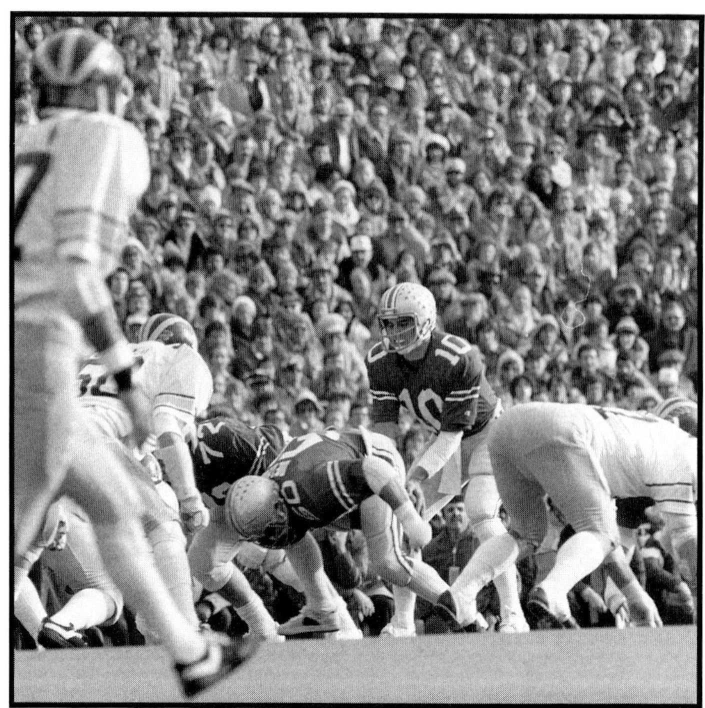

WASHINGTON

Photos by Chance Brockway

November 22, 1980

Columbus, Ohio

Wolverines Defeat Buckeyes 9-3 In Showdown For Conference Championship

Michigan Defense Shines In Victory

Once again, the Big Ten championship came down to the final game between the two conference powerhouses, Michigan and Ohio State. Both entered the game with identical 7-0 league marks and their eyes set on a Rose Bowl bid.

Capturing the ultimate prize were the Michigan Wolverines, who shattered Ohio State's bid for its second straight Big Ten title with a 9-3 victory over the Buckeyes before 88,827 in Columbus. In a game billed as a clash between the teams' offensive standouts, it was defense that ruled the day.

With the score tied 3-3 in the third quarter, Wolverine running backs Butch Woolfolk, Larry Ricks and Stan Edwards sparked the decisive Michigan touchdown drive. Michigan pounded out four first downs to reach the Ohio State 12. After two downs and a lost yard, the Wolverines looked to their main offensive threat - Anthony Carter. Carter angled towards the goal line on a post pattern, beating Ohio State linebacker Marcus Marek and safety Bob Murphy, and quarterback John Wangler nestled the ball in Carter's arms for a 13-yard touchdown. Ali Haji-Sheik's extra point try bounced off the left upright.

Michigan's defense took over from then on, squelching all of the Buckeyes' comeback attempts. Ohio State did manage to reach the Michigan 32-yard line on its final drive, first-and-10 with 51 seconds to play. Quarterback Art Schilchter, a Heisman Trophy hopeful, had just completed a 27-yard aerial to Doug Donley.

On first down, Schlichter was dropped for no gain. Then two passes went incomplete. Ohio State faced fourth down with almost no time remaining. Dropping back into the pocket, Schlichter didn't see UM linebacker Robert Thompson coming and he was sacked. The Michigan defense left the field triumphantly.

The first half scoring was limited to a 33-yard field goal by Ohio State's Vlade Janakievski and a 43-yarder by Michigan's Ali Haji-Sheikh, both coming in the second quarter.

Throughout the game, the Ohio State fans booed Coach Earle Bruce for what appeared to be a conservative game plan. The fans grew weary of Ohio State's ineffective ground game which netted only 114 yards. The aerial game wasn't much more productive as Schlichter completed only eight of 26 passes for 130 yards and had one intercepted.

Meanwhile, Woolfolk carried 31 times for 141 yards and Ricks added 54 more on 14 carries. Michigan's ground game allowed the Wolverines to control the clock most of the game, particularly in the second half with two drives eating seven minutes apiece on the clock.

Another telling statistic was third down conversions. Michigan was 10-for-20 as it gained 23 total first downs, while the Buckeyes could only convert four third downs in 17 chances for 14 total first downs.

STATISTICS

	UM	OSU
First Downs	23	14
Rushes-Yards	61-197	32-114
Passing Yards	120	130
Passes	11-23-3	8-26-1
Punts/Avg.	4-40	6-40
Fumbles-Lost	0-0	1-1
Penalties-Yards	4-31	2-31

SCORING

Michigan	0	3	6	0	- 9
Ohio State	0	3	0	0	- 3

1980			
Michigan	17	Northwestern	10
Michigan	27	Notre Dame	29
Michigan	14	South Carolina	17
Michigan	38	California	13
Michigan	27	Michigan State	23
Michigan	37	Minnesota	14
Michigan	45	Illinois	14
Michigan	35	Indiana	0
Michigan	24	Wisconsin	0
Michigan	26	Purdue	0
Michigan	9	Ohio State	3

Season Summary
Games won, 9; Lost, 2

ANTHONY CARTER
All-American Wide Receiver

GEORGE LILJA
All-American Center

MICHIGAN

No.	Name	Pos.	Wt.	Hgt.	Home Town
57	Anderson, Tim	LB	210	6-2	Pioneer, MI
27	Bean, Vincent	WR	179	6-1	Southfield, MI
65	Becker, Kurt	OG	252	6-6	Aurora, IL
19	Bergeron, Bob	PK	140	5-8	Ft. Wayne, IN
82	Betts, Norm	TE	230	6-5	Midland, MI
3	Body, Marion	DB	174	5-10	Detroit, MI
40	Boren, Mike	LB	210	6-2	Columbus, OH
13	Bostic, Keith	DB	190	6-1	Ann Arbor, MI
28	Bracken, Don	P	185	6-0	Termopolis, WY
25	Brockington, Fred	WR	200	6-4	West Bloomfield, MI
15	Burgei, Jerry	DB	182	5-11	Ottawa, OH
41	Cannavino, Andy	ILB	220	6-1	Cleveland, OH
9	Carpenter, Brian	DB	166	5-11	Flint, MI
63	Carraway, Winfred	MG	230	6-3	Detroit, MI
1	Carter, Anthony	WR	161	5-11.5	Riviera Beach, FL
83	Carthens, Milt	TE	236	6-3	Pontiac, MI
85	Christain, Chuck	TE	219	6-3	Detroit, MI
10	Cohen, Jeff	DB	185	5-11.5	Farmington Hills, MI
92	Coles, Cedric	DT	241	6-2	Detroit, MI
21	Cooper, Evan	DB	170	5-11.5	Miami, FL
29	Diggs, Geralkd	DB	182	6-0	Chicago, IL
64	DiOrio, Jerry	OG	243	6-2	Younstown, OH
69	Dixon, Tom	OG	228	6-1	Ft. Wayne, IN
88	Dunaway, Craig	TE	231	6-3	Upper St. Clair, PA
32	Edwards, Stan	TB	205	6-1	Detroit, MI
18	Feaster, Rodney	WR	191	6-1	Flint, MI
51	Felten, Jeff	C	234	6-2	Centerville, OH
54	Garrity, Tom	C	245	6-4	Grafton, WI
39	Gear, Kenney	WR	185	6-1	Madison, WI
50	Girgash, Paul	ILB	203	6-1	Lakewood, OH
22	Gosier, Harry	DB	185	6-1	Riviera Beach, FL
6	Haji-Sheik, Ali	PK	172	6-0	Arlington, TX
48	Hassel, Tom	DB	195	6-0	Cincinnati, OH
94	Herrmann, James	ILB	202	6-2	Dearborn Hgts, MI
2	Hewlett, Rich	QB	197	6-1	Plymouth, MI
76	Humphries, Stefan	DL	240	6-3	Broward, FL
35	Ingram, Jerald	FB	217	6-1	Beaver, PA
37	Jackson, Tony	DB	173	5-11	Cleveland, OH
73	James, Doug	DB	240	6-2	Louisville, KY
81	Johnson, Oliver	OLB	207	6-3	Detroit, MI
44	Joseph, Roger	K	180	6-0	Bellvue, OH
57	Keough, Kelly	KT	246	6-3	Merrilville, In
93	Lemirande, Mike	OLB	219	6-5	Grafton, WI
59	Lilia, George	C	255	6-5	Palos Park, IL
44	Lott, John	DB	176	6-0	Masury, OH
80	Lyles, Rodney	LB	214	6-2	Miami, FL
39	Melnyk, Mike	K	170	6-1	Warren, MI
86	Meredity, Dave	DL	233	6-3.5	Sterling Hgts., MI
30	Mitchell, Alan	WR	185	6-1.5	Detroit, MI
52	Motley, Fred	MG	227	6-2	Dayton, OH
72	Muransky, Ed	OT	270	6-7	Youngstown, OH
96	Nicolau, Dave	DT	243	6-5	Elk Grove Village, IL
78	Osbun, Tony	OT	258	6-5	Kenton, OH
53	Owens, Mel	OLB	236	6-2	Dekalb, IL
75	Paris, Bubba	OT	270	6-6.5	Louisville, KY
67	Powers, John	OG	265	6-3.5	Oak Park, IL
43	Reeves, Jeff	DB	192	6-1	Columbus, OH
46	Ricks, Lawrence	TB	191	5-10	Barberton, OH
89	Rose, Carlton	LB	199	6-1	Ft. Lauderdale, FL
95	Shaw, Jeff	DT	258	6-1	Matawan, NJ
23	Smith, Kerry	TB	190	6-.5	Grand Rapids, MI
6	Snith, Kevin	DB	191	6-2.5	Dallas, TX
16	Smith, Steve	QB	186	6-0	Grand Blanc, MI
68	Strenger, Rich	OT	245	6-7	Grafton, WI
55	Sweeney, Larry	C	225	6-1.5	Alma, MI
99	Thompson, Robert	OLB	215	6-3	Blue Island
77	Trgovac, Mike	MG	235	6-2	Austintown, OH
4	Wallace, Zeke	WR	184	6-4	Pompano Beach, FL
5	Wangler, John	QB	192	6-3	Royal Oak, MI
24	Woolfolk, Butch	TB	207	6-2	Westfield, NJ

OHIO STATE

No.	Name	Pos.	Wt.	Hgt.	Home Town
22	Anderson, Cedric	FL	177	5-11	Apopka, FL
30	Andrews, Bill	K	160	5-9	Cambridge, OH
58	Apke, Joe	C	212	6-5	Cincinnati, OH
1	Atha, Bob	QK-K	180	5-11	Worthington, OH
62	Balen, Alan	DT	234	6-1	Lackawanna, NY
82	Barwig, Ron	TE	248	6-8	Willoughby Hills, OH
25	Bell, Todd	ROV	203	6-1	Middletown, OH
34	Belmer, Cliff	FB	207	6-1	Mansfield, OH
94	Berner, Joe	LB	221	6-3	Avon Lake, OH
49	Braun, Don	DT	241	6-1	Columbus, OH
38	Broadnax, Vaughn	FB	230	6-3	Xenia, OH
52	Brown, Bernie	C	222	6-1	Marietta, OH
29	Brudzinski, T.J.	SE	177	5-11	Fremont, OH
53	Burris, Gary	C	200	6-1	Urbana, OH
63	Burris, Scott	OG	244	6-3	Point Pleasant, WV
4	Burrows, Norm	CB	184	5-11	Portsmouth, OH
71	Burrows, Scott	MG	221	6-2	Portsmouth, OH
42	Blythewood, Charles	QB	178	6-0	Dix Hills, NY
77	Carson, Jim	OT	254	6-5	Akron, OH
83	Cicero, Chris	OLB	205	6-0	Chagrin, Falls, OH
24	Cisco, Jeff	TB	182	5-11	St. Mary's, OH
35	Cobb, Glen	LB	208	6-3	Washington, DC
76	Corbin, Steve	OT	242	6-5	Lima, OH
11	Curtis, Clarence	OLB	207	6-3	Potomac, MC
66	Czyzynski, Rich	LB	216	6-2	Brook Park, OH
96	D'Andrea, Mike	MG	217	6-4	Akron, OH
50	DeLeone, Jim	C	214	5-11	Kent, OH
47	Donley, Doug	FL	180	6-1	Cambridge, OH
87	Dooley, Joe	TE	252	6-7	Cincinnati, OH
81	Dwelle, Brad	TE	215	6-4	Sandusky, OH
41	Eberts, Mark	CB	187	5-11	Canton, OH
73	Echols, Riggie	DT	234	6-1	Chardon, OH
5	Edwards, Karl	PT	203	6-3	Groveport, OH
27	Ellis, Ray	CB	196	6-2	Canton, OH
39	Ellison, Leon	OLB	218	6-2	Washinton, DC
59	Epitropoulos, Ernie	OG	230	6-2	Warren, OH
33	Epitropoulos, John	LB	231	6-2	Warren, OH
69	Ferguson, Carl	OLB	200	6-1	Portsmouth, OH
65	Ferguson Keith	OLB	234	6-5	Miami, FL
55	Foster, Jerome	DT	244	6-4	Detroit, MI
89	Frank, John	TE	216	6-3	Mt. Lebanon, PA
23	Furillo, Rich	PT	185	6-1	Brookfield, OH
17	Galloway, Tim	S	184	6-2	Columbus, OH
51	Gatewood, Russ	OG	231	6-3	Orlando, FL
26	Gayle, Jim	TB	192	5-10	Hampton, VA
2	Gayle, Shaun	ROV	200	6-0	Hampton, VA
16	Gorley, Rod	S	190	6-1	Cincinnati, OH
13	Gottron, Jeff	CB	182	5-11	Fremont, OH
85	Groza, Judd	TE	228	6-3	Berea, OH
67	Hafner, Bob	OLB	210	6-0	Sandusky, OH
54	Henson, Luther	OT	262	6-2	Sandusky, OH
55	Hernstein, Seth	LB	210	6-3	Chillicothe, OH
3	Hill, Doug	CB	182	6-1	Miami, FL
95	Hill, Timothy	LB	200	6-1	Columbus, OH
92	Hoocvar, Mark	MG	228	6-2	Warren, OH
57	Hutchings, John	C	202	6-0	Fremont, OH
13	Janakievski, Vlade	PK	160	5-8	Columbus, OH
88	Jemison, Thad	SE	186	6-2	Lincoln Heights, OH
21	Johnson, Ricky	TB	190	6-0	Santa Maria, CA
25	Kauth, Chris	CB	186	6-0	Clayton, OH
39	Keuchler, Lamar	ROV	186	5-10	Marion, OH
49	Kidd, Steve	K	208	6-2	Youngstown, OH
12	Lane, Garcia	FL	175	5-10	Youngstown, OH
14	Langley, Victor	TB	194	6-1	Richardson, TX
86	Lee, Ben	OLB	210	6-10	Canton, OH
23	Lewis, Doyle	CB	184	6-1	Canton, OH
20	Lindweys, Kelvin	TN	184	6-0	Sandusky, OH
37	Lowry, Orlando	OLB	222	6-4	Shaker Heights, OH
72	Lukens, Joe	OG	246	6-4	Cincinnati, OH
34	Manning, Rob	OLB	203	6-1	Columbus, OH
36	Marek, Marcus	LB	214	6-2	Masury, OH
97	Martin, Daryl	MG	210	6-1	Struthers, OH
96	McCall, Edward	SE	175	6-3	Cincinnati, OH
26	McCarthy, Jeff	SE	192	6-1	Sandusky, OH
41	McFarland, Dave	K	165	5-10	Oberlin, OH
37	McGlade, Dave	S	176	6-0	Zanesville, OH
8	McTier, Dave	QB	200	6-2	Eustis, FL
61	Medich, Dave	OG	242	6-2	Steubenville, OH
20	Medich, Rob	S	192	6-1	Steubenville, OH
90	Megaro, Tony	DT	242	6-2	Chicago, IL
99	Miller, Nick	MG	233	6-3	Upland, PA
60	Miller, Ron	OG	231	6-3	Auburn, NY
75	Moriarty, Tim	OG	244	6-3	Euclid, OH
28	Murphy, Bob	S	198	6-1	Santa Ynex, CA
43	Murray, Calvin	TB	182	5-11	Woodbine, N.J.
29	Myers, Ray	FB	227	6-2	Toledo, OH
18	O'Cain, Tim	TB	177	5-10	Gahanna, OH
98	Olman, Kevin	LB	228	6-3	Maumee, OH
19	Orosz, Tom	PT	196	6-1	Fairport Harbor, OH
53	Pack, Craig	C	227	6-2	Orrville, OH
79	Palhauk, Mike	OT	242	6-2	Hicksville, NY
84	Pauley, Doug	SE	182	6-1	Carpinteria, CA
95	Phillips, Larry	DT	236	6-3	Vienna, WV
1	Ranft, Brain	FL	157	5-11	Groveport, OH
93	Riehm, Chris	DT	244	6-7	Wadsworth, OH
70	Roberts, Bill	OT	248	6-5	Miami, FL
68	Sawicki, Tim	MG	218	6-0	Mayfield, OH
10	Schlichter, Art	QB	200	6-2	Bloomingburg, OH
89	Schmidt, Joe	OLB	195	6-1	Bradford, OH
56	Simpson, Steve	C	237	6-5	Temperance, MI
48	Skillings, Vince	CB	180	6-0	Brenizer, PA
67	Smith, Joe	OT	244	6-3	Cincinnati, OH
46	Spencer, Tim	FB	210	6-1	St. Clairsville, OH
6	Stephens, Tim	QB	194	6-2	Parkersburg, WV
97	Sullivan, Mark	MG	209	5-9	Timerlake, OH
32	Tatum, Rowland	LB	215	6-2	Inglewood, CA
9	Taylor, Alvin	FL	182	6-0	Newport News, VA
54	Utz, John	DT	215	6-2	New Washington, OH
15	Washington, Al	OLB	232	6-3	Cleveland, OH
44	Williams, Gary	SE	200	6-2	Wilmington, OH
69	Wilson, Bill	C	222	6-3	Columbus, OH
81	Woodruff, Mike	QB	175	6-0	Urbana, OH
74	Zalenski, Scott	OT	237	6-5	Bethel Park, PA

1980

Ohio State	31	Syracuse	21
Ohio State	47	Minnesota	0
Ohio State	38	Arizona State	21
Ohio State	0	U.C.L.A.	17
Ohio State	63	Northwestern	0
Ohio State	27	Indiana	17
Ohio State	21	Wisconsin	0
Ohio State	48	Michigan State	16
Ohio State	49	Illinois	42
Ohio State	41	Iowa	7
Ohio State	3	Michigan	9

Season Summary
Games won, 9; Lost, 2

BRUTUS BUCKEYE
Ohio State Mascot

STATE

MEDICH
10
61

55

November, 21, 1981

Ann Arbor, Michigan

Buckeyes Upset Wolverines 14-9 For Conference Co-Championship

OSU Ruins Michigan's Rose Bowl Hopes Through Clutch Defense

photos by Chance Brockway

Two well executed drives and a stubborn defense propelled Ohio State to a 14-9 upset over host Michigan and a share of the Big Ten championship with Iowa.

The Wolverines could have claimed an outright conference title and a trip to the Rose Bowl with a win, but the Ohio State victory secured a trip to Pasadena for Iowa. Understandably, Michigan Coach Bo Schembechler was disappointed with the defeat. "We shouldn't have lost. This is one game we should have won. We simply squandered too many opportunities. I didn't expect to lose," he said.

Four times Michigan landed within the Ohio State 10 yard line, only to be denied the end zone by Ohio State's much-maligned defense. It marked the first time since 1967 that Michigan failed to garner a touchdown at Michigan Stadium.

Ohio State entered the game with a pass defense that ranked worst in major college football. But on this day, the secondary came up with three key interceptions.

Offensively, the Buckeyes were stymied most of the game, except when it counted. "They only had two drives on us," Schembechler said. "Other than that, they didn't do anything."

Ex-Ohio State Coach Woody Hayes, watching his first Ohio State-Michigan battle since 1978, called the marches "two of the most perfectly executed drives I've ever seen."

The first came in the second period with Michigan leading 3-0 on an Ali Haji-Sheikh 1 9-yard field goal in the first quarter after the Buckeye defense had stopped the Wolverines at the 2-yard line. OSU tailback Tim Spencer carried the ball seven times on the 82-yard drive, which was capped by quarterback Art Schlichter's one-yard dive. The Buckeyes led 7-3 at intermission.

The Wolverines stormed back in the third quarter, gaining a 9-7 lead on two Haji Sheikh field goals from 26 and 23 yards. Still, Michigan was unable to crack the end zone despite moving down the field with ease. When the Wolverines crept within the 10, the Ohio State defense rose to the occasion.

Michigan was threatening again early in the fourth quarter with the ball on Ohio State's 8. This time freshman defensive back Kelvin Bell intercepted Michigan quarterback Steve Smith's pass, which was tipped by OSU's Shaun Gayle in the end zone.

Schlichter displayed great poise as he led the Buckeyes 80 yards for a touchdown and the final lead. Key plays in the drive were a 10-yard reception and l9-yard run by Tim Spencer, and a 17-yard pass to Gary Williams as Schlichter was about to be sacked.

With 2:50 to play, Ohio State faced a third down on Michigan's six. Schlichter rolled out on an option pass play but could find no receiver. He stopped, started again, ducked inside, then cut back out and into the end zone just inside the flag. A key block by fullback Vaughn Broadnax paved the way for Schlichter's decisive move.

Schlichter finished with 131 passing yards on 12 completions in 24 attempts. Spencer accounted for nearly all of Ohio State's 131 rushing yards with 110 of his own on 25 carries.

For Michigan, Smith completed nine of 26 passes for 136 yards while Butch Woolfolk pounded out 84 rushing yards on 19 carries.

With the win, Ohio State finished 8-3 overall and 6-2 in the Big Ten. Michigan ended up 8-3 overall and 6-3 in the Big Ten.

STATISTICS

	OSU	UM
First Downs	15	20
Rushes-Yards	39-126	51-231
Passing Yards	131	136
Passes	12-24-2	9-26-3
Punts/Avg.	5-40	1-20
Fumbles-Lost	1-0	1-1
Penalties-Yards	1-15	3-25

SCORING

Ohio State	0	7	0	7	- 14
Michigan	3	0	6	0	- 9

1981

1981			
Ohio State	34	Duke	13
Ohio State	27	Michigan State	13
Ohio State	24	Stanford	19
Ohio State	27	Florida State	36
Ohio State	21	Wisconsin	24
Ohio State	34	Illinois	27
Ohio State	29	Indiana	10
Ohio State	45	Purdue	33
Ohio State	31	Minnesota	35
Ohio State	70	Northwestern	6
Ohio State	14	Michigan	9

Season Summary
Games Won, 8; Lost 3

ANTHONY CARTER
All-American Wide Receiver

1981			
Michigan	14	Wisconsin	21
Michigan	25	Notre Dame	7
Michigan	21	Navy	16
Michigan	38	Indiana	17
Michigan	38	Michigan State	20
Michigan	7	Iowa	9
Michigan	38	Northwestern	0
Michigan	34	Minnesota	13
Michigan	70	Illinois	21
Michigan	28	Purdue	10
Michigan	9	Ohio State	14

Season Summary
Games Won, 8; Lost 3

OHIO STATE

No.	Name	Pos.	Wt.	Hgt.	Home Town
9	Alders, Gary	QB-PT	195	6-2	Centerville, OH
22	Anderson, Cedric	FL	172	5-10	Apopka Flk., PA
19	Andres, Bill	PK	160	5-9	Cambridge, OH
47	Anthony, Thomas	CB	186	6-1	Rockville, MD
58	Apoke, Joe	C	218	6-5	Maderia, OH
1	Altha, Bob	QB-PK	176	5-11	Worthington, OH
17	Backus, Clark	FB	206	6-0	Maitland, FL
62	Balen, Alan	DT	240	6-1	Lackawanna, NY
4	Bell, Kelvin	S	184	6-2	Richmond, VA
94	Berner, Joe	LB	226	6-2	Avon Lake, OH
38	Broadnax, Vaughn	FB	252	6-3	Xenia, OH
59	Burris, Gary	C	200	6-1	Urbana, OH
77	Carson, Jim	QT	267	6-4	Akron, OH
83	Cicero, Chris	OLB	212	6-0	Chagrin Falls, OH
24	Cisco, Jeff	CB	183	5-11	St. Marys, OH
35	Cobb, Glen	LB	210	6-3	Wash Crt. Hse., OH
97	Crecelius, Dave	DT	247	6-5	Ashland, OH
11	Curtis, Clarence	OLB	210	6-2	Potomac, MC
66	Czyzynski, Rich	LB	216	6-2	Brook Park, OH
96	D'Andrea, Mike	OLB	215	6-4	Akron, OH
50	DeLeone, Jim	C	222	5-10	Kent, OH
78	Dooley, Joe	C	258	6-7	Cincinnati, OH
42	Dunn, Craig	FB	228	6-3	Montclair, NJ
81	Dwelle, Brad	TE	228	6-4	Sanducky, OH
41	Eberts, Mark	CB	287	6-0	Canton, OH
4	Edwards, Karl	PT-SE	206	6-3	Groveport, OH
55	Foster, Jerome	DT	255	6-3	Detroit, MI
89	Frank, John	TE	216	6-3	Mt. Lebanon, PA
84	Gatwood, Russell	TE	229	6-3	Orlando, FL
26	Gayle, Jimmy	TB	190	5-10	Hampton, VA
2	Gayle, Shaun	CB	194	5-11	Hampton, VA
91	Gilmore, Jim	DT	250	6-5	Philadelphia, PA
28	Gottron, Jeff	CB	182	5-11	Fremont, OH
75	Graves, Rory	OT	262	6-6	Decatur, GA
48	Griggs, Anthony	OLB	224	6-2	Willingboro, NJ
60	Harvey, William	LB	227	6-2	Springfield, VA
27	Hill, Doug	ROV	190	6-1	Miami, FL
95	Hill, Tim	LB	246	6-1	Columbus, OH
92	Hocevar, Mark	C	242	6-2	Warren, OH
34	Holland, Jay	S	175	5-10	Columbus, OH
88	Jemison, Thad	SE	189	6-2	Lincoln Heights, OH
8	Keuchler, Lamar	ROV	189	5-11	Marion, OH
33	Kolic, Larry	LB	224	6-1	Smithville, OH
73	Krerowicz, Mark	OT	286	6-3	Toledo, OH
64	Lachey, Jim	OG	253	6-6	St. Henry, OH
12	Lane, Garcia	S	274	5-10	Youngstown, OH
14	Langley, Victor	FL	194	6-0	Dallas, TX
86	Lee, Ben	OLB	212	6-0	Canton, OH
23	Lewis, Doyle	CB	184	6-0	Canton, OH
20	Lindsey, Kelvin	TB	186	6-0	Sandusky, OH
63	Lowdermik, Kirk	OG	246	6-4	Salem, OH
37	Lowry, Orlando	OLB	222	6-3	Shaker Heights, OH
51	Lucente, John	DT	241	6-1	Struthers, OH
72	Lukens, Joe	OG	264	6-4	Cincinnati, OH
39	Manning, Joe	OLB	200	6-0	Columbus, OH
36	Marek, Marcus	LB	222	6-2	Masury, OH
61	Medich, Dave	OG	252	6-2	Steubenville, OH
99	Miller, Nick	MG	224	6-2	Upland, PA
57	Norrill, David	DT	245	6-3	Centerville, OH
29	Myers, Raymond	FB	227	6-2	Toledo, OH
54	Nelms, Spencer	DT	236	6-3	Decatur, GA
18	O'Cain, Tim	TB	177	5-10	Gahanna, OH
7	Offenbecher, Brent	QB	190	6-1	Massillon, OH
53	Pack, Craig	C	240	6-1	Orriville, OH
79	Palahnuk, Mike	OG	254	6-2	Hicksville, NY
87	Penn, Trent	FL	170	5-11	Columbus, OH
21	Richardson, Kevin	TB	190	6-0	Cleveland, OH
93	Riehm, Chris	DT	252	6-6	Wadsworth, OH
70	Roberts, William	OT	262	6-5	Miami, FL
10	Schlichter, Art	QB	208	6-3	Columbus, OH
56	Simpson, Steve	OT	236	6-5	Temperance, MI
67	Smith, Joe	OT	266	6-3	Cincinnati, OH
46	Spencer, Tim	TB	210	6-1	St. Clairsville, OH
6	Stephens, Tim	QB	208	6-2	Parkersburg, WV
90	Sullivan, John	DT	232	6-5	Chicago, IL
32	Tatum, Rowland	ROV	207	6-1	Inglewood, CA
15	Tomczak, Mike	QB	178	6-6	Calumet City, IL
44	Williams, Gary	SE	212	6-2	Wilmington, OH
74	Zalenski, Scott	OG	248	6-4	Bethel Park, PA

MICHIGAN

No.	Name	Pos.	Wt.	Hgt.	Home Town
57	Anderson, Tim	LB	220	6-2	Ann Arbor, MI
34	Armstrong, Greg	TB	195	6-2	Middletown, OH
27	Bean, Vincent	WR	185	6-1	Southfield, MI
65	Becker, Kurt	OG	260	6-6	Aurora, IL
19	Bergeron, Bob	PK	145	5-8	Ft. Wayne, IN
82	Betts, Norm	TE	230	6-5	Midland, MI
3	Body, Marion	DB	178	5-10	Detroit, MI
40	Boren, Mike	LB	217	6-2	Columbus, OH
13	Bostic, Keith	DB	207	6-1	Ann Arbor, MI
28	Bracken, Don	P	185	6-0	Thermopolis, WY
25	Brockington, Fred	WR	200	6-3	Detroit, MI
15	Burgel, Jerry	DB	182	5-11	Ottawa, OH
12	Burgess, Fritz	DB	183	6-0	Passadena, CA
9	Carpenter, Brian	DB	166	5-11	Flint, MI
83	Carthens, Milt	TE	235	6-3	Pontiac, MI
63	Carraway, Windred	DL	230	6-3	Detroit, MI
1	Carter, Anthony	WR	161	5-11	Riviera Beach, FL
10	Cohen, Jeff	DB	185	5-11	Farmington Hills, MI
92	Coles, Cedric	DT	237	6-2	Detroit, MI
21	Cooper, Evan	DB	170	5-11	Miami, Fl
36	Czarnota, Mike	ILB	220	6-2	Detroit, MI
56	Dana, Robert	MG	220	6-2	Brooklyn, NY
26	Davis, Nate	TB	191	5-10	Jamestown, NY
42	Davis, Ricky	TB	174	6-1	Detroit, MI
90	DeFelice, Vince	DT	228	6-2	Trenton, MI
18	Dickey, B.J.	QB	188	6-0	Ottawa, OH
64	Diorio, Jerry	OG	230	6-2	Youngstown, OH
69	Dixon, Tom	C	238	6-1	Ft. Wayne, IN
88	Dunaway, Craig	TE	226	6-3	Pittsburg, PA
32	Edwards, Stan	FB	208	6-0	Detroit, MI
29	English, Joe	FB	212	6-0	Detroit, MI
51	Felten, Jeff	C	223	6-2	Centerville, OH
17	Ferens, John	DB	190	5-11	Toledo, OH
20	Fischer, Brad	QB	201	6-0	Ortonville, MI
54	Garrity, Tom	C	245	6-4	Grafton, WI
50	Girgash, Paul	ILB	205	6-1	Lakewood, OH
22	Hanlon, Mickey	WR	150	5-9	Ann Arbor, MI
6	Haji-Sheikh, Ali	PK	172	6-0	Arlington, TX
7	Hall, David	QB	202	6-4	Livonia, MI
31	Harris, Stu	DB	196	6-2	Chargin Falls, OH
48	Hassel, Tom	FB	195	6-0	Cincinnati, OH
33	Haynes, Duke	FB	202	6-2	Bellevue, OH
94	Herrmann, Jim	ILB	212	6-2	Dearborn Heights, MI
2	Hewlett, Rich	DB	197	6-1	Plymouth, MI
76	Humphries, Stefan	OG	240	6-3	Broward, FL
35	Ingram, Jerald	FB	217	6-1	Beaver, PA
37	Jackson, Tony	DB	174	5-10	Cleveland, OH
73	James, Doug	DL	242	6-2	Louisville, KY
52	Kempthorm Eric	C	215	6-0	Canton, OH
93	Lemirande, Mike	OLB	220	6-4	Grafton, WI
44	Lott, John	DB	180	6-0	Masury, OH
80	Lyles, Rodney	LB	214	6-2	Miami, FL
39	Melnyk, Mike	K	170	6-1	Warren, MI
96	Meredith, Dave	DT	225	6-3	Sterling Heights, MI
72	Muransky, Ed	OT	275	6-7	Youngstown, OH
35	Nate, Jeff	P	180	5-11	Dowagiac, MI
79	Neal, Tom	QT	259	6-5	Orlando, FL
97	Needham, Ben	ILB	210	6-4	Groveport, OH
78	Osbun, Tony	DT	254	6-5	Kenton, OH
75	Paris, William	OT	270	6-6	Louisville, KY
8	Powell, Greg	QB	183	5-11	Ravenna, OH
70	Prusa, Ron	AT	242	6-2	Chicago, IL
43	Reeves, Jeff	DB	192	6-1	Columbus, OH
46	Ricks, Lawrence	TB	195	5-10	Barberton, OH
58	Roberts, Scott	ILB	213	6-2	Miami, FL
61	Rodgers, Nate	MG	223	6-0	Warren, OH
89	Rose, Carlton	OLB	205	6-1	Ft. Lauderdale, FL
99	Schlopy, Todd	PK	160	5-10	Orchard Park NY
89	Shaw, Vincent	TE	210	6-2	Wheaton, IL
36	Smih, Cedric	WR	180	5-10	Ann Arbor, MI
23	Smith, Kerry	TB	190	6-1	Grand Rapids, MI
6	Smith, Kevin	DB	191	6-2	Dalles, TX
16	Smith, Steve	QB	191	6-0	Grand Blanc, MI
68	Strenger, Rich	OT	254	6-7	Grafton, WI
55	Sweeney, Larry	C	230	6-1	Alma, MI
14	Tech, Karl	PK-P	180	6-0	Gross Pte. Shores, MI
99	Thompson, Robert	OLB	219	6-3	Blue Island, IL
91	Triplett, Todd	OLB	212	6-2	Detroit, MI
4	Wallace, Zeke	WR	188	6-4	Pompano Beach, FL
49	Washington, Sanford	OLB	203	6-2	Youngstown, OH
84	Wilson, Mike	TE	222	6-3	Detroit, MI
24	Woolfolk, Buch	TB	207	6-2	Westfield NJ
62	Yarano, Day	OG	231	6-3	Zanesville, OH
60	Zagnoli, Rolle	OL	235	6-2	Long Beach, IN

KURT BECKER
All-American Guard

ED MURANSKY
All-American Tackle

WILLIAM PARIS
All-American Tackle

BUTCH WOOLFOLK
All-American Tailback

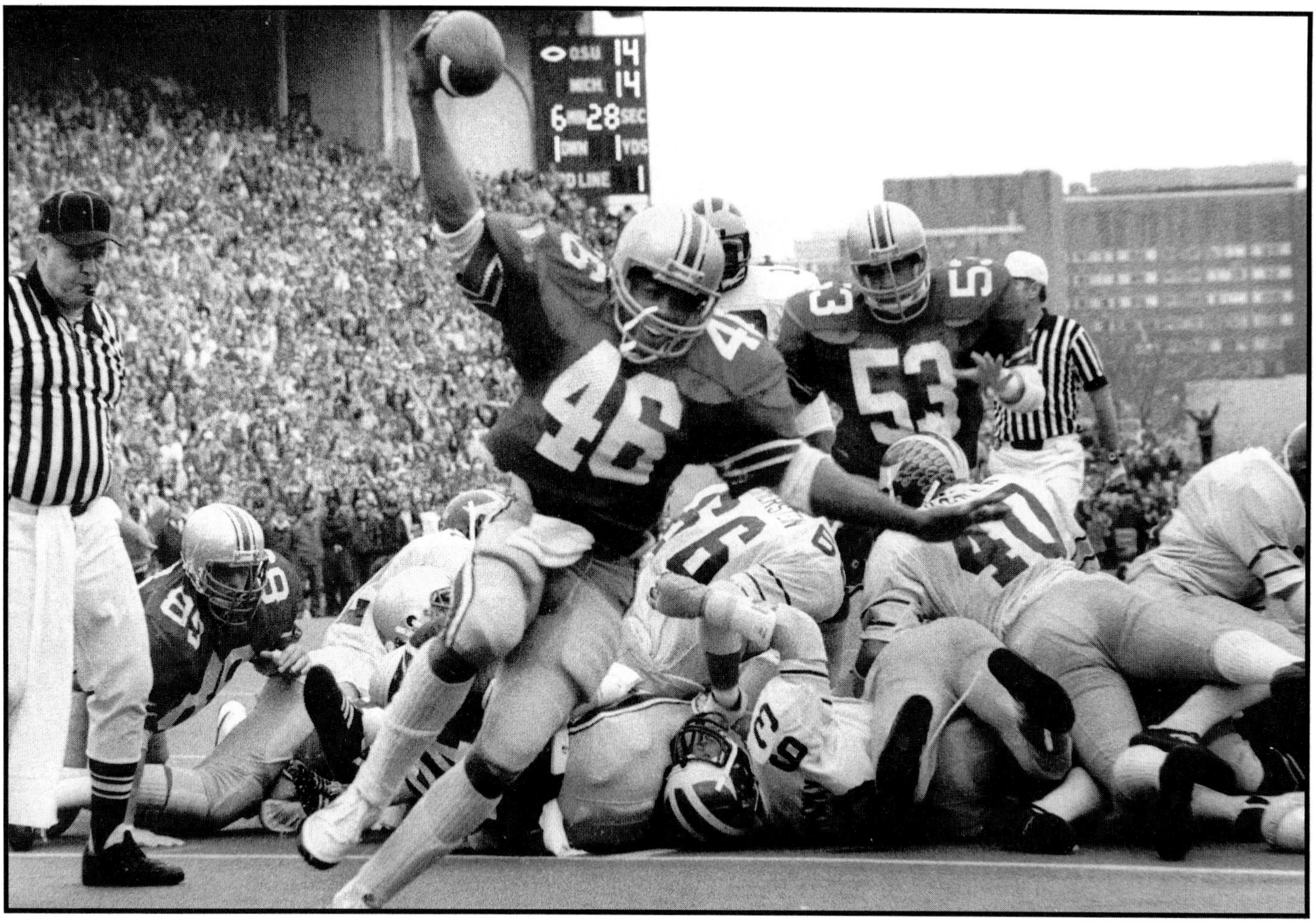
OSU 14
MICH 14
6 MIN 28 SEC
1 DWN 1 YDS
LINE 1

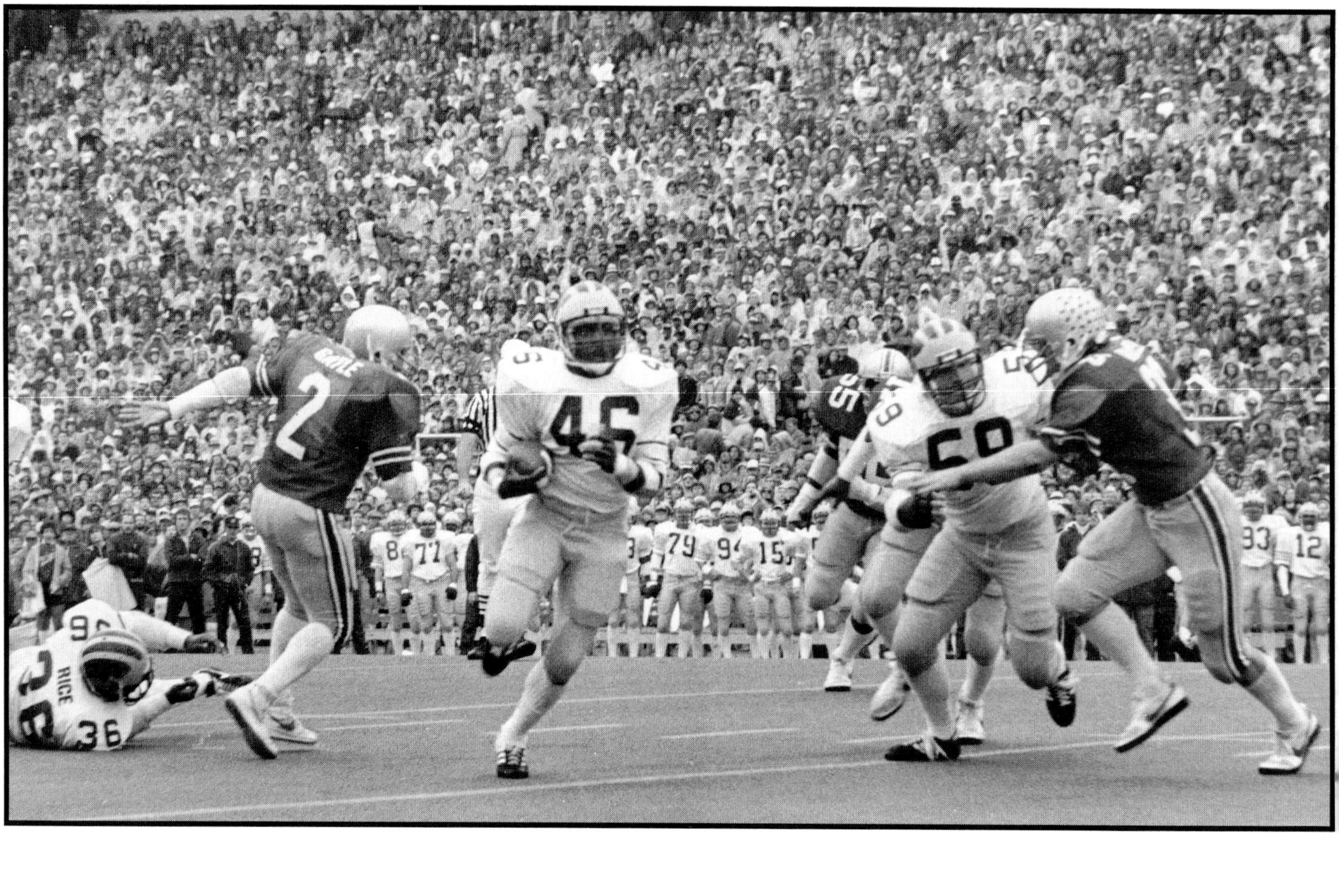

ɔhotos by Chance Brockway

November 20, 1982

Columbus, Ohio

Buckeyes Win 24-14, But Wolverines Advance To Rose Bowl

Ohio State Capitalizes On Costly Michigan Turnovers

Ohio State won the battle with a 24-14 victory over Michigan at Ohio Stadium, but Michigan won the war with a trip to the Rose Bowl.

Because of a scheduling quirk made years earlier, Michigan played more conference games than Ohio State and finished with an 8-1 Big Ten record, a league title and a Rose Bowl berth. The Buckeyes finished 7-1 in the league for second place, but gained the satisfaction of winning the head-to-head contest with their arch rivals.

Statistically the teams were almost equal, so the edge ultimately went to the team with fewer mistakes - Ohio State. Michigan suffered three interceptions and three lost fumbles to two lost fumbles for the Buckeyes.

Turnovers played a huge role in the decisive fourth quarter. With the score tied 14-14, Buckeye defenders Orlando Lowrey and Doug Hill caused Michigan receiver Anthony Carter to cough up the ball at the Michigan 14, and Hill recovered. Three plays later tailback Tim Spencer dove over the Michigan line from the one to give OSU a 21-14 lead with 6:27 to go.

On Michigan's next possession, Ohio State linebacker Marcus Marek intercepted a Steve Smith pass and returned it to the Michigan 19. Ohio State's freshman kicker Rich Spangler later split the uprights on a 33-yard field goal with 2:44 to play to guarantee the win.

Eager to celebrate the victory, the Ohio State fans flooded the field with five seconds to play and had to be urged off the field by the public address announcer so Michigan could run its final play.

The fans were more subdued earlier in the game as Michigan scored the lone touchdown of the first quarter on a l-yard sweep by tailback Larry Ricks. Ricks accounted for 50 of Michigan's 52 yards in that drive.

Ohio State then dominated the second quarter with a six-yard blast by fullback Vaughn Broadnax and a two-yard run by Spencer in the final two minutes. Michigan erased Ohio State's 14-7 halftime lead when Smith ran in from four yards out during the third quarter.

Smith's touchdown run was a bright spot in an otherwise frustrating day. He accounted for five of Michigan's six turnovers with three interceptions and two lost fumbles. He completed just 12 of 28 passes for 127 yards.

Leading the Michigan offense were Ricks with 110 yards on 27 carries and game breaking receiver Anthony Carter with seven catches for 78 yards and 48 yards in kick returns.

For Ohio State, quarterback Mike Tomczak was a solid 10 of 17 passes for 159 yards. Spencer led all rushers with 124 yards on 27 carries, pushing him past Ricks for the Big Ten rushing title.

The Buckeyes' Gary Williams caught four passes in the game, setting an NCAA record with at least one reception in all 44 regular season games he played.

STATISTICS

	UM	OSU
First Downs	20	18
Rushes-Yards	45-176	51-170
Passing Yards	127	159
Passes	12-28-3	10-18-0
Punts/Avg.	5-33	3-36
Fumbles-Lost	4-3	4-2
Penalties-Yards	2-15	4-35

SCORING

Michigan	7	0	7	0 -	14
Ohio State	0	14	0	10 -	24

1982

Michigan . . .	20	Wisconsin	9
Michigan . . .	17	Notre Dame	23
Michigan . . .	27	U.C.L.A.	31
Michigan . . .	24	Indiana	10
Michigan . . .	31	Michigan State . .	17
Michigan . . .	29	Iowa	7
Michigan . . .	49	Northwestern . . .	14
Michigan . . .	52	Minnesota	14
Michigan . . .	16	Illinois	10
Michigan . . .	52	Purdue	21
Michigan . . .	14	Ohio State	24

Season Summary

Games Won, 8; Lost 3

ANTHONY CARTER
All-American Wide Receiver

MICHIGAN

No.	Name	Pos.	Wt.	Hgt.	Home Town
1	Carter, Anthony	FLK	161	5-11	Riviera Beach, FL
2	Hewlett, Rich	DB	195	6-1	Plymouth, MI
3	Body, Marion	DB	180	5-10	Detroit, MI
4	Harbaugh, Jim	QB	195	6-3	Palo Alto, CA
5	McPhee, Riley	FB	225	6-2	Chicago, IL
6	Sessa, Mike	DB	172	6-1	St. Joseph, MI
6	Haii-Shelkh, Ali	PK	172	6-0	Arlington, TX
7	Hall, David	QB	190	6-4	Livonia, MI
8	Moons, Pat	PK	160	5-10	Coral Springs, FL
8	Powell, Greg	SE	190	6-2	Ravenna, OH
9	Decker, Dan	QB	180	6-2	Roseville, MI
10	Cohen, Jeff	DB	194	5-11	Farmington Hill, MI
12	Burgess, Fritz	DB	185	5-11	Pasedena, CA
13	Bostic, Keith	SS	205	6-1	Ann Arbor, MI
14	Pactorek, John	QB	177	5-9	Port Huron, MI
14	Gant, Tony	DB	175	6-2	Fremont, OH
15	Burgel, Jerry	DB	189	5-10	Ottawa, OH
16	Smith, Steve	QB	192	6-0	Grand Blanc, MI
17	Hicks, Ivan	DB	180	6-2	Pennsauken, NJ
17	Ferens, John	DB	190	6-0	Toledo, OH
18	Shevrin, Marc	DB	173	5-11	New York, NY
18	Makray, Triando	WR	185	6-2	Detroit, MI
19	Heren, Dieter	DB	190	6-3	Ft. Wayne, IN
19	Bergeron, Bob	PK	145	5-8	Ft. Wayne, IN
20	Rogers, Rick	RB	205	6-2	Inkster, MI
21	Cooper, Evan	DB	172	6-0	Miami, FL
22	Randall, Greg	DB	175	6-8	Chagrin Falls, OH
22	Hanlon, Mickey	WR	160	5-8	Ann Arbor, MI
23	Smith, Kerry	RB	190	6-2	Grand Rapids, MI
23	Kovacs, Lou	DB	195	5-10	Toledo, OH
24	Hood, Ed	DB	175	5-10	Toledo, OH
24	Johnson, Steve	WR	180	5-10	Youngstown, OH
25	Bean, Vincent	SE	190	6-3	Southfield, MI
26	Johnson, Gilvanni	WR	180	6-2	Detroit, MI
26	Davis, Nate	TB	195	5-10	Jamestown, NY
27	Wilcher, Thomas	TB	185	6-0	Detroit, MI
28	Bracken, Don	P	200	6-1	Thermopolis, WY
29	Woodmore, Derek	DB	190	6-1	Auburn Heights, MI
29	English, Joe	FB	198	5-9	Detroit, MI
31	Kimball, Bob	DB	170	6-0	Ypsilanti, MI
32	Garrett, Eddie	FB	220	6-2	Milwaukee, WI
33	Alkers, Jeff	ILB	220	6-2	Lynn, MA
34	Armstron, Greg	FB	195	6-2	Middleton, OH
35	Ingram, Jerald	FB	217	6-1	Beaver, PA
36	Rice, Dan	FB	215	6-2	Roxbury, MA
36	Samostuk, Andy	P	190	6-4	Lake Orion, MI
37	Perryman, Bob	FB	275	6-2	Buzzard's Bay, MA
38	Logue, Ben	RB	205	6-0	Atlata, GA
39	Melnyk, Mike	PK	170	6-1	Warren, MI
39	Fellin, Camp	DB	180	5-11	Ann Arbor, MI
40	Boren, Mike	ILB	228	6-3	Columbus, OH
41	Mercer, Brian	TB	200	6-2	Cincinnati, OH
42	Mallory, Mike	ILB	217	6-2	Dekalb, IL
42	David, Ricky	WR	174	6-1	Detroit, MI
43	Lewandowski, Phil	ILB	217	6-3	Solon, OH
44	Lott, John	DB	180	6-0	Masury, OH
45	Reinhold, Mike	ILB	215	6-3	Muskegon, MI
46	Ricks, Lawrence	TB	195	5-10	Barberton, OH
48	Hassel, Tom	OLB	212	6-0	Cincinnati, OH
49	Moeller, Andy	ILB	205	6-1	Ann Arbor, MI
50	Girgash, Paul	ILB	208	6-1	Lakewood, OH
51	Krauss, Mike	OL	235	6-0	Clinton, MI
52	Kempthorn, Eric	C	230	6-0	Canton, OH
52	Brooks, Kevin	DT	230	6-6	Detroit, MI
53	Sincich, Al	MG	227	6-1	Cleveland, OH
54	Harris, Robert	OLD	219	6-2	Palo Alto, CA
54	Garrity, Tom	OT	250	6-4	Grafton, WI
55	Sweeney, Larry	C	238	6-2	Alma, MI
56	Simon, Dave	C	220	6-7	Grosse Pointe, MI
57	Anderson, Tim	ILB	222	6-2	Ann Arbor, MI
58	Ghindia, John	OG	238	6-2	Trenton, MI
58	Cowan, Keith	OLB	205	6-0	Pittsburg, PA
59	Bakourdos, Art	C	230	6-2	Chicago, IL
60	Popowski, Bob	OG	240	6-3	Chicago, IL
61	Rogers, Nate	MG	230	6-0	Warren, OH
62	Yarano, Dan	OG	248	6-1	Zanesville, OH
63	Carraway, Winfred	DT	240	6-2	Detroit, MI
64	Diorio, Jerry	OG	244	6-3	Youngstown, OH
65	Mihic, John	OL	235	6-4	Lombard, IL
66	Hammerstein, Mike	DT	225	6-4	Wapakoneta, OH
67	Knoebel, Tom	OF	225	6-3	Chicago, IL
68	Strenger, Rich	OT	261	6-7	Grafton, WI
69	Dixon, Tom	C	247	6-2	Ft. Wayne, IN
70	Prusa, Ron	OT	242	6-3	Chicago, IL
71	Frazer, Rick	OL	230	6-4	Escanaba, MI
72	Zimmerman, Gil	OT	235	6-5	St. Louis, MO
73	James, Doug	OF	245	6-2	Louisville, KY
75	Quaerna, Jerry	OT	250	6-5	Ft. Atkinson, WI
76	Humphries, Stefan	OG	248	6-4	Broward, FL
77	Tabachino, Bob	OG	235	6-0	YOunstwon, OH
78	Hammerstein, Mark	OL	240	6-4	Wapakoneta, OH
79	Miller, Clay	OT	240	6-4	Norman, OL
80	Lyles, Rodney	OLB	225	6-3	Miami, FL
81	Kattus, Eric	TE	220	6-6	Cincinnati, OH
82	Schmerge, Paul	TE	210	6-2	Cincinnati, OH
83	Carthens, Milt	TE	240	6-3	Pontiac, MI
84	Wilson, Mike	TE	235	6-3	Detroit, MI
85	Scarcelli, Jim	DT	228	6-6	Warren, MI
86	Washington, Greg	OLB	215	6-3	Detroit, MI
86	Roberts, Scott	TE	212	6-1	Miami, FL
88	Dunaway, Craig	TE	233	6-2	Pittsburg, PA
89	Rose, Carlton	OLB	205	6-1	Ft. Lauderdale, FL
90	DeFelice, Vince	DT	245	6-2	Trenton, MI
91	Triplett, Todd	OLB	212	6-2	Detroit, MI
92	Gray, Joe	MG	225	6-1	Detroit, MI
93	Leminrande, Mike	OLB	226	6-4	Grafton, WI
94	Herrman, Jim	ILB	217	6-2	Dearborn Hgts., MI
95	Nelson, Sim	OLB	235	6-2	Ft. Hgts., MI
96	Meredith, Dave	DT	239	6-4	Sterling, Hgts., MI
97	Shimko, Marty	OLB	220	6-4	Bay Village, PA
99	Thompson, Robert	OLB	221	6-3	Blue Island, IL
99	Schlopy, Todd	PK	165	5-10	Orchard Park, NY

OHIO STATE

No.	Name	Pos.	Wt.	Hgt.	Home Town
1	Lansese, Mike	TB	185	6-0	Mayfield, OH
2	Gayle, Shaun	CB	194	5-11	Hampton, VA
3	Woolf, Scott	QB	180	6-1	Beloit, OH
4	Bell, Kelvin	S	190	6-2	Richmond, VA
5	Edwards, Karl	PT	206	6-3	Groveport, OH
6	Stephens, Tim	QB	210	6-2	Parkersburg, WVA
6	McFarland, Dave	PK	156	5-9	Oberlin, OH
7	Offenbecher, Brent	QB	190	6-1	Massillon, OH
8	Keuchler, Lamar	ROV	189	5-11	Marion, OH
9	Alders, Gary	OLB	196	6-2	Centerville, OH
10	Spangler, Rich	PK	200	6-2	Geneva, OH
11	Curtis, Curt	OLB	212	6-2	Potomac, MD
12	Lane, Garcia	CB	174	5-10	Youngstown, OH
13	Neff, Scott	FL/PK	180	5-11	Spring Valley, OH
14	Blair, Ken	FB	210	5-11	Newbury, OH
15	Tomczak, Mike	QB	184	6-1	Calumet City, IL
15	Willison, Randy	WR	180	6-0	New Lexington, OH
16	Karsatos, Jim	QB	218	6-3	Fullerton, CA
17	Backus, Clark	LB	206	6-0	Maitland, FL
18	Bates, Roman	TB	194	6-0	Memphis, TN
19	Hill, Steve	'S	190	6-1	Ft. Walton Bch., FL
20	Lindsey, Kelvin	TB	186	6-0	Sandusky, OH
21	Richardson, Kevin	CB	190	6-1	Cleveland, OH
22	Anderson, Cedric	FL	175	5-10	Apopka, FL
23	Lewis, Doyle	CB	184	6-0	Canton, OH
24	Cisco, Jeff	ROV	184	5-11	St. Mary's, OH
25	Wooldridge, John	TB	190	5-11	Akron, OH
26	Gayle, Jimmy	TB	192	5-10	Hampton, VA
26	Jordon, Ron	TB	180	5-9	Columbus, OH
27	Hill, Doug	ROV	192	6-1	Miami, FL
27	Keith-Jones, Emmett	TB	193	6-0	Xenia, OH
28	Gottron, Jeff	S	182	5-11	Fremont, OH
29	Myers, Ray	FB	227	6-2	Toledo, OH
30	Kee, Mike	LB	214	6-2	Columbus, OH
30	Coleman, Tim	CB	174	5-7	Buffalo, NY
32	Tatum, Rowland	OLB	218	6-1	Inglewood, CA
33	Kolic, Larry	LB	227	6-1	Smithville, OH
34	Holland, Jay	SE	184	5-11	Columbus, OH
35	Cobb, Glen	LB	212	6-3	Washington, C.H.
35	Wood, Mike	DB	185	6-0	N. Syracuse, NY
36	Marek, Marcus	LB	216	6-2	Masury, OH
36	Marsh, Tim	K	180	6-0	Worthington, OH
37	Lowry, Orlando	OLB	228	6-3	Shaker Hgts., OH
38	Broadnex, Vaughn	FB	248	6-3	Xenia, OH
39	Walker, Bary	FB	216	6-0	Lancaster, OH
41	Byars, Keith	FB	225	6-2	Dayton, OH
41	Caruso, Tom	ROV	173	5-11	Wappingers Falls, NY
42	Dunn, Craig	FB	240	6-3	Montclair, NJ
43	Palmer, Jim	CB	180	5-11	Williamsburg, VA
44	Williams, Gary	SE	212	6-2	Wilmington, OH
44	Pittman, Mark	SE	191	6-1	New Concord, OH
46	Spencer, Tim	TB	210	6-1	St. Clairsville, OH
47	Anthony, Tom	S	190	6-1	Rockville, MD
47	Clark, Sheldon	DB	180	6-0	Copley, OH
48	Cargile, Jeff	TB	203	5-11	Cincinnati, OH
49	Smith, Doug	SE	190	6-1	Atlanta, GA
50	Odom, Tim	C	237	6-3	Villa Hills, KY
51	Lucente, John	MG	245	6-2	Struthers, OH
52	Whitmer, Doug	C	191	5-11	Kettering, OH
53	Pack, Craig	C	238	6-1	Orrville, OH
53	Kidwell, Eric	C	210	6-1	Columbus, OH
54	Nelms, Spencer	MG	223	6-3	Decatur, GA
54	Hill, Tim	LB	226	6-1	Columbus, OH
55	Foster, Jerome	DT	258	6-3	Detroit, MI
56	Simpson, Steve	OT	236	6-5	Temperance, MI
57	Morrill, Dave	DT	246	6-3	Centerville, OH
57	Tomak, Ted	OG	180	6-0	Louisville, OH
58	Hueston, Dennis	OLB	204	6-1	Toledo, OH
59	Hutchinson, John	LB	208	6-3	Atwater, OH
60	Harvey, Bill	LB	227	6-2	Springfield, VA
61	Sullivan, John	DT	224	6-4	Chicago, IL
62	MCormick, Tom	OT	238	6-7	Lakewood, OH
63	Lowdermilk, Kirk	MG	248	6-4	Salem, OH
64	Lachey, Jim	OG	262	6-2	St. Henry, OH
65	Glancey, Tom	OGF	244	6-4	W. Palm Beach, FL
66	Czyzynski, Rich	OLB	216	6-2	Brook Park, OH
67	Smith, Joe	OT	275	6-3	Cincinnati, OH
68	Hocevar, Mark	C	250	6-2	Warren, OH
69	Giullani, Anthony	DT	250	6-0	Westerville, OH]
70	Roberts, Bill	OT	268	6-5	Miami, FL
71	Maggs, Bob	OT	262	6-5	Youngstown, OH
72	Lukens, Joseph	OG	262	6-4	Cincinnati, OH
73	Krerowicz, Mark	OT	278	6-4	Toledo, OH
74	Zalenski, Scott	OG	248	6-4	Bethel Park, PA
74	Chesbrough, Larry	DT	250	6-3	Mentor, OH
75	Graves, Rory	OT	267	6-6	Decatur, GA
76	Bachorski, Dan	OT	290	6-6	Bridgeville, PA
77	Carson, Jim	OT	268	6-5	Akron, OH
78	Dooley, Joe	C	262	6-6	Cincinnati, OH
79	Palahnuk, Mike	OF	251	6-2	Hicksville, NY
80	Delaney, Kevin	SE	190	6-1	Worthington, OH
81	Dwelle, Brad	TE	230	6-4	Sandusky, OH
81	Wagner, Dave	WR	174	5-11	Worthington, OH
82	Lee, Byron	OLB	226	6-3	Columbus, OH
83	Leach, Scott	ROV	185	6-3	Bridgeport, CT]
84	Andrews, Bill	PK	160	5-9	Cambridge, OH
85	Groza, Judd	TE	229	6-2	Beree, OH
86	Selvaggio, Rob	TE	210	6-4	Eagan, MN
87	Penn, Trent	FL	174	5-11	Columbus, OH
88	Jemison, Thad	SE	190	6-2	Lincoln Hgts., OH
88	Allen, Paul	PK	150	5-10	New York, NY
89	Frank, John	TE	217	6-3	Mt. Lebanon, PA
90	Braun, Don	DT	241	6-1	Columbus, OH
91	Gilmore, Jim	DT	248	6-5	Philadelphia, PA
92	Hulshult, Gene	DT	236	6-4	Hamilton, OH
93	Riehm, Chris	DT	266	6-5	Wadsworth, OH
94	Cicero, Chris	OLB	212	6-0	Chagrin Falls, OH
95	Lee, Darryl	MG	266	6-3	Columbus, OH
96	Bose, Tom	LB	221	6-4	Stow, OH
97	Credelius, Dave	DT	244	6-5	Ashland, OH
97	Elsenman, Terr	PT	195	6-11	Columbus, OH
98	Johnson, Thomas	LB	216	6-3	Detroit, MI
99	Pfister, Mark	LB	220	6-2	Columbus, OH

1982

Ohio State	21	Baylor	14
Ohio State	31	Michigan State	10
Ohio State	20	Stanford	23
Ohio State	17	Florida State	34
Ohio State	0	Wisconsin	6
Ohio State	26	Illinois	21
Ohio State	49	Indiana	25
Ohio State	38	Purdue	6
Ohio State	35	Minnesota	10
Ohio State	40	Northwestern	28
Ohio State	24	Michigan	14

Season Summary

Games Won, 8; Lost 3

MARCUS MAREK
All-American Linebacker

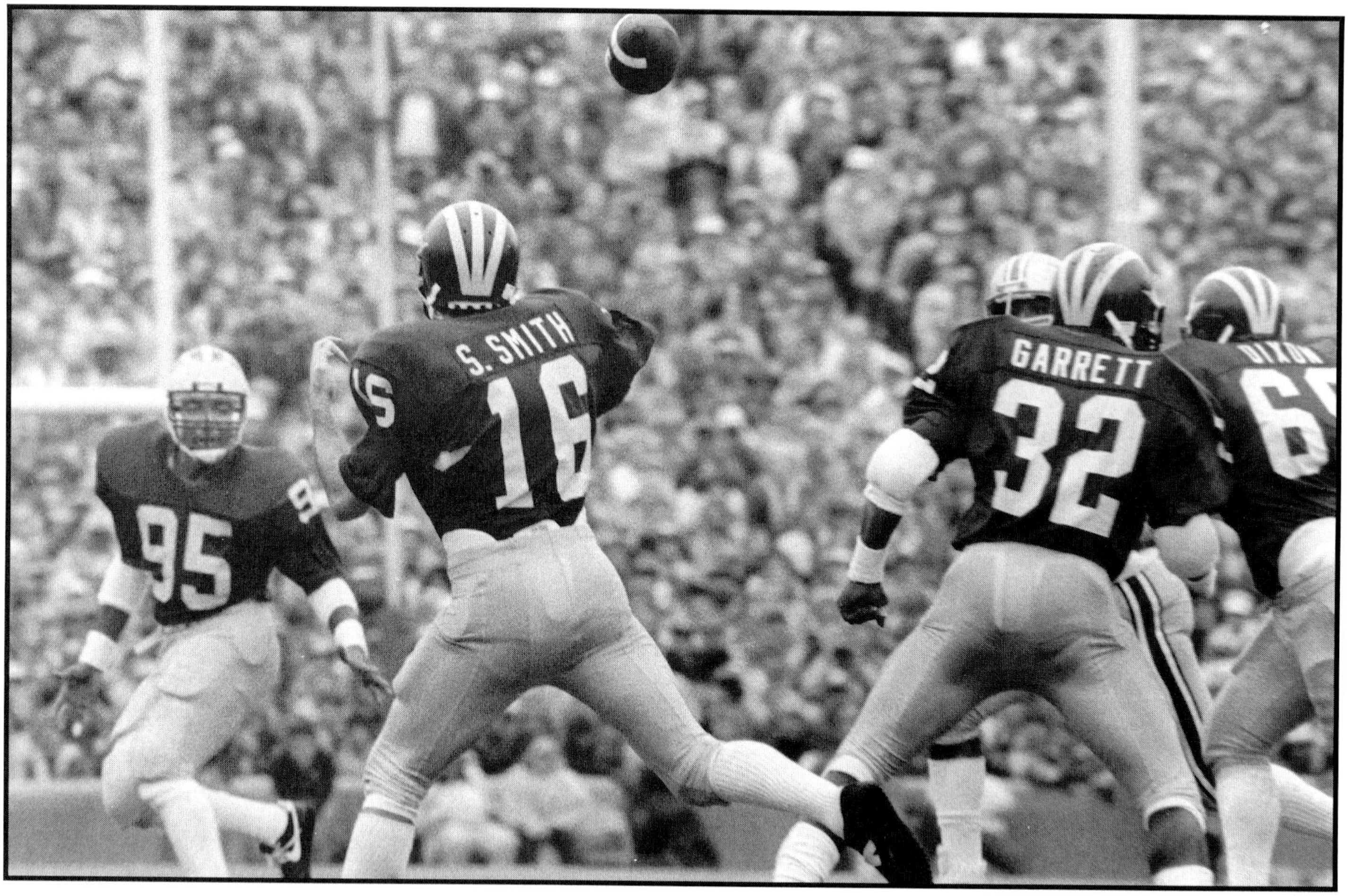
S. SMITH
16
95
GARRETT
32

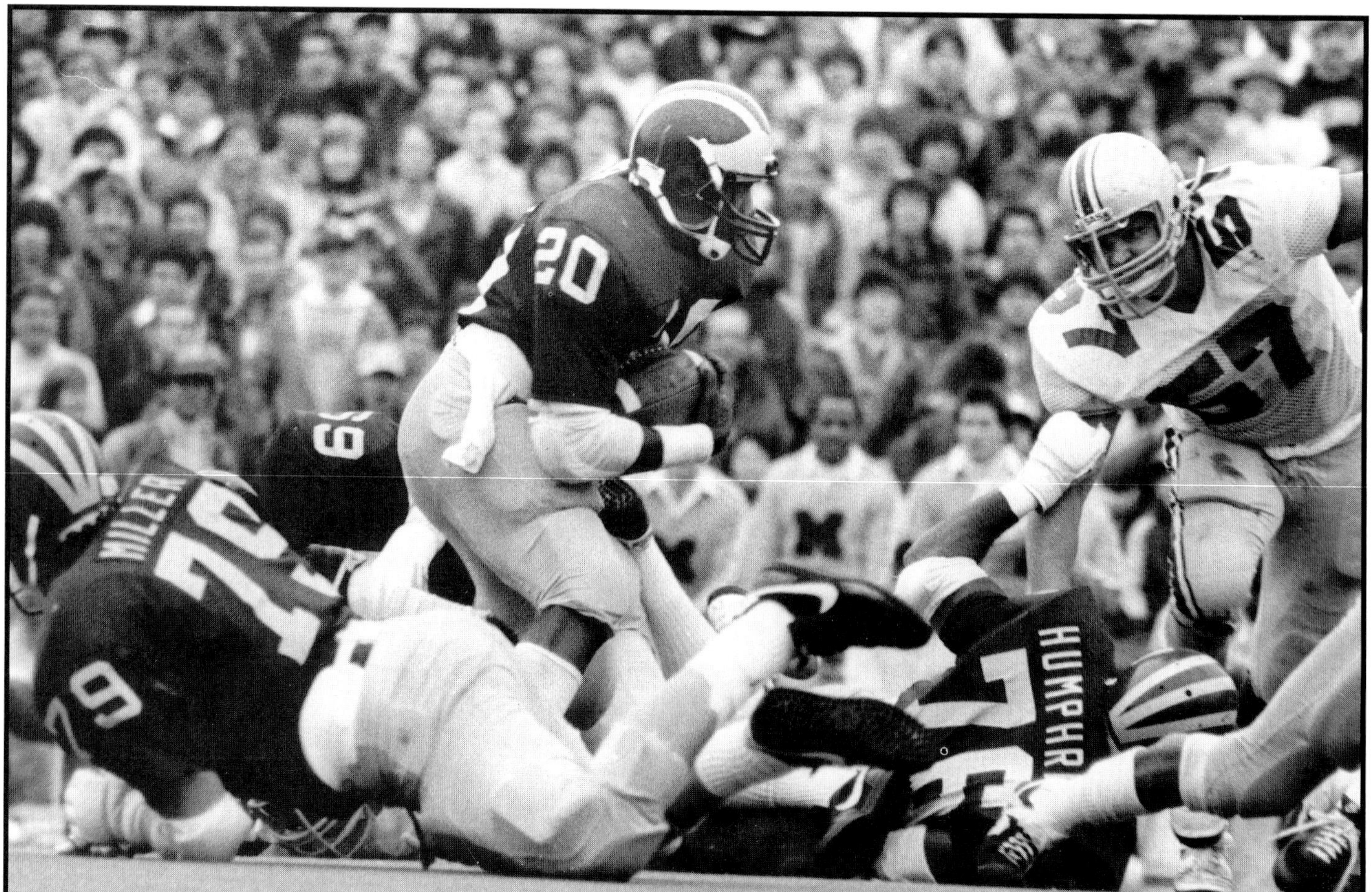
20
HUMPHR

photos by Chance Brockway

November 19, 1983

Ann Arbor, Michigan

Buckeyes Gamble and Lose As Wolverines Claim 24-21 Win

Michigan Foils Ohio's Surprise Play

During the week before the big contest, Ohio State Coach Earle Bruce insisted that he wouldn't use any trick plays in a game of the Ohio State-Michigan magnitude.

As it turned out, Bruce did gamble with a trick play and the ploy backfired. That, and Michigan's error-free ball, propelled the Wolverines to a 24-21 win in front of its home crowd.

Bruce decided to unveil his secret play with 10:51 remaining in the game and his team trailing 17-14. The Buckeyes had moved from their 20 to the Michigan 38 where they faced a second-and-10 situation. Ohio State quarterback Mike Tomczak took the ball from center Joe Dooley and then set the ball on the ground as he carried out a fake. Offensive guard Jim Lachey was supposed to pick up the ball and run while Michigan wondered what was happening.

Instead, Michigan nose guard Al Sincich submarined Dooley and Michigan's Mike Hammerstein fell on the ball.

"It was a bad call," Bruce said after the game. "It looked like a million dollars. It's worked all year in practice. Don't put the blame on anyone but me. "

Following the fumble recovery, the Wolverines drove 60 yards to paydirt with quarterback Steve Smith's one-yard run capping the drive. Michigan led at that point 24 14, and Ohio State was able to manage just one more touchdown before the game ended. Tomczak hit receiver Cedric Anderson with a 32-yard touchdown pass with 1 :52 to play. The Buckeyes did get the ball back with 32 seconds remaining, but could not advance beyond their 38-yard line.

The game featured several momentum shifts, with Michigan owning the early advantage. On their first offensive play, the Wolverines got a 47-yard run from Rick Rogers to set up a 26-yard field goal by Bob Bergeron. Michigan's next possession was even more fruitful as Smith connected with Triando Markray for a 67-yard scoring pass.

Trailing 10-0, Ohio State saw matters go from bad to worse as running back Keith

Byars lost a fumble at the Michigan six. The Buckeyes, however, gained strength in the second quarter with a one-yard touchdown run by Byars and a dramatic goal-line stand just before the half. Starting from the four, Michigan had four chances to score but the OSU defense, led by Orlando Lowry and Rowland Tatum, denied the Wolverines. On fourth down Bergeron missed a 22-yard field goal try.

Ohio State gained its only lead of the day early in the third quarter when Byars ran 18 yards for his second TD and a 14-10 Ohio State advantage. Michigan regained the lead later in the quarter when Brian Cochran picked off a Tomczak pass to the OSU 28, and Smith later ran it in from the one. Michigan's 17-14 lead set the stage for the Buckeye's bungled trick play.

Leading the Wolverines were Rogers with 91 yards in 16 carries and Smith with 11 of-20 passes for 207 yards. For the Buckeyes, Byars's two touchdowns gave him 19 for the season, breaking the Big Ten record set by Michigan State's Eric Allen in 1971. Byars gained 115 yards in 26 attempts. Tomczak completed 21 of 40 passes for 298 yards.

Tomczak was also intercepted twice which, coupled with Ohio State's two lost fumbles, gave the Buckeyes four turnovers to Michigan's none.

STATISTICS

	OSU	UM
First Downs	22	20
Rushes-Yards	36-150	54-208
Passing Yards	298	207
Passes	21-40-2	11-20-0
Punts/Avg.	6-40	4-34
Fumbles-Lost	3-2	1-0
Penalties-Yards	5-35	2-10

SCORING

Ohio State	0	7	7	7	21
Michigan	10	0	0	14	24

1983

Ohio State . . .	31	Oregon	6
Ohio State . . .	24	Oklahoma	14
Ohio State . . .	14	Iowa	20
Ohio State . . .	69	Minnesota	18
Ohio State . . .	33	Purdue	22
Ohio State . . .	13	Illinois	17
Ohio State . . .	21	Michigan State . .	11
Ohio State . . .	45	Wisconsin	27
Ohio State . . .	56	Indiana	17
Ohio State . . .	55	Northwestern . . .	7
Ohio State . . .	21	Michigan	24

Season Summary
Games Won, 8; Lost, 3

OHIO STATE

No.	Name	Pos.	Wt.	Hgt.	Home Town
9	Alders, Gary	OLB	203	6-2	Centerville, OH
87	Allen, Paul	PK	162	5-10	New York, NY
22	Anderson, Cedric	FL	170	5-10	Apopka, FL
76	Bachorski, Dan	OT	282	6-5	Bridgeville, PA
17	Backus, Clark	LB	210	6-0	Maitland, FL
28	Bates, Roman	TB	200	6-0	Memphis, TN
4	Bell, Kelvin	S	190	6-2	Richmond, VA
46	Blair, Ken	FB	210	5-11	Newbury, OH
96	Bose, Tom	OLB	232	6-3	Stow, OH
38	Broadnax, Vaughn	FB	252	6-2	Xenia, OH
94	Brown, Henry	DT	250	6-4	New York, NY
41	Byars, Keith	TB	226	6-2	Dayton, OH
48	Cargile, Jeff	ROV	203	6-0	Cincinnati, OH
77	Carson, Jim	QT	272	6-5	Akron, OH
97	Crecelius, Dave	DT	252	6-5	Ashland, OH
66	Czyzynski, Rich	OLB	218	6-2	Brook Park, OH
78	Dooley, Joe	C	268	6-6	Cincinnati, OH
5	Edwards, Karl	PT	190	6-2	Groveport, OH
89	Frank, John	TE	226	6-3	Mt. Lebanon, PA
2	Gayle, Shaun	CB	192	5-11	Hampton, VA
56	Gilmore, Jim	C	250	6-5	Philadelphia, PA
59	Giuliani, Tony	DT	244	6-0	Westerville, OH
39	Gordon, Sonny	CB	174	6-0	Milletown, OH
23	Gorley, Rod	S	194	6-0	Cincinnati, OH
75	Graves, Rory	OT	274	6-6	Decatur, GA
85	Groza, Judd	TE	227	6-2	Berea, OH
27	Hill, Doug	ROV	192	6-1	Miami,FA
19	Hill, Steve	S	190	6-1	Ft. Walton, Bch. FA
34	Holland, Jay	FL	174	5-11	Columbus, OH
55	Holliman, Ray	DT	240	6-5	Holland, MI
58	Hueston, Dennis	OLB	210	6-1	Toledo, OH
81	Hutchison, John	TE	221	6-3	Atwater, OH
88	Jemison, Thad	SE	195	6-2	Cincinnati, OH
98	Johnson, Thomas	LB	228	6-3	Detroit, MI
16	Karsatos, Jim	QB	226	6-3	Fullerton, CA
30	Kee, Mike	LB	210	6-2	Columbus, OH
33	Kolic, Larry	LB	235	6-1	Smithville, OH
73	Krerowicz, Mark	OT	278	OT	Toledo, OH
14	Kumerow, Eric	QB-PT	222	6-6	River Forest, IL
64	Lachey, Jim	OG	264	6-6	St. Henry, OH
12	Lane, Garcia	CB	178	5-10	Youngstown, OH
1	Lanese, Mike	TB	190	6-0	Mayfield, OH
8	Leach, Scott	ROV	191	6-3	White Plains, NY
82	Lee, Byron	OLB	223	6-3	Columbus, OH
95	Lee, Darryl	MG	262	6-3	Columbus, OH
20	Lindsey, Kelvin	TB	190	6-0	Sandusky, OH
63	Lowdermilk, Kirk	OG	256	6-3	Salem, TX
37	Lowry, Orlando	OLB	222	6-3	Shaker Heights, OH
71	Maggs, Bob	C	270	6-5	Youngstown, OH
62	McCormick, Tom	OT	254	6-6	Lakewood, OH
57	Morril, Dave	DT	262	6-3	Centerville, OH
53	Morris, Rich	C	242	6-4	Wheaton, IL
54	Nelms, Spencer	MG	242	6-3	Decatur, GA
50	Odom, Tim	C	240	6-3	Villa Hills, KY
7	Offenbecher, B	QB	190	6-1	Massillon, OH
3	Palmer, James	CB	182	5-11	Williamsburg, Va
99	Pfister, Mark	LB	218	6-2	Columbus, OH
21	Richardson, Kevin	CB	188	6-0	Cleveland, OH
70	Roberts, Bill	OT	278	6-5	Miami, FL
49	Smith, Doug	SE	190	6-1	Atlanta, GA
10	Spangler, Rich	PK	192	6-1	Geneva, OH
6	Stephens, Tim	QB	206	6-2	Parkersburg, WV
61	Sullivan, John	DT	251	6-4	Chicago, IL
80	Taggart, Ed	TE-PT	212	6-3	Akron, OH
32	Tatum, Rowland	LB	226	6-1	Inglewood, Ca
15	Tomczak, Mike	QB	190	6-1	Calumet City, IL
43	Walker, Barry	FB	214	6-0	Lancaster, OH
52	Whitmer, Doug	C	200	6-0	Kettering, OH
25	Wooldridge, John	TB	192	5-11	Akron, OH
74	Zalenski, Scott	OG	256	6-5	Bethel Park, PA

MICHIGAN

No.	Name	Pos.	Wt.	Hgt.	Home Town
33	Akers, Jeff	OLB	225	6-2	Lynn, MA
57	Anderson, Tim	ILB	218	6-2	Ann Arbor, MI
34	Armstrong, Greg	FB	195	6-2	Middleton, OH
59	Balourdos, Art	C/OG	240	6-2	Chicago, IL
50	Balourdos, John	ILB	215	6-2	Chicago, IL
25	Bean, Vincent	SE	190	6-3	Southfield, MI
19	Bergeron, Bob	PK	160	5-8	Ft. Wayne, IN
6	Bishop, Al	DB	180	5-10	Miami, FL
40	Boren, Mike	ILB	230	6-3	Columbus, OH
68	Borowski, Andrew	OL	250	6-4	Cincinnati, OH
99	Bostic, Carlitos	OLB	223	6-3	Ypsilanti, MI
28	Bracken, Don	P	205	6-1	Thermopolis, WY
52	Brooks, Kevin	DT	245	6-6	Detroit, MI
12	Burgees, Fritz	DB	192	5-11	Pasadena, CA
83	Carthens, Milt	TE	245	6-3	Pontiac, MI
94	Cecchini, Gene	DL	220	6-5	Farmington, MI
30	Cochran, Brad	DB	198	6-3	Royal Oak, MI
10	Cohen, Jeff	DB	198	5-11	Farmington Hills, MI
21	Cooper, Evan	DB	180	6-0	Miami, FL
58	Cowan, Keith	OLB	207	6-0	Pittsburg, PA
5	Dawson, William	WR	165	6-0	Evanston, IL
9	Decker, Dan	QB	200	6-2	Roseville, MI
90	Defelice, Vince	DT	246	6-2	Trenton, MI
64	Diorio, Jerry	OG	245	6-3	Youngstown, OH
69	Dixon, Tom	C	250	6-2	Ft. Wayne, IN
72	Elliott, John	OT	280	6-7	Lake Ronkonkoma, NY
39	Fellin, Camp	DB	174	5-11	Ann Arbor, MI
15	Ferens, John	DB	199	6-0	Toledo, OH
93	Folkertsma, David	ILB	248	6-5	Grand Rapids, MI
71	Frazer, Rick	OL	250	6-4	Escanaba, MI
9	Freeman, Dwayne	DB	185	6-3	W. Palm Beach, FL
14	Gant, Tony	DB	175	6-2	Fremont, OH
32	Garrett, Eddie	FB	220	6-2	Milwaukee, WI
58	Ghindia, John	OG	240	6-2	Trenton, MI
92	Gray, Joe	MG	230	6-1	Detroit, MI
7	Hall, David	QB	205	6-4	Livonia, MI
78	Hammerstein, Mark	OL	262	6-4	Wapakoneta, OH
66	Hammerstein, Mike	DT	239	6-4	Wapakoneta, OH
4	Harbaugh, Jim	QB	202	6-3	Palo Alton, CA
56	Harris, Billy	MG	230	6-1	Xenia, OH
48	Hassel, Tom	OLB	215	6-0	Cincinnati, OH
35	Heren, Dieter	DB	200	6-3	Ft. Wayne, IN
2	Hewlett, Rich	DB	195	6-1	Plymouth, MI
17	Hicks, Ivan	DB	180	6-2	Pennsauken, NJ
31	Higgins, Kenneth	WR	180	6-2	Battle Creek, MI
28	Hood, Ed	DB	178	5-10	Utica, MI
76	Humphries, Stefan	OG	262	6-4	Broward, FL
73	James, Doug	OT	267	6-2	Louisville, KY
38	Johns, Brandon	DB	175	6-2	Benton Harbor, MI
26	Johnson, Gilvanni	WR	175	6-2	Detroit, MI
24	Johnson, Steve	WR	170	5-10	Youngstown, OH
81	Kattus, Eric	TE	222	6-6	Cincinnati, OH
67	Knoebel, Tom	C	236	6-3	Chicago, IL
51	Krauss, Mike	DT	240	6-5	Clinton, MI
29	Lawson, Gene	WR	172	5-11	Ft. Lauderdale, FL
43	Lewandowski, Phil	ILB	222	6-3	Solon, OH
38	Logue, Ben	RB	195	6-0	Atlanta, GA
33	Logus, Phil	WR	165	5-10	Attamonte Springs, FL
44	Lott, John	DB	180	6-0	Masury, OH
80	Lyles, Rodney	OLB	226	6-3	Miami, FL
8	Mallory, Douglas	DB	185	6-1	Dekalb, IL
42	Mallory, Mike	ILB	217	6-2	Dekalb, IL
18	Markray, Triando	WR	182	6-2	Detroit, MI
54	McIntyre, Andree	ILB	245	6-1	Chicago, MI
39	Melnyk, Mike	PK	165	6-1	Warren, MI
41	Mercer, Brian	TB	205	6-2	Cincinnati, OH
96	Meredith, Dave	DT	245	6-4	Sterling Hgts., MI
65	Mihic, John	OL	258	6-4	Lombard, IL
79	Miller, Clay	OT	258	6-4	Norman, OK
49	Moeller, Andy	ILB	219	6-1	Ann Arbor, MI
74	Mogle, Glenn	OT	280	6-8	Sarasota, FL
8	Moons, Pat	PK	160	5-10	Ft. Lauderdale, FL
95	Nelson, Sim	OLB	235	6-2	Ft. Wayne, IN
84	O'Connor, Michael	SE	195	6-3	Kankakee, IL
14	Paciorek, John	QB	183	5-10	Port Huron, MI
37	Perryman, Bob	FB	230	6-2	Buzzard's Bay, MA
60	Popowski, Bob	OG	251	6-3	Chicago, IL
75	Quaerna, Jerry	OT	265	6-5	Ft. Atkinson, WI
22	Randall, Greg	DB	180	6-0	Chagrin Falls, OH
3	Rein, Russ	QB	188	6-1	Evergreen Park, IL
45	Reinhold, Mike	ILB	228	6-3	Muskegon, MI
36	Rice, Dan	FB	229	6-2	Raxbury, MA
13	Rivers, Garland	DB	182	6-2	Canton, OH
43	Robbins, Monte	P	195	6-4	Great Bend, KS
61	Rodgers, Nate	MG	234	6-0	Warren, OH
20	Rogers, Rick	RB	216	6-2	Inkster, MI
89	Rose, Carlton	OLB	218	6-1	Ft. Lauderdale, FL
36	Samosiuk, Andy	P	175	6-2	Lake Orion, MI
85	Scarcelli, Jim	OLB	216	6-6	Warren, MI
99	Schlopy, Todd	PK	163	5-10	Orchard Park, NY
82	Schmerge, Paul	TE	222	6-2	Cincinnati,OH
29	Schulte, Tim	DB	200	6-3	Ft. Thomas, KY
25	Schulte, Todd	ILB	210	6-3	Ft. Thomas, KY
6	Sessa, Mike	WR	175	6-1	St. Joseph, MI
18	Shevrin, Marc	DB	176	5-11	New York, NY
97	Shimko, Marty	DT	220	6-4	Bay Village, OH
56	Simon, Dave	C	230	6-7	Grosse Pte., MI
53	Sincich, Al	MG	222	6-1	Cleveland, OH
23	Smith, Kerry	RB	203	6-2	Grand Rapids, MI
16	Smith, Steve	QB	195	6-0	Grand Blanc, MI
55	Sweeney, Larry	C	255	6-2	Alma, MI
77	Tabachino, Bob	OG	255	6-0	Youngstown, OH
85	Thibert, Steven	TE	215	6-5	Union Lake, MI
91	Walker, Jack	DL	217	6-5	Westland, MI
46	Webb, Phil	RB	185	6-1	Romeo, MI
15	Wentworth, Peter	QB	215	6-2	Louisville, KY
22	White, Gerald	RB	205	6-1	Titusville, FL
5	Whitledge, John	QB	185	6-2	Delton, MI
27	Wilcher, Thomas	TB	185	6-0	Detroit, MI
84	Wilson, Mike	DT	240	6-3	Detroit, MI
12	Zurbrugg, Chris	QB	190	6-2	Alliance, OH

1983

Michigan	20	Washington State	17
Michigan	24	Washington	25
Michigan	38	Wisconsin	21
Michigan	43	Indiana	18
Michigan	42	Michigan State . .	0
Michigan	35	Northwestern	0
Michigan	16	Iowa	13
Michigan	6	Illinois	16
Michigan	42	Purdue	10
Michigan	58	Minnesota	10
Michigan	24	Ohio State	21

Season Summary

Games Won, 9; Lost, 2

STEFAN HUMPHRIES
All-American Guard

TOM DIXON
All-American Center

WALKER
TOMCZAK

BUCKEYES
SHOW DESIGN -
JON WOODS
ROGER CICHY
JAZZ
ARRANGER -
JOHN TAGENHORST
ANNOUNCER - DAVE KAYLOR
WBNS-TV
1:37
25
OHIO ST
OFFICIAL TIME
MICHIGAN
7
12:07
3
DOWN 3
TIME OUT LEFT 3
3 QTR
YDS TO GO
BALL ON
RUSHING 64
23 RUSHING
PASSING 70
72 PASSING
TOTAL 134
95 TOTAL
BIG BEAR
Get the Bear Minimum Price
Huntington Banks

CRECELIUS

November 17, 1984

Columbus, Ohio

Fourth Quarter Surge Sparks Buckeyes To 21-6 Victory

Lanese, Byars Lead OSU To Rose Bowl Berth

The heavily favored Buckeyes needed heroics from Mike Lanese and Keith Byars to stave off a stubborn Michigan team 21-6 at Ohio Stadium. The win enabled 9-2 Ohio State to advance to the Rose Bowl for the first time since 1979, while Michigan fell to its worst season under coach Bo Schembechler with a 6-5 record.

Ohio State needed two fourth quarter touchdowns to pull away from a narrow 7-6 lead and a momentum that was clearly in Michigan's favor. A spectacular catch by Lanese pulled the momentum back Ohio State's way.

With 10:30 to play in the game, Ohio State faced a third-and-12 situation at its own 43. Quarterback Mike Tomczak scrambled and got off a pass toward Lanese that sailed behind the cutting receiver. Lanese stopped suddenly and lunged back fully extended to catch the ball. The play kept the drive alive and sparked the Buckeyes towards the second of Byars' three touchdowns, this one on a hurdle from two yards out.

The Buckeyes widened their lead soon afterward when William White recovered Michigan receiver Sim Nelson's fumble at the Michigan 37, and Ohio State marched to the end zone with a two-yard blast from Byars.

Byars was the Buckeyes' workhorse, carrying 28 times for 93 yards. Tomczak displayed excellent passing efficiency as he completed 11 of 15 for 139 yards and no interceptions.

Even though the score appeared decisive in Ohio State's favor, the statistics indicated an even, hard-fought game. The Buckeyes' late surge enabled it to gain a 293-264 edge in total offense. Michigan's sophomore quarterback Chris Zurbrugg, performed well with 17 completions in 27 attempts for 164 yards.

Ohio State opened the scoring with a one-yard run by Byars in the first quarter. Then Michigan took control of the game for most of the second quarter and all of the third, edging closer to the Buckeyes on 37- and 45-yard field goals by Bob Bergeron. In fact, Michigan could have taken the lead going into the final quarter, but Bergeron missed a 34 yard field goal attempt.

In the post-game interview, Michigan Coach Bo Schembechler was bitter in defeat. "We should have won," he said. "Ohio State is a good team, but I concede nothing to it. We tossed away too many opportunities. The officials did not help. I am disappointed. "

Schembechler created a scene in the third quarter by storming onto the field and throwing a fit after his Wolverines were penalized for a delay of game call during an important drive.

Ohio State Coach Earle Bruce commended Schembechler's squad for a tough game. "Michigan, you know, is a well-coached team. Anytime you've beaten them and kept them out of your end zone, you've beaten a heckuva team. But that's what we are, too. "

STATISTICS

	UM	OSU
First Downs	15	17
Rushes-Yards	42-100	48-154
Passing Yards	164	139
Passes	17-27-1	11-15-0
Punts/Avg.	6-46	7-45
Fumbles-Lost	2-1	3-1
Penalties-Yards	4-13	2-10

SCORING

Michigan	0	3	3	0	- 6
Ohio State	7	0	14	0	- 21

1984

Michigan . . .	22	Miami	14
Michigan . . .	11	Washington	20
Michigan . . .	20	Wisconsin	14
Michigan . . .	14	Indiana	6
Michigan . . .	7	Michigan State . .	19
Michigan . . .	31	Northwestern . . .	0
Michigan . . .	0	Iowa	26
Michigan . . .	26	Illinois	18
Michigan . . .	29	Purdue	31
Michigan . . .	31	Minnesota	7
Michigan . . .	6	Ohio State	21

Season Summary

Games Won, 6: Lost, 5

MICHIGAN

No.	Name	Pos.	Wt.	Hgt.	Home Town
3	Rein, Russell	QB	190	6-2	Evergreen Park, IL
4	Harbaugh, Jim	QB	202	6-3	Palo Alto, CA
5	Campbell, Erik	DB	163	5-10	Gary, IN
5	Whitledge, John	QB	195	6-2	Delton, MI
6	Bishop, Allen	DB	180	5-10	Miami, FL
6	Sessa, Mike	WR	175	6-1	St. Joseph, MI
7	Mouton,Ken	DB	178	5-11	Naples, FL
8	Mallory, Douglas	DB	185	6-1	Dekalb, IL
8	Moons, Pat	PK	160	5-10	Ft. Lauderdale, FL
9	Freeman, Dwayne	DB	185	6-3	W. Palm Beach, FL
10	Randall, Greg	DB	187	6-1	Chagrin Falls, OH
12	Zurbrugg, Chris	QB	195	6-2	Alliance, OH
13	Rivers, Garland	DB	182	6-2	Canton, OH
15	Lessner, Don	DB	180	5-9	Trenton, OH
16	Evans, Keith	DB	180	5-10	Oakland Park, FL
17	Hicks, Ivan	DB	180	6-2	Pennsauken, NJ
18	Markray, Triando	WR	185	6-2	Detroit, MI
19	Bergeron, Bob	PK	149	5-8	Ft. Wayne, IN
20	Rogers, Rick	RB	216	6-2	Inkster, MI
20	Sites, Bob	LB	198	5-11	Ann Arbor, MI
21	Lawson, Gene	WR	172	5-11	Ft. Lauderdale, FL
22	White, Gerald	RB	205	6-1	Titusville, FL
23	Morris, Jamie	WR	170	5-7	Ayer, MA
23	Zingales, John	DB/K	185	5-10	Shaker Hgts., OH
24	Johnson, Steve	WR	172	5-10	Youngstown, OH
25	Bean, Vincent	SE	190	6-3	Southfield, MI
25	Sites, Rick	LB	197	5-11	Ann Arbor, MI
26	Johnson, Gilvanni	WR	180	6-2	Detroit, MI
27	Wilcher, Thomas	TB	185	6-0	Detroit, MI
28	Hood, Ed	DB	181	5-10	Utica, MI
29	Schulte, Tim	OLB	210	6-3	Ft. Thomas, KY
30	Cochran, Brad	DB	219	6-3	Royal Oak, MI
31	Higgins, Kenneth	WR	198	6-2	Battle Creek, MI
32	Garrett, Eddie	FB	220	6-2	Milwaukee, WI
33	Akers, Jeff	ILB	225	6-2	Lynn, MA
33	Logus,Phil	SE	172	5-10	Alt. Springs, FL
34	Armstrong, Greg	FB	215	6-2	Middletown, OH
35	Heren, Dieter	DB	205	6-3	Ft. Wayne, IN
37	Perryman, Bob	FB	225	6-2	Buzzard's Bay, MA
38	Logue, Ben	RB	195	6-0	Atlanta. GA
39	Meinyk, Mike	PK	165	6-1	Warren, MI
39	Willingham, John	ILB	213	6-2	Dayton, OH
40	Brown, James	RB	195	6-0	Cincinnati, OH
41	Mercer, Brian	TB	205	6-2	Cincinnati, OH
41	Schulte, Todd	ILB	220	6-3	Ft. Thomas, KY
42	Mallory, Mike	ILB	217	6-2	DeKalb, IL
43	Lewandowski, Phil	ILB	222	6-3	Solon, OH
43	Robbins, Monte	P	195	6-4	Great Bends, KS
44	Smith, Garret	FLK	149	5-6	Cleveland, OH
44	Hallow, Dan	OLB	255	6-2	Detroit, MI
45	Reinhold, Mike	ILB	228	6-3	Muskegon, MI
46	Webb, Phil	RB	180	6-1	Romeo, MI
48	Holloway, Ernie	RB	185	5-10	Detroit, MI
49	Moeller, Andy	ILB	219	6-1	Ann Arbor, MI
50	Balourdos, John	ILB	215	6-2	Chicago, IL
51	Krauss, Mike	OG	263	6-5	Clinton, MI
52	Brooks, Kevin	DT	245	6-6	Detroit, MI
53	Sincich, Alan	MG	230	6-1	Cleveland, OH
54	McIntyre, Andree	ILB	245	6-1	Chicago, IL
55	Hill, Mark	C	244	6-3	Holland, MI
56	Harris, Billy	MG	230	6-1	Xenia, OH
56	Simon, Dave	C	230	6-7	Grosse Pte., MI
57	Anderson, Tim	ILB	218	6-2	Ann Arbor, MI
57	Deveer, Dave	DT	234	6-4	Midland, MI
58	Cowan, Keith	OLB	210	6-0	Orchard Park, NY
58	Ghindia, John	OG	245	6-2	Trenton, MI
59	Balourdos, Art	C	250	6-3	Chicago, MI
60	Popowski, Bob	OG	265	6-3	Chicago, MI
60	Messner, Mark	DL	225	6-3	Milford, MI
61	Rodgers, Nate	MG	234	6-0	Warren, OH
62	D'Esposito, Chris	OG	258	6-2	Toledo, OH
63	Masters, Rick	OG	229	6-3	Nobelsville, IN
64	Chester, Dave	OG	275	6-2	Titusville, FL
65	Mihic, John	OL	258	6-4	Lombard, IL
66	Hammerstein, Mike	DT	239	6-4	Wapakoneta, OH
67	Vitale, John	OG	270	6-1	Detroit, MI
68	Borowski, Andrew	C	250	6-4	Cincinnati, OH
69	Herrick, Dave	OT/DT	255	6-3	Indianapolis, IN
70	Erhardt, Mark	OT	255	6-6	N. Olmstead, OH
71	Frazer, Rick	OL	250	6-4	Escanaba, MI
72	Elliott, John	OT	280	6-7	Ronkonkoma, NY
73	James, Doug	OG	267	6-2	Louisville, KY
74	Husar, Mike	OT	271	6-3	Chicago, IL
75	Gereg, Bud	DT	240	6-3	Mt. Clemens, MI
75	Quaerna, Jerry	OT	270	6-6	Janesville, WI
76	Dames, Michael	OG	251	6-2	Miami, FL
77	Tabachino, Bob	OG	263	6-1	Youngstown, OH
78	Hammerstein, Mark	OT	262	6-4	Wapakoneta, OH
79	Miller, Clay	OT	258	6-4	Norman, OK
80	Lyles, Rodney	OLB	226	6-3	Miami, FL
81	Kattus, Eric	TE	220	6-6	Cincinnati, OH
82	Schmerge, Paul	TE	222	6-2	Cincinnati, OH
83	Kovac, Mike	TE	262	6-5	Cleveland, OH
84	Jokisch, Paul	WR	240	6-8	Clarkston, MI
85	Scarcelli, Jim	OLB	220	6-5	Warren, MI
86	Thibert, Steven	OLB	225	6-5	Union Lake, MI
89	Adams, Chuck	TE	216	6-5	Detroit, MI
90	DeFelice, Vince	DT	245	6-2	Trenton, OH
91	Walker, Jack	TE	229	6-5	Westland, MI
92	Gray, Joe	MG	240	6-2	Detroit, MI
93	Folkertsma, David	DT	255	6-5	Grand Rapids, MI
94	Cecchini, Gene	DL	238	6-5	Farmington, MI
95	Nelson, Sim	TE	230	6-3	Ft. Wayne, IN
96	Meredith, Dave	DT	245	6-4	Sterling Hgts.., MI
97	Mandel, Dave	TE	205	6-3	Ann Arbor, MI
97	Shimko, Marty	DT	220	6-4	Bay Village, OH
99	Bostic, Carlitos	OLB	230	6-3	Ypsilanti, MI
99	Schlopy, Todd	PK	163	5-10	Orchard Park, MI

OHIO STATE

No.	Name	Pos.	Wt.	Hgt.	Home Town
1	Lanese, Mike	FL	190	6-0	Mayfield, OH
2	Carter, Chris	SE	184	6-3	Middletown, OH
3	Palmer, James	CB	180	5-11	Williamsburg, VA
3	Doty, Jeff	QB	197	6-4	Columbus, OH
4	Bell, Kelvin	S	200	6-2	Richmond, VA
5	Cargile, Jeff	ROV	209	6-0	Cincinnati, OH
6	Holland, Jamie	TB	185	6-2	Wake Forest, NC
7	Gordon, Sonny	CB	187	6-0	Middletown, OH
8	Leach, Scott	CB	200	6-3	White Plains, NJ
8	Gasper, Courtney	QB	186	6-1	Alexandria, VA
9	Alders, Gary	OLB	210	6-2	Centerville, OH
10	Spangler, Rich	PK	202	6-1	Geneva, OH
11	Hill, Steve	CB	196	6-1	Ft. Walton Bch., FL
11	Key, Keith	TB	186	5-11	Pittsburg, PA
12	White, Terry	S	170	5-9	Cambridge, OH
13	Powell, Scott	QB	205	6-4	North Canton, OH
14	Kumerow, Eric	OLB	228	6-6	River Forest, IL
15	Tomczak, Mike	QB	192	6-1	Calumet City, IL
16	Karasatos, Jim	QB	228	6-3	Fullerton, CA
17	Bell, Sean	CB	185	6-2	Middletown, OH
18	Clift, Gary	QB	190	6-2	Brunswick, OH
19	Tupa, Tom	QB	205	6-5	Brecksville, OH
20	Smith, Dwight	CB	180	5-11	Middletown, OH
21	Richardson, Kevin	ROV	192	6-0	Cleveland, OH
22	Dawson, Dino	FL	164	5-11	Detroit, MI
23	Compton, Jeff	PK	150	5-8	Ottawa, OH
24	Wood, Mike	S	187	6-0	Syracuse, NY
25	Wooldridge, John	TB	190	5-11	Akron, OH
26	Harris, Nate	FL	175	5-11	Akron, OH
26	Clark, Sheldon	DB	180	6-0	Copley, OH
27	Humphries, Hayden	DB	175	6-1	Worthington, OH
29	Rogan, Greg	CB	180	5-10	Urbana, OH
30	Kee, Michael	OLB	212	6-2	Columbus, OH
32	Anderzack, Tom	OLB	200	6-3	Toledo, OH
33	Kolic, Larry	LB	242	6-1	Smithville, OH
34	Holland, Jay	SE	181	5-11	Columbus, OH
35	Jenkins, Joe	LB	221	6-2	Chicago, IL
35	Royer, Mark	FB	212	6-0	Columbus, OH
36	Spielman, Chris	LB	223	6-2	Massillon, OH
37	White, William	CB	180	5-10	Lima, OH
38	McCray, Mike	OLB	210	6-3	Dayton, OH
39	Coleman, Tim	CB	177	5-9	Buffalo, NY
41	Byars, Keith	TB	233	6-2	Dayton, OH
43	Walker, Barry	FB	218	6-0	Lancaster, OH
44	Cooper, George	FB	234	6-2	Wyandanch, NY
46	Blair, Ken	FB	217	5-11	Newberry, OH
47	Jackson, Ray	CB	181	6-0	Akron, OH
48	Selvaggio, Rob	TE	217	6-4	Eagan, MN
49	Smith, Doug	SE	190	6-1	Atlanta, GA
49	Lishewski, Rick	DB	182	5-11	Toledo, OH
50	Odom, Tim	C	243	6-3	Villa Hills, KY
51	Zackeroff, Greg	OT	258	6-5	Warren, OH
52	Whitmer, Doug	C	200	6-0	Kettering, OH
53	Morris, Rich	C	245	6-4	Wheaton, IL
54	Foster, Tom	OLB	220	6-3	Worthington, OH
55	Holliman,Ray	DT	246	6-5	Holland, MI
56	Gilmore, Jim	OG	252	6-5	Philadelphia, PA
57	Morrill, Dave	DT	258	6-3	Centerville, OH
59	Giuliani, Anthony	NG	248	6-0	Westerville, OH
60	Harvey, Bill	LB	233	6-2	Springfield, VA
61	Sullivan, John	DT	253	6-4	Chicago, IL
63	Lowdermilk, Kirk	C	262	6-3	Salem, OH
63	Krill, Bill	OLB	203	5-11	Bryan, OH
64	Lachey, Jim	OG	280	6-6	St. Henry, OH
65	Glancey, Tom	OG	260	6-4	N. Palm Beach, FL
66	Madigan, Mike	OT	264	6-4	Wapakoneta, OH
67	Schaefer, Ed	LB	209	6-0	Columbus, OH
68	James, Tim	OG	260	6-2	Cincinnati, OH
69	Shaffer, Jay	OT	282	6-7	Youngstown, OH
70	Uhlenhake, Jeff	OG	230	6-4	Newark, OH
71	Maggs, Bob	OT	266	6-5	Youngstown, OH
72	Kotterman, Larry	OT	254	6-8	Crestline, OH
73	Krerowicz, Mark	OT	282	6-4	Toledo, OH
73	Foster, Tom	OLB	220	6-3	Worthington, OH
74	Zalenski, Scott	OG	257	6-5	Bethel Park, PA
75	Graves, Rory	OT	265	6-6	Decatur, GA
76	Bachorski, Dan	OT	276	6-5	Bridgeville, PA
77	Paulsen, Ron	OT	252	6-5	Long Beach, CA
78	Durham, Mike	OT	245	6-6	Evanston, IL
79	Bloemer, Mike	OT	250	6-4	Cincinnati, OH
79	Garber, Joe	DT	241	6-3	Columbus, OH
80	Taggart, Ed	TE	212	6-3	Akron, OH
81	Hutchinson, John	TE	228	6-3	Atwater, OH
82	Lee, Byron	OLB	230	6-3	Columbus, OH
82	Haller, Tim	SE	184	6-1	Columbus, OH
83	Delaney, Kevin	TB	198	6-1	Worthington, OH
84	Davidson, Jim	LB	225	6-5	Westerville, OH
85	Groza, Judd	TE	234	6-2	Berea, OH
86	Allen, Paul	PL	178	5-10	New York, NY
86	Longo, Gene	OLB	214	6-2	Winchester, OH
87	Carroll, Jim	TE	238	6-4	Brook Park, OH
88	Higdon, Alex	TE	234	6-5	Cincinnati, OH
89	Hoak, Frank	SE	205	6-2	Richeyville, PA
90	Ridder, Fred	LB	234	6-2	Eaton, OH
91	Klohn, Jim	NG	243	6-2	Ravenna, OH
92	Graves, Reggie	OLB	210	6-4	Decatur, GA
93	Conlin, Ray	DT	241	6-1	Turnersville, NJ
94	Brown, Henry	DT	250	6-4	New York, NY
95	Lee, Darryl	NG	267	6-3	Columbus, OH
95	Stukey, Todd	TE	210	6-4	Belpre, OH
97	Crecelius, Dave	DT	252	6-5	Ashland, OH
98	Johnson, Thomas	LB	242	6-3	Detroit, MI
98	Marcinick, Gary	FL	175	6-0	Brooklyn Hgts., OH
99	Pfister, Mark	LB	222	6-2	Columbus, OH
99	Niswander, Brent	WR	165	5-11	Findlay, OH

1984

Ohio State	22	Oregon State	14
Ohio State	42	Washington State	0
Ohio State	45	Iowa	26
Ohio State	35	Minnesota	22
Ohio State	23	Purdue	28
Ohio State	45	Illinois	38
Ohio State	23	Michigan State	20
Ohio State	14	Wisconsin	16
Ohio State	50	Indiana	7
Ohio State	52	Northwestern	3
Ohio State	21	Michigan	6

Season Summary

Games Won, 9: Lost, 2

JAMES LACHEY
All American Guard

KEITH BYARS
All American Tailback

Photos by Chance Brockway

November 23, 1985

Ann Arbor, Michigan

Harbaugh Paces Wolverines To 27-17 Romp

Michigan Breaks Away In Second Half For Impressive Win

Michigan quarterback Jim Harbaugh turned in a near-perfect performance in leading the Wolverines to a convincing 27- 17 victory over Ohio State at Michigan Stadium.

Harbaugh connected on 16 of 19 passes, three of them for touchdowns, for 260 yards in the air. He was especially effective in the second half when the game was tight, converting eight consecutive third down situations, many of them third-and-long situations.

No play, however, was as big as the one that broke Ohio State's back in the fourth quarter. The Buckeyes had just closed the gap at 20-17 on a 36-yard pass from quarterback Jim Karsatos to split end Cris Carter, who made a leaping catch over Michigan's Doug Mallory in the end zone. But two plays after the ensuing kick off with Michigan at its own 23, Harbaugh stepped back into the pocket and unleashed a bomb to John Kolesar. Kolesar beat Buckeye defender William White to catch the ball at the Ohio State 35 and outraced White to the end zone for a 77-yard TD reception.

Even though Michigan dominated the statistics, with 424 yards total offense to Ohio State's 265, the Wolverines didn't break away until the second half. The evenly-fought first half ended in a 10- 10 deadlock. Michigan drew first blood with a 34-yard field goal in the opening quarter by senior Pat Moons, the first in his four years at Michigan. Moons became the starting kicker the day before the big game when Schembechler suspended regular field goal kicker Mike Gillette and kickoff specialist Rick Sutkiewicz for unspecified violations of team rules.

The Buckeyes' Rick Spangler knotted the score at 3-3 early in the second quarter with a 48-yard field goal. Ohio State took its only lead of the game moments later after the Buckeyes' Eric Kumerow recovered a fumble by the Wolverines' Jamie Morris at Michigan's 19. Keith Byars later scored on a 2-yard touchdown dive.

Michigan tied the score before the half on a four-yard connection from Harbaugh to fullback Gerald White. White's touchdown was set up by a 40-yard pass from Harbaugh to tight end Eric Kattus.

The third quarter was dominated by the Wolverines, outgaining Ohio State 126-16 and running 26 plays to the Buckeyes' six. Harbaugh never missed a third down conversion and added to the scoring with a five-yard touchdown strike to Kattus. Moon added a 38-yard field goal, and Michigan entered the final period ahead 20-10.

After the teams traded touchdowns to open the fourth quarter, Michigan's highly regarded defense took over and thwarted the Buckeyes' comeback attempts. In Ohio State's remaining possessions, Michigan linebacker Mike Mallory recovered a Karsatos fumble and the final OSU drive stalled at the Michigan 46.

Overall, the Michigan defense held the Buckeyes to just 90 yards rushing . In fact, Ohio State was outrushed by Michigan's Gerald White, who carried 29 times for 1 10 yards.

With the win, Michigan (9-1-1 overall) ended up in second place in the Big Ten behind Rose Bowl-bound Iowa. Ohio State (8-3) finished fourth in the conference.

STATISTICS

	OSU	UM
First Downs	14	19
Rushes-Yards	30-110	46-210
Passing Yards	179	230
Passes	17-31-1	16-19-0
Punts/Avg.	3-42	2-48
Fumbles-Lost	3-1	1-1
Penalties-Yards	3-20	3-27

SCORING

Ohio State	0	10	0	7	- 17
Michigan	3	7	10	7	- 27

1985

1985

Ohio State	10	Pittsburg	7
Ohio State	36	Colorado	13
Ohio State	48	Washington State	32
Ohio State	28	Illinois	31
Ohio State	48	Indiana	7
Ohio State	41	Purdue	27
Ohio State	23	Minnesota	19
Ohio State	22	Iowa	13
Ohio State	35	Northwestern	17
Ohio State	7	Wisconsin	12
Ohio State	27	Michigan	27

Season Summary
Games Won, 8: Lost, 3

THOMAS JOHNSON
All-American Linebacker

OHIO STATE

No.	Name	Pos.	Wt.	Hgt.	Home Town
32	Anderzack, Tom	OLB	202	6-3	Toledo, OH
28	Bates, Roman	F	207	6-0	Memphis, TN
89	Beach, Keith	SE	190	6-2	Rawson, OH
3	Bell, Sean	ROV	188	6-2	Milletown, OH
9	Bolyard, Tom	QB	192	6-3	Orrivel, OH
27	Brown, David	S	182	6-0	Utica, NY
94	Brown, Henry	MG	268	6-4	New York, NY
41	Byars, Keith	TB	236	6-2	Dayton, OH
46	Canestraro, Joe	DB	195	6-0	Steubenville, OH
87	Carroll, Jim	TE	223	6-4	Brook Park, OH
2	Carter, Cris	SE	192	6-3	Middletown, OH
18	Clift, Gary	S	190	6-2	Brunswick, OH
66	Cole, Karl	DT	256	6-5	Gahanna, OH
23	Compton, Jeff	PK	160	5-8	Ottawa, MI
44	Cooper, George	FB	238	6-2	Wayandach, NY
84	Davidson, Jim	OLB	228	6-5	Westerville, OH
4	Dawson, Dino	FL	172	5-11	Detroit, MI
21	Delaney, Kevin	TB	203	6-1	Worthington, OH
78	Durham, Mike	OT	266	6-6	Evanston, IL
91	Fourman, Kent	TE	198	6-4	Burbank, OH
70	France, Steve	DT	251	6-5	Lancaster, PA
93	Frantz, Matthew	PK	155	5-8	Cincinnati, Oh
79	Garber, Joe	DT	242	6-3	Columbus, OH
56	Gilmore, Jim	OG	258	6-5	Philadelphia, PA
65	Glancey, Tom	OG	266	6-4	N. Palm Beach, FL
59	Gossett, Dennis	LB	221	6-2	Baden, PA
7	Gordon, Sonny	ROV	191	6-0	Middletown, OH
75	Graves, Rory	OT	280	6-6	Decatur, GA
76	Grubb, John	C	176	5-11	Whitehall, OH
26	Harris, Nate	FL	175	5-11	Akron, OH
28	Harshman, Andy	CB	183	5-11	Toledo, OH
88	Higdon, Alex	DT	233	6-5	Cincinnati, OH
11	Hill, Steve	CB	207	6-1	Ft. Walton Beach, FL
34	Hoak, Frank	FB	200	6-2	Richeyville, PA
6	Holland, Jamie	FL	184	6-2	Wake Forest, NC
55	Holliman, Ray	DT	256	6-4	Holland, MI
63	Howard, Dedrick	OLB	212	6-3	Middletown, OH
22	Humphrey, H.	TB	182	6-1	Worthington, OH
81	Hutchinson, John	TE	230	6-3	Atwater, OH
61	Isaman, Derek	OLB	203	6-3	Fremont, OH
47	Jackson, Ray	CB	188	6-0	Akron, OH
35	Jenkins, Joe	LB	224	6-2	Chicago, IL
98	Johnson, Thomas	LB	252	6-3	Detroit, MI
92	Jones, Tim	SE	182	5-11	Canton, OH
93	Jones, Ty	LB	230	6-0	Akron, OH
16	Karsatos, Jim	QB	220	6-3	Fullerton, CA
30	Kee, Mike	LB	218	6-2	Columbus, OH
62	Keenan, Charles	LB	211	6-2	Steubenville, OH
33	Kolic, Larry	LB	243	6-1	Smithville, OH
72	Kotterman, Larry	OT	282	6-7	Crestline, OH
14	Kumerow, Eric	OLB	237	6-6	River Forest, IL
64	Kuri, Mike	OG	260	6-5	Martins Ferry, OH
1	Lanese, Mike	FL	182	6-0	Mayfield, OH
8	Leach, Scott	LB	222	6-3	White Plains, NY
82	Lee, Byron	OLB	226	6-3	columbus, OH
95	Lee Darryl	DT	258	6-3	Columbus, OH
15	Lishewski, Rich	S	290	5-11	Toledo, OH
71	Maggs, Bob	C	286	6-5	Youngstown, OH
86	Marcinick, Gary	FL	172	6-0	Brooklyn Heights, OH
38	Matlock, Bill	FB	229	5-8	Columbus, OH
83	McConville, Jim	DT	248	6-4	Cleveland, Oh
81	McCray, Malcolm	CB	185	5-8	Yellow Springs, OH
99	McCray, Mike	OLB	229	6-3	Dayton, OH
52	Moore, Tom	C	235	6-3	Orrville, On
90	Morris, Don	FB	205	5-11	Xenia, OH
53	Morris, Rich	C	257	6-4	Wheaton, IL
74	Moxley, Tim	OT	290	6-7	Barnesville, OH
85	Palmer, James	TE	222	6-5	Loudonville, OH
77	Paulsen, Ron	OT	267	6-5	Long Beach, CA
39	Pfister, Mark	FB	214	6-2	Columbus, OH
13	Powell, Scott	QB	217	6-4	North Canton, OH
90	Ridder, Fred	DT	244	6-2	Eaton, OH
29	Rogan, Greg	CB	187	5-10	Urbana, OH
48	Ross, Everett	FL	180	5-11	Columbus, OH
97	Ryan, Jim	LB	222	6-0	Columbus, OH
60	Scholl, Tom	C	218	6-1	Columbus, OH
69	Shaffer, Jay	OT	284	6-7	Lakeside, OH
49	Smith, Doug	SE	192	6-1	Atlanta, GA
20	Smith, Dwight	CB	180	5-11	Middletown, OH
58	Solits, Edward	LB	215	6-3	Youngstown, OH
10	Spangler, Rich	PK	200	6-1	Geneva, OH
36	Spielman, Chris	LB	224	6-2	Massillon, OH
73	Staysniak, Joe	OT	286	6-5	Elyria, OH
95	Stukey, Brian	TE	210	6-4	Belpre, OH
57	Sullivan, John	OLB	219	6-0	Timberlake, OH
67	Sullivan, Mike	LB	234	6-0	Timberlake, OH
80	Taggart, Ed	TE	220	6-3	Akron, OH
64	Thomas, Pat	LB	225	6-1	Centerville, OH
19	Tupa, Tom	PT/QB	212	6-5	Brecksville, OH
68	Uhlenhake, Jeff	OG	246	6-4	Newark, OH
43	Walker, Barry	TB	206	6-0	Lancaster, OH
12	White, Terry	S	175	5-9	Cambridge, OH
37	White, William	CB	186	5-10	Lima, OH
24	Wood, Mike	ROV	190	6-0	Syracuse, NY
25	Wooldridge, John	TB	197	5-11	Akron, OH
42	Workman, Vince	TB	187	5-11	Dublin, OH
51	Zackeroff, Gregg	OG	256	6-5	Warren, OH
96	Zizakovic, Strecko	OLB	229	6-5	Weston, ONT

MICHIGAN

No.	Name	Pos.	Wt.	Hgt.	Home Town
24	Abrams, Bobby	DB	210	6-4	Detroit, MI
33	Akers, Jeff	ILB	221	6-2	Lynn, MA
57	Althouse, John	LB	250	6-3	Honolulu, HI
10	Anderson, Kyle	RB	206	6-1	Drayton Plns., MI
15	Arnold, David	DB	195	6-3	Warren, OH
29	Bissell, Beoff	WR	160	6-1	W. Bloomfield, MI
12	Bock, Ernie	DB	182	5-11	Northville, MI
68	Borowski, Andy	C	250	6-4	Cincinnati, OH
99	Bostic, Carlitos	OLB	231	6-2	Ypsilanti, MI
56	Boyden, Joel	C/LB	220	6-3	Grand Rapids, MI
6	Brown, Demetrius	QB	184	6-1	Miami, FL
80	Brown, Jeffrey	TE	230	6-4	Shaker Hhts., OH
35	Burrows, Brad	LB	220	6-3	Ionia, MI
5	Campbell, Erik	WR	168	5-10	Gary, IN
2	Cernak, Bob	QB	202	6-2	Lockport, IL
64	Chester, Dave	OG	248	6-2	Titusville, FL
30	Cochran, Brad	DB	205	6-3	Royal Oak, MI
92	Cooper, Keith	OLB	215	6-2	Detroit, MI
58	Cowan, Keith	OLB	206	6-2	Orchard Park, NY
16	Crawford, Scott	QB	190	6-3	Rawson, OH
62	D'Esposito, Chris	OG	267	6-2	Toledo, OH
76	Dames, Michael	OG	258	6-2	Miami, FL
14	DeBoer, Mike	P	165	6-2	Grand Rapids, MI
73	dePalma, Robert	OT	255	6-5	Pittsburg, PA
57	Dever, Dave	OG	245	6-4	Midland, MI
51	Duerr, John	OLB	219	6-3	Dearborn, MI
32	Edwards, Mike	DB	185	6-2	Cincinnati, OH
72	Elliot, John	OT	294	6-7	La. Ronkonkoma, NY
45	Fitzgerald, Patrick	SE	164	5-9	Vandalia, OH
93	Folkertsma, David	DT	263	6-5	Grand Rapids, MI
9	Freeman, Dwayne	DB	185	6-3	West Palm Beach, FL
14	Gant, Tony	DB	180	6-0	Fremont, OH
19	Gillette, Mike	P/PK	185	6-1	St. Joseph, MI
95	Grant, J.J.	ILB	226	6-1	Liverpool, NY
78	Hammerstein, Mark	OG	273	6-4	Wapakoneta, OH
66	Hammerstein, Mike	DT	269	6-4	Wapakoneta, OH
4	Harbaugh, Jim	QB	204	6-3	Palo Alto, CA
56	Harris, Billy	MG	257	6-0	Xenia, OH
25	Hassell, Rick	DB	180	6-0	Cincinnati, OH
35	Heren, Dieter	OLB	216	6-3	Ft. Wayne, IN
69	Herrick, Dave	C	258	6-4	Indianapolis, IN
96	Herrmann, John	DT	250	6-4	Sussex, WI
17	Hicks, Ivan	DB	174	6-2	Pennsauken, NJ
31	Higgins, Ken	WR	197	6-2	Battle Creek, MI
97	Holland, Joseph	OLB	215	6-3	Birmingham, MI
44	Holloway, Dan	OLB	245	6-2	Detroit, MI
48	Holloway, Ernie	RB	187	5-10	Detroit, MI
28	Hood, Ed	DB	183	5-10	Utica, MI
74	Husar, Mike	OG	283	6-3	Chicago, IL
26	Johnson, Gilvanni	WR	188	6-1	Detroit, MI
84	Jokisch, Paul	SE	240	6-8	Birmingham, MI
18	Jones, Mike	TE	220	6-3	Birdgeport, CT
81	Kattus, Eric	TE	223	6-6	Cincinnati, OH
26	Khan, Gulam	PK	145	5-8	Shaker Hts., OH
40	Kolesar, John	FLK	190	6-0	Westlake, Oh
51	Krauss, Mike	OT	269	6-4	Clinton, MI
34	LaFountaine, Sean	RB	190	6-0	Dearborn, MI
21	Lawson, Gene	WR	167	5-10	Ft. Lauderdale, FL
15	Lessner, Don	DB	182	5-10	Trenton, MI
33	Logas, Phil	SE	171	5-11	Altamonte Spgs., FL
8	Mallory, Doug	DB	191	6-1	DeKalb, IL
42	Mallory, Mike	ILB	223	6-2	DeKalb, IL
97	Mandel, Dave	TE	205	6-3	Ann Arbor, MI
88	Mandel, Scott	TE	201	6-2	Ann Arbor, MI
54	McIntyre, Andree	ILB	260	6-1	Chicago, IL
60	Messner, Mark	DL	243	6-3	Milford, MI
65	Mihic, John	DT	256	6-4	Lombard, IL
79	Miller, Clay	OT	273	6-4	Norman, OK
20	Mitchell, Anthony	WR	175	5-11	Titusville, FL
90	Mitchell, Keith	TE	225	6-4	Southgate, MI
49	Moeller, Andy	ILB	220	6-0	Ann Arbor, MI
8	Moons, Pat	PK	158	5-8	Ft. Lauderdale, FL
23	Morris, Jamie	RB/WR	175	5-7	Ayer, MA
38	Mouton, Ken	DB/FB	193	6-0	Naples, FL
21	Ogunfitidimi, Olatide	WR/DB	175	6-0	Washington, DC
71	Olszewski, Pat	OT	280	6-8	Conyers, GA
37	Perryman, Bob	FB	230	6-1	Buzzards Bay, MA
52	Petroff, Frank	DL	235	6-4	Parma, OH
61	Plantz, John	OT	246	6-5	Chicago, IL
75	Quaerna, Jerry	OT	276	6-7	Ft. Atkinson, WI
10	Randall, Greg	DB	187	6-1	Chagrin Falls, OH
59	Reid, Bryan	OG	235	6-5	Willoughby, OH
3	Rein, Russell	QB	190	6-0	Oak Lawn, IL
45	Reinhold, Mike	MG	253	6-3	Muskegon, MI
13	Rivers, Garland	DB	185	6-1	Canton, OH
43	Robbins, Monie	P	302	6-4	Great Bend, KS
85	Scarcelli, Jim	OLB	220	6-5	Warren, MI
82	Schmerge, Paul	TE	232	6-2	Cincinati, OH
29	Schulte, Tim	OLB	215	6-3	Villa Hills, KY
41	Schulte, Todd	ILB	223	6-2	Villa Hills, KY
97	Shimko, Marty	DT	235	6-4	Bay Village, OH
53	Simmons, Chris	OLB	230	6-2	Fremont, OH
20	Stites, Bob	LB	210	5-11	Ann Arbor, MI
25	Stites, Rick	LB	210	5-11	Ann Arbor, MI
7	Sutkiewicz, Rick	PK	195	6-3	Troy, MI
77	Tabachino, Bob	C/OG	267	6-1	Youngstown, OH
9	Taylor, Michael	QB	195	6-1	LIncoln Hts., OH
86	Thibert, Steve	OLB	230	6-5	Union Lake, MI
67	Vitale, John	OG	277	6-1	Detroit, MI
65	Walker, Derrick	ILB	229	6-1	Glenwood, IL
91	Walker, Jack	DT	235	6-4	Westland, MI
35	Washington, Vince	FLK	160	5-10	Atlanta, GA
46	Webb, Phill	RB	205	6-1	Romeo, MI
50	Weil, David	OG	235	6-4	Cincinnati, Oh
88	White, Brent	DT	220	6-5	Dayton, OH
22	White, Gerald	FB/RB	222	6-0	Titusville, FL
5	Whitledge, John	QB	198	6-2	Delton, MI
27	Wilcher, Thomas	TB	188	5-10	Detroit, MI
39	Willingham, John	ILB	228	6-3	Dayton, OH
43	Woronecki, Steve	DB	165	5-11	Kalmazoo, MI
23	Zingales, John	DB/K	183	5-10	Solon, OH
12	Zurbrugg, Chris	QB	201	6-1	Alliance, OH

1985

Michigan	20	Notre Dame	12
Michigan	34	South Carolina ..	3
Michigan	20	Maryland	0
Michigan	33	Wisconsin	6
Michigan	31	Michigan State ...	0
Michigan	10	Iowa	12
Michigan	42	Indiana	15
Michigan	3	Illinois	3
Michigan	47	Purdue	0
Michigan	48	Minnesota	7
Michigan	27	Ohio State	17

Season Summary

Games Won, 9; Lost, 1; Tied, 1

MIKE HAMMERSTEIN
All-American Tackle

BRAD COCHRAN
All-American Back

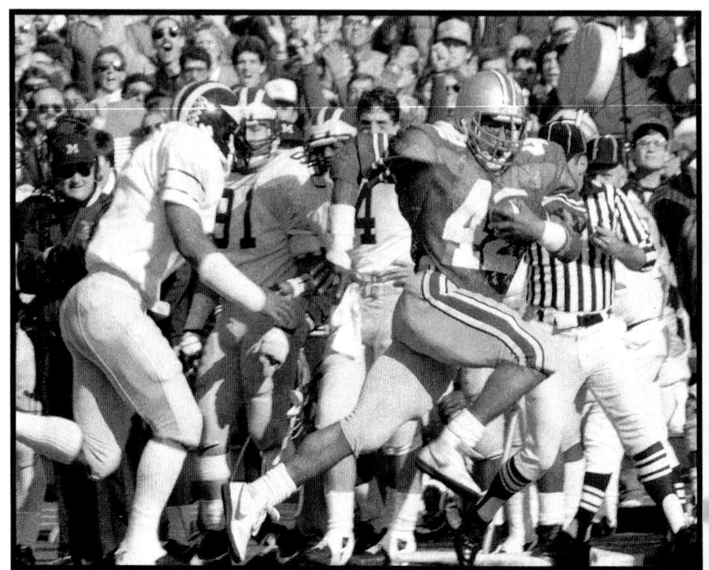

November 22, 1986

Columbus, Ohio

Michigan Holds Off Ohio State 26-24 For Trip To Rose Bowl

Harbaugh Guarantees Victory And Delivers On Promise

On the Monday before the Ohio State-Michigan showdown, Wolverines quarterback Jim Harbaugh boldly guaranteed a victory and a trip to the Rose Bowl. He was true to his word.

Michigan staved off a late Buckeye rally to post a 26-24 victory before 90,674 at Ohio Stadium. The win allowed Michigan to share the Big Ten title with Ohio State at 7-1 conference records, but Michigan received the Rose Bowl bid because of the head-to-head victory.

The game was decided by a failed 45-yard field goal attempt by Ohio State kicker Matt Frantz with 1 :06 to play. Ohio State faced a fourth down-and-two on the Michigan 28, and instead of running a play to gain the first down, Buckeye Coach Earle Bruce gambled on the field goal try. Bruce had consulted kicking coach Randy Hart before the decision and Hart felt confident that Frantz could deliver. Unfortunately for Ohio State, the ball was long enough but it sailed just wide of the left upright.

The men who did deliver for the Wolverines were Harbaugh and running back Jamie Morris. Harbaugh helped guarantee his guarantee by passing for 261 yards on 19 completions in 29 attempts. Morris darted for 210 yards in 29 carries for an average of 7.2 yards per attempt.

In the first half of the game, it seemed that Harbaugh would have to eat his words. The Buckeyes' Jamie Holland returned the opening kickoff 47 yards and in 10 plays, the Buckeyes posted a 7-0 lead on a four-yard lob pass from quarterback Jim Karsatos to receiver Cris Carter.

Michigan replied with a drive of its own and a 32-yard field goal by Mike Gillette. Ohio State took the ensuing kickoffand needed only three plays to move ahead 14-3. One play was a 32-yard pass from Karsatos to Everett Ross, another was a 46-yard touchdown gallop by Vince Workman.

The Wolverines got a 34-yard field goal by Gillette in the second quarter to narrow the gap to 14-6 at halftime.

Michigan dominated the third quarter to move ahead 19-17. The Wolverines took the second half kickoff, drove 83 yards in 14 plays and scored on Morris' four-yard run. Frantz tallied a field goal for Ohio State on its next series, and then back roared Michigan. Morris sprinted for a 52-yard gain, and three plays later blasted up the middle for an eight yard touchdown run.

The Wolverines carried their momentum into the final period as Thomas Wilcher ran eight yards to paydirt just five plays into the quarter. The drive, which made it 26-17 Michigan, was highlighted by a 20-yard run by Morris and a 23-yard screen pass from Harbaugh to Bob Perryman.

But the Buckeyes weren't finished yet. Daryl Lee blocked a 47-yard field goal try by Gillette, setting the stage for an Ohio State touchdown drive. Karsatos went to the air for a l9-yard completion to Nate Harris and later a 27-yard touchdown pass that Cris Carter dug out of the artificial turf in the end zone. That was to be Ohio State's last score as Coach Earle Bruce's late field goal gamble failed.

Standing out for the Buckeyes in the loss were Workman with 126 yards on 21 carries and linebacker Chris Spielman, who had 29 tackles. Karsatos completed 15 of 27 passes for 188 yards.

The 50 total points scored in the game were the most scored in the series since 1968 when Ohio State won 50-14.

STATISTICS

	UM	OSU
First Downs	27	17
Rushes-Yards	52-268	34-170
Passing Yards	261	188
Passes	19-29-2	15-27-1
Punts/Avg.	2+43	4-41
Fumbles-Lost	1-1	0-0
Penalties-Yards	7-44	4-26

SCORING

Michigan	3	3	13	7	- 26
Ohio State	14	0	3	7	- 24

1986

1986			
Michigan	24	Notre Dame	23
Michigan	31	Oregon State	12
Michigan	20	Florida State	18
Michigan	34	Wisconsin	17
Michigan	27	Michigan State	6
Michigan	20	Iowa	17
Michigan	38	Indiana	14
Michigan	69	Illinois	13
Michigan	31	Purdue	7
Michigan	17	Minnesota	20
Michigan	26	Ohio State	24

Season Summary
Games Won, 10; Lost, 1

GARLAND RIVERS
All American Back

JOHN ELLIOTT
All American Tackle

JIM HARBAUGH
All American Quarterback

MICHIGAN

No.	Name	Pos.	Wt.	Hgt.	Home Town
1	McMurtry, Greg	WR	200	6-3	Brockton, MA
2	Calloway, Chris	WR	170	5-10	Chicago, IL
3	Rein, Russell	QB	190	6-0	Ft. Lauderdale, FL
3	Moons, Pat	PK	165	5-8	Ft. Lauderdale, FL
3	Rein, Russell	QB	190	6-0	Oak Lawn, IL
4	Harbaugh, Jim	QB	307	6-3	Kalamazoo, MI
5	Campbell, Erik	DB	171	5-10	Gary, IN
6	Brown, Demetrius	QB	190	6-1	Miami, FL
7	Robinson, Huemartin	RB	180	6-0	Grand Rapids, MI
7	Sutkiewicz, Rick	PK	209	6-3	Troy, MI
8	Mallory, Doug	DB	194	6-1	DeKalb, IL
9	Taylor, Michael	QB	197	6-1	Lincoln Hgts., OH
10	Bishop, Allen	DB	185	5-10	Miami, FL
12	Zurbrugg, Chris	QB	207	6-1	Alliance, OH
13	Rivers, Garland	DB	187	6-1	Canton, OH
14	Gant, Tony	DB	180	6-2	Fremont, OH
15	Arnold, David	DB	196	6-3	Warren, OH
17	Hicks, Ivan	DB	178	6-2	Pennsauken, NY
19	Gillette, Mike	PK/P	185	6-1	St. Joseph, MI
20	Mitchell, Anthony	DB	176	5-11	Titusville, FL
21	Harris, Ted	WR	170	5-10	Detroit, MI
22	White, Gerald	FB/TB	220	6-0	Titusville, FL
23	Morris, Jamie	TB	179	5-7	Ayer, MA
24	Abrams, Bobby	DB	200	6-4	Detroit, MI
25	Hassel, Rick	DB	191	6-0	Cincinnati, OH
26	Key, David	RB	195	5-11	Columbus, OH
27	Wilcher, Thomas	TB	188	5-10	Detroit, MI
28	Jefferson, Allen	RB	205	6-2	Detroit, MI
29	Schulte, Tim	OLB	211	6-3	Villa Hills, KY
30	Ogunfiditimi, Olatide	WR	180	6-0	Washington, DC
31	Higgins, Ken	SE	190	6-2	Battle Creek, MI
32	Edwards, Mike	DB	177	6-2	Cincinnati, OH
32	Bunch, Jarrod	FB	214	6-2	Ashtabula, OH
33	Hoard, Leroy	FB	215	6-0	New Orleans, LA
34	LaFountaine, Sean	DB	186	6-0	Dearborn, MI
35	Heren, Dieter	OLB	219	6-3	Ft. Wayne, IN
36	Williams, Tracy	TB	200	6-0	Sarasota, FL
37	Perryman, Bob	FB	226	6-1	Buzzands Bay, MA
38	Mouton, Ken	DB	200	6-0	Naples, FL
39	Willingham, John	ILB	235	6-3	Dayton, OH
41	Schulte, Todd	ILB	223	6-2	Villa Hills, KY
42	Boles, Tony	RB	195	6-2	Westland, MI
43	Robbins, Monte	P	202	6-4	Great Bend, KS
44	Sites, Bob	LB	215	5-11	Ann Arbor, MI
46	Webb, Phil	TB	202	6-1	Romeo, MI
48	Holloway, Ernie	TB	199	5-10	Detroit, MI
49	Moeller, Andy	ILB	222	6-0	Ann Arbor, MI
50	Weil, David	OG	253	6-4	Cincinnati, OH
52	Petroff, Frank	DL	232	6-4	Parma, OH
53	Site, Rick	LB	211	5-11	Ann Arbor, MI
54	McIntyre, Andre	ILB	241	6-1	Chicago, IL
55	Spencer, Marc	LB	238	6-5	Troy, MI
56	Harris, Billy	MG	270	6-0	Xenia, OH
57	Dever, Dave	OT	264	6-4	Midland, MI
58	Smykowski, Scott	LB	210	6-4	Sterling Hghts., MI
60	Messner, Mark	DL	248	6-3	Hartland, MI
64	Chester, Dave	OG	255	6-2	Titusville, FL
66	Tubo, Jeff	OG	265	6-5	Akron, OH
67	Vitale, John	OG	289	6-1	Detroit, MI
68	Borowski, Andy	C	258	6-4	Cincinnati, OH
70	Erhardt, Mark	OT	270	6-6	Olmstead, OH
71	Olszewski, Pat	OT	272	6-8	Conyers, GA
72	Elliott, John	OT	306	6-7	Lake Ronkonkoma, MI
73	Dohring, Tom	OT	230	6-7	Dearborn, MI
74	Husar, Mike	OT	289	6-3	Chicago, IL
75	Quaerna, Jerry	OT	282	6-7	Ft. Atkinson, WI
76	Dames, Michael	OG	258	6-2	Miami, FL
78	Hammerstein, Mark	OG	285	6-4	Wapakoneta, OH
79	Manuel, Warde	DT	255	6-5	New Orleans, LA
80	Brown, Jeffrey	TE	224	6-4	Shaker Hgts., OH
82	Cernak, Bob	TE	221	6-2	Lockport, IL
83	Teeter, Mike	MG	240	6-4	Fruitport, MI
84	Jokisch, Paul	SE	239	6-8	Clarkston, MI
85	Williams, Timothy	OLB	225	6-4	Milwaukee, WI
86	Thibert, Steve	OLB	240	6-5	Union Lake, MI
88	White, Brent	DT	227	6-5	Dayton, OH
89	Walker, Derrick	TE	230	6-1	Glenwood, IL
90	Mitchell, Keith	TE	236	6-4	Southgate, MI
91	Walker, Jack	DT	260	6-4	Westland, MI
92	Cooper, Keith	OLB	216	6-2	Detroit, MI
93	Folkertsma, David	DT	263	6-2	Grand Rapids, MI
94	Osman, T. J.	DT	245	6-3	North Hills, PA
95	Grant, J. J.	ILB	237	6-1	Liverpool, NY

OHIO STATE

No.	Name	Pos.	Wt.	Hgt.	Home Town
1	Price, Lance	TB	180	6-1	Toledo, OH
2	Carter, Cris	SE	194	6-3	Middletown, OH
3	Bell, Sean	ROV	193	6-2	Middletown, OH
4	Dawson, Dino	FL	172	5-10	Detroit, MI
5	Ross, Everett	FL	178	5-11	Columbus, OH
6	Holland, Jamie	FL	186	6-2	Wake Forest, NC
6	Canestraro, Joe	CB	192	6-0	Steubenville, OH
7	Gordon,Sonny	ROV	192	6-0	Middletown, OH
8	Leach, Scott	LB	214	6-3	White Plains, NY
9	Morton, Mike	PK	194	6-2	Worthington, OH
10	Isaman, Derek	OLB	212	6-3	Fremont, OH
11	Matlock, Bill	FB	219	5-9	Columbus, OH
12	Frantz, Matthew	PK	162	5-8	Cincinnati, OH
13	Powell, Scott	QB	208	6-3	North Canton, OH
14	Kumerow, Eric	OLB	242	6-6	River Forest, IL
15	Frey, Greg	QB	186	6-2	Cincinnati, OH
16	Karsatos, Jim	QB	218	6-3	Fullerton, CA
17	Wagoner, John	QB	196	6-3	High Point, NC
18	Clift, Gary	SE	190	6-2	Brunswick, OH
19	Tupa, Tom	QB/PT	212	6-5	Brecksville, OH
20	Smith, Dwight	CB	180	5-11	Middletown, OH
21	Dumas, Zack	CB	190	6-2	Deptford, NJ
22	Cupe, Anthony	SE	186	6-0	Columbus, OH
23	Lishewski, Rich	S	188	5-11	Toledo, OH
24	Chancey, Mike	QB	208	6-4	Syracuse, OH
25	Wooldridge, John	TB	191	5-10	Akron, OH
26	Harris, Nate	SE	172	5-11	Akron, OH
26	Tuffin, Brian	ROV	202	6-0	Shaker Heights, OH
27	Brown, David	S	182	6-0	Utica, NY
28	Prelock, Steve	TB	200	5-10	Willowick, OH
29	Rogan, Greg	CB	187	5-10	Urbana, OH
30	Kee, Michael	LB	214	6-2	Columbus, OH
32	Anderzack, Tom	OLB	206	6-3	Toledo, OH
33	Gresock, Steve	FB	212	5-10	Boardman, OH
33	Cox, Todd	CB	166	5-11	Mentor, OH
34	O'Morrow, Pat	PK	177	5-11	Radford, OH
35	Jenkins, Joe	LB	220	6-2	Chicago, IL
36	Spielman, Chris	LB	232	6-2	Massillon, OH
36	Fenstermaker, Tony	FL	185	6-2	Powell, OH
37	White, William	CB	188	5-10	Lima, OH
38	Boddie, Chris	FB	224	6-2	Toronto, ONT
39	Graves, Reggie	OLB	236	6-4	Decatur, GA
41	Bryant, Jim	TB	212	6-0	Harrisburg, PA
42	Workman, Vince	TB	184	5-11	Dublin, OH
43	Walker, Barry	FB	209	6-0	Lancaster, OH
44	Cooper, George	FB	246	6-2	Wyandanch, NY
46	Peel, James	ROV	187	5-11	Beaver Falls, PA
47	Jackson, Ray	CB	184	6-0	Akron, OH
48	Pelini, Mark	S	182	6-2	Youngtown, OH
49	Robinson, Ceroy	CB	180	5-10	Bethesda, MD
50	Davidson, Jeff	OT	276	6-6	Westerville, OH
51	Zackeroff, Greg	OG	262	6-5	Warren, OH
52	Moore, Tom	C	220	6-3	Orrville, OH
53	Morris, Rich	C	248	6-4	Wheaton, IL
54	Thomas, Pat	NG	233	6-1	Centerville, OH
56	Craig, Orlando	LB	209	6-1	Detroit, MI
57	Sullivan, John	LB	233	6-0	Timberlake, OH
57	Saunders, Robert	OL	251	6-3	Newark, OH
58	Scholl, Tom	C	214	6-1	Columbus, OH
60	Hirneise, Dan	C	260	6-3	Marion, OH
61	Voll, Ken	C	268	6-3	Lakewood, OH
62	Keenan, Charles	NG	217	6-2	Steubenville, OH
63	Howard, Dedrick	OLB	218	6-3	Middletown, OH
64	Kuri, Mike	OG	268	6-5	Martins Ferry, OH
65	Grimm, Erik	OG	250	6-4	Sisterville, W. VA
66	Coles, Karl	OG	256	6-2	Gahanna, OH
67	Sullivan, Mike	NG	236	6-0	Timberlake, OH
67	Stephens, Paul	OL	244	6-3	Milan, OH
68	Uhlenhake, Jeff	OG	248	6-4	Newark, OH
69	Shaffer, Jay	OT	286	6-7	Lakeside, OH
70	France, Steve	C	265	6-5	Lancaster, PA
71	Maggs, Bob	C	292	6-5	Youngstown, OH
71	Williams, Steve	OLB	217	6-0	Fairborn, OH
72	Kotterman, Larry	OT	286	6-7	Crestline, OH
73	Kuczek, Jeff	OG	233	6-4	Boardman, OH
74	Moxley, Tim	OT	281	6-7	Barnesville, OH
75	Peterson, John	OT	278	6-4	Middletown, OH
76	Beatty, Dan	NG	242	6-4	East Liverpool, OH
76	Grubb, John	C	190	5-11	Whitehall, OH
77	Davidson, Jim	OG	238	6-5	Westerville, OH
78	Durham, Mike	OT	266	6-6	Evanston, IL
79	Staysniak, Joe	OT	274	6-5	Elyria, OH
80	Taggart, Ed	TE	223	6-3	Akron, OH
81	Hutchison, John	TE	234	6-3	Atwater, OH
82	Siegenthaler, Wes	FL	178	6-0	Massillon, OH
83	Hoak, Frank	TE	210	6-2	Richeyville, PA
84	Garber, Joe	DT	242	6-3	Columbus, OH
85	Palmer, James	TE	226	6-5	Loudonville, OH
86	Lickovitch, Gary	TE	217	6-3	Solon, OH
87	Huffman, Rich	TE	221	6-2	Salem, OH
88	Higdon, Alex	TE	238	6-5	Cincinnati, OH
88	Hartman, Tom	TE	170	6-1	Arlington, OH
89	Haller, Tim	TE	182	6-1	Columbus, OH
90	Ridder, Fred	DT	244	6-2	Eaton, OH
91	Benio, Brian	LB	222	6-2	Roswell, GA
92	Coleman, Kenneth	NG	240	6-2	Dayton, OH
94	Brown, Henry	DT	259	6-4	New York, NY
95	Lee, Darryl	DT	266	6-3	Columbus, OH
95	Manifold, Matt	TE	205	6-4	Kettering, OH
96	Zizakovic, Srecko	DT	236	6-6	Weston, ONT
97	Moore, Tony	DT	262	6-4	Amherst, OH
98	Showalter, Mike	DT	248	6-4	Bay Village, OH
99	McCray, Mike	OLB	239	6-3	Dayton, OH

1986

Ohio State	10	Alabama	16
Ohio State	7	Washington	40
Ohio State	13	Colorado	10
Ohio State	64	Utah	6
Ohio State	14	Illinois	0
Ohio State	24	Indiana	22
Ohio State	39	Purdue	11
Ohio State	33	Minnesota	0
Ohio State	31	Iowa	10
Ohio State	30	Northwestern	9
Ohio State	30	Wisconsin	17
Ohio State	24	Michigan	26

Season Summary

Games won, 9; Lost, 3

CRIS CARTER
All-American End

CHRIS SPIELMAN
All-American Linebacker

EARLE

hotos by Chance Brockway

November 27, 1987

Ann Arbor, Michigan

Buckeyes Rally To Overtake Wolverines 23-20

Ohio State Pulls Through In Coach Bruce's Final Game At OSU

Ohio State Coach Earle Bruce, fired after nine seasons the Monday before the Ohio State-Michigan game, received a final tribute from his players with a 23-20 come-from behind victory over the Wolverines in Michigan Stadium.

Wearing headbands emblazoned with "Earle" across the forehead, the Buckeyes pulled through with an emotional second half effort to overcome a 13-7 halftime deficit. "We didn't make a lot of adjustments (at halftime)," said OSU linebacker Chris Spielman, "We didn't have to. Someone mentioned that we had 30 minutes of our football season remaining. No one needed to say anything more. "

The shift in momentum was marked by a 70-yard touchdown connection between Ohio State quarterback Tom Tupa and running back Carlos Snow on the Buckeyes' first possession of the third quarter. Snow caught the pass five yards from the line of scrimmage, faked out Michigan's Doug Mallory and out-ran John Milligan to the end zone, giving Ohio State its first lead of the day at 14-13.

The Buckeyes stretched their advantage to 20-13 midway through the third period on a one-yard run by Tupa. Kicker Matt Frantz missed the extra point.

The Wolverines roared back when Mallory recovered a Snow fumble at the OSU 46 and Leroy Hoard later burst up the middle for a 1 0-yard touchdown run to deadlock the game at 20-20 late in the third quarter.

The rivals traded possessions without a score in the final quarter until Frantz hit the decisive 26-yard field goal with 5 :1 8 to play. From that point on, the charged-up Buckeye defense denied Michigan's comeback attempts, and when the final gun sounded, the Ohio State players carried Coach Bruce around the field for several minutes.

Such a scenario could hardly have been imagined after the opening half, in which Michigan led in first downs 16-6 and rushing yards 184-6.

The Wolverines struck paydirt on their first possession, travelling 73 yards in just seven plays as Jamie Morris rumbled in from the one.

Michigan added Mike Gillette field goals of 34 and 19 yards in the second quarter for a 13-0 lead. The Buckeyes finally lit the scoreboard at 1:36 remaining in the half when Tupa hit Everett Ross with a four-yard touchdown pass. The scoring opportunity arose after OSU linebacker Mike McCray recovered a Jarrod Bunch fumble at the Buckeyes' 39. The Wolverines had reason to feel confident in the locker room at halftime, leading 13-7 and dominating the first half, but they didn't expect the feverish emotion that carried Ohio State past them in the second half. As Spielman said, "They (the OSU administration) shouldn't have fired Coach Bruce when they did or the way they did, and we players came back and won the football game because none of us thought it was right. "

Leading Ohio State offensively were Tupa, who completed 1 8-of-26 passes for 219 yards, and Snow with 67 yards in 21 carries. For Michigan, Morris carried 23 times for 130 yards.

STATISTICS

	OSU	UM
First Downs	17	22
Rushes-Yards	44-106	56-271
Passing Yards	238	103
Passes	19-27-0	6-15-1
Punts/Avg.	6-42	4-38
Fumbles-Lost	2-1	4-3
Penalties-Yards	7-50	2-10

SCORING

Ohio State	0	7	13	3	- 23
Michigan	7	6	7	0	- 20

1987

Ohio State	24	West Virginia	3
Ohio State	24	Oregon	14
Ohio State	13	Louisiana State	13
Ohio State	10	Illinois	6
Ohio State	10	Indiana	31
Ohio State	20	Purdue	17
Ohio State	42	Minnesota	9
Ohio State	7	Michigan State	13
Ohio State	24	Wisconsin	26
Ohio State	27	Iowa	29
Ohio State	23	Michigan	20

Season Summary

Games Won, 6; Lost, 4; Tie, 1

CHRIS SPIELMAN
All-American Linebacker

TOM TUPA
All-American Punter

OHIO STATE

No.	Name	Pos.	Wt.	Hgt.	Home Town
32	Anderzack, Tom	OLB	212	6-3	Toledo, OH
76	Beatty, Dan	C	256	6-4	E. Liverpool, OH
3	Bell, Sean	ROV	194	6-2	Middletown, OH
91	Benio, Brian	LB	229	6-2	Roswell, GA
38	Boddie, Chris	FB	231	6-2	Toronto,ONT
27	Brown, David	S	188	6-0	Utica, NY
72	Brown, Henry	OG	262	6-4	New York, NY
41	Bryant, Jaymes	TB	214	6-0	Harrisburg, PA
16	Chancey, Mike	OLB	212	6-4	Syracuse, NY
18	Clift, Gary	SE	193	6-2	Brunswick,OH
92	Coleman, Kenneth	DT	244	6-4	Dayton, OH
66	Coles, Karl	OG	260	6-5	Gahanna, OH
44	Cooper, George	FB	246	6-2	Wyandanch, NY
56	Craig, Orlando	LB	224	6-1	Detroit, MI
22	Cupe, Anthony	SE	188	6-0	Cloumbus, OH
50	Davidson, Jeff	OG	276	6-6	Westerville, OH
21	Dumas, Zack	CB	192	6-2	Deptford, NJ
2	Edwards, Bernard	SE	195	6-5	Ft. Myers, FL
89	Ellis, Jeff	TE	225	6-4	Louisville, KY
90	Fenstermaker, Tony	SE	190	6-2	Powell, OH
70	France, Steve	OT	270	6-5	Lancaster, PA
12	Frantz, Matt	PK	162	5-8	Cincinnati, OH
15	Frey, Greg	QB	190	6-2	Cincinnati, OH
35	Graham, Scott	FB	207	5-10	Long Beach, NY
65	Grimm, Erik	OG	256	6-4	Sistersville, WV
62	Grubb, John	C	200	5-11	Whitehall,OH
49	Gurd, Andrew	LB	215	6-3	Chagrin Falls, OH
88	Higdon, Alex	TE	251	6-5	Cincinnati, OH
60	Hirneise, Dan	C	262	6-3	Marion, OH
83	Hoak, Frank	OLB	222	6-2	Richeyville, PA
55	Holliman, Ray	DT	262	6-4	Holland, MI
87	Huffman, Rich	TE	228	6-2	Salem, OH
10	Isaman, Derek	OLB	218	6-3	Fremont, OH
47	Jackson, Ray	ROV	190	6-0	Akron, OH
95	Kacherski, John	NG	240	6-3	Riverhead, NY
62	Keenan, Charles	LB	221	6-2	Steubenville, OH
82	Koch, Jay	TE	205	6-4	Cincinnati, OH
14	Kumerow, Eric	OLB	250	6-6	River Forest, IL
64	Kuri, Mike	OT	254	6-5	Martins Ferry, OH
81	Lease, Tom	OLB	229	6-5	Kenton, OH
86	Lickovitch, Gary	TE	226	6-3	Solon, OH
93	MacCready, Derek	DT	270	6-5	Montreal, Quebec
84	Manifold, Matt	TE	210	6-2	Kettering, OH
11	Matlock, Bill	FR	219	5-9	Columbus, OH
99	McCray, Mike	OLB	232	6-3	Dayton, OH
52	Moore, Tom	C	226	6-3	Orrville, OH
97	Moore, Tony	DT	271	6-4	Amherst, OH
74	Maxley, Tim	OT	284	6-7	Barnesville, OH
63	Nichols, Roy	OT	266	6-5	Jeannette, PA
39	Olive, Bobby	FL	155	6-0	Atlanta, GA
6	O'Morrow, Pat	PK	177	5-11	Radford, VA
85	Palmer, Jim	TE	230	6-5	Loudonville, OH
46	Peel, Jim	ROV	195	5-11	Beaver Falls, PA
48	Pelini, Mark	S	197	6-2	Youngstown, OH
75	Peterson, John	OT	282	6-4	Middletown, OH
13	Powell, Scott	QB	229	6-4	No. Canton, OH
1	Price, Lance	TB	190	6-0	Toledo, OH
90	Ridder, Fred	LB	230	6-2	Eaton, OH
29	Rogan, Greg	CB	187	5-10	Urbana, OH
5	Ross, Everett	FL	180	5-11	Columbus, OH
58	Scholl, Tom	C	224	6-1	Columbus, OH
69	Shaffer, Jay	OT	288	6-7	Lakeside, OH
78	Shoaf, Mike	OT	290	6-6	Orwell, OH
98	Showalter, Mike	DT	260	6-4	Bay Village, OH
4	Siegenthaler, Wes	SE	182	6-0	Massillon, OH
20	Smith, Dwight	S	180	5-11	Middletown, OH
8	Smith, Mark	PK-QB	202	6-2	Canton, OH
25	Snow, Carlos	TB	194	5-9	Cincinnati, OH
28	Spencer, John	TB	206	6-0	St. Clairsville, OH
36	Spielman, Chris	LB	236	6-2	Massillon, OH
79	Staysniak, Joe	OT	282	6-5	Elyria, OH
57	Sullivan, John	LB	235	6-0	Timberlake, OH
67	Sullivan, Mike	NG	238	6-0	Timberlake, OH
54	Thomas, Pat	NG	233	6-1	Centerville, OH
26	Tuffin, Brian	CB	202	6-0	Shaker Hgts, OH
19	Tupa, Tom	QB	222	6-5	Brecksville, OH
68	Uhlenhake, Jeff	C	250	6-4	Newark, OH
61	Voll, Ken	C	263	6-3	Lakewood, OH
17	Wagoner, John	FLK	200	6-3	High Point, NC
37	White, William	CB	192	5-10	Lima, OH
42	Workman, Vince	TB	194	5-11	Dublin, OH
51	Zackeroff, Greg	OG	268	6-5	Warren, OH
73	Zizakovic, Srecko	OT	240	6-6	Weston, Ontario

MICHIGAN

No.	Name	Pos.	Wt.	Hgt.	Home Town
24	Abrams, Bobby	OLB	200	6-4	Detroit, MI
37	Anderson, Erick	RB	205	6-3	Glenview, IL
15	Arnold, David	DB	196	6-3	Warren, OH
10	Bishop, Allen	DB	185	5-10	Miami, FL
29	Bissel, Geof	WR	160	6-1	W. Bloomfield, MI
12	Bock, Ernie	DB	185	5-11	Northville, MI
49	Bohn, Chris	LB	205	6-3	Traverse City, MI
42	Boles, Tony	TB	195	6-2	Westland, MI
68	Borowski, Andy	C	259	6-4	Cincinnati, OH
99	Bostic, Carlitos	OLB	231	6-2	Ypsilanti, MI
56	Boyden, Joel	C/LB	230	6-3	Grand Rapids, MI
6	Brown, Demetrius	QB	190	6-1	Miami, FL
80	Brown, Jeffrey	TE	238	6-4	Shaker Hgts., OH
32	Bunch, Jarrod	FB	227	6-2	Ashtabula, OH
4	Bush, Eric	QB	185	6-3	Quincy, IL
2	Calloway, Chris	WR	173	5-10	Chicago, IL
5	Campbell, Erik	DB	171	5-10	Gary, IN
58	Caputo, Dave	OG	235	6-2	Chelsea, MA
18	Carlson, J. D.	K	170	5-11	Tallahassee, FL
82	Cernak, Bob	TE	236	6-2	Lockport, IL
64	Chester, Dave	OG	260	6-2	Titusville, FL
92	Cooper, Keity	ILB	216	6-2	Detroit, MI
76	Dames, Michael	OG	265	6-2	Miami, FL
63	Daugherty, Doug	OT	265	6-4	Romeo, MI
14	DeBoer, Mike	P	169	6-2	Grand Rapids, MI
57	Dever, Dave	DL	270	6-4	Midland, MI
83	Diebolt, Dave	TE	240	6-5	Mayfield, OH
78	Dingman, Dean	OG	265	6-3	East Troy, WI
73	Dohring, Tom	OT	265	6-7	Dearborn, MI
22	Dottin, Lance	DB	195	6-3	Cambridge, MA
51	Duerr, John	OLB	230	6-3	Dearborn, MI
36	Duncan, Stuart	DB	197	6-1	New York, NY
5	Eastman, Sean	P/PK	159	5-10	Tom's River NJ
72	Elliott, John	OT	306	6-7	Lk. Ronkonkoma, NY
69	Elliott, Matt	OL	255	6-4	Carmel, IN
70	Erhardt, Mark	OT	280	6-6	North Olmsted, OH
61	Evans, Mike	DT	240	6-0	Roxbury, MA
48	Feaster, Curtis	LB	235	6-3	Flint, MI
41	Fichtner, Rusty	LB	205	6-2	Meadville, PA
45	Fitzgerald, Pat	WR	160	5-10	Vandalia, OH
93	Folkertsma, David	DT	263	6-5	Grand Rapids, MI
19	Gillette, Mike	PK	185	6-1	St. Joseph, MI
95	Grant, J. J.	ILB	237	6-1	Liverpool, NY
9	Gutzwiller, Mark	DB	170	5-10	Ann Arbor, MI
56	Harris, Bill	MG	270	6-0	Xenia, OH
25	Hassel, Rick	DB	191	6-0	Cincinnatti, OH
19	Herrala, Scott	DB	180	5-11	Muskegon, MI
96	Herrmann, John	DT	258	6-5	Sussex, WI
33	Hoard, Leroy	FB	215	6-0	New Orleans, LA
97	Holland, Joe	OLB	225	6-3	Birmingham, MI
18	Horn, Chris	RB/DB	205	6-0	Huntsville, AL
74	Husar, Mike	OT/G	279	6-3	Chicago, IL
84	Jokisch, Dan	WR	210	6-7	Clarkston, MI
61	Kerr, Michael	OG	258	6-4	Glen Ellyn, IL
26	Key, David	DB	200	5-11	Columbus, OH
12	Khan, Gulam	PK	150	5-8	Shaker Hgts., OH
21	Knight, Dave	RB	185	6-0	Riverview, MI
40	Kolesar, John	FLK	188	6-0	Westlake, OH
34	LaFountaine, Sean	DB	185	6-0	Dearborn, MI
44	Lawson, Byron	DB	190	6-3	Hanover Park, IL
15	Lessner, Don	DB	181	5-10	Trenton, MI
8	Mallory, Doug	SS	194	6-1	Dekalb, IL
97	Mandel, Dave	TE	228	6-3	Ann Arbor, MI
88	Mandel, Scott	TE	220	6-2	Ann Arbor, MI
79	Manuel, Warde	DT	260	6-5	New Orleans, LA
59	Marshall, Alex	DE	235	6-4	Detroit, MI
16	Matton, Doug	DB	180	6-0	Bloomfield, MI
1	McMurtry, Greg	SE	200	6-3	Brockton, MA
60	Messner, Mark	DT	248	6-3	Hartland, MI
30	Milligan, John	LB	218	6-3	Trenton, MI
20	Mitchell, Anthony	DB	176	5-11	Titusville, FL
90	Mitchell, Keith	TE	235	6-4	Southgate, MI
23	Morris, Jamie	TB	183	5-7	Ayer, MA
27	Murray, Vada	DB	185	6-4	Cincinnati, OH
13	Odom, Wilbur	QB	185	6-0	San Antonio, TX
38	Ogunfiditimi, Olatide	WR	188	6-1	Wahington, DC
71	Olszewski, Pat	OT	272	6-8	Conyers, GA
94	Osman, T. J.	DT	245	6-3	North Hills, PA
31	Owen, Kevin	DB	185	5-11	Moreland Hills, OH
52	Petroff, Frank	DL	232	6-4	Parma, OH
6	Plate, Todd	DB	185	6-1	Brooklyn, MI
62	Ramirez, Marc	C/G	265	6-2	Prairie View, IL
29	Ritter, Dave	DB	200	6-3	Hickory Hills, IL
43	Robbins, Monte	P	202	6-4	Great Bend, KS
43	Rudolph, Colin	OLB	200	6-4	Fortula Valley, CA
65	Simpson, Neil	LB	215	6-3	Highland Park, MI
20	Sinclair, Jim	ILB	200	6-2	Plymouth, MI
75	Skrepenak, Greg	OT	315	6-8	Wilkes Barre, PA
58	Smykowski, Scott	LB	225	6-4	Sterling Height, MI
35	Soehnlen, Mark	LB	232	6-2	Canton, OH
14	Sollom, Ken	QB	195	6-3	Canyon Country, CA
44	Stites, Bob	ILB	215	5-11	Ann Arbor, MI
53	Stites, Rick	ILB	215	6-0	Ann Arbor, MI
7	Sutkiewicz, Rick	PK	205	6-3	Troy, MI
9	Taylor, Michael	QB	195	6-0	Lincoln Heights, OH
91	Teeter, Mike	MG	255	6-4	Fruitport, MI
86	Thibert, Steve	OLB	240	6-5	Union Lake, MI
45	Townsend, Brian	LB	220	6-4	Cincinnati, OH
66	Tubo, Jeff	OG	265	6-5	Akron, OH
67	Vitale, John	C	289	6-1	Detroit, MI
89	Walker, Derrick	TE	239	6-2	Glenwood, IL
81	Walker, Trey	TE/P	218	6-5	Bradenton, FL
32	Walters, Mike	ILB	190	6-1	Kalamazoo, MI
35	Washington, Vincent	WR	165	5-10	Atlanta, GA
38	Watkins, Ra-Mon	DB	160	5-8	Detroit, MI
39	Watson, Shawn	RB	190	6-0	Somerville, NJ
46	Webb, Phil	RB	202	6-1	Romeo, MI
50	Weil, David	OG	265	6-4	Cincinnati, OH
3	Welborne, Tripp	WR	185	6-1	Greensboro, NC
88	White, Brent	DT	240	6-5	Dayton, OH
17	Williams, Otis	LB	215	6-3	Canton, OH
85	Williams, Tim	LB	229	6-4	Milwaukee, WI
36	Williams, Tracy	TB	205	6-0	Sarasota, FL
39	Willingham, John	OLB	236	6-5	Dayton, OH
27	Zacharias, Steve	QB	192	6-2	Sterling Hgts., MI
17	Ziegler, Greg	QB	190	5-11	McKinney, TX
77	Zielinski, Ron	DL	265	6-5	Sterling Hgts., MI

1987

Michigan	7	Notre Dame	26
Michigan	44	Washington State	18
Michigan	49	Long Beach State	0
Michigan	49	Wisconsin	0
Michigan	11	Michigan State	17
Michigan	37	Iowa	10
Michigan	10	Indiana	14
Michigan	29	Northwestern	6
Michigan	30	Minnesota	20
Michigan	17	Illinois	14
Michigan	20	Ohio State	23

Season Summary

Games Won, 7; Lost, 4

JOHN ELLIOTT
All-American Tackle

MARK MESSNER
All-American Tackle

HONDA
Huntington Banks
GRAHAM
84

Photos by Chance Brockway

November 19, 1988

Columbus, Ohio

Classic Battle Between Big Ten Titans Ends In 34-31 Michigan Victory

Kolesar's Clutch Plays In Final Minutes Lift Wolverines

The crowd at Ohio Stadium expected another thriller in the 85th meeting between the two rivals. They got everything they came for - and more.

This game, won by Michigan as expected 34-31, epitomized everything that the Ohio State-Michigan rivalry is all about. It also marked the first meeting between Michigan's legendary coach Bo Schembechler and first-year Ohio State mentor John Cooper.

The Buckeyes fought back from a 20-0 halftime deficit to lead three times in the second half before succumbing to the Big Ten champion and Rose Bowl-bound Wolverines, who finished with a league record of 7-0-1. Despite a gallant effort in this game, Ohio State ended with a 2-5-1 Big Ten mark, the first time in its history that it suffered five conference losses.

The hero for Michigan in this game was the same man who sparked its victory in 1985. That year John Kolesar caught a 77-yard pass for the winning touchdown in the Wolverines' 27-17 victory. This year, after the Buckeyes had taken a 31-27 lead with 2: 12 to play, Kolesar received the ensuing kickoff and ran it back 59 yards to the OSU 41. Two plays later, Michigan quarterback Demetrius Brown lobbed the ball into the end zone and Kolesar outleaped Ohio State defenders David Brown and Zack Dumas to grab the ball for the game-winner.

Ohio State had 1 :37 left to mount a comeback. The Buckeyes drove to the Michigan 39 but Michigan's Marc Spencer intercepted Ohio State quarterback Greg Frey's pass with 29 seconds remaining to seal the victory.

The wild ending was a fitting conclusion for a rare high-scoring game in the annual ritual. Michigan did most of its scoring in the first half on an 18-yard run by Leroy Hoard, a 57-yard pass from Brown to Greg McMurty and field goals of 22 and 56 yards by Mike Gillette. The 56-yarder set a Michigan school record, and more importantly, it came with one tick left on the first half clock.

The Buckeyes regrouped at halftime and came out strong in the third quarter. Carlos Snow scored on a four-yard run and Bill Matlock blasted nine yards to paydirt and Ohio State trailed just 20-14 entering the final quarter.

The Buckeyes grabbed their first lead at 21-20 when quarterback Greg Frey connected with Bobby Olive for a 14-yard TD pass play 3:30 into the fourth quarter. On its next possession, Ohio State faced a fourth-and-goal from the Michigan 3, but instead of gambling on running a play, Coach Cooper called on kicker Pat O'Morrow for a successful 21-yard field goal and a 24-20 lead.

Undaunted, the Wolverines roared back to regain the advantage 27-24 with an impressive 76-yard touchdown drive culminated by Leroy Hoard's eight-yard burst with 4: 14 remaining.

Ohio State earned its final lead of the game when Matlock capped an 88-yard drive with a 16-yard burst up the middle for a touchdown.

Like the champions they were, the Wolverines pulled through in the final two minutes to stave off the upset-minded Buckeyes - thanks to the clutch performances of Kolesar and Brown.

STATISTICS

	UM	OSU
First Downs	24	24
Rushes-Yards	51-276	44-277
Passing Yards	223	192
Passes	11-17-0	14-29-1
Punts/Avg.	3-35	5-33
Fumbles-Lost	3-1	2-1
Penalties-Yards	6-50	4-42

SCORING

Michigan	10	10	0	14 -	34
Ohio State	0	0	14	17 -	31

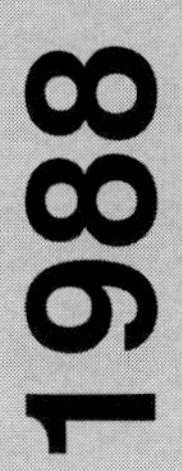

1988

Michigan . . .	17	Notre Dame	19
Michigan . . .	30	Miami	31
Michigan . . .	19	Wake Forest	9
Michigan . . .	62	Wisconsin	14
Michigan . . .	17	Michigan State . .	3
Michigan . . .	17	Iowa	17
Michigan . . .	31	Indiana	6
Michigan . . .	52	Northwestern . . .	7
Michigan . . .	22	Minnesota	7
Michigan . . .	38	Illinois	9
Michigan . . .	34	Ohio State	31

Season Summary

Games Won, 8: Lost, 2; Tie, 1

MARK MESSNER
All-American Tackle

JOHN VITALE
All-American Center

MICHIGAN

No.	Name	Pos.	Wt.	Hgt.	Home Town
1	McMurty, Greg	SE	197	6-3	Brockton, MA
2	Calloway, Chris	WR	176	5-10	Chicago, IL
3	Welborne, Tripp	DB	193	6-1	Greenboro, NC
3	Falander, Mike	PK	145	5-7	Indianapolis, IN
4	Bush, Eric	QB	190	6-1	Quincy, IL
5	Wallace, Coleman	CB	180	6-1	Willinboro, NJ
6	Plate, Todd	DB	191	6-1	Brooklyn, MI
7	Brown, Demetrius	QB	190	6-1	Miami, Fl
7	Maloney, Pat	S	190	6-3	LaGrange, IL
8	Ware, Dwayne	DB	185	6-0	Bloomington, IL
9	Taylor Michael	QB	202	6-0	Lincoln Hgts, OH
9	Gutzwiller, Mark	DB	183	5-10	Ann Arbor, MI
10	Albertson, John	PK	195	6-1	Portage, MI
12	Khan, Gulam	PK	155	5-8	Shaker Hgts., OH
12	Brbac, Elvis	QB	218	6-5	Willoughby Hills, OH
13	Odom, Wilbur	QB	187	6-0	San Antonio, TX
14	Sollom, Ken	QB	196	6-3	Canyon Country, CA
15	Arnold, David	DB	195	6-3	Warren, OH
16	Azcona, Eduardo	P	185	5-11	Montreal, QUE
17	Williams, Otis	DB	197	6-3	Canton, OH
18	Horn, Chris	RB	213	6-0	Huntsville, AL
19	Gillette, Mike	P/PK	194	6-1	St. Joseph, MI
20	Mitchell, Anthony	DB	176	5-11	Titusville, FL
20	Sinclair, James	FB	229	6-0	Plymouth, MI
21	Howard, Desmond	WR	172	5-10	Cleveland, OH
22	Dottin, Lance	DB	196	6-3	Cambridge, MA
23	Johnson, Levititus	TB	172	5-10	Chicago, IL
24	Abrams, Bobby	OLB	221	6-4	Detroit, MI
25	Hassel, Rick	DB	190	6-0	Cincinati, OH
26	Key, David	CB	200	5-11	Columbus, OH
27	Murray, Vada	DB	185	6-4	Cincinnati, OH
27	Zacharias, Steve	TE	220	6-2	Sterling Hgts., MI
28	Jefferson, Allen	RB	200	6-2	Detroit, MI
29	Ritter, Dave	DB	199	6-3	Hickory HIlls, IL
30	Milligan, John	LB	230	6-3	Trenton, MI
31	Owen, Kevin	DB	177	5-11	Moreland Hills, OH
32	Bunch, Jarrod	DB	240	6-2	Astabula, OH
33	Hoard, Leroy	RB	215	6-0	New Orleans, LA
34	LaFountaine, Sean	DB	193	6-0	Dearborn, MI
34	Van Dyne, Yale	WR	187	6-1	Kearney, MO
35	Soehnlen, Mark	LB	240	6-2	Canton, OH
35	Washington, Vincent	WR	175	5-10	Atlanta, GA
36	Williams, Tracy	RB	209	6-0	Sarasota, FL
37	Anderson, Erick	LB	215	6-3	Glenview, IL
38	Carlson, J.D.	PK	170	5-11	Tallahassee, FL
38	Watkins, Ra-Mon	DB	180	5-8	Detroit, MI
39	Mallory, Curt	ILB	205	5-11	Bloomington, IN
39	Watson, Shawn	RB	199	6-0	Somerville, NY
40	Kolesar, John	WR	191	6-0	Westlake, OH
41	Fichtner, Rusty	LB	212	6-1	Meadville, PA
42	Boles, Tony	RB	190	6-1	Westland, MI
42	Morton, Leon	OLB	194	6-1	San Diago, CA
43	Brown, Corwin	FS	175	6-2	Chicago, IL
44	Brown, D.J.	ILB	230	6-2	Alexandria, VA
45	Townsend, Brian	LB	233	6-4	Cincinatti, OH
46	Vaugh, Jon	DB	183	5-11	Florissant, MO
46	Knight, Dave	WR	189	6-0	Riverview, MI
48	McCoy, Matt	DT	247	6-2	Ypsilanti, MI
49	Bohn, Chris	LB	215	6-3	Traverse City, MI
50	Weil, David	OG	263	6-4	Cincinnati, OH
51	Everitt, Steve	OG	230	6-5	Miami, FL
52	Petroff, Frank	DL	248	6-4	Parma, OH
53	Schaffer, Bill	OT	280	6-4	Youngstown, OH
53	Hutchinson, Chris	DL	230	6-4	Houston, TX
54	Manning, Paul	OG	235	6-4	Bloomfields Hills, MI
55	Madden, Bill	C	245	6-2	Gaylord, MI
55	Spencer, Marc	LB	245	6-5	Troy, MI
56	Woodlock, John	C	294	6-3	Waynesburg, OH
56	Boyden, Joel	OLB	234	6-3	Grand Rapids, MI
57	Feaster, Curtis	LB	237	6-3	Flint, MI
58	Smykowski, Scott	LB	235	6-4	Sterling Hgts., MI
58	Wallace, Brian	OL	260	6-5	Parma, OH
59	Marshall, Alex	OLB	235	6-4	Detroit, MI
60	Messner, Mark	DT	244	6-3	Harland, MI
61	Caputo, Dave	MG	240	6-2	Chelsea, MA
61	Traupe, Eric	ILB	221	6-1	Ashland, MA
62	Ramirez, Marc	C/G	271	6-2	Prairie View, IL
63	Daugherty, Doug	OG	268	6-4	Romeo, MI
63	Pintel, Ira	DB	257	6-4	Fairlawn, NJ
64	Chester, Dave	OG	267	6-2	Titusville, FL
65	Simpson, Cornelius	LB	200	6-3	Highland Park, MI
66	Tubo, Jeff	OG	274	6-5	Akron, OH
67	Vitale, John	C	273	6-1	Detroit, MI
68	Cocozzo Joe	OT	300	6-5	Mechanicville, NY
69	Elliott, Matt	C	250	6-4	Carmel, IN
70	Doherty, Rob	OL	270	6-5	Sterling Hgts., MI
71	Olszeski, Pat	OT	285	6-8	Conyers, GA
72	Skene, Doug	OT	290	6-7	Fairview, TX
73	Dohring, Tom	OT	277	6-7	Dearborn, MI
74	Husar, Mike	OT	287	6-3	Chicago, IL
75	Skrepenak, Greg	OT	322	6-8	Wilkes Barre, PA
76	Dames, Michael	OG	268	6-2	Miami, FL
77	Zielinski, Ron	DL	255	6-5	Sterling Hgts., MI
78	Dingman, Dean	OG	280	6-3	East Troy, WI
79	Manuel, Warde	DT	262	6-5	New Orleans, LA
80	Brown, Jeffrey	TE	248	6-4	Shaker Hgts., OH
81	Walker, Trey	TE	231	6-5	Bradenton, FL
81	Kelley, Barry	LB	220	6-3	Bolingbrook, IL
82	Ellinson, John	WR	160	5-11	Delran, NJ
83	Diebolt, Dave	TE	250	6-5	Mayfield, OH
84	Jokisch, Dan	WR	215	6-7	Clarkston, MI
85	Williams, Tim	LB	237	6-4	Milwaukee, WI
86	David, Martin	OLB	230	6-3	Chesapeake, VA
88	White, Brent	DT	248	6-5	Dayton, OH
89	Walker, Derrick	TE	246	6-2	Glenwood, IL
90	Mitchell, Keith	TE	230	6-4	Southgate, MI
91	Teeter, Mike	MG	255	6-4	Fruitport, MI
92	Evans, Mike	DT	233	6-4	Roxbury, MA
93	Knuth, Erik	MG	230	6-4	Redfoed, MI
94	Osman, T. J.	DT	263	6-3	Pittsburg, PA
95	Grant, J. J.	O;B	234	6-1	Liverpool, NY
96	Herrmann, John	DT	267	6-5	Sussex, WI
97	Holland, Joe	P;G	225	6-3	Birmingham, MI
99	Stark, Randy	OLB	225	6-4	Mentor, OH

OHIO STATE

No.	Name	Pos.	Wt.	Hgt.	Home Town
1	Price, Lance	CB	185	6-0	Toledo, OH
2	Edwards, Bernard	FL	195	6-5	Ft. Meyers, FL
3	Beatty, Greg	SE	167	5-11	Missouri City, TX
4	Siegenthaler, We	WE	172	6-0	Massilon, OH
5	O'Morrow, Pat	PK	180	5-11	Radford, VA
7	Clear, Vincet	CB	180	6-0	Cincinnati, OH
7	Yoder, Mike	QB	176	6-1	Parma Hgts, OH
8	Olive, Bobby	FL	154	6-1	Atlanta, GA
9	Frank, Jason	QB	230	6-3	Anaheim, CA
10	McAllister, David	QB	195	6-2	Athens, OH
11	Matlock, Bill	FB	220	5-9	Columbus, OH
11	Giesler, Mike	QB	185	5-11	Woodville, OH
12	Cochran, Nick	QB	198	6-1	Girard, OH
13	Powell, Scott	QB	221	6-4	North Canton, OH
14	Stablein, Chris	FS	210	6-3	Erie, PA
15	Frey, Greg	QB	195	6-2	Cincinnati, OH
16	Chancy, Mike	LB	225	6-4	Syracuse, OH
16	Eisenberg, Brian	PL	159	5-10	Bloomfield Hilld, MI
17	Wagoner, John	QB	207	6-3	High Point, NC
17	Dinan, Doug	CB	175	6-0	Zanesville, OH
18	Clift, Gary	FL	195	6-2	Brunswick, OH
18	Hilsenroth, Troy	SS	180	6-2	Avon, OH
19	Herbstreit, Kirk	QB	204	6-1	Centerville, OH
20	Smith, Dwight	CB	180	5-11	Middletown, OH
21	Dumas, Zack	CB	192	6-2	Deptford, NJ
23	Hicks, Mark	SE	210	6-2	Davis, CA
24	Rugledge, Tim	SS	173	5-11	Youngstown, OH
24	Myrick, Charles	P	172	5-10	Coral, Springs, FL
25	Snow, Carlos	TB	200	5-9	Cincinnati, OH
26	Bohlman, Jeff	P	205	6-3	Centerville, OH
27	Brown, David	FS	180	6-0	Utica, NY
27	Kozel, Steve	P	165	5-10	New London, OH
28	Spencer, John	TB	200	6-0	St. Clairsville, OH
29	Cook, Bryan	FS	183	6-2	Youngstown, OH
30	Johnson, Brent	FB	198	6-1	Bexley, OH
32	Bals, Dave	LB	219	6-2	Eastlake, OH
33	Goodgame, Tony	TB	218	6-0	Roxbury, NJ
34	Metzger, Joe	LB	222	6-2	Centerville, OH
35	Graham, Scotty	FS	215	5-10	Long Beach, NY
35	Gibson, Eric	SS	203	5-11	Zanesville, OH
36	Herman, Judah	LB	207	6-1	Chagrin Falls, OH
37	Gaither, Steve	CB	185	5-11	Beckley, WV
38	Broddie, Chris	FB	234	6-2	Toronto, ONT
39	Harrison, Tyrone	LB	227	6-2	Highland Park, NJ
41	Bryant, Jaymes	FB	221	6-0	Harrisburg, PA
43	Martin, John	LB	214	6-1	Watseka, IL
44	Closson, Tony	LB	233	5-11	Delphos, OH
46	Peel, Jim	SS	196	5-11	Beaver Falls, PA
47	Rogan, Patrick	LB	212	6-1	Urbana, OH
48	Pehni, Mark	FS	185	6-2	Youngstown, OH
48	Torok, James	FL	165	5-10	Youngstown, OH
49	Gurd, Andrew	LB	215	6-3	Chagrin Falls, OH
49	Greer, Steven	SE	163	5-11	Delaware, OH
50	Davidson, Jeff	OG	285	6-6	Westerville, OH
51	Zackeroff	OG	265	6-5	Warren, OH
52	Moore, Tom	C	227	6-3	Orriville, OH
53	Long, Paul	DE	242	6-5	Highland Hts, OH
53	Sharp, Scott	OT	189	6-0	Stoutsville, OH
54	Thomas, Pat	NG	239	6-1	Centerville, OH
55	Warner, Stormy	SS	195	6-1	Columbus, OH
56	Craig, Orlondo	LB	220	6-1	Detroit, MI
56	DeWitt, James	OF	271	6-1	Lakewood, OH
57	Sullivan, John	LB	237	6-0	Timberlake, OH
58	School, Tom	C	220	6-1	Columbus, OH
59	Lachey, Ron	C	193	6-0	St. Henry, OH
60	Brown, Scott	LB	220	5-11	Dayton, OH
61	McCoy, James	LB	195	6-1	Wooster, OH
62	Keenan, Charles	LB	220	6-2	Steubenville, OH
62	Lutz, Travis	C	220	6-4	Bucyrus, OH
63	Nichols, Roy	OD	285	6-5	Jeanette, PA
64	Kuri, Mike	OT	270		Marins Ferry, OH
65	Grimm, Erik	OF	260	6-4	Sisterville, WV
66	Coles, Karl	OT	289	6-5	Gahanna, OH
67	Sullivan, Mike	NG	241	6-0	Timberlake, OH
68	Uhlenhake, Jeff	C	268	6-4	Newark, OH
69	Scholling, John	OT	267	6-2	Clinton, OH
70	France, Steve	OG	270	6-5	Lancaster, PA
71	Huddleston, Mike	C	270	6-5	Wooster, OH
72	Smith, Greg	NG	233	6-1	Canton, OH
73	Sherrick, Paul	OT	322	6-7	Middletown, OH
74	Moxley, Tim	OT	300	6-7	Barnesville, OH
75	Peterson, John	OG	285	6-4	Middletown, OH
74	Beatty, Dan	C	260	6-4	E. Liverpool, OH
77	Hartman, Len	NG	259	6-1	LaBrae, OH
78	Shoaf, Mike	OT	285	6-6	Orwell, OH
79	Staysniak, Joe	OT	287	6-5	Elyria, OH
80	St. John, Scott	TE	205	6-3	Mineral Rdg., OH
81	Lease, Tom	LB	230	6-5	Kenton, OH
82	Kock, Jay	FL	210	6-4	Cincinnati, OH
83	DeGraffenreid, Allen	FL	178	6-2	Cincinnati, OH
84	Graham, Jeff	SE	184	6-1	Dayton, OH
85	Palmer, Jim	TE	240	6-5	Loudonville, OH
86	Lickovitch, Gary	TE	240	6-3	Solon, OH
87	Huggman, Rich	TE	230	6-2	Salem, OH
88	Stablein, Brian	FL	169	6-1	Erie, PA
89	Ellis, Jeff	TE	230	6-4	Louisville, KY
90	Frimel, Rich	DG	232	6-3	No. Olsted, OH
91	Benio, Brian	LB	230	6-2	Roswell, GA
92	Coleman, Ken	DT	255	6-2	Dayton, OH
93	MacCready, Derek	DE	265	6-5	Montreal, Canada
94	Foster, Derrick	LB	226	6-4	Dayton, OH
95	Kacherski, John	LB	245	6-3	Riverhead, NY
96	Zizakovic, Srecko	LB	250	6-6	Weston, ON
97	Moore, Tony	DT	286	6-4	Amherst, OH
98	Showalter, Mike	DT	265	6-4	Bay Village, OH
99	McCray, Michael	LB	225	6-3	Dayton, OH

1988

Ohio State	26	Syracuse	9
Ohio State	10	Pittsburg	42
Ohio State	36	LSU	33
Ohio State	12	Illinois	31
Ohio State	7	Indiana	41
Ohio State	26	Purdue	31
Ohio State	13	Minnesota	6
Ohio State	10	Michigan State	20
Ohio State	34	Wisconsin	12
Ohio State	24	Iowa	24
Ohio State	31	Michigan	34

Season Summary

Games Won, 4; Lost, 6; Tie 1

JEFF UHLENHAKE
All-American Center

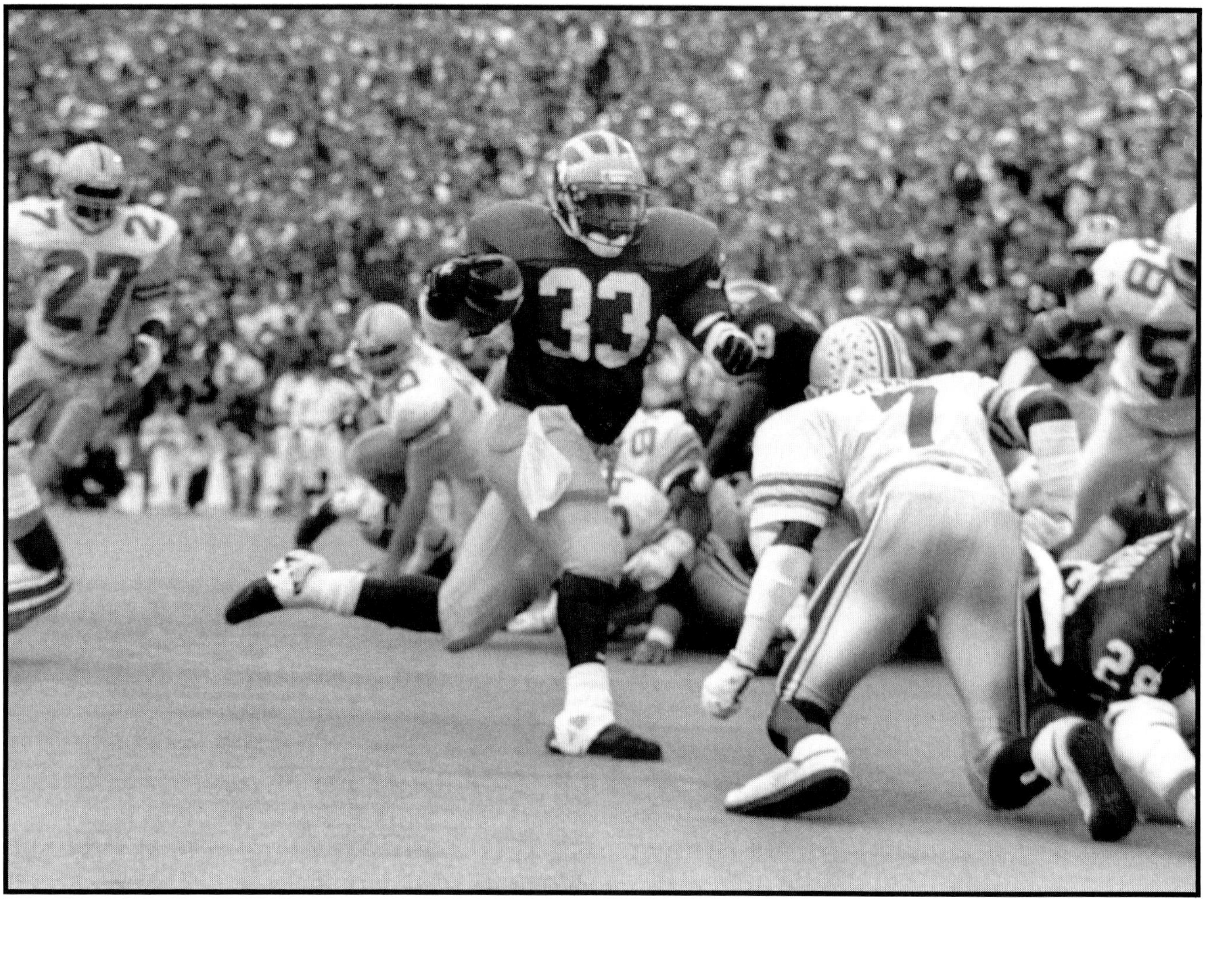

photos by Chance Brockway

November 25, 1989

Ann Arbor, Michigan

Wolverines Repeat as Big Ten Champions With 28-18 Victory Over Buckeyes

Michigan Leads From Start To Finish In Impressive Win

The favored Michigan Wolverines fended off a stubborn Ohio State squad to record a 28- 18 victory at Michigan Stadium that gave the Wolverines a Big Ten championship and a trip to the Rose Bowl.

Both teams were ranked in the Top 20 coming into the game, Michigan at No. 3 and Ohio State at No. 20. With its superior ranking and its home field advantage, Michigan was favored by 14 points to defeat the Buckeyes and win back-to-back Big Ten titles.

The Wolverines appeared to be heading for an even greater margin of victory by jumping out to a 14-3 lead at intermission. Michigan drew first blood with a one-yard touchdown blast by Leroy Hoard in the first quarter, followed in the second quarter with a 2-yard run by Allen Jefferson. Michigan's offense moved virtually at will in the first half, racking up 272 yards in total offense thanks largely to Hoard and fellow running back Jerrod Bunch. The Wolverines' lead might have been wider had it not been for two lost fumbles deep in Ohio State's territory.

All Ohio State could muster was a 20-yard field goal by Pat O'Morrow late in the half, after being unable to score on three tries from the Michigan four. The Buckeyes' rushing offense, No. 1 in the Big Ten entering the game, was held to 87 yards in the opening half by the tough Michigan defense.

The tide began to change in the third quarter as Ohio State's Vinnie Clark intercepted a pass by Michigan quarterback Michael Taylor on the second play of the period. The Buckeyes drove to the Michigan 7, but the Michigan defense dug in their heels and forced the Buckeyes to settle for a 22-yard field goal by O'Morrow.

On Michigan's next possession, punter Chris Stapleton shanked a 14-yarder that went out of bounds at the Michigan 40. Buckeye fullback Scottie Graham carried the ball seven times in the nine-play drive, including a three-yard romp into the end zone to make it 14-12 Michigan. Coach John Cooper decided to go for a two-point conversion to tie the game, but quarterback Greg Frey fumbled the snap and was tackled short of the goal.

The Wolverines answered with a 40-yard run by Hoard to set up a five-yard touchdown toss from Taylor to Bunch for a 21-12 advantage with 12:22 remaining.

Back came the Buckeyes with an 80-yard drive capped by Graham's four-yard burst. O'Morrow's extra point try was blocked by Michigan's All-American safety Tripp Welborne, and Michigan held a 21- 18 advantage.

Ohio State regained the ball with 5:18 to go and seemed to be moving toward a score, but Michigan cornerback Todd Plate picked off Frey's pass at the Michigan 41 with 2:48 to go. The Wolverines iced the game with a touchdown march that was culminated by Bunch's 23-yard romp.

Pacing the Michigan offense this day were Hoard with 152 yards on 21 carries and Bunch with 70 yards on 12 carries. Plate, who was substituting for injured cornerback Lance Dottin, came through with two interceptions and a a disruption of what appeared to be a certain touchdown pass.

Graham paced the Buckeyes' ground game with 133 yards in 28 attempts.

Both teams were without their leading rushers, Carlos Snow of Ohio State and Tony Boles of Michigan, because of injuries.

Michigan finished the regular season with an undefeated 8-0 Big Ten record, 10-1 overall. The Buckeyes wound up 8-3 overall, 6-2 in the conference.

STATISTICS

	OSU	UM
First Downs	25	22
Rushes-Yards	45-200	51-300
Passing Yards	220	100
Passes	14-25-2	8-16-1
Punts/Avg.	3-40	3-27
Fumbles-Lost	1-0	2-2
Penalties-Yards	4-29	2-10

SCORING

Ohio State	0	3	9	6	18
Michigan	7	7	0	14	28

1989

Ohio State . . .	37	Oklahoma State . .	13
Ohio State . . .	3	So. California	42
Ohio State . . .	34	Boston College . .	29
Ohio State . . .	14	Illinois	34
Ohio State . . .	35	Indiana	31
Ohio State . . .	21	Purdue	3
Ohio State . . .	41	Minnesota	37
Ohio State . . .	52	Northwestern . . .	27
Ohio State . . .	28	Iowa	0
Ohio State . . .	42	Wisconsin	22
Ohio State . . .	18	Michigan	28

Season Summary

Games Won, 8; Lost, 3

OHIO STATE

No.	Name	Pos.	Wt.	Hgt.	Home Town
76	Beatty, Dan	C	260	6-4	E. Liverpool, OH
3	Beatty, Greg	SE	175	5-11	Missouri City, TX
28	Berger, Jon	PK	180	5-11	Centerville, OH
26	Bohlman, Jeff	P	205	6-3	Centerville, OH
60	Borchers, Jim	C	204	6-0	Bellbrook, OH
27	Brown, David	CB	182	6-0	Utica, NY
41	Bryant, Jaymes	TB	215	6-0	Harrisburg, PA
53	Chancey, Mike	C	245	6-4	Syracuse, OH
7	Clark, Vinnie	CB	193	6-0	Cincinnati, OH
44	Closson, Tony	ILB	233	5-11	Delphos, OH
92	Coleman, Ken	DT	260	6-2	Dayton,OH
66	Coles, Karl	SG	295	6-5	Gahanna, OH
29	Cook, Bryan	FS	190	6-3	Youngstown, OH
56	Craig, Orlando	ILB	215	6-1	Detroit, MI
50	Davidison, Jeff	QG	300	6-6	Westerville, OH
60	Davis, Don	ILB	237	6-4	Gahanna, OH
83	DeGraffenreid, Allen	FL	178	6-2	Cincinnati, OH
21	Dumas, Zack	SS	192	6-2	Deptford, NJ
2	Edwards, Bernard	FL	200	6-5	Ft. Myers, FL
89	Ellis, Jeff	TE	250	6-4	Louisville, KY
25	Fields, Sean	DB	170	5-10	Dayton, OH
94	Foster, Derrick	OLB	250	6-5	Dayton, OH
70	France, Steve	QG	275	6-5	Lancaster, PA
9	Frank, Jason	QB	225	6-3	Anaheim, CA
15	Frey, Greg	QB	195	6-2	Cincinnaati, OH
90	Frimel, Rich	DE	250	6-3	No. Olmsted, OH
16	Giesler, Mike	CB	185	5-11	Woodvillee, OH
84	Graham, Jeff	SE	195	6-2	Dayton, OH
35	Graham, Scottie	FB	225	5-10	Long Beach, NY
49	Gurd, Andy	ILB	230	6-3	Chagrin Falls, OH
27	Hallway, Dave	K	161	6-1	Plymouth, MI
43	Halveland, Uwe	FB	210	5-11	Troy, MI
55	Harper, Rodric	OLB	225	6-1	Columbus, OH
24	Harper, Roger	FL	210	6-4	Columbus, OH
34	Harris, Raymont	TB	210	6-1	Lorain, OH
39	Harrison, Tyrone	FB	234	6-2	Highland Park, NJ
52	Hartman, Len	QG	270	6-2	LaBrae, OH
39	Hazelbaker, Joe	TE	220	6-1	Upr. Arlington, OH
4	Herbstreit, Kirk	QB	212	6-2	Centerville, OH
36	Herman, Judah	ILB	215	6-1	Chagin Falls, OH
12	Hilsenroth, Troy	SS	190	6-2	Avon, OH
62	Hirneise, Dan	C	290	6-3	Marion, OH
10	Houston, Dave	SS	185	6-2	Akron, OH
42	Houston, William	FB	235	6-1	Trotwood, OH
37	Howe, Buster	TB	180	6-0	Zanesville, OH
71	Huddleston, Mike	SG	280	6-5	Wooster, OH
87	Huffman, Rich	TE	230	6-2	Salem, OH
10	Isaman, Derek	ILB	220	6-3	Fremont, OH
30	Johnson, Brent	ILB	218	6-1	Bexley, OH
95	Kacherski, John	OLB	245	6-3	Riverhead, NY
67	Kline, Alan	QT	260	6-7	Tiffin, OH
82	Koch, Jay	OLB	220	6-2	Cincinnati, OH
64	Kuri, Mike	C	275	6-5	Martins Ferry, OH
55	Lachey, Ron	C	205	6-0	St. Henry, OH
81	Lease, Tom	OLB	230	6-5	Kenton, OH
20	Lee, Dante	TB	175	5-10	Dayton, OH
5	Lewis, Darrell	SS	180	6-2	San Diego, CA
86	Lickovitch, Gary	TE	235	6-3	Solon, OH
93	Long, Paul	DT	242	6-5	Highland Hgts., OH
32	Luna, Carlos	P	175	6-0	Willard,OH
47	Lutz, Travis	TE	220	6-4	Bucyrus, OH
38	McCoy, Matt	OLB	195	6-1	Wooster, OH
97	Metzger, Joe	OLB	222	6-2	Centerville, OH
77	Monnot, Dave	DT	245	6-5	Canton, OH
62	Moore, Tony	SG	275	6-4	Amherst, OH
65	Morgan, Eric	QG	260	6-6	Lorain, OH
74	Maxley, Tim	ST	310	6-7	Barnesville, OH
36	Myrick, Charles	PT	172	5-10	Coral Springs, FL
13	Nelson, Chico	DB	188	6-2	Sarasota, FL
63	Nichols, Roy	QT	295	6-5	Jeannette, PA
6	O'Morrow, Pat	PK	180	5-11	Radford, VA
8	Olive, Bobby	FL	160	6-1	Atlanta, GA
85	Palmer, Jim	TE	250	6-5	Loudonville, OH
72	Pargo, Corey	NG	280	6-3	Toledo, OH
22	Paulk, Foster	DB	170	5-11	Sarasota, FL
19	Payne, Aaron	SE	165	5-8	Louisville, KY
46	Peel, Jim	SS	190	5-11	Beaver Falls, PA
48	Pelini, Mark	FS	190	6-2	Youngstown, OH
94	Peterson, Billy	SE	175	5-11	Columbus, OH
75	Peterson, John	SG	285	6-4	Middletown, OH
1	Price, Lance	CB	195	6-1	Toledo, OH
80	Toy, Chris	OLB	245	6-3	Westerville, OH
69	Schilling, John	QT	275	6-4	Clinton, OH
28	Seach, Bill	OLB	225	6-3	Mingo Junction, OH
54	Sharp, Scott	C	189	6-0	Stoutsville, OH
73	Sherrick, Paul	ST	300	6-8	Middletown, OH
78	Shoaf, Mick	ST	285	6-6	Orwell, OH
98	Showalter, Mike	DT	272	6-4	Bay Village, OH
91	Simmons, Jason	DT	230	6-5	Akron, OH
57	Smith, Greg	NG	240	6-1	Canton, OH
59	Smith, Rod	C	290	6-3	Cleveland, OH
25	Snow, Carlos	TB	200	5-9	Cincinnati, OH
99	Spellman, Alonzo	OLB	255	6-6	Mt. Holly, NJ
88	Stablein, Brian	SE	180	6-1	Erie, PA
14	Stablein, Chris	QB	215	6-3	Erie, PA
79	Staysniak, Joe	QT	290	6-5	Elyria, OH
54	Thomas, Pat	NG	260	6-1	Centerville, OH
7	Thompson, Homer	FL	175	5-11	Cleveland, OH
61	Thrush, Jack	SG	255	6-4	Cincinnati, OH
58	Tovar, Steve	ILB	230	6-4	Elyria, OH
18	Walton, Tim	DB	170	6-0	Columbus, OH
15	Warner, Geoff	DB	160	5-11	Dellory, OH
23	Warner, Jason	DB	180	6-1	Columbus, OH
51	Williams, Mark	OLB	220	6-4	Forestville, MD
23	Williams, Tim	PK/P	155	5-9	Waynesville, OH
68	Winrow, Jason	ST	280	6-5	Bridgeton, NJ
96	Zizakovic, Srecko	DE	250	6-5	Weston, ONT., CAN

MICHIGAN

No.	Name	Pos.	Wt.	Hgt.	Home Town
24	Abrams, Bobby	OLB	229	6-3	Detroit, MI
90	Aghakkan, Ninef	DT	260	6-2	Mt. Prospect, IL
10	Albertson, John	PK	194	6-0	Portage, MI
40	Alenander, Derrick	WR	169	6-2	Detroit, MI
37	Anderson, Erick	OLB	234	6-1	Glenview, IL
16	Azona,Eduardo	P	189	5-9	Montreal, QUE
53	Barry, Joe	ILB	229	6-1	Boulder, CO
49	Bohn, Chris	ILB	210	6-2	Traverse City, MI
42	Boles, Tony	RB	187	6-1	Westland, MI
20	Brown, Corwin	FS	185	6-1	Chicago, IL
8	Buff, Ron	TB	207	6-0	Otisville, MI
32	Bunch, Jarrod	FB	241	6-2	Ashtabula, OH
7	Burch, Alfie	DB	174	6-0	Warren, OH
80	Burkholder, Marc	TE	225	6-3	Traverse City, MI
4	Bush, Eric	WC	190	6-0	Quincy, IL
2	Calloway, Chris	FLK	180	5-10	Chicago, IL
61	Caputo, Dave	MG	236	6-0	Chelsea, MA
38	Carlson, J.D.	PK	179	5-10	Tallahassee, FL\
68	Cocozzo, Joe	OT	294	6-3	Mechanicville, NY
10	Cohen, Doug	OLB	218	6-0	Farmington Hills, MI
63	Daugherty, Doug	OG	263	6-3	Romeo, MI
86	Davis, Martin	OLB	237	6-1	Chesapeke, VA
83	Diebolt, Dave	TE	256	6-4	Mayfield, OH
78	Dingman, Dean	OG	292	6-2	East Troy, WI
48	Dobreff, Dave	ILB	202	6-3	Mt. Clemens, MI
70	Doherty, Rob	OL	296	6-4	Sterling Hgts., MI
73	Dohring, Ron	OT	290	6-7	Dearborn, MI
22	Dottin, Lance	DB	201	6-1	Cambridge, MA
6	Elezovic, Peter	PK	299	5-10	Farmington Hills, MI
69	Elliott, Matt	C	269	6-3	Carmel, IN
19	Ellison, John	WR	181	5-10	Delran, NJ
92	Evans, Mike	DT	252	6-3	Roxbury, MA
51	Everitt, Steve	C	280	6-5	Miami, FL
57	Feaster, Curtis	LB	234	6-2	Flint, MI
41	Fichtner, Rusty	LB	213	6-0	Meadville, PA
19	Foster, Brian	DB	178	5-9	Columbia, MO
95	Grant, J.J.	ILB	245	6-0	Liverpool, NY
52	Graves, Eric	MG	244	6-2	Akron, OH
15	Grbac, Elvis	QB	220	6-5	Willoughby Hills, OH
17	Harbour, Robert	QB/P	203	6-0	Glen Ellyn, IL
99	Hedding, Kevin	TE	214	6-2	Waterford, MI
33	Hoard, Leroy	FB/TB	220	5-10	New Orleans, LA
21	Howard, Desmond	FLK	170	5-9	Cleveland, OH
97	Hutchinson,, Chris	DT	260	6-2	Houston, TX
28	Jefferson, Allen	TB	206	6-0	Detroit, MI
23	Johnson, Livetius	TB	172	5-10	Chicago, IL
84	Jokisch, Dan	SE	215	6-5	Clarkston, MI
35	Kelley, Barry	FB	224	6-5	Billingbrook, IL
26	Key, David	DB	198	5-10	Columbus, OH
12	Khan, Gulam	PK	159	5-8	Shaker Hgts., OH
48	Knight, Dave	WR	182	5-11	Riverview, MI
93	Knuth, Eric	MG	246	6-1	Redford, MI
46	Legette, Burnie	FB	221	6-1	Colorado Springs, CO
71	Lewis, Mike	OT	325	6-4	Brockton, MA
20	Looby, Terry	DB	181	5-11	Saginaw, MI
39	Mallory, Curt	ILB	206	5-10	Bloomington, IN
56	Maloney, Michael	OLB	199	5-11	Orland Park, IL
43	Maloney, Pat	S	194	6-2	LaGrange, IL
54	Manning, Paul	C	247	6-3	Bloomfield Hills, MI
59	Marshall, Alex	OLB	241	6-4	Detroit, MI
76	Martens, Todd	DL	260	6-2	Belvidere, IL
50	McCoy, Matt	DT	246	6-0	Ypsilanti, MI
82	McGee, Tony	TE	231	6-4	Terre Haute, IN
1	McMurty, Greg	SE	206	6-2	Brockton, MA
67	Milia, Marc	OG	250	6-2	Birmingham, MI
30	Milligan, John	LB	233	6-2	Trenton, MI
31	Morton, Leon	OLB	196	6-0	San Diego, CA
27	Murray, Vada	FS	193	6-3	Cincinnati, OH
12	Musgrave, Doug	QB	176	6-2	Grand Junction, CO
44	Nadlicki, Mike	FB	211	6-2	Traverse City, MI
13	Odom, Wilburr	QB	186	6-0	San Antonio, TX
29	Okezie, Alozie	WR	163	6-3	Detroit, MI
94	Osman, T.J.	DT	263	6-2	Pittsburg, PA
31	Owen, Kevin	WR	183	6-2	Moreland Hills, OH
6	Plate, Todd	WC	194	6-0	Brooklyn, MI
74	Plate, Troy	OT	270	6-6	Brooklyn, MI
62	Ramirez, Marc	OG	270	6-1	Prairie View, Il
66	Refowski, Steve	LB	231	6-5	Redford, MI
29	Ritter, Dave	SS	201	6-2	Hickory Hills, IL
53	Schaeffer, Bill	OT	278	6-2	Youngstown, OH
65	Simpson, Neil	OLB	222	6-1	Highland Park, Mi
72	Skene, Doug	OT	288	6-6	Fairview, TX
75	Skrepenak, Greg	OT	340	6-6	Wilkes Barre, PA
58	Smyrowski, Scott	ILB	239	6-4	Sterling Hgts. MI
14	Sollom, Ken	QB	192	6-0	Canyon Country, CA
55	Spencer, Marc	LB	243	6-5	Troy, MI
60	Stanley, Sylvester	DT	261	6-2	Youngstown, OH
18	Stapleton, Chris	P/PK	197	6-0	Springfield, IL
99	Stark, Randy	OLB	224	6-3	Mentor, OH
51	Steuk, William	DT	213	6-2	Sandusky, OH
9	Taylor, Michael	QB	180	5-11	Lincoln Hgts., OH
91	Teeter, Mike	MG	257	6-3	Fruitport, MI
45	Townsend, Brian	LB	228	6-3	Cincinnati, OH
96	Traupe, Eric	ILB	222	6-0	Ashland, MA
36	VanDyne, Yale	WR	186	6-0	Kearney, MO
25	Vaughn, Jon	TB	190	5-10	Florissant, MO
89	Walker, Derrick	TE	248	6-1	Glenwood, IL
64	Wallace, Brian	OL	275	6-4	Parma, OH
5	Wallace, Coleman	SC	178	5-11	Willingboro, NJ
8	Ware, Dwayne	WC	185	5-10	Bloomington, IL
41	Washington, Dennis	RB	193	5-9	Loraine, OH
39	Watson, Shawn	RB	190	5-10	Somerville, NJ
3	Welborne, Tripp	SS	201	6-0	Greensboro, NC
88	White, Brent	DT	253	6-4	Dayton, OH
17	Williams, Otis	SS	198	6-1	Canton, OH
85	Williams, Tim	OLB	237	6-3	Milwaukee, WI
56	Woodlock, John	OG	287	6-1	Waynesburg, OH
14	Wuerfel, Joshua	PK/P	139	5-3	Traverse City, MI
27	Zacharias, Steve	TE	224	6-3	Sterling Hgts., MI
77	Zielinski, Ron	DL	263	6-5	Sterling Hgts., MI

1989

Michigan	19	Notre Dame	24
Michigan	24	UCLA	23
Michigan	41	Maryland	21
Michigan	24	Wisconsin	0
Michigan	10	Michigan State	7
Michigan	26	Iowa	12
Michigan	38	Indiana	10
Michigan	42	Purdue	27
Michigan	24	Illinois	10
Michigan	49	Minnesota	15
Michigan	28	Ohio State	18

Season Summary

Games Won, 10; Lost, 1

TRIPP WELBORNE
All-American Safety

November 24, 1990

Columbus, Ohio

Carlson's Clutch Field Goal Gives Wolverines 16-13 Victory

Ohio State's Fourth Down Gamble Backfires As Big Ten Title Hopes Dashed

ɔhotos by Chance Brockway

Michigan placekicker J.D. Carlson capped a climactic ending to a classic Ohio State Michigan battle with a 37-yard field goal with three seconds to play to lift the Wolverines to a 16-13 triumph in Ohio Stadium.

As Carlson's kick sailed between the uprights, Ohio State's hopes of a Big Ten championship and Rose Bowl berth were destroyed. Those would have been the fruits of an OSU victory, but instead the Buckeyes fell to fifth place in the conference at 5-2-1.

Michigan improved its league record to 6-2 and finished in a four-way tie for the conference title with Iowa, Michigan State and Illinois. Iowa, however, advanced to the Rose Bowl based on the Big Ten's tie-breaking criteria.

Ohio State's need for a victory provided the background to a risky move by OSU Coach John Cooper that ultimately backfired, leading to Carlson's winning kick.

With 4:16 remaining in the game and the score tied 13-13, Carlson had just missed a 38-yard field goal attempt and Ohio State regained possession. The Buckeyes appeared to be on their way to field goal position when quarterback Greg Frey connected with receiver Bobby Olive for 15 yards to the OSU 44-yard line. The play was called back however, by a clipping call against flanker Jeff Graham. The ball was set at the OSU 29 where the Buckeyes faced a third-and-one situation.

Michigan's defense dug in and stopped Ohio State fullback Scottie Graham for a half yard on a third-down dive. Buckeye Coach John Cooper called his last timeout with :38 remaining to make a crucial decision: go for broke and run a play, or be safe and punt. He knew that the Buckeyes had to win to go to the Rose Bowl.

The Buckeyes chose a play in which Frey would fake to the fullback and either follow the fullback's block or take it to the outside. The alert Michigan defense spoiled any hopes of executing the play by swarming all over Frey before he could even start down the line. The Michigan tacklers were led by lineman Mike Evans.

The Wolverines took over and moved to the OSU 19 to set up Carlson's decisive kick.

Thus ended a well fought game in which both teams' defensive units shined. The Wolverines held Ohio State to just 131 rushing yards and intercepted Frey three times. The Buckeye defense held the Big Ten's top rushing team to 144 yards, all but 16 of them gained by Ricky Powers.

"I think it was a Woody Hayes-type game and that's the way it should be played," said Michigan Coach Gary Moeller. "And I think Bo Schembechler would agree."

Like most Ohio State-Michigan battles, the game was close throughout. The Buckeyes scored first when kicker Tim Williams booted a 38-yard field goal in the opening period. His kick was set up when defensive back Jim Peel forced a fumble by Michigan's Jerrod Bunch at mid-field, and OSU's Bryan Cook scooped up the ball and ran it 25 yards to the Michigan 20.

Early in the second quarter, the Wolverines marched to the OSU 3 before settling for a 27-yard field goal by Carlson for a 3-3 tie. Michigan moved ahead 6-3 on a 30-yard Carlson field goal after Michigan cornerback Lance Dottin intercepted a tipped Frey pass and returned it to the OSU 20.

The Buckeyes gained a 10-6 halftime lead when Frey connected with Jeff Graham for a 12-yard touchdown pass with 44 seconds remaining.

Ohio State opened the second half with a drive that led to a 43-yard field goal by Williams and a 13-6 lead. Michigan's Derrick Alexander returned the ensuing kickoff48 yards that set up a 1 2-yard touchdown pass from quarterback Elvis Grbac to split end Desmond Howard. That tied the score at 13-13 midway through the third quarter, and neither team could manage another score until Carlson's clutch field goal.

STATISTICS

	UM	OSU
First Downs	13	16
Rushes-Yards	40-144	36-127
Passing Yards	104	157
Passes	8-16-1	13-26-3
Punts/Avg.	3-33	3-43
Fumbles-Lost	1-1	3-0
Penalties-Yards	2-15	8-66

SCORING

Michigan	0	6	7	3	- 16
Ohio State	3	7	3	0	- 13

1990

Michigan	24	Notre Dame	28
Michigan	38	UCLA	15
Michigan	45	Maryland	17
Michigan	41	Wisconsin	3
Michigan	27	Michigan State	28
Michigan	23	Iowa	24
Michigan	45	Indiana	19
Michigan	38	Purdue	13
Michigan	22	Illinois	17
Michigan	35	Minnesota	18
Michigan	16	Ohio State	13

Season Summary
Games Won, 8; Lost, 3

TRIPP WELBORNE
All American Safety

DEAN DINGMAN
All American Guard

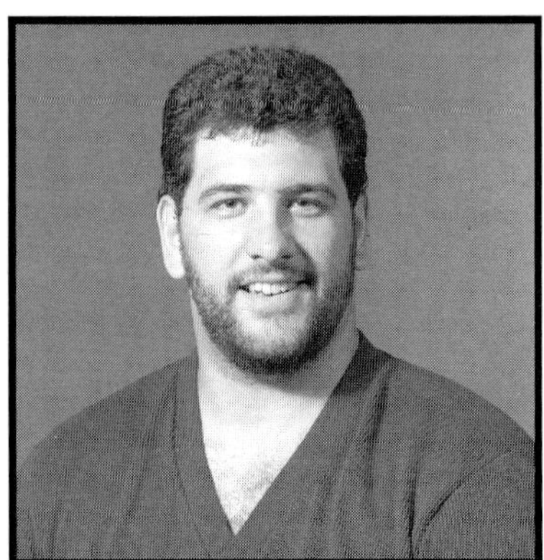

GREG SKREPENAK
All American Tackle

MICHIGAN

No.	Name	Pos.	Wt.	Hgt.	Home Town
1	Alexander, Derrick	WR	190	6-2	Detroit, MI
2	Smith, Walter	WR	190	5-11	Detroit, MI
3	Tripp, Welborne	SS	201	6-1	Greenboro, NC
4	Bush, Eric	FS	190	6-1	Quincy, IL
4	Holdren, Nate	QB	240	6-5	Richland, WA
5	Wallace, Coleman	DB	178	5-11	Willingboro, NJ
6	Plate, Todd	DB	194	6-0	Brooklyn, MI
7	Burch, Alfie	SE	190	6-2	Warren, OH
8	Ware, Dwayne	DB	191	5-10	Bloomington, IL
9	Azoona, Eddie	P	185	5-10	Montreal, QUE
10	Collins, Todd	QB	210	6-4	Walpole, MA
12	Powers, Ricky	RB	205	6-0	Akron, OH
13	Buff, Ron	FB	207	6-1	Otisville, MI
14	Sollom, Ken	QB	194	6-2	Canyon Country, CA
15	Grbac, Elvis	QB	218	6-5	Willoughby Hills, OH
16	Elezovic, Peter	PK	180	5-11	Farmington Hills, MI
17	Williams, Otis	DB	207	6-2	Canton, OH
18	Stapleton, Chris	P	200	6-1	Springfield, IL
19	Ellison, John	SE	181	5-10	Delran, NJ
20	Brown, Corwin	CB	185	6-2	Chicago, IL
21	Howard, Desmond	FL	176	5-0	Cleveland, OH
22	Dottin, Lance	DB	196	6-3	Cambridge, MA
23	Johnson, Livetius	WR	172	5-10	Chicago, IL
24	Washington, Dennis	RB	200	5-9	Lorain, OH
25	Vaughn, Jon	TB	200	5-11	Florissant, MO
26	Key, David	DB	202	5-11	Columbus, OH
27	Murray, Vada	FS	193	6-3	Cincinnati, OH
28	Jefferson, Allen	TB	206	6-0	Detroit, MI
28	Johnson, Dean	DB	210	6-2	Detroit, MI
29	Ritter, Dave	FS	199	6-2	Hickory Hills, IL
30	Milligan, John	ILB	233	6-3	Trenton, MI
31	Owen, Kevin	FL	183	5-10	Moreland Hills, OH
32	Bunch, Jarrod	FB	247	6-2	Astabula, OH
34	Van Dyne, Yale	SE	194	6-1	Kearney, MO
37	Anderson, Erick	ILB	234	6-2	Glenview, IL
38	Carlson, J. D.	PK	179	5-10	Tallahassee, FL
39	Mallory, Curt	ILB	206	5-10	Bloomington, IN
40	Legette, Burnie	FB	221	6-1	Colorado Springs, Co
41	McThomas, Greg	FB	240	6-4	Milwaukee, WI
42	Carlson, Justin	PK	177	5-11	Tallahassee, Fl
43	Maloney, Pat	DB	194	6-2	Lagrange, IL
44	Nadlicki, Mike	FB	220	6-2	Traverse City, MI
45	Townsend, Brian	OLB	228	6-3	Cincinnati, OH
46	Walker, Marcus	ILB	220	6-0	Chicago Hgts., IL
48	Dobreff, Dave	ILB	227	6-3	Mt. Clemens, MI
49	Bohn, Chris	ILB	215	6-2	Traverse City, MI
50	Traupe, Eric	ILB	222	6-1	Ashland, MA
51	Everitt, Steve	C	275	6-5	Miami, FL
52	Graves, Eric	MG	255	6-3	Akron, OH
54	Manning, Paul	OL	257	6-4	Bloomfield Hills, MI
55	Dudlar, Gannon	DL	235	6-4	Birmingham, MI
59	Marshall, Alex	OLB	241	6-4	Detroit, MI
61	Kendrick, Jason	LB	230	6-3	Louisville, KY
63	Elliott, Mark	OLB	225	6-2	Carmel, IN
64	Wallace, Brian	OT	275	6-4	Parma, OH
65	Simpson, Neil	OLB	230	6-3	Highland Park, MI
66	Rekowski, Steve	DT	240	6-5	Redford, MI
67	Milia, Marc	OL	265	6-2	Birmingham, MI
68	Cocozzo, Joe	OG	294	6-3	Mechanicville, NY
69	Elliot, Matt	OL	269	6-3	Carmel, IN
70	Doherty, Rob	OL	296	6-6	Sterling Hgts., MI
72	Skene, Doug	OG	288	6-6	Fairview, TX
73	Dohring, Tom	OT	290	6-7	Dearborn, MI
74	Plate, Troy	DT	270	6-6	Brolkyn, MI
75	Skepenak, Greg	OT	322	6-6	Wilkes Barre, PA
76	Martens, Todd	DT	260	6-3	Belvidere, IL
77	Zielinski, Ron	OT	262	6-5	Sterling Hgts., MI
78	Dingman, Dean	OG	292	6-3	East Troy, WI
79	Henderson, Troy	MG	265	6-2	Indianapolis, IN
80	Burkholder, Marc	TE	235	6-4	Traverse City, MI
81	Woodard, Allen	WR	190	5-10	Houston, TX
83	Diebolt, Dave	TE	250	6-5	Mayfield, OH
84	Jokisch, Dan	TE/WR	230	6-6	Clarkston, MI
86	Davis, Martin	OLB	240	6-3	Chesapeake, VA
88	McGee, Tony	TE	235	6-5	Terre Haute, IN
90	Aghakhan, Ninef	DT	260	6-2	Mt. Prospect, IL
92	Evans, Mike	DT	255	6-4	Roxbury, MA
93	Knuth, Erik	MG	253	6-1	Plymouth, MI
94	Osman, T. J.	MG	263	6-3	Pittsburg, PA
97	Hutchinson, Chris	DT	260	6-2	Houston, TX
99	Stark, Randy	OLB	234	6-4	Mentor, OH

OHIO STATE

No.	Name	Pos.	Wt.	Hgt.	Home Town
1	Price, Lance	CB	190	6-1	Toledo, OH
1	Vujevich, Steve	FB	212	6-2	Pittsburg, PA
2	Edwards, Bernard	FL	195	6-5	Ft. Myers, FL
3	Beatty, Greg	SE	175	5-11	Houston, TX
4	Herbstreit, Kirk	QB	212	6-2	Centerville, OH
4	Warner, Geoff	DB	160	5-11	Dellroy, OH
5	Lee, Dante	TB	180	5-10	Dayton,OH
6	Griffey, Craig	CB	170	5-11	West Chester, OH
7	Clark, Vinnie	CB	193	6-1	Cincinnati, OH
7	Thompson, Homer	FL	175	5-11	Cleveland, OH
8	Olive, Bobby	FL	165	6-1	Atlanta, GA
9	Frank, Jason	OLB	225	6-3	Anaheim Hills, CA
10	McLellan, Jenova	DB	183	5-9	Lima, OH
11	Graham, Kent	QB	235	6-5	Wheaton, IL
12	Pickens, Joe	QB	215	6-4	Brooklyn, OH
13	Nelson, Chico	SS	188	6-2	Sarasota, FL
14	Stablein, Chris	QB	215	6-3	Erie, PA
15	Frey, Greg	QB	195	6-2	Cincinnati, OH
16	Harrison, Preston	QB	230	6-4	Columbus,OH
17	Moore, Theodore	DB	156	5-9	Detroit, MI
18	Walton, Tim	CB	163	6-0	Columbus, OH
19	Payne, Aaron	SE	165	5-8	Louisville, KY
20	Berger, Jon	K	180	5-11	Centerville, OH
21	Patillo, Tim	CB	170	6-11	Aliquippa, PA
21	Lopes, Troy	FB	191	6-0	Columbus, OH
22	Paulk, Foster	CB	180	5-11	Sarasota, FL
22	Stewart, Patrice	WR	187	5-9	Anaheim Hills, CA
23	Williams, Tim	K/P	180	5-9	Waynesville, OH
23	Vickers, Tim	DB	176	6-0	Loudonville, OH
24	Harper, Roger	FS	224	6-4	Columbus,OH
24	Woodard, Shawn	WR	171	5-9	Detroit,MI
25	Capehart, Mark	RB	202	6-0	Reynoldsburg, OH
26	Bohlman, Jeff	P	205	6-3	Centerville, OH
27	Galloway, Joey	SE	170	5-10	Bellaire, OH
29	Cook, Bryan	SS	190	6-3	Youngstown, OH
29	Mahle, Andy	P	190	5-11	Columbus, OH
30	Johnson, Brent	ILB	218	6-1	Columbus, OH
32	Smith, Robert	TB	195	6-2	Euclid, OH
33	By'not'e, Butler	TB	185	5-11	St. Louis, MO
34	Harris, Raymont	TB	220	6-2	Lorain, OH
34	Stewart, Geoff	DB	165	5-8	Columbus, OH
35	Graham, Scottie	FB	220	5-10	Long Beach, NY
36	Herman, Judah	ILB	215	6-1	Chagrin Falls, OH
37	Brown, Deron	FB	202	5-9	Spring Valley, OH
38	McCoy, Matt	OLB	205	6-2	Wooster, OH
38	Graham, Andy	FB	189	5-6	Warren, OH
39	Harrison, Tyrone	FB	235	6-2	Highland Park, NJ
41	Rodriguez, Alex	FB	215	6-1	Chicago, IL
42	Houston, William	FB	245	6-1	Trotwood, OH
43	Williams, Norman	FL	185	6-0	Washington, DC
44	Harper, Rodric	ILB	225	6-1	Columbus, OH
46	Peel, Jim	SS	190	5-11	Beaver Falls, PA
47	Prewitt, Jesse	FL	182	5-11	Dayton, OH
48	Pelini, Mark	FS	195	6-2	Youngstown, OH
49	Gurd, Andy	ILB	230	6-3	Chagrin Falls, OH
50	Borchers, Jim	C	204	6-0	Bellbrook, OH
51	Williams, Mark	OLB	220	6-4	Upper Marlboro, MD
52	Hartman, Len	QG	280	6-2	Leavittsburg, OH
53	Seach, Bill	ILB	235	6-3	Mingo Junction, OH
53	Sharp, Scott	C	189	6-0	Stoutsville, OH
56	Brown, Randall	ILB	240	6-3	Detroit, MI
57	Smith, Greg	NG	255	6-2	Canton, OH
58	Tovar, Steve	ILB	240	6-4	Elyria, OH
58	Jenkins, Chris	OG	241	6-0	Morgantown, NC
59	Smith, Rod	SG	297	6-3	Cleveland, OH
60	Laurenson, Bill	C	229	6-1	Euclid, OH
61	Thrush, Jack	C	260	6-4	Cincinnati, OH
62	Moore, Tony	ST	296	6-4	Amherst, OH
63	Nichols, Roy	QT	295	6-5	Jeanette, PA
64	Dully, Mike	OG	280	6-5	Hamilton, OH
66	Long, Paul	C	242	6-5	Highland Hgts., OH
66	Goff, Carlos	OLB	208	6-1	Columbus, OH
67	Kline, Alan	QT	280	6-7	Tiffin, OH
68	Winrow, Jason	ST	300	6-5	Bridgeton, NC
69	Schilling, John	QT	265	6-4	Clinton, OH
70	Bonhaus, Matt	DT	240	6-5	Cincinnati, OH
71	Huddleston, Mike	QG	285	6-5	Wooster, OH
72	Pargo, Corey	NG	280	6-3	Toledo, OH
73	Sherrick, Paul	ST	300	6-8	Middletown, OH
74	Beckman, Pete	DE	225	6-5	Chesterland, OH
75	Peterson, John	SG	292	6-4	Middletown, OH
76	Beatty, Dan	C	285	6-4	East Liverpool, OH
77	Monnot, Dave	DT	261	6-5	Canton, OH
77	Iams, John	OG	244	6-2	Hamilton, OH
78	Shoaf, Mick	ST	285	6-6	Orwell, OH
79	Carden, Sean	NG	260	6-3	Berwick, PA
79	Lynch, Scott	C	190	5-9	Parma Hgts., OH
80	Roy, Chris	TE	245	6-3	Westerville, OH
81	Lease, Tom	ILB	230	6-5	Kenton, OH
82	Koch, Jay	OLB	220	6-2	Cincinnati, OH
83	DeGraffenreid, Allen	FL	197	6-3	Cincinnati, OH
84	Graham, Jeff	FL	195	6-2	Dayton, OH
85	Saunders, Cedric	TE	225	6-3	Sarasota, FL
86	Lickovitch, Gary	TE	245	6-3	Solon, OH
87	Huffman, Rich	TE	240	6-3	Salem, OH
88	Stablein, Brian	SE	186	6-1	Erie, PA
89	Ellis, Jeff	TE	250	6-4	Louisville, KY
90	Frimel, Rich	DT	250	6-3	North Olmsted, OH
91	Simmons, Jason	OLB	255	6-5	Akron, OH
92	Coleman, Ken	NG	260	6-2	Dayton, OH
94	Foster, Derrick	DE	250	6-5	Dayton, OH
95	Kacherski, John	OLB	240	6-3	Riverhead, NY
96	Lutz, Travis	TE	220	6-4	Bucyrus, OH
97	Metzger, Joe	TE	237	6-2	Centerville, OH
98	Bean, Mark	DE	240	6-5	Wichita, KS
99	Spellman, Alonzo	DE	265	6-6	Mt. Holly, NJ

1990

Ohio State	17	Texas Tech	10
Ohio State	31	Boston College	10
Ohio State	26	So. California	35
Ohio State	20	Illinois	31
Ohio State	27	Indiana	27
Ohio State	42	Purdue	2
Ohio State	52	Minnesota	23
Ohio State	48	Northwestern	7
Ohio State	27	Iowa	26
Ohio State	35	Wisconsin	10
Ohio State	13	Michigan	16

Season Summary

Games Won, 7; Lost, 3; Tie, 1

GARY MOELLER

Michigan's Head Coach

Birthdate: 1/26/41

Years on 'M' Staff: Starting 22nd

College: Ohio State '63

College Coaching Experience:

Miami (OH)	1967-68
Michigan	1969-76
Illinois (head)	1977-79
Michigan	1980-89
Michigan (head)	1990-

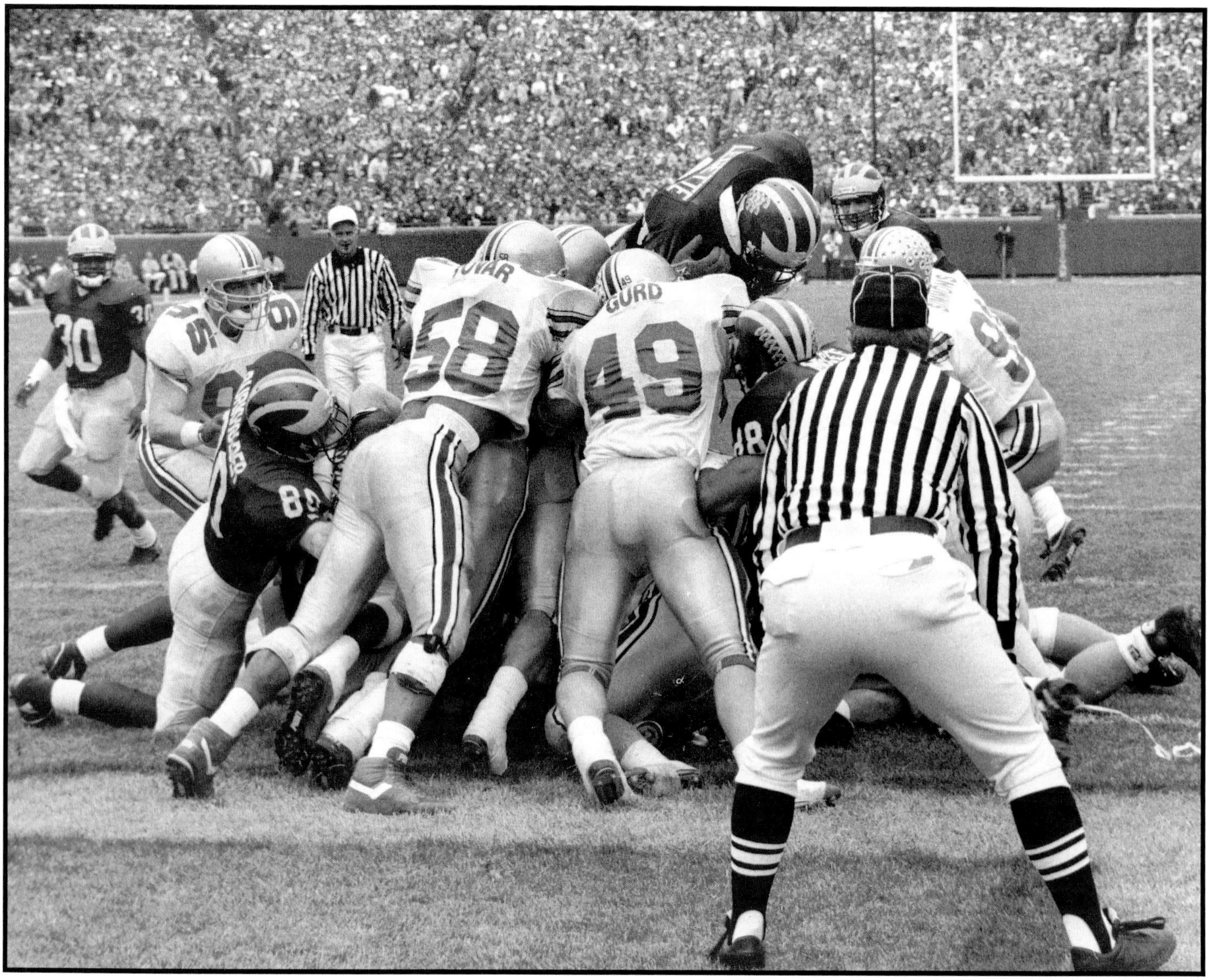

photos by Chance Brockway

November 23, 1991

Ann Arbor, Michigan

Wolverines Blow Out Buckeyes 31-3 Behind Heisman Trophy Winner Howard

Michigan Defeats Cooper's Squad For Fourth Time In A Row

Michigan standout Desmond Howard showed off his Heisman Trophy form with highlight film plays that sparked the Michigan Wolverines to a 31-3 battering of Ohio State. The Wolverines' victory was their fourth in a row over the Buckeyes. The win gave Michigan its 14th outright conference title with an 8-0 Big Ten record, 10-1 overall. The Buckeyes finished the regular season at 8-3 overall and 5-3 in the Big Ten, good for a third place tie with Indiana. The defeat was the worst for Ohio State in 45 years of the 88-year-old rivalry. Michigan crushed Ohio State 58-6 in 1946. Howard proved to the Buckeyes that all his publicity was well earned, finishing with 223 all-purpose yards including two sensational pass receptions of 50 and 42 yards. In the second quarter, Howard displayed his amazing quickness and speed on a 93-yard punt return touchdown. "He's a phenomenon," admitted OSU tailback Carlos Snow.

Michigan took control of the game from the outset, scoring on its first possession. The Wolverines faked a short field goal on fourth down at the OSU three as holder Ken Sollom threw a shovel pass to Greg McThomas, who reached a first down at the one. Fullback Burnie Legete scored on the next play.

Ohio State's lone score carne on a 50-yard field goal by Tim Williams early in the second quarter to close the gap at 7-3. Michigan struck back quickly when Lance Dottin intercepted a pass by OSU quarterback Kent Graham and returned it 18 yards to the OSU 12. Four plays later, tailback Jesse Johnson scored from the one. The first of two fumbles by Ohio State running back Carlos Snow was recovered by the Wolverines and set up a 38-yard field goal by J.D. Carlson, giving Michigan a 17-3 lead. Less than two minutes later, Howard exploded for his punt return, the longest in Michigan history. All told, the Wolverines scored 17 points within a span of 2 minutes and 21 seconds to put the game away. Michigan led 24-3 at halftime and added an insurance touchdown late in the third quarter when freshman tailback Tyrone Wheatly scored on a five-yard run. The Michigan defense thwarted the Ohio State offense all day, holding the Buckeyes to just 109 yards rushing and two yards per rush. In addition, the Wolverine defenders extended their streak of not allowing a rushing touchdown to 22 quarters.

"We were beaten by a great team," said Cooper. "They were as good as advertised. We wanted to run the ball and mix in some play-action passes, but their defense was exceptional. We never got anything started."

Many Ohio State fans and alumni, hungry for a champion, had been calling for Cooper's ouster much of the season. Athletic Director Jim Jones squelched the revolt by announcing just hours before the game that Cooper's contract had been extended for three years.

STATISTICS

	OSU	UM
First Downs	19	13
Rushes-Yards	52-109	39-198
Passing Yards	124	125
Passes	13-25-1	9-15-0
Punts/Avg.	4-45	4-36
Fumbles-Lost	3-2	3-1
Penalties-Yards	5-30	8-75

SCORING

Ohio State	0	3	0	0	- 3
Michigan	7	17	7	0	- 31

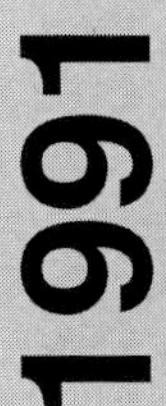

1991 - Ohio State

Ohio State	38	Arizona	14
Ohio State	33	Louisville	15
Ohio State	31	Washington State	19
Ohio State	7	Wisconsin	16
Ohio State	34	Illinois	10
Ohio State	38	Northwestern	3
Ohio State	27	Michigan State	17
Ohio State	9	Iowa	16
Ohio State	35	Minnesota	6
Ohio State	20	Indiana	16
Ohio State	3	Michigan	31

Season Summary
Games Won, 8; Lost 3

STEVE TOVAR
All-American Wide Linebacker

1991

Michigan	35	Boston College	13
Michigan	24	Notre Dame	14
Michigan	31	Florida State	51
Michigan	43	Iowa	24
Michigan	45	Michigan State	28
Michigan	24	Indiana	16
Michigan	52	Minnesota	6
Michigan	42	Purdue	0
Michigan	59	Northwestern	14
Michigan	20	Illinois	0
Michigan	31	Ohio State	3

Season Summary
Games Won, 10; Lost 1

OHIO STATE

No.	Name	Pos.	Wt.	Hgt.	Home Town
75	Bean, Mark	OG	270	6-5	Wichita, KS
3	Beatty, Greg	FL	180	5-11	Houston, TX
76	Bechman, Pete	NG	235	6-5	Chesterland, OH
20	Berger, Jon	K	190	5-11	Centerville, OH
70	Bonhaus, Matt	DT	250	6-5	Cincinnati, OH
50	Borchers, JIm	C	212	6-0	Bellbrook, OH
37	Brown, Deron	FB	202	5-9	Centerville, OH
56	Brown, Randall	DT	240	6-3	Detroit, MI
33	By'not'e, Butler	TB	185	5-11	St. Louis, MO
79	Carden, Sean	NG	260	6-1	Berwick, PA
29	Cook, Bryan	CB	190	6-3	Youngstown, OH
8	Cothran, Jeff	FB	220	6-2	Middletown, OH
83	DeGraffenreid, Allen	FL	200	6-3	Cincinnati, OH
64	Dully, Mike	OT	280	6-5	Hamilton, OH
2	Edwards, Bernard	FL	205	6-5	Ft. Myers, FL
89	Eillis, Jeff	TE	245	6-4	Louisville, KY
94	Foster, Derrick	DE	255	6-5	Dayton, OH
90	Frimel, Rich	DT	250	6-3	North Olmsted, OH
7	Galloway, Joey	SE	170	5-10	Bellaire, OH
93	Goff, Carlos	OLB	208	6-1	Columbus, OH
36	Graham, Andy	FB	190	5-6	Warren, OH
11	Graham, Kent	QB	220	6-5	Wheaton, IL
35	Graham, Scottie	FB	220	5-10	Long Beach, NY
55	Green, Keny	ILB	230	6-1	Pacoima, CA
49	Gurd, Andy	OLB	230	6-3	Chagrein Falls, OH
18	Haley, Earl	WR	180	5-9	Springdale, OH
24	Harper, Roger	SS	224	6-4	Columbus, OH
34	Harris, Raymont	TB	220	6-2	Lorain, OH
16	Harrison, Preston	OLB	235	6-4	Columbus, OH
39	Harrison, Tyrone	FB	232	6-2	Highland Park, NJ
52	Hartman, Len	OG	280	6-2	Leavittsburg, OH
4	Herbstreit, Kirk	QB	213	6-2	Centerville, OH
36	Herman, Judah	ILB	225	6-1	Chagrin Falls, OH
41	Hill, Will	FB	190	6-0	St. John, MO
42	Houston, William	TE/FB	240	6-1	Trotwood, MO
14	Hoying, Bob	QB	210	6-5	St. Hendry, OH
60	Iams, John	OG	244	6-2	Hamilton, OH
71	Jenkins, Chris	OG	242	6-0	Morganton, NC
30	Johnson, Brent	ILB	218	6-1	Columbus, OH
27	Johnson, Girmar	FS	185	6-2	Castaic, CA
95	Kacherski, John	OLB	240	6-3	Riverhead, NY
62	Kelly, C.J.	OG	250	6-5	Rowley, MA
46	Kerner, Marlon	CB	175	6-10	Columbus, OH
10	Kessell, Joel	P	170	6-0	Massillon, OH
67	Kline, Alan	OT	280	6-7	Tifin, OH
74	Kuszmaul, Greg	OT	290	6-5	Warren,OH
81	Lease, Tom	ILB	240	6-5	Kenton, OH
5	Lee, Dante	FL	185	5-10	Dayton, OH
63	Lige, Mike	C	250	6-2	Columbus, OH
66	Long, Paul	C	270	6-5	Highland Hgts, OH
28	Louis, Jason	FS	185	6-2	Lnaham, MD
96	Lutz, Travis	TE	220	6-4	Bucyrus, OH
56	Lynch, Scott	C	190	5-9	So. Parma Hgts., OH
37	Maag, Dennis	CB	180	6-1	Orrville, OH
82	Mazza, Joel	OLB	230	6-0	Mt. Vernon, OH
38	McCoy, Matt	OLB	205	6-2	Wooster, OH
92	McQueen, Therone	NG	260	6-3	Boston, MA
76	Meade, Jeff	OG	268	6-2	Reynoldsnburg, OH
97	Metzger, Joe	TE	235	6-2	Centerville, OH
93	Miller, Kent	K	160	5-9	Carmel, IN
77	Monnot, Dave	OG	265	6-5	Canton, OH
13	Nelson, Dave	FS	190	6-1	Sarasota, FL
6	Partee, Curt	FB	200	5-10	Defiance, OH
21	Patillo, Tim	FB/SS	170	5-11	Aliquippa, PA
9	Paul, Tito	CB	190	6-1	Kissimmee, FL
22	Paulk, Foster	CB	190	5-11	Sarasota, FL
19	Payne, Aaron	SE	165	5-8	Louisville, KY
12	Pickens, Joe	QB	220	6-3	Cleveland, OH
12	Pope, Brad	OLB	200	6-4	Westerville, OH
84	Powell, Craig	OLB	220	6-5	Youngstown, OH
47	Prewitt, Jesse	FL	182	5-11	Dayton, OH
48	Rodriguez, Alex	ILB	224	6-1	Chicago, IL
80	Roy, Chris	TE	245	6-3	Westerville, OH
17	Sanders, Chris	SE	170	6-1	Denver, CO
85	Saunders, Cedric	TE	238	6-3	Sarasota, FL
69	Schilling, John	OT	285	6-3	Clinton, OH
21	Shehee, Greg	FB	212	5-9	Akron,OH
73	Sherrick, Paul	OT	300	6-8	Middletown, OH
78	Shoaf, Mike	OT	280	6-5	Orwell, OH
91	Simmons, Jason	OLB	240	6-5	Akron, OH
57	Smith, Greg	NG	250	6-2	Canton, OH
59	Smith, Rod	OG	285	6-3	Cleveland, OH
25	Snow, Carlos	TB	200	5-9	Cincinnati, OH
99	Spellman, Alonzo	DE	186	6-1	Mt. Holly, NJ
88	Stablein, Brian	SE	186	6-1	Erie, PA
43	Taylor, Walter	SS	175	6-0	Dallas, TX
61	Thrush, Jack	C	260	6-4	Cincinati, OH
58	Tovar, Steve	ILB	240	6-4	Elyria, OH
18	Walton, Tim	CB	165	6-0	Columbus, GA
72	Wilkinson, Dan	OT	234	6-6	Dayton, OH
51	Williams, Mark	OLB	220	6-4	Upper Marlboro, MD
23	Williams, Tim	PK/P	180	5-9	Waynesville, OH
68	Winrow, Jason	OT	290	6-6	Bridgeton, NJ

MICHIGAN

No.	Name	Pos.	Wt.	Hgt.	Home Town
90	Agahakhan, Ninef	MG	274	6-3	Mt. Prospect, IL
27	Albertson, John	PL	190	6-1	Portage, MI
1	Alexander, Derrick	WR	190	6-2	Detroit, MI
37	Anderson, Erick	ILB	242	6-2	Glenview, IL
9	Azona, Eddie	P	189	5-10	Montreal, QUE
78	Barry, Paul	OL	289	6-3	Cincinnati, OH
31	Blankenship, Tony	DB	195	6-0	Detroit, MI
18	Brady, Matt	WR	180	6-2	Grosse Pointe, MI
20	Brown, Corwin	FS	190	6-2	Chicago, IL
58	Buda, James	OL	204	6-0	Plymouth, MI
25	Buff, Ron	TB	207	6-1	Otisville, MI
7	Burch, Alfie	DB	190	6-2	Warren, OH
80	Burkholder, Marc	TE	225	6-3	Traverse City, MI
38	Carlson, J.D.	PK	179	5-10	Tallahassee, FL
42	Carlson, Justin	PK	177	5-11	Tallahassee, FL
13	Carr, Jason	QB	191	6-1	Ann Arbor, MI
68	Cocozzo, Joe	OG	289	6-4	Mechanicville, NY
10	Collins, Todd	QB	219	6-5	Walpole, MA
26	Davis, Ed	TB	183	5-9	Detroit, MI
86	Davis, Martin	PLB	250	6-3	Chesapeake, VA
83	Diebolt, Dave	TE	243	6-5	Mayfield, OH
48	Dobrefe, Dave	ILB	230	6-3	Mt. Clemens, MI
70	Doherty, Rob	OT	298	6-6	Sterling Hgts., MI
22	Dottin, Lance	WCB	201	6-3	Cambridge, MA
55	Dudlar, Gannon	ILB	259	6-4	Birmingham, MI
91	Dyson, Matt	OLB	243	6-5	LaPlata, MD
16	Elezovic, Peter	PK	191	5-11	Farmington Hills, MI
63	Elliott, Marc	OL	246	6-2	Carmel, IN
69	Elliott, Matt	OL/C	269	6-3	Carmel, IN
19	Ellinson, John	WR	173	5-11	Delran, NJ
92	Evans, Mike	DT	269	6-4	Roxbury, MA
51	Everitt, Steve	C	275	6-5	Miami, FL
19	Foster, Brian	FS	184	5-10	Columbia, MO
33	Foster, Chè	RB	256	6-2	Edmond, OH
44	Gasperoni, Sergio	TE	230	6-2	Shelby Township, MI
52	Graves, Eric	MG	259	6-3	Akron, OH
15	Grbac, Elvis	QB	224	6-5	Willoughby Hills, OH
93	Hedding, Kevin	TE	220	6-2	Waterford, MI
79	Henderson, Tony	MG	259	6-2	Indianapolis, IN
38	Henkel, Dave	DB	179	6-0	Cleveland Hgts., OH
4	Holdren, Nate	ILB	238	6-5	Richland, WA
94	Horn, Jason	DL	242	6-5	Lafayette, IN
21	Howard, Desmond	WR	174	5-11	Cleveland, OH
97	Hutchinson, Chris	DT	260	6-2	Houston, TX
82	Jaeckin, John	TE	242	6-2	Cleveland, OH
77	Jenkins, Trezelle	OT	295	6-7	Chicago, IL
28	Johnson, Deon	CB	208	6-2	Detroit, MI
30	Johnson, Jesse	RB	216	5-9	Harper Wds., MI
23	Johnson, Livetius	WR	178	5-10	Chicago, IL
71	Julier, Mike	DL	232	6-0	Midlands
35	Kelley, Barry	FB	229	6-2	Bolingbrook, IL
50	Kendrick, Jason	ILB	252	6-2	Louisville, KY
93	Knuth, Eric	MG	253	6-1	Plymouth, MI
40	Legette, Burnie	FB	230	6-1	Colorado Springs, CO
71	Lewis, Mike	OT	287	6-5	Brockton, MA
17	Lovell, Eric	PK	187	6-0	Beavercreek, OH
62	Lyons, Mike	MG	250	6-1	Lake Orion, MI
39	Mallory, Curt	ILB	211	5-11	Bloomington, IN
43	Maloney, Pat	FS	194	6-2	LaGrange, IL
84	Malveaux, Felman	WR	166	6-0	Beaumont, TX
54	Manning, Paul	OG/C	260	6-4	Bloomfield Hills, MI
73	Marinaro, Leo	OL	272	6-4	Andover, MA
59	Marshall, Alex	DT	267	6-5	Detroit, MI
88	McGee, Tony	TE	241	6-5	Terre Haute, IN
41	McThomas, Greg	FB	238	6-4	Milwaukee, WI
49	Mignon, Jamie	LB	249	6-6	Appleton, WI
67	Milia, Marc	C/OG	268	6-3	Birmingham, MI
57	Miller, Shawn	OG	269	6-4	El Dorado, KS
36	Morrison, Steve	ILB	234	6-3	Birmingham, MI
44	Nadlicki, Mike	FB	230	6-2	Traverse City, MI
3	Peoples, Shonte	DB	224	6-1	Saginaw, MI
74	Plate, Troy	OT	278	6-6	Brooklyn, MI
95	Powers, Bobby	ILB	226	6-0	River Ridge, LA
12	Powers, Ricky	TB	200	6-0	Akron, OH
39	Pratt, Adam	DB	155	6-2	Bellaire, MI
8	Randall, Craig	QB	232	6-4	E. Kentwood, MI
96	Reggans, Walter	LB	223	6-1	Aurora, CO
66	Rekowski, Steve	DT	264	6-5	Redford, MI
29	Richards, Todd	SR	145	5-11	Reading, MI
16	Riemersma, Jy	QB	215	6-5	Zeeland, MI
29	Ritter, David	SS	205	6-3	Hickory Hills, IL
65	Simpson, Neil	OLB	228	6-1	Highland Park, MI
72	Skene, Doug	OG/OT	286	6-6	Farivie, TX
62	Skorput, Ante	OT	286	6-3	Toronto, ONT
75	Skrepenak, Greg	OT	325	6-8	Wilkes, Barre, PA
53	Smith, Brion	DL	278	6-2	Utica, MI
25	Smith, Lasker	DB	200	6-0	Ecorse, MI
2	Smith, Walter	WR	188	5-11	Detroit, MI
14	Sollom, Ken	QB	200	6-2	Canyon Country, CA
32	Southward, Damon	LB	214	6-3	Birmingham, AL
60	Stanley, Sylvestor	MG/DT	265	6-2	Youngstown, OH
18	Stapleton, Chris	P	210	6-1	Springfield, IL
99	Stark, Randy	PLB	236	6-4	Mento, OH
50	Steuk, William	PLB	221	6-4	Sandusky, OH
61	Sullivan, Mike	OT	299	6-7	E. Lansing, MI
81	Swearengin, Julian	WR	180	6-0	Madison Hgts., MI
33	Taylor, Dorian	DB	202	6-0	Detroit, MI
35	Tilmann, Michael	DN	190	5-11	West Branch, MI
45	Townsend, Brian	OLB	232	6-3	Cincinnati, OH
34	Van Dyne, Yale	WR	192	6-1	Kearney, MO
58	Vanderleest, Rob	DT	255	6-4	Muskegon, MI
46	Walker, Marcus	ILB	234	6-0	Chicago Hgts., IL
64	Wallace, Brian	OT	278	6-5	Parma, OH
5	Wallace, Coleman	CB	189	6-0	Willingboro, NJ
8	Ware, Dwayne	CB	188	5-11	Bloomington, IL
24	Washngton, Dennis	FB	192	5-10	Lorain, OH
6	Wheatley, Tyrone	RB	206	6-1	Dearborn Hgts., MI
17	Williams, Otis	SS	206	6-2	Canton, OH
56	Woodlock, John	OG	281	6-1	Waynesburg, OH
14	Wuerfel, Joshua	PL/P	148	5-6	Traverse City, MI
76	Zenkewicz, Trent	DL	249	6-5	Cleveland, OH

ERICK ANDERSON
All-American Linebacker

DESMOND HOWARD
All-American Wide Receiver

MATT ELLIOTT
All-American Gaurd

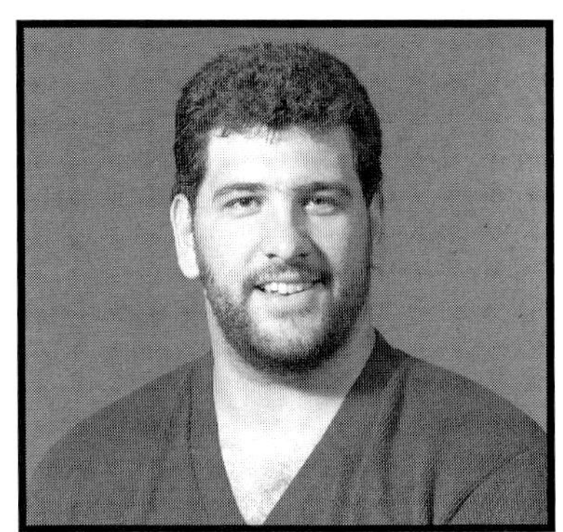

GREG SKREPENAK
All-American Tackle

10
30
BURKHOLDER
80
40

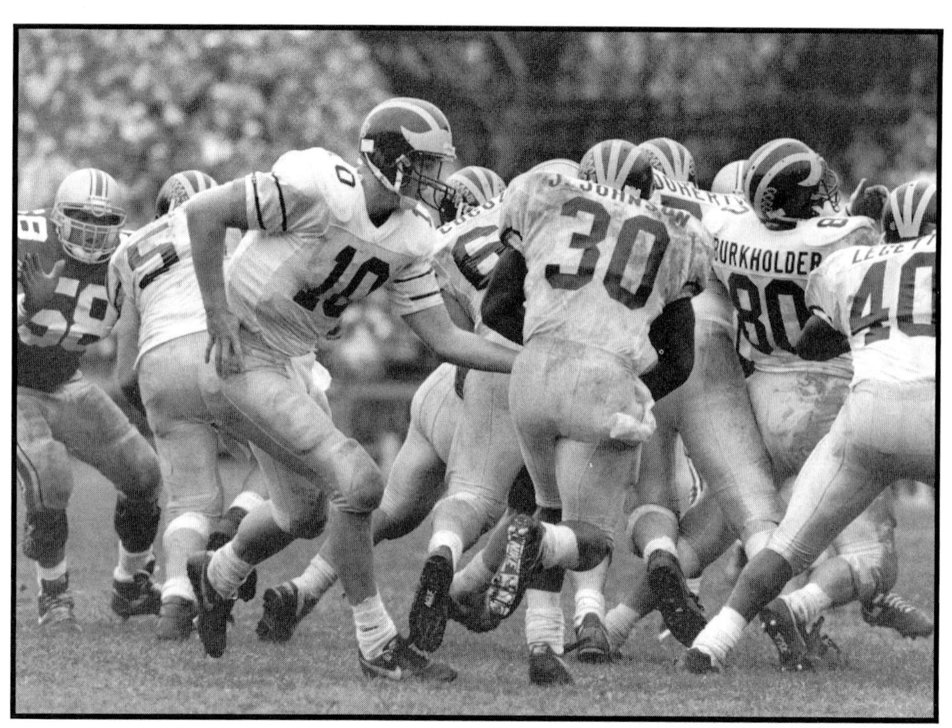

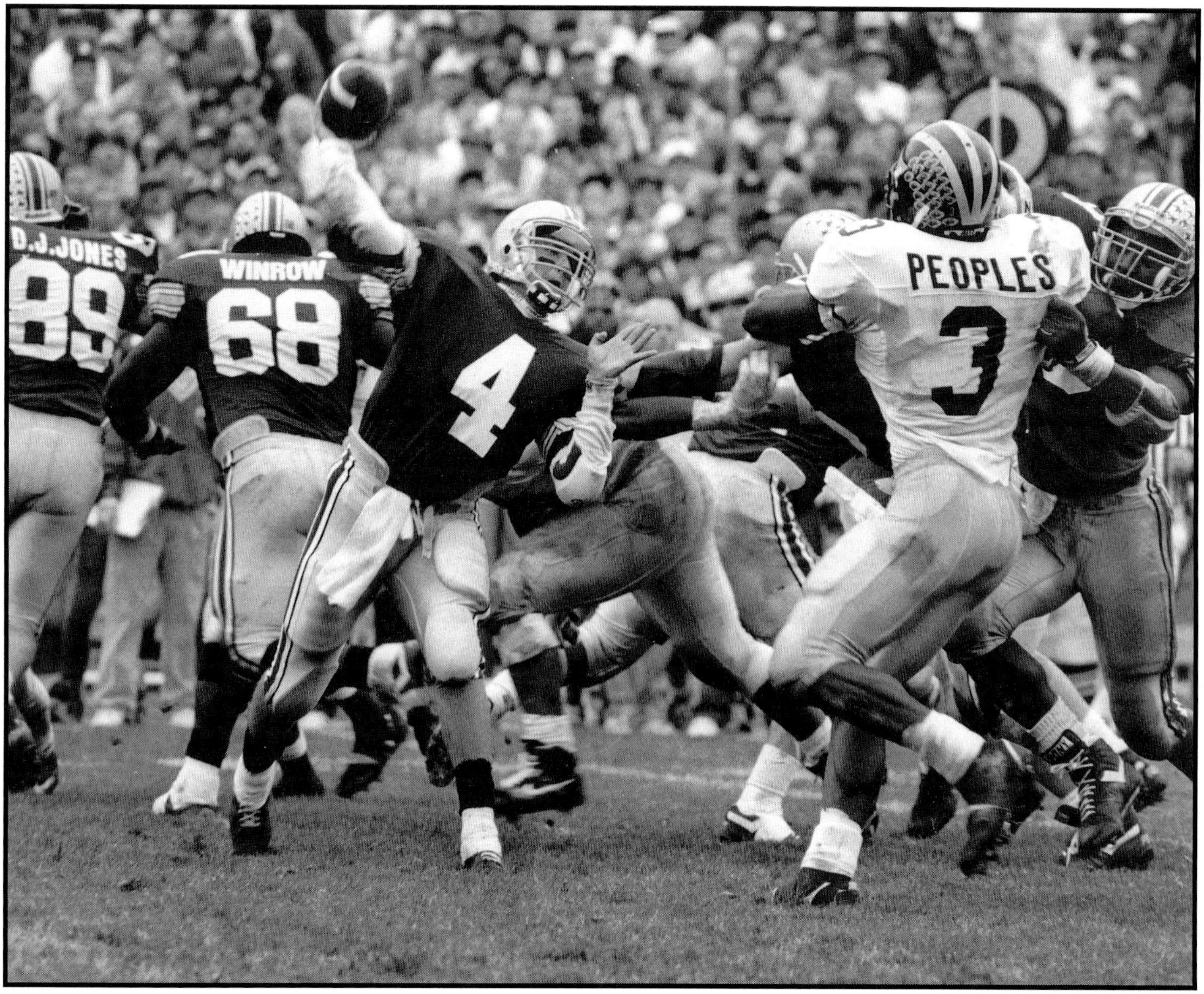
D.J.JONES
89
WINROW
68
4
PEOPLES
3

November 21, 1992

Columbus, Ohio

Buckeyes Rally For 13-13 Stalemate With Wolverines

Cooper Plays It Safe In Late Game Decisions

photos by Chance Brockway

The Ohio State Buckeyes ended their string of four straight losses to Michigan by rallying for a 13-13 deadlock. Still, the controversy surrounding embattled OSU Coach John Cooper intensified after fans second guessed his conservative decisions late in the game.

With 4:24 to play, the Buckeyes edged to within 13-12 on a fourth down, five-yard touchdown pass from Kirk Herbstreit to split end Greg Beatty. Instead of going for a two-point conversion for the lead, Cooper opted for a point-after-Touchdown kick by Tim Williams for the tie, unleashing a round of catcalls from Coopers critics.

"With over four minutes to play, it (a two-point conversion) never crossed my mind," said Cooper. "The idea was to hold them, get the ball back and kick a winning field goal."

Ohio State did receive another possession when its defense forced Michigan to punt on the next series. The Buckeyes started with good field position at their own 45, but could only move six yards in three downs. Facing a fourth-and-four at the Michigan 49 with 1:28 left, Cooper decided to punt rather than gamble for the first down.

Ohio State still received another ray of hope when Michigan's Derrick Alexander fumbled the punt near the Wolverines' goal line. After a mad scramble in which Ohio State's Steve Tovar narrowly missed the ball, Michigan's Shawn Collins saved the day for the Wolverines by pouncing on the fumble at the nine-yard line.

After the game, Ohio State University President Gordon Gee reinforced his support of Cooper, even though his perception of the outcome wasn't the same as the score. "It was one of our greatest wins," he said. "You don't have to read between the lines to see he (Cooper) is doing a good job."

As much as Cooper was fending off his critics, Michigan Coach Gary Moeller was enjoying the Wolverines' undefeated regular season record of 8-0-3. The Wolverines captured the Big Ten title and a trip to the Rose Bowl with a 6-0-2 conference record. Ohio State finished 8-2-1 overall, the best in Cooper's five-year tenure, and 5-2-1 in the Big Ten.

The Buckeyes lit the scoreboard first with a 3 9-yard field goal by Williams in the opening quarter. Ohio State's drive started with an interception by defensive back Chico Nelson.

Michigan gained a 6-3 lead in the second quarter when quarterback Elvis Grbac scored from the three on a quarterback draw play, but Peter Elezovic's conversion kick went wide right. Unfortunately for Michigan, Grbac suffered rib and head injuries on that touchdown run and was replaced for the rest of the game by freshman Todd Collins.

Ohio State had a chance to tie the game just before halftime, but Williams was just wide on his 56-yard field goal try.

The Wolverines expanded their lead late in the third quarter with an impressive 80 yard touchdown drive in 12 plays. Collins rolled out and ran in untouched for the final yard of the drive.

The Buckeyes began their fourth quarter comeback with a 30-yard field goal by Williams and the Herbstreit-to-Beatty touchdown connection.

Ohio State won the statistical battle with 362 yards total offense to Michigan's 271. The Buckeyes' advantage was primarily through the air, as Herbstreit completed 28-of-47 passes for 271 yards. His main target was Brian Stablein with 12 receptions for 111 yards.

Michigan could only muster 71 passing yards, but it rolled up 218 rushing yards to Ohio State's meager 91 yards.

STATISTICS

	UM	OSU
First Downs	16	24
Rushes-Yards	44-200	35-91
Passing Yards	71	271
Passes	6-15-2	28-47-0
Punts/Avg.	6-43	5-37
Fumbles-Lost	0-0	0-0
Penalties-Yards	6-59	5-34

SCORING

Michigan	0	6	7	0 -	13
Ohio State	3	0	0	10 -	13

1992

Michigan	17	Notre Dame	17
Michigan	35	Oklahoma State	3
Michigan	61	Houston	17
Michigan	52	Iowa	28
Michigan	35	Michigan State	10
Michigan	31	Indiana	3
Michigan	63	Minnesota	13
Michigan	24	Purdue	17
Michigan	40	Northwestern	7
Michigan	22	Illinois	22
Michigan	13	Ohio State	13

Season Summary

Games Won, 8; Lost, 0; Tied, 3

JOE COCOZZO
All-American Guard

CHRIS HUTCHINSON
All-American Tackle

DERRICK ALEXANDER
All-American Wide Receiver

MICHIGAN

No.	Name	Pos.	Wt.	Hgt.	Home Town
90	Aghakhan, Ninef	MGK	274	6-3	Mt. Prospect, IL
1	Alexander, Derrick	WR	190	6-2	Detroit, MI
17	Anderson, Deollo	DB	190	6-1	Youngstown, OH
9	Azoona, Eddie	P	189	5-10	Montreal, QUE
78	Barry, Pauly	OG	274	6-3	Cincinnati, OH
31	Blankenship, Tony	FS	195	6-0	Detroit, MI
99	Bolach, Mark	OL/DL	265	6-6	Muskegon, MI
8	Boykin, Eric	QB	205	6-4	Dayton, OH
20	Brown, Corwin	FS	193	6-2	Chicago, IL
25	Buff, Ron	FB	215	6-1	Otisville, MI
7	Burch, Alfie	CB	192	6-2	Warren, OH
80	Burkholder, Marc	TE	239	6-3	Traverse City, MI
38	Carlson, Justin	PK	177	5-11	Tallahassee, FL
13	Carr, Jason	QB	200	6-1	Ann Arbor, MI
34	Charles, Jean-Agnus	DB	200	5-11	Montreal, QUE
68	Cocozzo, Joe	OG	289	6-4	Mechanicville, NY
32	Collins, Shawn	OLB	215	6-3	Patterson, NJ
10	Collins, Todd	QB	223	6-5	Walpole, MA
26	Davis, Ed	TB	190	5-9	Detroit, MI
86	Davis, Martin	OLB	253	6-3	Chesapeake, VA
48	Dobreff, Dave	ILB	230	6-3	Mt. Clemens, MI
70	Doherty, Robando	OT	298	6-6	Sterling Hts., Mi
55	Dudlar, Gannon	DT	265	6-4	Birmingham, MI
91	Dyson, Matt	OLB	240	6-5	Laplata, MD
93	Edmonds, Ray	MG	278	6-3	Akron, OH
16	Elezovic, Peter	PK	191	5-11	Farmington Hills, MI
63	Elliott, Marc	OL	230	6-2	Carmel, IN
92	Evans, Stephen	LB	235	6-4	Roxbury, MA
51	Everitt, Steve	C	275	6-5	Miami, Fl
19	Foster, Brian	FS	184	5-10	Columbia, MO
33	Foster, Che'	FB	240	6-2	Edmond, OK
44	Gasperoni, Sergio	TE	230	6-2	Shelby Twnship., MI
56	Goodwin, Harold	OL	275	6-4	Hopkins, SC
52	Graves, Eric	MG	262	6-3	Akron, OH
15	Grbac, Elvis	QB	230	6-5	Willoughby Hills, OH
75	Guynes, Tom	OL	285	6-5	Kankakee, IL
19	Hamilton, Remy	PK	195	6-1	Boca Raton, FL
23	Hankins, Woodrow	RB	180	5-9	Owasso, OK
9	Hayes, Mercury	WR	180	5-11	Houston, TX
79	Henderson, Tony	MG	267	6-2	Indianapolis, IN
4	Holdren, Nate	ILB	238	6-5	Richland, WA
94	Horn, Jason	DL	253	6-5	Lafayette, IN
97	Hutchinson, Chris	DT	249	6-2	Houston, TX
37	Irons, Jarrett	LB	215	6-2	Conroe, TX
82	Jaeckin, John	TE	242	6-2	Cleveland, OH
77	Jenkins, Trezelle	OT	298	6-7	Chicago, IL
28	Johnson, Dean	CB	208	6-2	Detroit, MI
30	Johnson, Jesse	TB	209	5-9	Harper Woods, MI
85	Jones, Damon	TE	215	6-6	Evanston, IL
27	King, Steve	DB	180	6-1	Palm Beach Gardens, FL
22	Law, Ty	RB/DB	185	6-0	Aliquippa, PA
40	Legette, Burnie	FB	230	6-1	Colorado Springs, CO
71	Lewis, Mike	OT	270	6-5	Brockton, MA
21	Little, Earl	DB	185	6-0	Miami, FL
17	Lovell, Erik	PK	194	6-0	Beavercreek, OH
43	Maloney, Pat	SS	194	6-2	LaGrange, IL
84	Balveaux, Felman	WR	166	6-0	Beaumont, TX
54	Manning, Paul	OG/C	257	6-4	Bloomfield Hills, MI
73	Marinaro, Joe	OT	280	6-4	Andover, MA
88	McGee, Tony	TE	241	6-5	Terre Haute, IN
41	McThomas, Greg	OLB	233	6-4	Milwaukee, WI
49	Mignon, Jamie	OLB	241	6-6	Appleton, WI
67	Milia, Marc	C/OG	268	6-3	Birmingham, MI
57	Miller, Shawn	OG	269	6-4	El Dorado, KS
36	Morrison, Steve	ILB	242	6-3	Birmingham, MI
44	Nadlicki, Mike	OLB	220	6-2	Traverse City, MI
42	Noble, Tyrone	RB	185	6-1	Kankakee, IL
64	Payne, Rod	OL	280	6-4	Miami, FL
3	Peoples, Shonte	SS	227	6-1	Saginaw, MI
74	Plate, Troy	OT	272	6-6	Brooklyn, MI
95	Powers, Bobby	ILB	233	6-0	River Ridge, LA
12	Powers, Ricky	TB	215	6-0	Akron, OH
39	Pratt, Adam	DB	166	6-2	Bellaire, MI
96	Reggans, Walter	DT	233	6-1	Aurora, CO
66	Rekowski, Steve	DT	264	6-5	Redford, MI
29	Richards, Todd	WR	164	5-11	Reading, MI
16	Riemersma, Jay	QB	232	6-5	Zeeland, MI
69	Runyan, Jon	OL/DL	270	6-9	Flint, MI
72	Skene, Doug	OG/OT	294	6-6	Toronto, ONT
62	Skorput, Ante	OG	291	6-3	Toronto, ONT
53	Smith, Brian	MG	260	6-2	Utica, MI
25	Smith, Lasker	DB	200	6-0	Ecorse, MI
2	Smith, Walter	WR	190	5-11	Detroit, MI
60	Stanley, Buster	MG/DT	265	6-2	Youngstown, OH
18	Stapleton, Chris	P	210	6-1	Springfield, IL
51	Steuk, William	OLB	225	6-4	Sandusky, OH
61	Sullivan, Mike	OT	298	6-7	E. Lansing, MI
81	Swearengin, Julian	WR	180	6-0	Madison Hgts., MI
33	Taylor, Dorian	OLB	210	6-0	Detroit, MI
35	Tilmann, Michael	DB	177	5-11	W. Branch, MI
18	Toomer, Amani	WR	180	6-3	Concord, CA
45	Vanderbeek, Mike	LB	215	6-3	Hudsonville, MI
58	Vanderleest, Rob	DT	255	6-4	Muskegon, MI
59	Waldroup, Kerwin	DL	255	6-4	Chicago, IL
46	Walker, Marcus	ILB	234	5-11	Chicago Hgts., IL
5	Wallace, Coleman	CB	193	6-0	Willingboro, NJ
8	Ware, Dwayne	CB	193	5-11	Bloomington, IL
24	Washington, Dennis	FB	192	5-10	Lorian, OH
65	Wendt, Eric	OL	270	6-5	Cincinnati, OH
6	Wheatley, Tyrone	TB	225	6-1	Inkster, MI
35	Winters, Charles	RB	190	5-11	Detroit, MI
14	Wuerfel, Joshua	PK/P	148	5-6	Traverse City, MI
76	Zenkewicz, Trent	DL	256	6-5	Cleveland, OH

OHIO STATE

No.	Name	Pos.	Wt.	Hgt.	Home Town
3	Beatty, Gregy	SE	180	5-11	Houston, TX
76	Beckman, Pete	DTB	254	6-5	Chesterland, OH
95	Bell, Jim	OLB	230	6-6	Liberty, OH
70	Bonhaus, Matt	DT	250	6-5	Cincinnati, OH
50	Borchers, Jim	LS	212	6-2	Bellbrook, OH
37	Brown, Deron	FB	215	5-9	Spring Valley, OH
56	Brown, Randall	DE	260	6-3	Detroit, MI
33	By'not'e, Butler	TB	190	5-11	St. Louis, MO
39	Calhoun, Matt	FB	225	6-2	Heath, OH
1	Carter, DeWayne	SE	185	6-3	Youngstown, OH
36	Christopher, Matt	ILB	230	6-2	Uniontown, OH
38	Colson, Dan	DB	185	6-0	Middletown, OH
29	Cook, Bryan	CB	200	6-3	Youngstown, OH
8	Cothran, Jeff	FB	235	6-2	Middletown, OH
15	Crissy, Mike	P	175	5-11	Coral Springs, FL
96	Daniels, LeShun	MG	265	6-4	Warren, OH
87	Davis, Robbie	FL	175	6-2	Twinburg, OH
83	DeGraffenreid, Allen	FL	200	6-3	Cincinnati, OH
64	Dully, Mike	OT	280	6-5	Hamilton, OH
99	Fickell, Luke	DE	255	6-5	Westerville, OH
32	Finck, Dan	FS	187	6-0	Junction City, OH
94	Foster, Derrick	DE	260	6-5	Dayton, OH
7	Galloway, Joey	FL	180	5-10	Bellaire, OH
27	George, Eddie	TB	225	6-3	Philadelphia, PA
93	Goff, Carlos	ILB	208	6-1	Columbus, OH
55	Green, Keny	ILB	230	6-1	Pacoima, CA
49	Gwinn, Jayson	OLB	240	6-3	Columbus, OH
24	Harper, Roger	SS	224	6-4	Columbus, OH
34	Harris, Raymont	TB	226	6-2	Lorain, OH
16	Harrison, Preston	OLB	245	6-5	Columbus, OH
52	Hartman, Len	OG	280	6-2	Leavittsburg, OH
63	Hawkins, Neil	DT	245	6-5	Bucyrus, OH
4	Herbstreit, Kirk	QB	212	6-2	Centerville, OH
41	Hill, Will	TB	208	6-0	St. John, MO
42	Houston, William	FB	260	6-1	Trotwood, OH
20	Howard, Ty	DB	172	5-11	Columbus, OH
14	Hoying, Bob	QB	220	6-5	St. Henry, OH
11	Hurley, Bo	QB	210	6-3	McGuffey, OH
60	Iams, John	OG	244	6-2	Hamilton, OH
89	Jones, D. J.	TE	260	6-5	Lebanon, OH
98	Jones, R. C.	DE	238	6-3	Youngstown, OH
30	Johnson, Brent	ILB	220	6-1	Columbus, OH
62	Kelly, C. J.	C	285	6-5	Rowley, MA
25	Kelly, Rob	DB	195	6-3	Newark, OH
46	Marlon, Kernerh	CB	175	6-0	Columbus, OH
10	Kessel, Joel	P	170	6-0	Massillon, OH
67	Kline, Alan	OT	285	6-5	Warren, OH
74	Kuszmaul, Greg	OT	285	6-5	Warren, OH
82	Langenkamp, Max	TE	250	6-5	Cincinnati, OH
5	Lee, Dante	TB	185	5-10	Dayton, OH
66	Long, Paul	C	282	6-5	Highland Hgts., OH
28	Louis, Jason	SS	185	6-2	Lanham, MD
53	Lynch, Scott	LS	205	5-11	Parma Heights, OH
38	McCoy, Matt	OLB	205	6-2	Wooster, OH
6	McGuire, Travis	TB	195	6-0	Massillon, OH
92	McQueen, Therone	MG	260	6-3	Boston, MA
97	Metzger, Joe	TE	243	6-2	Centerville, OH
53	Mezgec, Mike	C	265	6-4	Eastlake, OH
43	Miller, Ryan	ILB	245	6-3	Allen Park, MI
77	Monnot, Dave	OG	275	6-5	Canton, OH
80	Moss, Eric	TE	270	6-6	Rand, WV
13	Nelson, Chico	FS	197	6-1	Sarasota, FL
86	Niekamp, Kevin	TE	248	6-6	St. Henry, OH
11	Niemeyer, Bryan	QB	192	6-1	Minster, OH
21	Patillo, Tim	SS	180	5-11	Aliquippa, PA
9	Tito, Paul	CB	195	6-1	Kissimmee, FL
22	Paulk, Foster	CB	185	5-11	Sarasota, FL
12	Pope, Brad	OLB	200	6-4	Westerville, OH
65	Porter, Juan	OT	305	6-5	Cleveland, OH
84	Powell, Craig	OLB	227	6-5	Youngstown, OH
47	Prewitt, Jesse	FL	182	5-11	Dayton, OH
48	Rodriguez, Alex	ILB	230	6-1	Chicago, IL
17	Sanders, Chris	FL	175	6-1	Denver, CO
85	Saunders, Cedric	TE	238	6-3	Sarasota, FL
71	Sheets, Steve	DT	265	6-5	Columbus, OH
91	Simmons, Jason	OLB	240	6-5	Akron, OH
60	Smith, Brian	OG	260	6-6	Crosss Lanes, WV
57	Smith, Greg	MG	250	6-2	Canton, OH
26	Smith, Robert	TB	195	6-2	Euclid, OH
59	Smith, Rod	OG	300	6-3	Cleveland, OH
88	Stablein, Brian	SE	186	6-1	Erie, PA
44	Stokes, Tommy	ILB	232	6-3	Houston, TX
54	Stoughton, Brian	ILB	210	6-2	London, OH
78	Stringer, Korey	OT	310	6-6	Warren, OH
90	Styles, Lorenzo	OLB	230	6-3	Farrell, PA
2	Taylor, Walter	FS	190	6-0	Dallas, TX
61	Thrush, Jack	OT	276	6-4	Cincinnati, OH
12	Tillman, Buster	WR	180	6-1	Steubenville, OH
58	Tovar, Steve	ILB	240	6-4	Elyria, OH
18	Walton, Tim	CB	170	6-0	Columbus, OH
72	Wilkinson, Dan	DT	299	6-5	Dayton, OH
35	Willard, Lou	TB	210	6-0	Grove City, OH
51	Williams, Mark	OLB	225	6-4	Upper Marlboro, MD
23	Williams, Tim	P/PK	180	5-9	Waynsville, OH
68	Winrow, Jason	OT	300	6-6	Bridgeton, NJ

1992

Ohio	20	Louisville	19
Ohio	17	Bowling Green	6
Ohio	35	Syracuse	12
Ohio	16	Wisconsin	20
Ohio	16	Illinois	18
Ohio	31	Northwestern	7
Ohio	27	Michigan State	17
Ohio	38	Iowa	15
Ohio	17	Minnesota	0
Ohio	27	Indiana	10
Ohio	13	Michigan	13

Season Summary

Games Won, 8; Lost, 2; Tied, 1

STEVE TOVAR
All-American Linebacker

M

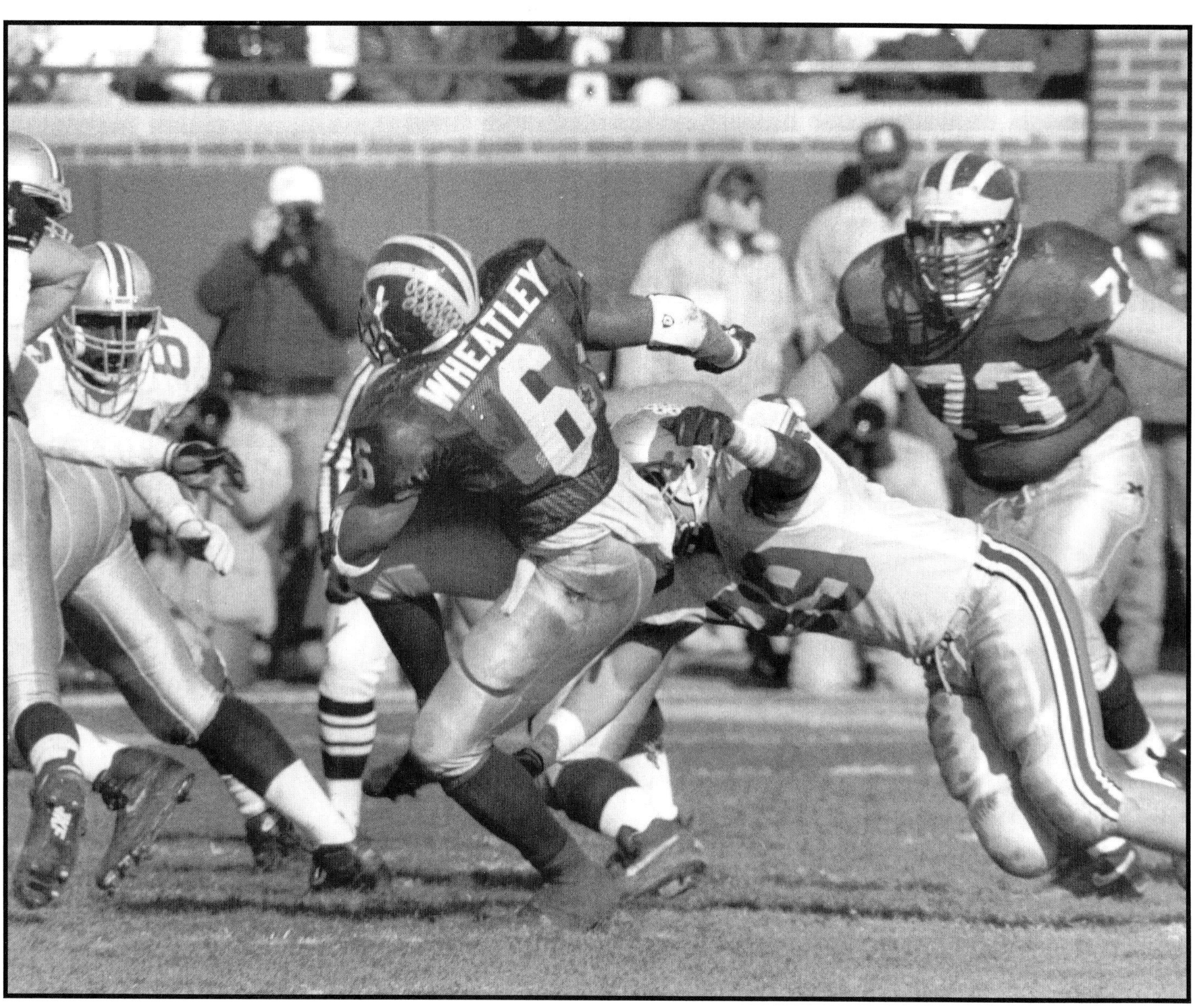

November 20, 1993

Ann Arbor, Michigan

Michigan Dominates Favored Buckeyes 28-0 Before Record Crowd

Wolverines Spoil Ohio State's Previously Unbeaten Mark

Photos by Chance Brockway

The largest crowd in NCAA history witnessed the Michigan Wolverines spoil the Rose Bowl hopes of the Ohio State Buckeyes with a 28-0 shellacking in Ann Arbor.

A crowd of 106,867 filled Michigan Stadium as the underdog Wolverines dominated every facet of the game against the previously undefeated Buckeyes. The Ohio State loss, coupled with a Wisconsin victory two weeks later, sent Wisconsin to the Rose Bowl.

The loss also marked the sixth straight year Ohio State Coach John Cooper hadn't defeated Michigan and its head coach, Gary Moeller. Cooper's 0-5-1 record against the Wolverines was brought up by a reporter in the post-game press conference. The OSU mentor threw up his hands, headed for the door and said "It's as frustrating as it could be" as he exited.

Cooper's emotions were understandable. On this day, everything went Michigan's way. "It was like Murphy's Law. Anything that could go wrong did," said Ohio State guard Jason Winrow.

Winrow might have been thinking about the reverse play by Michigan's Derrick Alexander, who fumbled the ball only to have it pop right back to him for a further gain.

Or maybe he was remembering when OSU punter Tim Williams let his knee hit the ground while fielding a low snap, giving the Wolverines the ball right there in Buckeye territory. Or perhaps it was the 15-yard sack by OSU's Randall Brown that was negated by a facemask penalty.

Most likely, it was a combination of all these plays and more that made it a nightmare for the Buckeyes and a bright spot in an otherwise disappointing season for 7-4 Michigan. The Wolverines committed just one turnover while intercepting Ohio State's quarterbacks, Bobby Hoying and Bret Powers, four times. Michigan almost doubled Ohio State's offensive output, 421 yards to 212. The Wolverine defense was especially stingy against the run, giving up just 58 yards in 28 tries.

"The shutout means a lot," said Michigan cornerback Ty Law. "We played the ball well and held their receivers down. This eases the pain for the seniors, but we still wanted that Rose Bowl. "

The Michigan offense was outstanding as well, with Tyrone Wheatley leading the way with 105 yards rushing, all in the first half. When Wheatley went down with a slight concussion, Ed Davis kept up the momentum with 96 yards on 22 carries.

Michigan established control with a touchdown midway through the first quarter. Soon after a 43-yard scamper by Wheatley, quarterback Todd Collins hit Mercury Hayes with a 25-yard aerial in the end zone. Hayes made a spectacular over-the-shoulder catch of a ball up for grabs.

The Wolverines upped their advantage to 14-0 in the second quarter with a five-play, 95-yard touchdown drive capped by Jon Ritchie's one-yard burst. A 50-yard completion from Collins to Derrick Alexander was the key play of the drive.

Soon afterward, Michigan's free safety Chuck Winters intercepted a Powers pass to set up a 3-yard touchdown pass from Collins to Che Foster. The Wolverines headed into the locker room at halftime with a 21-0 advantage.

The final score of the day occurred in the third quarter after Ohio State punter Williams was ruled down after fielding a low snap on the OSU 32. Four plays later, Davis scored from the five.

As the final gun sounded, the Buckeyes were saddled with their first loss of the season for a 9-1-1 regular season record. As Cooper aptly stated, "This puts a damper on the season. We were in a position to have a Cinderella-type season and we let it slip away."

For the winners, it was all smiles. "It was a big win. We played like we should have all season, with emotion, " said Michigan Coach Moeller.

STATISTICS

	OSU	UM
First Downs	14	22
Rushes-Yards	28-58	56-281
Passing Yards	154	140
Passes	14-30-4	14-20-1
Punts/Avg.	5-39	4-40
Fumbles-Lost	2-0	1-0
Penalties-Yards	4-19	6-45

SCORING

Ohio State	0	0	0	0	- 0
Michigan	7	14	7	0	- 28

1993

Ohio	34	Rice	7
Ohio	21	Washington	12
Ohio	63	Pittsburgh	28
Ohio	51	Northwestern	3
Ohio	20	Illinois	12
Ohio	28	Michigan State	21
Ohio	45	Purdue	24
Ohio	24	Penn State	6
Ohio	14	Wisconsin	14
Ohio	23	Indiana	17
Ohio	0	Michigan	28

Season Summary

Games Won, 9; Lost, 1; Tied, 1

KOREY STRINGER
All-American Wide Tackle

DAN WILKINSON
All-American Tackle

OHIO STATE

No.	Name	Pos.	Wt.	Hgt.	Home Town
89	Baker, Mike	DT	276	6-0	Louisville, OH
76	Beckman, Pete	DT	250	6-4	Chesterland, OH
95	Bell, Jim	DE	241	6-5	Liberty, OH
30	Bellisari, Greg	MLB	220	6-1	Boca Raton, FL
70	Bonhaus, Matt	NG	270	6-5	Cincinnati, OH
50	Borchers, Jim	LS	212	6-2	Bellbrook, OH
56	Brown, Randall	DE	250	6-3	Detroit, MI
33	By'not'e, Butler	TB	190	5-11	St. Louis, MO
39	Calhoun, Matt	FB	219	6-0	Heath, OH
32	Carlson, Gerald	K	157	6-0	Randolph, NY
1	Carter, DeWayne	SE	190	6-2	Youngstown, OH
36	Christopher, Matt	MLB	240	6-2	Uniontown, OH
22	Colson, Dan	SS	185	6-0	Middletown, OH
55	Connery, Will	OLB	228	6-1	Vandalia, OH
29	Cothran, Jeff	FB	231	6-2	Middletown, OH
96	Daniels, LeShun	NG	267	6-2	Warren, OH
87	Davis, Robbie	FL	200	6-0	Twinsburg, OH
97	Day, John	DE	230	6-3	Independence, OH
66	Dawson, Andy	OG	265	6-4	Shelby, OH
75	DeLong, Walt	OT	300	6-5	Ironton, OH
64	Dully, Mike	OT	280	6-5	Hamilton, OH
99	Fickell, Luke	NG	255	6-4	Westerville, OH
92	Finkes, Matt	DE	234	6-2	Piqua, OH
7	Galloway, Joey	SE	180	5-10	Bellaire, OH
27	George, Eddie	TB	227	6-3	Philadelphia, PA
83	Glenn, Terry	FL	180	5-11	Columbus, OH
59	Guiliani, Robert	NG	255	5-11	Columbus, OH
26	Gwinn, Anthony	FS	180	6-0	Columbus, OH
49	Gwinn, Jayson	DE	258	6-3	Columbus, OH
60	Harris, Ray	OG	325	6-3	Massillon, OH
34	Harris, Raymont	TB	225	6-2	Lorain, OH
16	Harrison, Preston	DE	244	6-5	Columbus, OH
63	Hawkins, Neil	OT	260	6-4	Bucyrus, OH
88	Houser, Bob	TE	230	6-4	Westlake, OH
42	Houston, William	FB	260	6-1	Trotwood, OH
20	Howard, Ty	CB	172	5-9	Columbus, OH
14	Hoying, Bobby	QB	223	6-4	St. Henry, OH
10	Hoying, Tom	QB	210	6-4	St. Henry, OH
95	Huntzinger, Rick	OG	236	6-3	Columbus, OH
9	Jackson, Josh	K	155	6-0	Logan, OH
8	Jackson, Stanley	QB	186	6-1	Paterson, NJ
13	Jacobs, Matt	SE	192	6-1	Amherst, OH
89	Jones, D. J.	TE	250	6-4	Lebanon, OH
98	Jones, R. C.	DE	263	6-2	Youngstown, OH
52	Keefer, Michael	OLB	219	6-1	Pigeon, MI
62	Kelly, C. J.	OG	288	6-4	Rowley, MA
25	Kelly, Rob	FS	192	6-2	Newark, OH
46	Kerner, Marlon	CB	188	5-11	Columbus, OH
67	Kline, Alan	OT	275	6-6	Tiffin, OH
74	Kuszmaul, Greg	OT	305	6-4	Warren, OH
82	Langenkamp, Max	TE	240	6-3	Cincinnati, OH
81	Langenkamp, Steve	TE	273	6-3	Cincinnati, OH
47	Long, Calvin	FB	237	6-3	Chagrin Falls, OH
28	Louis, Jason	SS	185	6-1	Lanham, MD
30	Lovely, Mark	FB	200	5-10	Columbus, OH
53	Lynch, Scott	LS	205	5-11	Parma Heights, OH
47	Maag, Dennis	CB	180	6-0	Orrville, OH
38	Malfatt, Mike	P	212	6-3	Dublin, OH
6	McGuire, Travis	TB	192	5-11	Massillon, OH
73	Meade, Jeff	OT	288	6-1	Reynoldsburg, OH
99	Merrick, Mike	WR	168	6-0	Galena, OH
56	Miller, Pete	OT	300	6-3	Mayfield Hts., OH
43	Miller, Ryan	OLB	220	6-2	Allen Park, MI
77	Monnot, Dave	OG	277	6-4	Canton, OH
80	Moss, Eric	TE	280	6-5	Charleston, WV
13	Nelson, Chico	SS	197	6-1	Sarasota, FL
25	Ost, Dave	HO	167	6-1	Akron, OH
21	Patillo, Tim	FS	170	5-10	Aliquippa, PA
9	Paul, Tito	CB	191	6-1	Kissimmee, FL
57	Payton, Timiko	NG	265	6-1	Alliance, OH
65	Porter, Juan	OG	296	6-4	Cleveland, OH
84	Powell, Craig	OLB	227	6-4	Youngstown, OH
3	Powers, Bret	QB	216	6-5	Glendale, AZ
86	Reid, Brad	DE	234	6-5	Rayland, OH
84	Robinson, Jeff	FL	176	6-0	Uniontown, OH
48	Rodriguez, Alex	MLB	240	6-1	Chicago, IL
58	Ross, James	OLB	225	6-4	Detroit, MI
17	Sanders, Chris	FL	175	6-1	Denver, CO
85	Saunders, Cedric	TE	241	6-3	Sarasota, FL
53	Schmidlin, Eric	FB	203	6-0	Dublin, OH
98	Shavers, Alonzo	WR	175	6-0	Columbus, OH
71	Sheets, Steve	C	244	6-4	Columbus, OH
21	Shehee, Greg	FB	219	5-9	Akron, OH
91	Simmons, Jason	DE	240	6-5	Akron, OH
69	Smith, Brian	C	275	6-6	Cross Lanes, WV
59	Smith, Rod	C	310	6-3	Cleveland, OH
24	Springs, Shawn	CB	180	5-11	Silver Springs, MD
35	Stanford, Jason	DB	200	6-1	Garland, TX
86	Stanley, Dimitrious	FL	180	5-10	Worthington, OH
19	Starks, Eric	SE	175	5-11	Columbus, OH
34	Stillwell, Obie	OLB	203	6-1	Mansfield, OH
44	Stokes, Tommy	MLB	220	6-2	Houston, TX
54	Stoughton, Brian	OLB	228	6-2	London, OH
78	Stringer, Korey	OT	310	6-6	Warren, OH
90	Styles, Lorenzo	OLB	242	6-2	Farrell, PA
37	Sualua, Nicky	FB	240	5-11	Santa Ana, CA
2	Taylor, Walter	FS	196	6-0	Dallas, TX
32	Terna, Scott	P	190	6-0	Kaneohe, HI
61	Thrush, Jack	C	270	6-5	Cincinnati, OH
12	Tillman, Buster	SE	175	6-1	Steubenville, OH
94	Vrabel, Mike	DE	260	6-4	Stow, OH
79	Waldon, Larry	OT	330	6-6	Detroit, MI
18	Walton, Tim	CB	180	5-11	Columbus, OH
57	Wargo, Mike	OG	260	6-0	Hudson, OH
4	Wilkerson, Keith	TB	185	5-9	Fort Lauderdale, FL
72	Wilkinson, Dan	DT	300	6-5	Dayton, OH
35	Willard, Lou	TB	214	5-11	Grove City, OH
51	Williams, Mark	OLB	227	6-4	Upper Marlboro, MD
23	Williams, Tim	K	180	5-9	Waynesville, OH
41	Willis, Tommy	SE	195	6-2	Griffin, GA
68	Winrow, Jason	OG	325	6-6	Bridgeton, NJ
11	Zban, Mark	QB	190	6-5	Huntington, WV

MICHIGAN

No.	Name	Pos.	Wt.	Hgt.	Home Town
68	Adami, Zach	OL	272	6-5	Maumelle, AR
90	Aghakhan, Ninef	DT	279	6-3	Mt. Prospect, IL
1	Alexander, Derrick	WR	190	6-2	Detroit, MI
20	Anderson, Deollo	SS	200	6-0	Youngstown, OH
78	Barry, Paul	OG	274	6-3	Cincinnati, OH
21	Biakabutuka, Tim	TB	187	6-1	Longueuil, QUE
24	Blackwell, Brent	DB	210	6-2	Anderson, IN
31	Blankenship, Tony	FS	196	6-0	Detroit, MI
70	Bolach, Mark	OT	260	6-5	Muskegon, MI
43	Brown, J. J.	LB	235	6-4	Chesterfield, SC
25	Buff, Ron	FB	230	6-1	Otisville, MI
7	Burch, Alfie	CB	192	6-2	Warren, OH
80	Burkholder, Marc	TE	244	6-3	Traverse City, MI
13	Carr, Jason	QB	200	6-1	Ann Arbor, MI
96	Carr, William	DT	275	6-2	Dallas, TX
34	Charles, Jean-Agnus	CB	200	5-11	Montreal, QUE
32	Collins, Shawn	OLB	228	6-3	Patterson, NJ
10	Collins, Todd	QB	240	6-5	Walpole, MA
88	Cooper, Pierre	TE	220	6-3	Alief, TX
26	Davis, Ed	TB	190	5-9	Detroit, MI
39	DeLong, Nate	P/PK	205	6-3	Wyandotte, MI
99	Denson, Damon	DT	270	6-5	Pittsburg, PA
48	Dobreff, Dave	ILB	230	6-3	Mt. Clemens, MI
55	Dudlar, Gannon	DT	267	6-4	Birmingham, MI
91	Dyson, Matt	OLB	252	6-5	LaPlata, MD
93	Edmonds, Ray	MG	275	6-1	Akron, OH
29	Elezovic, Peter	PK	197	5-11	Farmington Hills, MI
63	Elliott, Marc	OL	238	6-3	Carmel, IN
5	Elston, Mike	TE/LB	220	6-5	St. Mary's, OH
92	Evans, Stephen	OLB	219	6-4	Roxbury, MA
33	Foster, Che'	FB	240	6-2	Edmond, OK
24	Freeman, Zack	SS	193	5-10	Los Angeles, CA
44	Gasperoni, Sergio	TE	230	6-2	Shelby Township, MI
56	Goodwin, Harold	OG	282	6-2	Hopkins, SC
14	Griese, Brian	QB	215	6-2	Miami, FL
75	Guynes, Thomas	OT	298	6-5	Kankakee, IL
19	Hamilton, Remy	PK	190	6-0	Boca Raton, FL
23	Hankins, Woodrow	CB	188	5-9	Owasso, OK
9	Hayes, Mercury	WR	200	5-10	Houston, TX
79	Henderson, Tony	MG	256	6-2	Indianapolis, IN
94	Horn, Jason	MG/DT	253	6-5	Lafayette, IN
51	Howell, George	LB	230	6-3	Irving, TX
53	Huff, Ben	LB	234	6-4	Charlotte, NC
37	Irons, Jarrett	ILB	212	6-1	Conroe, TX
82	Jaeckin, John	TE	242	6-2	Cleveland, OH
77	Jenkins, Trezelle	OT	298	6-8	Chicago, IL
28	Johnson, Deon	CB	208	6-2	Detroit, MI
30	Johnson, Jesse	TB	215	5-9	Harper Woods, MI
85	Jones, Damon	TE	230	6-6	Evanston, IL
27	King, Steve	FS	189	6-0	Palm Beach Gardens, FL
39	Lancer, Jared	FB	213	5-10	Los Angeles, CA
22	Law, Ty	CB	184	6-0	Aliquippa, PA
15	Loeffler, Scot	QB	200	6-4	Barberton, OH
38	Lovell, Erik	PK	194	6-0	Beavercreek, OH
84	Malveaux, Felman	WR	171	6-0	Beaumont, TX
71	Mangan, Michael	ILB	214	6-0	Waukesha, WI
73	Marinaro, Joe	OG/OT	290	6-4	Andover, MA
41	McThomas, Greg	ILB	241	6-4	Milwaukee, WI
67	Milia, Marc	C/OG	272	6-3	Birmingham, MI
57	Miller, Shawn	OG	285	6-5	El Dorado, KS
36	Morrison, Steve	ILB	242	6-3	Birmingham, MI
42	Noble, Tyrone	CB	183	5-11	Kankakee, IL
50	Norment, Julian	ILB	241	6-0	Silver Spring, MD
4	Overton, Dayna	RB	197	6-1	Jeffersonville, IN
72	Partchenko, John	OT	285	6-4	Etobicoke, ONT.
52	Payne, Rod	C	280	6-3	Miami, FL
3	Peoples, Shonte	SS	227	6-1	Saginaw, MI
99	Peristeris, Paul	P	206	6-0	Lincoln Park, MI
43	Petterson, Chad	WR	189	6-2	Flint, MI
95	Powers, Bobby	ILB	233	6-0	River Ridge, LA
12	Powers, Ricky	TB	220	6-0	Akron, OH
8	Pryce, Trevor	LB	250	6-6	Caselberry, FL
66	Rekowski, Steve	DT	273	6-5	Redford, MI
83	Richards, Todd	WR	170	6-0	Reading, MI
16	Riemersma, Jay	QB	235	6-5	Zeeland, MI
54	Ries, Joe	C	260	6-4	Barberton, OH
40	Ritchie, Jon	FB	240	6-3	Mechanicsburg, PA
69	Runyan, Jon	OT	271	6-8	Flint, MI
49	Sanders, Earnest	DB	190	6-4	Flint, MI
17	Sanneh, Pap	PK	177	6-3	Detroit, MI
62	Skorput, Ante	OG	291	6-3	Toronto, ONT
86	Smith, Seth	WR	195	6-1	Murphysboro, IL
2	Smith, Walter	WR	190	5-11	Detroit, MI
60	Stanley, Buster	DT	273	6-2	Youngstown, OH
18	Stapleton, Chris	P	216	6-1	Springfield, IL
81	Steele, Glen	TE	255	6-5	Ligonier, IN
61	Sullivan, Mike	OT	298	6-7	East Lansing, MI
44	Swett, Rob	FB	225	6-3	Chalfont, PA
17	Thompson, Clarence	DB	180	6-2	Detroit, MI
18	Toomer, Amani	WR	190	6-3	Concord, CA
45	Vanderbeek, Mike	ILB	225	6-1	Hudsonville, MI
58	Vander Leest, Rob	OG	255	6-4	Muskegon, MI
59	Waldroup, Kerwin	DT	235	6-3	Chicago, IL
46	Walker, Marcus	ILB	234	5-11	Chicago, IL
65	Wendt, Eric	OG	287	6-3	Cincinnati, OH
6	Wheatley, Tyrone	TB	225	6-1	Inkster, MI
35	Winters, Chuck	FS	182	6-0	Detroit, MI
34	Zaeske, Jeff	WR	166	5-10	Okemos, MI
76	Zenkewicz, Trent	DT	263	6-5	Cleveland, OH

1993

Michigan	41	Washington State	14
Michigan	23	Notre Dame	27
Michigan	42	Houston	21
Michigan	24	Iowa	7
Michigan	7	Michigan State ...	17
Michigan	21	Penn State	13
Michigan	21	Illinois	24
Michigan	10	Wisconsin	13
Michigan	25	Purdue	10
Michigan	58	Minnesota	7
Michigan	28	Ohio State	0

Season Summary

Games won, 7; Lost, 4

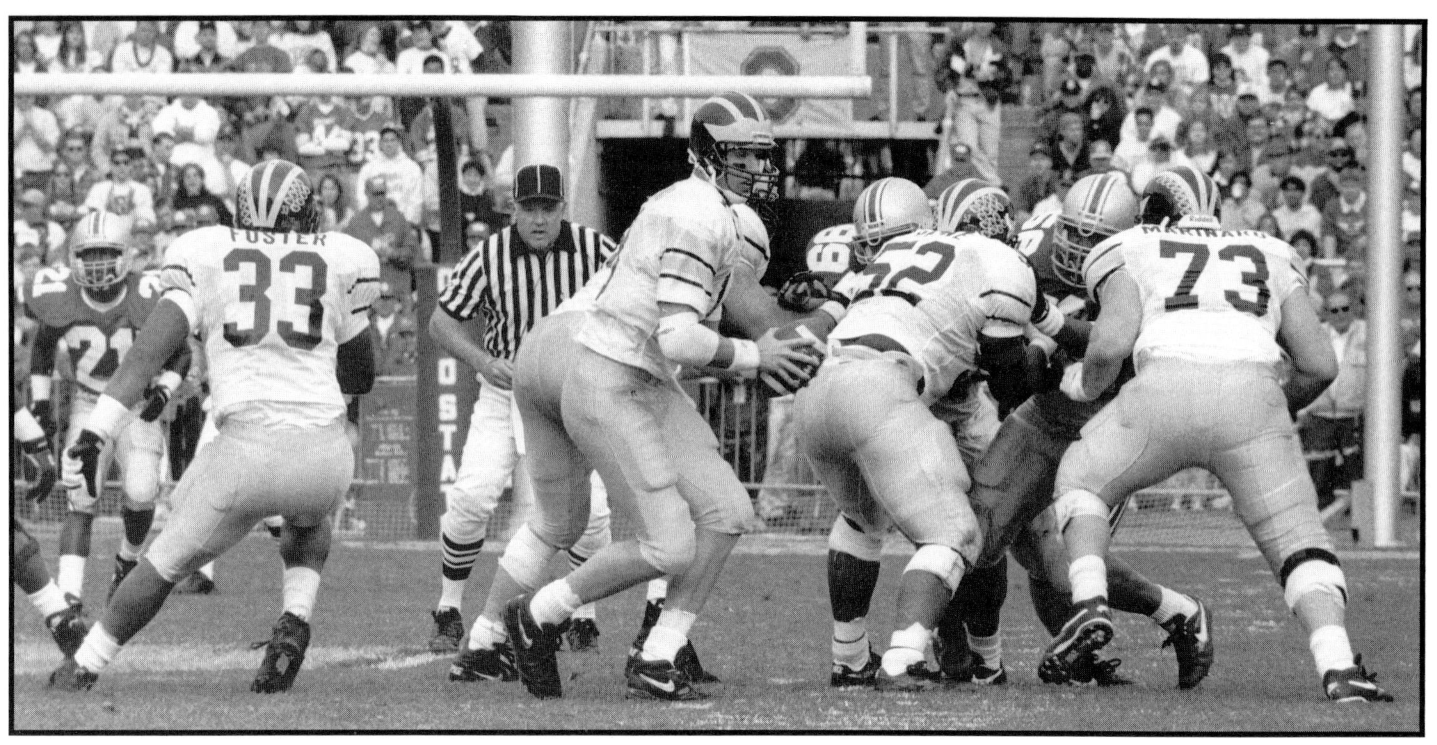
FOSTER
33
73
21

hotos by Chance Brockway

November 19, 1994

Columbus, Ohio

Cooper Ends Jinx With 22-6 Victory Over Michigan

Clutch Defensive Plays Spark Ohio State

Although Penn State had already clinched the Big Ten Title, Ohio State Coach John Cooper knew that this game against Michigan was crucial. Many observers believed his job was on the line based upon the outcome.

Michigan wide receiver Walter Smith fueled the controversy by this boast earlier in the week: "We want to get Cooper fired. That's what I want to do. We want to keep on beating them and beating them until he's not there."

Cooper, 0-5-1 against the Wolverines entering the 1994 contest, spoiled Smith's wishes by guiding the Buckeyes to a 22-6 romp before 93,869 at Ohio Stadium. Smith's remarks were just one of the sideshows leading up to the annual rivalry.

In an effort to stem the losing Ohio State tide, several former Buckeyes visited the team the week prior to the game to tell tales of their past victories over the Wolverines. The ex-Buckeyes formed a double line for the current players to run through just before the game.

In a teleconference with out-of-town reporters on the Tuesday before the game, Cooper refused to answer any questions except those he thought directly related to the game. When the questions began to deal with Smith's comments and Cooper's losing streak against Michigan, the testy coach abruptly ended the conference.

Then, the night before the game, thieves broke into the Michigan locker room and stole six helmets, including those of tailback Tyrone Wheatley and quarterback Todd Collins.

Replacement helmets and all, Michigan's woes continued early in the game as Collins tripped over the foot of left guard Jon Runyan and fell in the end zone for a safety.

Leading 2-0 entering the second quarter, the Buckeyes expanded their lead with a 40-yard drive in 10 plays, capped by a four-yard sweep by quarterback Bobby Hoying. Later, both teams traded field goals and Ohio State led 12-3 entering halftime.

recovered the ball at the Michigan 47. Seven plays later, Ohio State's Josh Jackson nailed a 36-yard field goal to put the Buckeyes up 15-6.

On the Wolverines next play from scrimmage, OSU nose guard Luke Fickell tipped a pass by Collins into the air and then made a diving interception at the Michigan 16. Ohio State capitalized on the turnover with a five-play drive for the decisive touchdown, a 2-yard run by tailback Eddie George.

After the game, George reflected on the importance of the OSU victory. "A lot of frustration is over. The atmosphere is going to be more relaxed. Not beating Michigan has lingered in people's minds. Now, the monkey is off our backs."

Although Ohio State lost the battle of statistics, netting just 210 yards to Michigan's 271, the Buckeye defense held the Wolverines without a touchdown for the first time since 1985.

The Ohio State victory ended another string: entering the game, Michigan Coach Gary Moeller was undefeated (14-0-2) in the month of November as head coach of the Wolverines.

Any questions about how badly Coach Cooper wanted to win this game were quickly answered when he put his fist through the blackboard in the locker room. "I've never seen him do anything like that," Hoying said afterward. "He's usually so businesslike at halftime."

Despite Cooper's outburst, Michigan took command in the third quarter, holding the Buckeye offense to just net six yards and no first downs. The offense, however, could only manage a 22-yard field goal by Remy Hamilton to close the gap to 12-6.

Hamilton was poised to boot another field goal early in the fourth quarter, but Ohio State's Marion Kerner, coming from the left corner, avoided a block by Che Foster and blocked the kick. The ball bounced downfield and OSU defensive end Mike Vrabel.

STATISTICS

	UM	OSU
First Downs	14	13
Rushes-Yards	34-111	45-85
Passing Yards	160	125
Passes	13-22-1	11-18-0
Punts/Avg.	3-35	5-44
Fumbles-Lost	0-0	1-1
Penalties-Yards	9-88	5-41

SCORING

Michigan	0	3	3	0	- 6
Ohio State	3	10	0	10	- 22

1994			
Michigan	34	Boston College	26
Michigan	26	Notre Dame	24
Michigan	26	Colorado	27
Michigan	39	Iowa	14
Michigan	40	Michigan State	20
Michigan	24	Penn State	31
Michigan	19	Illinois	14
Michigan	19	Wisconsin	31
Michigan	45	Purdue	23
Michigan	38	Minnesota	22
Michigan	6	Ohio State	22

Season Summary
Games won, 7; Lost, 4

REMY HAMILTON
All-American Place Kicker

TY LAW
All-American Cornerback

MICHIGAN

No.	Name	Pos.	Wt.	Hgt.	Home Town
2	Smith, Walter	WR	195	5-11	Detroit, MI
4	Williams, Anthony	WR	169	5-10	Terre Haute, IN
5	Elston, Mike	OLB	242	6-4	St. Mary's, OH
6	Wheatley, Tyrone	TB	226	6-1	Inkster, MI
7	Floyd, Chris	RB	221	6-1	Detroit, MI
8	Pryce, Trevor	OLB	255	6-6	Casselberry, FL
9	Hayes, Mercury	WR	195	5-11	Houston, TX
10	Collins, Todd	QB	216	6-5	Walpole, MA
12	Scott, Dreisbach	QB	192	6-4	Mishawaka, IN
13	Carr, Jason	QB	198	6-1	Ann Arbor, MI
14	Griese, Brian	QB	210	6-3	Miami, FL
15	Loeffler, Scot	QB	202	6-3	Barberton, OH
16	Riemersma, Jay	TE	252	6-6	Zeeland, MI
17	Thompson, Clarence	SS	190	6-1	Detroit, MI
18	Toomer, Amani	WR	194	6-4	Berkeley, CA
19	Hamilton, Remy	PK	196	6-0	Boca Raton, FL
20	Anderson, Deollo	SS	208	6-0	Youngstown, OH
21	Biakabutuka, Tim	TB	205	6-1	Longueuil, QUE
22	Law, Ty	CB	201	6-0	Aliquippa, PA
23	Hankins, Woodrow	CB	197	5-9	Owasso, OK
24	Blackwell, Brent	SS	221	6-2	Anderson, IN
26	Davis, Ed	TB	201	5-9	Detroit, MI
27	King, Steve	FS	193	6-1	Riviera Beach, FL
28	Johnson, Deon	CB	209	6-2	Detroit, MI
29	Ray, Marcus	SS	208	6-0	Columbus, OH
31	Sanders, Earnest	FS	199	6-3	Flint, MI
32	Howard, Chris	RB	216	5-10	River Ridge, LA
33	Foster, Chè	FB	245	6-2	Edmond, OK
34	Charles, Jean-Agnus	CB	197	5-11	Montreal, QUE
35	Winters, Chuck	FS	192	6-0	Detroit, MI
36	Morrison, Steve	ILB	242	6-3	Birmingham, MI
37	Irons, Jarrett	ILB	231	6-1	The Woodlands, TX
38	Lovell, Erik	PK	189	6-0	Beavercreek, TX
39	DeLong, Nate	P	214	6-2	Wyandotte, MI
40	Ritchie, Jon	FB	232	6-2	Mechanicsburg, PA
42	Noble, Tyrone	CB	196	5-11	Kankakee, IL
42	Petterson, Chad	WR	191	6-3	Flint, MI
44	Swett, Rob	ILB	229	6-2	Chalfont, PA
46	Baker, Kraig	P	168	6-0	Terre Haute, IN
50	Norment, Julian	MG	259	6-1	Silver Spring, MD
51	Howell, George	ILB	236	6-2	Irving, TX
52	Payne, Rod	C	288	6-4	Miami, FL
53	Huff, Ben	OLB	236	6-4	Charlotte, NC
54	Ries, Joe	C	288	6-3	Barberton, OH
56	Goodwin, Harold	OG	283	6-2	Hopkins, SC
61	Sullivan, Mike	OT	299	6-7	East Lansing, MI
62	Skorput, Ante	OG	284	6-3	Toronto, ONT
65	Wendt, Eric	C	286	6-4	Cincinnati, OH
68	Adami, Zach	OB	279	6-5	Maumelle, AR
69	Runyan, Jon	OL	299	6-8	Flint, MI
70	Bolach, Mark	OT	287	6-6	Muskegon, MI
71	Springer, Jeff	ILB	226	6-0	Detroit, MI
72	Partchenko, John	OT	291	6-4	Etobicoke, ONT
73	Marinaro, Joe	OG	290	6-4	Andover, MA
75	Guynes, Thomas	OL	299	6-5	Kankakee, IL
76	Zenkewicz, Trent	DT	270	6-6	Cleveland, OH
77	Jenkins, Trezelle	OT	298	6-8	Chicageo, IL
79	Henderson, Tony	MG	273	6-2	Indianapolis, IN
81	Steele, Glen	DT	270	6-5	Ligonier, IN
83	Richards, Todd	WR	172	6-0	Reading, MI
84	Vander Leest, Rob	TE	266	6-4	Muskegon, MI
86	Smith, Seth	WR	174	5-11	Carbondale, IL
88	Cooper, Pierre	TE	225	6-2	Aleif, TX
89	Parini, Sean	OLB	219	6-1	Grand Rapids, MI
90	Feazell, Juaquin	DT	253	6-4	Ft. Valley, GA
91	Dyson, Matt	OLB	246	6-5	LaPlata, MD
92	Evans, Steve	DT	261	6-4	Roxbury, MA
94	Horn, Jason	DL	277	6-5	Lafayette, IN
95	Powers, Bobby	ILB	229	6-0	Kenner, LA
96	Carr, William	DT	285	6-0	Dallas, TX
97	Holtry, Jeff	OLB	223	6-3	Salt Lake City, UT
99	Denson, Damon	DT	276	6-4	Pittsburg, PA

OHIO STATE

No.	Name	Pos.	Wt.	Hgt.	Home Town
1	Carter, DeWayne	SE	192	6-1	Youngstown, OH
2	Howard, Ty	CB	174	5-9	Columbus, OH
3	Stanley, Dimitrious	FL	181	5-10	Worthington, OH
4	Jackson, Josh	K	162	5-11	Logan, OH
5	Colson, Dan	FS	190	6-0	Middletown, OH
6	Baird, Steve	QB	190	6-1	Hillard, OH
7	Galloway, Joey	SE	186	5-11	Bellaire, OH
8	Jackson, Stanley	QB	198	6-1	Paterson, NJ
9	Paul, Tito	SS	196	6-1	Kissimmee, FL
10	Hoying, Tom	QB	221	6-4	St. Henry, OH
11	Zhan, Mark	QB	207	6-5	Huntington, WV
12	Tillman, Buster	FL	185	6-1	Steubenville, OH
13	Moore, Damon	DB	195	5-11	Fostoria, OH
14	Hoying, Bobby	QB	222	6-4	St. Henry, OH
15	Miller, Dee	SE	200	6-1	Springfield, OH
16	Harrison, Preston	OLB	245	6-5	Columbus, OH
16	Hatcher, Andre	TB	196	5-10	Silver Spring, MD
17	Sanders, Chris	FL	175	6-1	Denver, CO
18	Bryant, Che	FS	180	6-1	Canton, OH
19	Knisley, Heath	DB	190	6-3	New Philidelphia, OH
20	McClellion, Central	DB	185	5-11	Delray Beach, FL
21	Patillo, Tim	FS	178	5-10	Aliquippa, PA
23	Terna, Scott	P	196	5-11	Kaneohe, HI
24	Springs, Shawn	DB	181	5-11	Silver Spring, MD
24	Elmore, Carmie	FB	208	6-2	Smithtown, NY
25	Jackson, Jermon	TB	180	5-11	Ironton, OH
26	Gwinn, Anthony	SS	189	6-0	Columbus, OH
27	George, Eddie	TB	230	6-3	Philadelphia, OH
28	Louis, Jason	SS	192	6-1	Lanham, MD
29	Pearson, Pepe	TB	175	5-10	Euclid, OH
30	Bellisari, Greg	OLB	230	6-1	Boca Raton, FL
32	Stillwell, Obie	OLB	213	6-0	Mansfield, OH
34	Kelly, Rob	SS	200	6-2	Newark, OH
35	Rudzinski, Jerry	MLB	212	6-1	Centerville, OH
36	Christopher, Matt	MLB	235	6-2	Uniontown, OH
37	Sualua, Nicky	FB	245	5-11	Santa Ana, CA
38	Malfatt, Mike	P	210	6-3	Dublin, OH
39	Calhoun, Matt	FB	237	6-0	Heath, OH
41	Doyle, Patrick	K	185	6-0	Miamisburg, OH
42	Griffin, Kevin	TB	173	5-10	Redmond, WA
43	Miller, Ryan	OLB	217	6-2	Allen Park, MI
44	Jenkins, Josh	FB	220	6-1	Lorain, OH
44	Becker, Dave	DT	210	6-0	Cincinnati, OH
46	Kerner, Marlon	CB	188	5-11	Columbus, OH
47	Maag, Dennis	FS	176	6-1	Orrville, OH
48	Rodriquez, Alex	FB	225	6-1	Chicago, IL
50	Gohlstin, Eric	OG	300	6-3	Cleveland, OH
52	Miller, Pete	C	290	6-3	Mayfield Hts, OH
53	Lynch, Scott	IS	210	5-10	Parma Heights, OH
54	Stoughton, Brian	DE	240	6-2	London, OH
55	Connery, Will	MLB	235	6-1	Vandalia, OH
56	Brown, Randall	DT	276	6-3	Detroit, MI
57	Daniels, LeShun	OG	280	6-2	Warren, OH
58	Ross, James	DE	226	6-4	Detroit, MI
59	Kasparek, Robert	OT	314	6-3	Highland Park, IL
59	Giuliani, Robert	NG	245	5-8	Columbus, OH
60	Harris, Ray	OG	320	6-3	Massillon, OH
61	Baker, Matt	OLB	220	6-1	Louisville, OH
62	Clark, Shane	NG	268	6-2	Chillicothe, OH
62	Kozar, Jason	C	270	6-0	Amherst, OH
63	Cook, Jason	LB	220	6-2	Marysville, OH
64	Dully, Mike	OT	295	6-4	Hamilton, OH
65	Porter, Juan	C	285	6-4	Cleveland, OH
66	Gibbons, Dan	NG	300	6-4	Farmington Hills, MI
67	Burris, Brooks	OT	286	6-6	Logan, OH
68	Garnett, Winfield	DT	310	6-5	Riverdale, IL
69	Smith, Brian	C	294	6-6	Cross Lanes, WV
70	Bonhaus, Matt	DT	285	6-5	Cincinnati, OH
72	Summer, Jamie	OG	290	6-4	Wichita, KS
73	Meade, Jeff	OG	288	6-1	Reynoldsburg, OH
74	Kuszmaul, Greg	OG	294	6-4	Warren, OH
75	Pace, Orlando	OT	320	6-5	Sundusky, OH
76	Beckman, Pete	NG	255	6-4	Chesterland, OH
76	Kruezer, Dean	C	240	6-2	Columbus, OH
77	Moss, Eric	OT	310	6-4	Charleston, WV
78	Stringer, Korey	OT	315	6-5	Warren, OH
79	Waldon, Larry	OT	320	6-6	Detroit, MI
80	Dudley, Rickey	TE	240	6-7	Henderson, TX
81	Jacobs, Matt	SE	200	6-1	Amherst, OH
82	Langenkamp, Max	TE	253	6-3	Cincinnati, OH
83	Glenn, Terry	SE	180	5-11	Columbus, OH
84	Powell, Craig	OLB	224	6-4	Youngstown, OH
85	Lumpkin, John	TE	253	6-8	Dayton, OH
87	Davis, Robbie	FL	174	6-0	Twinsburg, OH
88	Houser, Bob	TE	240	6-4	Westlake, OH
89	Jones, D.J.	TE	250	6-4	Lebanon, OH
89	Baker, Mike	DT	287	6-1	Louisville, OH
90	Styles, Lorenzo	MLB	240	6-2	Farrell, PA
91	Wilson, Jeff	DE	235	6-3	Deerfield Beach, FL
92	Finkes, Matt	DE	258	6-2	Piqua, OH
93	Huntzinger, Rick	DE	238	6-2	Columbus, OH
94	Vrabel, Mike	DE	260	6-4	Stow, OH
95	Bell, Jim	DE	251	6-5	Youngstown, OH
97	Day, John	DE	245	6-3	Independence, OH
97	Heinen, Brian	FL	200	6-2	Louisville, KY
98	Spriggs, Marcus	DT	295	6-4	Washington, DC
98	Shavers, Alonzo	FL	170	6-0	Columbus, OH
99	Fickell, Luke	NG	260	6-4	Westerville, OH

1994

Ohio State	34	Fresno State	10
Ohio State	16	Washington	25
Ohio State	27	Pittsburg	3
Ohio State	52	Houston	0
Ohio State	17	Northwestern	15
Ohio State	10	Illinois	24
Ohio State	23	Michigan State	7
Ohio State	48	Purdue	14
Ohio State	14	Penn State	63
Ohio State	24	Wisconsin	3
Ohio State	32	Indiana	6
Ohio State	22	Michigan	6

Season Summary

Games won, 9; Lost, 3

KOREY STRINGER
All American Tackle

C. WILLIAMS
33
Riddell
86
HAYES

BIAKABUTUKA
21

November 25,1995

Ann Arbor, Michigan

Wolverines Thwart Buckeyes' Rose Bowl Plans . . . Again

Biakabutuka Romps For 313 Yards To Pace Michigan's 31-23 Win

Photos by Chance Brockway

For the second straight time, the Buckeyes arrived in Ann Arbor needing a victory over the underdog Wolverines for a Big Ten championship and a Rose Bowl berth.

And for the second straight time, Michigan spoiled Ohio State's party just as it had in 1993, this time with a 31-23 victory before 106,288 fans.

"Obviously, I'm very disappointed--" Ohio State Coach John Cooper said after the game. "I don't know if I've ever been so disappointed in my life."

The Buckeyes came into the game undefeated at 10-0, ranked second in the country and hopeful of a national championship. Ohio State's potent offense had averaged 39.8 points per game behind (quarterback Bobby Hoying, flanker Terry Glenn and its Heisman Trophy winner, running back Eddie George. Across the field, the 18th ranked Michigan had dropped three Big Ten games and were out of the conference championship race. Given the teams' records, the Buckeyes exuded confidence about the game, perhaps too much confidence.

Glenn committed the error of shrugging off Michigan's chances in a press conference earlier in the week. "They (the Wolverines) are nothing," he said "We expect to beat their butts like we've beaten everyone else this season."

Glenn's comments did nothing but inspire Michigan, especially running back Tshimanga Biakabutuka. On Michigan's first two plays from scrimmage, Biakabutuka carried for 22 yards and 19 yards on his way to 107 yards in the first quarter alone. When Biakabutuka wasn't sprinting through the gaping holes created by his offensive line, he was carrying Buckeye tacklers for several additional yards. In the greatest day that a running back has ever had against the Buckeyes, he finished with 313 rushing yards on 37 carries.

Sparked by Biakabutuka, Michigan took a 7-3 lead on its first possession with a 4-yard touchdown pass from quarterback Brian Griese to backup tailback Clarence Williams. The Wolverines never relinquished the lead from that point on and claimed a slim 10-g halftime advantage.

Ohio State's hopes of regaining the lead on the first possession of the second half were quickly dashed when Michigan's freshman cornerback, Charles Woodson, jumped in front of OSU's Glenn at the sideline for an interception at midfield. The Wolverines then marched on their scoring drive capped by Griese's 2-yard sneak.

The Buckeyes returned the favor when defensive end Mike Vrabel picked off a Griese pass and returned it to the Michigan 27. A 26-yard pass from Hoying to tight end Ricky Dudley set the stage for George's 1-yard touchdown dive with 1:14 left in the third quarter. That score pulled OSU within 1 7- 15 but George was stopped on the two-point conversion run.

Michigan wasted no time regaining the momentum with a 65-yard scoring drive, highlighted by a 3 8-yard run by Biakabutuka, 12 of those yards coming with Buckeye defenders Ty Howard and Shawn Springs clinging to his back. Williams later hit paydirt with a toss sweep from eight yards out to provide a 24- 15 lead early in the fourth quarter.

The Wolverines upped their lead to 31-15 when Griese hit tight end Jay Riemersma for a 35 yard gain to set up a 2 yard touchdown by Biakabutuka.

Ohio State attempted a comeback on the ensuing possession, driving 75 yards in seven plays for a 19 yard scoring pass from Hoying to wide receiver Buster Tillman. The Buckeyes added the two point conversion on a toss from Hoying to George to complete the scoring.

OSU's final drive ended when Woodson again picked off Hoying with 48 seconds remaining and the Wolverine celebration began.

First year Michigan Coach Lloyd Carr, who replaced Gary Moeller after Moeller"s drunken altercation with a police officer outside a Detroit area restaurant, was carried off the field by his team after the victory. "I don't think anyone in the country gave us an opportunity or much of a chance to win this game," he said. "It didn't matter what other people thought. The only thing that was important was the men who were going to play this game on our sideline believed. Any the believed."

Biakabutuka believed enough to become only the second Wolverine to gain more than 300 yards in a game (Ron Johnson tallied 347 yards against Wisconsin in 1968). Both Biakabutuka and George set single season rushing records for their respective universities, Biakabutuka finishing with 1,724 yards and George with 1,826 yards.

George carried 21 times for 104 yards against Michigan, his second lowest total of the season.

With the victory, Michigan leads the series 52-34-6, including eight victories in the last 11 meetings.

STATISTICS

	OSU	UM
First Downs	23	23
Rushes-Yards	29-106	57-381
Passing Yards	286	103
Passes	22-45-2	9-18-3
Punts/Avg.	7-44	4-36
Fumbles-Lost	0-0	0-0
Penalties-Yards	8-64	6-42

SCORING

Ohio State	3	6	6	8	23
Michigan	7	3	7	14	31

1995

1995			
Ohio State	38	Boston College	6
Ohio State	30	Washington	20
Ohio State	54	Pittsburg	14
Ohio State	45	Notre Dame	26
Ohio State	28	Penn State	25
Ohio State	27	Wisconsin	16
Ohio State	28	Purdue	0
Ohio State	56	Iowa	35
Ohio State	49	Minnesota	21
Ohio State	41	Illinois	3
Ohio State	42	Indiana	3
Ohio State	23	Michigan	31

Season Summary
Games won, 11; Lost, 1

EDDIE GEORGE
All-American Tailback

TERRY GLENN
All-American Flanker

ORLANDO PACE
All-American Tackle

OHIO STATE

No.	Name	Pos.	Wt.	Hgt.	Home Town
9	Baird, Steve	FS	190	6-1	Hillard, OH
61	Baker, Matt	MLB	220	6-1	Lousiville, OH
41	Bartholomew, Brent	P	198	6-2	Apopka, FL
16	Becker, Dave	OLB	220	6-1	Cincinnati, OH
95	Bell, Jim	DE	251	6-5	Youngstown, OH
30	Bellisari, Greg	MLB	230	6-1	Boca Raton, FL
70	Bonhaus, Matt	DT	285	6-5	Cincinnati, Oh
18	Bryant, Che	FS	180	6-1	Canton, OH
67	Burris, Brooks	OT	295	6-6	Logan, OH
39	Calhoun, Matt	FB	237	6-0	Heath, OH
1	Carter, DeWayne	SE	192	6-1	Youngstown, OH
62	Clark, Shane	NG	270	6-2	Chillicothe, OH
5	Colson, Dan	FS	190	6-0	Middletown, OH
55	Connery, Will	MLB	240	6-1	Vandalia, OH
63	Cook, Jason	LB	220	6-2	Marysville, OH
57	Daniels, LeShun	OG	285	6-2	Warren, OH
87	Davis, Robbie	FL	184	6-0	Twinsburg, OH
97	Day, John	DE	245	6-3	Injdependence, OH
41	Doyle, Patrick	P/K	185	6-0	Miamisburg, OH
80	Dudley, Rickey	TE	240	6-7	Henderson, TX
51	Dupree, Roedell	LB	240	6-3	Jersey City, NJ
96	Eisenhard, Tony	DE	220	6-7	Tiffin, OH
78	Elford, Drew	OL	277	6-4	Garfield, NJ
24	Elmore, Carmie	FB	208	6-2	Snithtown, NY
99	Fickell, Luke	NG	260	6-4	Westerville, OH
92	Finkes, Matt	DE	258	6-2	Piqua, OH
68	Garnett, Winfield	DT	310	6-6	Riverdale, IL
27	George, Eddie	TB	227	6-3	Philadelphia, PA
7	Germaine, Joe	QB	196	6-2	Mesa, AZ
66	Gibbons, Dan	OL	300	6-4	Farmington Hills, MI
83	Glenn, Terry	FL	185	5-11	Columbus, OH
50	Gohlstin, Eric	OT	295	6-3	Cleveland, OH
42	Griffin, Kevin	CB	183	5-10	Redmond, QA
26	Gwinn, Anthony	FS	200	6-0	Columbus, OH
60	Harris, Ray	OG	320	6-3	Massillon, OH
16	Hatcher, Andre	TB	196	5-10	Silver Spring, MD
97	Heinen, Brian	FL	200	6-2	Louisville, KY
53	Hester, Darron	LB	230	6-1	Dallas, TX
36	Homa, Randy	LB	250	6-2	Pottsville, PA
88	Houser, Bob	TE	240	6-4	Westlake, OH
2	Howard, Ty	CB	181	6-9	Columbus, OH
14	Hoying, Bobby	QB	223	6-4	St. Henry, OH
10	Hoying, Tom	QB	221	6-4	St. Henry, OH
93	Huntzinger, Rick	DE	242	6-3	Columbus, OH
61	Hyme, Kevin	C	298	6-4	Columbus, OH
25	Jackson, Jermon	TB	198	5-11	Ironton, OH
4	Jackson, Josh	K	173	5-11	Logan, OH
8	Jackson, Stanley	QB	203	6-1	Paterson, NJ
81	Jacobs, Matt	FL	200	6-1	Amherst, OH
44	Jenkins, Josh	FB	220	6-1	Lorain, OH
52	Johnson, Kevin	LB	220	6-2	Athens, GA
23	Keller, Matt	RB	200	6-0	Mason, OH
34	Kelly, Rob	SS	200	6-2	Neward, OH
17	King, Percy	DB	200	6-4	Columbus, OH
44	Kirk, Chris	LB	235	6-3	Westerville, OH
19	Knisley, Heath	SS	180	6-3	New Philidelphia, OH
62	Kozar, Jason	C	270	6-0	Amherst, OH
76	Kreuzer, Dean	C	240	6-2	Columbus, OH
74	Kuszmaul, Greg	OG	295	6-4	Warren, OH
48	LaVrar, Matt	LB	220	6-3	Maumee, OH
28	Louis, Jason	SS	192	6-1	Lanham, MD
85	Lumpkin, John	TE	260	6-9	Dayton, OH
38	Malfatt, Mike	K/P	205	6-3	Dublin, OH
20	McClellion, Central	CB	180	5-11	Delray Beach, FL
15	Miller, Dee	SE	190	6-1	Springfield, OH
43	Miller, Ryan	OLB	220	6-2	Allen Park, MI
33	Montgomery, Joe	RB	225	5-11	Robbins, IL
13	Moore, Damon	SS	195	5-11	Fostoria, OH
56	Murphy, Rob	OL	252	6-5	Cincinnati, OH
75	Pace, Orlando	OT	320	6-6	Sandusky, OH
29	Pearson, Pepe	TB	193	5-10	Euclid, OH
19	Plummer, Ahmed	DB	182	6-1	Wyoming, OH
65	Porter, Juan	C	285	6-4	Cleveland, OH
6	Redmond, Jimmy	WR	165	6-0	Lee's Summit, MO
58	Ross, James	DE	230	6-3	Detroit, MI
35	Rudzinski, Jerry	OLB	220	6-1	Centerville, OH
21	Sanders, Charlie	RB	215	5-9	Rochester Hills, MI
98	Shavers, Alonzo	SE	170	6-0	Columbus, OH
76	Smith, Eric	OL	300	6-5	Columbus, OH
98	Spriggs, Marcus	NG	295	6-4	Washington, DC
24	Springs, Shawn	CB	185	6-0	Silver Spring, MD
3	Stanley, Dimitrious	FL	181	5-10	Worthington, OH
32	Stillwell, Obie	OLB	220	6-1	Mansfield, OH
54	Stoughton, Brian	DE	240	6-2	London, OH
37	Sualua, Nicky	FB	245	5-11	Santa Ana, CA
72	Summer Jamie	OG	290	6-4	Wichita, KS
12	Tillman, Buster	SE	188	6-1	Steubenville, OH
94	Vrabel, Mike	DE	255	6-4	Stow, OH
79	Waldon, Larry	OT	330	6-6	Detroit, MI
46	Willis, Marc	OLB	215	6-3	Phoenix, AZ
91	Wilson, Jeff	DE	250	6-3	Deerfield Beach, FL
11	Winfield, Antoine	DB	178	5-9	Akron, OH
84	Wisniewski, Steve	TE	230	6-5	Timberlake, OH

MICHIGAN

No.	Name	Pos.	Wt.	Hgt.	Home Town
67	Acheson, Ron	OL	265	6-5	Lowell, MI
68	Adami, Zach	OG	279	6-5	Maumelle, AR
20	Anderson, Deollo	SS	208	6-0	Youngstown, OH
46	Baker, Kraig	P	168	6-0	Terre Haute, IN
21	Biakabutuka, Tshimanga	TB	205	6-1	Longueuil, QUE
24	Blackwell, Brent	OLB	221	6-2	Anderson, IN
70	Bolach, Mark	OT	287	6-6	Muskegon, MI
6	Bowens, David	ILB	230	6-3	Pontiac, MI
10	Brady, Tom	QB	215	6-4	San Mateo, CA
3	Brooks, Todd	WR	175	6-0	Freeport, IL
22	Bryant, Kevin	DB/WR	175	6-0	Farmington Hills, MI
1	Butterfield, Tyrone	WR	168	5-8	Miami, FL
82	Campbell, Mark	TE	241	6-6	Clawson, MI
13	Carr, Jason	QB	198	6-1	Ann Arbor, MI
96	Carr, Williams	NT	285	6-0	Dallas, TX
34	Charles, Jean-Agnus	CB	197	5-11	Montreal, QUE
74	Cockrell, Josh	OG	293	6-2	Evanston, IL
88	Cooper, Pierre	OLB	225	6-2	Alief, TX
43	Copenhaver, Clint	ILB	212	6-3	Brighton, MI
50	Crispin, David	ILB	220	6-0	Dearborn Heights, MI
26	Davis, Ed	TB	201	5-9	Detroit, MI
39	DeLong, Nate	P	214	6-2	Wyandotte, MI
51	Denson, Damon	OG	276	6-4	Pittsburg, PA
84	DeYoung, Matt	WR	190	5-10	Kalamazoo, MI
12	Dreisbach, Scott	QB	192	6-4	Mishawaka, IN
5	Elston, Mike	OLB	242	6-4	St. Mary's, OH
92	Evans, Steve	DE	261	6-4	Roxbury, MA
90	Feazell, Juaquin	DT	253	6-4	Ft. Valley, GA
49	Feely, Jay	PK	186	5-10	Odessa, FL
7	Floyd, Chris	RB	221	6-1	Detroit, MI
39	Ford, J. R.	RB/DB	165	5-8	Columbus, OH
64	Frazier, Steve	C	280	6-4	Kingwood, TX
14	Griese, Brian	QB	210	6-3	Miami, FL
75	Guynes, Thomas	OT	299	6-5	Kankakee, IL
56	Hall, James	OLB	245	6-3	New Orleans, LA
19	Hamilton, Remy	PK	196	6-0	Boca Raton, FL
23	Hankins, Woodrow	CB	197	5-9	Owasso, OK
9	Hayes, Mercury	WR	195	5-11	Houston, TX
34	Hill, Patrick	WR	181	5-10	Detroit, MI
94	Horn, Jason	DT/NT	277	6-5	Lafayette, IN
32	Howard, Chris	RB	216	5-10	River Ridge, LA
40	Howell, George	FB	236	6-2	Irving, TX
53	Huff, Ben	DT	236	6-4	Charlotte, NC
25	Hynes, Mike	CB	187	5-11	Southfield, MI
37	Irons, Jarrett	ILB	231	6-1	The Woodlands, TX
77	Jansen, Jon	OT	250	6-7	Clawson, MI
8	Johnson, DiAllo	QB	190	6-4	Detroit, MI
29	Keefer, Colby	QB	205	6-2	Holly, MI
27	King, Steve	FS	193	6-1	Riviera Beach, FL
17	Kiser, Ed	QB	197	6-3	Fremont, OH
95	Kratus, Pat	DE	240	6-4	Rocky River, OH
66	Kurpeikis, Chris	OT	281	6-6	Allison Park, PA
15	Loeffler, Scot	QB	202	6-3	Barberton, OH
73	Marinaro, Joe	OG	290	6-4	Andover, MA
16	Mayes, Eric	DB	195	5-11	Kalamazoo, MI
60	Miller, Nate	DT	257	6-3	Imlay City, MI
62	Moltane, Eric	DL	275	6-7	Bay City, MI
31	Mondry, Thomas	FB	196	6-1	Plymouth, MI
42	Noble, Tyrone	CB	196	5-11	Kankakee, IL
23	Parachek, Scott	WR	184	6-2	Temperance, MI
89	Parini, Sean	OLB	219	6-1	Grand Rapids, MI
78	Parker, Noah	OG	298	6-4	Milton, FL
72	Partchenko, John	OG	291	6-4	Etobicoke, ONT
52	Payne, Rod	C	288	6-4	Miami, FL
99	Peristeris, Paul	P	200	6-2	Lincoln Park, MI
45	Petterson, Darren	WR	156	5-10	Flint, MI
71	Potts, Jeff	OT	280	6-8	Three Rivers, MI
25	Quinn, Terrence	WR	178	5-10	Flint, MI
29	Ray, Marcus	SS	208	6-0	Columbus, OH
58	Renes, Rob	MG	275	6-2	Holland, MI
83	Richards, Todd	WR	172	6-0	Reading, MI
16	Riemersma, Jay	TE	252	6-6	Zeeland, MI
54	Ries, Joe	C	288	6-3	Barberton, OH
69	Runyan, Jon	OT	299	6-8	Flint, MI
31	Sanders, Earnest	SS	199	6-3	Flint, MI
36	Shea, Aaron	FB/TE	260	6-5	Ottawa, IL
55	Simmons, Rasheed	OLB	235	6-5	Edison, NJ
57	Singletary, Chris	OLB	230	6-1	Detroit, MI
59	Springer, Jeff	ILB	226	6-0	Detroit, MI
81	Steele, Glen	DT	270	6-5	Ligonier, IN
86	Streets, Tai	WR	185	6-4	Matteson, IL
61	Sullivan, Mike	OT	299	6-7	East Lansing, MI
44	Swett, Rob	ILB	229	6-2	Chalfont, PA
93	Sword, Sam	ILB	249	6-2	Saginaw, MI
63	Sygo, Matt	OG	298	6-2	Saginaw, MI
28	Taylor, Daydrion	DB	190	6-1	Longview, TX
17	Thompson, Clarence	CB/SS	190	6-1	Detroit, MI
18	Toomer, Amani	WR	194	6-4	Berkeley, CA
80	Tuman, Jerame	TE	238	6-4	Liberal, KS
45	Vanderbeek, Mike	FB	228	6-3	Hudsonville, MI
84	Vander Leest, Rob	TE	266	6-4	Muskegon, MI
38	Vinson, Jason	P	190	6-2	Troy, MI
38	Washington, Brent	DB	175	6-1	Inkster, MI
30	Weathers, Andre	CB	168	6-0	Flint, MI
65	Wendt, Eric	C	286	6-4	Cincinnati, OH
4	Williams, Anthony	WR	169	5-10	Terre Haute, IN
19	Williams, Bryan	CB	178	5-10	Detroit, MI
33	Williams, Clarence	RB	180	5-10	Detroit, MI
91	Williams, Josh	DL	260	6-4	Houston, TX
35	Winters, Chuck	FS	192	6-0	Detroit, MI
2	Woodson, Charles	DB	185	6-1	Fremont, OH
76	Zenkewicz, Trent	DT	270	6-6	Cleveland, OH
97	Ziemann, Chris	DL	250	6-7	Aurora, IL

1995

Michigan	18	Virginia	17
Michigan	38	Illinois	14
Michigan	24	Memphis	7
Michigan	23	Boston College	13
Michigan	38	Miami	19
Michigan	13	Northwestern	19
Michigan	34	Indiana	13
Michigan	52	Minnesota	17
Michigan	25	Michigan State	28
Michigan	5	Purdue	0
Michigan	17	Penn State	27
Michigan	31	Ohio State	23

Season Summary

Games Won, 9: Lost, 3

JASON HORN
All-American Tackle

THE BIG GAME It's Usually All on the Line When Wolverines-Buckeyes Meet

A LOOK AT THE BIGGER "BIG GAMES"

Since the Michigan-Ohio State game was moved to the final week of the conference season in 1935, the Wolverines and Buckeyes have decided the Big Ten championship between themselves 18 times. The following is a list of those classic matchups:

YEAR	'M'	OSU	RESULT
1944	14	18	Ohio State is Big Ten champion.
1949	7	7	Michigan and Ohio State are co-champions; OSU goes to the Rose Bowl because of a better overall record.
1950	9	3	Michigan is Big Ten and Rose Bowl champion.
1954	7	21	Ohio State is Big Ten and Rose Bowl champion.
1955	0	17	Ohio State is Big Ten champion (but by conference rules, cannot go to the Rose Bowl two consecutive years); Michigan State goes to Rose Bowl (Had Michigan won, U-M would have gone to bowl).
1964	10	0	Michigan is Big Ten and Rose Bowl champion.
1968	14	50	Ohio State is Big Ten and Rose Bowl champion.
1969	24	12	Michigan is Big Ten champion and goes to the Rose Bowl.
1970	9	20	Ohio State is Big Ten champion and goes to the Rose Bowl.
1972	11	14	Michigan and Ohio State are co-champions; Athletic Directors' vote sends OSU to the Rose Bowl.
1973	10	10	Michigan and Ohio State are co-champions; Athletic Directors' vote sends OSU to the Rose Bowl.
1974	10	12	Michigan and Ohio State are co-champions; Ohio State goes to Rose Bowl by beating Michigan.
1975	14	21	Ohio State is Big Ten champion and goes to the Rose Bowl.
1976	22	0	Michigan and Ohio State are co-champions; Michigan goes to the Rose Bowl by beating Ohio State.
1977	14	6	Michigan and Ohio State are co-champions; Michigan goes to the Rose Bowl by beating Ohio State.
1978	14	3	Michigan and Ohio State are co-champions; Michigan goes to the Rose Bowl by beating Ohio State.
1980	9	3	Michigan is Big Ten and Rose Bowl champion.
1986	26	24	Michigan and Ohio State are co-champions; Michigan goes to the Rose Bowl by beating Ohio State.
In addition, these 14 games had an effect in determining the Big Ten champion: .			
1935	0	38	Ohio State and Minnesota share Big Ten championship.
1942	7	21	Ohio State is Big Ten champion (Had Michigan won, Wisconsin would have won title).
1943	45	7	Michigan and Purdue are Big Ten co-champions.
1952	7	27	Wisconsin and Purdue are Big Ten co-champions (Had Michigan won,U-M would have won the title).
1956	19	0	Iowa is Big Ten champion (Had Ohio State won, OSU would have shared title).
1961	20	50	Ohio State is Big Ten champion (Had Michigan won, Minnesota would have won title).
1979	15	18	Ohio State is Big Ten champion (Had Michigan won, Ohio State, Purdue and U- M would have shared title).
1981	9	14	Ohio State and Iowa are Big Ten co-champions (Had Michigan won, U-M would have won title).
1984	6	21	Ohio State is Big Ten champion (Had Michigan won, Ohio State, Illinois, Purdue and U-M would have shared title).
1988	34	31	Michigan is Big Ten champion (Had OSU won, Michigan State and U-M would have shared title).
1989	28	18	Michigan is Big Ten champion (Had OSU won, Michigan, Illinois and Ohio State would have shared title).
1990	16	13	Michigan, Illinois, Iowa, and Michigan State are Big Ten co-champions (Had Ohio State won, OSU would have won the title outright).
1991	31	3	Michigan is Big Ten champion (Had OSU won, Michigan would have shared the title with Iowa).
1993	28	0	Wisconsin and Ohio State are Big Ten Co-Champions (Had OSU won, the Buckeyes would have gone to the Rose Bowl).

COLLEGE FOOTBALL'S GREATEST RIVALRY

An annual "prize" is not at stake in the Michigan-Ohio State game—though usually, the winner does receive the Big Ten Championship trophy.

The "Big Game" has decided the Big Ten championship 32 times since the contest was moved to the last Saturday in the season in 1935; on 18 of those occasions, Michigan and Ohio State settled the title between themselves. The throne atop the Big Ten, as well as a trip to the Rose Bowl, is usually the reward for a victory in this contest.

Michigan won the first game of the series in 1897 by a 36-0 score and then took 16 of the next 21 games (two were ties). However, the series has been one of the most evenly matched and intensely played rivalries in college football since Harry Kipke took over as 'M' coach in 1929. Kipke compiled an excellent 71-16-3 record and won a national championship in nine years at Michigan, but against Ohio State he was just 3-6. The rivalry had started.

Perhaps the most famous contest in the series was the "Snow Bowl" game of 1950. A snowstorm in Columbus obliterated the yard lines and turned the players into nothing but shadowy figures. Punting was the story of the game: Chuck Ortmann set a Big Ten record by punting 24 times, keeping OSU deep in its territory, and Michigan's points were all the result of Buckeye kicking errors. Michigan scored a 9-3 victory—without gaining a single first down—and went on to defeat California in the Rose Bowl, 14-6.

In 1969, Woody Hayes brought his top-ranked Buckeyes to Ann Arbor to meet the Wolverines and their first-year head coach, Bo Schembechler. Michigan intercepted six OSU passes and played error-free ball to score an incredible 24-12 upset and a trip to Pasadena.

The "Big Game" decided the conference champion each of the next six seasons. Over that span, Michigan came into the Ohio State game with an unbelievable 57-0-2 record, but the Wolverines came away with just one win and a single Rose Bowl trip in those six contests. The futility against OSU ended quickly, though, as Michigan won the ``Big Game" the next three years to earn three straight trips to the Rose Bowl and that special distinction—Big Ten Champions.

The Wolverines' 28-0 win in 1993 was Michigan's 26th shutout of the Buckeyes and first since 1976. The Wolverine win also kept OSU out of the Rose Bowl.

Reprinted from 1995 Media Guide with permission of Michigan Athletic Department

INDEX

This index covers the years, 1987 through 1992. The names for 1993 - 1994 - 1995 can be found on the appropriate pages.

-A-

Aartila 174
Abbott, George 150
Abrahams, Morris 2 4 6 , 250
Abrams, Bobby 315, 319, 323, 326 331
Ackerman, Cornelius 74, 79, 82
Adamle, Anthony 159
Adams 46
Adams, Chuck 311
Adams, Douglas 247, 250, 255
Adams, Thomas 234
Adams, William 135
Adderley, Nelson 231, 234
Addison 46, 50, 58, 63
Adulewicz, Casimir 207, 210
Agee, Michael 214
Aghakhan, Ninef 334, 339, 342
Agnew, Doug 291
Adkins, David 271, 274, 279, 282
Aghakhan, Ninef 330
Akers, Carl 247
Akers, Jeff 301, 307, 311, 315
Alber, George 79, 81, 82, 87
Alberti, Larry R. 147
Albertson, John 326, 331, 339
Albl 55
Alcorn 85
Alders, Gary 298, 302, 306, 312
Aleskus, Joseph 119, 122, 127
Alexander, Derrick 331, 334, 339, 342
Alexander, Joe 251
Alexinas, Edward 135
Aliber, James J. 147
Alix, Denis 219, 227
Allegro, Joseph 271, 274, 279, 282
Allen 17, 62
Allen, David 287
Allen, Jay 283
Allen, Paul 302, 306, 312
Allen, Richard 231, 234
Allen, Robert 98, 103
Allerdice, D.W. 33, 35, 37
Allis, Barry 169
Allis, Harry 165, 166, 171, 174
Allison, Bruce 227, 235
Allman, David 223
Allmendinger, Ernest J. 43, 45
Althouse, John 315
Ames, Robert T. 187
Amlin, George 234, 239
Amling, Martin 143
Amling, Warren 151, 154, 159
Amrine, Robert O. 110, 114
Amstutz, Ralph H. 139, 142
Ancona, Perry 227, 234
Anders, Billy 231, 233, 234, 239, 242
Anders, Richard 202, 207, 210
Andersen, John M. 155
Anderson 17, 58
Anderson, Cedric 296, 298, 302, 306
Anderson, Charles 130, 135, 137
Anderson, Deollo
Anderson, Erick 323, 326, 331, 334, 339
Anderson, Harry 134
Anderson, Jack 91
Anderson, John 270, 275, 278, 283
Anderson, John M. 163
Anderson, Kim 231, 234, 239
Anderson, Kyle 315
Anderson, Richard 170, 175, 183, 226, 231, 234
Anderson, Steve 270, 275, 278
Anderson, Thomas 167, 223, 231
Anderson, Tim 247, 250, 253, 255, 295, 299, 301, 307, 311
Anderzack, Tom 312, 314, 320, 322
Andrako, Steve 122, 126, 130
Andrew 54
Andrews, Bill 296, 298, 302
Andrews, Lawrence 178
Andrews, Phil 270, 275, 278
Andria, Ernie 274, 279, 282, 287, 290
Andrick, Theodore 226, 231, 234
Anetnucci, Frank 109, 111, 114, 119
Angood, David 283
Antennuci, Thomas 143, 151
Antell, Gunnard 102
Anthony, Melvin 222, 225, 227, 230
Anthony, Thomas 296, 302
Apoke, Joe 296, 298
Appleby, Gordon 143, 146
Applegate, Richard 266, 271, 274
Arbeznik, John 278, 283, 286, 291
Archambeau, Louis 210
Archer, Jack 191
Archer, S. 279
Arledge, Richard 170, 175, 178
Armour, Jim 262, 267, 270
Armstrong 17
Armstrong, Greg 299, 301, 307, 311
Armstrong, Jack 207
Armstrong, Michael 242
Armstrong, Ralph 169, 170, 175, 178
Armstrong, William 215, 218, 221, 223
Arnold, Allen 323
Arnold, Birtho 202, 207, 210
Arnold, David 315, 319, 326
Arnold, James 127, 135
Ashbeck, Fred 86
Ashton, Daniel 247, 250
Ashton, William 183, 186
Assman 46
Atchison, James L. 163, 166, 171
Atchison, John 214
Atha, Bob 285, 290, 296, 298
Atkins, Kevin 287
Auer, Howard 91, 94, 99
Auer, John 186
Aug, Vincent J. 110, 115
Augenstein, Jack 186
Austin, Thomas D. 102, 107, 110
Avery, Charles B. 142
Avery, Leslie 86, 93
Ayers, N.B. 17
Ayers, Ronald 266, 271, 274, 279
Azcona, Eduardo 326, 331, 334, 339, 342
Azok, Frank 207

-B-

Baas,James 231. 239
Babbin, George 115
Babcock, R.G. 67, 70, 75
Babcock, Sam 75, 78, 83
Babe, George 150
Babour, Frank 14
Babyak, John 150
Bach, Terry 282, 287
Bachman 37, 39
Bachorski, Dan 302, 306, 312
Backhus, Thomas 247, 250
Backus, Clark 298, 302, 306
Baer, Fred N. 182, 187, 190

Baer, Ray 75, 78, 83
Baffer, Stewart 218
Bahlow, Edward 158
Bailey 54
Bailey, Donald 230, 235, 238
Bailey, Ralph 199, 202, 207
Bain 17
Baines 46
Baird 15
Baker 23
Baker, Merle 70
Baker, Morgan 90
Baker, Ray 154
Baker, Scott 271
Baker, W.P. 17
Baldacci, Louis G. 185, 187, 190, 195
Baldacci, Thomas 194, 195, 199, 202
Baldwin, Ed 246, 251
Baldwin, Paul T. 189
Baldwin, William W. 142
Balen, Alan 296, 298
Ballau, Robert 158
Ballinger, Gary 199
Ballinger, Jerry 202
Ballmer, Paul 199, 207
Ballou, Robert 163
Balog, James T. 179, 182, 187
Balourdos, Art 301, 307, 311
Balourdos, John 307, 311
Bals, Dave 327
Balzhiser, Richard E. 179, 182, 185, 187
Banar, James 243
Banks 54, 58
Banks, Harry 259, 262, 270
Banks, John 210
Banks, Larry 262, 267, 270
Barabee, C.A. 17
Barasa, Joseph L. 115, 118
Barclay, William C. 115, 118, 123
Barger, Phil 206
Bargerstock, Douglas 271, 274
Bariklow 39
Barkenbus 19
Barklow, Carson 82
Barkeubus 19
Barley, A. 86
Barlow 29
Barmore, Edmund H. 15
Barna, Joseph 154
Barnes 51
Barnes, Ronald 194
Barnett 25
Barnett, David G. 110, 115
Barnett, James A. 115
Barnett, Tyrone 223, 226, 231
Barr, Terry A. 190, 193, 195, 197, 198
Barratt, Fred W. 85, 87, 89, 90
Barren, Henry 122
Barricklow, Don 41, 43
Barrington 29, 31, 33, 34, 38
Barrington, Tom 225, 231, 234
Barrington-Jones 35
Barrows, Arthur 106
Barrows, Professor 19
Barry, Joe 331
Barry, Paul 339, 342
Bartholomew, B.A. 174, 179, 182
Bartlett 29
Bartlett, William H. 166, 171
Bartley, Thomas 239, 242, 247
Bartnick, Greg 275, 278, 283, 286
Barton, Charles P. 43
Barton, John 191
Bartoszek, Michael 263, 266, 271
Bartschy, Ross 122, 126, 130
Barwig, Ronald 279, 282, 287, 290, 296
Baschnagel, Brian 266, 271, 273, 274
Basford, Michael 190, 195
Basinger, Edward 167, 170, 175
Bass, Michael 230, 233, 235, 238
Bates, Brad 291
Bates, James V. 182, 187, 190, 195
Bates, Roman 302, 306, 314
Bator, Kalman, Jr. 86
Batsakes, John 198, 203, 206
Battista, Thomas 254, 258, 263
Battle, Marvin 266
Baty, Donald 219
Bauer, Carl J., Jr. 86, 90
Bauer, Robert 95
Bauman, Charles 291
Bauman, Clement L. 147, 150,
Baumgarten, Eugene 95, 98
Baumgartner, Robert 238, 243, 250
Baxa, Tom 258
Baxter, Charles 263
Bay, Richard 222, 227
Beam, William 207, 210
Beamon, Eddie 271, 274, 279, 282
Beach, Keith 314
Bean, Mark 335, 338
Bean, Vicent 295, 299, 301, 307, 311
Beard, Chester C. 107, 110
Bearss, James 218, 223, 226
Beaty 39
Beatty 37
Beatty, Dan 320, 322, 327, 330, 335, 343
Beatty, Greg 327, 330, 335, 338, 343
Bechman, Pete 338, 343
Bechtel, Earl 178, 183
Beck, Herbert R. 71
Beck, P.E. 87
Becker, Kurt 286, 291, 295, 299
Beckman, Pete 335, 343
Beckman, Tom 251, 254, 259
Bednarek, Jeff 283
Beecroft, Charles 255, 258, 263
Beekley, Marts 175, 178, 183
Beel, Joseph G. 171
Beerman, Raymond 194, 199
Begle 19
Behrens, L. 170
Beier, Michael 238
Beison, Richard 187
Belgrave, Earl 255, 258, 263
Belko, Greg 274
Bell 17
Bell, Bob 74, 79, 82
Bell, Farley 274, 279
Bell, Gene 283
Bell, Gordon 267, 269, 270, 273, 275
Bell, Jim 343
Bell, Kelvin 298, 302, 306, 312
Bell, Robert 170
Bell, Robin 74, 79, 82
Bell, Sean 312, 314, 320, 322
Bell, Todd 282, 287, 290, 296
Bell, William 90, 95, 98, 130, 135
Belli, Roxie 114, 119
Belmer, Clifford 287, 290, 296
Belsky, Jerome 118, 123
Beltz, Richard 106, 111, 113, 114
Bembry, Dan 266
Benbrook 35, 37
Benbrook, Albert 36, 37, 38, 39
Bender, Edward 239, 242, 247
Benedict 16, 17
Benio, Brian 320, 322, 327
Benis, Joseph 90, 95, 98
Benis, Mike 207, 210, 215
Bennet, William 127, 130
Bennett, J.W.F. 17

Bennett, Arthur L. 123, 126
Bennett, Donald C. 179, 182, 187
Bennett, Richard C. 123
Benton, Julian 106
Bentz, Warren W. 150, 155
Berger, Jon 330, 335, 338
Berger, Thomas E. 195, 198, 203
Bergeron, Bob 295, 299, 301, 307, 311
Bergman, Milton 86, 91
Berkowitz, Albert 91, 94
Berline, James 235, 238, 241, 243
Bernard, Charles J. 99, 102, 105, 107
Berner, Joe 296, 298
Berner, Joseph 287
Berutti, William 251, 254
Bettis, Roger 275, 278, 283
Bettridge, John 111, 113, 114, 119
Betts, Jim 246, 251, 253, 254
Betts, Norm 291, 295, 299
Betz, Steve 250
Betz, Wayne 215, 218, 223
Bickle, Douglas G. 210
Biedenweg, C. 86
Biel, William 154
Bieson, Richard A. 179, 182
Bigelow 25
Bilbie, James N. 123
Bilkie, Edward 170, 175
Billings, William E. 174, 179, 182
Biltz, John 167, 170, 175
Birkholtz, Paul 119
Bishop, Al 307, 311
Bishop, Allen 319, 323
Bishop, H.S. 31
Bissell, Beoff 315
Bissell, Frank S. 110, 115, 118
Bisslee, Geof 323
Bittel, Robert 111
Bixler, Paul O. (Coach) 157
Black, D. 78
Blackburn, George 11
Blahnik 62
Blaine 36
Blaine, Ernie 41
Blair 55, 58, 63
Blair, Ken 302, 306, 312
Blanchard, Bruce 71, 74, 79
Blanchard, Donald 219, 222, 227
Blankenship, Tony 339, 342
Blazeff, Lalo 191
Bledsoe, John 255, 263
Blinco, Thomas 279, 282, 287, 290
Bliss 19, 50, 55
Bliss, Keith 119, 122, 127
Bloemer, Mike 312
Blose 17
Bloser, Parker 71, 79
Blott, Jack 62, 65, 67
Blowney, Henry 91
Blubaugh, Park 170
Blumenthal 55
Blumer, Gabe 71
Blythewood, Charles 296
Bobo, Hubert 189, 191
Bochnowski, Alex 195, 198, 203
Bock, Ernie 315, 323
Boddie, Chris 320, 322
Boden, M. H. 78, 83, 86
Bodenbender, George 223, 231
Body, Marion 291, 295, 299, 301
Boesel 37, 39
Bogle 39
Bogle, Thos. 41
Bohlman, Jeff 327, 330, 335
Bohn, Chris 323, 326, 331, 334
Boland 46
Bolach, Mark 342
Bolas, George A. 107, 110, 115
Bolden, Jim 270, 275, 278
Bolen, Charles 45
Boles, Tony 319, 323, 326, 331
Bolser, Harvey 127
Bolyard, Tom 314
Bombach, Jaren 239, 242
Bompeidi, Carl 98, 103, 106
Bond, Robert 183, 186, 191, 194
Bonhaus, Matt 335, 338, 343
Bonica, Charles 255, 258, 263
Bonnie, Dale 159, 162, 167
Bonnie, David 158, 162, 167
Bonser, Thomas 79
Boon 37
Boor, Donald P. 139, 142
Booth, William 117, 119, 186, 191, 194
Boren, Mike 295, 299, 301, 307
Borgmann, William F. 102, 107, 110
Borchers, Jim 330, 335, 338, 343
Borleske 37, 39
Borowski, Andrew 307, 311, 315, 319, 323
Borton, John 178, 181, 183, 185, 186, 190
Bose, Tom 302, 306
Boshoven, Robert 198, 203
Bostic, Carlitos 307, 311, 315, 323
Bostic, Keith 295, 299, 301
Boston, William 111, 114
Bosza, Joseph J. 131, 134
Boucher, Franklin A. 106, 111, 113, 114
Boudrie, James 186
Bough, Clarence 95
Boughner, Richard 119, 122
Bovard, Alan 83, 86, 91
Bovard, Theo. 86
Bovill 46
Bowermaster, Russell 199, 202, 207
Bowers, Brian 263, 266, 271
Bowers, Charles L. 123
Bowers, Dave 198, 203
Bowers, Glenn 179
Bowman, James 187, 190, 195
Bowsher, Jerry 199, 207, 210
Boxwell, Kenneth 151
Boxwell, Paul 71
Boyden, Joel 198, 203, 315, 323, 326
Boykin, Eric 342
Boyle, Michael H. 43
Boyle, William 258, 263
Bracken, Don 295, 299, 301, 307
Bradford, Wesley E. 177, 179
Bradley, R.T. 71, 74
Bradshaw, Jas. B. 66
Bradshaw, Morris 258, 263, 266
Brady, Matt 339
Braman, Mark 278, 283, 286, 291
Brandman, Charles 110, 115
Brandon, David A. 259, 262, 267
Brandstatter, James P. 251, 254, 259
Branoff, Tony 182, 185, 187, 189, 190, 195
Brashear, Richard 66
Braun, Don 296, 302
Breaky 51
Breaugh, Jim 286, 291
Breehl, Edward 194, 199, 202
Brefeld, Joseph 206
Bremen, George 94, 99
Brennan 33
Brennan, John C. 118, 123, 126
Breuleux, Jon 255
Brickman, Robert 167
Brieske, James F. 141, 142, 157, 158,

Brieske, James F. 161, 163
Brielmaier, Jerry 150
Brielmaier, G.D. 163
Briggs 43
Brigstock, Thomas 227, 235
Brilliant, George 186
Brindle 29
Broadnax, Stanley 235, 238, 243, 246
Broadnax, Vaughn 296, 298, 302, 306
Brockington, Fred 291, 295, 299
Brockington, John 247, 250, 255
Broddie, Chris 327
Broeseme 19
Brookfield 19
Brooks, Charles E. 190, 195, 198
Brooks, Kevin 301, 307, 311
Brophy 16, 17
Brown 19
Brown, Aaron 271, 274, 279, 282
Brown, Bernard 290, 296
Brown, Corwin 326, 331, 334, 339, 342
Brown, D. J. 326
Brown, David 203, 262, 267, 270, 314, 320, 322, 327, 330
Brown, Demetrius 315, 319, 323, 326
Brown, Dennis 238, 241, 243, 244, 245, 246
Brown, Deron 335, 338, 343
Brown, Frank P. 86, 91
Brown, H. 19
Brown, Harold 287
Brown, Henry 306, 312, 314, 320, 322
Brown, James 311
Brown, James J. 139
Brown, Jeff 258
Brown, Jeffrey 315, 319, 323, 326
Brown, Leo 193, 194, 199, 202
Brown, Matthew 146, 151, 154
Brown, Paul (Coach) 137, 138, 141
Brown, Phillip 270
Brown, Randall 335, 338, 343
Brown, Richard 158, 243, 251, 274, 279
Brown, Robert 67, 70, 74, 75
Brown, Robert 210, 214, 219, 222
Brown, Scott 327
Brown, Timothy 287, 290
Brown, Wilbur P. 187, 190
Brown, William A. 86, 91
Brown, Woody 275, 278, 283
Browns, Stanley 182
Brozic, Andrew 82
Brubaker, Richard 186, 189, 190, 191
Bruce, Earle 182, 290
Bruck, H.J. 66
Bruck, John 82
Bruckner, Edwin 130, 135, 138
Brudzinski, Robert 266, 271, 274, 279
Brudzinski, T. J. 296
Brugge, Robert 149, 151, 159, 162
Brumbaugh, Phil 270, 275
Bruhey, Fred 175, 178, 181, 183
Bruney, Robert 218, 223, 226
Brungard, David 242, 247
Brungard, George H. 106, 111, 114
Brunsting, Louis A., Jr. 155
Bryan, Fred J. 142, 147
Bryant, Bear 291
Bryant, Charles 210, 215, 218
Bryant, Gene 207
Bryant, Jaymes 322, 327, 330
Bryant, Jim 320
Bryant, John 95
Bryant', Robin 274
Bryce, Gary 214
Buda, James 339
Budd, D. 279
Buechsenschuss, A. 82, 87, 90
Buff, Ron 331, 334, 339, 342
Bugel, Thomas 226, 231, 234
Bulen 19
Bullock, William 119, 122, 127
Bunch, Alfie 334, 339
Bunch, Jarrod 319, 323, 326, 331, 334
Bunnell, Paul 210
Buonamici, Nicholas 266, 271, 274, 279
Burch, Alfie 331, 342
Burg, George 150, 158
Burgel, Jerry 295, 299, 301
Burger, Carl 103
Burgess, Fritz 299, 301, 307
Burgett, Richard 138
Burgin, Asbury 231, 234, 239
Burke, Tim 274, 279, 282, 287, 290
Burkholder, Marc 331, 334, 339, 342
Burks, Roy 262, 267
Burns 19
Burns, Jerry 171, 174
Burris, Gary 296, 298
Burris, Scott 279, 287, 290, 296
Burrows, Brad 315
Burrows, Norman 287, 290, 296
Burrows, Roger 255
Burrows, Scott 296
Burton, Arthur 247, 250
Burton, President 61
Bush, Eric 323, 326, 331, 334
Bush, Ken 275
Bushong, Jared 203, 206, 210
Bushong, Reid 206, 210, 213, 214
Bushnell, Thomas H. 43
Busich, Sam 106, 111, 113, 114
Butcher 16, 17
Butler 63
Butler, By' not' e 335, 338, 343
Butler, David W. 222, 227, 230
Butler, Jack W. 131, 134
Butts, Robert 215, 217, 221, 223
Buzynski, John 235
Byce 33
Byars, Keith 302, 306, 312, 314
Byers, David 235, 238
Byers, Jim 198, 203, 206
By' not' e, Butler 335, 338

-C-

Cachey, Theodore J. 182, 187, 190
Cady, Donald J. 142
Cahen, Herman 87
Cairns, Gary 231, 237, 239, 241, 242
Caldarazzo, Dick 243, 246, 251
Caldwell, Professor 19
Caley, W.H. 17
Calhoun 63
Calhoun, Matt 343
Calin, Peter, J. 259
Call, Norman D. 131, 134, 139
Callahan, Alex 198, 203, 206, 210
Callahan, Robert F. 155, 158
Calloway, Chris 319, 323, 326, 331
Cameron 63
Cameron, Geo. D. 66, 69, 71

Campana, Thomas 250, 254, 257, 258
Campanella, Joe 170, 175
Campbell 51, 55
Campbell, Charles A. 90, 95
Campbell, Charlie 15
Campbell, Erik 311, 315, 319, 323
Campbell, Jack 183, 186
Campbell, Paul 279, 282, 287, 290
Campbell, Robert D. 115, 118, 123
Canestraro, Joe 314, 320
Cannavino, Andy 286, 291, 295
Cannavino, Joseph 194, 199, 201, 202
Cannavino, Michael 159, 162, 167
Cantrill, Cecil, Jr. 99, 102
Capehart, Mark 335
Cappell, Richard 255, 258
Cappon 58, 62
Caputo, Dave 323, 326, 331
Caputo, Matt 267
Cargile, Jeff 302, 306, 312
Carian, Rob 275
Carden, Sean 335, 338
Carlin, Earl 130, 135
Carlin, Oscar E. 79, 81, 87, 90
Carlson, Herbert R. 66, 71
Carlson, J. D. 334, 339
Carlson, Justin 334, 339, 342
Carlson, Dave 323
Carlson, J. D. 326, 331
Carmody, Clarence 103
Carpell, Otto C. 41, 43
Carpenter, Al 251, 254, 259
Carpenter, Brian 291, 295, 299
Carpenter, Jack 158
Carpenter, John 262
Carr 15, 31, 33,
Carr, Carl W., Jr. 110, 115
Carr, Jason 339, 342
Carr, Leroy 202
Carraway, Winfred 295, 299, 301
Carroll, Ike 41, 43
Carroll, Jim 312, 314
Carroll, William 95, 97, 98, 103
Carson, Jim 296, 298, 302, 306
Carter 23, 27, 46, 62
Carter, Anthony 295, 299, 301
Carter, C.F. 83, 86
Carter, Cris 312, 314, 320
Carter, David W. 79, 87, 90
Carter, Dennis 218
Carter, DeWayne 343
Carter, Ronald 218
Carthens, Milt 295, 299, 301, 307
Cartwright 46
Cartwright, E. 119
Cartwright, Henry 235
Caruso, J. 279
Caruso, Tom 302
Carver 27
Cary 51
Casey, Kevin 259, 262, 267
Casey, William M. 33, 35
Cashell, Jack 106
Cassady, Craig 266, 271, 274
Cassady, Howard 183, 185, 186, 189, 191, 193, 194
Castignola, Gregory 279, 287, 290
Castle, Carl 94
Caswell, Harry H. 139
Catallo, Guido 246
Cato, Byron 274, 279, 282, 287
Cecchini, Gene 307, 311
Cecchini, Thomas 227, 230, 235
Cederberg, Jon C. 259, 262, 267
Ceddia, John 270, 278
Ceithami 137
Ceithaml, George 134, 139, 142
Cerecke, Charles 171
Cernak, Bob 315, 319, 323
Cervenka, Laddie F. 71
Chady, Otto E. 134, 139, 142
Chaeverini, Roger 150
Chambers 63
Chambers, H.E. 79, 82
Chancey, Mike 320, 322, 327, 330
Chandler 29
Chandler, Robert 214, 218, 222, 227
Chapman Gil 262, 267, 269, 270
Chapman, Harvey E. 99, 102, 107
Chapman, Harvey, Jr. 219, 222, 227
Chappuis, Robert R. 141, 142, 157, 158, 160, 161, 163, 164
Charles, Jean-Agnus 342
Chase, John 15
Cheney, David 247, 250, 255
Cheroke, George 138
Cherry 43
Cherry, John A. 259, 262, 267
Chesbrough, Larry 302
Chester, Dave 311, 315, 319, 323, 326
Chiames, George J. 155
Chiappini, Al 170
Chizek, Dave 93, 95
Chomicz, Casimir A. 182
Chonko, Arnold 223, 226, 231
Chrissinger, Warren 114, 119, 122
Christian, Chuck 286, 291, 295
Christopher, Matt 343
Christy, Edward 126, 131
Chubb, Ralph 149, 150, 157, 158
Churches 50
Cicero, Chris 296, 298, 302
Cipa, Larry 257, 259, 262, 267
Cisco, Galen 194, 199, 202
Cisco, Jeff 296, 298, 302
Claflin 31, 33
Claggett 31, 33
Clair, Frank 122, 127, 129, 130, 135
Clancy, Jack 225, 227, 230, 235, 237, 238
Clappison, Frank 214
Clare 39
Clark 25, 27, 29, 35, 37
Clark, Donald 199, 202, 205, 207
Clark, Gene 146
Clark, James 162, 167, 170
Clark, Myers A. 71, 73, 74, 77, 79
Clark, Oswald V. 166, 171, 174
Clark, Sheldon 302, 312
Clark, Vincent 327
Clark, Vinnie 330, 335
Clarke 27, 46
Clayton, Ralph 281, 283, 286, 291
Cleary, Thomas 143
Clement 29
Clement, C.H. 31
Clift, Gary 312, 314, 320, 322, 327
Cline, J. Daniel 182, 185, 187, 189, 190
Cline, Ollie 149, 151, 154, 162
Clohset, Fred 94, 99, 102
Closson, Tony 327, 330
Clotz, Dennis 210, 215, 218
Coakley, Gary 254, 259, 262

Cobb, Glen 290, 296, 298, 302
Coburn, Don 274, 279
Coburn, James 247, 250, 255
Coburn, Michael 210
Cochran, Brad 307, 311, 315
Cochran, Kenneth 98
Cochran, Nick 327
Cochran, Terrence 226, 231, 234
Cocozzo, Joe 326, 331, 334, 339, 342
Coffee, Charles 85, 87, 90
Coffey, Chas. B. 82
Cohen, Doug 331
Cohen, Jeff 295, 299, 301, 307
Cohn 46, 54
Coin, Dana 251, 253, 254, 257, 259
Cole 23
Cole, H.M. 43
Cole, Karl 314
Cole, Robert 191, 194, 199
Coleman, Don 259, 262, 267
Coleman, Horace 155
Coleman, Kenneth 138, 143, 320, 322, 327, 330, 335
Coleman, Paul 223
Coleman, Tim 302, 312
Coles, Karl 320, 322, 327, 330
Coles, Cedric 291, 295, 299
Collette, William H. 43
Collins, Chuck 219
Collins, Jerry 267, 270, 275
Collins, Shawn 342
Collins, Todd 334, 339, 342
Collmar, William 186, 191, 194
Colson, Dan 343
Colvin 58
Colzie, Cornelius 263
Colzie, Neal 266, 271
Compton, Jeff 312, 314
Conklin 39, 58
Conklin, F.L. 41
Conklin, Jon 214
Conklin, Robert 79
Conley, James 222, 227, 230
Conley, William 255, 258
Conlin, Ray 312
Connell 58
Connell, Dennis 251
Connor, Dan 218
Connor, Don 215
Conover, James 99
Conrad, Frederick B. 98, 103, 106
Conroy, James 247, 250, 255
Conroy, Robert 255
Contino, Amato 171
Conway, Blair 261, 263, 265, 266
Coode, James E. 254, 259, 262, 267
Cook, A. 78
Cook, Bryan 327, 330, 335, 338, 343
Cook, Donald 114, 119
Cook, James M. 71
Cook, Paul A. 83
Cook, Ronald 194, 199, 202
Cook, Thomas C. 147
Cooke, Thomas M. 86, 99
Cooley 23, 41
Cooper, Evan 295, 299, 301, 307
Cooper, George 312, 314, 320, 322
Cooper, Keith 315, 319, 323
Cooper, Kenneth 191
Cooper, Robert E. 115, 118
Coover 19, 21, 23
Cope, Captain 19
Cope, James 263, 266, 271
Corbin, Scott 270, 275
Corbin, Steve 296
Corbitt, Walter 183
Corey, George R. 187, 190, 195
Cornwell, Francis 86, 91, 94
Corona, Clement L. 190, 195, 198
Correll, John 135
Cory, Lincoln 82, 85, 87
Cothran, Jeff 338, 343
Cott 50, 55, 58
Cottrell, Ernest 151
Courtney, Hap 47
Cousineau, Tom 274, 279, 282, 287
Coventry, W.D. 70, 75
Cowan, Jerry 219
Cowan, Keith 203, 206, 210, 214, 301, 307, 311, 315
Cowans, Leroy 202
Cowell, G. 78
Cowman, Randall 255, 258, 263
Cox 37, 39
Cox, M. Budd 103, 106, 111
Cox, Garth 271, 274, 279, 282
Cox, Joe 41, 79, 82, 87
Cox, Larry G. 187
Cox, M. 279
Cox, Roderick 94, 99, 102
Cox, Todd 320
Coyer, William 122, 127, 130
Coyle, Thomas J. 254, 259, 262
Coyne, Mike 267, 270
Crabbe, Jack 127
Cragin, Ray 78, 83, 86
Craig 55
Craig, George 199
Craig, James B. 41, 43, 44
Craig, Orlando 320, 322, 327, 330
Cramer, Carl 97, 98, 101, 103, 105, 106
Crane, Fenwick J. 147, 158
Crane, James 154
Crane, Jameson 159, 162
Crapser, Steven 247, 250
Craw, Garvie 243, 246, 249, 251
Crawford 25
Crawford, Albert 199, 202, 207
Crawford, Frank 14
Crawford, Scott 315
Crawford, Thomas 194, 199, 202
Crecelius, Dave 298, 302, 306, 312
Crego, W.B. 83
Cress 51
Criames, George 153
Crisler, Fritz 112, 121, 125, 128, 141, 153
Crisler, Prescott A. 190
Crissy, Mike 343
Croft 63
Croft, Daniel R. 66
Cron, Robert 98, 103
Crow, Fred 114, 119, 122
Crownley, Ermin 203
Croy, Jack 183
Crumpacker 35
Cruse 46, 49, 51
Csuri, Charles 138, 141, 143, 159
Culbertson 16, 17
Culligan, William L. 147, 149, 150, 157, 158
Culver 51
Culver, Frank 44
Cumisky, Frank 109, 111, 114, 116, 117, 119
Cummings, John 258, 263
Cummings, William 191, 194, 199
Cummins, Thomas 223, 226, 231
Cunningham, Dan 255, 258
Cunningham, Harold 66, 69, 71, 72, 74
Cunningham, Lee 146
Cunningham, Leo P. 131, 134, 139

Cunningham, William Ralph 17
Cups, Anthony 320, 322
Curcillo, Tony 175, 178, 183
Curtis 25, 27, 29
Curtis, Clarence 296, 298
Curtis, Curt 302
Curtis, Guy 206, 210, 214, 218
Curtis, J.S. 31
Curtis, John 199
Curtis, Tom 243, 246, 251
Curto, Pat 274
Curran 27, 62, 65, 67
Curren, Robert B. 118, 123
Current, Michael 231, 234, 239
Curto, Patrick 266, 271
Cushing, Frederick 115
Cusick, Martin 271, 279
Cusick, Peter 263, 266, 271
Cutillo, Dan 258, 263, 266
Czak, Edward W. 126, 131, 134
Czarnota, Mike 291, 299
Czirr, Jim 267, 270, 275
Czoyz 54
Czysz 46, 49, 51
Czyzynski, Rich 296, 298, 302, 306

-D-

Dahlem, Alvin G. 78, 86, 91
Dailey, J. 279
Dale, Michael 255
D'Amato, John 271, 274
D'Andrea, Mike 296, 298
D'Angela, Mike 290
D'Andrea, Michael 287
Dames, Michael 311, 315, 319, 323, 326
Damm, Russell 94, 99, 102
Dana, Robert 299
Danhof, Jerome 235, 238
Daniell, James 130, 135, 138
Daniels, John 254, 262
Daniels, LeShun 343
Daniels, Norman 91, 94, 99
Dannelley, Scott 263, 266, 271, 274
Dansby, William J. 83, 86
Dansler, Kelton 274, 279, 282, 287
Darden, Thomas W. 251, 254, 257, 259
Darst, Lester 41, 43
Datish, Michael 266, 271, 274, 279
Daugherty, Doug 323, 326, 331
Daugherty, Harold 154
Dauksza, Antone 107
Davies 46, 47, 49, 50
Davies, James H. 190, 203
DaviesBoy, James J. 195, 198
Davidson 35
Davidson, James 223, 226, 231
Davidson, Jeff 320, 322, 327, 330
Davidson, Jim 312, 314, 320
Davis, Don 330
Davis, Ed 339, 342
Davis, H.L. (Governor) 61
Davis, Jeff 258, 263, 266
Davis, Jerome 266, 271
Davis, Martin 326, 331, 334, 339, 342
Davis, Michael 283, 286
Davis, Nate 299, 301
Davis, Paul 146
Davis, Ricky 299, 301
Davis, Robbie 343
Davis, Russel 70
Davis, Russell 278, 283, 286
Davis, Tim 267, 270, 275, 277
Davison, S.J. 31
Dawdy, Donald 183, 186
Dawley, Fred M. 134, 139
Dawson, Dino 312, 314, 320
Dawson, Jack 162, 167, 170
Dawson, William 307
Day, Floyd 227, 235
Day, Frank 134
Day, Michael J. 259, 262, 267
Dayton, Joseph 235, 238, 243
Dean, Harold 138, 143, 159
DeBaker, Charles 94, 99, 102
Debevc, Mark 247, 250, 255
DeBoer, Mike 315, 323
Decker, Art W. 86
Decker, Dan 301, 307
DeCree, Van 263, 266, 271
DeFelice, Vince 299, 301, 307, 311
DeFillippo, Joe 263
DeGraffenreid, Allen 327, 330, 335, 338, 343
Dahlin, Barry 235, 238
Dehlin, Charles 227, 230
Delaney, Kevin 302, 312, 314
Delich, Peter B. 98, 103, 106
DeLeone, James 282, 287, 290, 296, 298
DeLeone, Thomas 250, 255, 258
DeMark, Richard 150
DeMassa, Thomas 203, 206, 210
Demmel, Robert 162, 167, 175
DeMora 50, 55
DenBoer, Greg 262, 267, 270
Dendiu, Traian 151, 159, 162
Dendrinos, Peter C. 163, 166
Denise, Theodore E. 134, 139
Denker, Irv 183
Denzin, David 243, 246
dePalma, Robert 315
DePree 25
Depuy, Gay 15
D'Eramo, Paul 233, 235, 243
Derleth, Robert J. 142, 147, 155, 158
Derricotte, Eugene 141, 150, 157, 158, 163, 166
DeSantis, Mark 278, 283, 286
Deshler, Dana 199
Deskins, Donald 206, 210
D'Esposito, Chris 311, 315
DeStefano, Guy 210, 214
De Tar, Dave 15
Detrick, Roger 207, 210, 215
Detwiler, James 229, 230, 235, 237, 238
DeWitt, James 327
Dever, Dave 311, 315, 319
Devich, Dave 267, 270, 275
Devoe 65
De Voe, Keith B. 66, 71
Dewey, Sidney 70, 75, 78
Deyo, Charles 207
Diamond 58
Diamond, Charles 151
Dickey 23
Dickey, B.J. 286, 291, 299
Dickey, James A. 195, 198, 203, 206
Diebolt, Dave 323, 326, 331, 334, 339
Diefenthaler, D. 279
Diehl, William 95, 98, 103
Diel, Lloyd 21
Dierberger, Wesley 91
Dierdorf, Dan 246, 251, 254
Dietrich, Russell 122
DiFederico, Jules 239
Diggs, Gerald 283, 286, 291, 295
Dill, M. Reese 87, 90
Dillman, Thomas 191, 194, 199

Dillon, Dan 239
Dilts 25
Diltz 27
Dinan, Doug 327
Dingman, Dean 323, 326, 331, 334
Dingman, Robert W. 171, 174, 179, 182
Dingeman 25
DiOrio, Jerry 295, 299, 301, 307
DiPierro, Ray 151, 159, 162, 167
Disher, Larry 194, 199, 202
Dixon, Joseph 271, 274, 279, 282
Dixon, Kenneth 255, 258
Dixon, Stanley 159, 162
Dixon, Thornton 130, 135, 138, 154
Dixon, Tom 295, 299, 301, 307
Doane, Thomas 238
Dobbin, John 86,
Dobbs, Bennie 111
Dobeleit, Richard 66
Dobreff, Dave 331, 334, 339, 342
Dodd, William 219, 222, 227
Doersam, Paul 210
Doherty, Rob 326, 331, 334, 339, 342
Dohring, Ron 326, 331
Dohring, Tom 319, 323, 334
Doig 55
Domhoff, Victor 70, 75, 78, 81, 83
Donahue, Mark 275, 278, 283
Donham 63
Donley, Douglas 282, 287, 290, 296
Donnelly 67
Donovan Brenden 263
Donovan, Brian 247, 250, 255
Dooley, Joe 296, 298, 302, 306
Doolittle, William 157, 159, 162
Dorris, Victor 111, 114, 119, 122
Dorsey, Robert 162, 167
Dottin, Lance 323, 326, 331, 334, 339
Doty 25, 29
Doty, Alfred 235, 238, 242
Doty, Howard R. 155
Doty, Jeff 312
Dotzauer, Barry S. 259, 262, 267
Dougall, Bill 210, 219
Doughty, Glenn M. 251, 254, 259
Douglas 33
Douglass, Leslie 94, 99
Douglas-Green 35
Dove, Robert 151, 154
Downing, Walt 275, 278, 283
Doyle, Burton L. 90
Doyle, Richard 170, 175, 183
Drabicki, J.J. 83
Drake 23
Drake, Donald 150, 179, 182, 187, 190
Drake, Phillip 143
Drake, Thomas E. 259, 262, 265, 267, 270
Drakulich, Samuel 98, 103, 106
Draveling, Leo 83, 86, 91, 94
Dreffer, Stephen 223, 226, 231
Drehmann, Peter 243, 246
Drenik, Douglas 223, 226, 231
Dresser, John 202, 207
Dreyer, Carl A. 71
Dreyer, Walter O. 145, 147
Dudlar, Gannon 334, 339, 342
Duell 55
Duerr, John 315, 323
Dufek, Donald 166, 169,
Dufek, Donald 171, 174, 267, 270, 275
Dufek, William 270, 275, 278, 286
Duff, Robert 86
Duffy, James 243, 246
Duffy, Mark F. 254, 259
Dugger, Dean 183, 186, 191
Dugger, Donald R. 179, 182, 187
Dugger, Jack 143, 146, 149, 151
Dulin, Gary 279, 282, 28, 290
Dully, Mike 335, 338, 343
Dumas, Zack 320, 322, 327, 330
Dunaway, Craig 295, 299, 301
Duncan, Howard 159, 162
Duncan, Randy 205
Duncan, Stuart 323
Dunivant, Bill 146
Dunlap 29, 58, 63
Dunlap, John 79
Dunlap, Nelson 66
Dunleavy 62
Dunlop 23, 25
Dunn, Craig 298, 302
Dunn, D. 51, 53, 54
Dunn, D.L. 82
Dunn, J. 54
Dunne 46, 47, 58
Dunne, Arthur L. 171
Dunne, Maurice 150
Dunne, R.J. 51
Dunsford 27, 29
Dupay, Michael 203, 206, 210
Durant 19
Durham, Mike 312, 314, 320
Durtschi, H. 279
Durtschi, William 143
Dutcher, Gerald 251, 254
Dutter, George S. 179, 182, 187
Dwelle, Brad 290, 296, 298, 302
Dworsky, Daniel 155, 157, 158, 163
Dworsky, Don 166
Dwyer, Donald 234, 239, 242
Dye, William H.H.(Tippy) 109, 111, 113, 114, 117, 119
Dyer 16, 17
Dyson, Matt 339, 342

-E-

Eachus, William 231, 234, 239
Eaddy, Don 179
Eades 51
Early 46, 55
Eastlake, Charles 130
Eastman, Harry 94, 99
Eastman, Sean 323
Eaton, Donald R. 254, 259, 262, 267
Eberle 35, 37
Eberts, Mark 287, 296, 298
Ebinger, Elbert 186, 191, 194
Eby, Byron 77, 79, 81, 82, 85, 87
Echols, Reggie 290, 296
Eckstorm, Dr. John B. 18, 21
Ecrement, Thomas 247
Edgington, Harry 183
Edmiston, Charles 66
Edmonds, Ray 342
Edmunds 25, 37, 39
Edwards, Bernard 322, 327, 330, 335, 338
Edwards, Coach David 12
Edwards, Frank 183
Edwards, Karl 296, 298, 302, 306
Edwards, Mike 315, 319
Edwards, Stanley 286, 291, 295, 299
Edwards, Tom 15,
Edwards, T.L. 70, 75
Edwards, William 162, 167, 170

Archie Griffin is college football's only two-time Heisman Trophy winner. And while those two coveted bronzed statues are undoubtedly Griffin's most prized pieces of hardware, the Columbus native and Eastmoor High School graduate has a trophy case filled with numerous other tributes to his splendid four years with the Buckeyes.

Griffin was the Buckeyes' starting tailback for four years, leading Ohio State to a 40-5-1 record and four Big Ten titles between 1972 and 1975. He started in four consecutive Rose Bowls, the only player ever to do so, and was a three-time first-team All-American.

Griffin was a diminutive 5-9 and 180 pounds, small by college football standards even then, but he played with the heart of a lion and no football accomplishment was beyond his reach.

In just the second game of his freshman year, Griffin ran for a school record 239 yards. It was the start of a brilliant career that would see him amass an OSU record 5,589 yards and 26 touchdowns.

Excluding bowl games, Griffin rushed for 5,177 yards on 845 carries. The former figure ranks him fifth among all NCAA career ball carriers and his 6.13 yards per carry still stands as an NCAA record. And Griffin rarely played more than half a game, his coach, Woody Hayes, always opting to take his star out as soon as the Buckeyes were in control.

Between his sophomore and senior seasons, Griffin ran for 100 or more yards in 31 consecutive games. That, too, is still an NCAA record.

In addition to two Heisman Trophies, Griffin also has a pair of Silver Footballs, an award presented annually by the Chicago Tribune to the Big Ten's MVP. He won those as a sophomore and junior, in the process joining Minnesota's Paul Giel as the only player ever to win two. Griffin also was a two-time pick as National Player of the Year by both United Press International and the Walter Camp Foundation. He won those honors as a junior and senior.

Following his senior year, Griffin, who graduated a quarter early with a degree in industrial relations, received the NCAA's prestigious Top Five Award for combined excellence in athletics, academics and leadership. It is the highest award the NCAA can bestow.

After an eight-year career with the Cincinnati Bengals, Griffin is now an assistant athletic director at Ohio State. To this day, he remains one of the most popular and visible players ever to play for the Buckeyes.

Egan, J. E. 17
Egbert 39
Eggers, Pat 258
Ehrensberger, Carl 95
Ehrensberger, Fred 210
Ehrsam, Gerald 239, 242, 247
Ehrsam, John 151, 154
Eichwald, Kenneth 143
Eisenberg, Brian 327
Eizonas, John 166
Eldred, Dale L. 195
Eldridge, James E. 171, 174
Elezovic, Peter 331, 334, 339, 342
Elfers, Benjamin 207
Elgin 46, 47, 63
Elia, Bruce 266, 269, 271
Ellerby, Harold 99
Ellis, Jeff 327, 335, 338
Ellison, John 331
Elliott, Bruce N. 251, 254, 259
Elliott, Chalmers (Bump) 158, 160, 161, 163, 209, 245
Elliott, David L. 259, 262, 267, 270
Elliott, John 307, 311, 315, 319, 323
Elliott, Mark 334, 339, 342
Elliott, Matt 323, 326, 331, 334, 339
Elliott, Peter 153, 155, 157, 158, 161, 163, 165, 166
Elliott, Roy 127
Elliott, Samuel 239, 242
Ellis, Gregory A. 254, 259, 262
Ellis, Jeff 322, 330
Ellis, Joseph O. 110, 115
Ellis, Ray 282, 287, 290, 296
Ellis, Richard T. 13
Ellison, John 326, 334, 339
Ellison, Leon 282, 287, 290, 296
Ellwood, Frank 191, 193, 194, 197, 199
Ellwood, Richard 167, 170, 175
Elsenman, Terry 302
Ely, Roger 171
Elzinga, Mark 267, 270, 275
Embrey, Russell 98
Embs 29,34
Embs, Wm. 33
Emelianchik, Robert 207, 210
Endres, George 167, 170, 175
Endres, Robert 170, 175, 178
Engelhard 19
Engensberger 16, 17
England, Robert 227, 235
English, Joe 299, 301
Enos 16, 17
Epitropoulos, Ernest 282, 287, 290, 296
Epitropoulos, John 282, 287, 290, 296
Erben, Robert F. 163, 166, 171
Erhardt, Mark 311, 319, 323
Ernst, Richard 178, 183
Ervin, Terry 239, 242
Espy, Bennie 223, 226, 231
Evans, Benjamin F. 71
Evans, Donald K. 179, 182
Evans, Keith 311
Evans, Mike 323, 326, 331, 334, 339
Evans, Robert 87
Evans, Stephen 342
Evashevski, Forest 126, 128, 129, 131, 133, 134
Evashevski, Forest 222, 227, 230
Everhardus, Herm 99, 102, 105, 107,
Everhardus, Herm 110, 115
Everitt, Steve 326, 331, 334, 339, 342
Ewart 50
Eyke 25, 29
Eyke, W. L. 31
Ezzo, Billy 263, 266, 271

-F-

Fabyan, August E. 126
Facchine, Richard 194
Faehl, Paul 170, 175
Failer 55
Fair, Robert 218, 223
Fairbanks, Jack 267, 270
Falander, Mike 326
Falkenhagen, Curt 243
Farabee, Ben 222, 227, 230
Farabee, David 243
Farbizo, Thomas 231, 234
Farcasin 46, 50, 63
Farmer, Douglas A. 115, 118, 123
Farrall, John 207, 210, 215
Farrell 36
Farrer, Richard D. 166, 171, 174
Farrier, Marvin E. 90, 95
Fate, Donald 150
Faul, Lawrence J. 195, 198, 203
Fay 19, 21, 23
Fay, Stanley E. (C.) 99, 102, 107
Fazio, Charles 154, 159, 162, 167
Feaster, Curtis 323, 326, 331
Feaster, Rodney 285, 286, 291, 295
Fedderson, Jerry 146
Federico, Eric 243, 246. 251
Federle, Thomas 223, 226, 231
Fediuk, Arthur W. 259, 262, 267
Feinthal, Kenneth 186
Fekete, Gene 141, 143
Feldswich 43
Feldwisch, Hen 41
Fellin, Camp 301, 307
Felten, Jeff 291, 295, 299
Felver, Howard 17
Fender, Paul 234, 239
Fenner, Harry 79
Fenstermaker, Tony 320, 322
Ferbert, Gustave 16
Ferchau, Tom 254
Ferens, John 299, 301, 307
Ferenz 67
Ferguson, B. 279
Ferguson, Carl 296
Ferguson, Keith 282, 287, 290, 296
Ferguson, Robert 210, 213, 215, 216, 217, 218
Ferko, Richard 255, 258, 263
Ferral, Walter 87
Ferrall, Junius 95, 98, 103
Ferrelli, Jeff 271, 279
Fesler, Wesley 85, 87, 89, 90, 93, 95,
Fesler, Wesley, (Coach) 162, 173, 178, 209
Fertig, Dwight 242
Fess 23
Fette, Thomas 227
Fichtner, Rusty 323, 326, 331
Fickell, Luke 343
Fields, Jerry 202, 205, 207, 209, 210
Fields, Sean 330
Fiers, Alan 207, 210, 215
Filar, Robert 214, 219
Fill, John 231, 234, 239
Fillichio, Mike 203, 206, 210
Finck, Dan 343
Fioretti, A.R. 63, 66

Fisch, Frank 106, 109, 111, 114
Fischer, Brad 291, 299
Fischer, Louis 175, 178, 183
Fischer, Robert H. 147
Fish, Willard 86
Fisher, David 230, 233, 235, 237, 238
Fisher, Dick 138
Fisher, Jerome 98, 103, 106, 110
Fisher, John 274
Fisher, Max M. 87, 90
Fisher, Richard 130, 135, 137, 154
Fitch, Alan 163, 166, 171
Fitz, Thomas 223, 226, 231
Fitzgerald, Dennis 206, 210, 213, 214
Fitzgerald, Patrick 315, 323
Fitzgerald, Fred 98
Fivaz, Robert 87
Flajole, Paul 83
Flanagan, Dennis 230, 235
Flanagan, Richard 149, 151
Flanagan, Stephen 246
Flanagan, Steve 246,
Fleming, Mark 106, 111
Fletcher, Kevin 255, 263
Floersch, Harold 118, 123, 126
Flora, Robert 73, 75
Flora, Robert L. 126, 131, 134, 139
Flora, William 70, 78
Flower, Jim 49, 50
Flynn, Leo M. 171
Foley, David 239, 241, 242, 245, 247
Folkertsma, David 307, 311, 315, 319, 323
Follett, Richard 90
Foltz, James H. 155
Fonde, Henry 153, 155, 157, 158, 163, 217
Fontes, Arnold 234
Fontes, Leonard 207, 210
Fontess, Arnold 233, 239
Ford, Gerald 101, 102, 107, 110
Ford, John 239
Ford, Leonard 155, 157, 158, 163
Ford, Samuel 103
Ford, Thomas G. 126, 131
Fordham, Forrest 122, 127
Foreman, Charles 215
Forrest 23
Fortney, Douglas 218, 223
Fortune 46, 51, 54
Foster 62
Foster, Brian 331, 339, 342
Foster, Che' 339, 342
Foster, Derrick 327, 330, 335, 338, 343
Foster, Jerome 287, 290, 296, 298, 302
Foster, Rodney 215, 218, 223
Foster, Tom 312
Foss 23, 25, 39
Foss, Whitie 41
Fouch, George 82, 90
Foulk, Charles W. 13
Fourman, Kent 314
Fout, James 154
Fox 63, 87
Fox, James W. 187, 190, 195
Fox, Sam 130, 135, 137, 138
Fox, Tim 266, 271, 274
France, Doug 263, 266, 271
France, Matt 322
France, Steve 314, 320, 327, 330
Francis, Alan 243, 246, 251
Francis, David 215, 218, 221, 223
Frank 19
Frank, Dean 218
Frank, Donald 191
Frank, Jason 327, 330, 335
Frank, John 296, 298, 302, 306
Franklin, Dennis 261, 262, 265, 267, 269, 270
Franklin, Glenn 262, 267
Franklin, Wilbert 210
Franks, Dennis 262, 267, 270
Franks, Julius S. 139, 142
Frankowski, Wallace 107
Frantz, Matthew 314, 320
Franzen, Raymond 222
Frazer, Rick 301, 307, 311
Fraumann, Harlin E. 131, 134, 137, 139
Freehan, William 214
Freeman 46
Freeman, Bill 213
Freeman, Dwayne 307, 311, 315
Freeman, Eddie 79
Freeney 37
Freppel, F. 87
Frey, Greg 320, 322, 327, 330, 335
Fried, Lawrence 95
Friedman 46, 50, 69
Friedman, Ben 70, 73, 75, 77, 78, 93
Friehofer, Cecil 150, 155
Freihofer, Walter B. 139, 142, 158
Friend 58
Friend, Dwight 66
Frimel, Rich 327, 330, 335, 338
Frisco, Frank P. 147
Frisk, Leslie 94, 99, 102
Fritz 43
Fritz, Kenneth 279, 282, 287, 290
Fritz, Ralph 126, 131, 134
Fritzsche, James 162
Froemke 51
Froemke, Harlan 70
Fromme, Eloise 63
Fronk, Daniel 199, 202, 207
Frontczak, John 222
Frontczak, Nick 222
Frontczak, Stanley 227
Frost, Kenneth D. 118, 123
Frutig, Edward C. 123, 126, 131, 133, 134
Fry, Edgar Allen 82
Frye, Robert 138, 143
Frysinger, Terry 243
Fuggit, John 98, 103
Fuller, Fred 75, 83
Fulton 25
Funk, Robert 226, 231, 233, 234
Funk, William 131
Fuog, Russell J. 102, 107, 110
Furillo, Rich 296
Furtig, Ed 125

-G-

Gabel, Norman 75, 78, 83
Gabler, John 241, 243, 246, 251
Gabler, Wallace 230, 233, 235
Gaffney, Mike 258
Gagalis, Peri 182, 187, 190
Gage, Ralph 186, 191, 202, 207
Gage, Robert J. 142
Gailus, Joseph 103, 106
Gaither, Steve 327
Galbos, Richard 255, 258, 263
Galbraith, James 154
Galbraith, M.H. 71
Gales, Charles 114, 119, 122, 127
Gales, Rick 258
Galius, Joe 97, 98
Gallagher, David D. 259, 262, 267
Gallagher, John M. 147
Galles, James 131
Galloway, Joey 335, 338,

Galloway, Joey 343
Galloway, Tim 290, 296
Gambill, David 175, 178, 183
Gambis, Joe 86
Gandee, Charles 154, 167, 170, 175
Gandee, Sherwin 167, 175, 178
Gannatal, Paul 131, 134
Gans, William 142
Ganshaw 17
Gant, Tony 301, 307, 315, 319
Gappen 54
Garber 75
Garber, Jesse G. 110, 115, 118
Garber, Joe 312, 314, 320
Garcia, Joe 274
Gardner, Gardy 41, 43
Gardner, James 95
Garfield 62
Garrels 25, 29
Garrells, A.E. 41
Garrels, J.C. 31
Garrett, Eddie 301, 307, 311
Garrity, Tom 291, 295, 299, 301
Gasper, Courtney 312
Gasperoni, Sergio 339, 342
Gates, David W. 123
Gatewood, Russell 287, 296, 298
Gaudette, Roger 283, 286
Gaudio, Robert 159
Gayle, James 287, 290, 296, 298, 302
Gayle, Shaun 296, 298, 302, 306
Gear, Kenney 295
Gease 37
Gedeon, Elmer J. 118, 123, 126
Gee, Thomas 210, 214
Geffney, Mike 263
Geib 37, 43
Geib, Dad 41
Geib 175
Geise, J.R. 41
Geismann, Irving 41, 43
Geistert, Walter E. 83, 86
Gembis, Joe G. 81, 83, 85, 89, 91
Genebach 46
Gentile 175
Gentile, James 247, 250, 255
Gentry, Bob 271, 274
Genyk, George 203, 206, 210
George, August 111, 114, 119, 231, 234
George, Eddie 343
George, Edward 83
George, Samuel 87
Georgepoulos, Tom 111, 114
Gerald, Rod 274, 279, 281, 282, 285, 287
Gereg, Bud 311
Gerhard, Maurice 87
German, William 207, 210, 215
Geyer, Ronald 179, 182, 187, 190
Ghindia, John 301, 307, 311
Ghindia, John V. 163, 166, 171
Gibbs, Jack 186, 191
Gibson 31, 33, 34, 35
Gibson, Eric 327
Giesler, Jon 278, 286
Giesler, Mike 327, 330
Gilbert, Charles 167, 170
Gilbert, Louis 75, 78, 81, 83
Gill 27
Gillam 46, 50, 58
Gillette, Mike 315, 319, 323, 326
Gillian, Ray 242, 247, 250
Gillie 31
Gillman, Sidney 98, 101, 103, 106
Gilmore 54
Gilmore, Jim 298, 302,
Gilmore, Jim 306, 312, 314
Gilmore, Keith 283
Girgash, Paul 295, 299, 301
Gitman, William 86, 91, 94
Giuliani, Anthony 302, 306, 312
Glancey, Tom 302, 312, 314
Glasser, Chester 82, 87, 90
Glenn, C.L. 79
Glinka, Dave 213, 214, 217, 219
Godfrey 43
Godfrey, Chris 283, 286, 291
Goebel, Jerry P. 190, 195, 203
Goebel, Paul 58, 61, 62
Goeble 54
Goering, William 223
Goetz 46, 47, 51, 54
Goff, Carlos 335, 338, 343
Goldsmith, DuVal 94, 99
Golvach, Duane 203
Gondy, Professor 19
Gonser, Jerry I. 187, 190, 195
Gonzsalez, Eduardo 267
Goodgame, Tony 327
Gooding 23, 25
Goodsell, Douglas 178, 183
Goodwin, Harold 342
Gorby, Herbert 154
Gordon 17
Gordon, George 151, 162
Gordon, L. 279
Gordon, Sonny 306, 312, 314, 320
Gorley, Rod 290, 296, 302
Gorrill, C.V. 66, 71, 74
Gorte, Michael 227
Gosier, Harry 295
Goss, Thomas 235, 238, 243, 246
Gossett, Dennis 314
Gottron, Jeff 296, 298, 302
Gradishar, Randy 258, 263, 266
Grady, Robert 90, 95, 98
Graham 27, 29
Graham, Andy 335, 338
Graham, Jeff 327, 330, 335
Graham, Kent 335, 338
Graham, Scott 322, 327, 330, 335, 338
Graham, W.D. 31, 33
Graf 43
Graf, Campbell 122, 127, 130
Graf, Jack 130, 135, 137, 138
Graf, Larry 266
Grambau, Fredrick E. 251, 254, 259, 262
Granger, Ralph 103, 133
Grant, J. J. 315, 319, 323, 326, 331
Grant, Todd 210, 214, 219
Graper, Frank 151
Graper, Robert 110
Graven 25
Graver 19, 23, 25
Graves, Eric 331, 334, 339, 342
Graves, Reggie 312, 320
Graves, Rory 298, 302, 306, 312, 314
Graves, Steve 270, 275, 277, 278, 283
Gray, Charles 115, 118
Gray, James 195, 198, 203, 206
Gray, Joe 301, 307, 311
Grbac, Elvis, 331, 334, 339, 342
Green 39,
Green, "Jack" 15
Green, James 222, 227
Green, Keny 338, 343
Green, Mark 231
Green, Merritt II 174, 179,

Green, Merritt II 182
Greenberg, Jack 95, 98, 103
Greenblatt, Louis 103, 106
Greene, Anthony 287
Greene, Cornelius 265, 266, 269, 271, 273, 274
Greene, Edward 227, 230, 235
Greene, Horatius 247
Greene, John J. 139, 142, 147
Greenwald, Edward U. 115, 118
Greenwald, H.T. 78, 83
Greenwood, John C. 190, 195, 198
Greer, Curtis 278, 283, 286, 291
Greer, Edward 150
Greer, Steven 327
Gregory 21, 23, 25
Gregory, Bruce 70, 75
Greider, Robert 111
Grenkoski, Edward 155
Gresock, Steve 320
Grey, William 142
Grieves, Chris 278
Griffey, Craig 335
Griffin Archie 261, 266, 269, 271, 273, 274
Griffin, Duncan 274, 279, 282, 287
Griffin, Raymond 271, 273, 274, 279, 282
Griffith, Eugene 103
Griffith, William A. 90, 95
Griffith, William N. 71, 87
Griggs, Anthony 298
Grim, Fred 73, 74, 79, 81, 82
Grimm, Erik 320, 322, 327
Grimes, Robert 175, 178, 181, 183
Grinnell, Henry 75, 83
Grinnell, H.S. 78
Grinnell, Ira 91, 94
Grissen, James 131, 134
Griswold, Francis 74, 79, 82
Gritis, Peter 142
Groce, Alvin 203, 206
Grodsky, Isadore 86
Groom, Jeff 274
Grosebeck, (Governor) 60
Gross 46
Groza, Judd 296, 302, 306, 312
Grubb, John 314, 320, 322
Grube, C.W. 67, 79, 75
Grundies, Jerry 127, 130, 135
Guess, Michael 279, 282, 287, 290
Guild 63
Guild, W.P. 66
Gundry, George 86
Gunther 63
Gunther, Don 154
Gurd, Andrew 322, 327, 330, 335, 338
Gusich, Frank J. 251, 254, 259
Gustafson, Lawrence J. 259, 262, 267
Gustavson, Carl 130, 135
Guthrie, George 175, 178, 183
Gutzwiller, Mark 323, 326
Guzik, Frank 186
Guy, Richard 191, 194, 199
Guynes, Tom 342
Gwinn 58, 63
Gwinn, Jayson 343

-H-

Hackett, Jim 270, 275, 278
Hackett, William 143, 146, 151, 154. 242, 247, 250
Haddad, George 111, 114, 119, 122
Hafner, Bob 296
Hagar 19
Hagar, H. 86
Hague, James 159, 162, 165, 167,
Hague, James 169, 170
Hague, Thomas 178, 183, 186
Hahn, Dick 222, 227
Haines 46
Hainrihar, Gary 259, 262, 267
Haji-Sheikh, Ali 295, 299, 301
Hale, Coach 23, 25
Hale, Perry 22
Haley, Earl 338
Haley, John 210
Hall 15, 37, 39
Hall, David 299, 301, 307
Hall, B. Lee 206, 210, 214, 219
Hall, Clarence 134
Hall, D. 279
Hall, David 301
Hall, Foster 70
Hall, Jim 270, 275
Hall, John E. 90, 95
Hall, Robert 146
Hall, Ted 287, 290
Hall, Werner 243, 246, 251, 254
Hall, William 218, 223
Hallabrin, John 130, 135, 137, 138
Hallenbeck, John 210
Haller, Dave 198, 203
Haller, Tim 312, 320
Halloway, Dan 311
Halloway, Dave 330
Halstead, John 206, 209, 210, 214
Halveland, Uwe 330
Hamilton 51, 58
Hamilton, Clarence 79
Hamilton, Forest 154, 159, 162
Hamilton, H.L. 63
Hamilton, Howard 66
Hamilton, Ian B. 63, 66
Hamilton, M.N. 151
Hamilton, Ray 169, 170, 175, 178
Hamilton, Remy 342
Hamilton, W. 279
Hamilton, Walter 183
Hamlin, Stanley 239
Hammels 51
Hammerstein, Mark 301, 307, 311, 315, 319
Hammerstein, Mike 301, 307, 311, 315
Hammond, E. 25
Hammond, H. 27, 29,
Hammond, Harry 33
Hammond, H.S. 31
Hammond, T. 25, 27, 28, 29
Hammons, Roger 199
Hampton 17
Hamrick, Charles 111, 114, 119
Hankins, Woodrow 342
Hankwitz, Mike 243, 246, 251
Hanlon, Mickey 299, 301
Hanna, Henry 235, 238
Hannan, F.C. 17
Hannan, W.M. 15
Hannah, Donald 206, 210, 214
Hans, Joseph 186
Hanshue, Cloyce E. 110, 115
Hansley, Gary 210, 215
Hansley, Terence 210
Hanzlik, Robert 147
Harbaugh, Jim 301, 307, 311, 315, 319
Harbin, Jerry 210
Harbour, Robert 331
Harden, Linwood 262
Harden, Michael 283, 286, 291
Harding, Dave 275, 278, 283
Hardman, Von Allen 210, 215, 218
Hardway, L.E. 79
Hardy 19
Hardy, William 235, 238
Hare, Greg 258, 263, 266
Harley, Charles 45, 49, 50
Hargraves, William 114
Hargreaves, William 119, 122
Harkins, Donald 223, 226,

Harkins, Donald 231
Harkrader, Jerry 186, 189, 191, 194
Harmon, Tom 125, 126, 128, 129, 131, 132, 134
Harper, Darrell 203, 206, 209, 210
Harper, Rodric 330, 335
Harper, Roger 330, 335, 338, 343
Harpring, Jack 246, 251, 254
Harre, Gilbert 106, 111, 114
Harrell, James 271, 274, 279, 282
Harrigan, Frank 78, 83
Harrigan, John F. 139
Harris, Billy 307, 311, 315, 319, 323
Harris, George 82
Harris, Jasper 146
Harris, Jimmie 250, 255, 258
Harris, Nate 312, 314, 320
Harris, Raymont 323, 335, 338, 343
Harris, Robert 301
Harris, Stuart 286, 291, 299
Harris, Ted 319
Harris, Tyrone 271, 274, 279, 282
Harris, William 243, 244, 246, 249, 251, 254
Harrison, Gregory 251, 254
Harrison, H.C. 71, 74
Harrison, Preston 335, 338, 343
Harrison, Tyrone 327, 330, 335, 338
Harshman, Andy 314
Hart, Randy 242, 247, 250
Hart, William 254, 259, 262
Harter 58, 63
Harter, Albert G. 66
Hartley, Robert 223, 226
Hartman, Gabriel 207, 210, 215
Hartman, Gerald 243, 246
Hartman, Jerald 238
Hartman, Len 327, 330, 335, 338, 343
Hartman, Tom 320
Hartrick, James G. 142
Harvey, William 298, 302, 312
Hasenohrl, George 255, 258, 263
Haslam, Charles J. 139
Haslerig, Clinton E. 259, 261, 262, 267
Haslett, Bill 254
Hassel, Rick 315, 319, 323, 326
Hassel, Tom 295, 299, 301, 307
Hasselo, Albert 167
Hatfield 37
Haubrich, Robert C. 90, 95, 97, 98
Hauer, Oscar 207, 210, 215
Haupt, Richard 210, 215, 218
Haverstock, Thomas 227, 230
Hawkins, Captain 16, 17
Hawkins, Harry 67, 70, 75
Hawkins, Neil 343
Hayden E. 91
Hayden, Leophus 247, 250, 253, 255
Hayes, Chip 11
Hayes, Geoffrey 11
Hayes, Glenn E., III 11
Hayes, Mercury 342
Hayes, Matthew 11
Hayes, Millie 11
Hayes, Nyol 91, 94
Hayes, W.W. (Woody) (Coach) 17, 177, 178,181, 189, 192, 193, 229, 237, 249, 257, 273, 281, 290,
291
Haynes, Duke 299
Hayzen, Francis 99
Hazel, David 263, 266, 271
Hazelbaker, Joe 330
Healy, Brian 243, 246, 251
Heater, Chuck 261, 262, 267, 270
Heath, Charles 91
Heath, William 62, 70, 75, 78
Hecker, Bob 146
Hecklinger, Harold 130, 135, 138
Hedding, Kevin 331, 339
Heekin, Richard F. 103, 106, 109, 111, 113, 114
Heffelfinger, Clifford 130, 135
Heffelfinger, Jon 235, 243
Hefferman, Jack 270
Heffleman 29
Hefflinger, Ronnie 146
Hegler, David S. 13
Heid, Robert 170, 175, 178
Heiden, Richard 210
Heikkinen, Ralph I. 118, 123, 125, 126
Heilman, P. 279
Heiser, Vern 111
Heneveld, Bill 270
Heneveld, Lloyd A. 158, 163, 166, 171
Hendershot — 46
Hendershott, L.W. 66
Henderson 51, 53, 55, 62
Henderson, John 227, 229, 230
Henderson, Tony 334, 339, 342
Hendricks, Thomas, Jr. 187, 190, 195
Henkel, Dave 339
Hennessy, John 270, 275, 278
Henninger, W. 82
Henry 17
Henry, Joseph 162, 167, 170
Henry, Preston 251, 254
Henson, Harold (Champ) 261, 263, 271
Henson, Luther 282, 287, 290, 296
Heppberger, C.E. 82
Herbstreit, Jim 205, 207, 209, 210, 213, 215
Herbstreit, Kirk 327, 330, 335, 338, 343
Heren, Dieter 301, 307, 311, 315, 319
Herman, Judah 327, 330, 335, 338
Hermann, Jim 299
Hernstein 19,23
Hernstein, Seth 296
Hernstein, Wm. 67, 70, 75
Hernstein, Knight 21
Harrala, Scott 323
Herrala, Wallace 210, 214
Herrick, Dave 311, 315
Herrman, Harvey 207, 210
Herrman, Jim 301
Herrmann, James 295
Herrmann, John 315, 319, 323, 326
Herrnstein, A.E. 30, 34
Herrnstein, John 197, 198, 201, 203, 206
Herron, Kendall 151
Herschberger, Peter 130, 135, 138
Hershberger, Donovan P. 155, 158, 163, 166
Hesler, Robert 186
Hess, Albert 82, 87
Hess, Brice 210
Hess, Edwin 71, 74, 79
Hess, John H. 166, 171, 174
Hess, William 215, 218, 223
Heston 23, 25, 26, 27, 67, 75
Heston, John P. 99, 102, 105, 107

Heston, L.G. 78, 83
Heston, Shaw 21
Heston, William 24
Heston, Willie, Jr. 89, 91, 94, 97, 99,
Hetts, Chuck 286, 291
Hewitt, William 91, 94, 99
Hewlett, Rich 295, 299, 301, 307
Heyman, Joseph 103, 106
Heynen, Richard B. 195, 198, 203
Hickey, Coach Charles 12
Hickey, Edward L. 179, 182, 187, 190, 195
Hicks, Dwight 270, 275, 278, 283
Hicks, Ivan 301, 307, 311, 315, 319
Hicks, John 255, 263, 266
Hicks, Mark 327
Hicks, Tyrone 287, 290
Hieronymus 74, 82, 85, 87
Hietikko, James 175, 178, 183
Higdon, Alex 312, 314, 320, 322
Higgins 58
Higgins, Kenneth 307, 311, 315, 319
Highitt, Ernest F. 43
Hildebrand, Willard H. 102, 107, 110
Hildebrand, Willard 206, 210, 214
Hildebrandt, George H. 134, 139
Hilinski, Richard 186, 191
Hilkene, Bruce L. 147, 150, 156, 158, 160, 163
Hill 23,
Hill, David J. 174, 189, 190, 195, 198
Hill, Doug 296, 298, 302, 306
Hill, Henry 246, 251, 254
Hill, Joseph 231
Hill, Mark 311
Hill, Richard F. 190, 195
Hill, Steve 302, 306, 312, 314
Hill, Timothy 296, 298, 302, 306
Hill, Will 338, 343
Hilsenroth, Troy 327, 330
Himes, Richard 239, 242
Hinchman, Lewis 95, 97, 98, 101, 103
Hinchs 19
Hinebaugh 175
Hines 37
Hines, Snake 23
Hinshaw, Joseph M. 115
Hinton, Eugene 155, 171, 174
Hirneise, Dan 320, 322, 330
Hirsch, Elroy L. 145, 147, 150
Hlay, John 175, 178, 183
Hoak, Frank 312, 314, 320, 322
Hoard, Leroy 319, 323, 326, 331
Hoban, Bill 262, 267, 270, 275
Hoban, Michael A. 259, 262, 267
Hocevar, Mark 296, 298, 302
Hodder 46
Hodge, Glenn 239
Hodgman 17
Hodgson, Harold 91
Hodick, Mike 127
Hodnick, Paul 95
Hoey, George 238, 243, 246
Hoffer 95, 98
Hoffman, James 178
Hoffman, Leo 75, 78, 83
Hofmayer, Edward 119, 122, 127
Hogg, J.R. 17
Hohenberger, C. 119
Hoke, Hugh 203
Holcomb, Stuart K. 90, 93, 95, 97, 98
Holdren, Nate 334, 339, 342
Holdren, Richard 194
Holland, Jamie 312, 314, 320
Holland, Jay 298, 302, 306, 312
Holland, Joseph 315, 319, 323, 326
Holland, Kirk 91, 99
Holliman, Ray 306, 312, 314, 320
Hollingsworth, Morris 63, 66
Hollis, Peter 227, 235
Holloway, Dan 315
Holloway, Ernie 311, 315, 319
Holloway, Ralph 250, 255
Holloway, Randy 247
Hollway, Robert C. 163, 166, 171, 278, 283, 286
Holman, Allen 85, 87, 89, 90
Holmes, Danny. W. 86, 91, 94
Holmes, Mike 267, 270, 275
Holmes, Paul M. 63, 66
Holtkamp 50
Holycross, Timothy 263, 266, 271
Honaker 58, 63
Honaker, Frank 66
Honigsbaum, F. 158
Hood, Earl 214
Hood, Ed 301, 307, 311, 315
Hood, Edward 219, 222
Hook, R. Wallace, Jr. 118, 123, 126
Hook, Robert M. 126, 134
Hooper 15
Horn, Chris 323, 326
Horn, Jason 339, 342
Horn, Robert L. 87, 89, 90, 95
Hornbeck, William 210, 214, 219
Horner, William 99
Hornung, Paul 290
Honigsbaum, Frank 150
Hornik, Joe 274, 279, 282, 287
Horvath, Leslie 135, 138, 141, 143, 149, 151
Horwitz, Gilbert 94
Horwitz, Sam 111
Hosket, Wilmer 98
Hosking, John 103
Houck, Ronnie 210, 215, 217, 218
Houser, Thomas 250
Housteau, Joseph 223, 231
Houston, Dave 330
Houston, James 202, 207, 210, 287, 290
Houston, Lindell 138, 143
Houston, William 330, 335, 338, 343
Houtman, John 214, 219, 227
Howe, Buster 330
Howley, Edward 191
Howard, Dedrick 314, 320
Howard, Derek 270, 275, 278, 282
Howard, Desmond 326, 331, 334, 339
Howard, Fritz 130, 135, 138
Howard, Harry 250, 253, 255, 258
Howard, Ty 343
Howe, Frank 122, 127, 130
Howell 46,
Howell, Carroll 174, 178, 183, 186, 191
Howell, Frank 179, 181, 182
Howell, Raymond S. 66
Howenstine 46
Howman, Dennis 223, 231
Hoyer 27, 29
Hoying, Bob 338, 343
Hoyne, Jeffrey 227, 230, 235
Hozer, Stanley 86, 94, 99
Hribal, James 235, 238
Hubbard, Rudy 234, 239,

241, 242
Huckleby, Harlan 278, 282, 286
Huddleston, Mike 327, 330, 335
Hudson, A.M. 87
Hudson, Addison 95
Hudson, Paul 231, 234, 239
Hudson, Roy 91, 93, 94, 99
Huebel, Herbert H. 41, 43
Hueston, Dennis 302, 306
Huff, Marty 246, 251, 2545
Huff, Paul 242, 247, 250
Huffman 46, 49, 50, 53
Huffman, Iolas 55, 57, 58
Huffman, Rich 320, 322, 330, 335
Huggins, John E. 13
Huggman, Rich 327
Hughes, John 255, 263, 266
Hughes, A. Morris 78, 86
Huiskens, Tom 251, 254
Hulke, Scott E. 251, 254, 259
Hull, James 118, 122
Hullinger, Dennis 218, 223
Hulshult, Gene 302
Humberstone, H.J. 87, 90
Humbert, Stanley 191, 194, 199
Humphrey, H. 314
Humphries, Derrick 235, 238, 243
Humphries, Hayden 312
Humphries, Jame 291
Humphries, Stefan 295, 299, 301, 307
Hunington 25
Hunn, David S. 107
Hunt, L.W. 41
Hunt 69, 74
Hunt, Howser C. 71
Hunt, William 71, 79
Hunter, Charles 279, 282, 287, 290
Hurley, Bo 343
Hurley, Robert 174, 179, 182, 185, 187
Husar, Mike 311, 315, 319, 323, 326
Husband, John 263, 266
Huston, Arthur 82, 87, 90
Hutchings, John 287, 290, 296
Hutchinson, Chris 326, 331, 334, 339, 342
Hutchison, Charles 242, 247, 250
Hutchison, John 302, 306, 312, 314, 320
Hutter, George 155
Hutton, Thomas G. 123, 126
Hyatt, Robert 271, 274, 279
Hyde 25

-I-

Iams, John 335, 338, 343
Idle, Ralph 87, 95
Imsland, Jerry 246, 251
Ingalls, Robert D. 131, 134, 139
Ingle 67
Ingram, Jerald 295, 299, 301
Ingram, Michael 210, 213, 215, 218
Ireland, Glenn 134
Irons, Jarrett 342
Irwin, John 235
Isabel 63
Isabell, Wilbur 55, 57, 58
Isaman, Derek 314, 320, 322, 330

-J-

Jabbusch, Robert 141, 143, 159, 162
Jack, Alan 242, 247, 250
Jackson 27, 55, 58,
Jackson 63
Jackson, Allen M. 166, 171, 174
Jackson, Andy 275
Jackson, George H. 70
Jackson, Hardy 21
Jackson, Jeff 286
Jackson, M. 279
Jackson, Norman E. 162, 166, 171, 174
Jackson, Ray 312, 314, 320, 322
Jackson, Richard 151, 154
Jackson, Tony 291, 295, 299
Jackson, William 278, 282, 286
Jaco, William 279, 282, 287, 290
Jacobs, Benjamin P. 102, 107
Jacobs, Phillip H. 110
Jacobson, Tage O. 102, 107, 110
Jacoby, Bill 291
Jacoby, George 178, 181, 183, 186
Jacoby, Mark 262, 267, 270
Jaeckin, John 339, 342
James 25
James, Daniel 199, 202, 207
James, Doug 295, 299, 301, 307, 311
James, Richard H. 107, 110
James, Thomas 143, 159
James, Tim 312
Janakievski, Vlade 281, 282, 287, 290, 296
Janecke, Jerry 195
Janecko, Gene 151
Janke, Fred C. 118, 123, 125, 126
Jankowski, Bruce 247, 250, 253, 255
Janowicz, Victor 169, 170, 173, 175, 176, 178
Jeckell, Charles 79
Jefferson, Allen 319, 326, 331, 334
Jeffrey 74
Jekel, Rich 262
Jemison, Thad 296, 298, 302, 306
Jenkins, Chris 335, 338
Jenkins, Joe 312, 314, 320
Jenkins, Joseph 239, 242
Jenkins, Thomas 218, 223, 226
Jenkins, Trezelle 339, 342
Jenkins, William R. 71, 74
Jenks, John 198
Jennings, Ferris G. 110, 115, 118
Jennings, Jack 162, 167, 170
Jennings, William 166
Jensen, Tom 267, 270, 275
Jentes, Charles 207, 210, 215
Jilek, Dan 267, 270, 275
Jisa 63
Jobe, Theodore 238
Jobko, William 191, 194, 202
Jobson, E. Thomas 210, 214
Johns 54, 58, 62
Johns, Brandon 307
Johnson 23, 50, 51, 55
Johnson, Barry 271, 273, 274
Johnson, Brent 327, 330, 335, 338, 343
Johnson, Dean 334, 339
Johnson, Deon 342
Johnson, Gilbanni 315
Johnson, Grimar 338
Johnson, Jesse 339, 342
Johnson, Ricky 296
Johnson, C. Robert 155
Johnson, Earl 98, 103, 106
Johnson, Earl, Jr. 187, 190, 195
Johnson, Ernest C. 107, 110, 115

Ohio State Coaches' Records

Coach	Years	Won	Lost	Tied	Pct.
Alexander S. Lilley	1890-1891	3	5	0	.600
Jack Ryder	1892-1895, 1898	21	22	2	.479
Charles A. Hickey	1896	5	5	1	.500
David F. Edwards	1897	1	7	1	.167
John B. Eckstorm	1899-1901	22	4	3	.810
Perry Hale	1902-1903	14	5	2	.714
E. R. Sweetland	1904-1905	14	7	2	.652
A. E. Herrnstein	1906-1909	28	10	1	.731
Howard Jones	1910	6	1	3	.750
Harry Vaughn	1911	5	3	2	.600
John R. Richards	1912	6	3	0	.667
John W. Wilce	1913-1928	78	33	9	.688
Sam S. Willaman	1929-1933	26	10	5	.695
Francis A. Schmidt	1934-1940	39	16	1	.705
Paul E. Brown	1941-1943	18	8	1	.685
Carroll C. Widdoes	1944-1945	16	2	0	.889
Paul O. Bixler	1946	4	3	2	.556
Wesley E. Fesler	1947-1950	21	13	3	.608
W. W. "Woody" Hayes	1951-1978	205	61	10	.761
Earle Bruce	1979-1987	81	26	1	.755
John Cooper	1988-94	54	26	4	.667
All-Time Record	**105**	**667**	**270**	**53**	**.701**

1941 GAME ANN ARBOR, MICHIGAN

Johnson, Franham J. 147
Johnson, Gene 278, 283, 285, 286
Johnson, George 155, 163
Johnson, Gilvanni 301, 307, 311
Johnson, Irvin 283, 286, 291
Johnson, Keith 267, 270, 275
Johnson, Kenneth 215, 218
Johnson, Larry L. 259, 262, 267, 270, 273
Johnson, Livetius 326, 331, 334, 339
Johnson, Oliver 286, 291, 295
Johnson, Paul 235, 238, 243
Johnson, Pete 265, 266, 271, 274, 279
Johnson, Ray 275, 278, 279
Johnson, Ricky 282, 287, 290
Johnson, Robert 203, 206, 210, 214, 234, 239
Johnson, Ronald 238, 241, 243, 245, 246
Johnson, Stacy 278, 283
Johnson, Steve 301, 307, 311
Johnson, Thomas 171, 173, 174, 179, 302, 306, 312, 314
Johnson, Walter 198, 203, 206
Johnston 50
Johnston, Herbert L. 13
Johnston, James D. 259, 262
Johnston, Paul 255, 258
Johnstone, Collins H. 15
Jokisch, Dan 323, 326, 331, 334
Jokisch, Paul 311, 315, 319
Jolly, Mike 281, 283, 286, 291
Jolson, Tom 209
Jones 19, 23, 25, 27, 34, 37, 41
Jones, A.D. 71
Jones, Arnold 263, 266, 271
Jones, Ben 213, 214, 215, 218
Jones, Damon 342
Jones, Dave 103, 106, 111
Jones, David 223
Jones, Dennis 222, 227
Jones, D. J. 343
Jones, Gomer T. 106, 111, 113, 114
Jones Herbert 186, 199, 202
Jones, Herman 271, 274, 279, 282
Jones, Howard 36, 38
Jones, Jesse 13
Jones, Joe 246, 251
Jones, Larry 274, 283
Jones, Mike 315
Jones, Norman K. 71
Jones, Paul 271, 274
Jones, Rick 286
Jones, R. C. 343
Jones, Scott 258, 263
Jones, T.A.D. 72
Jones, Tim 314
Jones, Ty 314
Jones, William 91, 218
Jones-Bachman 35
Jordan 46
Jordan, Forrest R. 118, 126, 131
Jordan, Jhn D. 118
Jorday, William 94
Jordon, Ron 302
Joseph 71
Joseph, Roger 295
Joslin, Robert 178, 181, 183, 186
Judy, Edwin 63, 66
Julian, Fred 203, 206, 210
Julier, Mike 339
Jurin, Jeffrey 271
Justice, Thomas G. 91, 94
Juttner, C.F. 17

-K-

Kabealo, Charles L. 90, 95, 103
Kabealo, George 103, 106, 111, 113
Kabealo, John 105, 106, 111, 114
Kabealo, Michael 119, 122, 127
Kacherski, John 322, 327, 330, 335, 338
Kadela, Dave 278, 283
Kafury, Michael 239
Kain, Larry 266, 271, 273
Kamhout, Carl R., Jr. 182, 187, 190, 195
Kampe, Kurt 163, 262, 267, 270, 275
Kample, Kurt 158
Kanaga 29
Kane, Gary 206, 210
Kanitz, G. 83
Kanitz, Tharel 86
Kaplanoff, Carl 116, 119, 121, 122, 127
Kaplow 55, 58, 63
Karch, Robert 45
Karcher, James M. 103, 106, 111, 114
Karow, Marty 71, 73, 74, 77, 79
Karow, Robert 194
Karpus 46
Karsatos, Jim 302, 306, 312, 314, 320
Karvasales, James 130
Karwales, John J. 134, 139, 142
Kasparek, Ed 283, 286
Kasper, Capt. 17
Kasunic, Gerald 223, 226, 231
Katterhenrich, David 215, 218, 221, 223
Kattus, Eric 301, 307, 311, 315
Katula, Theodore 183, 199
Kauth, Chris 296
Kay, Don 146
Kaylor, Ronald 223, 226, 231
Kaynor, H.S. 41
Kavanaugh, Russell L. 155
Keane, Michael 154
Keane, Tom 149, 151
Keating, Tom 219, 222, 227
Keating, William 227, 230, 235
Keating, Wallace 134
Kee, Mike 302, 306, 312, 314, 320
Kee, Thomas G. 254, 259, 262
Keefe, Thomas C. 98, 103, 106
Keefer 62
Keeler, Walter 158
Keemsnyder 29
Keenan, Charles 314, 320, 322, 327
Keenan, William C. 142
Keene, Clifford 86
Keeton, Michael 271
Keith, Randy 258, 263, 266
Keith-Jones, Emmett 302
Keitz, Dale 278, 283, 286, 291
Keller, Dale 203
Keller, Michael P. 251, 254, 259
Keller, Tom 283, 291
Kelley, Barry 326, 331, 339
Kelley, Bethel 99, 102
Kelley, Dwight 226, 231, 234
Kelley, John 242
Kellum, W. 279
Kelly, C. J. 338, 343
Kelly, King 19
Kelly, J.J. 78
Kelly, John 234, 239
Kelly, Rob 343
Kelly, Robert 258

Kelsey, Thomas 154, 171, 174
Kelsey, Thomas 174
Kelsey, Ray Thomas 179
Kelsie, Tony 291
Kelto, Reuben 126, 131, 134, 139
Kemp, Stanley 229, 230, 235, 238
Kempthorn, Eric 299, 301
Kempthorn, Richard J. 163, 166, 171
Kenaga, Ray 187, 190
Kendrick, Jason 334, 339
Kenn, Mike 275, 278, 283
Kenna, L.S. 17
Kennedy 17
Kennedy, Arthur H. 13
Kennedy, Charles F. 139, 142
Kennedy, Robert W. 147
Kennedy, Theodore, Jr. 131, 134, 139
Keough, Kelly 286, 291, 295
Kern, Carl 263, 266
Kern, Frank J. 147
Kern, Rex 244, 245, 247, 249, 250, 253, 255
Kerner, Marlon 338, 343
Kerr 46
Kerr, Douglas 83, 86
Kerr, Michael 323
Kerr, Stan 41
Kerr, Thomas 206, 210, 214
Kerr, William 150
Kessell, Joel 338, 343
Kessler, Bud 146, 154
Kessler, Kaye 290
Ketteman, Dick 195, 198, 203
Ketz, W.H. 83
Keuchler, Lamar 296, 298, 302
Key, David 319, 323, 326, 331, 334
Key, Keith 312
Khan, Gulam 315, 323, 326, 331
Kidd, Steve 296
Kidston 23, 25
Kidston, James A. 107
Kidwell, Eric 302
Kiehfuss, Thomas 223, 226, 231
Kiesel, George C.F. 142, 147, 163
Kieta, Robert 238, 243, 246
Kile, Eugene M. 90, 95, 98
Kilgore, David 202, 205, 207, 210
Killian, Tim 245, 246, 249, 251, 254
Kimball, Bob 301
Kinel, Tony 119
Kines, Charles 227, 230, 235
King 16, 17
King, Dale 167, 170
King, Gerald 247, 255
King, Kevin 270, 275, 278, 283
King, Steve 262, 267, 270, 275, 342
Kinkade, Thomas 129, 130, 135, 137, 138
Kinsey, John H. 123, 126
Kinsey, Marvin 255
Kinyon, Peter C. 171, 174, 179
Kipke, Harry 58, 61, 62, 65, 67
Kipke, Coach 113
Kirby 29
Kirby, Craig 227, 230, 235
Kirk 59, 62
Kirk, Brenton 159, 162, 167
Kirk, James 98, 103
Kissell 58, 63
Kitti, Walter I. 126, 131
Kittle, Birdseye 21
Klaban, Tom 269, 271, 273, 274
Klee, Ollie 63, 66, 71
Klein 46, 74
Klein, A. 63
Klein, Alex 79
Klein, D. 63
Klein, Robert 213, 215, 217, 218, 223
Kleinfelder, K. 119
Kleinhans, John 111, 119
Kleinhaus, John L. 106
Klevay, Walter 170, 175, 178
Kligis, Mike 286, 291
Kline, Alan 330, 335, 338, 343
Klinge, Walter W. 195
Klofta, Dan T. 151
Klohn, Jim 312
Knapp, George 235
Knecht, Gilbert 183, 186
Knecht, John 119
Knickerbocker 63
Knickerbocker, S. 182, 187, 190, 195
Knickerbocker, Steve 275
Knight, Dave 323, 326, 331
Knight, Professor 19
Knoebel, Tom 301, 307
Knode 46, 47, 51, 62
Knuth, Erik 326, 334, 339
Knutson, Eugene P. 179, 182, 187
Kocan, Ronald 214, 222
Koceski, Leo R. 165, 166, 169, 171, 174
Koch, Jay 322, 327, 330, 335
Koder, Robert 183
Kodros, Archie J. 123, 125, 126, 131
Koegel, Steve 271
Koegel, Vic 258, 263, 266
Koepnick, Robert 175, 178, 183
Kohl, Harry E. 126, 131, 134
Kohl, Ralph A. 163, 166
Kohut, William 223, 231
Kolcheff, Donald 203
Kolesar, John 315, 323, 326
Kolesar, Robert C. 134, 139, 142
Kolesar, William P. 187, 190, 195
Kolic, Larry 298, 302, 306, 312, 314
Komer, Stuart 146
Kopach, Stephen 122
Korn, Gary 207, 210, 215
Kornowa, Donald 219
Korowin, James 210, 214, 219
Koschalk, Rich 267, 270, 275
Koss, Gregory 259, 262, 267
Kotterman, Larry 312, 314, 320
Kovacevich, Dave 222, 227
Kovac, Mike 311
Kovacs, Lou 301
Kowalik, John F. 99, 102, 107
Kowalik, John F., Jr. 214, 219, 221, 222
Kozel, Steve 327
Kozlowski, Jim 283, 286
Kraeger, George W. 147, 158
Kraglow 74
Krahl, Joseph W. 187, 190
Krahnke, Charles H. 187, 195
Krall, Gerald 154, 159, 167, 169, 170
Kramer, John 238, 243, 246
Kramer, Melvin G. 115, 118, 123
Kramer, Ronald 189, 190, 193, 195, 197, 198
Krauss, Mike 301, 307, 311, 315
Kreager, Carl A. 166, 171, 174
Krejsa, Robert 134
Kregel, Jim 258, 263,

266
Kreger, John 198, 203
Kreglow, James J. 71
Kreglow, Julius 79
Kremblas, Frank 199, 201, 202, 207
Krerowicz, Mark 298, 302, 306, 312
Kress, E.S. (Ted) 179, 182, 185, 187
Krieger, George 159, 162
Krill, Bill 312
Krisher, Jerry 178, 183, 186, 191
Kriska, Nicholas 214
Kriss, Frederick 191, 193
Kriss, Howard 79, 81, 82, 87
Kriss, Frederick 189, 194, 199
Kromer, Paul S. 126, 133, 134
Kromer, Philip F. 71
Kromer, Paul 125, 131
Krstolic, Raymond 215, 218, 223
Krueger, Frederick 195, 198, 203
Kruse 58
Kruskamp, Harold 79, 87
Kubicek, Louis 86
Kuchka, John M. 187, 190
Kuczek, Jeff 320
Kuhn, Dennis A. 123, 126, 131
Kuhn, Kenneth 266, 271, 274
Kuhn, Richard 247, 250, 255
Kuick, Donald O. 158, 163
Kuick, Stanley J. 155
Kuijala, Walfred 94
Kull, Herbert 98
Kulpinski, John J. 163
Kumerow, Eric 306, 312,
Kumerow, Eric 314, 320, 322
Kumler, Karl 215, 218 223
Kunow, Walter 67, 70
Kunsa, Joseph 243
Kupec, C.J. 262
Kuri, Mike 314, 320, 322, 327, 330
Kurtz, David W. 219, 222, 227
Kurz, Ted 247, 250
Kuszmaul, Greg 338, 343
Kutler, Rudolph J. 63, 66, 71
Kutsche, Arthur 94, 99
Kuyper, William E. 139, 142
Kuzma, Thomas G. 139, 141, 142
Kuzuma, 137
Kwiatkowski, Dan 286, 291
Kyle, George S. 63, 66

-L-

Labun, Nick 278, 283
Lachey, Jim 298, 302, 306, 312
Lachey, Ron 327, 330
Lacksen, Frank 74, 79
Ladwig, Eric 223
LaFountaine, Sean 315, 319, 323, 326
Lago, Gary 255, 258, 263
Laine, John T. 131, 134, 139
LaJeunesse, Omer 91, 94, 99
Lakin 54
Lamb, Steven 287
Lambert, Fred 222
Lambert, Howard 210, 215, 218
Lamka, Donald 250, 254, 258
Lancaster, George 235
Landsittel, Thomas 238
Landsnals, Linda 190
Lane, Garcia 296, 298, 302, 306
Lanese, Mike 302, 306, 312, 314
Lang, Bob 278
Lang, Mark 271, 274, 279, 282
Lang, Robert A. 66
Lang, Robert 270, 275
Langenkamp, Max 343
Langermaier, G. 207
Langguth, Elmer 70
Langhurst, James 127, 130, 135
Langley, Victor 296, 298
Lantry, Mike 261, 262, 265, 267, 269, 270
Lapuh, Edward 247
Larkins, Richard C. 87, 90, 95
Larson, Harry E. 90
Laser, Joel 279, 287
Lashufka, Gregory 234
Lashutka, Gregory 226, 231
Laskey, William 222, 227, 230
Laskey, Derwood D. 123, 126
Laskoski, Richard 215, 218
Laskowski, Richard 223
Laughlin, James 279, 282, 287, 290
Laurence 31
Laurenson, Bill 335
Lauterbach, Ronald 222
Lavelli, Dante 143
Law, Ty 342
Lawson, Byron 323
Lawson, Gene 315
Lawton 37
Lawrence 23, 25, 31
Lawson, Gene 307, 311
Lazetich, Milan 150
Leach, Rick 273, 278, 281, 283, 285, 286
Leach, Scott 302, 306, 312, 314, 320
Leadbeater, Arthur 118
Lease, Tom 322, 327, 330, 335, 338
LeBeau, Richard 199, 201, 202, 205, 207
LeClaire, Laurence E. 174, 179, 182
Ledman, Kenneth 194
Lee, Ben 287, 290, 296, 298
Lee, Byron 302, 306, 312, 314
Lee, Biffy 19
Lee, Dante 330, 335, 338, 343
Lee, Darryl 302, 306, 312, 314, 320
Lee, Felix 282
Lee, Louis 230, 235, 238
Legacki, Norman 227, 235
Legette, Burnie 331, 334, 339, 342
Leggett, David 178, 183, 186, 189, 191
Lehman 54
Lehman, Ernest 146
Lehr, H.E. 17
Lehr, John 214, 219
Leith, Jerry 203, 206, 210
Lemirande, Mike 291, 295, 299, 301
Lemley 63
Lemon, George D. 87
Lentz, Charles W., Jr. 163, 166, 169, 171
Leo, Thomas 178
Leonard 16, 17, 29
Leoni, Mike 283, 286, 291
Leoni, Tony 283, 286, 291
LeRoux, Arthur N. 147, 150
Leslie, Kent 235
Lessner, Don 311, 315, 323
Lett, Franklin 110
Lewandowski, Phil 301, 307, 311
Lewis, Mike 342
Levenick, Thomas 287, 290
Levine, Louis 118, 123, 126
Lewis, D. King 107
Lewis, Darrell 330
Lewis, Doyle 290, 296, 298, 302
Lewis, Kirk 267, 270, 275, 278
Lewis, Mike 331, 339
Leyburne 39
Lickovitch, Gary 320, 322,

327, 330,
Lickovitch, Gary 335
Lieberman 46
Liffiton, Jack K. 110
Lige, Mike 338
Light, James 287
Lightburn, Robert 106, 111
Lightner 55, 58, 63
Lilienthal, Robert 191, 194
Lilja, George 283, 286, 291, 295
Lille, Robert 271
Lilley, Alexander S. 12
Lillie, R. 279
Lillie, Walter I. 115
Lillvis, Gary 263, 266, 271
Lincoln 23, 25, 31, 58, 63
Lincoln, James H. 115, 117, 118, 123
Lincoln, Paul M. 13
Lind, Jack 119
Lindauer 63
Lindenfeld, Dick 251
Lindner, James 207, 210, 215
Lindsay, Harold 91, 94
Lindsay, Jean 130
Lindsey, Kelvin 290, 296, 298, 302, 306
Lindsey, Leon 223, 226, 231
Lindsay, Rock 278, 283, 286
Linhart, Dr. 19
Lininger, Jack 154, 162, 165, 167, 170
Linjak, Bill 146
Linkins, Arthur 135
Lintol, John F. 150, 155, 158
Lipaj, Cyril 143
Liptak, Steve 106
Lippert, Elmer 258, 263, 266
Lishewski, Rick 312, 314, 320
Lister, Robert 210, 215, 218
Little, Earl 342
Little, George 70
Livorno, Joseph 103, 106
Lloyd 19
Lockard, Harold C. 134, 139
Lockwood, R.S. 17
Loell, J.L. 31, 33
Loft, John 295, 307
Logan, Jeff 271, 274, 277, 279, 281, 282
Logan, Randolph 254, 259, 262
Logan, Richard 170, 175, 178
Logas, Phil 315
Logue, Ben 301, 307, 311
Logus, Phil 307, 311
Lohr, Wendell 119, 122, 127
Loiko, Alex 118
Long, David 255
Long, Norm 262
Long, Paul 327, 330, 335, 338, 343
Long, Thomas N. 63, 66
Long, William 239, 241, 242, 247
Longer, Robert 223, 231
Longman 25, 27, 29
Longo, Gene 312
Looby, Terry 331
Loofbourrow 46
Lopes, Troy 335
Lord, James 199
Lord, John 199, 207
Lott, John 299, 301
Loucks 51
Louis, Jason 338, 343
Lousma, Jack 198, 203
Lousman, Jack R. 195
Love 29
Lovell, Eric 339, 342
Lovell, Robert 219
Lovette, John H. 70, 75, 78
Lowdermilk, Kirk 298, 302, 306, 312
Lowry, Orlando 296, 298, 302, 306
Luby, Earle B. 115, 118,
123
Lucente, John 298, 302
Lucki, Martin 255
Luckino, Angelo 111
Ludwig, Dean 179
Ludwig, Paul 183, 186, 191
Luke, Steven 263, 266, 271
Lukens, Joe 290, 296, 298, 302
Lukens, William 266, 271, 274, 279
Lukz, Frank 95, 98, 103
Lukz, Joseph 251
Luna, Carlos 330
Lund, Donald A. 142, 145, 147, 150
Lundstrom, Al 215
Lusk 55
Lusk, Homer D. 66
Luther, William 126, 131
Lutomski, Harry J. 115
Luttner, Kenneth 250, 255, 258
Lutz, Travis 327, 330, 335, 338
Lyall, James M. 259, 262, 267
Lyles, Rodney 295, 299, 301, 307, 311
Lynch, John 243
Lynch, Scott 335, 338, 343
Lynn, George 135, 138, 143
Lyons, Douglas 218, 223
Lyons, Mike 339
Lykes, Robert 226, 231, 234
Lytle, Richard 86
Lytle, Rob 269, 270, 273, 275, 277, 278

-M-

Maag, Charles 127, 130, 135
Maag, Dennis 338
Maaker 23
MacConnachie, William 139
MacCready, Derek 322, 327
MacDonald W. 143
MacDougall, William J. 139
Machinsky, Francis 186, 191, 193, 194
Maciejowski, Ronald 247, 250, 255
Mack, Carl 66
Mack, Richard 263, 266, 271
Mack, Thomas 227, 230, 235
Mackall, Rex 275, 278
Mackie, Douglas 279, 282
MacKenzie, Doug 262, 267
Mackey 16, 17
Mackey, Douglas 287
Mackey, Fred C. 71, 74, 79
MacGinnis, C. 55
MacGinnis, D. 55
MacPhee, William 195, 198, 203
Madar, Elmer F. 131, 139, 142, 157, 158
Madden, Bill 326
Madden, Francis L. 102
Maddock 23, 25
Maddock, James A. 190, 193, 195, 197, 198
Mader, Gerald 222, 227, 230
Madigan, Mike 312
Madro, Joseph 122, 127, 130
Madsen, Edgar 70
Maentz, Scott 210, 214, 219
Maentz, Thomas 190, 195, 197, 198
Maggied, Sol 114, 119, 122
Maggs, Bob 302, 306, 312, 314, 320
Magidson 39
Magidsohn 37
Magoffin 29
Magoffin, P.P. 31, 33
Magruder, Professor 19

Mahaffey, Howard 150
Mahle, Andy 335
Mair, Peter 238, 243
Maki, Wesley 206
Malashevich, M. 107
Malinak, Tim 278, 283, 286
Mallory, Curt 326, 331, 334, 339
Mallory, Douglas 307, 311, 315, 319, 323
Mallory, Mike 301, 307, 311, 315
Maloney, Frank 210, 214, 219
Maloney, Michael 331
Maloney, Pat 326, 331, 334, 339, 342
Maltinsky, Paul 146, 151, 154
Malveaux, Felman 339, 342
Mamula, Charles 218, 221, 223, 226
Manalakas, George 134
Manchester, Frank 71
Mandel, Dave 311, 315, 323
Mandel, Scott 315, 323
Mandich, James 243, 245, 246, 249, 251
Mandich, John 275
Mandula, George 95, 98, 103
Mangiamelle, Richard 215, 218, 223
Manifold, Matt 320, 322
Mann, Jerry 167
Mann, Robert 157, 158, 160, 161, 163
Manning, Joe 298
Manning, Paul 326, 331, 334, 339, 342
Manning, Rob 296
Mans, George 210, 214, 219
Mans, John 210
Mantho, Henry 150
Mantz, Jerry 170
Manuel, Kenneth 94
Manuel, Warde 319, 323, 326
Manyak, John 175, 178, 183
Manz 175
Marcellus, Phillip 142
Marciniak, Jerry 198, 203, 206
Marcinick, Gary 312, 314
Marck, Elmer 73
Marcovsky, Abe 94, 99, 102
Marcum, John 222, 227, 230
Marek, Elmer 74, 77, 79, 82
Marek, Marcus 290, 296, 298, 302
Marendt, Tom 258, 263
Marenot, Thomas 266
Marinaro, Joe 339, 342
Mark, Martin 118
Marker 25, 27
Marklev, J. Charles 94
Markray, Triando 301, 307, 311
Marino, Victor 122, 127, 129, 130
Marion, A.W. 66, 67, 69, 71
Marion, P.E. 70
Marion, Robert L. 187, 190, 195
Marker, Jim 146
Markley 39
Markley, Hoss 41
Marks 17, 19
Marold, John 170, 175
Marquart 27
Marr, Joseph E. 71
Marsh, Doug 283, 285, 286, 291
Marsh, Jack 247, 255
Marsh, George C. 90
Marsh, Tim 302
Marshall, Alex 323, 326, 331, 334, 339
Marshall, Clyde 154, 167
Marshall, James 202, 207
Marshall, R.W. 163
Martens, Todd 331, 334
Martin, Daryl 296
Martin, Earl 138
Martin, Edward D. 13
Martin, John 194, 199, 202, 327
Martin, Paul 210, 215, 218
Marts, R.J. 63, 65, 66
Marzonie, George A. 118, 123
Mascio, Joe 151
Mason, Glen 250, 255
Masoner, Robert 119, 127
Massie, Edmund 135
Mastako, Frank 122
Masters, Rick 311
Masterson, Kevin J. 259, 262
Matheny 46, 50
Matheson, Robert K. 179, 182
Mathis, Lou 258, 263, 266
Matlock, Bill 314, 320, 322, 327
Matte, Thomas 207, 210, 213, 215
Mattey, George 162, 167, 170
Matton, Doug 323
Matulis, Charles 190, 195
Maturo, John 163
Matus, Paul 143
Matz, James 202, 207, 210, 215
Maulbetsch, John 44
Maurer, George J. 118
Maves, Earl C. 145, 147
Mayer, Richard 222
Mayes, Rufus 239, 242, 245, 247
Maynard 23
Mazaika, John 95
Mazeroski, David 271
Mazza, Joel 338
McAfee, John 103, 106, 111
McAleer, Pat 222, 227
McAllister 33, 35
McAllister, David 327
McBrayer, Tom 263, 271
McBride, Jennings 83, 86, 91
McBride, John R. 254, 259
McCafferty, Don 135, 138, 143
McCaffrey, Tom 246
McCall, Edward 296
McCarthy 37
McCarthy, Jeff 296
McCarthy, Patrick 199
McCarthy, Tim 71, 74, 79
McCarty 37
McCarty, Bill 146
McCauley, William 14
McClain 37, 39
McClain, Mark 262
McCleery, Tony 167
McClelland, Don B. 163, 166, 171
McClintic, William 102
McClure 25, 43
McClure, Donald 82, 87, 90
McClurg, Bum 23
McCombs, Alton 103
McConnell, Arden L. 87, 89, 90
McConville, Jim 314
McCormick, Robert 138, 143
McCormick, Tom 302, 306
McCormick, Wilson 86
McCoy, Earnest 86
McCoy, Ernie 198, 203
McCoy, James 327
McCoy, John 231, 234. 239
McCoy, Mac 41
McCoy, Matt 330, 326, 331, 335, 338, 343
McCoy, Richard 246, 251, 254
McCrath, L.E. 99
McCray, Malcolm 314
McCray, Mike 312, 314, 320, 322, 327
McCullough, Robert 167, 170, 175
McCune 46
McCutcheon, Gary 271
McDonald 31, 46, 50
McDonald, Duncan B. 179, 182, 187, 190
McDonald, James 114, 119, 121, 122
McDonald, Kenneth 227
McElheny, Norman 151
McEndree, Randy 274

McFaddin, Robert L. 139
McFarland, Dave 296, 302
McGee, Tony 331, 334, 339, 342
McGinnis 19
McGinnis, Robert 151, 154, 159
McGlade, Dave 296
McGrath 51
McGregor 55, 58
McGugin 19, 23
McGuire, Donald T. 99, 107
McGuire, Travis 343
McIntyre, Andree 307, 311, 315, 319
McIntyre, John 182
McIntyre, Kent C. 70, 75, 78
McKee, David 282, 287
McKee, Robert 210, 214
McKenna, James 154
McKenney, John 103
McKenzie, Reginald 251, 254, 259
McKinney, William 98, 103
McKinley, G. William 187
McKoan, Joseph H. 190, 195
McLaughlin, Donald 235
McLaren 19, 21, 23
McLean 17
McLeese, Ronald 222
McLellan, Jenova 335
McLenna, Bruce 217, 219
McMillan 39, 40
McMillan, Neil 41
McMillen, Harold 79
McMurry, Preston 199, 207
McMurtry, Greg 323, 326,
McMurtry, Greg 331
McNamer 63
McNamer, Arthur 71
McNeill, Edward D. 155, 158, 161, 163, 166
McNitt, Gary 206, 210, 214
Mcngeau, David 214
McPhee, Riley 301
McPherson, James 203, 206, 210
McPherson, Professor 19
McQuade, Bob 146
McQueen, Therone 338, 343
McRae, Benjamin 210, 214, 217, 219
McThomas, Greg 334, 339, 342
McTier, Dave 296
McWilliams, R. 166, 171, 174
Meacham, Howard 71, 79
Meade, Jeff 338
Meade, John 287, 290
Meads, G. Edgar 187, 190, 195
Medich, David 282, 287, 296, 298
Medich, Rob 296
Meeks, R.C. 41
Meese, Frank E. 78, 83, 86
Megaro, Anthony 282, 287, 290, 296
Megregian, Michael 126, 134
Mehaffey, Howard 126
Meinerding, Wesley 231, 234, 239
Meinke, Dick 146
Melchiori, Wayne F. 174, 179, 182
Meldman, Leonard 99, 102
Melita, Tom 278, 283, 286
Melnyk, Mike 295, 299, 301, 307, 311
Melzow, William 131, 134, 137, 139
Mercer, Brian 301, 307, 311
Meredith, Dave 295, 299, 301, 307, 311
Merrell, Bob 154
Merrell, James 178, 183
Merryman, Dick 247
Meshloh 58
Messner, Mark 311, 315, 319, 323, 326
Meter, Jerry 278, 283, 286
Metz, Dave 262, 267, 270
Metzger 58
Metzger, Joe 327, 330, 335, 338,
Metzger, Joe 343
Meyer, Jack 126, 131
Meyer, Ted 79, 82
Meyer, Terry 223
Meyers 50, 53, 74
Meyers, Earl J. 110, 115
Mezgec, Mike 343
Michael, Richard 202, 207, 210
Michael, William 191, 193, 194, 197, 199
Michaels 63
Middlebrook, John P. 259
Middleton, Rick 258, 263, 266
Middleton, Robert 215, 218, 223
Midlam, Max 271, 274, 279
Mielke, Robert 230, 235, 238
Mignon, Jamie 339, 342
Mihic, John 301, 307, 311, 315
Miklos, Gerald 243, 246
Milczuk, Henry 150
Miles, Les 267, 270, 275
Milia, Marc 331, 334, 339, 342
Miller 16, 17, 29, 46, 55, 67, 75
Miller, A.R. 71
Miller, Austin S. 139
Miller, Clay 301, 307, 311, 315
Miller, E.P. 66
Miller, Gary 226, 231, 234, 239
Miller, Harold 91
Miller, J.B. 66
Miller, James F., Jr. 78, 83
Miller, James 111, 114, 121, 122
Miller, J.K. 70
Miller, Kent 338
Miller, Nicholas 282, 287, 290, 296, 298
Miller, Robert 99, 102, 106, 111, 114, 119
Miller, Ronald 282, 287, 290, 296
Miller, Ryan 343
Miller, Shawn 339, 342
Miller, Wallace B. 91, 94, 99
Miller, Walter "Kansas" 13
Miller, William 146, 167, 170, 175
Milligan, John 323, 326, 331, 334
Milligan, Robert 187
Milliken, F.H. 63
Milliken, E.C. 63
Mills, Ed 279, 282,
Mills, Leonard 274, 279, 282, 287
Minko, John 214, 219, 222
Mires, David 135
Mirick, Wesley 218, 223, 226
Mitchel, Joe 82
Mitchell 74
Mitchell, Alan 286,291, 295
Mitchell, Anthony 315, 319, 323, 326
Mitchell, C.S. 15
Mitchell, Keith 315, 319, 323, 326
Mobley, Ben 223, 226, 231
Moeller 46
Moeller, Andy 301, 307, 311, 315, 319
Moeller, Gary 215, 218, 223
Mogle, Glenn 307
Moldea, Emil 162
Molenda, Bo 72, 73, 75, 78
Moler, William 79, 82
Molls, Larry 271, 279
Moloney, Robert 122, 130
Momsen, Anton, Jr. 155, 167, 171, 173, 174
Momsen, Robert 170, 173,

175
Monahan, J. Regis 103, 106, 109, 111
Monahan, Thomas 114, 119, 122
Monas, Alfons 127
Mongeau, David 219
Monnot, Dave 330, 335, 338, 343
Monthei, Dennis 238, 243
Mooney, Charles 215
Mooney, Philip K. 142
Moons, Pat 301, 307, 311, 315, 319
Moore 17
Moore, David 215
Moore, Ed 246, 251, 254
Moore, Frank 267, 270
Moore, Jimmy 279, 282, 287
Moore, James H. 82
Moore, Ross 255, 258
Moore, Theodore 335
Moore, Tom 314, 320, 322, 327
Moore, Tony 320, 322, 327, 330, 335
Moorehead 58, 63
Moorhead, Don 244, 246, 249, 251, 253, 254
Moran, John 207
Moran, William 254
Morgan, Dennis 235, 238, 243
Morgan, Eric 330
Morgan, Robert 83, 91, 94
Morgan, Thomas 199, 202, 207
Moriarty, Tim 296
Moritz, Roger 175, 178
Morlock, Emil 179
Morrill, David 298, 302, 306, 312
Morris, Don 314
Morris, Jamie 311, 315, 319, 323
Morris, Rich 312, 314
Morrison, Fred 159, 162, 167, 169, 170
Morrison, Steve 339, 342
Morrison, Steven 266, 271
Morrissey, Ed 41, 43
Morrey, Charles B. 13
Morris, Rich 302, 320
Morrison 46
Morrison, Fred 169
Morrison, Maynard 91, 94, 99
Morrison, Robert L. 139
Morrison, Steve 263
Morrow, Gordon H. 195, 198, 203, 206
Morrow, John M., Jr. 187, 190, 195
Morrow, Ned 131
Morse, James 183
Morton, Greg 267, 270, 275, 278
Morton, Leon 326, 331
Morton, Mike 320
Moseley 58
Moshier 175
Moss, Eric 343
Moss, Tom 291
Mosser, Murray 91
Motejzik, John 151
Motley, Fred 286, 291, 295
Mott, William 183, 186
Mouch, William 243
Mountz, Gregory 255
Mouton, Ken 311, 315, 319
Moxley, Tim 314, 320, 322, 327, 330
Moyer, Chas. P. 86
Mroz, Vincent P. 145, 147
Mrukowski, William 215, 218, 223
Muelder, Wesley W. 155
Muellich, George C. 182, 187
Muhlbach, John 239, 242, 247
Muir, William 219, 222, 227, 230
Muirhead 59, 62, 67
Mulholland, Harry K. 123, 126
Mummey, John 215, 217, 218, 223
Mumford, John 110, 115
Muransky, Ed 291, 295, 299
Murdock, Guy B. 251, 254, 259
Murphy, Loren A. 63, 66, 71
Murphy, Mike 14
Murphy, Robert 263, 282, 287, 290, 296
Murray 62
Murray, Calvin 282, 287, 290, 296
Murray, Charles A. 115
Murray, Dan 283, 291
Murray, Douglas 187
Murray, Vada 323, 326, 331, 334
Musgrave, Doug 331
Musser, James C. 43
Mutch, Craig A. 259, 262, 267
Muzyk, Alexander F. 115
Myers 46, 55, 58, 63
Myers, Bradley 203, 205, 206, 210
Myers, Ray 296, 298, 302
Myers, Robert 183, 201
Myers, Steven 263, 266, 271
Myll, Clifton O. 142, 147
Myrick, Charles 327, 330

-N-

Nadlicki, Mike 31, 334, 339, 342
Nagy, Alex 194, 199, 202
Nagy, John 111
Nakamura, Frank 150, 155
Naples, Carmen 143
Nardi, Richard 114, 119, 121, 122
Nasman, Bert 95, 98, 103
Nate, Jeff 299
Nauta, Steve 275, 278, 286
Navin 50, 55
NcNamer, A.V. 66
Neal, George V. 103, 106, 111
Neal, Tom 291, 299
Needham, Ben 286, 291, 299
Neff, George 146, 151
Neff, Scott 302
Negus, Fred W. 147
Neidert, John 87
Nein, James 231, 234, 239, 242
Neisch 62, 67
Nelms, Spencer 298, 302, 306
Nelson 54
Nelson, Chico 330, 335, 343
Nelson, Dave 338
Nelson, David M. 131, 134, 139
Nelson, Douglas 235, 238, 243
Nelson, Harry 103
Nelson, Sim 301, 307, 311
Nelson, Winfred 107, 110, 115
Nemecek 50, 55
Nesbitt 55
Nesser, John P. 79, 82, 87
Nesser, William 87, 90
Nestich, Martin 186
Neubreckt, K. 87
Newcomer, Mark 231, 234
Newell, Pete 246, 251, 254
Newell, William 159, 162, 167, 170
Newlin, John 127, 130, 135
Newlum 50
Newman, Harry 93, 94, 99, 101, 102
Newman, Harry, Jr. 206, 210
Newton 29
Newton, F.R. 31
Nichlaus, F.E. 87
Nichols, Donald M. 163
Nichols, Roy 327, 330, 335
Nicholson, John E., Jr. 123, 126, 131

1964 GAME   COLUMBUS, OHIO

1971 GAME   ANN ARBOR, MICHIGAN

Nichols, John H. 66, 71, 74
Nichols, Harold 135
Nichols, Ray 322
Nicholson, G.A. 78
Nicholson, George, Jr. 83
Nickerson, Max 75, 78, 83
Nickerson, Norman J. 118, 123, 126
Nicolau, Dave 286, 291, 295
Nicolls, Donald 154
Nida 63
Niederhauser, Don 194
Niekamp, Kevin 343
Niemeyer, Bryan 343
Nielsen, Brad 242, 247, 250
Nielsen, Paul 123, 126, 131
Nieman, Tom 251, 254
Niesz, Dale 207, 210, 215
Niswander, Brent 312
Nixon, Thomas 255, 258, 263
Noble, Tyrone 342
Noel 53
Nolan, Delbert 219
Nopper, Arnold 66
Norcross 25, 27, 28, 29
North, D.W. 87
Nosker, William 127, 130, 135
Noskin, Stanton 203, 206, 209, 210
Nosky, Richard 186
Nulf 174
Nunley, Frank 230, 233, 235, 238
Nussbaum, Lee 191
Nussbaumer, Robert J. 145, 147, 155
Novak, Joseph 135, 138
Novak, Richard 283, 286
Novotny, George 111, 119, 122
Nyland, H.Z., Jr. 78, 83
Nyren, Marvin R. 190, 195, 198, 203

-O-

Oade, J. 75, 78
Oates, James 231, 234
Oberlin, R.W. 58, 63, 66
Ochmann, Ward 94
Ochs, Lilburn M. 118
O'Cain, Timothy 287, 296, 298
O'Connor, Michael 307
O'Dea, Stephen 154
Odom, Tim 302, 306, 312
Odom, Wilbur 323, 326, 331
O'Donnell, Joseph 214, 219, 222, 227
O'Donnell, Raymond 235
Oehmann, Ward 99
Offenbecher, Brent 298, 302, 306
Ogunfitidimi, Olatide 315, 319, 323
O'Hanlon, Richard 159, 162, 167, 170
Ohlenroth, William 166, 171, 174
Ohsner, Clarence S. 79, 81, 82, 90
Okezne, Alozie 331
Okulovich, Andy 202
Oldham, Donald L. 174, 179, 182
Oldham, Michael 251, 254, 259
Olds 37, 39
Olds, Frederic C. 115, 118, 123, 126, 131
Oliphant, Marshall T. 98, 101, 103, 106
Olive, Bobby 322, 327, 330, 335
Oliver, Glen 146, 159, 162
Oliver, Russell D. 102, 105, 107, 110
Olken 46
Olm, Fred 203, 206
Olman, Kevin 296
Olshanski, Henry S. 147
Olson, Joel E. 86
Olszewski, Pat 315, 319, 323, 326
Oman, Donald 127, 130
O'Morrow, Pat 320, 322, 327, 330
O'Neal, Calvin 267, 270, 275, 278
O'Neil, Emmett 94
O'Neil, William 94
Oosterbaan, B. 73, 75, 77, 78, 81, 83
Oosterbaan, Bennie (Coach) 165, 173, 205
Oostroot, George 131
Oppermann, James 247, 250, 255
Oppman, Douglas 203, 206
Orazen, Edward 223, 226, 231
Orazen, Michael 231, 234, 239
Oren, Robert A. 142
Orosz, Thomas 282, 287, 290, 296
O'Rourke, James 271, 274
O'Rourke, Larry 263, 271
Ort, Paul J. 66, 71
Ortmann, Charles 165, 166, 169, 171, 173, 174
Orvis, Douglas 198
Orwig, James 86
Orwig, James B. 190, 195, 198, 203
Osbun, Tony 286, 291, 295, 299
Osburn 55
Osman, T. J. 319, 323, 326, 331, 334
Oster, Harvey 87
Osterman, Russell 171, 174, 179
O'Shaughnessey, T. 103
O'Shaughnessy, D. 187
O'Shaughnessy, J.J. 87, 90
O'Snaughnessy, R.E. 179, 182
Otis, Jim 241, 242, 245, 247, 249, 250
Ott, John A. 155
Ott, Richard 227
Ottoman, Louis J. 102
Owen, David G. 195
Owen, Kevin 323, 326, 331, 334
Owens, Mel 283, 286, 291, 295
Oyler, Thomas T. 110, 115

-P-

Pace, James E. 195, 197, 198, 200, 201, 203
Pacenta, James 271, 274, 279
Paciorek, Jim 291
Paciorek, John 307
Pack, Craig 287, 296, 298, 302
Packard, Ralph 71
Pactorek, John 301
Paddy, Arthur 126, 131
Padgen, John 166
Padjen, John 171, 174
Padlow, Max 103, 106
Pagac, Fred 258, 263, 266
Page, Craig 283
Page, Steven 247
Pagelson 17
Palahnuk, Michael 287, 296, 298, 302
Palmer, James 159, 162, 167, 170, 314, 320, 322
Palmer, Jim 302, 306, 312, 327, 330
Palmer, John 226, 231, 234, 239
Palmer, Lowell 67, 70, 75
Palmer, Paul 210
Palmer, Peter 166, 171, 174
Palmer, Richard 138, 143, 159
Palmeroli, John 75, 78, 83, 102
Palomaki, David 206, 210
Pampu, Virgil 210, 214
Paper 54
Paplomatas, James 195

Paquette, Donald M. 118
Parenti, Frank 146
Parfet, William 126
Pargo, Corey 330, 335
Paris, Bubba 291, 295
Paris, William 299
Parker, Albert 218, 223, 226
Parker, C.F. 86
Parker, H.F. 67, 70, 75
Parker, James 189, 191, 193, 194, 199
Parker, Orville 91
Parker, Ray 86, 91
Parker, Roy 83
Parkhill, Thomas 227, 230, 235
Parks, Dan 246, 251
Parks, Ernest 145, 146, 159
Parmelee 37
Parry, Ward 130
Parsons, Richard 263, 266, 271
Partee, Curt 338
Pasch, John 227
Pastorius, Tom 290
Patanelli, Matthew L. 110, 115, 117, 118
Patchel 55
Patchell 58, 63
Patchen, Brian 222, 227, 230
Patchin, Arthur B. 107
Patek, Bob 278
Paterson, G.C. 41
Patillo, Tim 335, 338, 343
Patrick 29
Patrick, H.E. 31
Pattengill 39
Patterson 55
Patterson, Geo. C. 43
Patton, Robert J. 86, 91
Paul, Charles R. 66
Paul, Tito 338, 343
Pauley 55, 58, 63
Pauley, Douglas 287, 296
Paulk, Foster 330, 335, 338, 343
Paulsen, Ron 312, 314
Paulson, Herbert C. 106
Pavey 39, 43
Pavey, Baldy 41
Pavloff, Louis 210, 214, 219, 222
Payne, Aaron 330, 335, 338
Payne, David 283, 291
Payne, Rod 342
Payton, Joel 282, 287, 290
Peach 49, 51
Pearson, Myron 146
Peckham, John 187, 190, 195
Pederson, B.L. 179, 182
Pederson, Chip 278, 286
Pederson, Ernest A., Jr. 110, 115, 118, 123
Peel, James 320, 322, 327, 330, 335
Peggs, Carl 199
Pelini, Mark 320, 322, 327, 330, 335
Pella, G. Roy 182
Penksa, Robert 238, 243, 246
Penn, Trent 298, 302
Penrod, James L. 71, 82
Penvenne, Paul F. 123
Peoples, Shonte 339, 342
Peppe, Louis 95, 97
Perdue, Thomas 210, 215, 218
Pergament, Milton 142
Perini, Pete 159, 162, 167, 170
Perlinger, Jeff 262, 265, 267, 270, 275
Perrin 46, 54
Perry 37,
Perry, Charles 194
Perry, Clarence 271
Perry, Lowell W. 174, 179, 182
Perry, Ronald 210
Perryman, Bob 301, 307, 311, 315, 319
Persky, LesLester 126
Person 25
Petcoff, Boni 58, 63, 66
Peterman, Billy 330
Petersen, William 170, 183
Peterson, Archie 66, 71
Peterson, Donald W. 171, 179
Peterson, John 320, 322, 327, 330, 335
Peterson, L.B., Jr. 90. 95
Peterson, Tom R. 163, 165, 166, 171, 174, 177
Peterson, Tom 150
Petoskey, Fred 99, 102, 107
Petroskey, Jack E. 139, 142
Petoskey, Ted 105
Petro 54, 58
Petroff, Frank 315, 319, 323, 326
Pettit, A.S. 15
Peyton, Leroy 239
Pfister, Mark 302, 306, 312, 314
Phelan, Robin 231
Phelps, Eric 270, 275, 278
Phillips, Clyde 106
Phillips, David 287
Phillips, Edward J., Jr. 118, 126
Phillips, Elmer 158
Phillips, Larry 287, 296
Phillips, Tomas 157, 159
Phillips, Raymond 235, 238, 243
Phillips, William 119, 122
Picard, F.A. 41
Piccinini, James 130, 135
Pickard, Frederick R. 171, 174, 179
Pickens, Jim 270, 275, 278, 283
Pickens, Joe 335, 338
Pierce 29
Pierson, Barry 243, 246, 249, 251
Pietrini, Louis 271, 274, 279
Pighee, John 254, 262
Pillinger, Harry J. 110, 115
Pincura, Stanley 105, 106, 111, 113, 114
Pingree, H.S., Jr. 17
Pintel, Ira 326
Piotrowski, Robert P. 118, 123
Pipoly, James E. 106, 111
Pisanelli, Fred 255, 258, 263
Pitlosh, Max 235
Pitstick, Anthony 255, 258, 263
Pittman, Mark 302
Pitton, Robert 135
Pixley 46, 50, 58, 63
Placas, John 135, 138
Place, Graham 66
Planck 54
Plank, Douglas 263, 266, 271
Plank, Ernest 146, 159
Plantz, John 315
Plate, Todd 323, 326, 331, 334
Plate, Troy 331, 334, 339, 342
Plesha, Robert 214
Podlewski, Arthur 94
Poe, Howard W. 83, 86, 91
Polaski, Michael 242, 247, 250
Poling, Luther 66, 71
Polister, Ed 262
Pollitt, William 242, 247, 250
Pommerening, Otto P. 78, 83, 86
Pond, Allen B. 15
Pond, Irving K. 15
Ponsetto, Joe L. 147, 149, 150, 155, 156
Pont, Johnny 11
Pontius, Miller H. 41, 43, 44
Ponto, Hilton A. 102, 107
Poorman, Edwin B. 83, 86, 91
Pope, Brad 338, 343
Popowski, Bob 301, 307, 311
Poplawski, Thomas 254, 259, 262
Popp, Leslie 171, 174, 179

Popp, Milton F. 82, 87
Porretta, Daniel 223, 226, 231
Porter, David 235, 238, 243, 279
Porter, Douglas 271, 274, 282
Porter, Juan 343
Portsmouth, Thomas 234, 239, 241, 242
Portz 37
Pothoff, William 66, 71
Poulos, Paul 203, 206, 210, 214
Powell 25, 35, 37, 39
Powell, Craig 338, 343
Powell, Greg 299, 301
Powell, Scott 312, 314, 320, 322, 327
Powell, Theodore 263, 266
Powelson, Myron 151
Powers, Bobby 339, 342
Powers, Jerome E. 147
Powers, John 166, 171, 174, 283, 286, 291, 295
Powers, Ricky 334, 339, 342
Powers, Ward 150
Powers, William 239, 242
Prahst, Gary 198, 203, 205, 206
Prashaw, Michael 155
Prather, Pete 271
Pratl, Ron 283
Pratt, Adam 339, 342
Pratt, William 155
Prchlik, Richard 162
Precobb, G.W. 86
Pregulman, Mervin 139, 142
Prelock, Steve 320
Prepolec, John 286
Preston, Fred 79
Preston, James O. 190
Prewitt, Jesse 335, 338, 343
Price, Charles 223, 226
Price, Charles R. 71
Price, Lance 320, 322, 327, 330, 335
Prichard, Thomas 219, 222, 227
Priday, Paul 143
Priday, Robin 154
Priest, Ray 91
Primeau 35
Pritula, William 139, 142, 158, 160, 163
Provenza, Russell 194, 199
Provost, Ted 242, 247, 250
Prusa, Ron 299, 301
Pryor, Cecil 243, 246, 251
Pryor, Ray 231, 234. 239
Przygodski, George 267, 270, 275
Ptacek, Bob 197, 198, 203, 205, 206
Puckelwartz, Wm. 83
Puckolwartz 75, 78
Pullen, Thomas 235, 238, 243
Purcell, George A. 131
Purdum, Claire 94
Purdy 16, 17
Purdy, David 263, 266, 271
Purucker, Norman B. 118, 121, 123, 126
Putich, William 171, 174, 176, 177, 179

-Q-

Quaerna, Jerry 301, 307, 311, 315, 319
Qualls, Larry 247
Quattrone, Joseph 159
Quinn, Clement P. 41, 43
Quinn, Gary 283, 286, 291
Quinn, Thomas 191, 194
Quist, Robert 227

-R-

Rabb, Johnny 115, 116, 119, 122, 130
Rabbers, Norman 155
Rabenstein, Howard 95, 98
Rader, O.W. 66
Rader, Ted 186
Radigan, Timothy 230, 235, 238
Radtke, Michael 242, 247, 250
Raeder, Paul 206, 210, 214, 219
Rahrig, Don 182
Raimey, David 214, 217, 219, 222
Ramirez, Marc 323, 326, 331
Ramser, Richard 191, 194
Rammey 35
Ramsey, Richard 186
Ramsey, Robert 98, 103
Randall, Craig 339
Randall, Greg 301, 307, 311, 315
Randolph, Chuck 267, 270 275
Rane, Frank W. 13
Ranft, Brian 296
Rankin 62
Ranney 23
Ranney-Lillie 35
Raskowski, Leo 79, 82, 87
Rath, Thomas 170, 175, 178
Rather, David E. (Bo) 254, 257, 259, 262
Ratterman, L.F. 107
Ray, David 171, 174, 179
Ray, Ernest 87
Rayford, Elwood 215, 218
Raymond 39, 43
Raymond, Bugs 41
Raymond, Harold 166
Raymond, Henry T. 107
Raynsford, James W. 43
Read 25
Ream, Charles 114, 119, 121, 122
Reboulet, Laverne 87, 90
Rector, Robert 223
Redd, Jack 146, 151, 154
Redden 19, 21, 23
Redden, C. 25
Redden, F. 25
Redman, F.A. 82
Redmond, William 150
Redner 19
Reed, Frank 15
Reed, Samuel 231, 234
Reed, William 79
Reed 71
Reeme 174
Rees, James 143
Rees, Trevor J. 106, 111, 114
Reese, D. 87
Reeves, Jeff 291, 295, 299
Refowski, Steve 331
Regeczi, John 101, 102, 105, 107, 110
Reggans, Walter 339, 342
Reichenbach, James 178, 183, 186, 189, 191
Reichman, Gerson 86
Reid, Brian 315
Reid, Dorle 227
Reid, Lawrence 283, 285, 286, 291
Reilly, Robert 103
Rein, Robert 229, 233, 234, 237, 239
Rein, Russ 307, 311, 315, 319
Reinhold, Mike 301, 307, 311, 315
Reiser 63
Rekowski, Steve 334, 339, 342
Rembiesa, Donald 195, 198
Remias, Steve 107, 110, 115
Remsnyder 27
Renard, Barney 266, 271, 279
Renda, Hercules 123, 126,

Renda, Hercules 131
Rennebohm, R.B. 147
Renner 91
Renner, Arthur W. 147, 150, 155, 156, 157, 158
Renner, Charles 151, 159, 162, 167
Renner, William W. 99, 102, 105, 107, 110, 113, 115
Rentschler, David F. 190, 195, 198
Renwick, William 203
Rescoria, Russ 177, 181
Rescorla, Russell G. 174, 179, 182
Rentschler, David P. 187
Rex, Richard U. 182
Reynolds, David 239
Reynolds, John 238
Rheinschilds 29
Rheinschild, W. M. 33
Rice, Dan 274, 301, 307
Rice, Elliott 255
Rice, Richard 210
Rich, George 78, 83, 86
Rich, Rocco 258, 263, 266
Richards 16, 17
Richards, David 191, 194, 199
Richards, J.D. 17
Richards, John R. 42
Richarsd, Todd 339, 342
Richardson 17
Richardson, Dennis 270, 275
Richardson, Hamilton H. 13
Richardson, Karl 91, 94
Richardson, Kevin 298, 302, 306, 312
Richardson, Max 270, 275, 278, 283
Richey, Frank 135
Richley, Richard 231, 234
Ricketts, Girard 91
Ricketts, Ormonde 217, 218, 223, 226
Ricks, Lawrence 295, 299, 301
Ridder, Fred 312, 314, 320, 322
Ridder, William 226, 231, 234
Riddle 21
Rieck, John A. 110, 115
Riehm, Chris 290, 296, 298, 302
Riemersma, Jay 339, 342
Ries, Richard 227
Rife 46, 47
Rifenburg, Richard 157, 158, 160, 163, 166
Rinaldi, Joseph M. 115, 116, 118, 123
Rindfuss, Dick 222, 225, 227, 230
Rio, Anthony 201, 203, 206, 209, 210
Risk, Robert D. 86
Ritchie, C. Stark 115, 116, 118, 123
Riticher, Ray 183, 186
Ritley, Robert 243, 251
Ritter, Charles A. 182, 187, 190
Ritter, Dave 323, 326, 331, 334, 339
Rivers, Garland 307, 311, 315, 319
Roach, Tom 91
Roach, Woodrow 266, 271, 274
Robbins, J.S. 83
Robbins, Monte 307, 319, 323
Robey 61
Roberts, Bill 296, 302, 306
Roberts, Harris W. 131
Roberts, Jack 210, 215, 218
Roberts, Robert 178, 183, 186
Roberts, Scott 299, 301
Roberts, Vernell 111
Roberts, William 298
Robertson, Bob 271
Robbins, Monte 311, 315
Robbinson, Huemartin 319
Robbinson, James 119
Robinson, Ceroy 320
Robinson, Don W. 139, 142, 155, 158
Robinson, Joseph 279, 282, 287
Robinson, Ortho 171
Robinson, Philip 199, 202, 207
Robson, Charles 186, 191
Roby 58, 62
Roche, Tom 271, 274, 277, 279, 282
Rockne, Knute 72
Rockwell, Tod 67, 69
Rockwall, F. 70
Roderick, H. 83
Rodgers, Nate 299, 301, 307, 311
Rodriquez, Alex 335, 338, 343
Roe, Jack 143, 154
Roe, John 138
Roesch, Karl A. 71
Roesch, Karl O. 66
Roff 58
Rogan, Greg 312, 314, 320, 322, 327
Rogers 37
Rogers, John 66
Rogers, Joseph C. 123, 131, 134, 139
Rogers, R.J. 66
Rogers, Rick 301, 307, 311
Rohrbach, William R. 147
Rohrback, William R. 142
Roman, James 239, 242, 247
Roman, Nicholas 135, 239, 242, 245, 250
Romoser, James W. 106
Ronemus, Thor 175, 178
Roper, William 150
Rosatti 62
Rose, Carlton 295, 299, 301, 307
Rose, H. 78
Rose, James 103
Rose, Milton 87
Roseboro, James 191, 194, 197, 199
Rosema, Robert J. 251, 254, 259
Rosema, Roger 235, 238, 243
Rosen, Andy 127, 130, 135
Rosen, John 138
Rosenthal, S.C. 118
Rosequist, Ted 98, 103, 106
Roshon, Ray 79
Rosofsky, Jacob 71
Ross, Everett 314, 320, 322
Ross, J.G. 66
Ross, Paul 279, 282, 287
Ross, Robert 114, 118
Ross, Tony 271
Ross, William 251, 254
Rosso, George 178, 183, 186
Roth, Michael 95
Rotunno, Michael J. 190, 195, 198
Roush, Ernest 106, 111, 114
Roush, Gary 239, 242, 247
Rowan, Deb 74, 79, 82
Rowland 54
Rowland, James 207, 210
Rowser, John 227, 235, 237, 238
Roy, Chris 335, 338
Royer, John 71
Royer, Mark 312
Rudness, George 107, 110
Rudolph, Colin 323
Ruehl, James 183, 186
Ruhl, Bruce 266, 271, 274, 279
Rumer 55
Rumney 29
Rumney, M.P. 31, 33
Runyan, Jon 342
Rusnak, Kevin 242, 247, 250
Russ, Carl 262, 267,

Russ, Carl 270
Russ, Donald 98
Rutan, Hiram E. 13
Ruth, Babe 72
Rutherford, William 231, 234, 239
Rutkay, Nicholas 119, 122, 127
Rutledge, Tim 327
Ruzich, Steve 170, 175, 178
Ruzicka, Charles 227, 230, 235
Ryan 43
Ryan, Jim 314
Ryan, Prentice 171
Ryan, Robert 151, 154
Ryder, Jack 12
Rye 51
Rye, Harold 49

-S-

Sack, Irving A. 87
Sakupckak, Paul 91
Salmi, Terry 235, 238
Salucci, Ralph 163
Salvaterra, Arnold 131
Salvaterra, Joe 103
Samostuk, Andy 301, 307
Samson, Paul C. 70
Sample, Fred 246
Sampson, Charles 150
Samuels, James 202
Samuels, Tom 91, 94, 99
Sander 233
Sanders, Chris 338, 343
Sanders, Daryl 215, 218, 221, 223
Sanders, Willard 226, 231, 234
Sandman, Russell 82
Sandrock 63
Sansom, Elijah 243, 246
Santora, Ernest 154
Santschi, John 127, 130, 135
Sanzenbacher 33, 35
Sapp, Michael 271
Sarantos, Peter 243, 246, 251
Sarkkinen, Eino 127, 130, 135
Sarkkinen, Esco 122, 127, 130
Sarnacke, Phil 227
Sarringhaus, Paul 138, 141, 143, 154
Sattler, C.L. 87
Sauls, Reginald 155, 171
Saunders, Cedric 335, 338, 343
Saunders, J. 279
Saunders, Robert 320
Savage 17
Savage, Carl M. 99, 102, 105, 107
Savage, Michael 110, 115
Savic, Pandel 162, 167, 169, 170, 175
Savilla, Roland 123, 126, 131
Savoca, James 271, 274, 279, 282, 287
Sawicki, Timothy 279, 287, 290, 296
Saxby 16, 17
Sayers, Peter 135
Scanlon 63
Scannell, Michael 255, 258, 263
Scarberry, William 130
Scarcelli, Jim 301, 307, 311, 315
Scarr 174
Schactel 35
Schachtel 33
Schaefer, Ed 312
Schaeffer, Bill 326, 331
Schaffer 37, 63
Schafrath, Dick 197, 199, 202, 205, 207
Schantz, Fred B. 91
Scharl, James 227
Schear, Herbert 82, 87
Scheffler, Lance 246, 251, 253, 254
Scheiderer, Paul P. 71
Schembechler, Glenn E. "Bo" 11, 245, 249, 257,
Schembechle, Glenn E. "Bo" 281, 291
Schenking, Fred 199, 202
Scherer, Belden 103
Schick, Gary 227, 230, 235
Schieber 37
Schiller, Richard 178, 183
Schilling, John 327, 330, 335, 338
Schimke, Louis 135
Schlichter, Art 285, 287, 290, 296, 298
Schlict, Leo 179, 187
Schlopy, Todd 299, 301, 307, 311
Schmerge, Mark 278, 283, 286
Schmerge, Paul 301, 307, 311, 315
Schmid, Herbert T. 99, 107
Schmidlin, Paul 241, 242, 247, 250
Schmidt, Francis A. (Coach) 108, 117
Schmidt, Joe 296
Schmidt, Paul 210, 214, 219
Schmidt, Robert 227
Schmidt, Walter 79, 82
Schmitt, Roger 219
Schmitz, Jim 251
Schneider, Michael 279, 282
Schneider, Wilbur 138, 143, 159
Schnittker, Max 151, 153, 154, 159
Schoenbaum, Alex 119, 122, 127
Schoenbaum, Leon 138
Schoenfeldt 75
Schoenfeld, J. 78
Scholl, Millard 111
Scholl, Tom 314, 320, 322, 327
Schopf, Jon 210, 214, 219
Schory 27, 29, 31, 33, 34
Schram, Bruce 202
Schram, Fred 253, 255, 257, 258
Schram, Richard 219, 222
Schule 25
Schulist, B.N. 63, 66
Schulist, Bernard 71
Schulte 25, 27, 29
Schulte, Tim 307, 311, 315, 319
Schulte, Todd 307, 311, 315, 319
Schulz 27, 28, 29, 35
Schultz, A.G. 32, 33
Schumacher 51
Schumacher, James 183, 186
Schumacher, Kurt 263, 266, 271
Schumacher, Gerald F. 254, 259, 262
Schuman, Stanton J. 110, 115
Schurrer, Charles 86
Schuster, George 159
Schwartz, Alan E. 147
Schwartz, Brian 279, 282, 287, 290
Schwartzbaugh 43
Schwarze, Bruce 83
Schweinsberger, H. 63, 66, 71
Scott 16, 17
Scott, Dan 258, 263, 266
Scott, Donald 127, 130, 133, 135
Scott, Doug 129
Scott, James 103, 105, 106, 111
Scott, Robert 223
Scott, Virgil 126
Scudder, A. 279
Seabron, Tom 278, 283, 286
Seach, Bill 330, 335
Seal, Paul N. 259, 262, 265, 267
Seamon, David 222
Searle 54
Sears, Harold W., Jr. 110
Secontine, Vincent C. 139, 142
Secrist 33
Sedor, William 138, 143
Segrist 16
Segrist, C. 19
Segrist, J. 19
Segrist, L.T. 17

Seiber, James 235
Seifert, Richard 255, 258, 263
Seiffer, Ralph E. 66, 71, 74
Seilkop, Kenneth 207, 210
Selby, David 207
Selby, Sam 87, 90, 95
Selby, Paul 143
Seltzer, Holbrooke 134
Selvaggio, Rob 302, 312
Semeyn, Roy A. 107
Sengel, Rudolph 134
Sensanbaugher, Dean 146, 162
Sensibaugh, Michael 247, 250, 254, 255
Sessa, Mike 301, 307, 311
Sexton, James 130, 135
Sexton, Joseph 127
Sexton, Walter E. 259, 262
Seyferth, John F. (Fritz) 251, 254, 257, 259
Seymour, Paul C. 251, 254, 259, 262
Seymour, Philip 243, 246, 251, 254
Shackson 46
Shafer 43
Shaffer, Jay 312, 314, 320, 322
Shaffer, Bernard 122
Shafor, Ralph 41
Shakarian, George 115, 118
Shannon, Edward J. 190, 195, 198
Shannon, James 242
Shannon, Richard 159, 162, 167
Shantz, Fred B. 83
Sharp, Scott 327, 330, 335
Sharp, William 250
Sharpe, Ernest 235, 238, 243
Sharpe, Philip E. 134, 139, 142
Shatusky, Mike 195, 198, 203
Shaw 19
Shaw, Donald 251
Shaw, Jeff 295
Shaw, Lee C. 102, 107
Shaw, Robert 138, 141, 143
Shaw, Vincent 291, 299
Shea, Sylvester C. 94, 102, 107
Shedd, Jan 186, 191, 194
Sheets, Steve 343
Shehee, Greg 338
Sheiber 39
Sheldon 31
Shelton, John 178
Shemky, Robert W. 139, 142
Sherrick, Paul 327, 330, 335, 338
Sherwood, Marion 86
Shevrin, Marc 301, 307
Shields, Kenneth H. 182, 187
Shifflette, Don F. 71, 79
Shimko, Marty 301, 307, 311, 315
Shingledecker, W. 191
Shoaf, Mike 322, 327 330, 335, 338
Shoenfeld, John 83
Shomsky, Joseph G. 182, 187, 190
Shorts 19, 21, 25
Showalter, Mike 320, 322, 327, 330
Shuster, Robert 210
Shuttlesworth, E. Ed 257, 259, 261, 262, 265, 267
Shwayder, Irving 134
Sickels, Quentin 150, 158, 163, 166
Sidell, Rolo 183
Siebert 58
Siegenthaler, Wes 320, 322, 327
Siegle, Don J. 118, 123, 126
Siferd, Charles 135
Sigler, William 147
Sigman, Al 193, 198
Sigman, Lionel A. 195
Sikkenga, Jay 91, 94, 99
Simione, John 122, 127, 130, 135
Simkus, Arnold 222, 227, 230
Simmons, Chris 315
Simmons, Jason 330, 335, 338, 343
Simon, Charles 271, 279
Simon, Dave 301, 307, 311
Simon, Richard 250, 255, 258
Simons 17
Simpson, Cornelius, 326
Simpson, Neil 323, 331, 334, 339
Simpson, Steve 296, 298, 302
Simrall, Harrison 94
Simrall, James O. 86, 91, 93
Simpkins, Ron 281, 283, 286, 291
Sims 19
Sims, A.H. 83
Sincich, Al 301, 307, 311
Sinclair, Jim 323, 326
Singer, Oscar A. 99, 102, 107
Sipp, Warren 238, 243, 246
Sirosky, Dennis 243, 246
Sisinyak, Eugene 198, 203, 206
Sites, Bob 315, 319
Sites, Rick 315, 319
Sivinski, Daniel 254
Skala, James 171, 174
Skeele 63
Skelly, Jack 183
Skene, Doug 326, 331, 334, 339, 342
Skepenak, Greg 334
Skillings, Vincent 282, 285, 287, 290, 296
Skladany, Thomas 266, 271, 279
Skorput, Ante 339, 342
Skrepenak, Greg 323, 326, 331, 339
Skvarka Bernie 175, 178, 183
Sladany, Tom 274
Slade, Thomas A. 257, 259, 262, 267
Slager, Richard 159, 162, 165, 167
Slagle, William 186
Slater, Roger 86
Slaughter, David R. 90
Slaughter, E.R. 62, 67, 70
Slemmons, Robert H. 71, 79
Slezak, David 210, 219
Slicker, Richard 191
Sloan, Gary 255
Slough, Gene 146
Slough, Herb R. 71, 74, 79
Slusser, George 143
Slyker 46, 50, 55, 58
Smale, Harry 171, 174
Small, Irwin 166
Smeja, Rudy M. 134, 139, 142, 147
Smick, Dan 116, 118, 123, 126
Smith 37, 39
Smith, Brian 343
Smith, Brion 342
Smith, Bryan 339
Smith, Butch 242, 247
Smith, Bruce 247, 250, 254
Smith, Carroll 170, 175, 178
Smith, Cedric 299
Smith, Cedrick 45
Smith, Doug 302, 306, 312, 314
Smith, Dwight 312, 314, 320, 322, 327
Smith, Earl 41
Smith, Francis L. 122, 127
Smith, Frank 122, 127, 130
Smith, Garrett 311
Smith, Gerald 203, 205, 206, 210, 214
Smith, Gilbert 171, 174
Smith, Greg 327, 330, 335, 338, 343
Smith, Hack 41
Smith, Harley 154
Smith Harsen A. 86

Smith, Inwood 111, 114, 119
Smith, Ivan 91, 94
Smith, Jack E. 103, 105, 106, 111, 155
Smith, James 273, 275, 278
Smith, Jeffrey 210, 214, 219
Smith, Joseph 287, 290, 296, 298, 302
Smith, Keith 218
Smith, Kerry 295, 299, 301, 307
Smith, Kevin 291, 295, 299
Smith, Larry 231, 234
Smith, Lasker 339, 342
Smith, Lewis 278
Smith, Mark 322
Smith, Mike 251, 254, 275, 278
Smith, R.G. 71
Smith, Richard 95, 97, 98, 103
Smith, Robert 134, 239, 242, 247, 250, 335, 343
Smith, Rod 330, 335, 338, 343
Smith, Roosevelt 281, 283, 285, 286, 291
Smith, Rudy 239. 242
Smith, Stephen 227, 230, 235
Smith, Steve 295, 299, 301, 307
Smith, Ted 266, 271, 274
Smith, Tony L. 254, 259,
Smith, Tony L. 262
Smith, Walter 334, 339, 342
Smith, William A. 123, 126, 131
Smith, Willie 198, 203
Smithers, John A. 115, 118
Smurda, John 258, 263, 266
Smykowski, Scott 319, 323, 326, 331
Sneddon 46
Snell, Matthew 218, 223, 225, 226
Snider, Eugene 190, 198, 203
Snow 19
Snow, Carlos 322, 327, 330, 338
Snow, M.B. 17
Snow, Neil 17, 21
Snyder, Larry 223, 231, 234
Snyder, Lawrence 66
Snyder, Tom 151, 161, 162, 167
Soboleski, Joseph R. 155, 158, 160, 163, 166
Sobolewski, John 239, 242, 247
Sobsey, Solomon 115, 123
Sobul, Sanford 66
Soehnlen, Mark 323, 326
Soelberg, Carlton 94
Sohacki, Edward 150
Sola, Olavi 95
Sollom, Ken 323, 326, 331, 334, 339
Soltis, Edward 314
Sommers, Karl 191, 194, 199
Soodik, Eli 107, 110
Sorenson, Eric 243
Sorensen, Thorwald 91
Souchek, Donald 166
Souders, Cecil 143, 146, 159
Southern, Clarence 66
Southward, Damon 339
Sowers, Ray B. 139
Spacht, Ronald 210, 214, 219
Spahn, Jeff 262, 267, 270
Spahr, William 223, 226, 231
Spangler, Rich 302, 306, 312, 314
Sparkman, R. Wayne 219, 222, 227
Sparks 51
Sparks, Cliff 49
Sparma, Joseph 217, 218, 223
Spearman, Clinton 254, 259, 262
Spears, Jerry 122, 127, 130
Spears, Thomas 186, 191, 194
Speed 55, 58, 63
Spellman, Alonzo 330, 335, 338
Spencer, George 159
Spencer, John 322, 327
Spencer, Marc 319, 326, 331
Spencer, Tim 296, 298
Spencer, Royce 235, 238, 243
Spencer, Tim 298, 302
Spichek, Willie 210
Spidel, John 198, 203, 206
Spielman, Chris 312, 314, 320, 322
Spiers 50, 55, 57, 58
Springs, Rod 279, 281
Springs, Ronald 282, 287
Spychalski, Ernie 197, 199, 202, 207
Squier, George 78, 86
Sriver, Robert E. 187, 190, 195
Stablein, Brian 327, 330, 335, 338, 343
Stablein, Chris 327, 330, 335
Stabovitz, Chester C. 115, 118
Stackhouse, Ray 146, 159
Stagg, Amos Alonzo 291
Stagg, Frank 227
Staker, Loren 138, 143
Stamman, Carl 70, 75
Stamos, John 210, 213, 214, 219
Stanford, Tad C. 179, 182, 185, 187
Stanley, Bernie 218, 223, 226
Stanley, Buster 342
Stanley, Sylvester 331, 339
Stanton, Edward C. 118, 123
Stapelton, Chris 331, 334, 339, 342
Stapp, William 171
Stark, Randy 326, 331, 334, 339
Staroba, Paul 246, 251, 253, 254
Staveren, Howard M. 259
Stawski, Willard 210, 214, 219
Staysniak, Joe 314, 320, 322, 327, 330
Stechkle, W.C. 17
Steel, Harry 63, 66
Steele, Dale 190
Steele, Harold O. 70
Steele 58, 62, 67
Steen, Kenneth 123
Stefan, Terry 275
Steger, Geoffrey C. 259, 267, 270
Steger, Herbert 62, 65, 67, 70
Steinberg, Don 138, 143, 154
Steinke, Al 86, 91
Steinle 17
Steinmeyer, William B. 190, 195
Steketee 46, 47, 53, 54, 55, 57, 58
Steketee, Jack N. 126
Stenberg, Robert P. 139, 142
Stephens, Larry 210, 215, 218
Stephens, Paul 320
Stephens, Tim 296, 298, 302, 306
Stephenson, Curt 270, 275, 278, 283
Stephenson, Jack 130, 135, 138
Sterry 19, 23
Stetson, Parker F. 107
Stetten, Maynard 198, 203, 206

OSU Football Dateline

1890 - Varsity football began, and the Buckeyes won their opener at Ohio Wesleyan, 20-14. OSU lost its other three games by a combined score of 96-10. Alexander Lilley was the first head coach.
1897 - The first game with Michigan was played and the Wolverines won, 34-0.
1899 - The Buckeyes won their first state title and recorded their first unbeaten season at 9-0-1. OSU outscored its foes 179-0 in the nine wins and tied Case, 5-5.
1902 - Fred Cornell wrote the words to "Carmen Ohio" on the back of an envelope as the team returned from Ann Arbor following an 86-0 loss. It was officially recognized as the alma mater in 1916.
1904 - E.R. Sweetland became the school's first "all-year" football coach. Ticket prices ranged from 25 cents to a dollar for "deluxe" games with Michigan and the Carlisle Indians.
1910 - The first spring practices were held on Mondays and Tuesdays. That same spring, the Athletic Board approved a $5 all-year, five-sport student pass. A student season football pass cost $2.50.
1912 - Ohio State joined the Western Conference, which later became the Big Ten. With five minutes remaining in the Penn State game and OSU trailing 37-0, coach John Richards took the Buckeyes off the field because of alleged rough play, and PSU was awarded a 1-0 win.
1915 - Varsity manager William A. Dougherty wrote the fight song "Across the Field." The song was dedicated to coach John Wilce and was first performed at the Illinois game.
1916 - Ohio State won its first Western Conference title, The Buckeyes set a school scoring mark in defeating Oberlin, 128-0.
1919 - The Buckeyes gain their first win over Michigan, 13-3.
1921 - Ohio State made its first trip to the Rose Bowl but lost to California to finish 7-1.
1922 - Ohio Stadium opened and the Buckeyes defeated Ohio Wesleyan, 5-0. The stadium was officially dedicated two weeks later against Michigan.
1934 - The tradition of an annual Captain's Breakfast began in which all former grid captains are invited to a breakfast and welcome the current team captains.
1936 - The Ohio State Marching Band performed "Script Ohio" for the first time at the Indiana game.
1942 - The Buckeyes won their first national championship. Head coach Paul Brown led the team to a 9-1 record and the Big Ten title.
1943 - With the game apparently ending in a 26-all tie, Ohio State and Illinois left the field. But the teams were called back 20 minutes later when it was discovered the Illini were called for a penalty on the Buckeyes' final play. With little of the crowd remaining, John Stungis kicked a 27-yard field goal for a 29-26 win.
1944 - Les Horvath became the school's first Heisman Trophy winner.
1947 - Ohio State was afforded three plays after time had expired due to Northwestern penalties and came away with a 7-6 victory in Ohio Stadium.
1949 - OSU beat California, 17-14, for its first Rose Bowl win.
1950 - Vic Janowicz won the Heisman Trophy and the famous "Snow Bowl" game with Michigan was contested.
1951 - Woody Hayes began his 28-year tenure as head coach. His initial Buckeye squad finished 4-3-2.
1954 - Hayes led OSU to the national championship and perfect 10-0 season, beating Southern Cal in Rose Bowl.
1955 - The first athletic scholarships were available at OSU.
1956 - Offensive guard Jim Parker won the Outland Trophy.
1957 - The Buckeyes were national champions after a 9-1 campaign and a Rose Bowl win over Oregon.
1958 - Defensive tackle Jim Marshall scored both Buckeye touchdowns in a 14-14 tie with Purdue. He returned a blocked punt and interception for scores.
1960 - Following a 7-0 win over Michigan, Head Coach Woody Hayes held an impromptu practice at dusk with Paul Warfield and Matt Snell south of the stadium. After a third place Big Ten finish, he was concerned about the 1961 season.
1961 - Ohio State finished 8-0-1, defeated Michigan, 50-20, won the Big Ten and was named national champion by the Football Writers. The school's faculty council voted to reject Ohio State's Rose Bowl bid.
1963 - Ohio State defeated Michigan in Ann Arbor, 14-10. The game was delayed a week as the nation mourned the death of President John F. Kennedy. The attendance of 36,424 was the smallest at Michigan Stadium in 20 years.
1968 - Ohio State's last undefeated (10-0), national championship team culminated the season with a 27-16 win over Southern Cal in the Rose Bowl.
1969 - A season-ending loss to Michigan ended OSU's 22-game unbeaten streak.
1970 - Jim Stillwagon won the Outland Trophy and the initial Lombardi Award as the Buckeyes finished 9-1, losing only to Stanford in the Rose Bowl. Ohio State ended a three-year span with a record of 27-2.
1971 - Artificial turf was installed in Ohio Stadium at a cost of $533,544.
1972 - Tailback Archie Griffin came off the bench in his debut against North Carolina and rushed for a then-Ohio State record 239 yards.
1973 - Offensive tackle John Hicks won the Outland Trophy and Lombardi Award and finished second in the Heisman voting.
1974 - Griffin won the Heisman Trophy, becoming the fifth non-senior to win the award.
1975 - Griffin became the first two-time winner of the Heisman Trophy. He led the Buckeyes to their conference-record fourth straight Rose Bowl.
1977 - OSU won a share of its sixth straight Big Ten title and ended the six-year span with a 58-10-2 record.
1978 - Tom Cousineau was the first player taken in the NFL draft.
1979 - A 17-16 loss to Southern Cal spoiled a perfect mark (11-1) in Earle Bruce's first season as head coach.
1980 - Illinois' Dave Wilson passed for an NCAA record 621 yards and six touchdowns, but the Buckeyes held on for a 49-42 win.
1981 - Art Schlichter completed 31 of 52 passes for 458 yards — all OSU records — but the Buckeyes fell to Florida State.
1984 - Keith Byars rushed for a school-best 274 yards and scored five TDs in leading the Buckeyes to a 45-38 win over Illinois. OSU won the conference championship and earned a Rose Bowl trip.
1985 - The first night game in Ohio Stadium history — thanks to portable light standards — saw the Buckeyes defeat Pittsburgh, 10-7. Flanker Mike Lanese became the first OSU gridder to win a Rhodes Scholarship. Iowa comes to Columbus ranked No. 1, but OSU sends the Hawkeyes home with a 22-13 loss.
1987 - OSU becomes the first Big Ten team to play in the Cotton Bowl and defeats Texas A&M. Linebacker Chris Spielman won the Lombardi Award.
1988 - John Cooper was named the school's 21st head football coach.
1989 - Ohio State celebrated its 100th season of intercollegiate football. The Buckeyes overcome a 31-0 deficit to win 41-37 at Minnesota. OSU competed in the Hall of Fame Bowl, its 10th different postseason bowl appearance.
1990 - Natural grass returned to Ohio Stadium. Robert Smith gained 1,126 yards to break Archie Griffin's OSU freshman rushing record.
1991 - Thanks to 5,000 new bleacher seats, home (654,500), average home (90,500) and single game (95,357 vs. Iowa) attendance records fell.
1993 - OSU recorded its best record since 1979 by going 10-1-1, capturing a share of the Big Ten title and winning the Holiday Bowl.
1994 - The Buckeyes defeat Michigan 22-6, ending a six-game winless streak against the Wolverines.

Steuk, William 331, 339, 342
Stewart 51
Stewart, G.D. 17
Stewart, Geoff 335
Stewart, Patrick 335
Stewart, Roland 186
Stewart, Thomas 102
Stewart, William E. 71
Stieler, Stephen 210
Stienecker, C. 78
Stienle 16
Stier, Mark 239, 242, 247
Stillwagon, James 245, 247, 250, 255
Stinchcomb, Gaylord 49, 50, 53, 55
Stincic, Thomas 238, 243, 246
Stine, William 206, 210, 214
Stinespring, Harry 99
Stites, Bob 315, 323
Stites, Rick 315, 323
St. John, Scott 327
Stock, Robert 226, 231
Stoeckel, Donald 186, 191, 193, 194
Stokes, Tommy 343
Stoll, Claude 94
Stolp 29, 31
Stone, Charles 99
Stone, Edward A. 107, 110
Stora, Joe 146
Storer, Gregory 271, 274, 279, 282
Stottlemyer, Victor 239, 242, 247
Stoudenmire, Malory 255
Stoughton, Brian 343
Stovall, Jack 198
Stover, A. 279
Stover, Dutch 41, 43
Stowe, John 239, 242, 247
Strabley, Mike 267, 270, 275
Straffon, Ralph A. 166, 171, 174
Strahine, Michael 279, 282, 287, 290
Strait, Lynn 210
Straka, Mark 263, 266
Stranges, Tony 151
Straub, G.H. 83
Straub, Harvey 86, 91
Strausbaugh, James 127, 130, 135
Strauss, Richard 163
Strenger, Rich 291, 295, 299, 301
Stribe, Ralph 171, 174, 179, 182
Strickland, Phillip 247, 250, 255
Striegel, Daniel 219
Stringer, Korey 343
Strinko, Greg 267, 270, 275
Strinko, Steve 262, 267, 270
Strobel, Jack 214, 219, 222
Strong, David A. 126, 131
Strong, Terry 255, 258
Strozewski, Richard J. 174, 182, 187
Stuart 17, 27, 29
Stuart, Henry 206
Stuart, Johnny 57, 58
Studabaker 63
Stukey, Brian 314
Stukey, Todd 312
Stump, Wilson 111, 114, 119
Stungis, John 145, 146, 159, 162
Sturges, Ray E. 147
Sturtz, Karl 167, 170, 175
Styles, Lorenzo 343
Suber, Vince 247
Sukup, Milo F. 123, 126, 131, 134
Sukupchak, Paul 86
Sullivan 33
Sullivan, John 298, 302, 306, 312, 314, 320, 322, 327
Sullivan, Mark 274, 279, 282, 287, 290, 296, 327
Sullivan, Mike 314, 320, 322, 339, 342
Sullo, Dominic 83
Summers 39
Summeers 37
Sunderhaus, Dale 218, 223
Sundra, John 87
Surina, Cyril 79, 82, 87
Sutherin, Donald 192, 193, 194, 199, 201, 202
Sutherland, G. 166, 171
Sutkiewicz, Rick 315, 319, 323
Swan 27, 62, 67
Swan, Bob 254
Swank, Thomas 271
Swanson, Robert 155, 206
Swanson, Robert G. 107
Swartz, Donald 183, 186, 191
Swartzbaugh, Jack 146
Swearengin, Julian 339, 342
Sweeley 19
Sweeley, Everett 23
Sweeley, Redner 21
Sweeney, Larry 295, 299, 301, 307
Sweeney, Paul 135, 138
Sweet, Cedric C. 110, 115, 117, 118
Sweetland, E.R. (Coach) 26
Sweitzer 50
Swift, Thomas 150
Swinehart, Rodney 157, 159, 162, 167, 170
Sygar, Richard 230, 233, 235, 237, 238
Sykes 16, 17
Syring, Richard 206, 214
Sytek, Jim 198, 203, 206
Szabo, Tom 258, 266
Szafranski, Roger 270, 275, 278
Szara, Gerry 270, 275, 278, 283
Szydlowski, Ron E. 259, 262, 267
Szymanski, Richard 219, 222, 227

-T-

Tabacca, Jernoe 239, 242
Tabachino, Bob 301, 307, 311, 315
Tabener, Joe 167
Tageson, William 219, 222
Taggart, Ed 306, 312, 314, 320
Takach, Thomas 251
TaTabkacs, Michael 178, 183, 186
Talcott 17
Tandjourian, R. 171, 174
Tangeman 21
Tanner, Charles C. 71
Tanski, Victor 98, 103
Tarr, Robert 82
Tatum, Jack 250, 255
Tatum, John 245, 247
Tatum, Rowland 296, 298, 302, 306
Tayler 55
Taylor 46, 50, 55
Taylor, Alvin 282, 287, 290, 296
Taylor, Billy 249, 251, 254, 255, 259
Taylor, Charlie 57, 58
Taylor, Dorian 339, 342
Taylor, L.H. 83
Taylor, Lonnie 259
Taylor, Michael 315, 319, 323, 326, 331
Taylor, Mike 251, 254, 256, 257, 259
Taylor, Russell E. 87, 90, 95
Taylor, T. 53
Taylor, Tom 143
Taylor, Walter 338, 343
Teague, Marvin 255, 263
Tech, Karl 291, 299
Tedesco, Dominic 275, 278, 283
Teeter, Mike 319, 323,

Teeter, Mike 326, 331
Teetzel, C.T. 17
Teifke, Howard 146, 159, 162, 167
Templeton, David 159, 162, 167
Teninga, Walter H. 155, 163, 165, 166, 169, 171
Tennant, Byron 227, 235
Ternent, William 175, 183
Terry, Carl 130
Tessmer, Estil 94, 99, 107
Teuscher, Charles 203
Theis, Franklyn 191, 194, 199
Thibert, Steven 307, 311, 315, 319, 323
Thies, Wilford 103, 106
Thisted, C.E. 75, 83
Thom, Leonard 130, 135
Thomas 17, 39
Thomas, Alfred S. 139
Thomas, Aurelius 194, 199, 202
Thomas, David 210
Thomas, Earl 111, 114
Thomas, James 159, 167, 170, 175
Thomas, Joe 103, 106
Thomas, John 238, 243, 246, 267
Thomas, John E. 259, 262
Thomas, Pat 314, 320, 322, 327, 330
Thomas, Professor 19
Thomas, Richard 178, 183
Thomas, Robert 131, 134
Thomas, Russell 146, 151, 154
Thomas, Will 231, 234, 239
Thomson 25
Thomson, Geo. C. 41, 43
Thompson 37, 58
Thompson, Ed 274, 279
Thompson, Homer 330, 335
Thompson, Kenneth 191, 194, 199, 271
Thompson, Monty 263
Thompson, President 19, 61
Thompson, Robert 291, 295, 299, 301
Thone, Franklin 79
Thornbladh, Robert 259, 262, 267
Thornton, Richard 186
Thornton, Robert 183. 189, 191
Thrower 23, 25, 27
Thrush, Jack 330, 335, 338, 343
Tidmore, Samuel 207, 213, 215, 217, 218
Tillman, Buster 343
Tilmann, Michael 339, 342
Tilton 19
Tilton, Westwater 21
Timberlake, Bob 222, 225, 227, 229, 230
Timko, Richard 239
Timm, Robert F. 174, 179, 182
Tingley, David 210, 218
Tinker, Horace C. 123, 126, 131
Titas, Frank 243, 246, 249, 251
Tinkham, David J. 174, 179, 182
Tobik, Andy 127, 130, 135
Tolford, George 210, 215, 218
Tomagno, Chelso 107
Tomak, Ted 302
Tomasi, Dominic 155, 158, 160, 163, 166
Tomczak, Mike 298, 302, 306, 312
Toneff, George, 151, 162, 167, 170
Toomer, Amani 342
Topor, Ted 174, 177, 179, 182
Topp, E. Robert 179, 182, 187
Torbet, Roy H. 41, 43
Torok, James 327
Torrance, James 111
Torzy, Mark 278, 283, 286
Totzke, H.G. 78
Totzke, John H. 86
Tovar, Steve 330, 335, 338, 343
Townsend 23
Townsend, Brian 323, 326, 331, 334, 339
Toy, Chris 330
Traber, Pete 270
Trabue, Jerry 191
Tracy 31
Tracy, F.S. 62
Trapuzzano, Robert 247, 250
Traugott, Alan 158
Traupe, Eric 326, 331, 334
Trautman, Red 41, 43
Trautwein, William 167, 170, 175
Treat 39
Trepanier, Edwin 263
Trgovac, Mike 286, 291, 295
Triplehorn, Howard 107, 110
Triplett, Todd 299, 301
Tripp, Welborne 334
Trittipo, John 194, 199
Trivisonno, Joseph 194, 199, 202
Trogan, Angelo, E. 139,142
Troha, Richard 247, 250
Trombetti, Raymond 79,
Trosko, Fred 123, 125, 126, 128, 129, 131
Troszak, Douglas 259, 262, 267
Trott 50, 55, 58
Truitt, Darrell 270, 275
Trump, Jack 147
Truskowski, Joe 78, 86, 91
Truster, Jerry 223, 231
Tuba, Jeff 319, 326, 323
Tucci, Amel 122, 127, 130
Tucker, Curtis J. 259, 262, 267
Tuffin, Brian 320, 322
Tumpane, Pat 262, 267, 270
Tunicliff, William 210, 214, 217, 219
Tupa, Tom 312, 314, 320, 322
Tureaud, Kenneth 210, 214, 219
Turner, Edward 94
Tuttle, Jerry 151
Tuttle, George 87
Twining, Robert 163
Tyrer, James 207, 210, 215

-U-

Uhjelyi, Joseph 90
Uhlenhake, Jeff 312, 314, 320, 322, 327
Ujhelyi, Joe 87
Ulevitch, Herman H. 123, 126
Ullery, Jack 74, 79, 82
Ullman, Wm. S. 70
Ulmer, Ed 215, 218
Unger, William 94, 218, 223
Unverferth, Donald 225, 226, 229, 231, 233, 234
Urban 16, 17
Urbanik, William 239, 242, 247, 250
Uridil, Leo 74, 79, 82
Urquhart 19
Usher 46, 47, 53, 54, 58
Uteritz 57, 58, 62, 65, 67
Utz, John 296
Uzis, Alfred R. 190

-V-

Valek, Vincent 123, 126
Valpey, Arthur L. 115, 118, 123
Van Blaricom, Kirk 227
VanBlaricom, Paul 235
VanBlaricom, Robert 95, 98, 103
Vanderbeek, Mike 342

Vanderleest, Rob 342
Vandervoort 62, 67
VanderZeyde Ray 182, 187
VandeWater, C. 117, 118, 123
VanDyne, Yale 326, 331, 334, 339
Vanderleest, Rob 339
VanFossen, Jesse 231
Van Dyne, Rudd 210, 214
Van Heyde, George 87
Van Horn, Douglas 226, 231, 234
Van Mater, Howard 114
Van Ness 29
Van Ordan 54, 58, 62
VanPelt, James S. 195, 197, 198, 201, 203
Van Raaphorst, Richard 217, 218, 223, 225, 226
Vanscoy, Jerry 215
Van Scoyk, E.N. 63, 66
Van Summern, J.S. 142
Van Summern, R. 166, 171
VanTongeren, Rick 262
Van Wagoner 51
Vargo, Kenneth 186, 191, 193, 194
Vargo, Thomas 231, 234
Varner, Martin 95, 98, 103
Varner, Thomas 207, 210, 215
Vaselenak, John 179
Vauchinich, Mike 97, 98, 103
Vaughn, Harry 39, 43
Vaughn, Jon 326, 331, 334
Vavroch, John 203
Vavroch, William 175, 178. 183
Vecanski, Milan 250, 255, 258
Vercel, Jovan 259, 262, 267
Verdova, Alex 154, 159, 162, 167
Verhoff, Jack 186
Vernier, Robert W. 142, 158
Veselenak, John 182, 187, 190
Vial, A. Burgess 123, 126
Vicic, Donald 191, 193, 194, 199
Vick 46, 49, 51, 54, 67
Vickers, Tim 335
Vickroy, William 135, 138, 143
Vidis, Henry 58
Vidis, Martin 98, 103, 105
Vidmer, Richard 235, 237, 238, 243
Viergiver, John D. 107, 110, 115
Virgil, Bryan 291
Vitale, John 311, 315, 319, 323, 326
Vittek, Paul 127
Vogel, Robert 215, 218, 221, 223
Vogele, Jerry 270, 275, 278
Vogelgesang, Don 207, 210, 215
Vogelgesang, James 106
Vogler, Terry 279, 282, 287
Vogler, Tim 274, 279, 282, 287
Volk, Richard 229, 230, 233, 235, 238
Voll, Ken 320, 322
Volley, Ricardo 279, 282, 287, 290
Vollmar, James 206
Vollmer, William E. 126, 131
Volzer 50, 55
Von Derau, John 90
VorenKamp, Richard 187, 190
Vuchinich, Michael , 106
Vujevich, Steve 335
Vuocolo, Michael 219

-W-

Wable, Robert 194, 199
Wachter 54
Wadhams, Timothy 243, 251
Wagner, Dave 302
Wagner, David 202, 207
Wagner, Jack 170, 175, 178
Wagner, Jim 179
Wagner, Van 47
Wagnoner, John 320, 322, 327
Wahl, Allen 166
Wahl, Charles 150
Wahl, Robert Allen 155, 171, 174
Waite 16, 17
Wakefield, Richard 250, 255, 258
Walbolt, George 154
Walden, Robert 231, 233, 234, 237, 239
Walder, Harold 83
Waldroup, Kerwin 342
Walker 25, 46, 55
Walker, Alan (Cowboy) 259
Walker, Arthur D. 179, 182, 187, 190
Walker, Barry 302, 306, 312, 314, 320
Walker, Derrick 315, 319, 323, 326, 331
Walker, Gordon 82, 87
Walker, Jack 307, 311, 315, 319
Walker, John 206, 214, 219
Walker, Marcus 334, 339, 342
Walker, Mike 323
Walker, Trey 326
Walker, W.P. 19
Walkup, Mos. K. 87
Wall 67
Wall, Kenneth 243, 246
Wallace 58
Wallace, Brian 326, 331, 334, 339
Wallace, Coleman 326, 331, 334, 339, 342
Wallace, Jack 210, 215, 218
Wallace, Robert 151
Wallace, Zeke 291, 295, 299
Wallenhurst, Douglas 231
Waller, Francis 114
Walls, Grant 206, 210, 214
Walsh, Christy 72
Walsh, Leo 199
Walter, David 207
Walters 27
Walters, Niles 223
Walters, Trey 323
Walther, Richard 175, 178
Walther, L.R. 66
Walton, Tim 330, 335, 338, 343
Wambold, Ed 154
Wandersleben, Tom 286, 291
Wandke, Richard 1 5 1 ,
Wangler, John 283, 286, 291, 295
Wansack, Andy 130
Ward 43
Ward, Carl 230, 233, 235, 237, 238
Ward, Christopher 271, 274, 279, 282
Ward, David H. 190
Ward, Jack 217
Ward, James 214, 219, 222
Ward, Willis F. 102, 105, 107, 110
Wardley, Frank L. 142
Ware, Dwayne 326, 331, 334, 339, 342
Warfield, Paul 217, 218, 223, 225, 226
Warner, Donald R. 259, 262, 267
Warner, Duane 207, 210, 215
Warner, Geoff 330, 335
Warner, Glenn 72
Warner Glen "Pop" 291
Warner, Jason 330
Warner, Stormy 327
Warns, James 115
Warth, Mark 291
Warwick 27

Washington, Alvin 282, 287, 290, 296
Washington, Dennis 331, 334, 339, 342
Washington, Greg 301
Washington, Martin 238, 243, 246
Washington, Sanford 291, 299
Washington, Vincent 315, 323, 326
Waslik, Nicholas 114
Wasmund, Wm. 33, 35, 37
Wassmund, James 191, 194, 199
Wasson, Harold 58, 63, 66
Wasylik, Nicholas 113, 117, 119, 121, 122
Watkins 37
Watkins, E.H. 66, 71
Watkins, Jene 210, 215
Watkins, Ra-Mon 323, 326
Watkins, Robert 178, 183, 185, 186, 189, 191
Watters, Thomas 219
Watson, Otha 287, 290
Watson, Shawn 323, 326, 331
Watson, Thomas 154, 167, 170, 175
Watts, E. D. 63
Watts, Harold 147, 149, 150, 155, 158
Watts, R.S. 66, 71
Waugh, Charles 247, 255
Waugh, Thomas 279, 282, 287, 290
Weadock 51
Weaver 50, 55, 58
Weaver, Buck 57
Weaver, David 186, 191, 193, 194
Weaver, J. Edward 90, 95, 98
Weaver, J.H. 103
Weaver, William 82
Webb, Phil 307, 311, 315, 319, 323
Weber 17
Weber, Gary 283, 286, 291
Weber, Marwood A. 131
Webber, H. 75, 78, 83
Webber, W. 75, 78
Wedebrook, Howard 119, 122, 127, 130
Wedge, Robert 238, 243, 246
Weed, Thurlow 183, 186, 189, 191
Weeks 19, 23, 27
Weeks, Graver 21
Weeks, Harrison 22, 25, 29
Weeks, W. 19, 23, 25, 36
Weiche 55
Weil, David 315, 319, 323, 326
Weiland, Jeffery 266, 274
Weiman 54
Weinmann, Tom 243, 246
Weisenburger, Jack 150, 155, 158, 160, 161, 163
Weiss 50, 55
Welbaum, Thomas 119, 122, 127, 130
Welborne, Tripp 323, 326, 331
Welch, George 147
Weldy, Ronald 210
Welever, Watson 98
Wells 37, 39
Wells 145
Wells, Rex C. 147
Wells, Richard 227, 230, 235
Wells, Robert L. 107
Wells, S.M. 41
Wells-Funkhouser 35
Wells, Stanfield 38
Welz 17
Wendell 25
Wendler, Harold 66, 71, 73, 74
Wendt, Emerson 119, 122
Wendt, Eric 342
Wendt, Merle 109, 111, 114, 116, 119
Wenner 39
Wentworth, Peter 307
Wentz, Burke 71, 74
Wentz, William 202, 207, 210, 213, 215
Weprin, Abram 82, 87
Werner, Irving 103
Werner, Mark 243, 246, 251
Wersel, Timothy 255, 263
Wertz, George 162, 167, 170
West, Alfred L. 259
West, Edward 114, 119
Westfall, Robert B. 128, 131, 133, 134, 137, 139
Weston 51
Weston, Daryl 271
Westover, Louis W. 99, 102, 107
Westwater 19
Wetzel 35
Wetzel, Damon H. 103, 106, 109, 111
Weyers, John 150, 155
Wharton 19
Wheatley, Tyrone 339, 342
Wheeler, Alan 267
Wheeler, Jack 85, 86, 91, 93, 94
Wheeler, Jack C. 187
Wheeler, Lewis 147
Whetstone, Robert 186, 194
Whinnery, Glenn 106
Whisler, Joseph 157, 159, 162, 165, 167
Whitaker, Larry 207, 210
White, Brent 315, 319, 323, 326, 331
White, Captain 21
White 62, 67
White, Claude 122, 127, 130, 135, 137
White, Gerald 307, 311, 315, 319
White, H.S. 70
White, H. 19
White, Jan 247, 249, 250, 255
White, John T. 156, 158, 160, 163
White, John 143
White, M. 19
White, Paul G. 139, 141, 142, 157, 158, 161
White, Rick 275, 278, 283
White, Robert 201, 202, 205, 207, 209, 210, 243, 246, 251
White, Stan 249, 250, 253, 255, 258
White, Terry 312, 314
White, William 312, 314, 320, 322
Whiteford, Dave 270, 275
Whitehead, Stuart 122, 127, 130
Whitfield, David 242, 245, 247, 250
Whitledge, John 307, 311, 315
Whitmer, Doug 302, 306, 312
Whittle, John D. 78, 83, 86
Wible, Cal 154
Wiche 50
Wickes 17
Wickter, Larry D. 126, 131
Widdoes, Carroll C. (Coach) 149
Widdoes, Dick 165, 167, 170, 175
Widman, John C. 86, 91
Wieman, Elton "Tad" 81
Wiese, Robert L. 141, 142, 145, 147, 155, 158
Wiggens, Lawrence 263
Wikel, Howard 147
Wilce, John W. 46, 65, 85
Wilcher, Thomas 301, 307, 311, 315, 319
Wilcox, John 171
Wilder 55
Wiley, James 219
Wilhite, Clayton 230, 235, 237

Wilhite, James 243, 246
Wilkins, Dwight 262
Wilkins, F. Stuart 155, 158, 163, 166
Wilkinson, Dan 338, 343
Wilks, William 178, 183
Willaman, Sam S. 90
Willaman, Willie 41, 50, 53, 55
Willard, Lou 343
Willard, Robert 266
Williams, Albert 146
Williams, David 183, 186, 187, 191
Williams, Derek 283
Williams, Everett 91
Williams, Gary 287, 290, 296, 298, 302
Williams, Gerald H. 187, 190
Williams, Joseph 114, 119
Williams, Kyron 278
Williams, Lee 191, 194, 207
Williams, Mark 330, 335, 338, 343
Williams, Norman 335
Williams, Otis 323, 326, 331, 334, 339
Williams, Quentin 130, 135
Williams, R.J. 83, 86
Williams, Randy 302
Williams, Raymond 191
Williams, Ronald M. 179, 182, 187
Williams, Shad 255, 263
Williams, Steve 320
Williams, Tim 326, 331, 335, 338, 343
Williams, Timothy 319, 323, 330
Williams, Tracy 319, 323, 326
Williams, Virgil 283, 286,
Williamson, Ivan 94, 97, 99, 101, 102
Williamson, Richard 238, 243
Williamson, Walter L. 259, 262, 267
Williman 74
Willingham, John 311, 315, 319, 323
Williott, Louis 266, 271, 274
Willis, Leonard 271, 273, 274
Willis, William 143, 145, 146, 151
Williston 63
Willner, Gregg 278, 281, 283, 285, 286
Wills, Ralph 91, 94
Wilson 19, 21, 46, 51, 54, 59, 63
Wilson, Bill 296
Wilson, Clifford 199, 207
Wilson, Don A. 106
Wilson, Donald 91, 98
Wilson, Franklin 87
Wilson, J.B. 71
Wilson, Jack 159, 162, 167, 170
Wilson, John F. 66
Wilson, John L. 131
Wilson, Mike 299, 301, 307
Wilson, Tug 19
Wiltse, Robert 150
Windle, Gary 231
Wine, Raymond L. 182, 198, 203
Wingert, Charles 95
Wink, Jack S. 145, 147
Winrow, Jason 330, 335, 338, 343
Winston, J. Leo 94, 99
Winters, Charles 342
Winters, Paul C. 71
Winters, Samuel 154
Wiper 47, 58
Wiper, D. 46, 50, 55
Wiper, H. 46, 50
Wiragos, Lewis 87
Wise, Clifford C. 134, 142
Wisniewski, Irvin 158, 163, 166, 169, 171
Wisterman, John M. 66, 71
Wistert, Albert A. 131, 134, 139, 142
Wistert, Alvin 163, 166, 171
Wistert, Francis M. 99, 102, 107
Wiswell, Owen 79, 82
Witherspoon 67,
Witherspoon, T. W. 174, 177, 179, 182
Wittmer, George 210, 215, 218
Wittman, Julius 170, 175, 178
Woerlein, George 71, 79
Wojtys, Ed 262
Wolery, Scott 271, 279
Wolf, Ralph 114, 117, 119, 121, 122
Wolf, Ronald 167
Wolfe 25
Wolfe, C. 279
Wolfe, Russell 159
Wolff, John S., Jr. 83, 91, 246, 251, 254
Wolgast, Pete 187
Wolter, James R. 166, 171, 174, 175, 179
Wood, Mike 302, 312, 314
Wood, Robert 270, 273, 275, 277, 278
Wood, Rolland P. 63, 66
Woodard 19
Woodard, Allen 334
Woodard, Shawn 335
Woodbury 29
Woodford, Tony 278
Wooding, Peet 210
Woodlock, John 326, 331, 339
Woodmore, Derek 301
Woodruff, Charles 66
Woodruff, Mike 296
Woods, G.C. 71
Woodward, Paul 222, 227
Woolfolk, Butch 291, 295, 299
Woolley, Edwin 243, 246
Wooldridge, John 302, 306, 312, 314, 320
Woolf, Scott 302
Worden, Dirk 239, 241, 242, 247
Work 29
Workman 29, 53, 58,
Workman, Hoge 61
Workman, N. 55
Workman, Harry 55, 63, 66
Workman, H.A. 31
Workman, Vince 314, 320, 322
Wormser 58
Woromecki, 315
Worstell, Hillis 90
Wortman, Robert 223, 231
Woytek, Louis 134
Wrenn, Robert 19
Wright 37, 39
Wright, Bill 41
Wright, David 255
Wright, Ernest 207, 210
Wright, Harry T. 110, 115
Wright, Kenneth 227, 230, 235, 238
Wright, Ward 154
Wuellner, Richard 119, 122, 127, 130
Wuerfel, Joshua 331, 339, 342
Wunderli, Greg 286, 291
Wyer, P.H. 87
Wymer, D. 279
Wynn, Herbert 135
Wynn, Philip 210

-Y-

Yaap, Warren E. 142
Yanz, John 219, 222
Yanz, Richard 243
Yanz, Richard 235, 238
Yards, Ludwig 103, 106, 111
Yarano, Dan 299, 301
Yearby, William 227, 230, 235
Yedinak, Martin 235
Yedinak, Michael 158
Yerges, Howard F., Jr. 146, 150, 153, 155, 157, 158, 160, 161,

Yerges, Howard S., Jr. 163
Yingling, Walter 79, 82, 87
Yoder, Mike 327
Yonclas, Nicholas 223, 226, 231
Young, Don 207, 215
Young, Frank D. 58, 63, 66, 71, 74
Young, James 191
Young, Louis 119, 122, 127
Young, Richard 186, 191
Young, William 82, 87
Youngblood, Dennis E. 155
Yost, Coach 21, 23, 24, 25, 31, 33, 47, 49, 72
Yost, Fielding, Jr. 94, 99

-Z-

Zacharias, Steve 323, 326, 331
Zachary, Jack 206
Zachary, John 198, 203
Zackeroff, Greg 312, 314, 320, 322, 327
Zadworney, Frank 122, 127, 130
Zaenglein, C.M. 63, 66
Zagnoli, Rolle 299
Zalenski, Scott 296, 298, 302, 306, 312
Zanfagna, Donald M. 177, 179, 182
Zangara, Don 154
Zarnas, Gus 114, 119, 121, 122
Zatkoff, Roger 174, 179, 182
Zavistoske, George 130, 135, 138
Zawacki, Charles 194, 199
Zeigler, Andrew 159
Zelina, Lawrence 245, 247, 249, 250, 255
Zendzian, Frank P. 102
Zenkewicz, Trent 339, 342
Zervas, Stephen J. 195, 198, 203
Zetts 255
Zeune, Roger 255
Ziegler, Greg 323
Zielinski, Ernest P. 126, 131
Zielinski, Ron 323, 326, 331, 334
Ziem, Fred C. 115, 118, 123
Zima, Albert 218, 223
Zimmerman, Dick 138
Zimmerman, Gil 301
Zimmerman, Robert 131, 134
Zingales, John 311, 315
Zirkle, Lewis G. 106, 111
Zizakovic, Srecko 314, 320, 322, 327, 330
Zubkus, E. James 210, 214, 219
Zuccarelli, David C. 251, 254, 259, 262
Zuchegno, Albert 127
Zuganellis, George 251
Zuhars, David 202
Zurbrugg, Chris 307, 311, 315, 319
Zuver, Jerry 270, 275, 277, 278

WOODY HAYES REFLECTS

Former Head Coach Wayne Woodrow Hayes, MA'48 (LM), last month addressed the annual meeting of the Columbus Area Chamber of Commerce. An enthusiastic crowd of nearly 1,200 filled the Neil House ballrooms to hear his speech. Some excerpts:

"I've been asked by several newsmen, and I don't say this humorously at all, by newsmen who are my real friends, who are my personal friends, have asked me how I feel toward this entire incident and I haven't told them. That's why I feel sorry that a story was released yesterday that was not to be released until next week. But I didn't work through my secretary or my wife on it and the story was to be released next week in a serial of five issues. I went ahead and gave this man an interview. Evidently, we didn't understand one another.

"That happens occasionally and that story broke today, so a lot of good newsmen who are friends of mine, men like Paul Hornung, Tom Pastorius, Kaye Kessler, the man on the UPI, those fellows who I could confide a story to and I've talked to several times but I could not give the story, I cheated them out of that story. I did not mean to. I'm very, very sorry for that. 'Cause I did not treat them right, but I did not do it purposefully.

"The incident down at Jacksonville was a matter of an instant. It was my attitude not to apologize, 'cause I don't apologize for anything. When I make a mistake, I take the blame for it and go on from there. I've seen too many people who quickly apologize and sorta cop out. I just don't think there are easy ways out of anything like that. And yet, the thing that makes me apologize is this: I feel very, very sorry for it, because of the wonderful people it has affected, my coaches, five of whom are without jobs. And several graduate students. Men with no problems of their own, because they work 14 to 16 hours a day, seven days a week, enormously loyal, yet they do not have a job. So, we've got to help them get jobs. We've got to do that . . .

* * *

"How good a coach is Coach Bruce? He's a great coach. Am I qualified to say? Yes, I know. He coached with us for seven years. He's honorable, he's smart, he's tenacious, he'll work, he'll get the job done, you can be sure of that. Will he make mistakes? Who doesn't? We all make mistakes. Sure, he's not perfect, but he's a mighty fine coach. A man you'll be proud of. My guess is he'll improve on the record that's been established in the last 28 years. Excepting one thing he won't do. My guess is, he will not last as long as the previous incumbent.

* * *

"Do I carry bitterness toward the organization? No, I carry bitterness toward me, because we got that game, we got beaten down there when I thought we were going to win.

"And nobody in this world despises to lose like I do. No one in this world. It's been a failing of mine. It's got me in trouble more than once. But it's also taken a man with mediocre ability and made a pretty good coach out of him. 'Cause I despise to lose.

"How about my attitude toward this university? I've given this university about everything I have. For me to be bitter, I'm bitter at losing, because I thought we had that darn thing coming our way. I'm bitter at losing. In the last two years, I felt we lost games where my luck wasn't what it used to be, 'cause I've always believed in Woody's luck.

"That one we lost against Oklahoma — nothing ever hurt me more than that, because we had that darn thing (won). When I lose a ball game like that, I'm the stupidest coach that ever lived. I am the stupidest coach that ever lived when I blow one like that. And we haven't won some of those close ones, so I paid for it. I paid for it.

"But I'll never take it out on this university because I love it too much. I know what it means.

"You know, when I was a kid, there was only one thing in our home that was important and that was education. That's all. We sacrificed everything for that. My dad nor mother neither had gone to high school. There was no high school in the county. But my dad graduated from college and when he went to high school he went there as a principal. That's the first time he was ever there. From that time on, we were gonna get an education.

"And the wonderful thing about our education was this, and I've tried to hammer it into every player we've had: When you get an education, it's merely an opportunity to see how many people you can help. The implication is, sure you'll make a good living. With an education, how can you miss? But you don't sell it on just making a good living. You think in terms of how many other people you can help that need help, how much better you can help your family, how much broader you can think.

"You know, we've got a crazy expression on our football squad . It's homely, but I hope it's meaningful. It's simply this — since I saw my best friend die of lung cancer, I've liked to use this expression because he smoked too much. I tell my squad this almost every week: 'Put the wrinkles on your brain, not on your face.' 'Cause when you think and learn, you put wrinkles on your brain. When you smoke, you start right here and you put 'em on your face. Don't make that mistake. It's a homely expression but the kids know what we are talking about.

But we're always talking about education. For a man to be looking up, because that's where you get somewhere, never looking down. And this is a great university of ours. I don't know how I can help it, but I guarantee I'll never hurt it . . .

* * *

"Am I bitter? Yeah, losing the darn ball game. Yeah, yeah. And I'll stay that way forever, because I felt we could win it. I thought we played good enough in that game to win and we were the underdog. I love to win when we are underdogs. But we didn't.

But bitterness? Naw, I got what was coming to me. Let's just let it go that way. And let's just have good thoughts for everybody at that University and I said EVERYBODY . . ."

* * *

(These excerpts represent approximately one-fifth of his total speech, which also touched on the loyalty of his players; the importance of a good home life in the development of character of youngsters; how playing to win is the essence of any game; and references to those in the coaching profession who had been inspirational to his career.)

Hayes, after the Bauman incident, rebelled against Buckeye Ken Fritz, who sought to break-up the ensuing battle.

THE END OF AN ERA

This football season which included the 75th battle between Ohio State and Michigan will be forever overshadowed by the unfortunate situation which developed in a post season game between Ohio State and Clemson in the 34th Gator Bowl in Jacksonville, Florida, on December 29, 1978.

Clemson linebacker, Charles Bauman, intercepted an Art Schlichter pass. Dodging Ohio State players as he danced up the sidelines, Bauman was driven out of bounds by Schlichter in front of the Ohio State bench. Millions of TV viewers watched as Coach Woody Hayes grabbed Bauman and slugged him in the throat. Thus ended the 28 year reign of Woody Hayes at Ohio State.

As difficult as it is for anyone to understand such a reaction, Michigan Coach Bo Schembechler had this comment: "It's saddened those of us who have been associated with him as players and coaches. We wouldn't want this to happen. You should take into consideration the enormity of the pressure a coach is under. Sometimes you do things you shouldn't. I know I have." Perhaps the "enormity of the pressure" finally had to be released after 33 years of college coaching. The tragedy is that Hayes' magnificent coaching career ended with such a downturn.

The three-time coach of the year, who was inducted into the OSU Sports Hall of Fame in 1978, was college football's second most successful active coach, behind Alabama's Bear Bryant. His Buckeye teams amassed a 205-61-10 record, and won or shared 13 Big Ten championships, including an unprecedented string of six. His teams won three national championships and he coached 58 All-Americans and three Heisman Trophy winners. During his 33 years in college coaching (including three years at Denison and two at Miami of Ohio) his teams posted a 238-72-10 tally. The record ranks fourth best in NCAA history; only Glen "Pop" Warner, Amos Alonzo Stagg, and Bear Bryant are ahead of him.

Woody Hayes believed in winning, not only on the field, but in life. The few negative qualities of this man seem minor indeed when weighed against his concern for fellow human beings less fortunate than himself. The times he went to Vietnam to visit with men in the Armed Forces, speaking to demonstrating students in 1970, the countless times he stopped in to see patients in hospitals to cheer them up, and many other humanitarian ventures contrast sharply with the anger and frustration which unleashed his temper. For Woody Hayes winning wasn't the only thing, it was everything, and a lonely thing.

Reprinted from First Edition One Game Season, (1978)

THE BIG TEN CONFERENCE

Celebrating 100 years of Intercollegiate Athletics

A meeting of seven Midwest university presidents on January 11, 1895 at the Palmer House in Chicago to discuss the regulation and control of intercollegiate athletics, was the first development of what would become one of organized sports' most successful undertakings.

Those seven men, behind the leadership of James H. Smart, president of Purdue University, established the principles for which the Intercollegiate Conference of Faculty Representatives, more popularly known as the Big Ten Conference, would be founded. At that meeting, a blueprint for the control and administration of college athletics under the direction of appointed faculty representatives was outlined. The presidents' first-known action "restricted eligibility for athletics to bonafide, full-time students who were not delinquent in their studies."

Eleven months after the presidents met, one faculty member from each of those seven universities met at the same Palmer House, and officially established the mechanics of the "Intercollegiate Conference of Faculty Representatives", or "Big Ten Conference" or "Western Conference." Those seven universities were: University of Chicago, University of Illinois, University of Michigan, University of Minnesota, Northwestern University, Purdue University and the University of Wisconsin.

Indiana University and the State University of Iowa were later admitted in 1899. Ohio State joined in 1912. Chicago withdrew in 1946 and Michigan State College (now Michigan State University) was added three years later in 1949. On June 4, 1990, the Council of Presidents voted to make Pennsylvania State University the 11th member of the Conference.

Football and baseball were the most popular sports prior to 1900. Wisconsin won the first two football championships in 1896 and '97. Chicago claimed the first three baseball titles also beginning in 1896. The first "official" sponsored championship event was in outdoor track and field, held at the University of Chicago in 1901. Michigan won from amongst a field of nine teams competing at Marshall Field in Chicago.

Since then, there have been many different athletic events popularized on Big Ten campuses. Some became extremely popular - football and basketball, for example. Others, like boxing, fell by the wayside. After the first Conference champions were named in football and men's basketball, most of the existing men's championships began during the first 20 years of this century. Although women competed in unofficial Conference championships dating back to the 1970s, the first official Big Ten championships for women were sanctioned during the 1981-82 school year. Today the Big Ten sponsors 24 sports, 12 each for men and women.

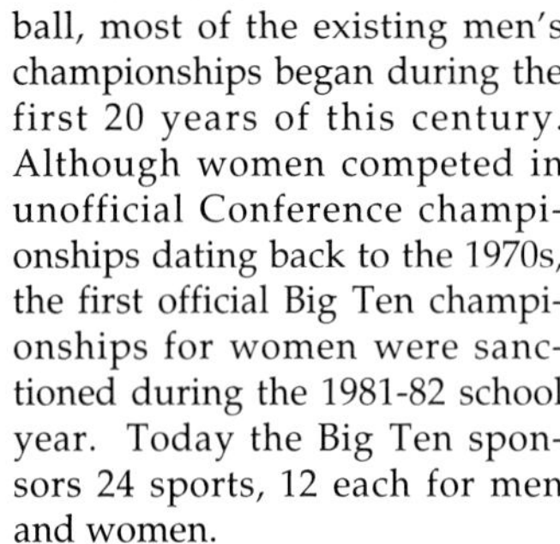

During the 20th century, the Big Ten has seen many stages in the world of athletics: The crisis of rough play in college football in 1906, almost causing its demise; the "Golden Age of American Sport" in the 1920s, where the Big Ten played a major role with all-American heroes such as Red Grange and Bennie Oosterbaan; the emerging Olympic movement (which continues today) where Conference athletes like Jesse Owens and Mark Spitz dominated in such sports as track and swimming; the campus civil unrest of the 1960s, which profoundly affected collegiate athletics; the American fitness boom that began in e 1970s; the emergence of women in collegiate sports in the '80s, including such athletes as track star Suzy Favor; and the intercollegiate athletics reform movement led by university presidents. All this comes to mind when looking back upon the legacy of the Big Ten.

The office of the commissioner of athletics was created in 1922 "to study athletic problems of the various Western Conference universities and assist in enforcing the eligibility rules which govern Big Ten athletics." Major John L. Griffith was appointed as the first commissioner and served in that position until his death in 1944. Kenneth L. "Tug" Wilson, former director of athletics at Northwestern, served from 1944 until he retired in 1961. Bill Reed, an assistant commissioner since 1951, succeeded Wilson until his death in 1971. Wayne Duke became the fourth Big Ten commissioner in 1971 and retired June 30, 1989. Duke was succeeded by current Commissioner James E. Delany on July 1, 1989.

Delany came to the Big Ten with a legal background that also includes having worked as an enforcement representative for the NCAA and served as the Ohio Valley Conference Commissioner for 10 years. Delany oversees the operation of the Big Ten Conference office and its 23-member staff that work out of the Conference office headquarters and meetings center in Park Ridge, Illinois. The Conference office building is 10 minutes from O'Hare International Airport and has been designed to fully service the needs of the Conference's 60-plus different committees, coaches and governance groups that hold over 125 meeting days per year.

From the Conference office headquarters, Delany and his staff manage more than 200 live television events (more than any other sports entity), provide legislative and compliance services to member institutions and their personnel, manage championships and inseason competitive schedules for 24 sports, provide staff services to over 400 coaching and administrative personnel on Big Ten campuses, and service the needs and interests of media and fans.

The 1995-96 school year marks the Big Ten's 100th anniversary. The Conference's history of accomplishments and contributions will be spotlighted, as well as its potential for future success. The anniversary year will provide an opportunity to commemorate the many ways in which the association of Conference member universities have provided opportunities for individuals and teams to contribute not just to the world of athletics but also to society in various different fields.

The Centennial celebration begins with "Big Ten Centennial Week," July 31 through August 2, 1995 in Chicago. The week's highlight will be the Centennial Gala Reception and Dinner at the Palmer House Hilton, where the Big Ten held its first meetings. Garrison Keilor, renowned author and humorist, National Public Radio personality and host of "Prairie Home Companion", will be the distinguished guest speaker for the Dinner. The 50th anniversary of the Big Ten's partnership with the Rose Bowl will also be observed with a celebrity golf outing. The week wraps up with the 24th annual Big Ten Kickoff Luncheon at the Chicago Marriott Downtown on August 2.

The celebration continues throughout the 1995-96 academic year as Big Ten institutions host special Centennial events on their own campuses. Some of these events will take place in conjunction with football games, Homecoming celebrations and other campus happenings.

February 8, 1996 is the actual date of the Big Ten Conference's 100th anniversary and a Conference-wide celebration is planned to honor the Conference's birth date. Celebration plans for that date are continuing to unfold.

The Conference has undertaken many projects in preparation for the Centennial celebration. Throughout the year, the league will air television public service announcements, produce special publications, and present articles in alumni magazines, game programs and other school publications. In addition, the Centennial logo will appear on team uniforms and warmups, at campus athletic events and on Conference and institutional materials prior to and throughout the celebration. Commemorative merchandise, publications, artwork and video cassettes will be available to the public during Centennial period.

Reprinted from 1995 Michigan Media Guide with permission

BO SCHEMBECHLER

"The Team, The Team, The Team."

That was Bo Schembechler's winning philosophy over the course of his 27 years as a collegiate head football coach. Schembechler used that philosophy to build successful teams out of individuals, to make men out of boys, and to create a coaching legend out of a prep football all-stater from Barberton (Ohio) High School.

His loyalty to Michigan was matched only by the success he enjoyed at the Ann Arbor campus. Schembechler's ability to motivate his players to perform as a disciplined, cohesive unit is displayed in the long list of achievements that follow:

*A career won-lost record at Michigan of 194-48-5. Including his six year tenure as coach of Miami of Ohio (1963-68), he had an overall record of 234-65-8, a figure that places him fifth in all-time NCAA Division 1-A coaching victories. At the time of his retirement, Schembechler was the winningest active coach in college football.

*A sparkling 143-24-3 (.850) record in Big Ten games.

*His 194 wins at Michigan make him the winningest football coach in school history.

*13 of his 21 Michigan football teams either won or tied for the Big Ten Championship.

*Schembechler never had a losing season in 27 years as head coach.

*17 of his 21, and each of his last 15, Wolverine teams went to bowl games.

*17 of his 21 Michigan teams were ranked in the top ten of the final wire service polls (AP and/or UPI).

*39 different players earned All-America honors and 97 different Wolverines earned first team All-Big Ten honors during his coaching reign.

*Eleven of his 21 teams won ten or more games in a season.

*During the 1970s, his regular season record of 96-10-3 was the finest in the nation.

*Schembechler was named National Coach of the Year in 1969, was selected as Big Ten Coach of the Year four times (1972, 1976, 1980, and 1985), was honored as Ohio Coach of the Year in 1966, and won the MAC Coach of the Year in 1965.

*Schembechler is a past-president of the American Football Coaches Association.

Schembechler also upheld Michigan's tradition of excellence in athletic administration when he assumed the role of athletic director on May 5, 1988. As athletic director, Schembechler oversaw 21 varsity sports with a $20 million budget. Under Schembechler, Michigan produced several nationally ranked teams and a generous supply of championship trophies, including the 1989 NCAA Basketball and Rose Bowl Championships. He initiated construction of a $12 million football complex and sports services building that, upon its dedication on May 21, 1991, stands in his honor as Schembechler Hall.

Schembechler resigned as athletic director on January 7, 1991 to become President of the Detroit Tigers, a role he is still serving in today.

Schembechler played his college football at Miami of Ohio where he was an offensive tackle for three seasons. He played under George Blackburn and Woody Hayes. Schembechler graduated in 1951 and received a master's degree in 1952 at Ohio State where he served as a graduate assistant coach. After serving in the U.S. Army, Schembechler was named an assistant coach at Presbyterian College in 1954 and Bowling Green in 1955, and then joined Ara Parseghian's staff at Northwestern in 1958 before serving for the next five seasons as an assistant to Ohio State. Bo was appointed head football coach at Miami of Ohio in 1963, a position he held until taking over the Michigan program prior to the 1969 season.

BORN:	April 1, 1929—Barberton, Ohio
COLLEGE:	Miami (OH) '51
COACHING:	Miami (OH), 1963-68
	Michigan, 1968-89
RECORD:	Overall 234-65-8 (.775)
	Michigan 194-48-45 (.796)

THE MICHIGAN COACHES

Years	Coach	Record	Pct.	First Season	Record	Pct.
1879-90	No Coaches	23-10-1	.691	—	—	—
1891	Mike Murphy & Frank Crawford	4-5-0	.444	1891	4-5-0	.444
1892-93	Frank E. Barbour (Yale '92)	14-8-0	.632	1892	7-5-0	.583
1894-95	William L. McCauley (Princeton '94)	17-2-1	.875	1894	9-1-1	.864
1896	William Douglas Ward (Princeton '95)	9-1-0	.900	1896	9-1-0	.900
1897-99	Gustave H. Ferbert (Michigan'97)	24-3-1	.875	1897	6-1-1	.813
1900	Langdon 'Biff' Lea (Princeton)	7-2-1	.750	1900	7-2-1	.750
1901-3, 25-6	Fielding H. Yost (W. Virginia)	165-29-10	.833	1901	11-0-0	1.000*
1924	George Little (Ohio Wesleyan '12)	6-2-0	.750	1924	6-2-0	.750
1927-28	Elton E. 'Tad' Wieman (Michigan '21)	9-6-1	.593	1927	6-2-0	.750
1929-37	Harry G. Kipke (Michigan '24)	46-26-4	.631	1929	5-3-1	.611
1937-49	H.O.'Fritz' Crisler (Chicago '22)	71-16-3	.805	1938	6-1-1	.813
1948-58	Bennie G. Oosterbaan (Michigan '28)	63-33-4	.650	1948	9-0-0	1.000*
1959-68	Chalmers W.'Bump' Elliott (Michigan '48)	51-42-2	.547	1959	4-5-0	.444
1969-89	Glenn E. 'Bo' Schembechler (Miami '51)	194-48-5	.796	1969	8-3-0	.727*
1990-	Gary O. Moeller (Ohio State '63)	28-5-3	.819	1990	9-3-0	.750*

* Won Big Ten Championship in inaugural season

Reprinted from 1995 Michigan Media Guide with permission.

THE RECORD

Michigan 52

Ohio State 34

Ties 6

As the teams and coaches return to their locker rooms to plan for the next regular season and the next Big Game at Columbus, I would like to take this opportunity to thank several people and offices for their help in completing this project.

From the Ohio State University

OSU Photo Archives
Sports Information Office
Athletic Director's Staff
OSU Alumni Magazine
University Archives

From the University of Michigan

Sports Information Office
Athletic Director's Office
Alumni Magazine Staff
Bentley Historical Library

The following newspapers

The Toledo Blade
The Cleveland Plain Dealer
The Ann Arbor News
The Columbus Dispatch
The Napoleon (OH) Northwest Signal

The printing company

Walsworth Publishing, Marceline, MO

For special help

Brent Bowen, writing and marketing
Thomas Cousino, marketing
Bonnies Printing Plus, St. Cloud, MN, typesetting/promotional materials
Chance Brockway, Sports Photos for use of photographs

All comments, criticism, corrections and inquiries on this book should be sent to:

Steve White
One Game Season
P.O. Box 5633
Collegeville, MN 56321

MICHIGAN STADIUM